Securing Cisco IP Telephony Networks

Akhil Behl

Cisco Press

800 East 96th Street

Indianapolis, IN 46240

Securing Cisco IP Telephony Networks

Akhil Behl

Copyright © 2013 Cisco Systems, Inc.

Published by:

Cisco Press

800 East 96th Street

Indianapolis, IN 46240 USA

Printed in the United States of America 1 2 3 4 5 6 7 8 9 0

First Printing September 2012

Library of Congress Cataloging-in-Publication data is on file.

ISBN-13: 978-1-58714-295-6

ISBN-10: 1-58714-295-3

Warning and Disclaimer

Trademark Acknowledgments

Corporate and Government Sales

The publisher offers excellent discounts on this book when ordered in quantity for bulk purchases or special sales, which may include electronic versions and/or custom covers and content particular to your business, training goals, marketing focus, and branding interests. For more information, please contact

U.S. Corporate and Government Sales
1-800-382-3419
corpsales@pearsontechgroup.com

For sales outside of the U.S. please contact:
International Sales
international@pearsoned.com

Feedback Information

At Cisco Press, our goal is to create in-depth technical books of the highest quality and value. Each book is crafted with care and precision, undergoing rigorous development that involves the unique expertise of members from the professional technical community.

Readers' feedback is a natural continuation of this process. If you have any comments regarding how we could improve the quality of this book, or otherwise alter it to better suit your needs, you can contact us through e-mail at feedback@ciscopress.com. Please make sure to include the book title and ISBN in your message.

We greatly appreciate your assistance.

Publisher: Paul Boger

Business Operation Manager, Cisco Press: Anand Sundaram

Associate Publisher: Dave Dusthimer

Manager Global Certification: Erik Ullanderson

Executive Editor: Brett Bartow

Development Editor: Eleanor C. Bru

Managing Editor: Sandra Schroeder

Copy Editor: Apostrophe Editing Services

Project Editor: Seth Kerney

Technical Editors: Zeeshan Farees, Alvin Laguerta

Editorial Assistant: Vanessa Evans

Cover Designer: Gary Adair

Composition: Mark Shirar

Proofreader: Sheri Cain

Indexer: Larry Sweazy

Americas Headquarters	**Asia Pacific Headquarters**	**Europe Headquarters**
Cisco Systems, Inc.	Cisco Systems (USA) Pte. Ltd.	Cisco Systems International BV
San Jose, CA	Singapore	Amsterdam, The Netherlands

Cisco has more than 200 offices worldwide. Addresses, phone numbers, and fax numbers are listed on the Cisco Website at **www.cisco.com/go/offices.**

CCDE, CCENT, Cisco Eos, Cisco HealthPresence, the Cisco logo, Cisco Lumin, Cisco Nexus, Cisco StadiumVision, Cisco TelePresence, Cisco WebEx, DCE, and Welcome to the Human Network are trademarks; Changing the Way We Work, Live, Play, and Learn and Cisco Store are service marks; and Access Registrar, Aironet, AsyncOS, Bringing the Meeting To You, Catalyst, CCDA, CCDP, CCIE, CCIP, CCNA, CCNP, CCSP, CCVP, Cisco, the Cisco Certified Internetwork Expert logo, Cisco IOS, Cisco Press, Cisco Systems, Cisco Systems Capital, the Cisco Systems logo, Cisco Unity, Collaboration Without Limitation, EtherFast, EtherSwitch, Event Center, Fast Step, Follow Me Browsing, FormShare, GigaDrive, HomeLink, Internet Quotient, IOS, iPhone, iQuick Study, IronPort, the IronPort logo, LightStream, Linksys, MediaTone, MeetingPlace, MeetingPlace Chime Sound, MGX, Networkers, Networking Academy, Network Registrar, PCNow, PIX, PowerPanels, ProConnect, ScriptShare, SenderBase, SMARTnet, Spectrum Expert, StackWise, The Fastest Way to Increase Your Internet Quotient, TransPath, WebEx, and the WebEx logo are registered trademarks of Cisco Systems, Inc. and/or its affiliates in the United States and certain other countries.

All other trademarks mentioned in this document or website are the property of their respective owners. The use of the word partner does not imply a partnership relationship between Cisco and any other company. (0812R)

About the Author

Akhil Behl, CCIE No. 19564, is a Senior Network Consultant in Cisco Services, focusing on Cisco Collaboration and Security Architectures. He leads collaboration and security projects worldwide for Cisco Services and the Collaborative Professional Services (CPS) portfolio for the commercial segment. Prior to his current role, he spent ten years working in various roles at Linksys as a Technical Support Lead, as an Escalation Engineer at Cisco Technical Assistance Center (TAC), and as a Network Consulting Engineer in Cisco Advanced Services.

Akhil has a bachelor of technology degree in electronics and telecommunications from IP University, India, and a master's degree in business administration from Symbiosis Institute, India. He is a dual Cisco Certified Internetwork Expert (CCIE) in Voice and Security. He also holds many other industry certifications, such as Project Management Professional (PMP), Information Technology Infrastructure Library (ITIL) professional, VMware Certified Professional (VCP), and Microsoft Certified Professional (MCP). Over the course of his career, he has presented and contributed in various industry forums such as Interop, Enterprise Connect, Cloud Connect, Cloud Summit, Computer Society of India (CSI), Cisco Networkers, and Cisco SecCon. He also has several research papers published to his credit in various international journals.

About the Technical Reviewers

Alvin M. Laguerta, CCIE Voice # 13976, is a Senior Network Consulting Engineer for Cisco Advanced Services Unified Communications (UC) Practice at Cisco Systems. He is the Virtual Team technical lead focused on Unified Communications Security for Voice and Video technologies and helped many customers in planning, designing and deploying UC Security over the past 11 years. Alvin's experience extends into other networking technologies over the course of his 20+ years and holds various industry certifications. Alvin holds a Bachelor of Science in Electronics and Communications Engineering from the University of Santo Tomas, Philippines and MBA in IT Management from WGU, Utah.

Zeeshan Farees, CCIE # 20963, is a Technical Marketing Engineer for Unified Communications Security in the Collaboration and Communications Group at Cisco. Her focus is on security for Voice and Video technologies within the Cisco Unified Communications Solution. She has authored the security content of multiple design guides, including the Cisco Unified Communications Solution Reference Network Design (SRND) document. Prior to becoming a TME, Zeeshan was an Escalation Engineer for Voice related products at the Cisco Technical Assistance Center (TAC). Zeeshan holds a Bachelor of Science degree in Computer Science from the University of Illinois, Urbana-Champaign.

Dedication

This book is dedicated first to my family, my dear wife Kanika and my lovely son, Shivansh, for without their support, encouragement, and patience, it would not exist. Secondly, to my parents Vijay and Ravi Behl, who provided resources and direction when I was young, and inspiration and support as I got older. Lastly, to my brothers, Nikhil and Ankit, who have always been there when I needed them.

Acknowledgments

I would like to thank the following amazing people and teams for helping me create this book.

I would like to thank my wife Kanika. She sacrificed many days and weekends over the past year so that I could work on this book. Without her patience and support, this book would not have been possible.

The technical reviewers, Alvin Laguerta and Zeeshan Farees, for their invaluable feedback and providing exceptional technical coverage.

The Cisco Press team: Brett Bartow, the executive editor, for seeing the value and vision in the proposed title and providing me the opportunity to build this title. Eleanor Bru, development editor, and Christopher Cleveland, senior development editor, for their support and guidance to edit and polish my rough manuscript and develop it into a fine piece of technical literature. It is my sincere hope to work again with them in the near future. Lastly, everyone else in the Cisco Press production team for their support and commitment.

Contents at a Glance

Contents

Icons Used

 Voice-Enabled Switch

 Core Switch (Secure)

 Core Switch

 Data Center Switch with Firewall Module

 Access Layer Switch

 Voice-Enabled Access Router

 IDS / IPS

 Cisco ASA 5500 Series Firewall

 Router with Firewall

 Distribution Layer Switch

 Data Center Switch

 DHCP Server

 AAA Server

 Mail Server

 XMPP Enterprise Server

 Web Server

 LDAP Server

 Microsoft OCS

 Cisco Unified Communications Manager

 Cisco Unity Connection

 Cisco Unified Presence Server

 Cisco Unified Communications Manager Express

 Cisco Unity Express

 Cisco Unity

 TFTP Server

 Cisco Unified Border Element

 CAPF Server

 Cisco Unified Personal Communicator

 Cisco Unified IP Phone

 Cisco Conference Phone

 Cisco IP Communicator

 Voice-Enabled Router

 Voice Gateway / Gatekeeper

 Wireless IP Phone

 PC

 Attacker / Hacker

 Wireless Access Point

 Cisco Wireless LAN Controller

 Lightweight Access Point

 WAN / Internet

PSTN

MPLS WAN

 IT Service Provider

 Management Endpoint

 Voice Service Provider Soft Switch

End User

Certificate Authority

Headquarters (Main Data Center)

Remote / Backup Data Center

 Branch Office / Remote Site

Telecommuter

Advance Telecommuter (Remote Worker)

Command Syntax Conventions

The conventions used to present command syntax in this book are the same conventions used in the IOS Command Reference. The Command Reference describes these conventions as follows:

- **Boldface** indicates commands and keywords that are entered literally as shown. In actual configuration examples and output (not general command syntax), boldface indicates commands that are manually input by the user (such as a **show** command).

- Italic indicates arguments for which you supply actual values.

- Vertical bars (|) separate alternative, mutually exclusive elements.

- Square brackets ([ ]) indicate an optional element.

- Braces ({ }) indicate a required choice.

- Braces within brackets ([{ }]) indicate a required choice within an optional element.

Introduction

Over the past several years, I have seen security becoming a key component in network design. With more organizations using IP Telephony as a business instrument today, security is more important than ever. Keeping pace with the rapid security technology evolution and the growing complexity of threats is a challenge, even in the best of times. Understanding and deploying IP Telephony network security is a key factor to determine whether your business, which relies on the same, will succeed.

The past couple of years have witnessed a dramatic increase in the threats to IP Telephony network security in corporate, financial, healthcare, education, and government institutions. The invent of IP Telephony has fundamentally changed the way organizations conduct business and communicate. Reliance on access to collaboration and communication resources has never been greater, which, in turn, makes the impact of IP Telephony network downtime increasingly devastating.

The costs that businesses have incurred over the past few years because of security vulnerabilities are staggering. In addition to the direct costs to your business if you suffer a network security compromise, you can also put other businesses or Internet users at risk because the compromise you suffered can be leveraged to attack against other network devices.

The purpose of this book is to explain an End-to-End IP Telephony Security approach and architecture and to show how each piece of the puzzle fits together. This book is focused on providing you with an in-depth understanding of the Cisco IP Telephony Security principles, features, protocols, and implementation best practices. Most topics start with the basics to help keep the discussion complete. This helps you read the book more easily and comprehend the topics.

The book provides an introduction to the key tools and techniques essential for securing a Cisco IP Telephony network of any size. This book answers the need for an easy-to-understand manual for IP Telephony engineers, managers, and architects seeking the knowledge to make important business and technical decisions. Unlike books that revolve around generic VoIP security concepts, this book is focused on Cisco IP Telephony Security. It addresses the important task of enabling you to implement and maintain a secure, stable, and robust Cisco IP Telephony network. This book provides the answers you need by showing you how to use a layered security approach to secure your Cisco IP Telephony network. This book will be an indispensable resource for anyone who needs to understand, build, and maintain Secure Cisco IP Telephony networks.

Objectives of This Book

The most important and obvious objective of this book is to explain not only the rationale behind securing your Cisco IP Telephony network, but also the best ways to do so to achieve a secure, robust, and resilient IP Telephony network. This book is focused on providing you with an in-depth understanding of the various IP Telephony network security principles, features, protocols, and implementations in today's networks. The goals of this book are as follows:

- Provide a complete discussion at a basic to an advanced level for all topics involved in the implementation of IP Telephony Security in today's networks.

- Provide detailed and in-depth discussion and insight into the workings of the protocols behind Cisco IP Telephony Security implementations.

- Detailed step-by-step walkthroughs of various Cisco IP Telephony application and underlying network gear configuration to achieve the ultimate goal of a secure network, which can evade and restrain attacks from within and outside your organization.

- Discuss security principles and leading practices that form the basis of successful Cisco IP Telephony Security implementations.

- Provide an insight into the operational needs and requirements to set up and maintain a Secure Cisco IP Telephony network.

Who Should Read This Book?

The answer to this question is uncomplicated: Everyone. Anyone who is interested in Cisco IP Telephony and network security should become familiar with the information included in this book. That includes audience from IP Telephony engineers and security engineers to architects to administrators to management and executives. The principles and leading practices covered in this book apply to almost every organization and every business vertical. This book covers not only numerous technical topics and scenarios, but also covers a wide range of operational best practices. This book is a valuable asset to anyone who is tasked with securing IP Telephony networks. In addition to technology perspective, this book provides an all-around business impact perspective of securing what is an asset and the lifeline of the modern-day organizations: IP-based communications. To get the most value from this book, you should have a basic knowledge of IP Telephony, networking, and security.

How This Book Is Organized

This book is both a reference and a guide. It begins by describing the quintessence of IP Telephony Security and by examining the threats that thwart today's IP Telephony networks. As technologies are dramatically changing the way we work and collaborate, there are associated risks and threats that you must think about. This book follows a logical path that begins by giving you a quick introduction to the reasons why you must secure your Cisco IP Telephony network followed by IP Telephony network security mechanisms, and continues by showing you what you need to do to have your Cisco IP Telephony network secured, end-to-end.

You learn about the challenges and threats that today's organizations and businesses face as they struggle to fully embrace the value that Cisco IP Telephony has to offer, without sacrificing enterprise security.

This book contains sixteen chapters and two appendixes that cover the core areas of Cisco IP Telephony Security, from basic concepts to advance configurations to leading practices. An overview of each chapter follows.

Part I: Introduction to Cisco IP Telephony Security

- **Chapter 1, "What Is IP Telephony Security and Why Do You Need It?":** This chapter covers an introduction to IP Telephony as a technology and provides an insight to rationale as to why you should be concerned about the security of your IP-based communications. In addition, it gives an overview of the threats that pester the sanctity of your Cisco IP Telephony network. Moreover, it gives an overview of the attack vectors and follows footsteps of an attacker/hacker to give you an insight to how they go about attacking an IP Telephony network. Finally, this chapter concludes with introduction to IP Telephony Security and penetration tools and addresses questions relevant to business challenges associated with adoption and secure operation of IP Telephony.

- **Chapter 2, "Cisco IP Telephony Security Building Blocks":** This chapter starts with an introduction to Cisco IP Telephony Security methodology and delves into demystifying the otherwise perceived complex IP Telephony Security methodology. The chapter covers concepts pertinent to layered security, from the physical layer up to the application layer. In addition, Cisco IP Telephony network components that should be secured to attain a robust and secure Cisco IP Telephony network are explored.

- **Chapter 3, "What Can You Secure and How Can You Secure It?":** In this chapter you learn the layered security approach (Defense-in-Depth strategy), which is instrumental to secure your Cisco IP Telephony network. This chapter details the various components that form the basis of a Cisco IP Telephony network and walks you through their relevant security controls. The chapter presents a case study in which you are introduced to Cisco IP Telephony Security in context to an organization, which has geographically diversified IP Telephony deployment at a main data center, and at a remote (backup) data center, a remote site, and must also support telecommuters.

- **Chapter 4, "Cisco IP Telephony Security Framework":** This is one of the most important chapters of this book. It covers many important topics such as Cisco IP Telephony Security life cycle, risk assessment, IP Telephony Security strategy, cost of security, and so on. The intent is to help you create a well-defined IP Telephony Security Framework, which acts as a blueprint for planning, deployment, and management of your secured Cisco IP Telephony network. This chapter starts with insight to specifics of Cisco IP Telephony Security life cycle and then guides you through the risk assessment and IP Telephony Security strategy (policy) development. Topics such as the cost of security (the cost of deploying security versus assuming the risk of security breach) and determining the level of security for your Cisco IP Telephony network are covered in this chapter. A case study fortifies the concept on level of security required and helps you decide what should and shouldn't be considered while planning and deploying security for your IP Telephony network. This chapter concludes with the IP Telephony Security Framework demystified and defined.

Part II: Cisco IP Telephony Network Security

- **Chapter 5, "Cisco IP Telephony Physical Security"**: This chapter covers the topic of physical security as it pertains to Cisco IP Telephony to help you better prepare your network infrastructure, security policies, procedures, and organization as a whole against physical security threats from within and outside of your organization. You will learn numerous tips on how to increase the security of your Cisco IP Telephony network infrastructure and how to better secure critical network assets from human or environmental induced threats.

- **Chapter 6, "Cisco IP Telephony Layer 2 Security"**: This chapter starts with an introduction to OSI Layer 2 security issues as they pertain to Cisco IP Telephony. This chapter explores various threats to Cisco IP Telephony Layer 2 network infrastructure and their mitigation techniques. This is complemented by an introduction of 802.1x technology, followed by a detailed walk-through, which enables you to keep out those rogue endpoints from being admitted into your IP Telephony network. In addition, this chapter provides leading practice recommendations for Layer 2 security.

- **Chapter 7, "Cisco IP Telephony Layer 3 Security"**: This chapter starts with an overview of the OSI Layer 3 security fundamentals. It explains the various kinds of threats that you'll face in securing your Cisco IP Telephony network (Layer 3) infrastructure and the solutions that you can use to deal with these threats. The chapter categorizes security threats and lists some common and not so common security threats you'll face, and an in-depth approach to how you can mitigate them. Cisco router control plane, management plane, and data plane security specifics are discussed in great detail as they pertain to IP Telephony networks. The chapter concludes with leading practice recommendations that you can leverage to secure your IP Telephony network.

- **Chapter 8, "Perimeter Security with Cisco Adaptive Security Appliance"**: This chapter introduces Cisco Adaptive Security Appliance (ASA) as an IP Telephony Firewall and shows you how to implement your organization's security policy, leveraging the features that the Cisco ASA offers. The chapter builds on Cisco ASA Firewall's functionality as a data center perimeter firewall followed by an introduction and detailed configuration of IP Telephony-centric features such as TLS Proxy, Phone Proxy, VPN Phone, and Telecommuter VPN features. All these features are detailed and their relevant configuration examples are presented in an easy-to-follow manner. This chapter lays the groundwork for the firewall technologies that Cisco offers to protect the perimeter of your IP Telephony network.

Part III: Cisco IP Telephony Application and Device Security

- **Chapter 9, "Cisco Unified Communications Manager Security":** The cost-savings and features introduced with Voice over IP (VoIP) solutions can be significant. However, these benefits can be heavily impacted if you do not have the appropriate security mechanisms in place to control the heart and soul of your Cisco IP Telephony network, the call control, which makes this chapter an indispensable companion to the security of your IP Telephony network. This chapter covers detailed steps to secure a multitude of technologies pertaining to the Cisco UCM and its integration with applications and endpoints, for example, secure phone conversations, secure trunks to ITSP and gateways, thwart toll fraud, secure CTI/JTAPI connections, and fighting SPIT. In addition, this chapter addresses the requirements to enable auditing on your Cisco UCM and to integrate it with a Single-Sign On solution for your organization.

- **Chapter 10, "Cisco Unity and Unity Connection Security":** This chapter covers both Cisco Unity and Cisco Unity Connection voice messaging solution security, from an application and from a platform perspective. In this chapter you learn how to secure Cisco Unity/Unity Connection voice messaging platforms to curb toll fraud, eavesdropping, Man-In-The-Middle, and account hijacking attacks. In addition, you are introduced to secure integration of Cisco Unity/Unity Connection with Cisco Unified Communications Manager, Cisco Unified IP Phones, Cisco Unified Personal Communicator, and other applications. This chapter details how you can reinforce end user-to-administrator rights at granular level and how to enable audit for the voicemail system.

- **Chapter 11, "Cisco Unified Presence Security":** This chapter starts with a discussion around the security of Cisco Unified Presence solution. It then delves deep into the Secure Presence Federation – Intra-domain and Inter-domain for Cisco Unified Presence servers and the Microsoft OCS Server respectively, where detailed examples help you comprehend secure federation fundamentals as well as associated advance topics. The chapter concludes with a deep dive into the Cisco Unified Personal Communicator Security, which ensures that you have all the ammunition you need from a knowledge standpoint to protect the softphone client.

- **Chapter 12, "Cisco Voice Gateway Security":** This chapter starts with an introduction to Cisco IOS Voice Gateway platform security. It then walks you through one of the most drastic issues, toll fraud – its intricacies and remediation. This chapter provides guidance and detailed examples to implement secure conferencing and securing voice media and signaling streams pertinent to protocols and applications on Voice Gateways for SIP to H.323 to MGCP to SRST. In addition, you will learn about strategies and methodologies for monitoring your Cisco Voice Gateways.

- **Chapter 13, "Cisco Voice Gatekeeper and Cisco Unified Border Element Security":** This chapter builds on Cisco IP-IP Gateway Security, which becomes of paramount importance when you liaise with third-party and IT Service Provider (ITSP) networks. It covers Cisco Voice Gatekeeper and Cisco Unified Border Element security. It presents easy-to-comprehend concepts and examples to ensure that you are well equipped to restrain threats originating from your partner organizations and ITSP network.

- **Chapter 14, "Cisco Unified Communications Manager Express and Cisco Unity Express Security":** This chapter provides a comprehensive coverage of security of Cisco Unified Communications Manager Express call-control solution and Cisco Unity Express voice-messaging solution. Detailed configuration examples help you build on a plan and execute the plan to secure the express communication solution from Cisco. You will comprehend solutions to security issues such as toll fraud, user authentication/authorization, insecure configuration and management access, rogue endpoint admission, and so on.

- **Chapter 15, "Cisco IP Telephony Endpoint Security":** This chapter covers the security of Cisco Unified IP Phones, Cisco Wireless IP Phones, and Cisco IP Communicator. The chapter starts with a discussion about the importance of endpoint security and walks you through various attack vectors pertinent to Cisco Unified IP Phones and softphones. You will learn about securing Cisco Unified IP Phones (wired and wireless) by hardening the endpoints as well as securing the network connectivity. In addition, you will comprehend voice media and signaling security as it pertains to wired and wireless Cisco Unified IP Phones. You will find comprehensive coverage of wireless Cisco Unified IP Phones as well as underlying wireless infrastructure security. The chapter concludes with addressing security concerns around Cisco IP Communicator as a softphone from an administrative and system perspective.

Part IV: Cisco IP Telephony Network Management Security

- **Chapter 16, "Cisco IP Telephony: Network Management Security":** This chapter focuses on securing IP Telephony network and application management aspect. The chapter starts with an insight to various network management options such as In-Band, Out-Of-Band, and Hybrid management setups. Then it covers the wide spectrum of management protocols for Cisco IP Telephony network and applications, for example Telnet, SSH, VNC, RDP, SNMP, Syslog, ASDM, Cisco Configuration Professional, and so on, and the particulars about how you can ensure the security of these management protocols in a sustainable and efficient manner. Detailed practical examples help you plan for and execute secure management setup for your IP Telephony network. The last part of the chapter briefly discusses the Security Event Management System (SEMS) that you can envision and deploy for attack event correlation and central logging leading to event aggregation.

Part V: Cisco IP Telephony Security Essentials

- **Appendix A, "Cisco IP Telephony: Authentication and Encryption Essentials":** This appendix covers the basics of Cisco IP Telephony Security. It covers basic to advance concepts such as authentication, encryption, Public Key Infrastructure (PKI), certificates, and everything else that as a technology component helps you secure your Cisco IP Telephony network. This appendix is a great primer for people who are new to the world of Cisco IP Telephony and network security, and a refresher for veterans.

- **Appendix B, "Cisco IP Telephony: Firewalling and Intrusion Prevention":** This appendix leads you into a deep insight of the Cisco Firewall and Intrusion Prevention and Detection technology as it pertains to Cisco IP Telephony network and application security. This appendix helps you be cognizant of the Cisco ASAs advance firewall features as well as Cisco IOS Firewall benefits and features for small organizations. Detailed configuration examples combined with real-life experiences help you achieve optimum security without sacrificing performance or features. Moreover, leading practice recommendations on deployment of Intrusion Prevention Solutions (network and host) pave the way for you to make tactical decisions to secure your Cisco IP Telephony network.

Introduction to Cisco IP Telephony Security

"If you know your enemies and know yourself, you will not be imperiled in a hundred battles." –Sun Tzu

Chapter 1

What Is IP Telephony Security and Why Do You Need It?

In last few decades, communication systems have evolved, and one such major evolution is in the field of telecommunications in which increasingly, there has been adoption of Internet Protocol-based communications or in other words, Internet Protocol Telephony. Internet Protocol Telephony (IP Telephony) leverages the power of a converged network that is, a network where data and voice can co-exist, thereby helping organizations to reduce the Total Cost of Ownership (TCO) and increase the Return On Investment (ROI).

IP Telephony is a real-time technology that virtually encompasses an organization's communication channels and dependent lines of business and processes. This fact makes it vulnerable and susceptible to attacks and exploits. It is unfortunate, but true that there are many threats to your IP Telephony network's safety and security. If you feel intimidated by the mere idea of securing your IP Telephony network, don't worry. In this chapter, you will learn about the rationale behind securing your IP Telephony networks and get an insight to the various types of threats to modern-day telephony (IP Telephony networks). By the end of this chapter, you will know about the tools that can be used to exploit and attack an IP Telephony network, and how you can address the various business challenges posed against IP Telephony Security in the best possible manner. This chapter is intended to provide you an introduction to the world of IP Telephony Security.

This chapter covers the following topics:

- Defining IP Telephony Security
- Understanding various threats to IP Telephony
- An insight to VoIP security tools
- Understanding business challenges and Cisco IP Telephony Security responses

Defining IP Telephony Security

What is IP Telephony Security and why do you need it? How can you secure your IP Telephony network?

The following sections answer these questions and more.

What Is IP Telephony?

IP Telephony has been prevalent since the 1990s and seen as the future of communications, enabling various business verticals to transport multimedia over the IP network. The major reason behind the prevalence of IP-based communications is the key benefits such as cost-savings, rich media service, mobility, portability, ease of integration with other applications, and rich features. With the ever-increasing awareness and adoption of IP Telephony, IP-based communication networks are now gaining popularity, and businesses continue to leverage VoIP platforms to handle all their communication traffic, whether it is voice calls, Instant Messaging, or voicemail. As IP Telephony technology matures, new voice services and applications will be offered and therefore resulting in yet broader acceptance and implementation of IP-based communication networks.

IP Telephony is slowly becoming an integral part of the modern day organization's day-to-day operations. However, the benefits of IP Telephony do not come without cost. The openness of modern day IP-based communications introduces new ethical, financial, and business continuity demands to protect networks and enterprises from internal and external threats and attacks.

What Is IP Telephony Security?

IP Telephony and other pertinent services are real time in nature and a vital focal point for an organization adopting it, security of the same becomes of paramount importance. Moreover, because of IP Telephony's inherent nature (which acts both in its favor and against it) it depends on the underlying network (OSI Layers 1 through 7) for its successful operation and functioning. In essence, IP Telephony networks are built on top of underlying network infrastructure and share the strengths and weaknesses of the data networks. This implies that IP Telephony networks are susceptible to attacks as much as its basic foundation: the data networks. To make matters worse, Voice over IP has its own set of security requirements, which can be exploited if left exposed.

IP Telephony Security by definition is "Securing the 'IP Telephony components' on top of a 'Secure data network infrastructure' to provide a resilient, stable and scalable IP Telephony network."

Cisco IP Telephony operates at a system level by interacting with many different components: Call Control, IP Phones, voicemail, gateways, other IP Telephony applications, and underlying network infrastructure.

IP Telephony Security includes (and is not limited to) securing Call Control, Voice Messaging, Voice/Video calls, Network Infrastructure (LAN/WAN), Wireless, Perimeter network defenses, and so on. In short, IP Telephony Security is securing—a conversation from an IP endpoint (IP Phone) to another endpoint or an end device (IP Phone, gateway, application server, and so on).

Figure 1-1 gives a 10,000 feet view to how a Cisco IP Telephony network is built and leverages underlying network infrastructure for converged communications.

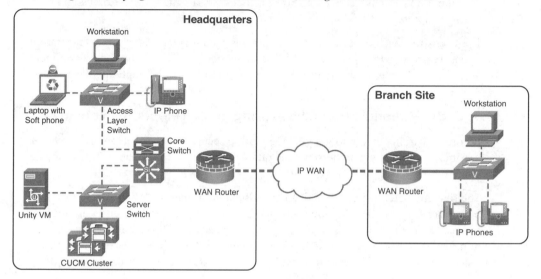

Figure 1-1   *IP Telephony Network Built on Top of a Data Network*

Securing data networks is the first and foremost step taken by almost all organizations. However, they tend to ignore the IP Telephony Security aspect because of lack of confidence to secure a relatively new technology. Although, this is a major loophole in overall organizational security, it is an opportunity for the hackers and attackers to exploit the vulnerabilities.

The most prominent question is, "Why would anyone attach a VoIP/IP Telephony network?" The answer is, "To benefit financially via information and identity theft, toll fraud, and espionage and to disrupt service."

Because of the converged nature of VoIP/IP Telephony (that is, to leverage the underlying data network for voice applications), the same types of attacks that plague the data networks can also impact the IP Telephony environment as well. Thus, the content of VoIP network is vulnerable to being attacked, hacked, altered, re-routed, or intercepted. An attack on the IP Telephony system could eventually compromise the entire IP network, leading to a business's inability to communicate via either voice or data. In addition to external threats, internal threats also need to be prohibited. Appropriate security policies need to be implemented to ensure that employees cannot abuse or misuse the IP Telephony network.

Consequently, developing a culture of security is not limited to physical, application, or network security measures; it also extends to an organization's core values and ethics.

The concepts of security controls, processes, and framework for IP Telephony and developing a culture of security awareness are discussed in-depth in Chapter 2, "Cisco IP Telephony Security Building Blocks," Chapter 3, "What Can You Secure and How Can You Secure It?" and Chapter 4, "Cisco IP Telephony Security Framework." Moreover, the basics pertinent to IP Telephony network and application security as well as detailed configuration examples along with best practices for safeguarding are discussed in following chapters.

The Cisco approach to securing IP Telephony is a 'multilayer security' implementation to ensure protection of the critical IP Telephony components. Security mitigation techniques are available starting from the network periphery to IP Telephony devices.

What Is the Rationale Behind Securing an IP Telephony Network?

Before embarking on our journey on the road to secure Cisco IP Telephony networks, it is imperative that you understand the rationale behind securing the IP Telephony networks.

The first and foremost question that may arise in your mind is, "Why should I even bother securing my IP Telephony network? It has been running fine, and I do not want to break something which is working by applying security." It is a common misconception that applying security to an IP Telephony network will break it! The reality being that, a non secure IP Telephony network is open to attacks and is prone to breakdowns.

Now, let's consider some IP Telephony Security breach incidents that have occurred in the past and understand the overall impact. As illustrated in Figure 1-2, there have been incidents in which unsecured or poorly secured VoIP/IP Telephony networks were exploited and the consequences were disastrous.

VoIP Telecom Billing Fraud shakes telecom industry…

Miami: The federal government arrested Edwin Andrew Pena, 23, owner of Fortes Telecom Inc. and Miami Tech & Consulting Inc., for hacking into other providers' networks, routing his customer's calls onto those platforms, then billing those companies and pocketing the proceeds. He reaped more than $1 million.
Source –
http://nolastname.articlealley.com/voip-telecom-billing-fraud-shakes-telecom-industry-67797.html

Small business gets $120,000 phone bill after hackers attack VoIP phone!

Sydney: A small business landed with a $120,000 phone bill after criminals hacked into its internet phone system and used it to make 11,000 international calls in just 46 hours.

Source –
http://news.hitb.org/node/29587

Figure 1-2 *IP Telephony Networks Attacked*

These cases are public examples of attacks on IP Telephony networks.

As you can see, attacks on the IP Telephony network may result in monetary and reputation loss. Interruption of communication service equates to dollar loss, and a business that was hacked is most likely to lose consumers and will not be expecting new customers for a while. It is the overall business value of security everybody overlooks until they become a victim of an attack. Besides, attacks can adversely impact the organization's business continuity. Overall, the consequences can be devastating.

You should secure your IP Telephony networks for the following reasons:

- **Secure IP Telephony infrastructure:** Securing what is an asset to an organization's daily life operations, without which the organization's communications will crumble. This in turn has a domino effect as; the organization can experience disrupted communications with peers, amongst employees, with customers, and so on.

- **Secure the conversation:** Ensure that your conversation is private and protected from eavesdropping or hacking of voice calls. Securing voice or video calls can help evade any chances of confidential information (being conveyed over an IP Telephony system) being eavesdropped, leading to Intellectual Capital theft, for example, eavesdropping of a conversation between a CEO and a CIO of a financial institution could otherwise reveal a lot of confidential information if it weren't secure.

- **Business continuity:** Ensures that the business continuity is maintained and the chances of disruption and losses are minimized. If voice and video conversations are secure, it helps ensure the business continuity and minimize disruption leading to monetary and credibility losses.

- **Business value:** Protect your company's privacy and intellectual property by protecting your IP Telephony communications. Lost business and trade-secret information, for example, pursuant to a man-in-the-middle (MITM) attack, could be worth a million dollars to your company.

Keeping your voice communications safe from the same threats that can impact your data network is essential. In a world plagued with attackers and hackers, IP Telephony Security is an even more critical issue than ever before.

A secure voice network is the foundation of a successful organization.

What Can You Do to Safeguard Your IP Telephony Network?

Before taking any action to safeguard an IP Telephony network, it is imperative for organizations and businesses to understand the key security threats to their IP Telephony network and the proactive solutions they can adopt to mitigate these threats. The key lies in recognizing the problem before finding the solution.

Not all threats are present in all organizations. A commercial organization may be concerned primarily with toll fraud, whereas a government agency may need to prevent disclosure of sensitive information because of privacy or integrity concerns. Thus, organizations must evaluate what is the right level of security for them; what is the cost versus risk trade-off for them, and so on.

No single solution protects a network from a variety of threats. You need multiple layers of security. If one fails, others still stand. Therefore, you need to understand how to secure a Cisco IP Telephony network using a layered approach. Throughout this book, you discover ways to apply security measures in a step-by-step and layered approach, that is, leveraging defense-in-depth with—physical security, network security, application security, and endpoint security to secure your Cisco IP Telephony network.

In the next section, you will explore and understand the various types of attacks or hacks that can be launched against an IP Telephony network. Moreover, in next few chapters you will explore the step-by-step approach to develop an IP Telephony Security plan and understand how you can implement end-to-end security by developing an IP Telephony Security framework, evaluating cost versus risk, and understanding the level of security required for your organization.

IP Telephony Security Threats

Advances and trends in Information Technology have always outpaced the corresponding realistic yet necessary security requirements. These security requirements are often tackled only after these technologies have been widely deployed.

IP Telephony is no different. As IP Telephony adoption increases, so will its exposure to current and emerging security threats. Both "phreakers" (voice) and "hackers" (data) lurk around all the time, trying to find vulnerabilities and security slacks to do what they do the best—disrupt the IP Telephony network.

The following section gives you an insight to how hackers can attack an IP Telephony network.

How Do Hackers Attack an IP Telephony Network?

It is worthwhile to know about the ways a hacker can break into your IP Telephony network so that you know how to deter an attack. A hacker may use the following sequence of events to break into your IP Telephony network:

- **Foot printing:** Gather information about the target organization.

- **Scanning:** Search for an active or open target.

- **Enumeration:** Extract information from target(s) found during the scanning phase.

- **Exploit:** Eavesdrop, hijack streams, install backdoors, and debilitate an IP Telephony network.

- **Cover tracks:** Evade any detection by making a legible user accountable.

Let's go through these steps in detail to understand what happens behind the scenes and how a hacker can possibly breach your network defenses.

Foot Printing

A hacker typically starts with finding as much information as possible through the Internet by:

- Looking into WHOIS records

- Performing Internet searches

- Probing blog posts and boards where employees leave any information pertinent to their organization structure, phone numbers, extensions, and so on

- Researching the organization's websites for contact details

These searches give the hacker enough ammunition to launch the next wave of attack, which is scanning.

Scanning

The hacker will now try to scan for any active targets (live hosts) that can be compromised, by leveraging:

- Host discovery via ping sweeps

- SNMP sweeps

- TCP ping scans

- Port scans

The most common tools used for scanning are Nessus, Nmap, hping, snmpwalk, and so on.

Enumeration

During this stage, the hacker tries to extract usernames and passwords from hosts who were identified to be reachable and live on the victim's network using the following:

- SIP option, registration, and invite (automated or manual)

- Enumerate TFTP server

- SNMP enumeration

The most common VoIP security tools used for enumeration are SIPVicious, Nastysip, and Nmap to name a few.

Exploit

During this phase, the hacker or attacker exploits the IP Telephony network and compromises its integrity. The following attacks or hacks can be used to extract invaluable and confidential information:

- Eavesdropping

- DoS/DDoS attack

- Call redirection and hijacking

- Toll fraud

- Flooding attack

- Call pattern tracking

- Signaling and media manipulation

- Registration removal and rejection

This phase is the most devastating for the IP Telephony network and is a "Gold Mine" phase for the hacker/attacker. On one hand, calls can be eavesdropped, blocked, and manipulated, and on the other hand, calls can be hijacked and redirected. The IP Telephony platform now is vulnerable to toll fraud, registration rejection, flooding, and DoS attacks.

Covering Tracks

This is the last phase in which the hackers tries to cover their tracks to ambush the integrity of an IP Telephony network. Essentially, the hackers or attackers attempts to cover the detection of their presence by erasing any logs, using IP spoofing tools, using ARP spoofing tools, and by imitating valid user credentials, so the victim is someone innocent (a legal employee or member of organization). Moreover, Trojans and backdoor programs are usually installed on victim machines to allow for easy entry the next time an intrusion is attempted.

Equipped with the knowledge on how your IP Telephony network can be compromised by an insider or an outside attacker or hacker, let's now go over some of the key security threats and their mitigation techniques.

What Are IP Telephony Security Threats and Countermeasures?

It is a war out there between Cisco IP Telephony administrators and phreakers or hackers. To be successful, you must know your enemy as well as your own strengths and weaknesses. As you know by now that IP Telephony networks share the same weaknesses as their underlying foundation data networks, it is time to explore the cause that phreakers or hackers can leverage to take advantage of any weakness in your IP Telephony network. To truly know the threats, you must consider both external and internal threats. Internal security threats are perceived by the employees or from within the secure zone, and the external security threats originate from public network(s) or nonsecure zone.

The next section highlights the main threats targeting the IP Telephony system.

Let's understand what each one of these threats is all about and how you can counter them, as explained in the next section, following which you'll be introduced to various commercial and free tools available that can be used to exploit and attack an IP Telephony network.

Threats

This section highlights the various threats that can adversely distress your IP Telephony network:

- **Eavesdropping:** Refers to loss of private or confidential information because of sniffing, scanning, and interception (tapping) of voice calls. If calls can be sniffed, conversations can be replayed or eavesdropped; there is a monumental risk associated with non-secure IP Telephony systems and ample opportunity for phreakers and hackers. While hacking calls, a hacker, for example, could acquire access to financial material. Because of the open nature of IP networks and especially the low trust level in the Internet, privacy is a commonly raised concern when comparing IP Telephony solutions against traditional telephony solutions. Free and paid tools are available on the Internet that can be used to sniff or passively scan the voice traffic.

- **Manipulation:** Integrity of information means that information remains unaltered by unauthorized users. In the context of IP Telephony, this refers to the loss of integrity of voice communications (alteration of voice or video traffic) by hijacking calls and injecting or altering the contents of voice packets (man-in-the-middle attack). If voice call signaling or media messages can be intercepted, they can be modified, and the recipient (listener) can be made to listen to what the attacker or hacker wants and not what the original party (speaker) conveyed.

- **Impersonation:** Identity spoofing is not limited to humans (for instance, the person behind a telephone) but can also extend to devices, such as Cisco CallManager, a voice gateway, or an IP Phone. Impersonation in the form of frame-tagging (VLAN-hopping) and MAC or IP address spoofing gives attackers the ability to impersonate a VoIP phone.

- **Denial-of-service (DoS):** This refers to the prevention of access to voice network services by bombarding voice servers, proxy servers, or voice gateways with malicious or malformed voice packets. This leaves users deprived of the services or resources they would normally expect to have. For example, voicemail, IM, and SMS (notification) services in IP Telephony systems can be the targets of message flooding attacks. These attacks cause loss of functionality.

- **Toll fraud:** Refers to when an individual or an organization devises method(s) to gain unauthorized or unsolicited access to IP Telephony resources to gain the ability to dial long-distance calls. When access is gained, it can lead to large telephone bills, accumulating in a period of days or even hours.

■ **SPIT and Vhishing:** Spam over Internet Telephony (SPIT) is equivalent to unnecessary e-mail (SPAM). A dedicated hacker can release a flurry of calls to a targeted IP Telephony system and a particular IP Phone. This can cause that IP Phone to be overloaded (unable to take any calls) and the IP Telephony system to be busy for that endpoint. Now, imagine this attack scaled to multiple IP Phones. Not only can it leave the IP Phones unusable (because per line capability for taking calls will be well overshot), it will also busy out the PSTN channels and the IP PBX's capacity to handle calls. If SPIT were not enough, hackers can also ploy Vhishing to lure IP Telephony users into yielding personal information such as credit card number, bank accounts, Social Security numbers, and so on under the disguise of needing this information for a legitimate reason.

Countermeasures

At a high level, following suggestions can help prevent loss of integrity, privacy, and threats arising out of impersonation, DoS attacks, toll-fraud, and so on.

■ Be up to date on new and changing threats.

■ Follow best practices for VoIP network security (as mentioned throughout this book).

■ Implement tools to monitor and report of IP Telephony use.

■ Follow a layered security approach instead of only a network or an application security approach.

■ Implement an IP Telephony Security policy for your organization.

To overcome the concern of loss of privacy, DoS attacks, hijacking of media, signaling streams, and so on,, it is highly recommended to use the defense-in-depth (also known as layered security) approach (as detailed throughout this book) because there is no single system or way to stop or evade privacy threats. Cisco IP Telephony applications, endpoints, and Cisco network gear empowers you to leverage the built-in security features. These features and associated leading practice recommendations on planning, designing, deployment of secure IP Telephony networks are described and discussed in detail in following chapters.

You will learn more about the end-to-end security methodology for IP Telephony and layered security approach throughout this book. As we explore the world of Cisco IP Telephony Security, you will discover the best practices and ways to secure your Cisco IP Telephony network.

An Insight to VoIP Security Tools

This section gives you insight to various VoIP security tools. These tools are meant to test an IP Telephony network's resilience and susceptibility against attacks. However, they can be used by hackers and phreakers to attack an IP Telephony network. These tools can be used to launch attacks against VoIP systems, such as hijacking media and signaling streams (MITM attack), sniffing RTP traffic (eavesdropping), rebooting phones (DoS attack), flooding phones with calls (DoS attack), and reassigning the devices (impersonation) unlawfully to other users.

There are many VoIP security tools available on the Internet, some free, whereas other are commercial tools. As discussed earlier, on one hand these tools can be used to compromise integrity of an IP Telephony network, and on the other hand, they can be used to assess the security posture of an IP Telephony network, find any security gaps, and fill them.

The following section gives you an insight to various VoIP security and penetration tools available which can be used in favor of or against your IP Telephony network's security.

IP Telephony Security/Penetration Tools

Now, that you know about the possible ways a hacker could possibly compromise your IP Telephony network as well as the threats which lurk around your IP Telephony network, it is time to go over different VoIP security tools that can be used effectively for and against your IP Telephony network.

Following is the list in which the VoIP security tools can be broadly categorized:

- Sniffing tools

- Scanning and enumeration tools

- Flooding/DoS tools

- Signaling and media manipulation tools

Sniffing Tools

Sniffing tools are some of the most popular tools available to promiscuously sniff the data off your IP Telephony network:

- **Cain & Abel:** It can reconstruct RTP media calls. This tool has features such as APR (ARP Poisoning Routing), which enables attackers to sniff on switched LANs and perform MITM attacks.

- **UCSniff:** An assessment tool that enables users to rapidly test for the threat of unauthorized VoIP eavesdropping. UCSniff supports SIP and SCCP signaling. It supports G.729, G.723, G.726, G.722, G.711 u-law, G.711 a-law voice codecs, and H.264 Video codecs. It can reconstruct the voice conversation and has features such as MITM (ARP Poisoning mode).

- **VOMIT:** Can convert a Cisco IP Phone dialogue into a wave file that can be played with any ordinary sound player. It however works only with G.711 codecs.

- **VoIPong:** Detects VoIP calls on a pipeline (only G.711 codec) and can dump actual conversation into wave files. It supports SIP, H.323, SCCP, RTP, and RTCP protocols.

- **VoIP Hopper:** A GPLv3 licensed security tool that rapidly runs a VLAN Hop into the Voice VLAN on specific Ethernet switches. VoIP Hopper does this by mimicking the behavior of an IP Phone.

- **Wireshark:** One of the most famous network traffic analyzer, which can capture RTP and VoIP signaling traffic (SIP, SCCP, H.323, MGCP, and so on). It can reconstruct the voice conversation and play it back as a .wav file.

Scanning and Enumeration Tools

Scanning and enumeration tools can not only be used by an attacker to scan for active and live targets for IP, ports, services, and so on, they can also to gain valuable information about your IP Telephony network.

- **Nessus:** One of the most famous vulnerability scanners that supports credentialed or un-credentialed port scanning and network-based vulnerability scanning leading to vulnerability analysis. It can be used to scan for outdated services, vulnerability, and security exploits.

- **Nmap:** An open source utility for network exploration or security auditing. It supports Advance techniques for mapping networks filled with IP filters, firewalls, routers, and other obstacles. This includes many port scanning mechanisms (both TCP and UDP), OS detection, version detection, ping sweeps, and so on.

- **SIPVicious:** A set of tools used to audit or attack SIP-based IP Telephony systems. It has a SIP scanner, a SIP phone extension range finder, and an online password cracker for SIP PBX and provides the ability to manage sessions and generate reports.

Flooding/DoS Tools

The information or session flooding and DoS attack tools present a new attack vector to bring down a functional and healthy IP Telephony system. Thus, you should be aware of the various tools available, which hackers bring into play to carry out their dirty work, so that you can take preventive measures:

- **Scapy:** Forges or decodes packets of a wide number of protocols and send them on the wire, capture them, and match requests and replies. It can send invalid frames, combine techniques (for example, VLAN hopping plus ARP cache poisoning) and perform VoIP decoding.

- **RTP Flooder:** Creates RTP packets that can flood a phone or proxy thereby leaving the target unusable for the legal user.

- **UDP Flooder:** Used to send numerous UDP packets at a pre-selected speed. It uses a specific port to attack and also uses some imaginary source address.

- **Nastysip:** A simple Linux-program that generates bogus SIP-messages and can send them to any peer.

Signaling and Media-Manipulation Tools

These tools help an attacker or hacker to manipulate the information and have the listener listen to what the attacker or hacker wants and not what the original party conveyed. Moreover, these tools can be used to hijack calls:

- **RTP Injector:** An attack tool that can be used to inject random audio into established RTP connections. The tool can identify active conversations and can enumerate the media codec in use, allowing for the injection of an arbitrary audio file that is automatically transcoded into the necessary format required.

- **Fuzzy Packet:** Used to manipulate messages through the injection, capturing, receiving, or sending of packets generated over a network. It can fuzz RTP and includes built-in ARP poisoning option.

- **H225regregject:** Enables you to disconnect H.323 calls. It can watch a network to figure out whether a call is happening. When it finds a call, it can send a Registration Reject packet, which will effectively end the call.

- **SIP-Kill:** Simple yet effective, this tool can sniff for SIP-INVITEs and tear down the call.

Business Challenges and Cisco IP Telephony Security Responses

Where there is security, there are challenges ranging from ethical concerns to technical or procedural complexity for the application of security. It is not unusual to face a multitude of challenges when you prepare to secure your IP Telephony network.

There are quite a few questions, which unfold during conception phase, while developing an approach to IP Telephony Security. The majority of these revolve around various technical, solution, and business goals.

Common Business Challenges Associated with IP Telephony Security

Let us look at some of the major business challenges, which are likely to be encountered while preparing for planning, executing, and optimizing IP Telephony Security:

- **Solution challenge:** The major challenge is to identify the customer security risks and vulnerability, how to develop a security policy around it, and how to maintain stability and robustness of the IP Telephony solution.

- **Ethical challenge:** Every IP Telephony user has a responsibility to promote ethical use of the IP Telephony system and any relevant information. However, what is the remediation when people overlook ethics?

- **Technical challenge:** How to implement IP Telephony Security and develop similar standard(s) applicable to corporate users dispersed over multiple region or locations.

- **Environmental challenge:** How to deploy IP Telephony Security around a network which is not all Cisco equipment (inter-operating with other vendors), which can be difficult or sometimes, impossible.

Cisco IP Telephony Security Responses

There's no "silver bullet" to address all these issues. However, Cisco IP Telephony offers the following best practice recommendations and solutions to address these issues:

- **Solution challenge:** This can be addressed by understanding the needs of the organization or business, through security risk assessment, working on a detailed security plan with internal and external customers or stakeholders, followed by a phased deployment approach to implement just the right level of security. (You learn more about an IP Telephony Security policy development approach and determining the right level of IP Telephony Security required in Chapter 4).

- **Ethical challenge:** Although there is no black-and-white procedure to tackle this challenge, IP Telephony Security policy can help clear out many grey areas. As an IP Telephony Security policy is driven by the corporate security policy, it should lay down specifics of the level of access, ease of access, information access review or audit, and so on. Moreover, employees' awareness of the corporate security policies helps reduce the likelihood of insider threats.

- **Technical challenge:** This can be addressed via the Cisco leading practices to deploy and secure IP Telephony technologies across the globe. Cisco Advance Services (AS) teams have deployed IP Telephony Security solutions for many organizations worldwide in different market segments ranging from finance to manufacturing to government to pharmaceuticals.

- **Environmental challenge:** This can be addressed by keeping the IP Telephony Security solution based on industry standards. The Cisco IP Telephony Security implementation conforms to the industry wide standards (for example SSL and AES) and can be leveraged by third-party vendors and products for secure integration with Cisco IP Telephony network.

Summary

Just as you wouldn't leave your doors unlocked and your precious belongings in the open, you do not want to leave your IP Telephony network open to attacks from within and outside the organization either. In This chapter, we tried to unfold the meaning of IP Telephony Security and understand the logic behind securing an IP Telephony network.

This chapter looked at some of the basic yet important logical measures you can take to ensure the security of your IP Telephony network, and the rationale behind why you should secure your Cisco IP Telephony network. You learned about the security threats that lurk around your IP Telephony network, the detrimental effects of leaving an IP Telephony network unsecured, how attackers or hackers can attack an IP Telephony network, and the ways in which various security tools can be used or abused.

This book is primarily focused on understanding the Cisco IP Telephony network security principles, features, and protocols that can help you in the successful implementation of comprehensive end-to-end Cisco IP Telephony Security. As you go through the various chapters of this book, you will learn about ways by which you can secure your Cisco IP Telephony network. This will ultimately result in you gaining a deep level of understanding of IP Telephony network security-related issues and their resolution. At this point, you have a brief understanding of IP Telephony network security and its importance to your organization.

In following chapters, you learn in depth how you can go about securing your Cisco IP Telephony network in a holistic manner and build a concrete understanding on Cisco IP Telephony Security fundamentals.

Chapter 2

Cisco IP Telephony Security Building Blocks

Now that you have a fair idea about the need to secure your IP Telephony network and the threats that pester the sanctity of your IP Telephony network, it is time to look into the methodology that lays out the path to define how end-to-end IP Telephony Security can be achieved. It takes a little work, but this chapter shows you how to protect your IP Telephony network from external and internal threats. This rudimentary information can help you make the right choices to best suit your needs.

This chapter covers the following topics:

- Introduction to IP Telephony Security methodology
- IP Telephony Security architecture
- Define IP Telephony components that should be secured

Introduction to IP Telephony Security Methodology

Let's try to figure out the IP Telephony (Cisco IP Telephony) Security methodology because this will be your ammunition against IP Telephony Security threats, issues, and challenges.

Understanding the IP Telephony Security Methodology

As discussed in Chapter 1, "What Is IP Telephony Security and Why Do You Need It?," the better the reach and availability of the IP Telephony network, the greater its vulnerability and exposure to threats from within and outside the organization. Thus, it is important to understand that IP Telephony Security is neither a one-time nor a one-step process. Chapter 1 briefly discussed multilayer security strategy (defense-in-depth approach) and how one layer of security should be built upon another.

IP Telephony Security is a broad topic, which can be best summed up by the abbreviation CIA, that is:

- **Confidentiality:** Ensures that a voice conversation cannot be intercepted by anyone not authorized to do so

- **Integrity:** Ensures that a voice conversation and its contents cannot be modified

- **Availability:** Enables system availability to support voice conversations to take place as and when required

Keeping CIA in mind, let's explore the Cisco IP Telephony layered security approach in detail, which gives a 360° robust and scalable security.

A secure network is the foundation for a secure IP Telephony network.

A secure IP Telephony network is an asset for an organization.

Figure 2-1 shows the methodology of stepwise and layered approach to IP Telephony Security. However, because it is empty (for now), it gives you a chance to deduce how different components can be interlinked to provide end-to-end security to your IP Telephony network.

Can you guess what goes in each layer or block of the pyramid structure (see Figure 2-1)?

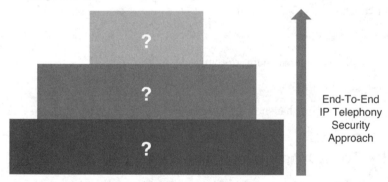

Figure 2-1 *Layered Security Approach for End-to-End Security*

Write down what you think will fit into each block and why it should be there. This will help you realize the importance of each component and the underlying principle of it being in that order.

Now that you have translated your thought process into black-and-white on paper, let's go over the IP Telephony Security methodology, step by step and try to understand how you can defend your IP Telephony network from vivid threats and sort out where each piece of the puzzle fits.

When you visualize IP Telephony, what do you think of? Call control, voice messaging, PSTN connectivity, IP endpoints, and so on. Now, when you want to secure these components, what do you think should be the approach to secure them and to ensure that the security applied is foolproof? The immediate answer that would come to you might be to apply encryption and authentication for signaling and media, CAPF, class of restriction, secure conferencing, secure trunks, and so forth.

How about when someone breaks into the perimeter router or attempts an IP spoof or MAC spoof attack, or manipulates ARP table on a switch? Did you think about that?

In addition, did you consider how you are going to deploy security, if the level of security you want to deploy is sufficient, for your IP Telephony network? Will applying security break something crucial in your environment?

If you did not consider any of these points, read further to understand how IP Telephony Security builds from ground up, and how you can successfully secure your Cisco IP Telephony network. In the next section, you will find the IP Telephony Security methodology demystified and explained.

Demystifying IP Telephony Security Methodology

Figure 2-2 shows the methodology of a stepwise and layered approach to IP Telephony Security.

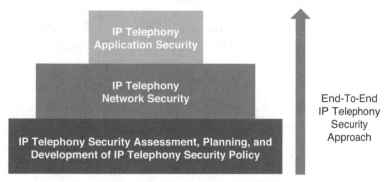

Figure 2-2   *IP Telephony Network Security Methodology*

This methodology is a clear indication that the IP Telephony Security will be only stable, supple, robust, and scalable if the smaller block is placed on top of a larger block (here blocks are representative of various activities and their order of execution) and not vice versa. The idea behind adopting this methodology is to provide pervasive security to protect the corporate assets.

This methodology helps lay a foundation for end-to-end IP Telephony Security. Let us look into the various steps to secure an IP Telephony network and understand the rationale behind each step. More details on an end-to-end security approach, IP Telephony

Security life cycle, and IP Telephony Security policy are covered in Chapter 4, "Cisco IP Telephony Security Framework."

The next section explores the IP Telephony Security methodology to understand the importance of each layer and how you can adopt this layered approach to secure your IP Telephony network.

Essentially, even before an IP Telephony network is secured, it will be worthwhile to ask yourself the following questions:

- **The level of security required:** What is the level of security, which is right for my IP Telephony network?

- **The security policy to govern the overall process:** Do I have an effective security policy to govern the security of my IP Telephony network?

- **Planning and preparation to deploy security:** Have I done the right amount of planning and preparation before I leap into securing my IP Telephony network?

The answers to these questions will determine the need, the level of security, and the prerequisites to secure your IP Telephony network. Chapter 4 helps you answer these questions and much more.

After these questions have been answered, the next obvious step is to start deployment of IP Telephony Security adopting bottom-up approach:

- Understand IP Telephony Security architecture as pertinent to your IP Telephony network, perform Risk assessment, and formulate an IP Telephony Security policy.

- Assess the current security level (if any security has been deployed) to highlight the security gaps.

- Secure the underlying network and enable device security (physical, Layer 2, Layer 3, and perimeter security).

- Secure IP Telephony applications (Call-control, voice messaging, presence, end-points, and so on).

The next section covers the IP Telephony Security architecture and its importance in unifying the security processes vital to the sanctity of your IP Telephony network.

IP Telephony Security Architecture

Security architecture is the unifying construction and services that help implement security policy, standards, and risk management decisions. In other words, it is the capability of a system (network) to protect the confidentiality and integrity of data (or processed information) as well as to bring the key areas of concern for the enterprise to focus, thereby highlighting the decision criteria. In context of IP Telephony Security, the security architecture should ideally lay down a security framework, following which the IP Telephony and security administrators can define IP Telephony Security mechanisms, define IP Telephony Security strategy, follow the IP Telephony Security life cycle, and consequently, apply the framework to secure the IP Telephony environment so that a robust and resilient IP communications network is achievable. Security architecture, risk management, and security policy govern the security processes and the defense-in-depth posture.

You may ask, "Why is security architecture important for IP Telephony Security?" The simple answer is this: to defend against ever evolving, organized, and complex attacks from within or outside the organization; arbitrary security mechanisms or solutions do not fare well. To safeguard the organization's assets and information, it is essential to have a reference architecture in place which acts as a bible for the network administrators, IP Telephony administrators, engineering team, and key decision makers.

"Network Security is only as strong as the weakest link."

Source: http://www.cisco.com/cisco/web/solutions/small_business/resource_center/ articles/secure_my_business/as_strong_as_the_weakest_link/index.html.

Note: You learn more about IP Telephony Security policy/strategy and risk management in Chapter 4.

In a nutshell, the IP Telephony Security architecture is an iterative process that unifies the business, technical, and security domains.

The four supporting pillars of IP Telephony Security architecture are as following:

- **IP Telephony architecture risk assessment:** Assess the business impact to critical business assets, the probability, and the impact of security threats and vulnerabilities. Essentially, definition of assets and their relevant risk appetite is the stepping stone to developing a successful IP Telephony Security strategy. Risk assessment specifics are discussed in Chapter 4.

- **IP Telephony Security architecture and design:** The organizational security policies, standards, and risk management decisions drive the security architecture, and the blueprint of the security processes.

- **Implementation of IP Telephony application and network security:** In this phase, security processes and services are implemented, operated, and managed. Implementation of IP Telephony (network or application) security, following IP Telephony Security strategy for a green field project or organic growth can be done during the design phase (conceptual security specifics converted to actual on-ground security measures), in a phased approach, or concurrently with network security deployment.

- **IP Telephony network operation and monitoring:** It's an ongoing process, which monitors and manages the operations of system security. This implies that any new or existing vulnerabilities will be discovered during this phase.

You will see these building pillars and stages reflected in the next sections, as well as in the next two chapters. Let's now explore the security methodology and understand how it paves the path for implementing end-to-end security.

Exploring IP Telephony Security Methodology and Defining Security Architecture

Let's explore each block of the IP Telephony Security methodology pyramid to understand why every block of the pyramid is important in its own self, and the reason behind its order of placement, to achieve end-to-end security.

Let's start with the fundamental building block and the base, that is, IP Telephony Security assessment, planning, and policy development; then we will progress upward to IP Telephony network security block, and finally, explore the last block, IP Telephony application security.

IP Telephony Security Assessment and Security Policy Development

This section focuses on the basic and most critical layer of the security pyramid, where an organization would follow its corporate security strategy, mixed with the IP Telephony Security requirements to assess the IP Telephony network security followed by planning and ultimately leading to development of the IP Telephony Security strategy/policy (The words security policy and security strategy will be used interchangeably. Although, both mean the same semantically, some organizations prefer using one over other.)

IP Telephony Security policy development is a critical step, and a substantial amount of time needs to be spent to develop an effective policy, which revolves around the corporate security policy. The process of developing IP Telephony Security policy as well as an in-depth analysis of the same is done in Chapter 4. IP Telephony risk assessment is also covered in Chapter 4.

As depicted in Figure 2-3, the base block is composed of IP Telephony Security assessment, followed by planning, and development of an IP Telephony-specific security strategy.

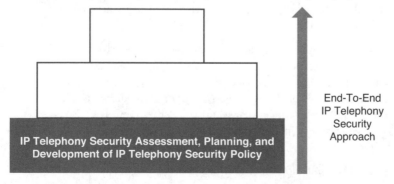

Figure 2-3   *IP Telephony Security Methodology: Layer 1*

Network security assessment may mean different things for network administrators, engineers, or architects, depending on their perception. For some, it more or less corresponds to inventory management. For others, it is a process similar to penetration testing, which enables them to see a network through the eyes of the attacker or hacker.

There is a fine line between a full penetration study (in which vulnerabilities are detected) and an assessment procedure (in which an overall picture of the potential vulnerabilities and weaknesses is drawn). Some of the tools are common in both activities, including network scanners, manipulation tools, and enumeration tools (NMAP, Nessus, and so on). However, security assessment is less invasive and focuses more on providing the overall security level and opportunities for improvement for an IP Telephony network and its available services.

Figure 2-4 shows the IP Telephony Security strategy planning and development, as driven by corporate security strategy.

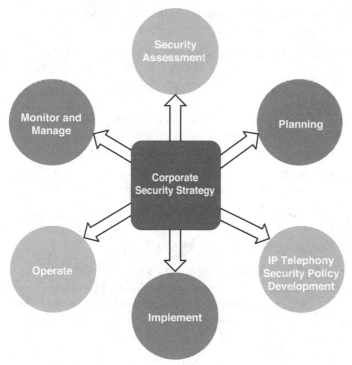

Figure 2-4 *IP Telephony Security Cycle*

A typical IP Telephony Security assessment ideally embraces the following:

■ **Discovery and data gathering:** Review overall IP Telephony Security requirements in accord with an organization's business goals, objectives, and technical requirements.

■ **Information analysis:** Evaluate the effectiveness of each IP Telephony Security control and its designated security function.

■ **Recommendations:** Provide a comprehensive report that documents IP Telephony network security control gaps (application and network level security), security risk analysis, and recommendations for remediation.

Note: All these activities can be carried out by using either automated tools or manually.

Cisco offers an IP Telephony Security assessment and Security Strategy development service. For more details, visit the following URL:

http://www.cisco.com/en/US/services/ps10658/security_architectureassessment_servfeds.pdf

By this service, clients can benefit from recommendations focused on alleviating risk mitigation concerns and addressing required security controls and countermeasures.

Visit the following URL to find out more details about all Cisco security service offerings:

http://www.cisco.com/en/US/products/svcs/ps2961/ps2952/serv_group_home.html

The next obvious step in the cycle is to plan for and develop a viable IP Telephony Security strategy. As described earlier, it is an essential component of the overall IP Telephony Security framework and is described in great detail in Chapter 4.

After an IP Telephony Security strategy is formulated, and IP Telephony Security implementation planning is in place, it is time to proceed with deployment of next phase: network security.

IP Telephony Network Security Implementation

It has been discussed numerous times previously: "Without a secure network an IP Telephony application cannot be considered to be secure." It's more or less like an inverted pyramid, which is unstable and vulnerable. As important as it is to secure the IP Telephony application itself, it is yet more important to secure the basis to implement the application, the underlying network.

Let's try and understand what falls in this block of security methodology and forms another layer of a robust and supple secure IP Telephony network. Figure 2-5 shows the network security implementation phase.

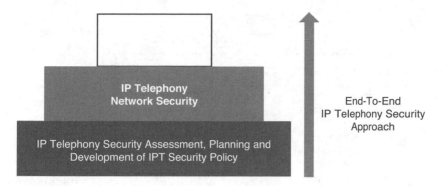

Figure 2-5 *IP Telephony Security Methodology: Layer 2 (and lower Layer)*

It is important to understand that network security implementation can be done parallel to IP Telephony application security. It is not necessary to divide these in phases, that is, network security followed by application security if the level of IP Telephony Security has been deployed is easy to medium, and if the security strategy and planning have been done truthfully. You learn more about IP Telephony network security levels in Chapter 4.

The following components form the second layer: the network security layer of IP Telephony Security methodology:

1. Physical security

2. Layer 2 security

3. Layer 3 security

4. Perimeter security

Let's consider security implementation at the different network layers and their importance.

Figure 2-6 gives an insight to the various OSI layers between two systems participating in a Voice over IP call, and which component of security is significant to what layer. Moreover, it also illustrates an end-to-end security approach, encompassing all layers.

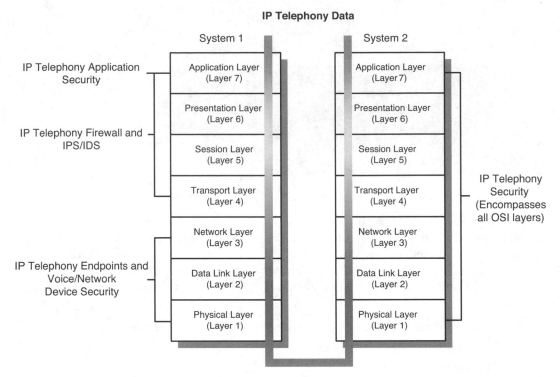

Figure 2-6   *IP Telephony Security Across OSI Layers*

Physical Security

When you think about physical security, what do you think of? Most people think of locks, cameras, security card readers, and maybe even security guards. In context of Cisco IP Telephony, physical security implies that the network gear (routers, switches, IP Telephony servers, endpoints, and so on) are secured from unauthorized access, by means of one or more tools described earlier. In other words, it refers to the task to ascertain that only authorized people have physical access to your IP Telephony and underlying supporting network systems.

You may ask, "What are the main threats to physical security?" The most frequent threats are as follows:

- Theft of equipment or related data or information

- Destruction of equipment

Depending on the physical location and criticality of the site and information, some of these threats may rank higher on the list than others. Even organizations with the most modern network security standards can remain vulnerable to some physical and low-tech threats. This topic is covered in depth in Chapter 5, "Cisco IP Telephony Physical Security."

What is the importance of physical security?

Physical security is an important and vital component for the protection of corporate information. The ability to gain physical access to IP Telephony servers and network equipment by unauthorized people can be devastating.

Layer 2 Security

Layer 2 security is one of the most disregarded aspects of information security because most of the logical security efforts are concentrated on Layer 3 and above. Why, you may ask? Because, Layer 2 network the secure zone (inside) without any direct interaction with the outside world unlike, for example, Layer 3 routing traffic. The consequences for not deploying Layer 2 security mechanisms (such as DHCP snooping, 802.1x, VLAN trunk locked down, and so on) would mean that hackers who manage to break in to a single switch or endpoint in your network can expand their reach in no time, and the results are quite evident.

The hackers or attackers can

- Sniff LAN for passwords and break into critical systems (including IP Telephony servers and endpoints).

- Erase your LAN switch or router configuration.

- Change the root bridge causing network to reconverge as they may please.

- Lock out IP Telephony endpoint ports, causing the system to de-register phones or reject endpoint registration, and so on.

These are only a few examples of Layer 2 threats. Implementing security measures to the upper layers (Layers 3 and higher) does not benefit your IP Telephony network if Layer 2 is compromised. Although, understanding and preparing for network threats is important, hardening Layer 2 is imperative. Chapter 6, "Cisco IP Telephony Layer 2 Security," covers the topic of Layer 2 security in detail.

Layer 3 Security

Network layer is where the packets are routed and connections are made and concluded. An endpoint or a host typically has a network layer address, in other words, an IP address (per interface). This address is not only the identity of the node, it also tends to make Layer 3 addressing critical to network topology. The network layer is, however, vulnerable to the following attacks:

- DoS attacks

- IP spoofing attacks

- Man-in-the-middle attacks

- Route poisoning attacks

- Information privacy tribulations and so on.

Because voice media (UDP) and signaling (TCP/UDP) data grams are encapsulated in IP packets at Layer 3, it not only becomes crucial to secure the network layer, but also its essential to secure the layers above it. This is because network layer security provides end-to-end security across a routed network, providing services such as data integrity, authentication, and encryption.

You will learn about Layer 3 security mechanisms in Chapter 7, "Cisco IP Telephony Layer 3 Security," and this gives you a prospect about how you can go about securing your IP network infrastructure.

Perimeter Security

Perimeter in context to IP networks is defined as the transition point where information or data from an internal (trusted and protected) network transits to an outside (uncontrolled and untrusted) network or vice versa; in other words, a point of interaction where the internal network interfaces with the rest of the world. In the context of IP Telephony network's perimeter security, it's the point of interaction of your internal network with outside network(s). Cisco IOS routers, Cisco ASA Firewalls, and Intrusion Prevention Systems (IPS) or Intrusion Detection Systems (IDS) are mostly deployed at the perimeter and take care of Layer 3 to Layer 7 security concerns. Thus, the trust condition(s) must be well defined to apply security strategy appropriately. You will comprehend the trust conditions and perimeter security specifics in Chapter 8, "Perimeter Security with Cisco Adaptive Security Appliance" and Appendix B, "Cisco IP Telephony: Firewalling and Intrusion Prevention."

Note: Firewalls and IPS/IDS can also be deployed within the network to shield the IP Telephony equipment from internal attacks.

When the data transits to/from outside world, multiple attack vectors and various threats come into play. Threats that originate from the outside (untrusted environment) can be broadly classified as follows:

- Intrusion attempts

- Malware (viruses, Trojans, and worms)

- Exploited vulnerabilities

- Information privacy and integrity attacks

An in-depth approach to perimeter security is covered in Chapter 8.

IP Telephony Application Security Implementation

Finally, it's time to pay a visit to the last block in the security methodology pyramid. With a well-though-out and laid-out security plan and strategy and an underlying network secured, now it is time to secure your IP Telephony applications.

Let's see what goes in this block of security methodology and forms the final layer of a secure IP Telephony network. Figure 2-7 illustrates the IP Telephony application security implementation layer/phase.

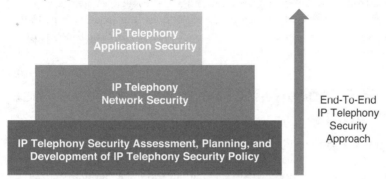

Figure 2-7   *IP Telephony Security Methodology: Layer 3 (and Lower Layers)*

It all comes down to IP Telephony application security that you have applied excellent security through the underlying layers. From the point of view of IP Telephony Security, the application layer can be considered as the dominion where user interaction takes place and the high-level processes function, above the network layer.

It is essential to understand that if the vulnerabilities lie within the application, then firewalls, IPS/IDS, or any underneath layer mechanisms will not be sufficient to protect the system from a host of attacks. The security controls at lower layers would only be able to address their relevant layer of protocol(s), and not the issues that transpire above. The services and the applications themselves need to be secured. Updated or patched software, server hardening, secure (encrypted) communications, and strong authentication mechanisms provide for resilient and robust application layer security.

IP Telephony application layer deals with the high-level functions of the user interface, application programs accessing the network, and interaction with and between endpoints (signaling and media). In a nutshell, all functions not pertaining directly to network operations occur at this layer. These can be divided into application protocol layer and IP Telephony application layer. From a protocol layer perspective, the following user-oriented and endpoint protocols all fall within the application layer:

- HTTP/HTTPS
- TFTP/SFTP

- DNS
- SMTP
- Telnet/SSH/RDP/SNMP
- SCCP/SIP
- MGCP/H.323/SIP

On the other hand, from an IP Telephony application layer perspective, the security of IP Telephony servers (server hardening) and relevant applications (for example, Call Control, voice messaging, and so on) running on top of appliance or virtualized environment are considered part of the application layer.

Defining the IP Telephony Network Components That Should Be Secured

It is implicit that the various elements of IP Telephony network are well defined in order to have a crystal clear picture of what you must secure. Let's go over the different IP Telephony network components (both network and application) that should be secured to enable end-to-end IP Telephony Security.

IP Telephony Network Elements That Should Be Secured

A Cisco IP Telephony network broadly consists of the following elements, which in an ideal world should be secured against internal and external threats:

- Call Control (Cisco Unified Communications Manager, Cisco Unified Communications Manager Express, and Survivable Remote Site Telephony)
- Voice messaging (Cisco Unity, Cisco Unity Connection, and Cisco Unity Express)
- Presence information (Cisco Unified Presence Server)
- Voice gateway
- Voice gatekeeper
- Session Border Controller (Cisco Unified Border Element)
- Endpoints (Cisco Unified IP Phones—wired and wireless, Cisco IP Communicator, and Cisco Unified Personal Communicator)
- Underlying network equipment (Cisco Catalyst switches, Cisco IOS routers, Cisco ASA Firewall, and Cisco Intrusion Prevention and Detection Systems)
- Physical components (rack, cameras, card readers, and so on)

Table 2-1 lists the various components and elements that comprise the IP Telephony network, which should be secured. Notice that each IP Telephony network component has been associated with the following:

- **Component reference:** Explains where in the hierarchy of the IP Telephony network that component fits, for example, if the component is an application, voice equipment, or a network device

- **Type of security applicable for each component:** Explains whether security applicable is physical security, Layer 2 security, Layer 3 security, Layer 4 to Layer 7 security or application layer security

- **Possible locations:** Explains where a particular IP Telephony component is expected to be found in the network

Table 2-1   *IP Telephony Network Elements That Should Be Secured*

IP Telephony Network Component	Component Reference	Type of Security Applicable	Possible Location(s)
IP Telephony equipment rack	IP Telephony servers, network equipment	Physical security	IP Telephony data center, remote site
IP Telephony server switch	IP Telephony servers, network equipment	Layer 2 security	IP Telephony data center, remote site
IP Telephony server router	Network equipment	Layer 3/IOS security	IP Telephony data center, remote site
IP Telephony firewall	Network equipment	Perimeter security (Layer 3 to Layer 7)	IP Telephony data center, remote site
CUCM server	IP Telephony application	Application security	IP Telephony data center, remote site
Unity/CUC server	IP Telephony application	Application security	IP Telephony data center, remote site
CUPS server	IP Telephony application	Application security	IP Telephony data center, remote site
CUCME /CUE module	Voice Router	Application/IOS security	IP Telephony data center, Remote site, home office
Voice gateways	Voice router	Application/IOS security	IP Telephony data center, remote site, home office
Gatekeeper	Voice router	Application/IOS security	IP Telephony data center
CUBE	Voice router	Application/IOS security	IP Telephony data center

IP Telephony Network Component	Component Reference	Type of Security Applicable	Possible Location(s)
IPS/IDS	Network equipment	Perimeter security	IP Telephony data center, remote site
IP Phones (endpoints)	End user	Endpoint security	IP Telephony data center, remote site, home office
Soft phones (endpoints)	End user	Endpoint security	IP Telephony data center, remote site, home office, telecommuters
IP Telephony endpoint switch	Network equipment	Layer 2 security	IP Telephony data center, remote site, home office
IP Telephony remote site router	Network equipment	Layer 3/IOS security	IP Telephony data center, remote site, home office

As it is apparent, each IP Telephony network component has a pre-determined role to play and in its own rights should be secured.

Summary

When designing a secure IP Telephony network, some objectives need to be taken into consideration. The aim of implementing IP Telephony network security is to protect Cisco IP Telephony networks against attacks, while ensuring data and system confidentiality, availability, and integrity.

This chapter covered the basics of IP Telephony Security methodology and architecture and the physical layer, Layer 2, Layer 3, perimeter, and application layer security issues. In a nutshell, the IP Telephony Security methodology is neither a one-time nor a one-step process. The three layers/phases that form the security pyramid also outline the basis of IP Telephony Security methodology and architecture. Moreover, now you know that although each layer is accountable for the security of its own protocol(s), it is indirectly responsible for the security of the layers above it.

Now that you learned about IP Telephony Security methodology and the various components that are the building pillars of a secure IP Telephony network, it is time to know about the security controls for each of these elements. In the next chapter, you will comprehend the various security controls for the different IP Telephony components and get an insight to how end-to-end security can be achieved in a typical Enterprise Cisco IP Telephony network.

Chapter 3

What Can You Secure and How Can You Secure It?

The key to secure an IP Telephony network requires taking into account voice, data, and video communications as a coherent system (converged communications network) and employing a multilayered, homogeneously applied defense construct for the system infrastructure. This goes uniformly for call control, management, applications, and endpoints. The security solution should be layered with multiple controls and fortifications at various network levels. This minimizes the possibility that a single point of failure could compromise overall security. In other words, if one security layer is contravened, other defensive barriers are still available to deter the attack.

This chapter helps you work with your network security design so that you can apply a layered approach to secure your IP Telephony network. In this chapter, you will learn about the layered security approach (defense-in-depth) and the security controls that can be applied to your IP Telephony network to enable layered security. Furthermore, you will comprehend how to secure a typical enterprise grade IP Telephony network by implementing these IP Telephony Security controls.

This chapter covers the following topics:

- Explore layered security approach to IP Telephony Security

- Cisco IP Telephony Security controls

- Overview of Cisco IP Telephony Security

Layered Security Approach for IP Telephony Security

Preceding chapters discussed the importance of a layered security approach for securing your Cisco IP Telephony network. It is time that we take a deep dive into the defense-in-depth concept, in other words layered security approach and understand how security can be implemented layer by layer in your IP Telephony network.

IP Telephony Layered Security Approach

You can argue, "Why should an organization invest in multiple security options instead of deploying just one solution that is cost-effective, easy to deploy, and manage?" Let's go over a case study and try to find a viable answer to this question.

Case Study

Organization XYZ has a Unified Threat Management (UTM) security appliance installed at its IP Telephony data center to prevent any outside threats to its IP Telephony network. The organization chose the UTM security appliance because it offered cost benefits and ease of configuration and management. The IT department routes all inside, outside, and demilitarized zone (DMZ) traffic through this appliance to ensure that all traffic is inspected for any suspicious behavior.

Note: Topics of UTM and security zones (inside, outside, and DMZ) are covered in Chapter 8, "Perimeter Security with Cisco Adaptive Security Appliance."

Although, XYZ's IT and IP Telephony personnel treasure its UTM appliance and baseline all security measures on the same, somewhere in a dark room, a determined hacker is conspiring and staging an attack against XYZ's IP Telephony network. The hacker has been busy gathering information about the UTM appliance by virtue of reconnaissance (passive scans and monitoring) and social engineering. The motive behind the staged attack is to earn a hefty amount from a competitor of XYZ by selling the tapped and captured conversations, CDR data, and customer details.

One fine day, the hacker launches a flurry of attacks and breaks through the organization's primary (and only) defense line. Now, XYZ's IP Telephony network stands defenseless against this individual, begging to be plundered.

Do you think that the IT department and decision makers at XYZ did justice to its IP Telephony network by implementing a solo defense mechanism?

No matter how good any solitary network security application/appliance (for example, a UTM security appliance) is, there is always someone out there adequately equipped with knowledge and experience who will eventually get past it. It is for this reason that you should consider deploying multiple lines of defense. By establishing a layered security approach, you have a good chance to keep out all but the most committed hackers. For the latter, at least you know if your network is under attack and can take an evasive action against it.

Layered security, at the network perimeter, core, distribution, and access layers ensures optimum protection. You should take a layered approach when securing your IP Telephony infrastructure.

Defense in depth, is the approach to use a layered approach to network security.

The most ideal approach is to build security layer upon layer starting at the user-facing access ports where workstations and IP Phones connect, and work your way to the distribution, core, and data center distribution and finally to the data center access layer.

In all these layers you realize that all IP Telephony elements that should be secured will be secured by virtue of the defense-in-depth approach. At a broad level, these elements can be best organized in the following categories:

- **Call Control:** Cisco Unified Communication Manager (CUCM), Cisco Unified Communications Manager Express, and Survivable Remote Site Telephony

- **IP Telephony applications:** Cisco Unity/Unity Connection Voice Messaging, Cisco Unified Unity Express, Cisco Unified Contact Center Express, and so on

- **IP Telephony endpoints:** IP Phones (wired, wireless), soft phones, Cisco IP Communicator, Cisco Unified Personal Communicator, VT Advantage, Voice Gateways, and so on

- **Network infrastructure:** Layer 2/3 switches, routers, internal and perimeter firewalls, IPS, and everything else that is not an IP Telephony application or an endpoint

The next section walks you through the various layers of an enterprise grade IP Telephony network that should be secured to achieve end-to-end IP Telephony Security.

Enabling IP Telephony Security: Layer upon Layer

Let's understand how you can build layer-by-layer security so that your IP Telephony network is seemingly impervious to external and internal threats. In order to attain such a security stance, the five elements of building a layered IP Telephony Security construct must be realized. These five elements are as follows:

- **Secure user facing access layer:** Access layer switches provide connectivity to user workstations and IP Phones. This layer can also include wireless access points (for supporting wireless handsets or wireless workstations and laptops with voice software). At this layer primarily, Layer 2 of the OSI model (data link layer) is used to carry data and voice traffic in their respective VLANs to their relevant destination. At this layer, most of the attacks emerge because of either a poorly designed network, or failure to follow the Cisco best practices to secure Layer 2. These attacks and their mitigation are covered in Chapter 6, "Cisco IP Telephony Layer 2 Security."

- **Secure distribution layer:** At this level, the network layer (Layer 3) of the OSI model comes into the picture. It is the demarcation point between the access and core layers, and it is in this sector of the IP Telephony network where routers and Layer 3 switches can be found. It is in this layer where you can implement Layer 3 policies (ACLs and Layer 3 QoS). The routers and Layer 3 switches ensure that packets are properly routed between subnets and VLANs. The various security issues and their mitigation at Layer 3 (that is, the network layer) are covered in Chapter 7, "Cisco IP Telephony Layer 3 Security."

- **Secure the network core:** The network core usually consists of high-end routers and Layer 3 switches, which are optimized for availability and performance. At the core, the intention is usually to do switching only of packets flowing in and out of the network, barring any policies or filtering (which can impact the performance of core layer and can be detrimental for high-volume traffic voice and data networks). Routers and Layer 3 switches in the core layer should use routing features that optimize packet throughput, and the core should be optimized for low latency. This implies that security policy-based decisions to filter out unwanted traffic must be carried out in access (user and data center) and distribution layers.

- **Secure data center distribution layer:** This is where the IP Telephony data center connects to the rest of the network. Although, this layer is not much different from the network distribution layer, it does have its own share of services to host. At this layer, it is usual to find a connection to the outside world via the public Internet, lease lines, or MPLS. The purpose is to connect with other sites outside the IP Telephony data center that host IP Telephony endpoints so that these endpoints can leverage the services off the data center. Also, at this layer firewall and other security components can be found because traffic to remote sites and the outside world traverse through the data center distribution switches and routers and must be filtered and inspected for malicious information and attacks.

- **Secure data center access layer:** This layer hosts the access switches to which all the IP Telephony servers and application servers are connected. These servers and services can be classified broadly as the following:

  - Call Control (Cisco Unified Communications Manager, Cisco Unified CME)

  - Voice Messaging (Cisco Unity/Unity Connection)

  - Presence (Cisco Unified Presence Server)

  - Session Border Controller (SBC/CUBE)

  - CDR, SFTP servers, DNS, NTP, and other applications/network services

  - Media resources (conferencing, transcoding, and MTP hardware resources)

The data center access layer is unlike the user access layer because in the data center, the servers are trusted for the purpose that they exist; therefore the range of security threats is considerably reduced. You will learn about each IP Telephony application's security issues and mitigation techniques in Part III, "Cisco IP Telephony Application and Device Security."

Note: This construct is based on the Cisco popular Core Distribution Access (CDA) network design approach. Even though some of the networks may have a collapsed core and distribution or an altogether collapsed core, distribution, and access layers, these principles are still valid because they not only represent the layers in their entirety, but also represent the relationship and coherence between layers.

Figure 3-1 shows the different layers and their relationship.

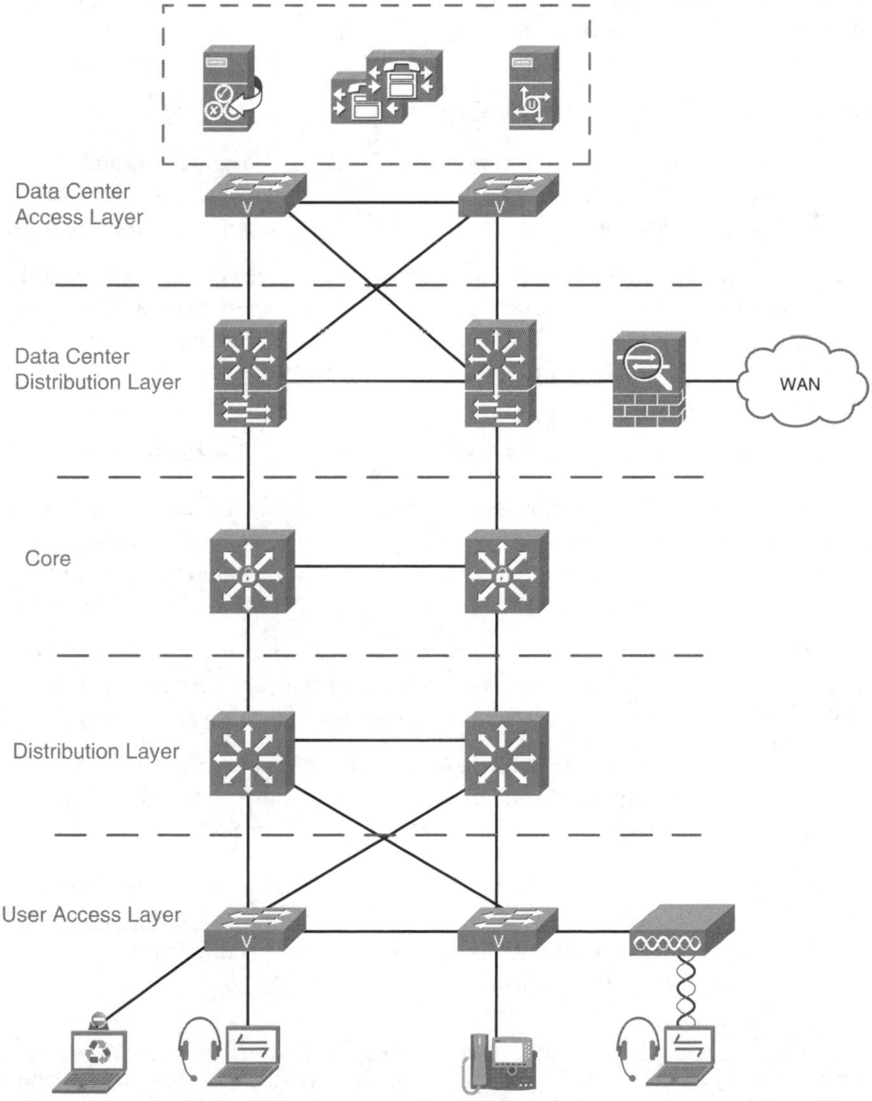

Figure 3-1 *IP Telephony Layered Security Approach*

Cisco IP Telephony Security Controls

To reduce the risk of an attack to your IP Telephony network, adequate layered network security is required. This in turn requires the proper combination of IP Telephony Security policy (more on IP Telephony Security policy in Chapter 4, "Cisco IP Telephony Security Framework"), procedures, and suitable security controls in place. The defense-in-depth approach or holistic IP Telephony Security requires multiple layers of network security controls and IP Telephony Security controls along with network security best practices to minimize the risk of attack or compromise while providing acceptable functionality and performance.

Discovering IP Telephony Security Controls

Before defining IP Telephony network security controls, let's spend some time understanding what exactly a security control is. A Security control is a technical or administrative thwart to shun, neutralize, or minimize losses due to threats arising from security risks.

Security controls can be broadly classified as either administrative controls or technical (also known as logical) controls. Administrative controls entail where people take action in favor of or against an event, as guided by corporate policy, a standard, or a procedure. Technical (also known as logical) controls are the ones implemented by IT systems to deter a known or unknown threat.

Logical or administrative security controls can be further classified as the following:

- **Prevention or precautionary controls:** As the name suggests, these controls are logical controls placed in networks to stop the threat in its tracks. In other words, proactive controls. A well-known example is Cisco CSA (now SELinux), which is a Host Intrusion Prevention System (HIPS) that helps prevent day-0 threats from blossoming.

- **Correction or remedial controls:** These are the opposite of preventive controls and the action is a reaction to the threat. For example, using an antivirus program to clean a virus from a PC is a corrective action rather than preventive.

- **Detection or revealing controls:** These controls are neither preventive nor corrective in nature. They are simply detection security controls that detect that an attack has happened or is on its way. The example is IDS, Syslog, or SNMP alarms.

It's unfortunate, however true, that security controls are referenced all the time in security frameworks, but they are not often defined. Thus, it is of the utmost importance to define the IP Telephony Security controls and implement them, as directed by the corporate or IP Telephony Security policy.

Note: Effective security controls provide for protecting the confidentiality, integrity, and availability of critical information and resources.

Cisco IP Telephony Security Controls

Let's go over the various IP Telephony network and application security controls. Although, most of the controls discussed in the following section are technical or logical controls, it is an organization's security policy that enforces the administrative controls. (IP Telephony Security policy and related sub policies and controls are covered in great detail in Chapter 4.)

While this list of technical controls may not be extensive, it can give you an insight of what security controls you can implement at several levels within the network and at the IP Telephony application level.

Note: Some IP Telephony Security controls are common among various IP Telephony network elements and applications, yet vital (for example, authentication and encryption controls at network and application layers). Also, not all security controls are required in all networks because, every network is unique and thus, its requirements and appetite for security is also unique.

Cisco IP Telephony Network Security Controls

IP Telephony network security controls refer to the available network security features in the underlying network infrastructure, that is, switches and routers. Cisco switches (Catalyst switches) and IOS routers have security features that can be leveraged to secure the network on which the IP Telephony applications and voice streams (signaling and media) rely. Secure physical connectivity for IP Telephony endpoints is extended to wireless via wireless devices, for example, access points, wireless LAN controller, enabling wireless endpoints to connect securely to Call Control, and other voice services. Moreover, at the network perimeter Cisco Adaptive Security Appliance Firewall can help shun external attacks via application of perimeter security controls and by segregating network into different security zones.

Table 3-1 describes Layer 2 (switching layer) security controls.

Table 3-1 *Cisco IP Telephony Network Switch Security Controls*

Cisco IP Telephony Network Switches
Port security
802.1x for endpoints
DHCP snooping
DAI
IP source guard
Different voice and data VLANs

Cisco IP Telephony Network Switches
Selective VLAN trunking (VLAN pruning)
Logging and monitoring
AAA/RADIUS authentication, authorization, accounting
Encrypted passwords
Support for SSH
Secure SNMP
NTP authentication
QoS scavenger model
VLAN ACLs

Table 3-2 gives an insight to the various Layer 3 (routing/IP layer) security controls.

Table 3-2   *Cisco IP Telephony Network Router Security Controls*

Cisco IP Telephony Network (Non-Voice) IOS Routers
Ensure router IOS version is not deferred
Disable unnecessary IOS services
Logging and monitoring
AAA/RADIUS authentication, authorization, accounting
Encrypted passwords
Support for SSH and HTTPS
QOS scavenger model
Layer 3 ACLs
Secure SNMP
NTP authentication

Table 3-3 illustrates the various security controls that come into play with wireless infrastructure.

Table 3-3   *Cisco IP Telephony Network Wireless Security Controls*

Cisco Wireless Access Points/Controllers
Wireless encryption (for example, WPA or WPA2)
802.1x for wireless endpoints
Wireless SSID segregation (different SSID for voice and data)

Table 3-4 gives an insight to the security controls which can be applied at the network perimeter.

Table 3-4 *Cisco IP Telephony Network Firewall/Perimeter Security Controls*

Cisco Adaptive Security Appliance (Cisco ASA Firewall)
TLS-Proxy
Phone Proxy
Presence Proxy
IPSec or SSL-based VPN for remote node connections/public Internet/telecommuters
Inspects for voice protocols (H.323, MGCP, SCCP, and SIP)
Zone concept to protect IP Telephony servers/services
Logging and monitoring
Traffic filtering with ACLs (Layers 2–4)
Network Address Translation (NAT)

Table 3-5 is an outline of IP Telephony network security controls that are not specific to a technology or device but can be leveraged to reduce the attack surface and increase immunity to internal or external attacks.

Table 3-5 *Cisco IP Telephony Network (Generic) Security Controls*

Cisco IP Telephony Server/Phone Placement
IP Telephony server placement in IP Telephony server-only VLAN
IP Phones placement in voice-only VLAN
Broker connections from user VRF to IP Telephony server/application VRF using Firewalls (Cisco ASA)

Cisco IP Telephony Device Security Controls

In essence, IP Telephony device security controls can be described as the available security features in the IP Telephony devices, which can be deployed to deter internal and external attacks. These range from Cisco Voice Gateway to Cisco Unified Communications Manager Express to Cisco Unified Border Element pertinent security controls. These and other Cisco voice devices have built-in security features that can be leveraged to secure the device itself as well as connectivity to the underlying network and IP Telephony applications. This complements both the network and application layer security because these components are logically amid the two layers.

Table 3-6 summarizes the Cisco Unified Communications Manager security controls.

Table 3-6   *Cisco Unified Communications Manager Express Security Controls*

Cisco Unified Communication Manager Express (Cisco Unified CME)
Ensure Cisco Unified CME IOS version is not deferred
CAPF
Disable unnecessary IOS services
Logging and monitoring
Different voice and data VLANs are separate (if using Etherswitch module)
AAA/ RADIUS authentication, authorization, accounting
Secure SNMP
NTP authentication
QoS scavenger model

Table 3-7 exemplifies the security controls pertinent to Cisco Unity Express.

Table 3-7   *Cisco Unity Express Security Controls*

Cisco Unity Express (CUE)
Ensure CUE IOS Version is not deferred
Logging and monitoring
AAA/RADIUS authentication, authorization, accounting
Secure SNMP
NTP authentication

Table 3-8 emphasizes Cisco Voice Gateway security controls.

Table 3-8   *Cisco Voice Gateway Security Controls*

Cisco Voice Gateways (Analog/Digital)
IPSec tunnels to CUCM (H.323 and MGCP)
TLS to CUCM (MGCP and SIP)
AAA/RADIUS authentication, authorization, accounting
Disable unnecessary services
Logging and monitoring

Cisco Voice Gateways (Analog/Digital)
Secure SRST
Secure SNMP
NTP authentication

Table 3-9 gives an insight to Cisco voice gatekeeper security controls.

Table 3-9   *Cisco Voice Gatekeeper Security Controls*

Cisco Voice Gatekeeper
IPSec tunnels to CUCM (H.323)
AAA/RADIUS authentication, authorization, accounting
Secure gatekeeper registration (default subnet)
Secure gatekeeper Trunk
Logging and monitoring
Secure SNMP
NTP authentication

Table 3-10 illustrates Cisco Unified Border Element security controls.

Table 3-10   *Cisco Unified Border Element Security Controls*

Cisco Unified Border Element (CUBE)
Secure SIP trunks
Signaling and media encryption
Secure registration
ACL-based traffic filtering
Logging and monitoring
Secure SNMP
NTP authentication

Cisco IP Telephony Application Security Controls

Like network and IP Telephony devices, Cisco IP Telephony servers also have built-in security mechanisms (aka controls) that can be activated or deployed to help ensure that the IP Telephony applications and servers are safeguarded from internal and external attacks or exploits. The following tables outline the IP Telephony Application security controls as pertinent to Cisco IP Telephony.

Table 3-11 gives a detailed outline of the various security controls pertinent to Cisco Unified Communications Manager.

Table 3-11 *Cisco Unified Communications Manager Security Controls*

Cisco Unified Communications Manager (CUCM)
Ensure that CUCM OS version is updated (Cisco provided OS version)
Ensure that the OS and application patches are applied on an ongoing basis (as per corporate policy)
CSA/SELinux-based HIPS solution
Ensure that a strong OS, Security, and Application Password is used and that these passwords are different
CAPF (cluster mixed mode)
External Certificate Authority for CAPF/HTTPS certificates
Secure Integration with LDAP
Multilevel access/User Group access
Voicemail Port(s) and Pilot Point(s) in an isolated partition
Secured Third-Party SIP Phones
Secure ICT/GK/SIP Trunk
Logging, monitoring, and auditing
Secure conferencing
Secure SNMP
Credential policy
VPN Phone

Table 3-12 illustrates the security controls relevant for Cisco Unity.

Table 3-12 *Cisco Unity Security Controls*

Cisco Unity
Ensure that Unity OS version is updated
Ensure that OS and application patches are applied on an ongoing basis (as per corporate patching/security policy)
Supported HIPS solution (CSA)
Supported antivirus solution

Cisco Unity
Disable unnecessary windows services
HTTPS for PCA and Web SA (External Certificate Authority for digital certificates)
Secure voicemail port(s)
Password aging
Restricted out calling (as per organization policy)
Logging, monitoring, and reporting

Table 3-13 provides an insight to the security controls pertinent to Cisco Unity Connection.

Table 3-13   *Cisco Unity Connection Security Controls*

Cisco Unity Connection (CUC)
Ensure Cisco Unity OS version is updated
Ensure that OS and application are upgraded on ongoing basis (as per corporate policy)
CSA/SELinux-based HIPS solution
HTTPS for PCA and Web Admin access (External Certificate Authority for digital certificates)
Secure Voicemail Port(s)
Secure Integration with LDAP
Password aging
Restricted out calling (as per organization policy)
Logging, monitoring, and reporting/auditing
Secure SNMP

Table 3-14 briefly describes the security controls for Cisco Unified Presence Server.

Table 3-14   *Cisco Unified Presence Server Security Controls*

Cisco Unified Presence Server (CUPS)
Secure CUPS Federation (ASA CUPS Proxy)
CSA/SELinux-based HIPS solution
Secure Integration with CUCM
Secure Integration with LDAP

Cisco Unified Presence Server (CUPS)

HTTPS for Web Admin and user access (external certificate authority for digital certificates)

Secure SNMP

Logging and monitoring

Cisco IP Telephony Endpoint Security Controls

Cisco IP Telephony endpoint security controls can be defined as the security features found in IP Telephony endpoints that enable Cisco IP Telephony administrators to help ensure that the endpoints are protected from malicious attacks or exploits. Moreover, safeguarding the endpoints from rogue users helps evade any attacks targeting voice servers, devices, and media and signaling streams.

Table 3-15 lists the various security controls pertinent to wired IP Phones.

Table 3-15 *Cisco Unified IP Phone (Wired) Security Controls*

Cisco Unified IP Phones (Wired)

Disable IP Phone web access

Disable GARP

Disable video support (where it is not needed)

Disable PC voice VLAN access

Restrict phone settings access (as per organizational policy)

CAPF (for secure signaling and media)

Class of Restriction (COR – CSS and Partitions)

Locally Significant Certificates (LSC)

802.1x

VPN Phone

Table 3-16 illustrates the security controls pertinent to Cisco IP Communicator.

Table 3-16 *Cisco IP Communicator/Soft Phone Security Controls*

Cisco IP Communicator

Disable video support (where not needed)

Restrict Settings access

Cisco IP Communicator
CAPF (for secure signaling and media)
Class of Restriction (COR – CSS and Partitions)
Locally Significant Certificates (LSC)
802.1x
Extension mobility for additional security
Restrict phone RTP range (as per organizational policy)
Disable changes to the Registry on user machine

Table 3-17 summarizes the security controls available for Cisco Unified Wireless IP Phones.

Table 3-17 *Cisco Unified IP Phone (Wireless) Security Controls*

Cisco Unified IP Phones (Wireless)
Disable phone web access
Disable GARP
Restrict phone settings access (as per organizational policy)
Disable PC Voice VLAN access
CAPF (for secure signaling and media)
Class of Restriction (COR – CSS and Partitions)
Locally Significant Certificates (LSC)
Use Wireless Encryption (WPA and WPA2)
802.1x
Separate voice and data SSIDs

The security controls defined in earlier sections describe the basis of securing Cisco IP Telephony networks and are an integral part of overall IP Telephony Security strategy and framework. Once, the security controls have been defined, it is time that they are implemented to secure your IP Telephony network. However, you still have some work to do before applying the previously defined security controls:

- You should follow the corporate security policy guidelines to put together an IP Telephony Security policy or build an IP Telephony Security policy from scratch (more on IP Telephony Security policy in Chapter 4).

- You should weigh the cost of implementing a security control versus risk of not implementing the same. Remember, not all networks are alike, and consequently not all security controls may be required in your IP Telephony network.

- You should look into the level of security required for your IP Telephony environment because not all networks are same, and they require different levels of security. (For example, a government organization IP Telephony network requires higher security than a school's IP Telephony network.)

These topics and other crucial information that can help you plan and implement security for your Cisco IP Telephony network is covered in Chapter 4.

Cisco IP Telephony Security Overview

You have learned about layered security (defense-in-depth) approach. You know about the security controls that can be applied at various network, application, endpoint, and information transition points to secure your IP Telephony network. Now, you are going to learn about how and where you can apply these controls. The following section gives you both a high-level overview and a deep-dive insight to help you understand the intricacies behind deploying successful IP Telephony Security solution.

Discovering End-to-End IP Telephony Security

This section gives you a solid understanding of the various elements that form the basis of a secure IP Telephony network. We deliberately take the use case of an enterprise network to understand the "Where's" and the "What's" of Cisco IP Telephony Security, since such a network has extensions, which covers the following network deployment models:

- IP Telephony data center/headquarter where most of the IP Telephony applications and equipment (and employee work force) are concentrated

- Remote data center, where there may be local call processing, other IP Telephony services, and a few hundred users are located

- Remote site(s), which may feature local survivability (such as SRST or CUCME) with a small population of users

- Telecommuters that use either the SOHO VPN solution or VPN software-based solutions

Let's now build on the example for the fictitious organization: XYZ that has approximately 20,000 IP Telephony users, and demystify the various components and their relative security requirements. This case study embodies all Cisco IP Telephony deployment models (centralized, distributed, and hybrid) to showcase where and how IP Telephony Security can be applied.

Figure 3-2 showcases Cisco IP Telephony Security at an enterprise level.

Note: This example considers that the IP Telephony data center is collocated at XYZ's headquarters (as well as remote data center).

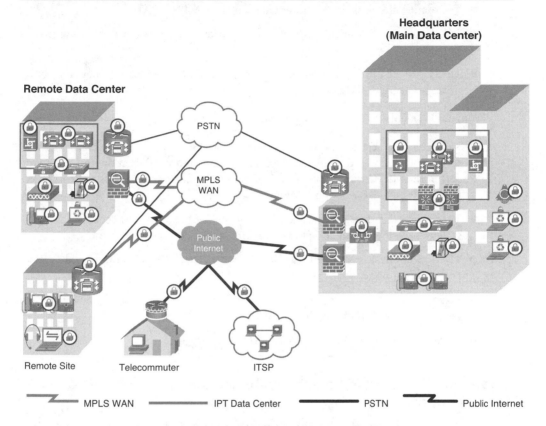

IP Telephony Security Overview

Figure 3-2 *Enterprise Grade IP Telephony Security Overview*

From an architectural perspective, at a high level, XYZ has the following network architecture:

- Main data center (also the headquarters)
- Remote data center
- Remote site with a couple hundred phones
- Telecommuters
- IT service provider (PSTN SIP trunk)

From a connectivity perspective organization, XYZ has following connectivity scheme:

- The data centers connect with each other by MPLS WAN.

- The remote site connects to either data center by MPLS WAN.

- Telecommuters leverage the IP Telephony services using a public network or the Internet.

- The IT service provider's (ITSP) connection is via ITSP-provided Internet connection or via public network(s).

From an IP Telephony services perspective, XYZ has following IP Telephony services:

- The main data center has Call Control, voice messaging, conferencing, and Presence services. Along with these, users are offered wired and wireless endpoints, PCs with soft phones (IP Communicator), and other IP Telephony applications (such as Cisco Unified Presence Client and VMO).

- The remote data center, which acts as a backup for the main data center however is scaled down in size and complexity, providing all services except presence.

- The remote site has endpoints that leverage local CUCME Call Control and CUE voice messaging services.

- Telecommuters have soft phones on their PCs and laptops, which enable them to be mobile and work from their home office.

- Third-party ITSP provides SIP-based PSTN access.

Understanding Each IP Telephony Component and its Relative Security Control

Now that you understand the basics of the organization XYZ's enterprise network, let us try to break down the network into smaller components to realize each component's deployment model to see how you can effectively use the Cisco IP Telephony Security controls to secure them.

XYZ Headquarters (Main Data Center)

To start with, XYZ's headquarters can be classified as a standalone data center. In effect, it has all the elements that comprise a standard Enterprise IP Telephony data center and end-user site from Core IP Telephony applications to endpoints. This, in a different frame of reference, could be represented as a single cluster, single-site model (centralized call processing).

Figure 3-3 gives an insight to the IP Telephony Security specifics at XYZ's corporate headquarters.

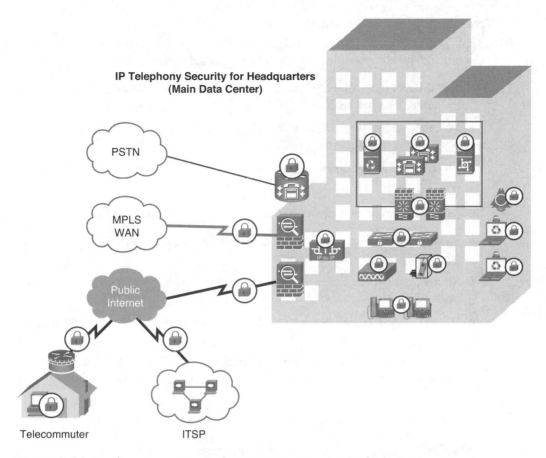

Figure 3-3 *Headquarters vis-à-vis the Main Data Center IP Telephony Security*

Let's now classify the various IP Telephony components in play here and match them with their respective security controls.

Note: For all IP Telephony network elements, applications, endpoints, and devices, the security controls are referred from the previous section—Cisco IP Telephony Security Controls. Each element's security controls will not be reiterated for brevity; however, if an element is leveraging a security control not covered before, it will be explicitly mentioned.

IP Telephony Data Center Security Insight

Application and network security is in action at the HQ (IP Telephony main data center). Cisco IP Telephony application security includes the following:

- **Call Control (CUCM):** For CUCM, Call Control Security controls are applicable (including SIP trunk security for ITSP).

- **Voice messaging (Unity/CUC):** Voice Messaging Unity or Unity Connection security controls come into play here.

- **Presence (CUPS):** Security controls for Presence are applicable (optional for federation if deployed).

Cisco IP Telephony underlying network security includes the following:

- **Switching infrastructure:** Layer 2 security controls are applicable for the switching infrastructure at the HQ data center.

- **Routing infrastructure:** Security controls for Layer 3 and routing protocols are relevant for routers and Layer 3 switches.

- **Wireless infrastructure:** Security controls for secure wireless infrastructure are pertinent.

- **Cisco ASA Firewalls:** Firewall rules and security controls are of interest here (including telecommuter security and encryption of voice and data traffic on the Internet link).

Cisco IP Telephony device security includes the following:

- **Voice Gateways:** Security controls for voice gateway are applicable.

- **CUBE:** Security controls for CUBE/SBC are applicable.

Cisco IP Telephony endpoint security includes the following:

- **IP Phones and Soft Phones:** Security controls for wired and wireless IP Phones and soft phones are relevant.

IP Telephony Remote Data Center Security Insight

Application and network security comes into the picture at IP Telephony remote data center. Figure 3-4 details the IP Telephony Security specifics at XYZ's remote data center.

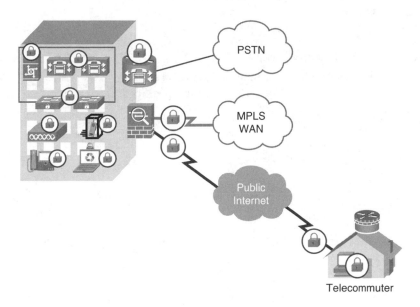

**IP Telephony Security for
Remote Data Center**

Figure 3-4   *Remote Data Center IP Telephony Security*

Cisco IP Telephony application security includes the following:

- **Call Control (CUCM):** Call Control Security controls are pertinent

- **Voice messaging (Unity/CUC):** Voice Messaging Unity or Unity Connection security controls come into play here

Cisco IP Telephony underlying network security includes the following:

- **Switching infrastructure:** Layer 2 security controls are pertinent for the switching infrastructure at the remote data center.

- **Routing infrastructure:** Security controls for Layer 3 and routing protocols are of interest for routers and Layer 3 switches.

- **Wireless infrastructure:** Security controls for secure wireless infrastructure are significant.

- **Cisco ASA Firewall:** Firewall rules and security controls are relevant here (including telecommuter security and encryption of voice and data traffic on the Internet link).

Cisco IP Telephony device security includes the following:

- **Voice Gateway(s):** Security controls for voice gateway are applicable.

Cisco IP Telephony endpoint security includes the following:

- **IP Phones and soft phones:** Security controls for wired and wireless IP Phones and soft phones are relevant.

IP Telephony Remote Site Security Insight

Application and network security is yet again in action at IP Telephony remote site. Figure 3-5 gives an overview of the IP Telephony Security specifics at the remote site.

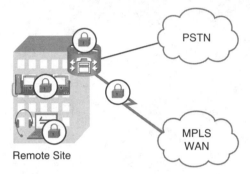

Figure 3-5   *Remote Site IP Telephony Security*

Cisco IP Telephony application security includes the following:

- **Call Control (CUCME):** Cisco Unified CME Call Control security controls are persuasive for remote site Call Control.

- **Voice messaging (CUE):** CUE security controls come into play here.

Cisco IP Telephony underlying network security includes the following:

- **Switching infrastructure:** Layer 2 security controls are relevant for the switching infrastructure.

- **Routing infrastructure:** Security controls for Layer 3 are significant for edge router (CUCME).

Cisco IP Telephony endpoint security includes the following:

- **IP Phones and soft phones:** Security controls for wired IP Phones and soft phones are applicable.

Telecommuter Solution Security Insight

As depicted in Figure 3-6, endpoint and network security is pertinent for the telecommuter solution.

Figure 3-6 *Telecommuter IP Telephony Security*

Cisco IP Telephony underlying network security includes the following:

- **VPN Client (IPSec):** Encryption for all traffic from telecommuters traversing to the HQ or alternatively to remote data center is the highlight for telecommuter endpoints.

- **IOS Firewall:** This provides protection for smaller sites and telecommuters.

Cisco IP Telephony endpoint security includes the following:

- **Soft phones:** Security controls for soft phones are applicable.

- **VPN phones:** Security controls for Cisco Unified IP Phone (wired) are applicable.

Summary

Security is one of the most important and probably complex elements of IP Telephony networks. The complexity can be reduced with proper planning and ensuring that the system is secure at various layers, instead of a single secure mechanism waiting to be breached. Although, some hackers attack with malicious intent for profit, others do it for fun. Either way, it is your IP Telephony network, and it is you who must be in control of it, not an outside or inside attacker.

This chapter began with a generic discussion about the layered security approach (or defense-in-depth) in which you were familiarized with layers of security that you can deploy in the real world in your Cisco IP Telephony network. These layers are your friend and a nightmare for your foes—the hackers and attackers out there and within your network. Next, you visited the security controls for enabling security at various layers to help you select the right controls for your Cisco IP Telephony environment. You were also introduced to end-to-end security approach for an enterprise-grade Cisco IP

Telephony network that enabled you to understand the positioning of different security controls at various places in your Cisco IP Telephony network.

In the next chapter, you will learn about tactics, tools and processes such as—risk assessment, security strategy, cost of security, level of security, and so on, which will help you build a viable and succinct Cisco IP Telephony Security Framework for your organization.

Chapter 4

Cisco IP Telephony Security Framework

The threats, the remediation, IP Telephony Security methodology and much more has been discussed in previous chapters. However, the objective has always been to amalgamate IP Telephony and conventional data services onto a shared network infrastructure, without compromising the security of either service. The intention has been to apply protective mechanisms against all types of attacks that must be applied in a holistic manner throughout the enterprise network. The two main principles of an IP Telephony Security Framework are the simplification of design and configuration, and the limitation of exposure.

It is time to start putting together your IP Telephony network security strategy together. With the basics of what makes your secure IP Telephony network out of the ordinary, it is time to move on and choose the best style of security network to suit your needs. In many ways, this can be a subjective process because you might prefer one type of network security rather than another regardless of objective criteria. There's nothing wrong with taking that approach as long as you're armed with the facts, and that's what this chapter is all about.

This chapter covers the following topics:

- Cisco IP Telephony Security life cycle

- Develop an IP Telephony Security policy

- Evaluate cost versus risk

- Determine the level of security required for your IP Telephony network

- Develop Cisco IP Telephony Security Framework

Cisco IP Telephony Security Life Cycle

Cisco understands and values the importance of network security and continuously drives toward building robust, scalable, and secure products, and networks. It is vital that security is induced in design wherever possible (rather than implemented post-deployment of the network). The process of developing and securing your IP Telephony network should follow what is popularly known as a *security wheel*. After developing an IP Telephony Security policy, you can secure your IP Telephony network. (An IP Telephony Security policy acts as a guide for implementing various security measures without which the IP Telephony network security will neither be complete nor based on the ethics and principles of your organization.)

The security wheel, as shown in Figure 4-1, projects the verity that IP Telephony network security is a continuous process built around your corporate security policy.

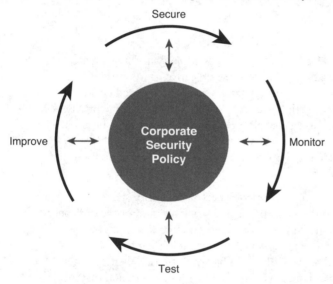

Figure 4-1 *Cisco Security Wheel*

After the IP Telephony network is secured, it should be monitored for any deviations from normal behavior, for example, abnormal usage of services, network and application level attacks, illicit scans, and log analysis to ensure that it stays secure.

After the monitoring phase comes the testing phase. Testing can be done by an organization, or it can be outsourced to a third-party, such as the Cisco Advanced Services. Network and IP Telephony administrators and engineers should use the information from the monitoring and testing phase to make improvements to the security implementation. They should also adjust the IP Telephony Security policy as new vulnerabilities and risks are identified.

For more details on the security services offered by Cisco Advance Services and other security groups within Cisco, visit http://www.cisco.com/en/US/products/svcs/ps2961/ps2952/serv_group_home.html.

Enabling IP Telephony Security

Implementing and enabling IP Telephony Security is neither a single step nor a one-time process. It is a constant and continually improving cycle, which must be reiterated time and again as and when new threats evolve or new requirements need to be addressed. Figure 4-2 illustrates the IP Telephony Security cycle and its various phases.

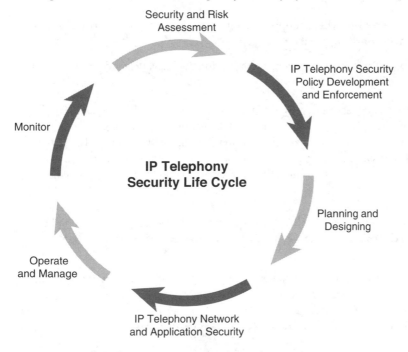

Figure 4-2   *IP Telephony Security Life Cycle*

At the core, this cycle is based on the Cisco security wheel; however, it is more detailed and explicit toward the IP Telephony network security process.

Security and Risk Assessment

The process begins at security and risk assessment; during this stage any new or existing vulnerabilities and security loopholes are discovered. During this phase, a rigorous process consisting of multiple objectives is carried out. These include however not limited to the following:

- Evaluating and identifying the principle assets

- Identifying any existing security concerns

- Exploring any possible new threats or attack vectors

- Evaluating the cost of security

The security assessment of the enterprise IP Telephony network infrastructure helps support key business processes. The IP Telephony Security assessment should cover the following elements of your IP Telephony environment:

- Network devices (routers and switches) vulnerabilities

- Network and security services (firewall, routing protocols, and anti-spoofing services)

- Network access layer, where endpoints connect to the network, and the distribution and core layers of the internal network

- IP Telephony services, endpoints, and applications, such as Presence, IP Phones, Call Control, gateways, and so on

The objective of security assessment is to identify potential weaknesses in your IP Telephony network, which may lead to toll fraud, denial-of-service (DoS), eavesdropping on voice calls, and unauthorized access to voice mail systems within your IP Telephony environment. The result is a report on the network security posture, including recommendations for network infrastructure and IP Telephony application security improvements.

Note: The assessment report should ideally include a priority list of suggestions on how to decrease risks, adapted to the environment and special needs of an organization.

Risk assessment helps identify the vital assets of your IP Telephony network and evaluate the potential cost of security. The topic of risk assessment is covered in detail in the section "Risk assessment." The completion of the risk assessment phase triggers the next phase, in which IP Telephony Security policy (strategy) is developed.

IP Telephony Security Policy Development and Enforcement

The process of development and enforcement of IP Telephony Security policy is baselined on corporate security policy and objectives. An IP Telephony Security policy is much like a network security policy. However, the major difference is that the IP Telephony Security policy is explicitly developed for IP Telephony network covering the network, applications, and services relevant to IP Telephony infrastructure and services. You must recognize that the development of an IP Telephony Security policy is not a lone effort by the IP Telephony team. Instead, it should be done in collaboration with the network and security teams to ensure that all aspects and view points are covered as they pertain to IP Telephony Security.

Note: Do not be surprised if your organization does not have any existing IP Telephony Security policy because most organizations tend to apply or extend the network security policy to their IP Telephony network. It is however vital to have a specific IP Telephony Security policy to tackle the issues that a network security policy just cannot address.

Planning and Designing

The subsequent phase is the planning and designing phase, in which you plan and design the blueprint for deployment of your IP Telephony network. As a best practice, it is in this phase that you should integrate security with the design being developed instead of deploying security after your IP Telephony network has been deployed. The design should be such that the IP Telephony network and the services based on it are scalable, robust, supple, and most obviously, secure. The planning for deployment should include security as the integral component and should be done in such a manner that a layered security approach is adopted instead of concentrating security at one point, for example, at enterprise perimeter.

Note: If an IP Telephony network is a green field deployment, it is optimum to incorporate security in design. If the IP Telephony network is already set up, then following assessment and policy phases, you can skip to the application and network security phase.

IP Telephony Network and Application Security Deployment

This is the phase where maximum action can be expected. It goes right from deploying and enabling security on IP Telephony applications (Call Manager and Unity Connection) on servers to IP Telephony network (access layer switches, routers) to IP Telephony endpoints. As mentioned earlier, if security is planned into the design, it becomes much easier to implement in coherence with the underlying functional network. In other words, implementing security for IP Telephony network becomes seamless.

IP Telephony network security can be organized into the following categories:

- Hardware and device security (endpoints and servers)
- Network security (Layers 2 and 3 and upper layers)
- Application security (Call Control, voice messaging, presence, and so on)
- Management and monitoring (SSH and logging)

Operate and Manage

In this penultimate phase, you leverage the services offered by your IP Telephony network. It is time to reap the benefits of your hard work! Your IP Telephony network is fully operational, and you could bring it into production. However, it is also time to ensure that things go the way they were planned and that there are minimal hiccups from the intended operational and management perspective. Ensure that proper administrative and other privileges are assigned to the intended authorized staff. Furthermore, ensure that only the legitimate users can leverage the IP Telephony services without any loss of service or disruption in the IP Telephony environment. This phase almost amalgamates with the last phase, that is, monitor the IP Telephony network.

Monitor

At this point, your IP Telephony network should be under ideal conditions fully functional, and to ensure that it remains that way, you must consistently keep an eye on the health of your IP Telephony network. IP Telephony monitoring tools, techniques, security, and best practices are discussed in Chapter 16, "Cisco IP Telephony: Network Management Security." Monitoring and responding to potential threats is a manifold process and requires monitoring and reporting any 'deviations'. Now, let's consider the scope of word deviation in perspective of IP Telephony network management and monitoring. Deviation could be described on one hand as the anomaly induced by improper or unjustified use of the services provided by your IP Telephony network. On the other hand it can be described as the threats that have matured and cause the loss of integrity, confidentiality, and availability of your IP Telephony network. Thus, it becomes paramount to have proper monitoring mechanisms in place and have these deviations reported as soon as they are discovered so that they can be dealt with either via an automatic defense system (for example, Firewall, Network IPS, or Host IPS) or manually.

Developing an IP Telephony Security Policy

This section covers the intricacies behind building an IP Telephony Security policy because without one you cannot enforce IP communications' pertinent security effectively.

Building an IP Telephony Security Policy/Strategy In line with Your Corporate Security Policy

An IP Telephony network security policy (the words policy and strategy will be used interchangeably) defines a construct to protect the assets connected to a network that supports IP Telephony, based on a risk assessment analysis. It defines the access limitations and rules for accessing various assets connected to an IP Telephony network. It is the source of information for users and administrators as they set up, use, and audit the network.

It is imperative that the IP Telephony network security policy is general and broad in scope. This implies that it should provide a high-level view of the corporate ideology based on which security-related decisions should be made. However, it should not go into the details of how the policy should be implemented. The rationale is that the details can change overnight, but the general principles of what these details must achieve should remain the same. An IP Telephony Security policy needs to balance between ease of use and ease of implementation, network performance, and the security aspects in defining the rules and regulations.

Building an IP Telephony Security policy is not a one-time process. It requires adjusting policy as per new requirements, objectives, threats, or challenges. Also, IP Telephony Security policy is not an isolated or a single team effort. It requires participation and support from all segments: the IP Telephony team, network team, security team, and most importantly, management (executive sponsor). The security policy needs to be supported by management and other respective engineering teams within an organization; otherwise, it is difficult to have user buy-in.

Note: A security policy is not a static document and must be updated on a regular basis depending on the need to address new security challenges or to meet organizational objectives. For example, if an organization supports remote working (telecommuters), it is not feasible to chalk off remote access. Furthermore, a security policy is intended to harden the system with rules however not to deteriorate any process or production potential.

The first step toward developing an effective IP Telephony Security policy is to assess the risk associated with the network assets to be protected. Risk assessment in quintessence is a method to outline why the resources in your IP Telephony network should be protected. The next section investigates risk assessment and the fundamentals of the risk assessment process for an IP Telephony network.

Risk Assessment

Let us go over this intriguing topic to understand what goes behind performing a risk assessment exercise and why it might just save you from a certain catastrophe.

Note: As pointed out earlier in Chapter 2, "Cisco IP Telephony Security Building Blocks," the IP Telephony Security assessment includes the plans for areas that have scope for improvement. Risk assessment is partially covered in almost every security assessment.

At a high level, the risk management process helps you attain the following goals:

- **It helps achieve the organization's objectives (vision and goals):** By highlighting the assets that are important or central to an organization's functions. This helps protect those vital assets.

- **It ensures the network and infrastructure availability for rightful users:** By helping categorizing network assets in terms of their importance for the network to be up and running, thereby helping with the scale of economy.

- **It assists in maintaining a strong security posture:** To deter attacks against an organization's vital assets by deploying appropriate security controls against identified and potential threats.

- **It ensures compliance with organization's rules, regulations, standards, and policies:** By helping to understand the various components of the network that could be exploited and misused, thereby building policies, rules, and regulations around their use or access mechanisms.

Figure 4-3 gives an insight to the various benefits perceived by carrying out the risk management process.

Figure 4-3   *Risk Management: Areas Addressed*

A typical IP Telephony risk assessment activity may well be outlined via the following steps:

Step 1.   Identify sensitive information and critical systems.

Step 2.   Estimate the value of IP Telephony system (information and components).

Step 3.   Identify potential threats and vulnerabilities to your IP Telephony network (covered in security assessment).

Step 4.   Estimate the likelihood of a potential attack or penetration being realized.

Step 5.   Identify countermeasures against perceived threats and vulnerabilities (covered in security assessment).

Step 6.   Estimate the cost of implementing countermeasures versus not implementing them.

Step 7. Select suitable countermeasures for implementation (covered in security assessment).

Before taking a deep dive to understand the different processes that work within a risk assessment exercise, you must realize an important fact. Not all risks are present and applicable in all different types of IP telephony implementations; every IP Telephony network is unique and has its own set of strengths and weaknesses. However, it is important to create an overall IP Telephony Security policy or strategy in which all assets, potential risks, existing issues, and mitigation methods are listed. Although, it is advisable to perform a risk assessment on existing IP telephony implementation(s), it is equally important to perform an initial risk assessment, including a review of the impact on the data network for new implementations.

Step 1. Identify Sensitive IP Telephony Information and Critical Systems

Organizations should pinpoint the various systems that form the baseline for IP Telephony, from internal servers to external network components, to understand where their critical information may potentially be stored, processed, managed, or viewed.As a disseminated system, IP Telephony network has many individual components that must be protected. Any attack vector realized at any point of time can render the system unusable for legit users. This includes and is not limited to the following:

■ Endpoints and servers targeted for DoS/DDoS or MITM attacks

■ Changes in routing protocols, leading to failed or hijacked calls

■ Change in the IP Telephony application or device configuration

Step 2. Estimate the Value of IP Telephony System (Information and Components)

After identifying the critical information and systems, organizations can then estimate the value of data loss based on where sensitive information is sent, depending on who sends it, and how often it happens. For example, an organization may find that the majority of data loss risks are associated with employees inside the organization who unconsciously put information at risk in the course of their day-to-day activities at work, for example, placing CDR data on a USB drive in preparation to work at home. Also, an estimate of loss of revenue because of a loss of communication or unavailability of the IP Telephony system should be evaluated.

Step 3. Identify Potential Threats and Vulnerabilities to Your IP Telephony Network

Identifying the threats to your IP Telephony network and understanding the vulnerabilities (gaps) is the key to secure your network. Threats can be various, such as the following:

■ Inside attacks from malicious users

■ Outside attacks from hackers and phreakers

- Viruses, Trojan horses, and worms
- DoS or DDoS
- Man-in-the-middle attacks
- Hardware or software failures
- Loss of critical systems

Vulnerability can range from a simple software defect to a sophisticated implementation for application and network security. A gap could be introduced because of a defect that may allow an attacker to implant a back door or because there was no host protection applied, as the system was supposed to be insulated.

Step 4.   **Estimate the Likelihood of a Potential Attack/Penetration Being Realized**

To assess the probability of an attack from malicious individuals who are either inside or outside the organization and network, application security or penetration tests could be carried out. No matter if these tests are conducted by security professionals inside the organization or outside (for example, third-party security consultants), the end result should be to identify the specific attack vectors that may be used by malicious users or outsiders to gain access to critical information and, in turn, identify and validate potential vulnerabilities that could lead to data loss.

Step 5.   **Identify Countermeasures Against Perceived Threats and Vulnerabilities**

At the termination of an information security revelation or a penetration assessment, an organization should develop an alleviation plan based on their risk tolerance. This plan should detail the findings of the information exposure risks and explain the estimated business impact in case a vulnerability is exploited or an attack is established. The report must also address an assessment of the security measures currently in place.

Most importantly, organizations must also formulate a prioritized action plan for remediation together with a list of recommendations to enhance security and reduce risk.

Step 6.   **Estimate Cost of Implementing Countermeasures Versus Not Implementing Them**

Always remember that security is a balance between risk and cost. To achieve a balance, there must be a plan well in advance and resources to put the plan in action. Too less or too much security can be a serious disadvantage to your IP Telephony network because it will either pave a way for the attackers to invade your network or may cost much more than you expected it to (in terms of financial and performance cost). For example, elevated operational costs because of fraudulent usage of the system by unauthorized users and high-usage bills can ensue.

Note: Since the equation of cost versus risk is a delicate one, you need to comprehend it and understand what you can do within your budget to apply the best possible yet effective security. This topic is covered in detail in the section, "IP Telephony Security Cost Versus Risk."

No two networks and their security needs could possibly be similar, and the same applies to IP Telephony network as well. Thus, to cover this topic, that is the level of security required, there's a dedicated section that explains the level of security required for your IP Telephony network to enable you to make the right decisions for your network.

Step 7.   **Select Suitable Countermeasures for Implementation**

The last part of the risk assessment process is the contingency plan. The contingency plan usually consists of what to do if the systems do not work as expected, or in other words, they backfire. For example, if there is a natural or unnatural disaster, what should be done to contain the damage to a minimum. Fortified with the data collected during risk assessment and the final outcome, an organization should have a precise understanding of where its exposures are and how it can leverage this information to take a risk-based, prioritized approach to create a secure IP Telephony environment.

Note: It is important that you classify the data resident on the various servers, end user workstations, and so on. Classification can be done in terms of the type of data "Company Confidential," "Company Public," or sensitive client data.

It is important to understand that although risk assessment requires high-level participation and decision making, it's actually a team effort. The process of risk assessment should be initiated and fronted by the top management in an organization. However, feedback from all levels is required, and everyone right from inventory maintenance to network administration to IP Telephony (telecom) team to CTO should be involved as stakeholders during risk assessment.

Identifying risk and conducting risk assessment are vital components of any successful and comprehensive security strategy. This significantly helps to underline what is valuable and at risk. It helps to ensure that the security planned and applied is effective and is aligned with the organization's objectives.

Components of IP Telephony Security Policy

There are standards around which a security policy should be built and implemented. These standards are guided by RFC 2196, which lists the elements of a security policy. Although RFC 2196 provides a generic security policy outline, an IP Telephony Security policy should follow these guidelines and be built on the lines of either an existing corporate security policy or developed from scratch.

As described in RFC 2196, "The Site Security Handbook:"

A security policy is a formal statement of the rules by which people who are given access to an organization's technology and information assets must abide.

IP Telephony Security Policy/Strategy

Following is an example of an IP Telephony Security policy built to protect not only the underlying network, but also the IP Telephony servers, applications, endpoints, and related assets.

Note: We are going to consider an example of a fictitious organization XYZ, trying to formulate its IP Telephony Security policy or strategy.

An IP Telephony Security policy statement follows:

It shall be the responsibility of the IP Telephony/IT Department to provide adequate protection and confidentiality of all IP Telephony-specific corporate data and proprietary software systems, whether held centrally, on local storage media, or remotely, to ensure the continued availability of IP Telephony data, network access, and programs to all authorized members of staff and to ensure the integrity of all data and configuration controls.

The security policy for IP Telephony must address the following areas:

- Acceptable use of organizational IP Telephony equipment (for example, hard phones, soft phones, WLAN phones, voicemail, and conferencing). The acceptable use includes calling plan restrictions (for example, calls to 900 numbers or international calls). These restrictions are also translated to configuration parameters on the respective IP Telephony components (for example, IP-PBX or SIP proxy). Acceptable use of IP Telephony equipment pertains also to contractors, vendors, and other third parties who interact with the organization.

- Protection of IP Telephony services, including the following:

  - Service access (for example, password-protected conferencing sessions and voice mailbox access controls)

  - Signaling and media encryption for interactions in which sensitive information is handled (for example, calls or videoconferencing in which customer or patient health information or financial information is communicated)

- Media retention based on the minimum duration that media should be kept based on regulatory or other industry, state, or federal requirements. The types of media include, but are not limited to, CDRs (call detail records), voicemail, call or video-conferencing recordings, instant messages, or backup.

- Signaling or media interception to satisfy law enforcement requirements (for example, CALEA). Although the requirement for lawful intercept pertains to carrier networks, it is helpful to provide such capability in an enterprise network to support the investigation of unforeseen incidents or circumstances.

- A vulnerability management process should be in place to categorize and prioritize the impact of vulnerabilities that may affect the organization's IP Telephony infrastructure and service.

Summary of Main IP Telephony Security Policies:

- Confidentiality of all data is to be maintained through discretionary and mandatory access controls.

- No Internet and other external service access is allowed to or from IP Telephony data center.

- Calling restrictions access will be implemented globally on all call-control clusters.

- Only authorized IP Telephony and IT staff are allowed to enter the data center. (The only exception is third-party and vendor employees escorted by IP Telephony and the IT team).

- Voice communication will be secured by using encryption techniques and by Layer 2 or Layer 3 mechanisms where possible and required.

- Voice equipment will be placed behind firewalls restricting access to users. A dedicated management VLAN will be used to manage IP Telephony devices.

- Antivirus and HIPS products will be installed and enabled wherever applicable.

- OS and administrator passwords must consist of a mixture of at least eight alphanumeric characters must be changed every 30 days, and must be unique.

- IP Telephony configurations may be changed only by IP Telephony and the IT staff.

- To prevent the loss of availability of IP Telephony resources, measures must be taken to back up data, applications, and configurations of IP Telephony equipment.

- A business continuity plan will be developed and tested on a regular basis.

- Technology purchasing guidelines must be well laid out and defined to ensure that only a vendor that passes certain criteria is to be considered for the IP Telephony solution.

- The authentication, accountability, and access (AAA) policy should clearly define the level of access, authorization for different work levels, and monitoring requirements for the access to IP Telephony system.

- Availability Statement.

- Information Technology Systems and Network Maintenance Policy.

- Supporting information.

Policy General Guidelines and Statements

Following are organization XYZ's IP Telephony Security policy general statements and guidelines.

IP Telephony Technology Purchasing Guidelines:

- All IP Telephony and network-related equipment must be purchased keeping in mind XYZ's requirements for confidentiality, integrity, and availability (CIA).

- It is essential for the equipment to incorporate mechanisms for secure and confidential administration.

Availability Statement:

- The network is available to bona fide users at all times of the day except for outages that occur for various reasons. When a trade-off must be made between confidentiality and network availability, confidentiality is always given priority.

Supporting Information:

- All information regarding XYZ IP Telephony operations must be kept confidential and must never be divulged to sources outside the company. All publicity-related matters should be handled through the Corporate Press Relations office.

- Any later conflicts and issues about the security policy must be resolved with the intervention of the chief security officer, who bears the ultimate responsibility for the security policy.

Policy Enforcement

Any employee found to have violated this policy may be subject to disciplinary action up to and including termination of employment.

Core IP Telephony Security Policies

Accountability Policy:

- All users (end users and administrators) of the network are accountable for their actions that may result in network security concerns.

- It is the responsibility of every user to be familiar with the guidelines for the services offered through the XYZ network. Also, every user is responsible to report to the system administrator about any suspected inappropriate use of IP Telephony endpoints or malicious activity on the network.

- All users are accountable for use of their phone and in the manner it is used.

Authentication Policy:

- All information assets on the IP Telephony network require authentication before someone is given access to them. Access attempts are logged for auditing.

- Remote-access users need to go through two layers of authentication to authenticate themselves to the access servers connecting them to the network and then to gain access to individual resources on the network.

- Authentication is carried out using security servers on the network. Steps must be taken to safeguard the security servers against attacks and intrusions from the outside or inside network.

- Authentication should be carried out using one-time passwords. Authentication must be accompanied by authorization and accounting on the security servers. Authorization should be used to restrict user access to resources that are intended for users based on their belonging to a certain group. Accounting should be used to further track authorized user activities. This is a basic safeguard that must be supplemented along with intrusion detection systems.

Acceptable Usage Policy:

- XYZ's IP Telephony network is available for use by employees any time of the day or night for the sole purpose to address business-related conversations.

- Using telephony, voicemail, and all IP Telephony resources for any function that is non business-related or for personal use is prohibited.

Access Policy:

- Data center access will be strictly restricted. Access will be allowed by assuming that all access is denied unless specifically required. Access to IP Telephony data center will be given to only the following:
  - IP Telephony administrators
  - IP Telephony network administrators
  - IP Telephony management team
  - Authorized vendors or third-party employees

- The IP Telephony resources must be accessed while an authorized IT or IP Telephony staff employee is located on the local network or from one of the remote sites or by one of the authorized telecommuters (only through company-approved procedures for remote-access users). Access from any other location is prohibited.

- Access to network resources will be on an as-needed basis. Information assets are protected by giving access to specific groups and denying access to all others. Increasing access privileges for a given asset requires approval from the management.

- All remote users must get management approval before they can use the resources to remotely access the corporate network. Users from the remote sites and telecommuters are treated the same as local users who use network resources. Similar access restrictions are placed on these users for accessing the various network resources.

- Remote-access users must comply with corporate guidelines to make sure that their PCs are safe to connect to the corporate network.

- It is the responsibility of the employees using remote access to ensure that their remote-access equipment is not used by unauthorized individuals to gain access to the resources on the corporate network.

IP Telephony Network Maintenance Policy:

- All IP Telephony and related network equipment is to be managed only by the full-time and authorized employees of XYZ Inc. who have the privileges to do so. Giving an individual permission to work on any network equipment for administrative purposes requires management approval.

- Remote access to administer the networking equipment is allowed, but it requires that the access be done using encryption and that authentication for login access takes place against the security servers. All management sessions, internal and external, must be encrypted.

Violations and Security Incident Reporting and Handling Policy:

- Documented processes must be set up to identify when intrusions and network attacks take place. These processes of detection must include manual reporting and automatic reporting tools.

- The following processes need to be set up for incident reporting and handling:

  - As soon as it has been confirmed that a breach has taken place or an attack is taking place, a process must be invoked to inform all the necessary network administrators of the problem and what their role is in tackling the situation.

  - A process needs to be set up to identify all the information that will be recorded to track the attack and for possible prosecution.

  - A process must be in place to contain the incident that has occurred or that is occurring. The process must be written keeping in mind that confidentiality and integrity is a bigger concern for XYZ than availability.

- A process must be in place to follow up on attacks that have occurred to make sure that all the vulnerabilities exposed through the attack are corrected and that similar attacks can be avoided in the future.

Physical Security of IP Telephony Equipment

Physical Security of IP Telephony equipment must comply with the guidelines as detailed:

- **Data center equipment:** All IP Telephony equipment, which includes IP Telephony servers, appliances, routers, switches, firewalls, and any IP Telephony related data center equipment.

- **High-risk situations:** This refers to any IP Telephony data center area that is accessible:

    - At the ground floor level

    - At the first floor level, but accessible from the adjoining roof

    - At any level via external fire escapes or other features providing access

    - Rooms in remote, concealed, or hidden areas

- **Lockdown devices:** The IP Telephony equipment will be locked down by placing it in dedicated racks placed in the secured data center.

Physical Security Policy

The following section summarizes the required physical security features for an IP Telephony data center or remote sites hosting IP Telephony equipment.

- IP Telephony servers, routers, and switches locked down to rack.

- Racking of equipment away from windows.

- High-risk situations should be addressed by window locks, shutters, and bars.

- Blinds should be deployed for observable windows.

- Intruder alarm installed by an approved company.

- Install movement detectors where applicable and possible.

- Door specification for entry/exit to/from data center.

- Visual or audio alarm confirmation.

- Strict badge access to data center.

- Access to only authorized Network Operation Center (NOC) and IP Telephony or IT team personnel.

- Break glass alarm sensors.

- Anti masking intruder alarm sensors in the data center and access routes.

- Alarm shunt lock on door.

- Superior protection of alarm signal transmission.

- Security marking.

    - All IP Telephony and related hardware should be prominently security marked by branding or etching with the name of the establishment and area postcode. Advisory signs informing that all property has been security marked should be prominently displayed externally. The following are considered inferior methods of security marking: text composed solely of initials or abbreviations, marking by paint or ultra violet ink (indelible or otherwise), or adhesive labels that do not include an etching facility.

Local-Area Network Security Policy

This section details the essential LAN security mechanisms that should be implemented to safeguard IP-based communications.

- LAN equipment

    - IP Telephony LAN equipment, hubs, bridges, repeaters, routers, and switches will be kept in secure hub rooms.

    - Hub rooms will be kept locked at all times.

    - Access to hub rooms will be restricted to IT and IP Telephony staff only.

    - Other staff and contractors requiring access to hub rooms will notify the IT department in advance so that the necessary supervision can be arranged.

    - All unused ports on switches must be in administrative shut down mode.

    - Trunk ports will allow only specific VLANs to traverse the switch trunks.

    - All VTP domains should be password protected, and VTP should be pruned.

    - Essential port security should be enabled allowing only three MAC addresses on the access port.

    - DAI and DHCP snooping should be implemented.

    - Appropriate provisions for preventing CAM table overflow, IP, and MAC spoofing attacks should be implemented.

- Workstations

    - Users must logout of their workstations when they leave their workstation for any length of time. A password protected screen saver will be implemented on all user workstations (helps prevent CIPC, sniffer-based attacks).

    - All unused workstations must be switched off outside working hours.

- LAN wiring

    - All network wiring will be fully documented.

    - All unused network points will be deactivated when not in use.

    - All network cables will be periodically scanned and readings recorded for future reference.

    - Users must not place or store any item on top of network cabling.

    - Redundant cabling schemes will be used where possible.

- Monitoring software

    - The use of LAN analyzer and packet sniffing software is restricted to the IT department.

- LAN analyzers and packet sniffers will be securely locked up when not in use.

- Intrusion detection systems will be implemented to detect unauthorized access to the network.

- Servers and other related equipment

  - All IP Telephony switches and routers will be kept securely under lock and key in the hub room. All IP Telephony servers will be kept in a secure data center.

  - Access to the system console and server disk, tape, and network share drives will be restricted to the authorized IT/IP Telephony staff only.

- Electrical security

  - All IP Telephony servers will be fitted with UPS, which also condition the power supply.

  - In the event of a mains power failure, the UPSs will have sufficient power to keep the network and servers running until the generator takes over.

  - All UPSs will be tested periodically.

- Inventory management

  - The IT/IP Telephony department will keep a full inventory of all servers, network gear, computer equipment and software in use throughout the organization.

- Audit

  - IP Telephony and underlying hardware and software audits will be carried out periodically. These audits will be used to track unauthorized changes to hardware and software configurations and to trace the source of change.

Wide-Area Network and Perimeter Security Policy

This section details the WAN and network perimeter security guidelines:

- IP Telephony equipment will be based off XYZ HQ and Remote data center, protected by firewalls.

- Remote users' alias telecommuters will be required to connect over IPSec or SSL VPN connections to the corporate VPN server for any IP Telephony services to be availed.

- Wireless LANs will make use of the most secure encryption and authentication facilities available (for example, WPA and WPA2).

- Users will not install their own wireless equipment, switches, and phones under any circumstances.

- Unnecessary protocols and services will be disabled on routers.

- The preferred method of connection to outside organizations is by a secure VPN connection, using IPSec or SSL connections.

- Permanent connections to the Internet will be via a firewall to regulate network traffic.

- Permanent connections to other external networks for offsite processing and so on will be via a firewall to regulate network traffic.

- Where firewalls are used, a dual-homed firewall (a device with more than one TCP and IP address) will be the preferred solution.

- Firewall redundancy in Active/Standby mode is preferred.

- Network equipment will be configured to close inactive sessions.

IP Telephony Server Security Policy

This section details security policy as it applies to Windows and Linux IP Telephony servers:

- The operating system will be kept up to date and patched on a regular basis.

- Servers will be checked daily for viruses (applicable to Windows servers only).

- Servers will be locked in a data center.

- Where appropriate the server console feature (HP ILO or IBM RSA) will be activated.

- Remote management passwords will be different from the application and OS administrator passwords.

- Users possessing administrator rights will be limited to trained members of the IT/IP Telephony staff only.

- Use of the Administrator accounts will be kept to a minimum. MLA/Roles will be enabled.

- Assigning security equivalences that give one user the same access rights as another user will be avoided where possible.

- Users' access to IP Telephony applications will be limited by the access control features (ACL).

- Intrusion detection and lockout will be enabled.

- The system auditing facilities will be enabled.

- All accounts will be assigned a password of a minimum of eight characters, alphanumeric.

- Administrators will change the server passwords every 180 days. (180 days is an example here; the number of days for changing passwords for servers may differ for different organizations and business verticals.)

- Unique passwords will be used for OS administrator and the web application administrator.

- FTP or SFTP facilities will be restricted to authorized staff only.

- SSH facilities will be restricted to authorized users.

Voice Application Security Policy

This section details the specifics of IP Telephony application level security:

- Call accounting will be used to monitor access and abnormal call patterns.

- Internal and external call forwarding privileges will be separated to prevent inbound calls being forwarded to an outside line.

- The operator will endeavor to ensure that an outside call is not transferred to an outside line.

- Use will be made of multilevel passwords and access authentication where available on IP Telephony applications.

- Voicemail accounts will use a password with a minimum length of six digits.

- The voicemail password should never match the last six digits of the phone number.

- Caller to a voice mail account will be locked out after three failed attempts at password validation.

- Dialing paid numbers will be prevented.

- Telephone bills will be checked carefully to identify any misuse of the telephone system.

- A conference call will be dropped when the initiator leaves.

- The phones of all executive level employees and managers and above must be encrypted.

- Use of encrypted conferences is preferred.

- CFA CSS can forward only calls to internal VoIP numbers.

- Auto registration of phones is not permitted; manual registration should be used.

Endpoint Security Policy

This section details the specifics of endpoint security (applies to wired and wireless IP Phones and soft phones):

- Web access to IP Phones will be disabled. (If web access is enabled, it should be either restricted by ACLs or should leverage HTTPS URLs.)

- Video capabilities where not needed should be disabled.

- Settings button access should be restricted or disabled.

- PC Voice VLAN access should be always disabled.

- PC port should be disabled on lobby, elevator, and rest room phones.

- GARP should be disabled on all IP Phones.

Conclusion

As apparent in various sections of the sample security policy, each asset in the IP Telephony network needs to be protected right from the perimeter to endpoints. It is essential that your IP Telephony Security policy covers all components as, leaving anything unguarded can possibly open up flood gates to attacks.

After you formulate your IP Telephony Security policy, it is time to look into some common questions that would mushroom in any IP Telephony or network security administrator's mind. Two of the most burning questions are as follows:

- What is the cost of implementing security in my Cisco IP Telephony network?

- What is the right level of security for my Cisco IP Telephony network?

In the following sections, you will be introduced to the facts that can help you decide both the level of security and the cost to implement (versus not implementing) security for your Cisco IP Telephony network.

Evaluating Cost of Security—Cost Versus Risk

The best way to put forth cost versus risk in implementing IP Telephony Security is a single phrase, "There's no such thing as a free lunch."

There's a cost for everything whether it is setting up your IP Telephony network or securing it. In the context of cost, consider the following:

- What do you think is the cost to secure your IP Telephony network?

- What should you do to minimize the cost and to maximize the security? In other words, not to put at risk what is the lifeline of your organization, the communications network, yet decrease the cost of securing this asset.

It is sometimes complicated to calculate the ROI for security implemented for your IP Telephony network. However, the damage sourced by the absence of efficient security controls is far greater than the cost to implement them. Figure 4-4 depicts the analytic details of the cost of security.

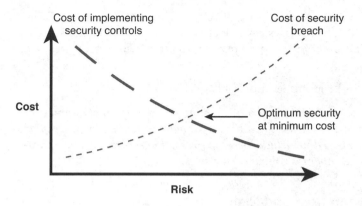

Analysis of cost vs. risk
Cost of implementing security vs. cost of security breach

Figure 4-4   *Cost vs. Risk Evaluation*

Note: Cost is in context of two major factors: monetary and human resource. In other words, how much it costs to deploy a security control or process and how many man-hours does that exercise demands.

Two factors contribute to the overall cost of security for an IP Telephony system:

■ Cost of IP Telephony Security

■ Cost of IP Telephony Security breach

Cost of Implementing IP Telephony Security

The first factor is the cumulative cost of all system security components. For example, the costs to set up Certificate Authentication Proxy Function (CAPF) with a third-party certificate to encrypt media and signaling, administer user accounts and passwords, and to set up and operate routine data backup and recovery procedures. In the long run, if planned properly this cost pays off quite well.

Cost of a Security Breach

The second cost factor arises from the expected cost (damages) resulted by IP Telephony Security breaches. For example, the organization's reputation damage, cost of recovering damaged IP Telephony information, and cost of losing data to a competition. This is the cost that would be incurred if the IP Telephony system was compromised and sensitive and critical data about call records, recordings, and customer's data were destroyed or exposed to the wrong people.

Thus, it is expected that any organization using IP Telephony would invest rationally in security controls for its IP Telephony system (as long as you invest your money judiciously), and as a result the cost of the expenditure for damages from security breaches should go down.

As described in RFC 2196, "The Site Security Handbook:"

One old truism in security is that the cost of protecting yourself against a threat should be less than the cost of recovering if the threat were to strike you. Cost in this context should be remembered to include losses expressed in real currency, reputation, trustworthiness, and other less obvious measures.

How to Balance Between Cost and Risk

With the preceding discussion about cost of security in context, let's look at the cost versus risk evaluation and understand how this can affect your decision to implement security controls in your IP Telephony network. Figure 4-5 depicts the verity that "Security is a balance between cost and risk."

Increasing Cost, Decreasing Risk

Low Default Security, No Additional Cost	Medium Moderate Security, Nominal Cost	High Highly Secure, Cost Increase
Separate Voice and Data VLANs	IP Telephony-aware Network Firewalls	TLS/Phone Proxy
Port Security	Develop IP Telephony security policy	Third-party certificate (e.g., CAPF)
Layer 2, Layer 3 ACLs	Wireless infrastructure security	Telecommuter solution
Server hardening	Host Intrusion Prevention System	802.1X
Class of Restriction (Toll Fraud)	Encrypted TFTP transfer	Network IPS
Antivirus	TLS/SRTP - Phones, Applications	Security Event Management
Scavenger QOS	IPSec/SRTP to Gateways, Trunks	
Signed Firmware		
Phone Security Settings		

IP Telephony Security: A Balance Between Risk And Cost

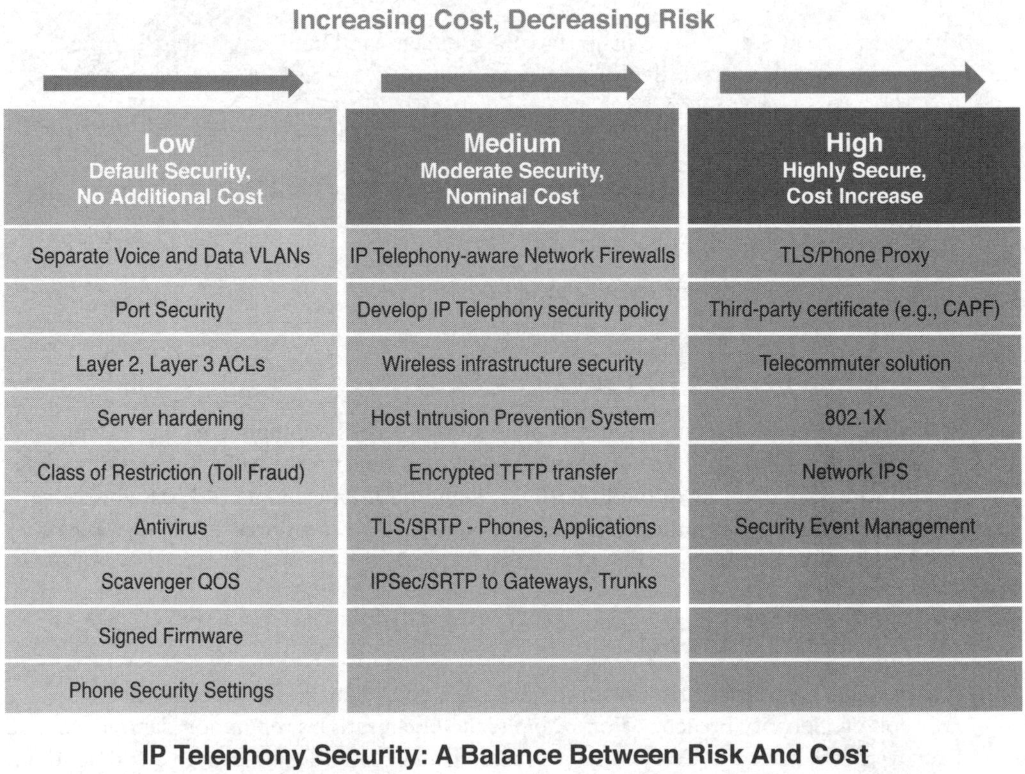

Figure 4-5   *Security Is a Balance Between Cost and Risk*

As you can discern, the cost of implementing a security control and process increases from left to right. The security implemented in an IP Telephony network can be broadly categorized in three categories: low, medium and high.

Let's explore what each one of these cover and the trade-off to invest heavily versus not investing in IP Telephony Security:

- **Low (or default level of) security:** As it is evident, a low-level of security costs nothing to minimum. This level of security is provided at a default level by IP Telephony applications and network elements. As a matter or fact, it is just about enabling it on an IP Telephony application or an underlying network component. Although this level of security might be right for networks considered to be low profile or networks where intrusion and breaches would not interest hackers, it is also an open invitation for attacks.

- **Medium (or moderate level of) security:** This level requires a moderate level of investment (not only in terms of cost however, also in terms of increasing complexity). At this level, the investment into security (fiscal and manpower) is higher than the default security level; however, it provides a much better security level to organizations (for example, SMBs to enterprises) where security breaches into IP communication network are almost imminent. The investment, both manpower and cost, pays in the long terms as, the assets are protected, and the chances of damage as a result of malicious attacks from inside or outside are minimized.

- **High (or maximum level of) security:** This is the most secure level that an IP Telephony network can be elevated to and may require a lot of planning and investment. The result is an IP Telephony solution that is secure, end-to-end. This kind of deployment is recommended for highly secure environments; however, it can be opted for by organizations where cost and manpower are next to security concerns. At the maximum security level, the monetary cost also goes up to ensure that the performance does not take a dip because of encryption overhead. To counter the same, more equipment might be required (for example, an increase in CUCM cluster size or the use of dedicated hardware encryption modules in IOS gateways instead of software encryption).

With this discussion in view, you can start thinking about the cost of implementing versus not implementing security in your IP Telephony network and make a conscious decision on how you will go about securing your IP Telephony network.

To address the second question about the level of security, let us go through the next section of evaluating the level of security required for your IP Telephony network before you can comprehend the cost versus risk equivalence with complexity versus security level. The same matrix would be leveraged to describe the level of security, complexity, and manpower or man-hours required to implement various levels of security for different IP Telephony networks.

Determining the Level of Security for Your IP Telephony Network

Let' start with a fundamental fact: Not all five fingers of a hand are equal. The same applies to IP networks, organizations, and people. No two people or two organizations are precisely identical. And the same applies to IP Telephony networks as well; no networks are ever exactly the same.

With that said, more likely than not, you must be thinking about your own IP Telephony network and how dissimilar it is to another IP Telephony network you've had a chance to work with (or designed). The question here is, "How can you compare the security applied in that other IP Telephony network to your network?" And consider if the level of security applied was perhaps too much for your network, or maybe it was lesser than what you would like to have employed in your network.

To help you with these questions, let's take an example of different organizations and their expectations from their IP Telephony network. Let's go through a series of brief case studies to help you understand which level of security may be right for your organization.

Note: The levels of security and their constituents are illustrative. These levels and their constituents may be different or represented differently by your organization. Refer to Figure 4-5 to see a broad perspective of the various security levels that can be adapted to your network and requirements, respectively.

Case Study

The following organizations are considering securing their Cisco IP Telephony network:

- A university
- Sport store with multiple branches
- Financial institution
- Government agency

All these institutions want to leverage Cisco's world-class IP Telephony solution for addressing their telecommunications requirement. They are all very excited to experience IP Telephony and IP-based collaboration solutions. However, they are also concerned about the security of their communication channels, stored call records, rogue devices, unauthorized access, and other practical issues that plague the integrity and confidentiality of their IP Telephony network. They are all striving to secure their IP Telephony network. Let's analyze the level of security each one of them should logically and practically implement. The following examples are based on assumptions relevant to IP Telephony network security that different organizations or business verticals might plan for.

Before beginning, we will use the same matrix we used in the section, "How to Balance Between Cost and Risk," for reference. However, now the discussion is no longer about the cost of security or risk. Instead, it revolves around the level of security and the associated complexity, as shown in Figure 4-6.

Increasing Complexity, Security Level, Manpower

Low Default Security, Provides Minimum Protection	Medium Moderate Security, Provides Reasonable Protection	High Highly Secure, Provides Maximum Protection
Separate Voice and Data VLANs	IP Telephony-aware Firewalls	TLS/Phone Proxy
Port Security	Develop IP Telephony Security policy	Third-party certificate (e.g., CAPF)
Layer 2, Layer 3 ACLs	Wireless infrastructure security	Telecommuter solution
Server hardening	Host Intrusion Prevention System	802.1X
Class of Restriction (Toll Fraud)	Encrypted TFTP transfer	Network IPS
Antivirus	TLS/SRTP - Phones, Applications	Security Event Management
Scavenger QOS	IPSec/SRTP to Gateways, Trunks	
Signed Firmware		
Phone Security Settings		

IP Telephony Security: Level of Security

Figure 4-6 *IP Telephony Security Levels*

Note: Security levels on the right (refer to Figure 4-6) include the features from the left, that is, moving from left to right, it is imperative that the right (successor) security level has all features from its left counterpart (predecessor).

University: At the university, because of openness and availability of resources, it is essential to prevent unauthorized access to IP Telephony facility. Moreover, any rogue devices should be barred from registering to the CUCM cluster. Also, the university IT staff would like to have the wireless communication encrypted because many students will be using Cisco Unified Presence Client (CUPC) or Cisco IP Communicator soft phones installed on their laptops. No remote access via VPN is allowed. Maintaining the IP Telephony network and cost are some of the challenges for the university's IP Telephony department.

Given the details, what do you think is the right level of security for the university's IP Telephony network? Could it be low, medium, or high? Give it a thought and write down your answer.

Sport Store: The sport store organization has multiple branches and hosts a decentralized IP Telephony network with clustering over WAN and SRST support at remote sites. The employees are allowed to access the network remotely enabling them to work from home. Thus, VPN is also part of the solution. Thanks to stiff competition, the organization wants to protect its communication streams from any possible tapping or service outage. Also, the organization intends to safeguard its IP Telephony network resources from any intrusion attempt. The security must be within a set budget and implemented in a predefined timeline.

Can you guess what level of security this organization is aspiring for, by referring to Figure 4-6?

Financial institution: A popular and successful financial institution plans to secure its Cisco IP Telephony deployment. Although it does not want to let go of any native security feature, it does not want to increase the complexity level too much. One important aspect is that as per the security policy of the organization, no endpoints can register unless they have been authenticated by the AAA server on its premises. Also, no autoregistration of the endpoints is allowed. The IP Telephony staff of the organization maintains a separate IP Telephony Security policy that it must follow meticulously. Cost is not an issue and neither is manpower.

Equipped with this information, what do you think is the level of security this financial institution is planning for?

Government agency: A government agency is considering implementing its new IP Telephony network. It chose Cisco as its vendor. It wants to have it secured end-to-end with no exception. The level of security must meet guidelines set by its telecom and network security department security policy. Also, it has a contingency plan to address any security issues that may show up during normal operations. Cost, manpower, and time have virtually no frills.

With this information, can you think of the right security level to satisfy the government agency's need for end-to-end security (based on security levels depicted in Figure 4-6)?

The Riddles Are Over

It is time to put all these riddles to an end and explore the options these institutions should "ideally" opt for.

University: Because the security needed is minimal and basic, a low or default level of security should suffice for the university IP Telephony network. This can enable it to secure its IP Telephony network with minimal additional cost and manpower. (The only exception is the addition of wireless security that overlaps with a medium or moderate security level.)

Sport store: The store is aspiring for a non-default level of security because the requirement was to encrypt the communication (media and signaling) streams and to evade any DoS attacks (use of a firewall to prevent malicious attack attempts). Thus, a medium or moderate level of security will be an ideal fit for it.

Financial organization: The financial organization does not want a complex solution yet one that provides maximum protection. This calls for a medium or moderate security level with the exception that it is requires that the endpoints use its AAA server (for 802.1x). This overlaps with the high or maximum security level.

Government agency: A government agency, as you might have guessed, is a maximum protection facility. Also, keeping in view the end-to-end security requirements along with a contingency plan (security event management), only the highest level of IP Telephony Security can satisfy its requirements.

As you can probably figure out, it is not always that the need for security is addressed by a static set of security controls defined within a security level. Sometimes, these may overflow or overlap to the next level as some of the security requirements cannot be satisfied by the current level. However, at the same time it is important to note that, the cost, time to plan or deploy, and man-hours also increase.

Putting Together All the Pieces

It is finally time to put together all the pieces to outline a security framework for your Cisco IP Telephony network:

- Security strategy

- Risk assessment

- Security controls

- Identified threats, attacks and vulnerabilities, and mitigations

- Organization objectives

The driving force is that an IP Telephony Security Framework should help in the enrichment of IP Telephony services, enabling the users to feel confident in the privacy and integrity of their communication. In other words, a security framework should enhance and not form an obstruction to the IP-based communications.

IP Telephony Security Framework

The main ideologies that drive an IP Telephony Security Framework are as following:

- Supports simplification of design and configuration for security for IP Telephony network

- Ascertains confidentiality, integrity, and availability of IP Telephony network

- Provides defense in opposition to internal and external threats and diverse attacks

- Provides for scalable IP Telephony architecture by integrating multiple layers for security
- Based on corporate security policies and strategy
- Should function in a mixed environment of secured and unsecured IP Telephony components

To describe the security framework for your IP Telephony network, a useful approach would be to divide the tangible IP Telephony solution into logical domains and to pin down threats and vulnerabilities within each domain. The logical domains in which an IP Telephony solution can be broken down into following categories:

- IP Telephony Call Control servers (CUCM)
- IP Telephony media servers (Unity and Unity Connection)
- IP Telephony application servers (Attendant console and UCCX)
- IP Telephony billing, user data servers (CDR and LDAP)
- IP Telephony end-user devices (IP Phone, soft phone, and CUPC)
- IP Telephony operational and management access
- Peripheral servers (voice gateways)
- Communication transit in internal networks (Intranet or Extranet)
- Communication transit in a public network (Internet)

Note: Each domain must be fortified and equipped with authentication, encryption, authorization, accounting, and security mechanisms.

Figure 4-7 outlines the logical domains pertinent to an IP Telephony Security Framework.

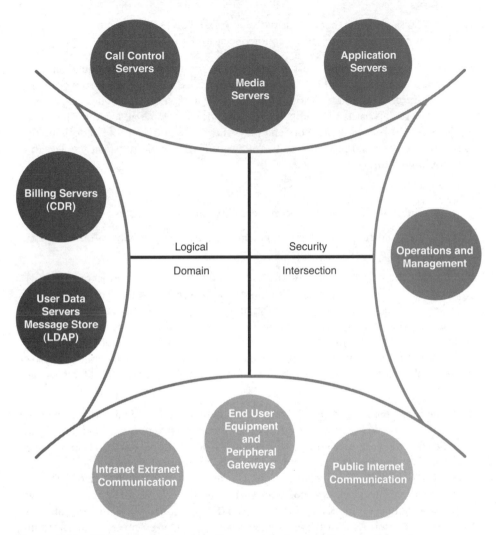

Figure 4-7 *IP Telephony Security Framework: Logical Security Domains*

In essence, at a high level, the IP Telephony Security Framework can be envisioned as a blend of the following elements:

- Technology involved

- Management support

- Regulatory aspects

- Organization processes

- Training requirements

It is around these elements that a security framework revolves. Let's comprehend what each element contributes to the IP Telephony Security Framework:

- **Technology involved:** The most critical element for maintaining confidentiality, integrity, and availability of IP Telephony services. Technology goes from evading passive intrusion attempts to sophisticated attack mitigation techniques (as discussed in Chapter 1, "What Is IP Telephony Security and Why Do You Need It?"). It is the core of an IP Telephony network and plays the most significant role in defining the security controls and processes to be followed. The technology aspect involves (but is not limited to) the following:

  - Attack mitigation

  - Pre- and Post-deployment risk, vulnerability, and security assessment

  - Define standards for encryption, key management, and authentication within the organization

- **Management support:** As a well-known fact, no (IP Telephony) project will commence devoid of apt funding and support by higher management. The decision makers, stakeholders, and executives should be supportive to have a secure and robust IP Telephony network in place. In other words, they should be better informed about the cost of security breaches and the ROI so they not only support the financial cause, but also support from a leadership and involvement perspective. (Remember risk assessment and security strategy requires participation from stakeholders.)

- **Regulatory aspects:** The U.S. Communications Assistance for Law Enforcement Act (CALEA) may require access at various security levels. A service provider is obliged to provide the necessary session keys to law enforcement personnel. Despite that private companies may be exempt, a 2007 U.S. government regulation, CALEA, requires public VoIP carriers to comply with federal wiretapping standards. There are other regulatory acts that come into action pertinent to VoIP systems, for example, the Fighting Internet and Wireless Spam (FISA) Act and USA Patriotic (also known as Patriot) Act. Moreover, some organizations (for example, financial institutions) are required to meet global certifications. See the following URL for more information on how Cisco products cater to these requirements:

  http://www.cisco.com/web/strategy/government/sec_cert.html

- **Organization processes:** The organization processes have a strong influence on the security framework because they drive the organization's objective to which the security framework should be aligned with. Furthermore, a security strategy must be aligned with organization's mission and vision, objectives, and goals. IP Telephony Security requires continuous vigilance and should be integrated into existing processes rather than viewed at as a one-time task. In essence, the processes elements include the following:

  - Security strategy

  - Organization objectives and goals

■ **Training requirements:** The Cisco IP Telephony system provides users with an extensive range of security features. These features are however useless if users of IP Telephony do not understand how to use them. Thus, it is important that end users are involved early in the implementation phase and IP Telephony administrators are involved during planning phase. Furthermore, cross-training should also be provided by the organization to the IT and telecom staff who may not have worked together prior to an IP Telephony implementation. Because IP Telephony systems are more complex than traditional telephone systems and use the underlying network, getting IT, telecom, and network teams aligned and training collectively is crucial to build and maintain a secure IP Telephony system.

Therefore, it is the accumulation of all the elements discussed (in Chapters 1 through 4), that derive the security framework for an IP Telephony network, as illustrated in Figure 4-8.

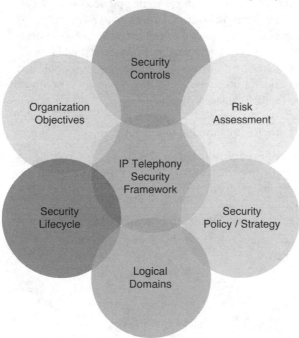

Figure 4-8   *IP Telephony Security Framework*

The IP Telephony Security Framework (refer to Figure 4-8) should serve as the baseline to protect your IP Telephony network and its services. The implementation of this framework is detailed in the subsequent chapters via security construct in design, configuration, and implementation.

Summary

While forming a security framework for your Cisco IP Telephony network, it is vital to have a handle on the various components that form the security framework. The Cisco security life cycle must be followed meticulously to implement the four phases and fit them to your IP Telephony network. This should be followed by the planning and designing of security into your IP Telephony network. Then is the rigorous exercise of risk assessment, countermeasures, and a contingency plan for every recognized asset for your IP Telephony system and underlying network equipment the organization or business owns or operates. IP Telephony Security policy is an imperative component of your IP Telephony Security Framework, without which you simply cannot position proper security controls even if you have them penned down.

A security policy is not a fixed document because it needs to be updated on a regular basis to counter any new security challenge or to address a new requirement. When designing a secure IP Telephony network, some goals (for example, objectives an organization; intent to ensure IP Telephony system availability, confidentiality, and integrity; readiness for lawful interception; alignment with overall organization security objectives; and so on) need to be taken into consideration. This chapter also discussed how much it costs when threats are realized and the IP Telephony system is out of service, that is, the cost of security. Also, you can work out the right level of security for your IP Telephony network based on the covered case studies presented in this chapter.

Part II, "Cisco IP Telephony Network Security", shows you how to protect your IP Telephony network by securing Layer 1 (physical layer), Layer 2 (switching infrastructure), Layer 3 (routing infrastructure), and network perimeter. You will learn about the importance of network security pertinent to IP Telephony, and the ways in which you can secure your IP Telephony network against internal and external threats.

Cisco IP Telephony Network Security

"If you have built castles in the air, your work need not be lost; that is where they should be. Now put the foundations under them." –Henry David Thoreau

Chapter 5

Cisco IP Telephony Physical Security

Now that you have your IP Telephony Security Framework worked out, it is time to apply the same to the technology element and to start with the first fundamental step, physical security. It is your IP Telephony network, so there's no reason why it cannot be secure at the basic layer.

In the past, protecting network and telecom equipment with an utmost level of reliability was not necessary because of the clear demarcation between telecom and network domains. Today, however, with network convergence and the importance of IP-based communications, the paradigm has shifted, and it is essential to protect your IP Telephony systems. If the network is not physically secure, many attack vectors are left open, which can lead to significant loss of information and system availability. All other security is far-fetched if physical security is scarce.

This chapter covers the following topics:

- IP Telephony physical security: What is it all about?
- IP Telephony physical security challenges
- Locking down IP Telephony equipment
- Environmental factors

IP Telephony Physical Security

Physical security for IP Telephony is defined as the process of employing all the actions necessary to protect an IP Telephony data center or facility. In other words, defend against physical damage (or abuse) the facility (whether it is a data center, a remote site, or an end user location, such as a home office) where IP Telephony servers and endpoints are located. This process includes internal and external security measures, disaster-recovery plans, and personnel training.

What Is IP Telephony Physical Security All About?

You may ask, "Why is there a dedicated chapter on physical security in this book?" Alternatively, you can argue that it is something that is done at a minimum level across all organizations. Then, why read or think about something so fundamental? The answer depends on how seriously you take physical security, and if you understand the consequences of not doing things you are supposed to.

IP Telephony users anticipate converged communication networks to preserve the high level of availability, as was provided by the traditional phone systems. To ensure that the end users get this level of availability, it is critical that you plan physical security for the IP Telephony application servers, switches, routers, firewalls, endpoints, and so on, that construct a converged network.

All organizations, whether small or large, must consider the ramifications of stolen or lost data, principally in terms of monetary and reputation losses as well as in terms of legal costs. Not only are the modern-day organizations more susceptible to malicious attacks, but also losses as a result of competition, openness because of the reach of networks, and possible incapability to follow rapid technology changes, they are also further susceptible to legal action against them on account of lost customer or internal information. Although, the negative image can certainly cause damage to a business, lawsuits can be very costly and can even dictate an organization going broke.

The best way to describe physical security is to look at the concept as a sequence of concentric circles, as shown in Figure 5-1, with each layer more secure than the previous one.

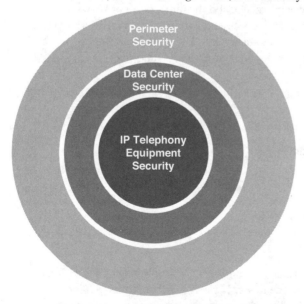

Figure 5-1   *IP Telephony Physical Security: Conceptual View*

Physical security is the first line of defense and the first step to build a secure and robust IP Telephony network. However, as easy as it can be defined using a blueprint or a standard, it is much more difficult to put into action in the real world. Let's figure out the various physical security challenges which are subsequently addressed in succeeding sections.

Physical Security Issues

Exploiting the physical security of any organization requires at a minimum, if at all, technical knowledge by the trespasser or attacker. Many times, physical security is compromised inadvertently by a well-meaning employee, in the process of carrying out a routine job, for example, someone working in the server room may unknowingly plug out the power cable to a rack instead of his laptop's power adaptor cable.

The realization of physical security can fall short for various reasons. Major reasons are usually financial constraints and lack of planning. If not proactively planned for, it becomes difficult to establish a secure data center (or a facility) where the IP Telephony equipment and endpoints could be locked down to evade any physical threats. It applies equally to resources (fiscal or human) being realized because without proper budget or human resources, it becomes extremely difficult to apply the level of security you want for your IP data center (or remote sites).

Note: The terms data center and facility are used interchangeably.

The four main areas of concern follow:

- Restricting access to IP Telephony facility
- Security at the perimeter of IP Telephony facility and within the IP Telephony data center
- Personnel training
- Disaster recovery and survivability

Apart from these four major areas of concern, there's another candidate for the most obnoxious category of risks, the environmental factor. Environmental factors consist of natural or man-made risks.

Let's delve deeper into each of these to understand how these concerns can be addressed.

Restricting Access to IP Telephony Facility

Let's begin by addressing the physical security issues rising off the perimeter and within the IP Telephony facility.

Securing the IP Telephony Data Center Perimeter

When implementing physical security, the first thing to look into is the location of your site and the characteristics of that location. For example, if the location is on the seismic line, whether there's a forest nearby, and if there could be a risk of a wild forest fire, and so on. After this, comes the facility perimeter, which is the demarcation between the external world and your IP Telephony facility. Now, the question is, "How can you secure the boundary beyond which you may not have any exercisable control; however, on the inside it is your domain to protect?"

At the physical perimeter, multiple layers of security are required to repel any attempt to attack the facility. You have read about the physical security elements in the IP Telephony Security Strategy (Chapter 4, "Cisco IP Telephony Security Framework"). Let's go through the extended list of physical security controls and mechanisms that can be put in place to safeguard your IP Telephony facility.

The following list is an overview of available layers and options for external physical security:

- Security guards always should be stationed on the fringe (enter and exit points).

- Windows (if any) should be secured by locks, shutters, and bars as applicable.

- Blinds should be provided for observable windows.

- An electromagnetic intrusion detection system must be installed.

- An intruder alarm should be installed by an approved company.

- Movement detectors should be installed.

- Visual or audio alarms must be available.

- Access only to authorized personnel or accompanied individuals upon display of ID cards at the perimeter gate.

- Protection of alarm signal transmission must be ensured (insulated alarm cables).

- An electronic fence should be deployed at perimeter walls.

- Use of motion sensing and infrared supporting camera/CCTV systems should be promoted.

- Control entrance security (smart cards and PIN codes).

- There should be a well-defined limit on access to the delivery and loading areas and other publically accessible areas, in accordance with the required operational requirements.

- Isolation of loading, publically accessible areas from information processing facilities and areas where information is stored, where possible.

- Inspection of incoming and outgoing materials must be performed by authorized staff.

Note that achieving maximum external physical security according to these specifications may be compromised in many situations because not all layers can be easily implemented. It could be because of situational, procedural, financial, or lack of planning issues.

IP Telephony Data Center Internal Security

Comparable to a network being more susceptible to internal attacks, an IP Telephony data center is also most vulnerable to inside threats. Internal physical security techniques can be defined by following a layered model approach. Some areas protected by both the external and internal measures overlap. For instance, camera systems can be installed all over the campus and as entrance security for mission-critical areas, such as lab space, communication rooms, and server rooms. Just as with external security, internal security must follow the layered security approach. Entrance to low-security areas requires only a PIN code or card reader, and entrance to high-security areas requires card readers in combination with biometrics. High-level security areas can also be equipped with smoke, temperature, and humidity sensors.

In addition to previously defined security controls for securing an IP Telephony data center perimeter, the following list gives an overview of available layers and security controls and options for internal (data center) physical security:

- IP Telephony servers, routers, firewalls, gateways, and switches should be locked down to racks, and racks should be secured by lock and key.

- Racks should be placed away from windows.

- Visual or audio alarms must be installed and active.

- Fire suppression systems (foam extinguishers and sprinklers) must be installed.

- RFID-based badge access to the data center must be implemented. (A biometric access system is preferred, for example, fingerprint access.)

- Access should be restricted to only authorized NOC and IP Telephony or IT Team personnel.

- Break glass alarm sensors must be installed.

- Alarm shunt lock on door must be installed.

- Guidelines for authorized staff working in sensitive areas should be implemented.

- Prohibit unsupervised or unmonitored work in sensitive areas for safety reasons and to evade any opportunity for intended or unintended misconduct.

- Alternative routing or transmission media (cabling and wireless) should be provisioned where appropriate, particularly for critical systems.

- Clearly identify cable and equipment markings, except where security may be enhanced by removing such markings.

■ If the information needs to be erased, secure information removal by appropriately trained personnel should be done.

Personnel Training

A well-built IP Telephony Security policy helps protect your crucial IP Telephony resources only if all staff members and employees are well trained and are aware of all aspects and processes of the policy. More often than not, organizations have their employees sign a proclamation confirming that they have read and understood the security policy. As mentioned in Chapter 4, it is essential that the IP Telephony, network, security, and telecom teams are together in training to understand what is expected of them and how they can complement each other in their areas of expertise. This helps not only build a robust and secure IP Telephony network however, also leads to coherence in the work force, motivated for a common goal, that is, the protection and security of IP Telephony network from internal and external threats.

Security education contents should include IT management establishing policies around operational security best practices when performing maintenance work on IP Telephony systems. Security education at the least should provide guidance to establish physical access restriction rules, protecting access cards and keys, emphasis on maintaining a security log of activities performed, use printed materials pertinent to location, and access details of physical equipment.

Security education-related information could be delivered via various channels such as newsletters, e-mails, campaigns, and posters. This helps nurture the sense of need for security at all levels enabling support from an executive level descending to clerks to operators to cleaning staff.

Disaster Recovery and Survivability

Murphy's law states, "If anything can go wrong, it will." However, it does not mean that you should not be prepared! With that said, a strong disaster-recovery plan needs to be in place, even for the most protected and secure areas. The likelihood of things going wrong should be addressed upfront to minimize disruption and losses.

From the point of view of survivability (under normal operational and disaster recovery circumstances), some basics must be followed consistently. For example, Uninterruptible Power Supply (UPS) is the implicit standard for protection against power outage. Furthermore, only one connection to the service provider accounts for a single point of failure and cannot be tolerated in a crucial communication network. Provisioning of SRST at remote sites, cold backup server(s), load balancers, and so on can be incorporated in design to provide a resilient solution.

Disaster recovery is the de-facto standard for a highly available IP Telephony network. It calls for the implementation of a complete fail-over site (redundant data center) or decentralized IP Telephony network (multiple clusters or clustering over WAN). This may be a radical approach for some organizations. However, it all makes sense when you consider the loss of not only the IP Telephony services, but also the loss of vital IP Telephony data. The cost of losing your critical infrastructure and IP Telephony services is nothing compared to the cost of installing a fail-over site.

Note: The critical infrastructure consists of IP Telephony servers, supporting network systems (routers, switches, and firewalls), that is essential to the minimum operational needs and communications of your organization.

To complement the IP Telephony Security policy, a backup and recovery policy must be in place. In essence, the constituents of such a policy define the processes to safeguard the information and service availability. This is necessary to ensure the IP Telephony network is restored to an operational status as quickly as possible after an attack or other events that may cause the network to fail.

A backup and restore policy must be formed around these principles:

- Backups must be stored in a secure location.

- Backups that leave the physical premises of the organization should be encrypted.

- Ensure that a reasonable provision for redundant equipment and backups is made available to support utility failure.

- Incidents should be managed and reported as per the Security Incident Management Policy of the organization.

Locking Down IP Telephony Equipment

Racks and enclosures help keep your network equipment (IP Telephony servers, routers, switches, gateways, and so on) out of harm's way and also shield it from meddlesome audience. The enclosures protect equipment from accidental spills and enable controlled access by providing the ability to lock the cabinets.

A useful approach to lock down IP Telephony equipment is to have an operational model as follows:

- Follow the IP Telephony Security policy.

- Protect all core IP Telephony components (servers, gateways, and underlying network devices).

- Controlled access to public area IP Phones.

Note: Public area refers to the lobby, rest rooms, elevators, break rooms, front desk, smoking zones, and so on that are unreservedly accessible.

IP Telephony equipment should be appropriately locked down and maintained to ensure its continued availability and integrity. This may include the following:

- IP Telephony servers and supporting network equipment should be properly planned and stacked in racks.

- CCTV cameras should be deployed in the vicinity of the critical infrastructure.

- Only authorized staff should have physical access, including locks and keys to IP Telephony racks.

- Appropriate preventive maintenance should be carried out only by authorized, certified employees or contracted third parties under strict supervision.

- An inventory of equipment should be maintained and audited at regular intervals.

- Appropriate security measures should be applied to off-site equipment, taking into account the different risks of working outside the organization's premises. Moreover, security controls for equipment in transit and in off-site premises should be appropriately applied.

- Employee and contractor awareness of their responsibilities for protecting information and the devices, and the particular risks of off-premises environments must be addressed.

Environmental Factors

When you live in a world where nature and its elements have a strong influence on your daily life activities, it becomes vital to safeguard your IP Telephony infrastructure from any certain known or possibly unknown natural or humanly induced risks.

Protection against damage from fire, flood, earthquake, explosion, civil unrest, sabotage, and other forms of natural and man-made (artificial) risks should be designed and implemented. This could include the following:

- Taking into account the security threats posed by nearby facilities or structures.

- Exclusive controls as appropriate to minimize physical threats, for example, damage from defacement, fire, water, dust, smoke, vibration, electrical supply variance, or electromagnetic radiation.

- Appropriate equipment, such as fire-fighting devices and other counter-measures provided and suitably located on site.

- Appropriate arrangements for remote location for backup facility.

- Guidelines for eating, drinking, smoking, or other activities in the vicinity of equipment.

- Facilities equipped with emergency equipment (for example, emergency lighting and first aid boxes) to ensure the safety for those working within a facility.

Summary

Without a well-built base, a strong structure cannot be erected. The same applies to all networks, and IP Telephony networks are no exception. Without the basic security at the physical level, higher logical level/layer security proves pointless. No amount of network security helps if a malicious user or an attacker breaks into the IP Telephony facility and walks off with the call detail records (CDR) or vandalizes the equipment. Thus, it becomes essential to have all physical security issues dealt with in a holistic way to counter the threats originating from inside and outside the IP Telephony facility.

This chapter gave you a sound understanding of the various physical threats that lurk around your IP Telephony network and how you can curb these threats. Physical security has many challenges to be addressed; however, most of these can be overcome with proper planning, training, and participation by all working technology groups and higher management support.

The next chapter helps you grasp Layer 2 security issues and their mitigation mechanisms to help ensure that those pesky rogue endpoints and attackers are kept at bay.

Chapter 6

Cisco IP Telephony Layer 2 Security

Layer 2 is one of the favorite places to attack by a hacker or attacker! The reason, you ask? It gives them access to virtually everything within your IP Telephony network! Also, Layer 2 attacks are the first ones a hacker will position, after getting access to a victim machine within your network. However, it should not make you feel anxious because this chapter addresses various Layer 2 threats. By the end of this chapter, you will know about the security attacks that can be used to exploit Layer 2 of your Cisco IP Telephony network and how you can deal with them.

This chapter covers the following topics:

- Layer 2 security overview

- IP Telephony Layer 2 security issues and mitigation

- Dealing with rogue endpoints: 802.1x

- Layer 2 security best practices

Layer 2 Security Overview

The OSI model was built to allow the different layers to work without awareness of each other. This means that if one layer is breached, the communication is compromised without the other layers being aware of the problem. And the logical security implementation begins at Layer 2: the data link layer. The data link layer is the second layer of the OSI model and has the primary functions such as communication with the network layer above and the physical layer below and changing upper-layer packets into frames before transmission. The security of Layer 2 is of utmost importance because a collapse in the switching infrastructure will lead to the disruption of all upper layer functions (Layers 3–7). This chapter discusses the various threats to Layer 2 (data link layer) of your Cisco IP Telephony network and how you can go about remediation of these threats.

Cisco IP Telephony Layer 2 Topology Overview

This section is dedicated to an overview of Layer 2 topology for IP Telephony environment. It is vital to understand what Layer 2 for your IP Telephony network may look like in order to effectively plan and secure it.

For every voice-enabled network, two VLANs at the access layer, one each for data and voice, are highly recommended, as shown in Figure 6-1.

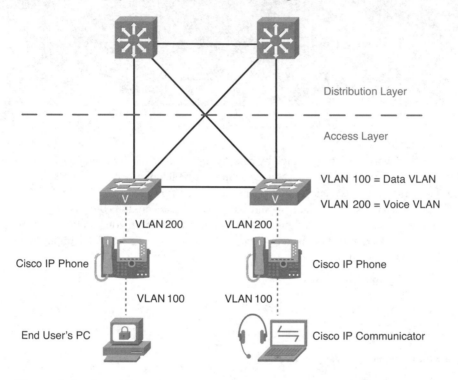

Figure 6-1 *Access Layer Overview*

As you can observe in Figure 6-1, Cisco Unified IP Phones are connected to two Cisco Catalyst 3550 switches. User PCs or laptops (optionally running IP Communicator) connect to the IP Phones. VLAN 100 is reserved for data endpoints whereas VLAN 200 is reserved for voice endpoints.

Having two unique VLANs, one for data and the other for voice, is recommended for various security reasons:

- It enables separation of voice and data traffic; therefore, any threats looming from data VLAN are automatically mitigated (best practice from network security perspective).

- Voice traffic can get its own QoS treatment in Voice VLAN.

- Helps limit exposure to DoS attacks on data traffic from affecting voice.

It is essential to understand that the switching infrastructure at the access layer must meet some minimum requirements such as the following:

■ Power over Ethernet (PoE) support for IP Phones

■ 802.1Q, 802.1p, or ISL support

■ Fast link convergence

■ CDP support for Cisco Unified IP Phones and LLDP-Med support for third-party IP Phones

Note Cisco Discovery Protocol (CDP) is the Cisco proprietary protocol to detect the type of device attached to the network. It is key when implementing Cisco IP Phones. Third-party switches may not support CDP, and in such a case, every phone must be configured manually and assigned to Voice VLAN. In case no IP Phones are connected to a switch, CDP can be disabled.

The next section helps you explore the rationale behind implementing Layer 2 security.

Why Bother with Layer 2 Security?

You may possibly ask, "Why should I worry about Layer 2 security in my IP Telephony network? Layer 2 is something that may never be extended across the boundary of my network, and it is Layer 3 that is hitting the WAN, going outside of the network, so why should I bother securing something that is possibly never exposed to the outside world and is always under my domain?"

Even though the latter is true, the former requires your immediate attention in case you do not have proper security controls applied at Layer 2. This is because when you consider Layer 2 security, you are anticipating that in a LAN you have users you can trust. Now, that very thought violates the fact that most of the attacks emerge from within the organization.

Try to answer the following question:

Are you sure that every employee in your organization is doing the right thing in the favor of network security?

If your answer is no, then it is time to reconsider your security implementation construct. As a matter of fact, even well-meaning employees can inadvertently induce flaws in your IP Telephony network. For example, an employee can plug in a switch brought from home to connect more devices at the workplace or can become a victim of social engineering, which puts your IP Telephony network in harm's way.

Layer 2 security is often one of the most overlooked aspects in most networks as explained earlier in Chapter 2, "Cisco IP Telephony Security Building Blocks." This is primarily because of the common misbelief that Layer 2 does not interact with the external world and therefore cannot be exposed to or vulnerable to threats, which on the contrary is not true because insider threats are always present. Moreover, with converged networks for collaboration technologies and the mobile workforce, the physical boundaries of a network are rather blurred, where resources are available at anytime, from anywhere.

A switch operating at Layer 2 does not need to know about the devices (for example, servers and physical transmission media) running at higher or lower layers. This further augments the need to secure Layer 2. Layer 2 without proper security measures is a weak link in the hierarchy of an IP Telephony network.

Remember, security is only as strong as the weakest link.

IP Telephony Layer 2 Security Issues and Mitigation

There are many threats that creep around your switching infrastructure. Let's investigate the diverse security issues that plague Layer 2 implementation and understand how you can address these issues in your IP Telephony network.

Let's go over the Layer 2 security threats and their mitigation techniques. Following is a list of various Layer 2 attacks that can be positioned by a talented and motivated hacker against your IP Telephony network:

- VLAN hopping
- STP manipulation
- DHCP server spoofing
- ARP spoofing
- MAC address spoofing
- IP address spoofing
- CAM table overflow and DHCP starvation

To repel and curb these threats, you need to understand each threat and its mitigation technique.

Note The commands and configuration examples assume Cisco IOS Software is the baseline. Cisco IOS version 12.2 for Cisco Catalyst switches is used for all configuration examples in this book.

VLAN Hopping Attack and Mitigation

This section explores the VLAN hopping attack, which is a serious threat to IP Telephony networks. By virtue of this attack, an attacker can own the voice segment and sniff or capture voice communication streams (signaling and media).

Attack Details

A VLAN hopping attack (as the name suggests) enables an attacker to hop between VLANs and access a native or an auxiliary VLAN. This attack poses a serious threat to voice segments because a malicious insider or outsider can hop between VLANs and access confidential information such as the following:

- Voice conversations can be sniffed and recorded or replayed.

- Voice signaling can be intercepted to trace the location/IP of the call control or voice messaging systems to unleash the next series of attacks.

A VLAN hopping attack can be accomplished in two ways: by negotiating a trunk with a legitimate switch and by double tagging. Let's explore the two approaches to understand how you can evade these attacks.

VLAN Hopping by Trunk Negotiation

In this attack, which is also known as 802.1Q and ISL tagging attack, an attacker tricks the network switch into believing that it is a legitimate switch on the network and requires trunk access, as shown in Figure 6-2.

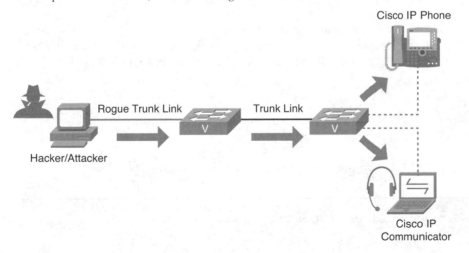

Figure 6-2 *VLAN Hopping Attack by Negotiating Trunk with Switching Infrastructure*

> **Note**   Connections between two Cisco switches are usually configured as trunk ports. The trunk ports are designed to connect two switches to allow VLAN traffic across the trunk. Also, note that Cisco switches have the capability to dynamically negotiate a trunk port.

An attacker connected to your IP Telephony network could then run the dynamic trunking protocol (DTP) in his machine or switch and attempt to negotiate a trunk link instead of a regular access layer connection. After the trunk is negotiated, all trunk-allowed VLANs (and their traffic) are accessible.

> **Note**   A trunk port can carry traffic from all trunks by default or only certain trunks, as configured by the switch administrator.

VLAN Hopping by Double Tagging (802.1Q)

Another way to initiate a VLAN hopping attack is to use double tagging, also known as a nested VLAN attack. In this attack, the attacker attempts to send double encapsulated 802.1Q frames.

> **Note**   802.1Q and ISL are the supported trunking protocols on Cisco switches. Although 802.1Q is open standard, ISL is Cisco proprietary.

Because a switch performs only one level of decapsulation, the switch cares only about the first tag and removes it, and then the second one is processed and sent out to other switches over the trunk links. The attack process is depicted in Figure 6-3.

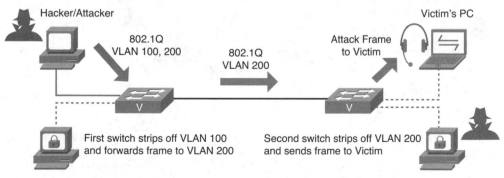

Figure 6-3   *VLAN Hopping Attack by Double Tagging*

The attacker sends double-tagged frames with VLAN 100 and 200. The first switch strips off VLAN 100 and forwards the frame to the trunk link for VLAN 200. The second switch strips off VLAN 200 and sends the frame to the destination port with the destination MAC address (that which was programmed by the attacker).

Mitigation

To alleviate a VLAN hopping attack using trunking or double-tagging mechanisms, ensure that you have the switch ports assigned to an access VLAN and all these ports are in mode access. In Example 6-1, we use VLAN 999, which is an unused VLAN and a non-Native VLAN. If a port is enabled, ensure that the mode of the port is set to access if it is user-facing (use to connect end-user devices) or set to trunk mode if it is switch-facing (carrying trunk traffic). Moreover, any unused ports on user or server facing switches should be disabled to elevate the risk of connection of any rogue devices.

In Example 6-1, the switch ports 0/2–0/24 are set to access mode (hard coded) and assigned VLAN 999.

Note Cisco IOS version 12.2.40 is used for all configuration examples in this book. For your Catalyst IOS version or switch model, refer to http://www.cisco.com.

Example 6-1 *Setting Cisco Catalyst Switch Port(s) to Hard-Coded Access Mode*

```
IPTSW(config)# interface range FastEthernet 0/2 - 24
IPTSW(config-if)# switchport mode access
IPTSW(config-if)# switchport access VLAN 999
```

In Example 6-2, the switch port 0/1 is set to trunk mode (hard coded) with the 802.1Q standard, not to negotiate any DTP, and the switch administrator is allowing only VLANs 50 and 51 through the trunk to the other switch.

Example 6-2 *Setting Cisco Catalyst Switch Port(s) to Hard-Coded Trunk Mode*

```
IPTSW(config)# interface range FastEthernet 0/1
IPTSW(config-if)# switchport mode trunk
IPTSW(config-if)# switchport nonegotiate
IPTSW(config-if)# switchport trunk encapsulation dot1q
IPTSW(config-if)# switchport trunk allow 50-51
```

Spanning Tree Protocol (STP) Manipulation

STP is the mechanism to prevent loops in a switching network. Loops can be dangerous, which motivates hackers to manipulate STP and re-converge IP Telephony network to their advantage.

Attack Details

On booting a Cisco switch, STP identifies one switch as a root bridge. STP uses Bridge Protocol Data Units (BPDU) to maintain a loop-free topology by blocking redundant paths. Now, a hacker can send spoofed BPDU packets to assume the role of the root bridge, as illustrated in Figure 6-4.

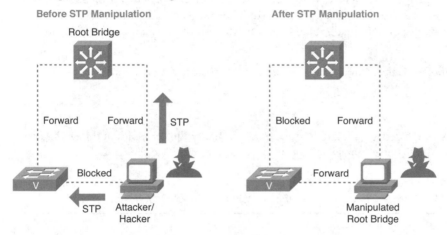

Figure 6-4   *STP Manipulation*

The motive is to spoof the root bridge to capture all traffic, launch DoS attacks, or initiate MITM attacks. By sending BPDU traffic, hackers can force VLAN STP recalculations and change STP topology, which can take a minimum of 30 seconds. This, in turn, enables them to perform a DoS attack indefinitely by keeping the switching infrastructure re-converging. On the other hand, a hacker (as previously mentioned) can also hijack traffic by pretending to be a root bridge and launch a man-in-the-middle (MITM) attack to change the data/RTP streams as he pleases.

Mitigation

The BPDU guard and root guard can prevent the Dos or MITM attacks originating as a result of STP manipulation. Portfast instructs switch port(s) not to go through the four stages, that is, listening, learning, blocking, and forwarding. On the other hand, this combined with bpduguard helps stop STP manipulation by enabling port(s) for not accepting any BPDU. The root guard ensures that when the root (or root bridge) is elected, a new

BPDU on a designated port that you apparently trust is not entertained, and the port is moved to a root-inconsistent STP state.

The commands shown in Example 6-3 help curb the STP manipulation attempts.

Example 6-3 *STP BPDU and Root Guard Configuration*

```
IPTSW(config)# spanning-tree portfast bpduguard
IPTSW(config)# spanning-tree guard root
```

DHCP Spoofing

DHCP spoofing can be used to launch a DoS attack, an MITM attack, or a reconnaissance attack against your voice network. The following section gives details about the attack and its mitigation technique.

Attack Details

In the DHCP spoofing attack, the attacker enables a rogue DHCP server on a valid network segment. When a client (IP Phone or PC running IP Communicator) broadcasts a request for DHCP configuration information, the rogue DHCP server responds before the genuine DHCP server can respond, assigning assailant-defined IP configuration information, as shown in Figure 6-5.

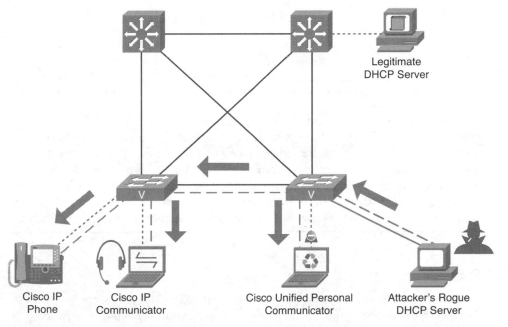

Figure 6-5 *DHCP Spoofing Attack*

DHCP spoofing enables an attacker to put unwary clients on a bogus IP range that must flow through the assailant's set up DHCP server to get to the rest of the network. In other words, the host packets are redirected to the attacker's machine because it can emulate a default gateway for the invalid DHCP address provided to the client. This enables the attacker to unleash MITM or DoS attacks.

Mitigation

The DHCP spoofing attack can be alleviated by enabling DHCP snooping on the switch. DHCP snooping enables the ports to be set as either trusted or untrusted. Trusted ports can send DHCP requests and acknowledgments. Untrusted ports can only forward DHCP requests. DHCP snooping enables the switch to build a DHCP binding table that maps a client MAC address, IP address, VLAN, and port ID. Example 6-4 outlines the DHCP snooping configuration, which can be done to enable DHCP snooping on the switch, set an interface to trusted (DHCP server-facing interface), and set an interface as untrusted (end-user facing interface).

Example 6-4   *DHCP Snooping Configuration*

```
IPTSW(config)# ip dhcp snooping VLAN 100 101
IPTSW(config)# no ip dhcp snooping information option
IPTSW(config)# ip dhcp snooping
!
IPTSW(config)# interface FastEthernet 0/10
IPTSW(config-if)# ip dhcp snooping trust
!
IPTSW(config)# interface FastEthernet 0/20
IPTSW(config-if)# no ip dhcp snooping trust
IPTSW(config-if)# ip dhcp snooping limit rate 10
```

The configuration illustrated in Example 6-4 enables DHCP snooping for VLANs 100 and 101 and disables adding option 82 in the DHCP request packet. Interface FastEthernet 0/10 is set as the trusted interface where a legitimate DHCP server is known to be connected, whereas interface FastEthernet 0/20 has been set to an untrusted interface so that any machine acting as a DHCP server on this interface will not be trusted, and the DHCP requests or replies on this specific port will be dropped by the switch. Furthermore, you can have the port rate-limited to drop excessive DHCP request or acknowledgment traffic.

ARP Spoofing

ARP spoofing attacks are deteriorating to the network. The following section describes the ARP spoofing attack and the simple way to defend your IP Telephony network against it.

Attack Details

In this attack, the hacker poisons the Address Resolution Protocol (ARP) table. The intention is to conceal, in order to become the default gateway for the IP Telephony subnet. This can be done by replying to and poisoning the network in such a way that the attacker's MAC address seems to be mapped to the default gateway IP address, by the IP Phones and PCs alike. Attackers usually use Gratuitous ARP to poison the ARP table, as shown in Figure 6-6.

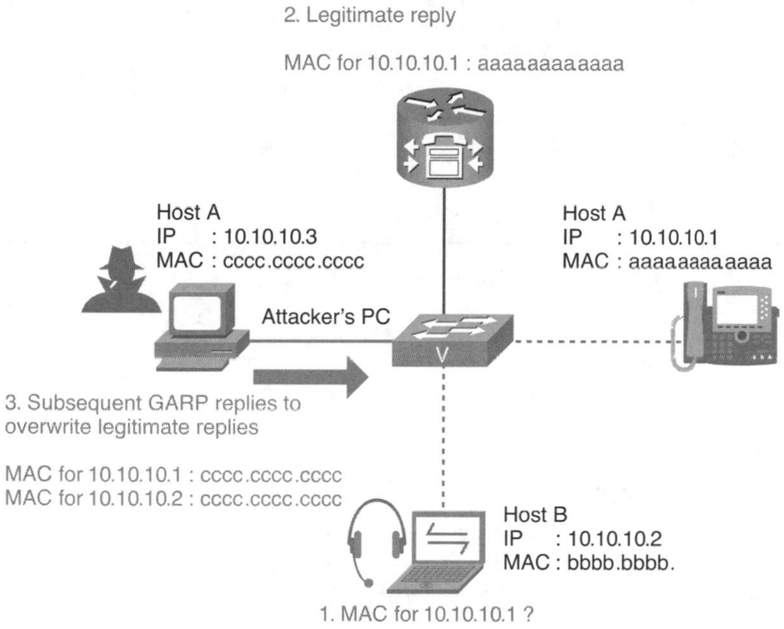

Figure 6-6 *ARP Spoofing Attack*

Note An ARP entry maps a MAC address to an IP address in the switch ARP table.

This way, the attacker receives all the traffic designated to the default gateway, which gives the attacker the possibility to perform an MITM attack. Because the switch does not care about Layer 3 (in this chapter, we limit ourselves to Layer 2, even though Cisco Catalyst switches can operate at Layer 3, which is IP-aware), the attacker can use a legitimate IP address, which is an untruthful MAC address. In a nutshell, the attacker becomes a proxy for everyone on that LAN segment forcing them to send all communication traffic through the attacker's machine.

Mitigation

An ARP attack can be mitigated by implementing Dynamic ARP Inspection (DAI). In DAI, the switch checks the IP/MAC mappings in the DHCP snooping binding table.

Note   This implies that DHCP snooping is enabled.

DAI inspection establishes the legitimacy of packets by performing an IP-to-MAC address binding inspection stored in the DHCP snooping binding database before forwarding the packet to the destination. DAI drops all ARP packets that do not pass the inspection process. Example 6-5 outlines the process to enable DAI on a global as well as per interface basis.

Example 6-5   *DAI Configuration*

```
IPTSW(config)# ip arp inspection vlan 100
!
IPTSW(config)# interface FastEthernet 0/5
IPTSW(config-if)# ip arp inspection trust
```

MAC Address Spoofing Attack

MAC spoofing is yet another type of spoofing attack, which is equally dangerous and potent as ARP and IP spoofing attacks. In the following section, you will learn about the MAC address spoofing attack and the techniques to restrain it.

Attack Details

Media Access Control (MAC) address spoofing attack can be used to overtake a valid identity at Layer 2, that is, the attacker spoofs the identity of an existing machine on the network such that the switch switches all frames destined for that specific MAC address to the attacker. MAC spoofing is the technique to change an assigned MAC address of a networked device to a different one by using freely available tools, such as macmakeup, SMAC, and so on. In this attack, the attacker effectively sends packets with an incorrect source MAC address such that, now the switch recognizes the attacker's machine as the valid destination MAC address and forwards the frames sent by the source to this spoofed destination. Changing MAC address allows hackers and attackers to bypass the access control lists (ACLs) on the switches or routers and to impersonate another IP Phone/PC (running CIPC, CUPC), as shown in Figure 6-7.

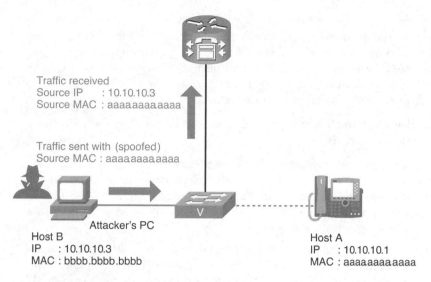

Figure 6-7 *MAC Spoofing Attack*

Mitigation

Cisco Catalyst switches have a feature called port security, which can help downsize MAC spoofing attacks (and various other attacks as explained in next few sections). This feature restricts the input to an interface by limiting and identifying MAC addresses of end devices. The MAC addresses can be introduced to the switch's address table in one of following ways:

Static Secure MAC address: This enables an administrator to manually limit the MAC addresses to be allowed on a switch port. An administrator can statically configure which MAC addresses exist off specific ports. In turn, these hand-picked MAC addresses are added to the switch's running configuration and CAM table.

Sticky Secure MAC address: This enables the port to dynamically configure secure MAC addresses with the MAC addresses of connected devices (sticky). This approach is similar to static secure MAC addresses; however, in this case an administrator does not need to configure all MAC addresses statically. A switch port dynamically learns the MAC addresses that exist off its ports configured for sticky secure MAC addresses and stores these MAC address-to-port associations in its running configuration and CAM table.

Dynamic Secure MAC address: This mechanism is similar to sticky secure MAC addresses, however, with a major difference. The MAC addresses learned from the switch port setup for dynamic secure MAC addresses are stored only in a switch's CAM table and not in the running configuration.

Finally, you can configure violation rules as applicable (and as defined by your security policy) to express what you want a port to do when things do not seem to be in order, such as when more than the wanted number of MAC addresses are appearing on a port or the same MAC address is appearing more than once on different ports. These rules help suppress any attack attempt and at the same time can inform the admin (via logs or SNMP) if anything suspicious happens on a switch.

You can configure the switch port to respond in one of following three ways when a port security violation occurs:

Protect: With this option, when the switch port reaches its configured maximum number of secure MAC addresses, it starts dropping frames with an unknown source MAC address. The frames with the known (learned) source MAC addresses are however still allowed on the switch port. In protect mode, no notifications are sent if a port security violation occurs.

Restrict: This option is similar to the protect option, that is, it allows the transmission of frames from known MAC addresses when the limit of the configured maximum MAC addresses is breached, however, drops packets from any unknown MAC addresses. The major difference is that the restrict option can send an SNMP trap and a Syslog message. Also, it increments the violation counter when a port security violation occurs.

Shutdown: When a switch port is configured with the shutdown option, after a port security violation occurs, no traffic transmits on that port. In other words, the port is shut down and put in err-disable state. Although, this option may seem to be extreme, it is also most effective against any intrusion (MAC spoofing, CAM table overflow, and so on) attempts and attacks. This option also allows generating the SNMP and Syslog notifications identical to the restrict option, and it will also increment a violation counter when a port security breach is attempted.

Example 6-6 illustrates enabling port security for interface FastEthernet 0/10 on a Cisco Catalyst switch. The maximum number of MAC addresses is set to 3 on this particular interface. On exceeding the maximum count (that is, connecting more than two devices—daisy chained, for example, a IP Phone daisy-chained with a PC that may be further connected to a hub or another switch), the port fires a violation message to administrators (SNMP or Syslog) and is put in error disable mode (shut down). The MAC-address command sets a static MAC on the port and can also be used to make the port remember the MAC addresses which were connected to it (sticky).

Example 6-6 *Switch Port Security Configuration*

```
IPTSW(config)# interface FastEthernet 0/10
IPTSW(config-if)# switchport port-security
IPTSW(config-if)# switchport port-security maximum 3
IPTSW(config-if)# switchport port-security violation shutdown
IPTSW(config-if)# switchport port-security mac-address aaaa.aaaa.aaaa
IPTSW(config-if)# switchport port-security mac-address sticky
```

Example 6-7 shows the output of the **show port-security** command.

Example 6-7 *Port Security* **show** *Command Output*

```
IPTSW# show port-security

Secure Port MaxSecureAddr CurrentAddr SecurityViolation Security Action
            (Count)       (Count)     (Count)
-----------------------------------------------------------------------
Fa10         3             1           0              Shutdown
-----------------------------------------------------------------------
Total Addresses in System (excluding one mac per port) : 0
Max Addresses limit in System (excluding one mac per port) : 6176
```

IP Spoofing Attack

IP spoofing attack (although) at Layer 3 is included in this chapter to cover and complete the spoofing attack group. In an IP spoofing attack, as you might have guessed, the attacker spoofs the IP of the victim machine/IP Phone to redirect traffic. More details and mitigation mechanisms are covered in the subsequent section.

Attack Details

In addition to MAC address spoofing, a capable hacker can also spoof IP, that is, the attacker can spoof the IP address of a valid network element (IP Phone or PC) and have all traffic destined for the legitimate device redirected to his own machine, thereby launching a MITM or a DoS attack. Figure 6-8 gives an insight to the specifics of an IP spoofing attack.

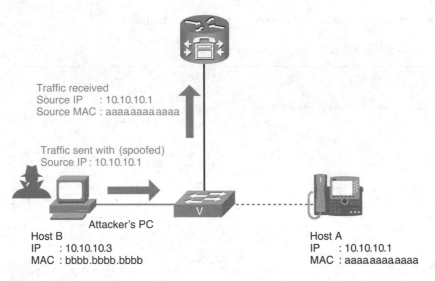

Figure 6-8 *IP Spoofing Attack*

Mitigation

To shun IP spoofing attack, IP source guard can enabled on untrusted Layer 2 ports. After you enable IP Source Guard feature, all IP traffic is initially blocked, except for DHCP packets captured by the DHCP snooping process. When a client receives a valid IP address from the DHCP server, a PACL is applied to the port. This restricts the client IP traffic to those source IP addresses configured in the binding. Any other IP traffic with a source address other than the addresses in the binding is filtered. Example 6-8 outlines the configuration steps required to enable the IP Source Guard on interface FastEthernet 0/10.

> **Note** This implies that IP source guard requires DHCP snooping to be enabled.

Example 6-8 *IP Source Guard Configuration*

```
IPTSW(config)# interface FastEthernet 0/10
IPTSW(config-if)# ip verify source
```

CAM Table Overflow and DHCP Starvation Attack

Overflow attacks are another category of malicious (DoS and MITM) attacks where, the network is deprived of certain resources, leaving the legit devices unable to request service.

Attack Details

Because switches and DHCP servers can hold a finite number of MAC and IP addresses respectively, hackers can take advantage and overload a switch's Content Addressable Memory (CAM) table. On the other hand, hackers can overload a DHCP server by requesting multiple IP addresses based on bogus MAC addresses. And how does a hacker accomplish these two tasks you may ask?

Let's first understand the CAM table overflow attack. The hacker can change his machine's MAC address rapidly to quickly fill up the CAM table on any Ethernet switch, as shown in Figure 6-9. (This type of attack can be easily launched with the macof utility, which can generate random bogus MAC addresses to flood the network.). Now, after the CAM table is full on an Ethernet switch, the switch is essentially converted to an Ethernet hub, that is, the switch can now flood every port with every incoming frame because it does not have any space to store any MAC addresses in its CAM table to map a MAC address to a port.

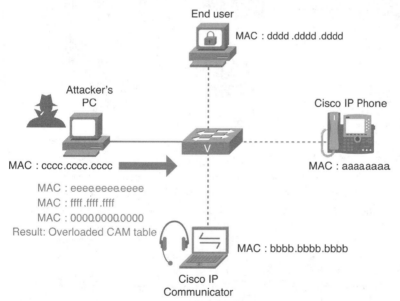

Figure 6-9 *CAM Table Overflow Attack*

This in turn causes massive performance degradation. As the switch is forced to broadcast every frame on every port, it allows the hacker to eavesdrop on all connected devices (including IP phones and PCs running CUPC and CIPC) and to record the conversations, capture signaling, and open gates for further attack. This type of attack can be categorized under both DoS and MITM attacks.

Now, let's turn our attention to DHCP starvation attack, which is not that different from CAM table overflow (only that the cause is at Layer 2 and the effect is at Layer 3), to understand how this can be carried out by an attacker and its implications. Because the attacker uses a software tool to generate random (and bogus) MAC addresses, the DHCP server tends to lease an IP to all these cosmetic MAC addresses, as portrayed in Figure 6-10.

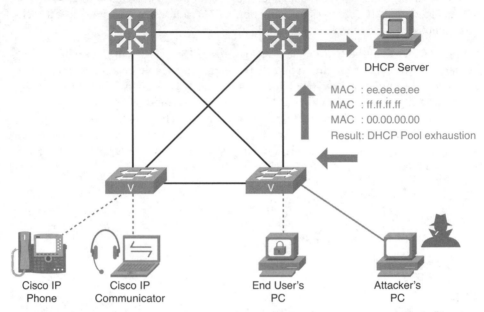

Figure 6-10 *DHCP Starvation Attack*

This ultimately results in the exhaustion of the DHCP pool designated for native or auxiliary VLAN (depending on where the hacker's machine is at work) and renders the legitimate devices unable to receive any IP. This type of attack is service disrupting (DoS attack).

Mitigation

The Port security feature comes to your rescue yet again. It helps prevent CAM table and DHCP starvation attacks by restricting input to an interface by limiting and identifying MAC addresses of end devices (as explained earlier in the "Mitigating MAC Spoofing Attack" section).

Also, a DHCP starvation attack can be stopped in its track by DHCP snooping and by IP source guard switch security features. The topics of DHCP snooping and IP source guard have been covered earlier in this chapter in detail.

Dealing with Rogue Endpoints: 802.1x

Have you ever thought of someone walking into your home, without your knowledge and playing around with things that belong dearly to you? It would certainly be painful to see things that are valuable to you be manhandled by an anonymous person who did so with malicious intent. This would be similar to the painstaking experience of being bitten by an attacker, who may secretly walk into your organization's premises, plugs-in his PC with a soft phone (or an IP Phone simulating software) to a switch port, and starts distorting and manhandling the communication streams. This very thought forces IT administrators and security engineers alike to think of a solution to the problem of unauthorized network access and unauthorized placement of endpoints or IP Phones.

Cisco does not leave any stone unturned to combat this dreadful issue. The 802.1x or Dot1x mechanism comes to your aid to keep out the rogue endpoints and to ensure that your network's integrity is maintained.

At a high level, the concept of Identity Based Network Service (IBNS) or 802.1x is as shown in Figure 6-11.

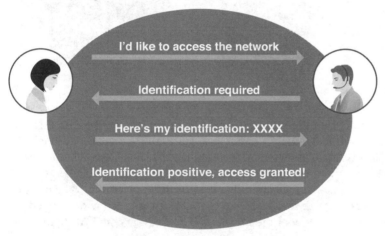

I'd like to access the network

Identification required

Here's my identification: XXXX

Identification positive, access granted!

Identity-Based Network Access

Figure 6-11 *802.1x Concept (High Level)*

Essentially, when an endpoint requests network access, in an IBNS scheme, the identity of the endpoint is the key to be granted or denied access. The identity can be in the form of a username and password, one-time password (OTP), or certificates (X.509 v3 certificates).

What Is 802.1x and How Does it Work?

802.1x is the fail-safe mechanism to kick out all unauthorized endpoints at the onset of the introduction of a rogue device in your network. 802.1X provides port-based authentication, which involves communications between a supplicant, an authenticator, and an authentication server. Let's decrypt these terms so that you can understand the components of an 802.1x-enabled network:

- The supplicant is software on a client device, such as a PC, a laptop, or an IP Phone.

- The authenticator is a wired Ethernet switch or a wireless access point.

- An authentication server is a RADIUS server, for example, Cisco TACACS+ in RADIUS mode.

The 802.1x process and components (supplicant, authenticator, and authentication server) are shown in Figure 6-12.

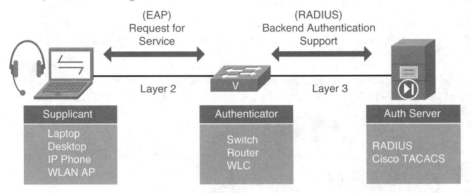

Figure 6-12 *802.1x Process Overview*

Upon detection of a new client (supplicant), the port on the switch (authenticator) is enabled and set to an unauthorized state. In this state, only 802.1X traffic is allowed, and other traffic, such as DHCP or DNS, is blocked at the data link layer. The authenticator (switch) sends out the EAP-Identify-Request to the supplicant (IP Phone/PC). In response, the supplicant sends an EAP-Identify-Response to the authenticator. Now, the supplicant and the authentication server (Cisco TACACS+) use one of the predefined EAP methods to verify the identity of the supplicant. The message is an EAP-Auth-Exchange with a RADIUS server.

Note Actual authentication is between the supplicant (client) and the authentication server (Cisco TACACS+) using EAP. The authenticator (switch) is more like an EAP conduit; however, it is aware of what is going on between these entities.

Upon an identity match, the Auth-success message is sent by the authentication server (or alternatively the Auth-fail message). Upon reception of Auth-success message, the authenticator (switch) puts the switch port in an authorized state and sends the

EAP-Success message to the supplicant. (Alternatively, upon receipt of the Auth-fail message from the authentication server, the authenticator puts the device in an Auth-fail VLAN.) Once the port is in an authorized state, the traffic from the client is allowed on the network and behaves like a normal client connected to switch port.

When the supplicant logs off, it sends an EAP-logoff message to the authenticator. The authenticator then sets the port to the unauthorized state, once again blocking all non-EAP traffic.

EAP Authentication Methods

As explained earlier, the supplicant, authenticator, and authentication server can use one of the many EAP options available for authenticating the identity of the supplicant. The following EAP authentication options are available with Cisco infrastructure:

- **Challenge-response-based:**

  - **MD5:** MD5-based challenge-response for authentication

  - **LEAP-MD5EAP:** Uses username/password authentication

  - **EAP-MSCHAPv2:** Uses username/password MSCHAPv2 challenge-response authentication

- **Cryptographic-based: EAP-TLS:** Uses x.509 v3 PKI certificates and TLS mechanism for authentication (used for IP Telephony endpoints with MIC or LSC)

- **Tunneling methods:**

  - **PEAP:** Protected EAP tunnel mode. (EAP encapsulates other EAP types in an encrypted tunnel, much like web-based SSL.)

  - **EAP-TTLS:** Other EAP methods over an extended EAP-TLS encrypted tunnel.

  - **EAP-FAST:** Tunneling method designed to not require the deployment of certificates.

- **Other:**

  - **EAP-GTC:** Generic token and OTP authentication

  - **GSS-API:** Kerberos

With the basics of 802.1x covered in the previous sections, let us look into 802.1x implementation specifics for an IP Telephony infrastructure (endpoints).

802.1x for IP Telephony

With voice ports, a port can belong to two VLANs, while still allowing the separation of voice/data traffic while enabling you to configure 802.1X. An access port can handle two VLANs that is:

■ **Native or Port VLAN Identifier (PVID):** Authenticated by 802.1X

■ **Auxiliary or Voice VLAN Identifier (VVID):** Authenticated by CDP

Before comprehending a Multi-Domain Authentication (MDA) approach to allow IP Phones or IP Telephony endpoints on an 802.1x enabled network, it is important that you understand some key mechanisms that are integral to 802.1x for IP Telephony. These are as following:

■ **MAC Authentication By-Pass (MAB):** MAB is an authentication mechanism that enables a Cisco Catalyst switch to check the connecting device's MAC address. IP Phones (for example, third-party IP Phones that cannot perform IEEE 802.1X) can be authenticated based on a MAC address, statically configured in authentication server.

■ **Guest VLAN:** Guest VLAN by definition allows limited access to network resources. An 802.1x-enabled switch port can send EAPoL-Identity-Request frames on the wire. Any device connected (for example, a visitor's laptop) on this switch port will be deployed into the Guest VLAN based on the lack of response to the switch's EAP-Request-Identity frames.

■ **Auth-Fail VLAN:** This VLAN as the name suggests is for devices that fail authentication. It is different from Guest VLAN since the scenario is different when the device is not capable of doing IEEE 802.1x authentication than when it fails the same. For example, an IP Phone that was authorized on the network by virtue of certificates (LSC) just got revoked, that is, the certificates are no longer valid. Thus, this entity becomes invalid and unauthenticated on the network and is assigned to Auth-Fail VLAN.

■ **Critical VLAN:** A critical VLAN is the backup VLAN created for unavailability of a RADIUS server. With this feature configured, when all the AAA servers are unreachable from a switch, the 802.1x hosts are put into this preconfigured VLAN that would typically provide more limited network services. The existing sessions retain authorization status.

With knowledge of various 802.1x components and tools to help you with 802.1x deployment, let's understand the ins and outs of 802.1x for Cisco Unified IP Phones. Figure 6-13 shows the 802.1x deployment leveraging MDA.

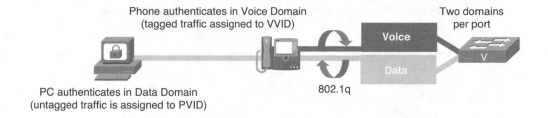

Figure 6-13 *802.1x for Voice Endpoints*

As shown in Figure 6-13, Multi Domain Authentication (MDA) helps you define two domains on same physical switch port: VVID and PVID. The 802.1x process for voice using an MDA approach is as follows:

- Cisco Unified IP Phone learns VVID from CDP. (Third-party phones use LLDP.)

- 802.1X times out.

- The switch initiates MAC Authentication Bypass (MAB).

- Cisco TACACS+ (RADIUS server) returns Access-Accept with Phone Vendor Specific Attribute (VSA).

- IP Phone traffic is allowed on either VLAN until it sends the tagged packet; then only voice VLAN is allowed for the IP Phone.

- (Asynchronous) PC daisy-chained to IP Phone authenticates using 802.1X or MAB.

- PC traffic is allowed on Data VLAN only.

Note Guest-VLAN, Auth-Fail-VLAN, and Critical VLAN work for PVID only, that is, they are limited to only data devices. If an IP Phone is placed in any of these VLANs, it will not work properly.

When MDA is enabled, both the IP Phone and the device behind the phone can authenticate using IEEE 802.1x. Cisco IP Phones can authenticate via X.509 certificates using the EAP-TLS or EAP-FAST.

Note X.509 certificates can be either Cisco Manufacturing Installed Certificates (MIC) or Locally Significant Certificates (LSC).

Phone certificate, CAPF, and TLS concepts are covered in detail in Chapter 9, "Cisco Unified Communication Manager Security."

Example 6-9 demonstrates the switch and TACACS configuration for MDA.

Example 6-9 *Switch Port Configuration for 802.1x (MDA)*

```
IPTSW(config)# interface FastEthernet1/10
IPTSW(config-if)# switchport mode access
IPTSW(config-if)# switchport access vlan 100
IPTSW(config-if)# switchport voice vlan 200
IPTSW(config-if)# authentication event fail action next-method
IPTSW(config-if)# authentication host-mode multi-domain
IPTSW(config-if)# authentication order dot1x mab
IPTSW(config-if)# dot1x pae authenticator
IPTSW(config-if)# authentication port-control auto
IPTSW(config-if)# dot1x timeout tx-period 10
IPTSW(config-if)# dot1x max-req 2
IPTSW(config-if)# mab
IPTSW(config-if)# spanning-tree portfast
```

Example 6-10 demonstrates the **show** command output to verify 802.1x identification success.

Example 6-10 *Show dot1x Command Output*

```
IPTSW# show dot1x interface Fastethernet 1/10 details


Dot1x Authenticator Client List
----------------------------------------------------
Domain                    = DATA
Supplicant                = 0014.5e42.66df
   Auth SM State          = AUTHENTICATED
   Auth BEND SM State     = IDLE
Port Status               = AUTHORIZED
Authentication Method     = Dot1x
Authorized By             = Authentication Server
Domain                    = VOICE
Supplicant                = 001bd513031c
   Auth SM State          = AUTHENTICATED
   Auth BEND SM State     = IDLE
Port Status               = AUTHORIZED
Authentication Method     = MAB
Authorized By             = Authentication Server
```

The following section highlights the configuration required on the Cisco Terminal Access Controller Access Control Server (TACACS+). Cisco TACACS+ is an authentication, authorization, and accounting (AAA) server/solution that can work in Cisco proprietary TACACS mode as well as open standard RADIUS mode.

Note   The configuration examples in this chapter are based on Cisco TACACS+ version 5.2.

Step 1.   As shown in Figure 6-14, configure Identity Group for Cisco Unified IP Phones, for example, Phone Group. It is under this group that all phones will be added as users and hosts.

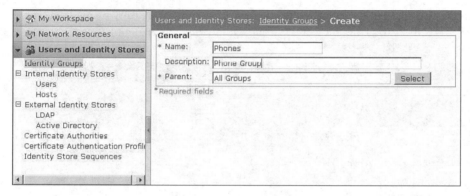

Figure 6-14   *Cisco TACACS+ Configuration: Phone Group*

Step 2.   As depicted in Figure 6-15, add the Cisco IP Phone's description under users, with the password that will be entered on the IP Phone to 802.1x to authenticate.

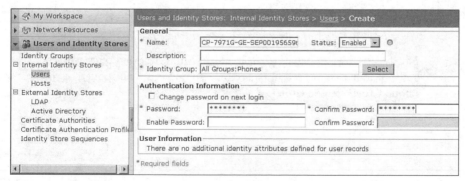

Figure 6-15   *Cisco TACACS+ Configuration: Identity Store IP Phone (as User) Addition*

Step 3.   Add Cisco IP Phone's MAC address under hosts, as shown in Figure 6-16.

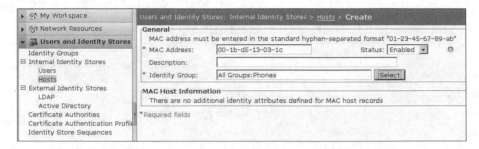

Figure 6-16   *Cisco TACACS+ Configuration: Host Configuration*

> **Step 4.**   Create an Authorization profile with an authorization rule, as shown in Figure 6-17, to permit the Phone Group with permission to join the static Voice VLAN.

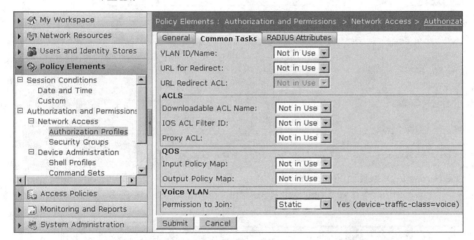

Figure 6-17   *Cisco TACACS+ Configuration: Authorization Profile*

> **Step 5.**   Finally, as shown in Figure 6-18, create an Authorization Policy with the authorization rule created in Figure 6-17 so that it can be applied to the Phone Group created earlier.

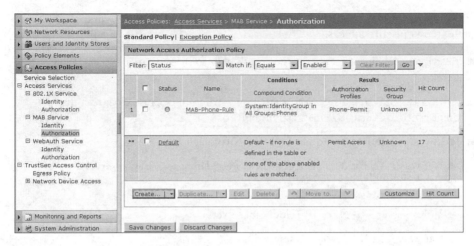

Figure 6-18 *Cisco TACACS+ Configuration: Authorization Policy*

Following are the minimum requirements for supporting 802.1x for IP Telephony end-points:

- CDP must be enabled on the switch to support Cisco IP Phones.

- LLDP should be enabled for third-party (and non-CDP supporting) IP Phones.

- You must use multi-VLAN access ports, that is, separate VLANs for voice and data (access and voice/auxiliary VLAN on same port).

For more information on 802.1x and Cisco TACACS+, visit http://www.cisco.com/go/acs.

Layer 2 Security: Best Practices

You have been through the various Layer 2 attacks and their mitigation mechanisms in this chapter. Let us now look into some of the key Layer 2 security best practices that can enable you to ascertain that your network is not only protected, but is protected based on the Cisco best practices.

Note Not all security mechanisms apply to all networks because no two networks are alike. For more information on how to determine the right level of security required for your network, revisit the topic "Determining the Level of Security for Your IP Telephony Network" in Chapter 4, "Cisco IP Telephony Security Framework."

Following are the best practices to ensure that the Layer 2 of your network is secure from external/internal attacks:

■ Restrict management access for the switch only to the authorized management team.

■ Always use SSH to manage your switch infrastructure because clear text management protocol, such as Telnet, can be sniffed.

■ Ideally, there should be a dedicated VLAN for each of following:

   ■ Native VLAN for data devices such as PCs, databases, or web servers

   ■ Voice VLAN for IP Phones

   ■ Voice server VLAN for IP Telephony servers

   ■ Gateway VLAN for voice gateways

   ■ Management VLAN for OOB management

   ■ Void VLAN for assigning any (dot1x) unauthenticated devices

■ Always enable port security on user-facing access switches to limit the number of allowed MAC addresses. It is recommended to keep this value to 3 for a switch corresponding to an IP Phone and a daisy-chained PC (because the switch port has its own MAC address, another one from IP Phone's switch port, and finally one from the PC connected behind the IP Phone, which makes it 3).

■ Adopt and maintain a port-security stature in terms of the action you take in case a port-security violation occurs. Although the shutdown option is recommended for highly secure environments, it is best to put it as a restrict option for IP Telephony deployments.

■ Use a dedicated VLAN ID for all trunk ports.

■ Always shut down unused ports. (Ensure that there is an inventory record of what ports are used from which switch to ensure that no unused ports are left active.)

■ Assign all shut down ports in an unused (void) and non-routed VLAN.

■ Use MD5 authentication for VTP.

■ Enable VTP pruning to allow only intended VLANs across trunks.

■ Enable BPDU guard and Root guard for STP protection.

■ Never use VLAN 1 for any traffic. It is highly recommended to shut down VLAN 1.

■ Set all user-facing ports to non-trunking, that is, access ports (turn off DTP). If using Cisco IP Phones, ensure that the port has a native VLAN and an auxiliary (or voice) VLAN to support voice and data traffic.

- Enable DHCP snooping and DAI to mitigate MITM attacks. (Although it may seem to be an overhead in a medium-to-large switching infrastructure, it pays to have DHCP snooping enabled in the longer run.)

- Enable IP source guard with DHCP snooping, to evade IP spoofing and DHCP starvation attack(s).

- Infrastructure management (inclusive of switching infrastructure) should be done securely via either Out-Of-Band (OOB) or In-Band management process. For more details on these management methods, refer to Chapter 16, "Cisco IP Telephony: Network Management Security."

- If using SNMP for switch management, ensure that the community strings are equivalent to strong passwords (at least eight characters, alphanumeric).

- If possible, enable Dot1x on user-facing switch ports to curb any unauthorized attempt to register a rogue device in your IP Telephony network.

- Ensure that voice endpoints get proper QoS treatment. This can be done by enabling the switch port to accept packets from a trusted device (Cisco IP Phone) marked at COS 5, with no rewriting.

- Enable CDP on switches where Cisco IP Phones are connected; otherwise, if not required by your IT Department, shut down CDP. CDP is a Cisco proprietary protocol that can reveal a lot of information about network infrastructure (switches and routers), for example, model, IP address, hostname, IOS version, and so on.

- In case CDP is not supported by third-party IP Phones and switches, it is recommended to use LLDP-MED instead and disable CDP for reasons mentioned earlier.

Summary

In this chapter, you were introduced to the concept of Layer 2 security, which is often forgotten because of more attention given to defend against attacks at high layers. It is never bad to be paranoid when matters involve the security of your communication channels. While, spoofing attacks such as ARP spoofing, MAC spoofing, IP spoofing or DHCP spoofing can result in voice traffic sniffing and disruption, there are worse attacks such as DHCP starvation and CAM table overflow attacks that may render your IP Telephony network to stand still. Moreover, flooding and spoofing attacks combined, summon a deadly duo as they are simple to carry out and yet so powerful. An attacker can not only collect valuable information or record voice streams and replay conversations but also can impact the stability of the targeted LAN segment. Then, there were attacks such as STP manipulation and VLAN hopping, which would serve all voice and data information alike to the attacker, on a sliver platter. Last, but certainly not the least, you had 802.1x (IBNS) to your rescue, to get rid of those pesky rogue endpoints on your network.

Backed up with Layer 2 security best practices, you should now be in a much better position to counter the attacks emerging from inside and outside of your IP Telephony network. Although there are tools and mechanisms to keep out the Layer 2 security threats from your network, it is essential to plan for the security construct carefully and implement the right security tools and controls where required.

In the next chapter, you will comprehend the basics of Layer 3 (network layer) security.

Chapter 7

Cisco IP Telephony Layer 3 Security

The vice president (VP) of organization XYZ checked the Intranet home page again—still nothing. All he got was an error message. For some reason, the Intranet site was not responding. He tried calling the Chief Technology Officer (CTO) to inquire what is going on, and to his surprise, his IP Phone displayed an unregistered message! The VP walks into the office of the CTO, where he finds the IT manager and other top brass officials, all with a common expression, troubled. He is briefed that it is a network wide attack. An attacker had invaded and was assaulting the network links. The attacker, whether internal or external, did not matter for now. All that mattered is to get the applications and communication back up.

Nobody wants to be in such a situation. Although, the end users want their applications and communications to work normally, the same notion is shared by IT (network and IP Telephony teams) to ensure that things keep rolling. A single weakness in the network can become an attack vector and a possible point of penetration into the wider network, affecting applications, underlying the network, and what matters the most—communications!

This chapter covers the following topics:

- Layer 3 security fundamentals
- IOS platform security
- Restricting management access
- Disabling unnecessary services
- Securing routing protocols
- Securing Hot Standby Routing Protocol (HSRP)
- Safeguarding against ICMP attacks

- Securing user passwords

- Controlling user access and privilege levels

- Antispoofing measures

- Banner messages

- Securing Network Time Protocol (NTP)

- Blocking commonly exploited ports

- Extending the Enterprise Security Policy to your router

- Layer 3 traffic protection

- Layer 3 Security—best practices

Layer 3 Security Fundamentals: Securing Cisco IOS Routers

Routers and routing protocols are central to any network's infrastructure and its operation. Concentrating security on the perimeter and at the server level does not help if the network links are the weak point. Without routing, voice signaling or media traffic cannot go anywhere. The least that IP Telephony applications need from an underlying network is the next hop that until the destination, the traffic travels on network links.

Remember, network security is only as strong as the weakest link in your network.

Since every OSI layer has its significance; Layer 3 certainly is something not to be left aside for the security of your IP Telephony network. In the following sections, you will learn about the different ways to safeguard your IP Telephony network's Layer 3.

Cisco IOS Platform Security

Whenever there is a discussion about securing a Windows or Unix server or terminal, the first thing on the list is the operating system (OS). A Cisco IOS router also has an OS that must be secured and should be resilient to attacks. Being a software program, almost every OS has vulnerabilities; Cisco IOS is no exception. Unless secured, certain vulnerabilities can enable an attacker to launch a DoS attack or manipulate information flowing in or out of the router.

To mitigate any chances of being exploited because of a known defect, ensure that you check the Cisco website for new releases and keep an eye out for any security advisory. Moreover, move from a deferred version and immediately (or at least plan to) upgrade to the next available, stable release. You can find more information about your current IOS release by using the **show version** command, as shown in Example 7-1.

Example 7-1   show version *Command*

```
IPTRouter# show version
Cisco IOS Software, 2800 Software (C2800NM-ADVENTERPRISEK9-M), Version 15.1(3)T,
 RELEASE SOFTWARE (fc1)
 <output omitted>
System image file is "flash:c2800nm-adventerprisek9-mz.151-3.T.bin"
```

Visit www.cisco.com to get a new IOS version for your router.

Visit http://tools.cisco.com/security/center/publicationListing to get updates on security advisories. You can also subscribe to Cisco Notification Service at http://www.cisco.com/cisco/support/notifications.html to get updates on Security Advisories, Field Notices, End of Sale/Support statements, Software Updates, and Known Bugs.

Apart from OS security, the other thing that comes to mind when talking about platform security is the hardware. To protect Cisco router hardware from becoming a target of vandalism, you must have an appropriate physical security plan and implementation (detailed in Chapter 5, "Cisco IP Telephony Physical Security").

Restricting Management Access

This section will help you understand the threats that are always present around the Cisco router management and how you can hold them down. The most commonly used access methods to manage a Cisco IOS Router are as following:

- Line Console (CTY), Auxiliary Port (AUX), Virtual Terminal Line (VTY), and Asynchronous Line (TTY) access

- HTTP Access

- SNMP

Note Network management can be defined in terms of physical access, electronic access, administrative hardware and software maintenance, network monitoring, and troubleshooting. The earlier mentioned access methods (depending on network management methods) can be used for some or all of these activities. For in-depth information on various IP Telephony network management (security) best practices refer to Chapter 16, "Cisco IP Telephony: Network Management Security."

Although the first two methods are used for management, SNMP is used for both management and monitoring. Because of its unique nature, the security of SNMP is covered in Chapter 16. Let us comprehend the basics behind securing access to your Cisco router's management plane.

Securing the Console Port

The console port is an Out-Of-Band (OOB) management method, which is used for physically accessing the router via a serial cable and a terminal emulation program. Illegitimate access to this port can spell disaster for the router because an attacker can reset the system passwords and gain full control over the router. To protect console access, at a minimum assign a line password, as shown in Example 7-2.

Example 7-2   *Enable Console Port Login*

```
IPTRouter(config)# line console 0
IPTRouter(config-line)# login
IPTRouter(config-line)# password <omitted>
```

To enhance console port security, have a local login or AAA-based login, that is, configure usernames and associated passwords on a Cisco router or in Cisco TACACS+ server. In both cases the next time you log in to the router to enter enable mode, you will be asked for the username and password instead of just the password. For more details on local and AAA-based login, refer to the section "Controlling User Access and Privileges." Moreover, IOS passwords can be encrypted such that even when an unauthorized person accesses the running configuration of the router, the passwords are encrypted. For more details on encrypting passwords, refer to the section "Securing User Passwords."

The most secure, however not the most intuitive, way to secure a console is to disable logins to the console port using the command shown in Example 7-3.

Example 7-3   *Disable Console Port Login*

```
IPTRouter(config)# line console 0
IPTRouter(config-line)# login
IPTRouter(config-line)# no password
```

Note   Disabling console access can prove detrimental for certain networks because it limits the ability to troubleshoot. It's worthwhile to note that disabling logins to the console port does not help protect against an attacker reloading the system and performing a password recovery unless the physical access to the router is secured. Chapter 5 addresses physical security issues and mitigations in detail.

Last, however certainly not the least, you should to limit the period of time that a user can be connected to an IOS router for a management session. This is particularly useful when an administrator forgets to log off. You obviously would not want the session hijacked or used by someone who is unwelcome. Time limit for a line can be set by the command shown in Example 7-4.

Example 7-4 *Limit Timeout for Console Port*

```
IPTRouter(config)# line aux 0
IPTRouter(config-line)# exec-timeout <minutes> <seconds>
```

Securing the Auxiliary Port

The auxiliary port is yet again dedicated for Out-Of-Band (OOB) management; however, it is different from the console port because the latter requires direct physical connection and the former does not. Usually, a modem or a terminal server is connected to this port for remote access. Although, this method was originally devised for remote access to the router in an OOB management system, it also increases the attack surface as anyone who has access to the public phone system and can figure out the phone number via which the system is managed, can attack the router remotely. Thus, it is highly recommended that a terminal server be used to control access to this port, instead of a dial-in modem.

To secure the port with a password, issue the commands from the privileged, enable mode, as shown in Example 7-5.

Example 7-5 *Enable Auxiliary Port Login*

```
IPTRouter(config)# line aux 0
IPTRouter(config-line)# login
IPTRouter(config-line)# password <omitted>
```

The commands to disable login to auxiliary port or to enable local/AAA-based login are same as shown in the previous section for the console port.

Securing the VTY Ports

The VTY ports are virtual TTY ports, and these are used for In-Band management of the router. Since these are virtual ports and are usable with the logical IP address of the router, they are logically reachable from anywhere on the network wherever there is IP connectivity. Either Telnet or SSH protocols can be used to manage the device on VTY ports.

Even though Telnet should be ideally be the last resort for a management protocol, if it must be used, use it either OOB or within an encrypted tunnel. Using Telnet In-Band may just land you up in the team explaining to the VP what happened to the network links. Secure Shell (SSH) should be the choice of protocol, which provides encryption for management traffic in transit and should be used wherever possible.

By default, Cisco IOS router provides five TTY ports that can be extended to 15 per device. Example 7-6 shows how you can allow the line VTY to accept incoming connections securely.

Example 7-6   *Enable VTY Login*

```
IPTRouter(config)# line vty 0 4
IPTRouter(config-line)# login
IPTRouter(config-line)# password <omitted>
IPTRouter(config-line)# transport input telnet
IPTRouter(config-line)# transport input ssh
```

The commands to disable login to VTY port(s) or to enable local login are same as illustrated in the previous section for console port. Because the VTY ports are accessible using IP addresses allotted to the IOS router, they can be accessed from any IP address that can reach the router. While this may mean ease of management access for you, it also means an easy access for an attacker to conduct his attack from anywhere within or outside your network. Thus, it becomes essential to limit the range of IP addresses to specific hosts or networks using access lists. Example 7-7 details the process to enable ACL-based access control.

Example 7-7   *Limiting Access to Line VTY Using ACL*

```
IPTRouter(config)# access-list 51 permit 10.100.100.100
IPTRouter(config)# access-list 51 permit 10.100.100.201
IPTRouter(config)# access-list 51 deny any any log
!
IPTRouter(config)# line vty 0 4
IPTRouter(config-line)# access-class 51 in
```

Note   The log option allows you to see denied connection attempts. It is equivalent to implicit **deny any any** at the end of an ACL; however, it will log the failed attempts from any hosts other than those allowed.

Securing the HTTP Interface

As with most Cisco network devices and applications, you have the ability to remotely manage (and monitor) a Cisco IOS router using a standard web browser.

Note   The Cisco Configuration Professional (Cisco CP) tool leverages an IOS router's HTTP web server.

Although the access using the HTTP browser may seem convenient (and it certainly is for users who prefer GUI over CLI) this access channel inherits the insecurity of the HTTP protocol, that is, all data, including usernames and passwords, is transmitted across the network in clear text. Moreover, by default, the web access uses the router's enable password to log in and grants the user privileged level rights.

You can secure the HTTP access in various ways. You can disable the HTTP access and enable the secure HTTP server instead, which uses RSA keys to transmit data in an encrypted channel, as shown in Example 7-8.

Example 7-8   *Enabling HTTP Secure Server*

```
IPTRouter(config)# no ip http server
IPTRouter(config)# ip http secure-server
IPTRouter(config)# ip http authentication local
```

If you decide to go ahead with non-secure HTTP, you can adopt a twofold approach to limit the web access to your router from specific hosts or networks. You can limit access based on:

- ACLs

- Non-default HTTP port numbers

Example 7-9 shows how you can enable the IOS HTTP server to accept incoming connections on a non-default (any other port than TCP 80) port and how you can restrict the connection coming from certain IP addresses:

Example 7-9   *IOS Router HTTP Server Security Measures*

```
IPTRouter(config)# ip http port <port number>
!
IPTRouter(config)# access-list 10 permit 10.100.100.151
IPTRouter(config)# access-list 10 deny any log
IPTRouter(config)# ip http access-class 10
```

To further lockdown the use of HTTP for web access to your router, you can configure HTTP authentication using either the local username and passwords or TACACS+ server, as shown in Example 7-10. Using these methods, privilege levels can be limited via user accounts.

Example 7-10 *Enabling IOS Router HTTP Server—User Authentication*

```
IPTRouter(config)# ip http authentication (local | tacacs | aaa)
```

Note The local option has been discussed earlier in the secure HTTP server configuration. Cisco TACACS+ and AAA (RADIUS) are the other two options to validate user credentials against Cisco ACS or any other third-party AAA server.

Disabling Unnecessary IOS Services

Cisco IOS enables some services and protocols by default. If these services are not needed, it is highly recommended that they be turned off. Every unneeded service active on the router can give a hacker an opportunity to attack your network layer. Example 7-11 illustrates how many services may be enabled on your Cisco router.

Example 7-11 *Cisco IOS Router Open Ports*

```
IPTRouter# show control-plane host open-ports
Active internet connections (servers and established)
Prot   Local Address    Foreign Address       Service      State
 tcp    *:22             *:0                   SSH-Server    LISTEN
 tcp    *:23             *:0                      Telnet    LISTEN
 tcp    *:23      10.105.127.213:25089       Telnet ESTABLISH
 tcp    *:80             *:0                   HTTP CORE     LISTEN
 tcp    *:2443           *:0         Skinny Socket Server    LISTEN
 tcp    *:1720           *:0                   H.225   LISTEN
 tcp    *:5061           *:0           CCSIP_TLS_SOCKET    LISTEN
 tcp    *:2000           *:0         Cisco Call manager serve    LISTEN
 tcp    *:5060           *:0                   SIP   LISTEN
 udp    *:1975           *:0                   IPC   LISTEN
```

Small Services

Cisco defined small UDP/TCP services such as

- Echo: TCP/UDP

- Chargen: TCP/UDP

- Discard: TCP/UDP

- Daytime: TCP

These are just a few small TCP/IP services, similar to those provided by the inetd process on UNIX systems. These small service daemons are enabled by default on Cisco IOS routers and should be disabled using the commands shown in Example 7-12.

Example 7-12 *Disabling TCP and UDP Small Servers*

```
IPTRouter(config)# no service udp-small-servers
IPTRouter(config)# no service tcp-small-servers
```

Finger Service

Finger service is a service from the UNIX world. It is an administrative utility that allows an administrator to remotely find out who is currently logged into the router. The attackers can use this feature to gather valid login names. As with all small services, the Finger service should also be disabled on your IP Telephony network's routers and switches as described in Example 7-13, if you do not have a need for it in your network.

Example 7-13 *Disabling Finger Service*

```
IPTRouter(config)# no ip finger
```

BootP

If you have ever booted a Cisco IOS router off of an IOS image located on another Cisco IOS router, you used the BootP service. Although, this service could be useful in a small environment (5 to 10 routers), that is, to get around installing and maintaining a dedicate SCP or TFTP server, in a medium-to-large enterprise setup, it is recommended to disable this service. The reason being that this can also be used by a hacker or an attacker to spoof and make your router boot from his machine using a tampered image. Alternatively, it enables the attacker to download a copy of your IOS image. BootP is enabled by default and should be disabled by issuing the command shown in Example 7-14.

Example 7-14 *Disabling BootP Server*

```
IPTRouter(config)# no ip bootp server
```

Note Any network device that has UDP, TCP, BOOTP, or Finger services should be protected by a firewall, ACLs, or have the services disabled to protect against DoS attacks.

Cisco Discovery Protocol (CDP)

Cisco Discovery Protocol (CDP) allows Cisco devices to learn about their neighbor Cisco devices. It is not trivial information; however, and a lot of information is gained by

CDP. For example, Example 7-15 shows a snippet from an IP Telephony switch.

Example 7-15   *Exploring CDP Detail*

```
IPTSW# show cdp neighbors detail
-------------------------
Device ID: Management-Sw
Entry address(es):
   IP address: 10.105.127.199
Platform: cisco WS-C3750G-24TS,  Capabilities: Router Switch IGMP
Interface: FastEthernet1/0/48,  Port ID (outgoing port): GigabitEthernet1/0/1
Holdtime : 154 sec

Version :
Cisco IOS Software, C3750 Software (C3750-IPBASEK9-M), Version 12.2(58.0.32)SE TEST
ENGINEERING ESTG_WEEKLY BUILD, synced to V150_2_10_SID
Copyright (c) 1986-2010 by Cisco Systems, Inc.
Compiled Wed 22-Dec-10 06:31 by abhakat

<output omitted>
-------------------------
Device ID: IPTRouter.XYZ.com
Entry address(es):
   IP address: 192.168.3.2
Platform: Cisco 2821,  Capabilities: Router Switch IGMP
Interface: FastEthernet1/0/33,  Port ID (outgoing port): GigabitEthernet0/0
Holdtime : 133 sec

Version :
Cisco IOS Software, 2800 Software (C2800NM-ADVENTERPRISEK9-M),
Version 15.1(3)T, RELEASE SOFTWARE (fc1)
Technical Support: http://www.cisco.com/techsupport
Copyright (c) 1986-2010 by Cisco Systems, Inc.
```

As you can see, the level of detail presented by **show cdp neighbors detail** command can be quite revealing. If an attacker were to get his hands on this information, for example, from a compromised switch, he might use this information to launch a DoS attack against the newly discovered targets. It is recommended that CDP be disabled when it is not needed. CDP is enabled by default and can be disabled globally or per interface basis, for example, globally by issuing the **no cdp run** command, as shown in Example 7-16.

Example 7-16   *Disabling CDP Globally*

```
IPTRouter(config) # no cdp run
```

CDP can be disabled per interface basis by issuing the commands shown in Example 7-17.

Example 7-17   *Disabling CDP per Interface Basis*

```
IPTRouter(config)# interface Fastethernet1/0
IPTRouter(config-if)# no cdp enable
```

Note   Cisco IP Phones depend on CDP to get VVID or Voice VLAN ID/Auxiliary VLAN. Therefore, in a Cisco IP Telephony network, at access layer, the switches should have CDP enabled provided that they have Voice VLAN configured and are expected to have IP Phones connected. For third-party phones, LLDP is required, and in that case, CDP can be disabled.

Proxy ARP

As the name suggests this is a Proxy feature provided by Cisco IOS routers. A router replies to a device's ARP request for the MAC address of a remote node with its own MAC address. In other words, Proxy ARP is a feature that enables a network device, which is not configured with a default gateway, to send packets outside of its network by means of a Cisco IOS router substituting the its interface's MAC address in the ARP reply.

Proxy ARP enables transparency across multiple network segments, and because of this reason, it can blur the LAN security demarcation boundary. Proxy ARP is enabled by default on Cisco routers, and it is highly recommended to disable it unless there is any effective requirement for it in your IP Telephony network, which is highly unlikely as all IP Telephony devices, endpoints, servers, and underlying network equipment should have a hard-coded network address. You can use the commands shown in Example 7-18 to disable proxy ARP, on a per interface basis.

Example 7-18   *Disabling Proxy ARP*

```
IPTRouter(config)# interface Fastethernet1/0
IPTRouter(config-if)# no ip proxy-arp
```

Directed Broadcast

A directed broadcast allows a device on one network segment (subnet) to send a broadcast to a different network segment (subnet). The broadcast is sent from a different network, directed via IP, not a unicast address. This technique is used in Smurf attack (which is a form of DoS attack). Smurf attacks leverage ICMP. An attacker spoofs the IP address of the broadcast, which is actually the IP address of the victim the attacker chooses. When every computer on the network responds to the ICMP request, all these requests go to the computer the attacker borrowed the IP address from. In this instance, the network acts only as an amplifier to the attack, not necessarily the victim. Figure 7-1 portrays Smurf attack in action.

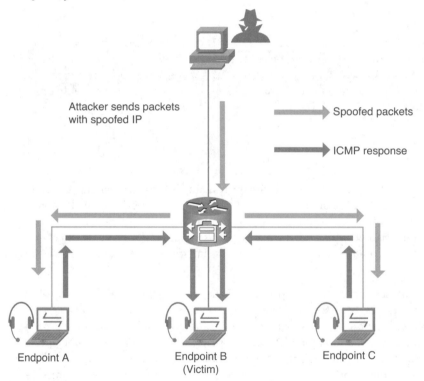

Figure 7-1 *Smurf Attack*

As a rule, directed broadcasts should be disabled. (It is disabled in IOS version post 12.0; however, it does not hurt to disable it explicitly.) To disable directed-broadcast on a per interface basis, issue the commands in Example 7-19.

Example 7-19 *Disabling Directed Broadcast*

```
IPTRouter(config)# interface Fastethernet1/0
IPTRouter(config-if)# no ip directed-broadcast
```

Source Routing

Source routing is a feature whereby the sender (source) of a packet can specify the route that a packet should take throughout the IP network. This is done against the internal network routing protocol decisions.

Note In source routing, the sender/source may make some or all these decisions.

Now, an attacker can use source routing to route his own malicious traffic around your network defenses choosing the path with minimal obstructions, for example, around a firewall. Also, an attacker can obtain information about a network's topology to gather information, which could be useful to launch an attack. (During an attack, the attacker could use source routing to direct packets to bypass existing security restrictions, for example, ACLs.) Figure 7-2 depicts a hacker or attacker executing a source routing attack.

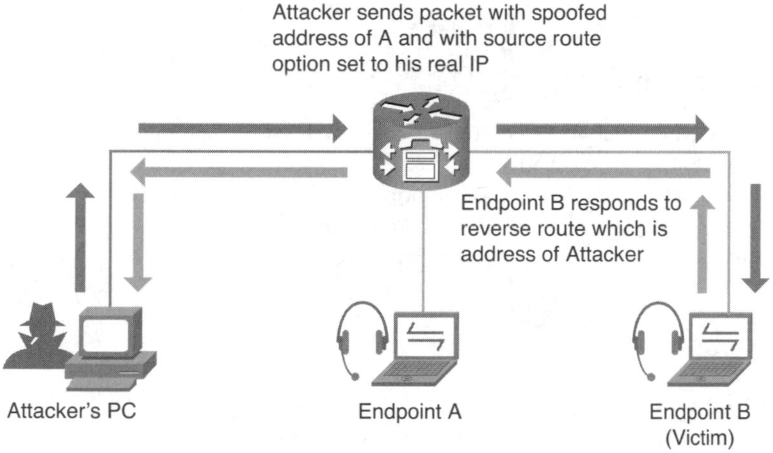

Attacker sends packet with spoofed
address of A and with source route
option set to his real IP

Endpoint B responds to
reverse route which is
address of Attacker

Attacker's PC   Endpoint A   Endpoint B
                                              (Victim)

Figure 7-2 *Manipulating Routing Using Source Routing*

Source routing is enabled by default on Cisco IOS routers. If you do not need source routing, it is recommended that it be disabled using the **no ip source-route** command, as shown in Example 7-20.

Example 7-20 *Disabling Source Routing*

```
IPTRouter(config)# no ip source-route
```

Classless Routing

If a router has classless routing enabled (RFC 4632), when it receives a network packet for which there is no configured route, the router forwards the packet to the best destination. In other words, with classless routing enabled, a router forwards packets even if it does not have an existing firm route defined for its destination. Classless routing is enabled by default on Cisco routers. It gives an attacker the opportunity to launch traffic injection/hijacking attacks. Consequently, classless routing should be disabled (Example 7-21) if it is not needed in your IP Telephony network.

Note   Do not disable this feature if you use classless routing in your network.

Example 7-21   *Disabling Classless Routing*

```
IPTRouter(config)# no ip classless
```

Configuration Autoloading

Cisco IOS routers have the capability to automatically load their configuration file from a remote TFTP server or from their NVRAM. The remote loading of a configuration file is an insecure way because an attacker has the opportunity to spoof the TFTP server (IP spoofing) and can load a configuration file (as shown in Figure 7-3), which allows a flurry of attacks to be launched against the whole network infrastructure.

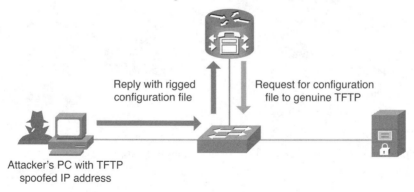

Reply with rigged
configuration file

Request for configuration
file to genuine TFTP

Attacker's PC with TFTP
spoofed IP address

Figure 7-3   *Configuration Autoloading (Spoofing and Intercept Attack)*

This feature should be disabled in almost every network because configuration management should be done securely to reduce the risk of attacks. Example 7-22 highlights the configuration steps to disable Autoloading in an IOS router.

Example 7-22 *Disabling IOS Configuration Autoloading*

```
IPTRouter(config)# no boot network
IPTRouter(config)# no service config
```

Securing TFTP

The most commonly used file management protocol, Trivial File Transfer Protocol (TFTP) is also used with Cisco routers to transmit IOS firmware and configuration files to and from the router. Natively, TFTP protocol does not provide for any authentication mechanism. Although, in an administrator's hands, this tool can be very powerful, it is as devastating when used by an attacker. Even more so when the Cisco IOS router is configured to download its configuration file from a remote TFTP server during system boot. In this case, if an attacker can compromise the TFTP server or spoof the identity of the TFTP server, he can load a faulty or attack prone configuration file. On the other hand, an attacker can connect to the router and download the configuration file (emulating itself as another IOS router) thereby exploiting the inherent weakness of TFTP protocol. This feature is disabled by default. However, you should explicitly disable it by issuing the **no tftp-server** command, as shown in Example 7-23:

Example 7-23 *Disabling IOS TFTP Server*

```
IPTRouter(config)# no tftp-server
```

To mitigate the inherent TFTP authentication issue, you can alternatively use SCP or FTP protocols, which provide the same file transfer functionality, however, provide for minimal security measures.

> **Note** Chapter 16 discusses Secure Copy Protocol (SCP).

You can use FTP to transfer configuration files to and from the router. FTP is preferred over TFTP because it gives you an option to define the user credentials to be verified before transfer or accept operation. The commands shown in Example 7-24 can be used to enable FTP on Cisco IOS routers.

Example 7-24 *Enabling IOS FTP Support*

```
IPTRouter(config)# ip ftp source-interface Fastethernet 1/0
IPTRouter(config)# ip ftp username adminuser
IPTRouter(config)# ip ftp password <omitted>
```

Securing Routing Protocols

At Layer 3, routers do what they are meant to do, they route IP packets. Routing protocols are the mechanisms through which routers communicate with each other and determine the routes that your network's traffic takes. As routers must do what they are meant for, the attackers will do what they want. Simply said, an attacker can manipulate the routing tables of your routers by injecting his own malicious routes causing the router to send all your voice and data network traffic along a path or destination of his preference. The traffic can be dropped, manipulated, hijacked, or sniffed when your router's routing tables yield to an attacker's choosing.

It is certainly something, which not only sounds scary when such an attack succeeds, but also it can cause a great magnitude of damage to your network. To protect against such a situation, all your routing protocols must be secured by configuring them to use authentication. Cisco routers can use two types of routing protocol authentication:

- Plain text authentication
- Message Digest 5 (MD5) authentication

In plain text authentication, the authentication key is sent across the network in clear text, thereby opening up venues for eavesdropping. On the other hand, MD5 authentication creates a hash value from the key and sends it to the neighbors where the neighboring router recalculates the hash value with the configured key to verify the integrity of the message. Hence, we are going to concentrate on securing routing protocols with MD5.

MD5 authentication is supported with the following routing protocols:

- RIPv2
- EIGRP
- OSPF
- BGP4

Routing protocol authentication is a symmetric process, that is, both peers must use the same algorithm for identification verification (authenticity). In other words, all peers participating in routing protocol update exchange (advertisement or acceptance) must be configured with same key/password.

The following routing topology (see Figure 7-4) will be used for all routing protocol authentication examples, with respective protocols. IPTRouter is advertising 10.0.0.0/8 to the DCRouter. Only the configuration of IPTRouter for each protocol's authentication example is covered, knowing that DCRouter will have a mirror configuration to support advertisement and acceptance of routing updates.

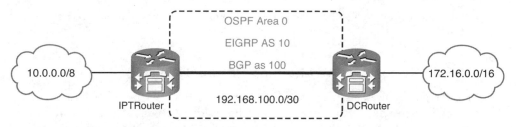

Figure 7-4 *Routing (Authentication) Topology*

> **Note** The intent here is to provide knowledge of basic security measures that must be implemented in your network to ensure protection of the routing protocol used in your IP Telephony network.

Routing Information Protocol v2 (RIPv2)

RIP is a distance vector protocol. RIPv1 does not provide any support for authentication of routing protocol updates. RIPv2 offers both plain text and MD5 authentication. RIPv2 uses the concept of a keychain to store passwords on the router. To enable MD5 authentication of RIPv2 updates, follow the steps outlined in Example 7-25.

Example 7-25 *Enabling RIPv2 Authentication*

```
IPTRouter(config)# key chain ciscoipt
IPTRouter(config-keychain)# key 1
IPTRouter(config-keychain-key)# key-string IPTRouter
!
IPTRouter(config)# interface Fastethernet 1/0
IPTRouter(config-if)# ip rip authentication mode md5
IPTRouter(config-if)# ip rip authentication key-chain ciscoipt
!
IPTRouter(config)# router rip
IPTRouter(config-router)# version 2
IPTRouter(config-router)# network 10.0.0.0
IPTRouter(config-router)# no auto-summary
```

> **Note** There is an option via which you can configure the period for which the key can be sent and received by using the **send-lifetime** and **accept-lifetime** commands. By default the time is infinite; you can configure it to be in compliance with your organizational security policy.

In the next section, you will comprehend securing EIGRP protocol using MD5 authentication.

Enhanced Interior Gateway Routing Protocol (EIGRP)

EIGRP is an advanced distance-vector Cisco proprietary routing protocol. Its authentication is almost on the same lines as RIPv2; however, EIGRP protocol authentication supports only the MD5 (RIPv2 also supports text only authentication), and you need to specify the EIGRP autonomous system number in which the router advertises and accepts routing updates. You can enable EIGRP routing protocol authentication using the commands shown in Example 7-26.

Example 7-26   *Enabling EIGRP Authentication*

```
IPTRouter(config)# key chain ciscoipt
IPTRouter(config-keychain)# key 1
IPTRouter(config-keychain-key)# key-string IPTRouter
!
IPTRouter(config)# interface Fastethernet 1/0
IPTRouter(config-if)# ip authentication mode eigrp 10 md5
IPTRouter(config-if)# ip authentication key-chain eigrp 10 ciscoipt
!
IPTRouter(config)# router eigrp 10
IPTRouter(config-router)# network 10.0.0.0
IPTRouter(config-router)# no auto-summary
IPTRouter(config-router)# eigrp log-neighbor-changes
```

In the next section you will learn about securing OSPF protocol using MD5 authentication.

Open Shortest Path First (OSPF)

OSPF is a link vector protocol that supports both plain text and MD5 authentication. In the interest of secure communications, only the MD5 approach is discussed. You can change the key used for authentication of OSPF protocol updates without disabling authentication. This is done based on the command shown in Example 7-27.

Example 7-27   *OSPF MD5 Authentication Syntax*

```
IPTRouter(config)# interface Fastethernet 1/0
IPTRouter(config-if)# ip ospf message-digest-key <key-id> md5 <key>
```

You can enable a different key by the key-id or key under the interface participating in OSPF routing updates without disabling authentication. The best practice is to configure another key-id with a different key and let the OSPF neighbors synchronize with that key before removing the earlier key. Example 7-28 outlines the course of action to enable MD5 authentication for OSPF protocol for OSPF area 0 exchange with other OSPF areas.

Example 7-28   *Enabling OSPF Authentication*

```
IPTRouter(config)# interface Fastethernet 1/0
IPTRouter(config-if)# ip ospf message-digest-key 1 md5 IPTRouter
!
IPTRouter(config)# router ospf 10
IPTRouter(config-router)# area 0 authentication message-digest
IPTRouter(config-router)# network 10.1.1.0 0.0.0.255 area 0
IPTRouter(config-router)# network 10.10.10.0 0.0.0.255 area 10
```

Border Gateway Protocol (BGP)

Border Gateway Protocol (BGP) is used at the network edge, where your Autonomous System (AS) meets ISP, partner, or any third-party AS. BGP protocol supports authentication mechanism using MD5 algorithm. When MD5-based authentication is enabled, any TCP segment exchanged between the BGP peers is verified and accepted only when the authentication is successful. Example 7-29 outlines the configuration required to enable BGP (MD5) authentication.

Example 7-29   *Enabling BGP Authentication*

```
IPTRouter(config)# router bgp 100
IPTRouter(config-router)# neighbor 172.16.10.10 password IPTRouter
```

Securing Hot Standby Routing Protocol (HSRP)

If your router participates in an HSRP configuration, it should be configured to use authentication. Why, you may ask? The reason is that an attacker can use freely available software tools such as Scapy to form malicious packets and inject them into your network such that his virtual router overrides the original HSRP preferred node (higher-priority member) and assumes the position of the HSRP primary router. HSRP supports plain text and MD5 authenticated packet exchange. With MD5 hash authentication configured, each router will append a secure one-way hash at the end of each HSRP packet. Example 7-30 shows the configuration required to establish MD5-based authentication between HSRP peers.

Example 7-30   *Enabling HSRP Authentication*

```
IPTRouter(config)# interface Fastethernet 1/0
IPTRouter(config-if)# standby 1 authentication md5 key-string IPTRouter
```

Safeguarding Against ICMP Attacks

Internet Control Message Protocol (ICMP) is a well-known network troubleshooting protocol. As helpful as it is to the network administrators to sort out connectivity or reach ability issues, hackers also find it an equally lucrative protocol to aid in their attacks. ICMP provides various services, of which some can be used against your network and should be disabled.

ICMP Unreachables

When a host sends a packet to another host or a network which the router is not aware of, an ICMP unreachable message is returned to the originating host. While this is a gracious feature that lets the source host know that the connection attempt failed, it can be used by an attacker to map your network as the scanning software will not have to wait for the attempt to time out since your router will quickly respond with an ICMP unreachable message. This feature is enabled by default and should be disabled on interfaces, which face untrusted networks, for example, the Internet. You can disable ICMP unreachables on a per interface basis by issuing the commands shown in Example 7-31.

Example 7-31 *Disabling ICMP Unreachables*

```
IPTRouter(config)# interface Fastethernet 1/0
IPTRouter(config-if)# no ip unreachables
```

ICMP Mask Reply

This is yet another feature that malicious insiders or outsiders can use to map your IP Telephony network. This feature allows the router to tell a requesting endpoint what the correct subnet mask is for a given network. ICMP Mask reply should be explicitly disabled on a per interface basis, as shown in Example 7-32.

Example 7-32 *Disabling ICMP Mask Reply*

```
IPTRouter(config)# interface Fastethernet 1/0
IPTRouter(config-if)# no ip mask-reply
```

ICMP Redirects

A router can send an IP redirect to notify the sender of a better route to the destination. The inventive purpose of this feature was for a router to send redirects only to the hosts on its directly connected networks. However, an attacker can leverage this feature to send an ICMP redirect message thereby luring nodes into sending all traffic through a (simulated perhaps) router, which is owned by the attacker.

ICMP redirects are enabled by default and should be disabled at least on the interfaces which face a potentially untrusted network, for example, an Internet or extranet interface. Example 7-33 illustrates how you can disable the router from sending ICMP redirects on **interface Fastethernet 1/0.**

Example 7-33   *Disabling ICMP Redirects (Outbound)*

```
IPTRouter(config)# interface Fastethernet 1/0
IPTRouter(config-if)# no ip redirects
```

In addition to sending ICMP redirects, to disable the router from receiving ICMP redirects on a particular interface, you must configure an ACL, as shown in Example 7-34.

Example 7-34   *Disabling ICMP Redirects (Inbound)*

```
IPTRouter(config)# access-list 200 deny icmp any any redirect
IPTRouter(config)# access-list permit ip any any
!
IPTRouter(config)# interface Fastethernet 1/ 0
IPTRouter(config-if)# ip access-group 200 in
```

Constraining ICMP

In a highly secure environment, the best practice might be to block all ICMP traffic to reach the network routers. Although, it is best practice to block all ICMP in such circumstances; however, it is necessary to still allow ICMP Type 3 Code 4 packets through because these packets help deal with Path MTU Discovery (PTMTUD) functions. An explanation of various ICMP options for Type 3 is shown in Example 7-35.

Example 7-35   *ICMP Type 3 Codes*

```
ICMP Fields: Type 3
Code:
0 = net unreachable
1 = host unreachable
2 = protocol unreachable
3 = port unreachable
4 = fragmentation needed and DF set
5 = source route failed
```

To deny all ICMP, with the exception of Type 3 Code 4, the commands shown in Example 7-36 should be issued on your router.

Example 7-36   *Disabling all ICMP Requests with Exception of Type 3 Code 4*

```
IPTRouter(config)# access-list 200 permit icmp any any 3 4
IPTRouter(config)# access-list 200 deny icmp any any
IPTRouter(config)# access-list 200 permit ip any any
IPTRouter(config)# interface Fastethernet 1/0
IPTRouter(config-if)# ip access-group 200 in
```

Securing User Passwords

As the Cisco IOS default method of authentication is reliant on passwords only (unless AAA is enabled), it is very important to protect all your passwords. Following some general rules when creating passwords help achieve at least a minimal level of security:

■ Ensure that passwords either are a minimum of eight characters long or are as per your security/IP Telephony Security policy.

■ Passwords should always combine letters, numbers, and symbols.

■ Change passwords as directed by your organization's security policy.

Remember, strong passwords are the primary defense against unauthorized access to your network devices.

Although using the normal enable password is not recommended, you can set a secret password (see Example 7-37) using an MD5 hash, which is the strongest option available on the Cisco IOS router.

Example 7-37   *Enable Secret Command*

```
IPTRouter(config)# enable secret <secret password>
```

For all other passwords, you can encrypt them on the IOS router using the Vigenere cipher. You must enable the service password-encryption command (see Example 7-38) that will encrypt all passwords on your IOS router:

Example 7-38   *Password Encryption Service*

```
IPTRouter(config)# service password-encryption
```

Note   Although, a Vigenere cipher is not a secure cryptographic algorithm and is not as safe as MD5, which is used for the **enable secret** command, it is still better than plain text passwords in IOS configuration.

Controlling User Access and Privilege Levels

When you log in to a router, you are asked for a password (if configured) from a console, telnet, SSH, or reverse telnet session. How secure do you think it is to have just a password defined without a simultaneous authorization level or accounting? Well, you might have guessed it already; it is not a secure way to just have a password to log in to the devices on which your IP Telephony network depends. You need to enable security such that anyone logging in to your network devices is properly authenticated, is authorized to run the set of commands, is authenticated for, and finally, be audited (accounting) for the activities performed on the device.

While some basic functionality of authentication, authorization, and accounting (AAA) is provided by IOS, using an access control server such as:

■ Cisco Terminal Access Control Access Control Server (TACACS+) or

■ RADIUS

is the preferred option for any medium-to-large enterprise environment. An AAA server not only authenticates the users logging into your network routers/devices, but it also authorizes them to use a certain command set and allows you to keep track of the sessions via the accounting feature. The 3 A's are explained as follows:

■ **Authentication:** Identifies users before admitting them into a network

■ **Authorization:** Dictates what a user can accomplish on the network

■ **Accounting:** Tracks the user's actions and logs them on the AAA server

Enabling Local Authentication and Authorization

Example 7-39 demonstrates how you can enable local authentication and command authorization on your Cisco router.

Example 7-39 *Local Authentication and Authorization*

```
IPTRouter(config)# username IPTAdmin password <password>
IPTRouter(config)# username RouterAdmin password <password>
!
IPTRouter(config)# username IPTAdmin privilege 5
IPTRouter(config)# username RouterAdmin privilege 15
!
IPTRouter(config)# privilege exec level 15 telnet
IPTRouter(config)# privilege exec level 5 ping
IPTRouter(config)# privilege exec level 5 show access-lists
IPTRouter(config)# privilege exec level 5 show ip access-lists
!
IPTRouter(config)# aaa authentication login default local
```

```
!
IPTRouter(config)# line vty 0 4
IPTRouter(config-line)# login local
!
IPTRouter(config)# line con 0
IPTRouter(config-line)# login local
```

At this point, your router is ready to accept connections from Line VTY and console. However, upon login, the user IPTAdmin will be authorized to only exec level 5 commands, whereas user RouterAdmin will be with full privilege level of 15.

Enabling External Server-based Authentication, Authorization, and Accounting (AAA)

Cisco routers offer you the functionality to enable AAA using an external server. This server can be Cisco ACS (TACACS+), RADIUS, or Kerberos. The AAA architecture is robust, and with redundancy it provides maximum protection against rogue users when it comes to device security. You can not only authenticate the users but also limit them to a certain set of commands (as previously shown in the local authentication section) and enable accounting that is, logging the actions and duration of the user connection for billing/audit functions. The following sections show how you can enable AAA on your Cisco router using Cisco-proprietary TACACS+ protocol.

Configuring Cisco TACACS+ Based Authentication

Example 7-40 illustrates how you can enable TACACS+ based authentication.

Example 7-40   *Configuring TACACS+ Based Authentication*

```
IPTRouter(config)# aaa new-model
!
IPTRouter(config)# tacacs-server host 10.200.200.250
IPTRouter(config)# tacacs-server key <shared password>
IPTRouter(config)# aaa authentication login default group tacacs+ local
IPTRouter(config)# aaa authentication enable default group tacacs+ enable
!
IPTRouter(config)# ip http authentication aaa
!
IPTRouter(config)# line vty 0 4
IPTRouter(config-line)# login authentication default
!
IPTRouter(config)# line con 0
IPTRouter(config-line)# login authentication default
!
IPTRouter(config)# line aux 0
IPTRouter(config-line)# login authentication default
```

The **aaa new-model** instructs the router to enable itself for AAA. The **tacacs-server host** command defines the AAA server location, password is to authenticate between router and TACACS+ server. While on the line(s) the **authentication default** command enables authentication via defined AAA server, **authentication enable default** enables authentication for entering into the privilege mode, and **ip http authentication** invokes any HTTP access to the router to use the AAA database for the username and password.

Configuring Cisco TACACS+ Based Authorization

Cisco TACACS+ offers two types of authorization:

- EXEC
- Command

Although EXEC authorization controls the level of access for an authenticated user to the IOS command line shell (EXEC prompt), the command authorization restricts the user's ability to issue certain commands while in EXEC mode. To enable EXEC and command authorization, follow the commands listed in Example 7-41.

Example 7-41 *Configuring TACACS+ EXEC and Command Authorization*

```
IPTRouter(config)# aaa authorization exec default group tacacs+ if-authenticated
IPTRouter(config)# aaa authorization commands 1 default group tacacs+ if-authenti-
  cated
IPTRouter(config)# aaa authorization commands 15 default group tacacs+ if-authenti-
  cated
```

Essentially, by executing Example 7-41, you instruct the router to allow the user into EXEC prompt and issue privilege level 1 and 15 commands 'if' the user were authenticated and 'if' the TACACS+ server was unavailable for some reason. Although this is a backdoor into the router if your ACS server is offline, it also means that it can be used as a way to get into your network devices by an attacker, wherein the attacker can bring down the ACS server. There are two remedies to this issue:

- Substitute **if-authenticated** with **none**
- Have redundancy for Cisco ACS server (high availability)

Configuring Cisco TACACS+ Based Accounting

To configure accounting, follow the commands in Example 7-42.

Example 7-42 *Configuring TACACS+ Based Accounting*

```
IPTRouter(config)# aaa accounting exec default start-stop group tacacs+
IPTRouter(config)# aaa accounting system default start-stop group tacacs+
IPTRouter(config)# aaa accounting connection default start-stop group tacacs+
```

```
IPTRouter(config)# aaa accounting network default start-stop group tacacs+
IPTRouter(config)# aaa accounting command 1 default start-stop group tacacs+
IPTRouter(config)# aaa accounting command 15 default start-stop group tacacs+
```

The various arguments used in Example 7-42 are as following:

- **System:** Logs all system events.

- **Network:** Logs all network service requests.

- **EXEC:** Logs all router EXEC commands

- **Connection:** Logs all outbound connections.

- **Commands:** Logs all commands of a given level.

- **Default:** Indicates that the accounting methods specified serve as the default list.

- **Start-stop:** The router sends an accounting notice to the AAA server when a process starts and when a process stops.

Note   AAA accounting provides additional detail beyond what Syslog can log and thus should be enabled wherever directed by your corporate security policy or as mandated by your environment.

Antispoofing Measures

As big as an annoyance it is with Layer 2 spoofing (MAC address spoofing, DHCP server spoofing) as you read about it in previous chapter, it remains a significant issue with Layer 3, too. Attackers often use spoofing to defeat network defenses and access control measures. Imagine an attacker on the outside of your IP Telephony network sending manipulated or crafted IP packets to your routers, with a source address that belongs to your internal IP Telephony network range. Your network will not stand a chance without anti spoofing measures in place because this attack would bypass access controls, thereby opening flood gates into your network. There are three major ways to suppress the spoofing attacks:

- RFC 2827 filtering

- uRPF

- IP Source Guard

The next sections detail each of these mechanisms. IP Source Guard has been discussed in Chapter 6, "Cisco IP Telephony Layer 2 Security."

RFC 2827 Filtering

A well-established system exists to identify and control a Layer 3 spoofing attack, emerging especially from outside your organization. Though this mechanism based on RFC 2827 might not be as flexible as uRPF (which you will learn next) it still gets the job done. The mechanism works as follows:

■ Create an ACL that denies all internal, known multicast and (possible) networks from outside while allowing all other traffic.

■ Apply this ACL list inbound on an interface, which is facing a potentially untrusted network.

The following example assumes that interface Fast Ethernet 1/0 is facing the Internet, where all possible spoofing attacks from outside originate. Eliminate inbound traffic from RFC 1918 addresses that are private non-routable IP addresses and major IANA reserved addresses:

■ 10.0.0.0/8

■ 172.16.0.0/12

■ 192.168.0.0/16

■ 0.0.0.0/8

■ 127.0.0.0/8

■ 169.254.0.0

In addition, the multicast range of 224.0.0.0/4, 239.0.0.0/8, and 240.0.0.0/5 and the broadcast address of 255.255.255.255 should be blocked.

The ACL 160 as stated in Example 7-43 should help you contain any Layer 3 spoofing attacks.

Example 7-43 *Antispoofing Using ACLs*

```
IPTRouter(config)# access-list 160 deny ip 0.0.0.0 255.255.255.255 any log
IPTRouter(config)# access-list 160 deny ip 10.0.0.0 0.255.255.255 any log
IPTRouter(config)# access-list 160 deny ip 127.0.0.0 0.255.255.255 any log
IPTRouter(config)# access-list 160 deny ip 172.16.0.0 0.15.255.255 any log
IPTRouter(config)# access-list 160 deny ip 169.254.0.0 0.0.255.255 any log
IPTRouter(config)# access-list 160 deny ip 192.168.0.0 0.0.255.255 any log
IPTRouter(config)# access-list 160 deny ip 224.0.0.0 15.255.255.255 any log
IPTRouter(config)# access-list 160 deny ip 239.0.0.0 0.255.255.255 any log
IPTRouter(config)# access-list 160 deny 240.0.0.0 7.255.255.255 any log
IPTRouter(config)# access-list 160 deny ip 255.255.255.255 0.0.0.0 any log
IPTRouter(config)# access-list 160 permit ip any any log
!
IPTRouter(config)# interface Fastethernet 1/0
IPTRouter(config-if)# ip access-group 160 in
```

> **Note**   Example 7-43 assumes that you are not using multicast routing or multicast MoH in your IP Telephony network.

Example 7-43 exemplifies the need to secure the Ingress traffic to prevent spoofing. However, a malicious user on the inside of your network can also try to attack someone on the outside. Thus, it is advisable to have egress filtering applied on the interface that connects to the Internet or any external network not under your domain.

Unicast Reverse Packet Forwarding (uRPF)

uRPF is an IOS feature that can be implemented on your Cisco IOS routers to thwart attempts to send packets with spoofed source IP addresses. uRPF adjusts to routing and topology changes automatically, thereby reducing the overhead associated with static ACLs.

uRPF looks for the source IP address of a packet arriving inbound on an interface of a router, in its routing table. If the source IP address belongs to the network behind the router, and the routing table contains an entry for the same, the packet is allowed. Nonetheless, if the IP address is spoofed, there is a good chance that an entry in the routing table does not exist. Because the router does not find the source IP address when it does the lookup, it drops the packet.

> **Note**   uRPF is the preferred method of anti spoofing because it results in less of a performance hit than using ACLs; it dynamically configures itself to changing network topologies; and it is simple to configure. Also, the uRPF feature requires Cisco Express Forwarding (CEF) to function properly.
>
> Moreover, uRPF does not work with asymmetrical routing and can cause problems. Thus, it is recommended that uRPF be used only on routers or interfaces that connect to possibly untrusted networks, where asymmetrical routing is not expected or configured.

Example 7-44 gives an insight to the configuration of uRPF.

Example 7-44   *Configuring uRPF*

```
IPTRouter(config)# ip cef
!
IPTRouter(config)# interface Fastethernet 1/0
IPTRouter(config-if)# ip verify unicast reverse-path
```

Router Banner Messages

Although login banners can be treated as informational messages, they are undoubtedly important for router security from a legal standpoint but not from a technical stand-point. You would certainly not want people who are not authorized to log in to your router and execute commands at their will. In such a case, you can let a possible intruder be aware of the legal prosecution and that he can be held liable if he continues to oper-ate in your environment. The banner should at a minimal express the following condi-tions:

- Only authorized users are allowed to use the system.

- All activities, configuration, and access will be monitored and recorded.

- Use of the system implies that the person accessing it agrees to the displayed condi-tions, and if the person does not agree to the conditions, he should immediately log off.

There are four types of banners that can be configured on your Cisco router:

- **Message of the Day (MOTD):** Displayed at login

- **Login:** Displayed after the Message of the Day banner appears and before the login prompts

- **EXEC:** Displayed when an EXEC process is commenced (post authentication of user)

- **Incoming:** Displayed on terminals connected to reverse Telnet lines

Of these at least MOTD should be enabled. To configure a banner, Example 7-45 out-lines the options.

Example 7-45 *Banner Syntax*

```
IPTRouter(config)# banner exec | motd | login | incoming <delimiting character>
* <Banner Content>
* <Banner Content>
<delimiting character>
```

Example 7-46 exemplifies how you can configure an MOTD banner on your Cisco rout-er; here $ is used as delimiting character.

Example 7-46 *Sample Banner*

```
IPTRouter(config)# banner MOTD $
Enter TEXT message. End with the character '$'.
****************************************************
*    WARNING!
```

```
* THIS IS A RESTRICTED SYSTEM!
* USE OF THIS SYSTEM WITHOUT PRIOR AUTHORIZATION IS STRICTLY PROHIBITED!
* LOGOFF IMMEDIATELY IF YOU ARE NOT AUTHORIZED TO USE THIS SYSTEM!
* THIS SYSTEM IS UNDER ACCESS CONTROL MONITORING AND UNAUTHORIZED USE
* WILL LEAD TO LEGAL ACTION!
********************************************************
$
```

Securing Network Time Protocol (NTP)

As good time management helps you keep your schedule in control, for Cisco routers it is a must for various services and support activities, some of which follow:

- Have log files with right timestamp to help with correlating log files from different systems, such as the Security Event Management System (SEMS), to analyze an attack. (For details on SEMS refer to Chapter 16.)

- Perform AAA-based accounting and time-based authentication and authorization.

- Use fault analysis for debugs and traces with right timestamps.

In a nutshell, good time management is essential to keep your network secure, and this is where NTP pitches in. All routers on the network can be enabled to reference a singular time source for accurate time keeping and synchronization. NTP server can be an IOS router, a Windows server, or a Linux server or a public server on the Internet (atomic time clock).

Although there are definite benefits to leverage from NTP, there are loopholes that an attacker can exploit if NTP is not secured. An attacker can compromise your systems by spoofing your network time server, thereby manipulating the clock of your routers. To safeguard against such attacks, NTP clients and servers should be configured to use an authentication mechanism. Example 7-47 details the configuration to enable NTP authentication on Cisco IOS routers.

Example 7-47   *Configuring NTP Authentication*

```
IPTRouter(config)# ntp authenticate
IPTRouter(config)# ntp authentication-key 1 md5 <password>
IPTRouter(config)# ntp trusted-key 1
IPTRouter(config)# ntp server 10.10.10.1 prefer key 1 source Fastethernet 0/1
```

IPTRouter has been configured to get time from the NTP server at the IP address 10.10.10.1 with the key configured and the source interface as Fastethernet 0/1 (refer to Example 7-47). This can not only ensure that the router gets time from a source that is authenticated via the key configured, but also that it gets time from a pre-designated source interface thereby reducing chances of spoofing by an attacker.

Blocking Commonly Exploited Ports

With almost every vulnerability scanner able to scan the open ports on a network device, it is futile to leave the commonly exploited ports open. It is as good as inviting a hacker to get in and show his magic!

Ensure that an extended ACL restricts all internal and external access to some ports of the router. These ports may be used for reconnaissance attacks. Example 7-48 shows how you can block unwanted ports on your IOS devices.

Example 7-48 *Using Access Control Lists (ACL) to Block Unwanted (Reconnaissance) Ports*

```
IPTRouter(config)# access-list 101 deny tcp any host 10.100.100.200 eq 7
IPTRouter(config)# access-list 101 deny tcp any host 10.100.100.200 eq 9
IPTRouter(config)# access-list 101 deny tcp any host 10.100.100.200 eq 13
IPTRouter(config)# access-list 101 deny tcp any host 10.100.100.200 eq 19
IPTRouter(config)# access-list 101 deny tcp any host 10.100.100.200 eq 23
IPTRouter(config)# access-list 101 deny tcp any host 10.100.100.200 eq 69
IPTRouter(config)# access-list 101 deny tcp any host 10.100.100.200 eq 79
IPTRouter(config)# access-list 101 deny tcp any host 10.100.100.200 eq 80
!
IPTRouter(config)# interface Fastethernet1/0
IPTRouter(config-if)# access-group in 101
```

Note   The consideration here is that ICMP ECHO, Discard, daytime, Chargen, Telnet, TFTP, Finger, and HTTP in that order (along with other non frequently used protocols) are not in use. In place of Telnet, SSH should be used, and in place of HTTP, HTTPS should be used. In place of TFTP, FTP or SCP can be used.

Extending Enterprise Security Policy to Your Cisco Router

Have you ever imagined your network devices without any security policy applied to them? How will the network roll out when there is no guideline for what to do, how to do, when to do, and so on? Well, you have just been saved from a definite nightmare because Cisco gives you the power to extend your security policies to the IOS platform.

Password Minimum Length

You can force a minimum password length of, for example, eight characters on your IOS router (using Example 7-49), just like you would on any application server. This is just like enforcing an enterprise wide minimum password length policy.

Example 7-49 *Enforcing Minimum Password Length*

```
IPTRouter(config)# security passwords min-length 8
```

Note This command affects user and enable passwords, secrets, and line passwords. It is important to note that existing router passwords remain unaffected and only new passwords will inherit the policy.

Authentication Failure Rate

You can also configure the number of unsuccessful login attempts and simultaneously generate the Syslog messages after the maximum preconfigured threshold number of unsuccessful login attempts have exceeded.

Example 7-50 shows how to configure your router to generate a Syslog message after five failed login attempts (a 15-second delay timer starts after the number of login failed is reached).

Example 7-50 *Setting Authentication Failure Parameters with Logging*

```
IPTRouter(config)# security authentication failure rate 5 log
```

Block Logins

Most of the times there are brute force or dictionary-based attacks attempted from within or outside your IP Telephony network on the network devices. Cisco IOS routers give you an option to thwart these attacks by rate limiting the login attempts (for example via an automated tool-based attack). Example 7-51 shows how you can block login access for 60 seconds after three failed login attempts within 20 seconds:

Example 7-51 *Blocking Automated Malicious Login (Dictionary Based or Brute Force Attack) Attempts*

```
IPTRouter(config)# login block-for 60 attempts 3 within 20
```

Disable Password Recovery

Have you been in a situation when you or the router administrator forgot the password to get to the enable mode? Well, although most of us have been there, neither it is a pretty situation nor is it friendly to the security of your network routers. Password recovery presents a potential security threat because anyone who gains physical access to the router console port can try and enter ROMMON and reset the enable password (password recovery does not apply to encrypted passwords.) Once done, the nonfriendly personnel will have full access to this router and can launch an attack on other network routers, nodes, or devices reachable from this compromised router.

To mitigate this threat, there is a somewhat "harsh" method, that is, to disable the password recovery procedure.

Note This command is particularly dangerous if you do not have a password management system, or you are not sure of why you should do it. Always, have a good password management system as defined and directed by your organization's security policy.

Example 7-52 shows the procedure to disable password-recovery, and it is interesting to follow the subsequent prompts.

If you are not sure that you need to disable password recovery DO NOT PROCEED.

Example 7-52 *Disabling Password Recovery*

```
IPTRouter(config)# no service password-recovery

WARNING:
Executing this command will disable password recovery mechanism.
Do not execute this command without another plan for
password recovery.

Are you sure you want to continue? [yes/no]: yes
```

Now, while it clearly states that there should be another backup plan to ensure that you, "the lawful'" user of the router, can get into in case you forget the password, it does not state how you can do it. There are two major options to break through the security you have set up.

- Either reseat the nonvolatile RAM (NVRAM) chip to reset the configuration, that is, to break the connection between the NVRAM and battery so that it loses its configuration.

- Or reload the router with console access, and press Ctrl-Break within 5 to 10 seconds (when Cisco IOS Software image starts decompressing) and try to reset the router to the factory default. This action will erase the start-up configuration.

If nothing works, contact Cisco TAC. In extreme conditions, your device may need a RMA!

Layer 3 Traffic Protection—Encryption

If your Layer 3 traffic (IP packets) must traverse a possibly unsafe territory or an untrusted network, encryption is your best friend in such a situation. Deploying Layer 3 encryption using IPSec protocol is a must when VoIP or crucial data traffic leaves the trusted frontier of your organization's network and ventures onto the Internet, where all possible dangers from a cyber-world perspective exist.

Although having IPSec tunnels within a network (same VRF or private network) is not common, it could be a mandatory task to undertake, as stated in your security policy. On the periphery, Cisco ASA can help you protect your traffic (voice media, signaling, and data traffic) streams from meddling audience because it enables you to create

- LAN to LAN IPSec tunnel with static IP's or DMVPN topology
- LAN to LAN IPSec tunnel, with one side as dynamic IP (EzVPN)
- Server-Client IPSec/SSL tunnel for telecommuters

Note   Usually, the tunnels are terminated on the peripheral firewall to minimize the performance impact on the edge router.

The role of Cisco ASA as a perimeter/corporate firewall is covered in Chapter 8, "Perimeter Security with Cisco Adaptive Security Appliance." Cisco IOS routers can also initiate and terminate IPSec tunnels to and from a Cisco IOS router or Cisco ASA. IOS Firewall is covered in Appendix B, "Cisco IP Telephony: Firewalling and Intrusion prevention."

Layer 3 Security—Best Practices

Cisco has empowered you with many Layer 3 security features so that you can safeguard your voice and data traffic. Let's look at some of the Layer 3 security best practices.

- Restrict management access for the router only to the authorized management subnet/team.
- Wherever possible instead of telnet, use SSH to manage your routing infrastructure.
- Enable secure Telnet access to a router user interface by limiting the access from trusted network subnets and by switching to SSH. Also, limit exposure to Console and AUX ports.
- Turn off all unnecessary services (small services TCP/UDP).
- Enable an audit trail by turning on Syslog logging and use AAA accounting.
- Wherever possible, enable routing protocol authentication with MD5 authentication.

- If using HSRP in your environment, ensure that HSRP messages are MD5 authenticated.

- Shut down unused router physical interfaces (explicit administrative shutdown).

- Always implement a non deferred and stable IOS release to minimize the attack surface.

- Implement encryption for Layer 3 traffic when the traffic is expected to traverse suspicious networks and the Internet.

- Extend your organization's security policy to your IOS routers and do it by enforcing a minimum password length, lockout time intervals, and so on.

- Always use **enable secret** instead of **enable password** for encrypted passwords and enable password encryption service to secure all user passwords.

- Wherever possible, deploy AAA for restricting user access and command-level authorization to your routing infrastructure, and if it is not possible to deploy Cisco TACACS+ or a RADIUS server, consider local authentication and authorization.

- Deploy anti spoofing mechanisms (RFC 2827 filtering, uRPF, or IP source guard).

- Reduce exposure to ICMP attacks by disabling ICMP redirects, mask replies, and unreachables.

- Implement (at the least) MOTD banner. It is recommended to configure EXEC banner as well.

- If using SNMP for switch management, ensure that the community strings are equivalent to strong passwords (at least eight characters, alphanumeric).

- Disable access to commonly, well-known exploited ports and services by using ACLs.

- Always ensure that a trusted NTP source (whether internal or external) is used and that MD5 authentication is enabled for NTP server and clients.

Summary

Because a complete book could be written on securing Cisco IOS routers, this chapter was a candid attempt to highlight the diverse threats that daunt your routing infrastructure and how you can go about mitigating them. Layer 3 is one of the most important layers in the OSI reference model, and practically, without Layer 3 availability, your IP Telephony network will be down to null. All Cisco IP Telephony applications leverage the underlying network for their functionality (the purpose they were built for) and hence, it is vital that the underlying network is robust, resilient, and non yielding to various attacks.

This chapter introduced Layer 3 security threats and their mitigation techniques. Although, not every threat and its prevention mechanics may come into play in your

IP Telephony network, rest assured your network will not be left untouched by many. Thus, it is time that you look into various attack vectors and existing vulnerabilities to safeguard the routing layer of your network. This can be as simple as enabling an ACL on the egress or ingress interface of your router or can be as complex as determining the services your network does not need. Some key features that you should consider deploying are routing protocol authentication, hardening IOS routers (user passwords, service disablement, and access control), safeguarding information traversing untrusted links, restricting management access, and limiting exposure to unwanted traffic, especially from untrusted sources.

In the next chapter, you will understand the perimeter security for your Cisco IP Telephony network. You will discover Cisco Adaptive Security Appliance, which will be your primary ammunition against threats originating from outside of your line of control in cyber world. You will be introduced to various mechanisms such as, VPN Phone, TLS Proxy, ALG firewall, and much more.

Chapter 8

Perimeter Security with Cisco Adaptive Security Appliance

It is 7 a.m. and your mobile rings. An onsite IP Telephony engineer is online with you explaining that there was an attack attempted on organization XYZ's IP Telephony network. The attackers tried contravening the network perimeter security, but Cisco Adaptive Security Appliance (ASA) Firewall was unyielding and saved the day! You feel relaxed but anxious as to who might have attempted the attack. Paranoia about how you can ensure that next time they cannot break into your IP Telephony data center and wreak havoc.

While it is true that an organization can lose money and important data because of lack of security, it is more vital to sustain a good reputation so that the clientage isn't affected. Information losses can include identity theft, information theft, lost business, and lost productivity from internal and external attacks. While internal attacks can be contained from media hype, attacks originating from the outside are the ones that can cause the most damage to an organization's reputation.

This chapter covers the following topics:

- Introduction to Cisco Adaptive Security Appliance
- Securing an IP Telephony data center with Cisco ASA
- Implementing Cisco ASA TLS proxy
- Implementing Cisco ASA Phone proxy
- Implementing VPN IP Phones with Cisco ASA
- Remote worker and telecommuter voice security

IP Telephony Data Center's Integral Element: Cisco Adaptive Security Appliance

Every organization has a network perimeter where its domain (or network) ends and the public domain (or the Internet) begins. Thanks to telecommuters and wireless and VPN technology, this frontier seems to be blurred. However, at this border, if security is fuzzy, you risk losing productivity, confidential data, money, clientage, and most importantly, your organization's reputation. Thus, it is not only extremely important to safeguard the boundary of your IP Telephony network, but it's also essential to curtail any attempts to break into your IP Telephony network.

Before leaping into the how's and what's of securing your IP Telephony data center, let's first get a basic know-how of your new friend, the Cisco Adaptive Security Appliance (ASA) Firewall.

An Introduction to Cisco ASA Firewall

Cisco ASA 5500 series firewalls are enterprise grade, robust, and resilient devices. The Cisco ASA 5500 series are a key element in the overall Cisco end-to-end security solution. Cisco ASA offers Unified Threat Management (UTM) by virtue of bundling multiple security solutions such as – an Intrusion Prevention System (IPS), content security (antivirus, URL filtering, antispyware, and so on), and VPN (SSL/IPSec) technologies. The Cisco ASA 5500 series is built on proven the Cisco Firewall technology.

Cisco ASA Firewalls are the soul mate of your IP Telephony network as they provide unmatched security for your IP Telephony network by protecting the IP Telephony services (for example Call Control and messaging), endpoints (gateways and IP Phones), and IP Telephony data (CDR records). Cisco ASA Firewalls are available in different configurations and flavors to suit your IP Telephony network's needs, whether it is the number of simultaneous connections through the firewall, the quantity of endpoints to which it can scale, or the services you want to leverage. Cisco ASA Firewalls range from compact plug-and-play desktop firewalls for a Small Office Home Office (SOHO) atmosphere to carrier-class gigabit firewalls for the most demanding enterprise and service-provider environments.

Cisco ASA is available in the following models (Cisco ASA 5500 series, as shown in Figure 8-1):

- **Cisco ASA 5505:** Delivers enterprise-class security for SOHO and a mobile worker environment

- **Cisco ASA 5510:** Delivers enterprise-class security for small-to-medium-sized businesses

- **Cisco ASA 5520:** Delivers enterprise-class security for small-sized enterprises

- **Cisco ASA 5540:** Delivers enterprise-class security for mid-sized to large enterprises

- **Cisco ASA 5550:** Delivers enterprise-class security for large enterprises

■ **Cisco ASA 5580/5585:** Delivers enterprise-class security for a data center, campus, and large enterprises

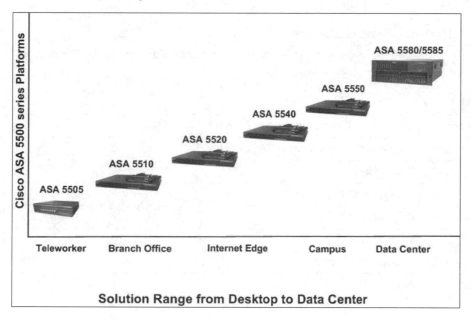

Figure 8-1 *Cisco ASA Firewall Models*

Some of the highlight features of Cisco ASA are as follows:

■ Reliability, security, and performance in an appliance format (hardware-based firewall)

■ Stateful packet inspection, including support for Cisco SCCP, H.323, SIP, FTP, and various other UPnP protocols

■ Built-in inspection engines that examine packet streams at Layers 4 through 7

■ Multiple security contexts within a single appliance to support virtual or multitenant environments

■ Robust IPSec VPN for secure site-to-site and remote access connections

■ SSL VPN for remote clients, including IP Phones

■ Stateful failover competence to guarantee network availability

■ Routed and transparent modes for deployment into existing network environments, as required

■ Integrated intrusion prevention to guard against malicious attacks

■ Remote manageability via Telnet, Secure Shell Protocol (SSH), and Cisco Adaptive Security Device Manager

In essence, the Cisco ASA 5500 series enables valid business traffic to flow while keeping out unwelcome visitors.

Cisco ASA Firewall and OSI layers

As discussed earlier, Cisco ASA can provide security services at various OSI layers, from Layer 2 through Layer 7, as shown in Table 8-1.

Table 8-1   *Cisco ASA Security for OSI Layers*

OSI Layer	Cisco ASA Firewall Security Feature
Application	Application Level Gateway (ALG), VPN (SSL)
Presentation	Encryption
Session	Proxy, stateful firewall
Transport	Port filtering
Network	VPN (IPSec), ACLs, NAT, routed firewall
Data Link	Transparent firewall
Physical	N/A

Cisco ASA performs application inspection for the protocols listed in Table 8-2. Although this is a list of the most commonly used protocols (including IP Telephony protocols), for an in-depth list, refer to the Cisco ASA web page at http://www.cisco.com/go/asa/.

Table 8-2   *Application/Protocol Inspection*

Protocol	Description
DNS	Domain Name Services: Used to translate names to IP addresses
TFTP	Trivial File Transfer Protocol: Used by IP Telephony endpoints to download or update firmware, configuration, and so on
H225	H.323 signaling protocol
H323 RAS	Gatekeeper registration, admission, and statistics services protocol
RTSP	Real Time Streaming Protocol: Standard for delivering real-time video and audio streaming
SKINNY	Skinny Client Control Protocol (SCCP): Cisco proprietary communication protocol
SIP	Session Initiation Protocol: Another voice signaling and media protocol
CTIQBE	Computer Telephony Interface Quick Buffer Encoding: IP telephony encoding standard

Protocol	Description
SQLNET	Protocol for allowing the delivery of queries to SQL-compliant databases over the network
NETBIOS	Microsoft Windows Network Protocol: To connect PCs running Windows operating systems
ICMP	Internet Control Message Protocol: Protocol used to communicate status and error messages between network devices using the TCP/IP stack
SNMP	Simple Network Management Protocol: Used to manage network devices
FTP	Standard protocol for file operations (move, copy, and so on)
HTTP	Hypertext Transfer Protocol: The Internet standard for browsing websites

Cisco ASA Basics

This section briefly walks you through Cisco ASA basics. This is so you can understand the capability of Cisco ASA as a firewall, and how you can configure interfaces for basic startup and security zones for your IP Telephony network.

Cisco ASA: Stateful Firewall

Cisco ASA is a stateful firewall, that is, it supports stateful inspection. Stateful inspection implies that the security appliance keeps a track of connections going out and coming in. This helps Cisco ASA enforce the concept that traffic sourced only from the inside or explicitly allowed with an ACL (on the outside) will be let back through the appliance.

Cisco ASA Firewall: Interfaces

Cisco ASA 5500 series security appliances have multiple interfaces (the number of interfaces differs depending on the model) that you can dedicate for isolating your internal network from the outside and from the Internet-facing servers (DMZ). These interfaces can be assigned to logical zones, which allow or disallow traffic by zone security levels (as per your security policy). Figure 8-2 shows this arrangement.

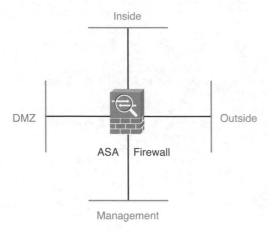

Figure 8-2   *Cisco ASA Physical/Logical Interfaces and Zones*

Although any interface can be configured as Inside, Outside, or DMZ, the usual practice is to configure the following:

■ Interface 0 (Fast Ethernet or Gigabit) as outside

■ Interface 1 (Fast Ethernet or Gigabit) as inside

■ Any other (or consecutive) interface as DMZ

Note   This assumes that your Cisco ASA model does not have any interfaces labeled as inside, outside, and so on. If so, it is best to configure the labeled interfaces as inside, outside, and so on, respectively.

This helps identify the interfaces physically on the appliance and to follow a logical sequence for interfaces.

Let's understand what each of these interfaces means to your IP Telephony network.

Inside Interface: Where the entities intended to be secured are placed; this interface is your friend. It helps protect the lifeline for your IP Telephony network, the call control servers, voice messaging servers, presence servers, transcoding, conferencing resources, and so on.

Outside Interface: Where all the crooks and rogue devices are supposed to be located. In other words, it is where your foes thrive, on the Internet and on the outside of your network domain. This interface is meant to liaise with the outside world, whether it is your ISP, a partner, or anyone on the Internet.

Demilitarized Zone (DMZ): Used to host servers that are required by users on the Internet. Because Internet servers are often the devices that hackers attack, even if they manage to compromise a host on the DMZ, they still must face the security appliance to get to the inside devices.

Management Interface: Provides an out-of-box management capability to the Cisco ASA administrator. Although a common practice by Cisco ASA administrators is to use the inside interface as the management interface, the management interface, however, is the recommended choice for managing the security appliance. The reason is that this interface does not route. This interface accepts traffic intended for only Cisco ASA and not the traffic destined for other networks.

Note   This interface can support routing protocols so that it can be set as a peer with other routers in the network.

Cisco ASA Firewall: Security Levels

Each physical or logical interface must be assigned a security level that dictates the level of trust that an interface is embraced with. Security levels can be defined within a range of 0–100 with 0 being least secure and 100 being most secure, as depicted in Figure 8-3.

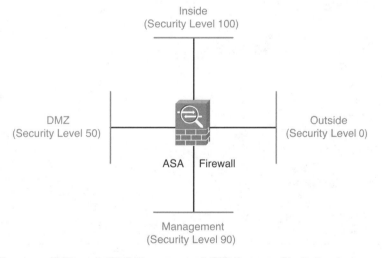

Figure 8-3   *Cisco ASA Physical/Logical Zones and Security Levels*

As you can observe, the inside interface is given a security level of 100 because this is the most secure interface where the core components of your IP Telephony network resides. On the other hand, the outside interface is assigned security level 0 because it faces the most untrusted network, the Internet, and the users of IP Telephony services (where a potential attacker could be resident). DMZ is assigned level 50 because it is semi-trusted and lies between the bounds of the inside and outside. The management interface is assigned a security level of 90 because it is supposed to be a secure interface, assigned to management VLAN where only trusted machines can connect for managing Cisco ASA.

Example 8-1 explains how these interfaces can be configured (see Figure 8-3).

Example 8-1 *Cisco ASA Interface Configuration*

```
IPTASA(config)# interface fastethernet 0
IPTASA(config-if)# description Outside Interface for Internet
IPTASA(config-if)# nameif outside
IPTASA(config-if)# security-level 0
IPTASA(config-if)# ip address 1.1.1.1 255.255.255.0
IPTASA(config-if)# no shutdown
!
IPTASA(config-if)# interface fastethernet 1
IPTASA(config-if)# description Inside Interface for IP Telephony servers
IPTASA(config-if)# nameif inside
IPTASA(config-if)# security-level 100
IPTASA(config-if)# ip address 10.1.1.1 255.255.255.0
IPTASA(config-if)# no shutdown
!
IPTASA(config-if)# interface fastethernet 2
IPTASA(config-if)# description DMZ Interface for application servers
IPTASA(config-if)# nameif DMZ
IPTASA(config-if)# security-level 50
IPTASA(config-if)# ip address 172.16.1.1 255.255.255.0
IPTASA(config-if)# no shutdown
!
IPTASA(config-if)# interface management 0/0
IPTASA(config-if)# description Management Interface
IPTASA(config-if)# nameif management
IPTASA(config-if)# security-level 90
IPTASA(config-if)# ip address 192.168.1.1 255.255.255.0
IPTASA(config-if)# no shutdown
```

By default, interfaces on the same security level cannot communicate with each other since allowing communication between the same security interfaces would let traffic flow freely between all the same security interfaces without any access control (ACL). This, however, can be enabled by the **same-security-traffic permit inter-interface** command.

Cisco ASA: Firewall Modes

Cisco ASA can work in the following modes:

- Routed
- Transparent
- Multi context

In routed mode (Layer 3 firewall), Cisco ASA is considered to be a hop in the network. Routed mode supports many interfaces, and each interface should be on a different subnet. Cisco ASA, on the other hand, can also work in transparent mode. In this mode, it is a Layer 2 firewall that acts like a bump in the wire and is not seen as a hop to connected devices.

While depending on a network or an organization's requirement, Cisco ASA can be configured in transparent or routed mode; for an IP Telephony network to leverage Cisco ASA as an ALG Firewall, it should be configured in routed mode. As a transparent (mode) firewall, Cisco ASA has following limitations:

- When the firewall is set to transparent mode, you are limited to the use of two traffic forwarding interfaces.
- Sharing of contexts, when in multiple context mode, is not possible in transparent mode.
- A transparent firewall does not support QoS or Network Address Translation (NAT). Former is a pre-requisite for acceptable voice quality across network links.
- A transparent firewall does not offer multicast routing support.
- A transparent firewall supports site-to-site VPN configuration, however only for its own management traffic. This proves to be limiting factor for telecommuters or remote workers.

Note   A transparent firewall can save you from changing your IP addressing scheme or readdressing the IP network, for example, for inside/outside subnets. For large enterprise networks, Cisco ASA as an internal firewall can be used in routed or transparent mode; however, at the perimeter, Cisco ASA is best used in routed mode for reasons mentioned earlier.

Cisco ASA supports firewall Multiple Context, also known as Firewall Multimode. Multiple Context mode can be viewed as having multiple separate virtual firewalls on the same physical hardware. Each context is its own security entity with its own security policy specifics and interfaces. Following firewall features are not supported in multiple context mode, such as

- VPN services (remote access or site-to-site VPN tunnels)
- Phone-Proxy

- Dynamic routing

- QoS

- Multicast routing

- Threat detection

For Cisco IP Telephony deployments, Cisco ASA should be configured in single (default) context, and multiple context mode should be avoided for the aforementioned reasons.

Cisco ASA: Network Address Translation

Cisco ASA can provide Network Address Translation (NAT) services, that is, it can change the IP address or port number or both for traffic going out of network (from a higher security interface to a lower security interface) and for traffic coming into your IP Telephony network (a lower security interface to a higher security interface). You can turn off NAT control, allowing packets to traverse Cisco ASA unaltered. This is particularly useful if you do not want to manipulate inside IPs to an outside address range (highly recommended for VoIP because RTP does not play well with NAT) or use RFC 1918 (private) addresses on internal servers, instead use the globally routable (public) network addresses on the IP Telephony and other servers (which is not a recommended practice). NAT control is disabled by default on Cisco ASA. Therefore, when you configure an out-of-the-box Cisco ASA, there's no NAT enabled on the security appliance.

Note   For Cisco IP Telephony applications, servers, and network devices, use of RFC 1918 addresses is highly recommended and use of publicly routable addresses is discouraged.

Cisco ASA: UTM Appliance

As previously mentioned, Cisco ASA Firewall is a UTM bundle and can optionally provide IPS, content security, and VPN services. Some of these services (for example, IPS signatures and VPN) are indigenous to Cisco ASA, other services such as content security (antivirus engine, antispyware engine, proxy, and so on) are optional and can be enabled using an AIP-SSC module. Also, an AIP-SSM module gives Cisco ASA the capability for enhanced IPS functionality (hardware acceleration). These services are not essential for IP Telephony Security and are optional (depends on a network architecture and traffic analysis and filtering requirements). For details on Cisco ASA advance inspection features and intrusion prevention/detection for voice signaling and media traffic, see Appendix B, "Cisco IP Telephony: Firewalling and Intrusion Prevention."

Cisco ASA: IP Telephony Firewall

Cisco ASA provides comprehensive access control, threat protection, network policies, service protection, and voice/video confidentiality for real-time IP Telephony traffic.

Voice (and related) protocols supported by Cisco ASA are listed as following:

- SIP
- SCCP (Skinny)
- H.323 v1 - 4
- GTP (3G mobile wireless)
- MGCP
- TRP/RTCP/RTSP
- TAPI/JTAPI
- HTTP
- TFTP
- DNS
- TCP
- UDP
- LDAP

Cisco IP Telephony applications and third-party applications supported by Cisco ASA follow:

- Cisco Unified Communications Manager
- Cisco Unity/Unity Connection
- Cisco Unified Presence Server
- Cisco Unified IP Phones
- Cisco Unified Personal Communicator
- Cisco IP Communicator
- Cisco Unified Meeting Place
- Cisco Unified Contact Center Enterprise and Express
- Microsoft Windows Messenger, NetMeeting
- Real Player

Again, this is not an exhaustive list of applications supported by Cisco ASA. Figure 8-4 shows the various IP Telephony Security services that a Cisco ASA Firewall can deliver.

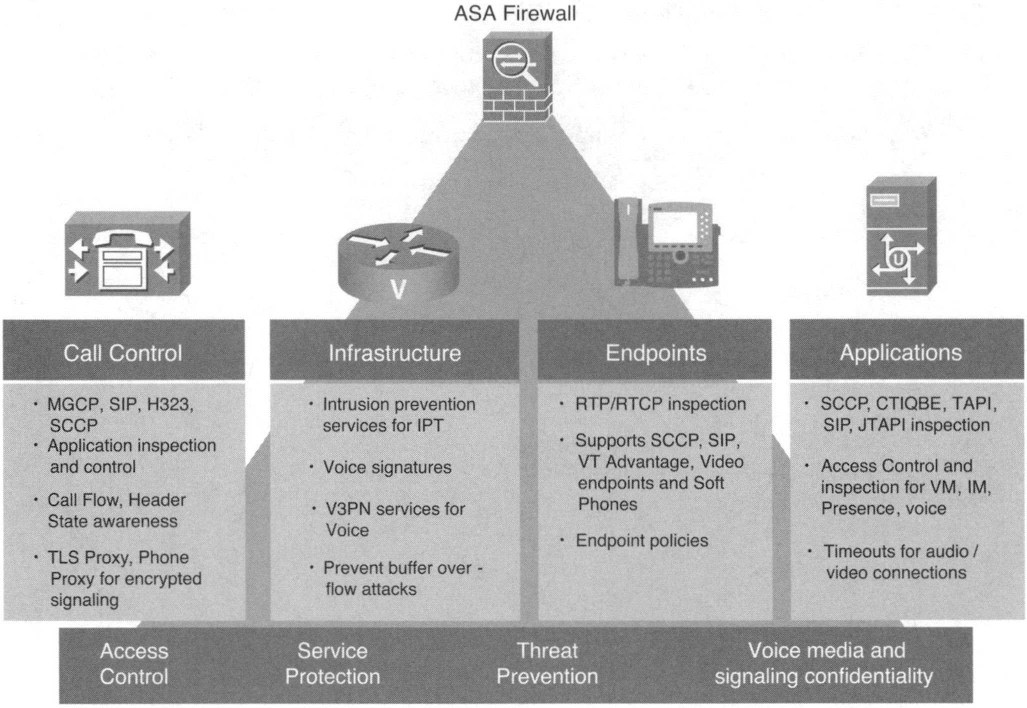

ASA Firewall

Call Control	Infrastructure	Endpoints	Applications
• MGCP, SIP, H323, SCCP • Application inspection and control • Call Flow, Header State awareness • TLS Proxy, Phone Proxy for encrypted signaling	• Intrusion prevention services for IPT • Voice signatures • V3PN services for Voice • Prevent buffer over - flow attacks	• RTP/RTCP inspection • Supports SCCP, SIP, VT Advantage, Video endpoints and Soft Phones • Endpoint policies	• SCCP, CTIQBE, TAPI, SIP, JTAPI inspection • Access Control and inspection for VM, IM, Presence, voice • Timeouts for audio / video connections

Access Control	Service Protection	Threat Prevention	Voice media and signaling confidentiality

Figure 8-4   *Cisco ASA Firewall IP Telephony Security Features*

Fortified with the basics of Cisco ASA, now you can dwell deep into the advance IP Telephony protection mechanisms that Cisco ASA has to offer. The following sections will help you understand the concepts behind IP Telephony data center security with Cisco ASA, proxy features, telecommuter solutions, and VPN Phone solutions. Configuration examples will help you set up the Cisco ASA perimeter defense to protect your IP Telephony network.

Securing IP Telephony Data Center with Cisco ASA

The perimeter of an organization is the first line of defense, both physically and logically from outside attacks. (You have read about physical security in Chapter 5, "Cisco IP Telephony Physical Security"). Firewalls are fundamental to the security of any business. The perimeter of an organization establishes the boundary between the inside of the organization and the outside. Although organizations may be susceptible to insider and outsider threats, both of which are significant, the enterprise perimeter and the firewalls are intended to protect the inside from outsider attacks. No matter if an IP Telephony network is tightly locked down from the inside or if the system administrators are on top of security issues, a weak perimeter security turns an otherwise secure IP Telephony system into a platter served to hackers and attackers.

To understand the implication of Cisco ASA as the first line of defense at the perimeter, refer to Chapter 3, "What Can You Secure and How Can You Secure It?," where you first understood the basics of Cisco ASA as a perimeter firewall, brokering connections from the outside world to protect IP Telephony applications, servers, and devices in the data center. For IP Telephony data center security, we will refer to same setup as we did earlier and expand further on it. Figure 8-5 provides a recap of the security zones and the various elements in each zone.

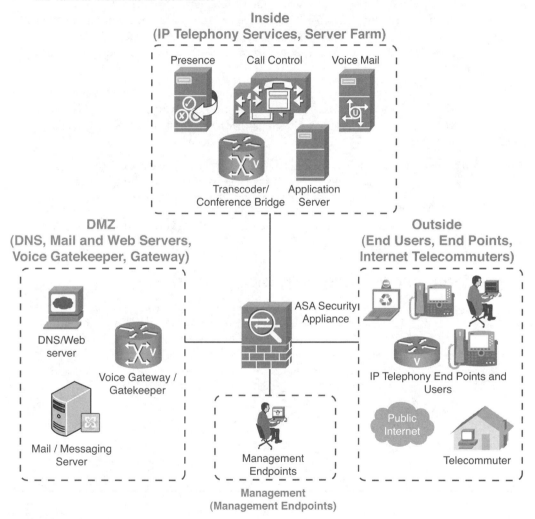

Figure 8-5 *Cisco ASA Security Zones*

As you know by now, Cisco ASA allows you to set up at least three basic zones. (You can set up more than three zones; however, for most networks three zones suffice.) These zones are as follows:

- Inside or secure zone

- Outside or non-secure zone

- DMZ or semi-secure zone

Each zone has its own characteristics and utilization, as follows:

- **Inside zone:** This is the zone where the IP Telephony servers and applications should be ideally placed. This zone is deemed to be most secure because by default (and ideally) all traffic leaving from this zone can traverse through DMZ and outside zones. However, vice versa is not allowed unless explicitly enabled by an access-rule (ACL).

- **DMZ zone:** This zone is semi-trusted, and the Internet- or extranet-facing devices should be placed here (for example, voice gateways, which are serving as an interconnect between your network and partner network) such as DNS, Mail, and web services.

- **Outside zone:** This is the untrusted ground, where you clearly cannot trust any connection or entity. Simply put, in this zone everything you cannot trust to be in your data center is to be placed, from endpoints to users to Internet access.

Let us explore how the perimeter defense via Cisco ASA works with the help of a case study.

Case Study: Perimeter Security with Cisco ASA

Organization XYZ is setting up its IP Telephony network and wants to protect the IP Telephony servers and other applications hosted in its data center. The IT department of XYZ has decided to go with Cisco ASA 5540 Firewall for IP Telephony data center perimeter protection. The system will be divided broadly in two Virtual Routing and Forwarding (VRF) domains: data center VRF (inside) and user VRF (outside), as shown in Figure 8-6.

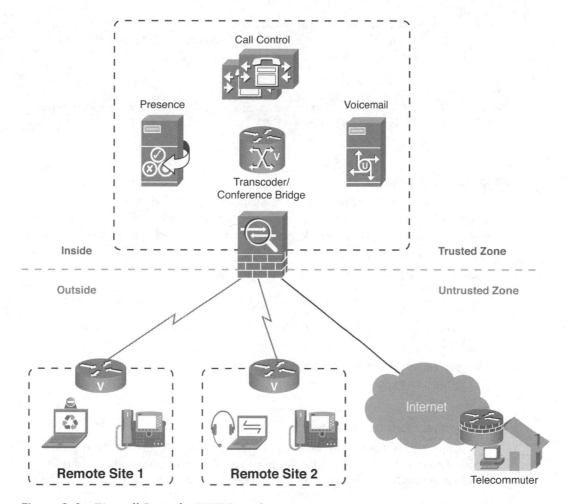

Figure 8-6   *Firewall Setup for XYZ Data Center*

Organization XYZ has adopted the following firewall deployment scheme:

■ Cisco ASA Firewall(s) should be placed between IP Telephony servers and end-points, at the data center edge (data center distribution layer) to protect the IP Telephony servers and services from external attacks and to inspect the incoming traffic for any malicious content (deep packet inspection).

■ For communication between endpoints and IP Telephony servers, specific ports and protocols should be configured to permit traversal through Cisco ASA Firewall(s), which in turn can dynamically open and close connections for media (RTP) streams, leveraging deep packet inspection capabilities (based on signaling streams).

■ Management traffic will originate from a dedicated management subnet (for Cisco ASA and for managing IP Telephony servers). Thus, all traffic necessary to manage IP Telephony servers should be allowed through the Cisco ASA Firewall.

Note   Without the support of deep packet inspection, the firewall must open a full set of UDP ports between the range 16384–32767. This is required for RTP traffic.

Cisco ASA QoS Support

Because Cisco ASA 5540 Firewalls will be the point of transition from XYZ's data centers to the outside world, where end users and endpoints reside, it is important that firewalls follow the QoS markings set by CUCM and other IP Telephony applications for signaling and media traffic going from the data center to the user VRF.

The QoS markings will be as follows:

■ Voice media traffic will be classified as DSCP EF and will be assigned to LLQ.

■ Voice signaling traffic will be classified as DSCP CS3/AF31 and will be assigned to LLQ.

■ The rest of the traffic will be considered as nonmission critical and will get best-effort treatment.

Firewall Transiting for Endpoints

Since there is a requirement to support IP Telephony endpoints outside the firewall at XYZ's data center, the traffic will flow through the Cisco ASA from outside to inside (from endpoints to IP Telephony servers) and vice versa, as shown in Figure 8-7.

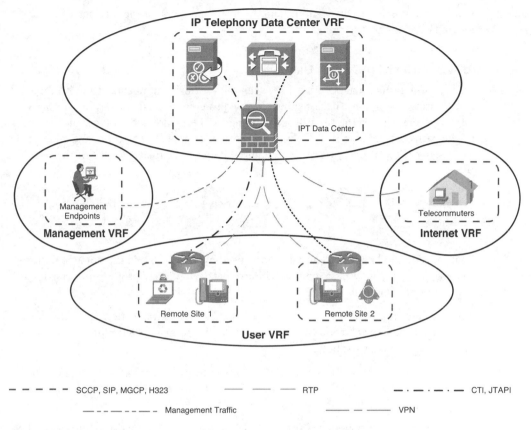

Figure 8-7   *Cisco ASA Firewall IP Telephony Traffic Transition*

> **Note**   This is a conceptual view of the network where WAN, PSTN, and ITSP connections have not been shown to emphasize the actual signal and media flows.

The following Cisco IP Telephony devices are located outside the data center VRF, in the user VRF:

- IP Phones (SCCP and SIP)

- IOS voice gateways (MGCP, H323, SIP, and SCCP)

- VG224 and VG202 analog gateways (MGCP, SCCP, and SIP)

- CUPC and CIPC clients (SCCP, SIP, and CTI)

In addition, the management subnet and the telecommuters (or the Internet VRF) are located outside the data center VRF.

Cisco ASA Firewall (ACL Port Usage)

This section outlines the ports used between the various components of the XYZ data center firewall solution. This list should be used to configure adequately the network infrastructure, namely the firewall and filtering (ACL) requirement in the signaling or media paths between the IP Telephony servers and endpoints. The following tables provide an overview of the ports that are required between various elements of the solution.

Note   This port list covers the ports required between endpoints and IP Telephony servers.

You can find the latest TCP and UDP ports used by CUCM 8.x in the documentation roadmap at http://www.cisco.com/en/US/products/sw/voicesw/ps556/products_documentation_roadmaps_list.html.

You can find the latest TCP and UDP ports used by Unity Connection 8.x in the documentation roadmap at http://www.cisco.com/en/US/products/ps6509/products_documentation_roadmaps_list.html.

And you can find the latest TCP and UDP ports used by CUPS 8.x in the documentation roadmap at http://www.cisco.com/en/US/products/ps6837/products_documentation_roadmaps_list.html.

For the latest port requirements for both CUCM and Unity, these documents should be reviewed on time to time basis.

Intracluster Ports

Because all IP Telephony servers including CUCM are within the same data center and in the same network subnet, the ICCS traffic will not be filtered. Thus, XYZ does not need to consider the ICCS ports.

Ports Used Between Endpoints and CUCM

The ports shown in Table 8-3 are common and may be required to be opened on the data center firewalls between the CUCM core servers and the endpoints and services on the outside of these firewalls.

Table 8-3 *CUCM Ports Used*

From (Sender)	To (Listener)	Destination Port and Protocol	Description
CUCM	Endpoint	TCP 22	SFTP and SSH
Endpoint or gateway	CUCM	69, 6969, and then Ephemeral UDP	TFTP service for phones and gateways
CUCM	NTP Server	UDP 123	Network Time Protocol (NTP)
SNMP server	CUCM	UDP 161	SNMP service response (requests from management applications)
SNMP server	CUCM	TCP 199	Native SNMP agent listening port for SMUX support
SNMP server	CUCM	TCP 7999	Cisco Discovery Protocol (CDP) agent communicates with CDP executable
CUCM	External Directory	Ephemeral TCP	LDAP query to external directory
External directory	CUCM	Ephemeral TCP	LDAP query to external directory
Browser	CUCM	TCP 80, 8080	Hypertext Transport Protocol (HTTP)
Browser	CUCM	TCP 443, 8443	Hypertext Transport Protocol over SSL (HTTPS)
Browser or CLI	CUCM	TCP 2355, 2356	Log audit events from the CLI and web applications
CUCM	Phone	TCP 80	Hypertext Transport Protocol (HTTP)
Phone	CUCM	TCP 8080	Phone URLs for XML applications, authentication, directories, services, and so on
Phone	CUCM	TCP 2000	Skinny Client Control Protocol (SCCP)
Phone	CUCM	TCP 2443	Secure Skinny Client Control Protocol (SCCPS)
Phone	CUCM (CAPF)	TCP 3804	Certificate Authority Proxy Function (CAPF) listening port for issuing Locally Significant Certificates (LSC) to IP phones

From (Sender)	To (Listener)	Destination Port and Protocol	Description
Phone	CUCM	TCP and UDP 5060	Session Initiation Protocol (SIP) phone
Phone	CUCM	TCP and UDP 5061	Secure Session Initiation Protocol (SIPS) phone
IP VMS	Phone	UDP 16384-32767	Real-Time Protocol (RTP), Secure Real-Time Protocol (SRTP)
Gateway	CUCM	UDP 2427	Media Gateway Control Protocol (MGCP) gateway control
Gateway	CUCM	TCP 2428	Media Gateway Control Protocol (MGCP) backhaul
CTL Client	CUCM CTL Provider	TCP 2444	Certificate Trust List (CTL) provider listening service in Cisco Unified Communications Manager
Cisco Unified Communications App	CUCM	TCP 2748	CTI application server
Cisco Unified Communications App	CUCM	TCP 2749	TLS connection between CTI applications (JTAPI/TSP) and CTIManager
Cisco Unified Communications App	CUCM	2789/TCP	JTAPI application server
Cisco Unified Communications App	CUCM	TCP 8443	AXL/SOAP API for programmatic reads from or writes to CUCM

Ports Required by Voice Gateways

The ports shown in Table 8-4 may be required to be opened on the firewall for signaling and media traffic to and from the voice gateways and CUCM.

Table 8-4   *Voice Gateway to IP Telephony Servers*

From (Sender)	To (Listener)	Destination Port and Protocol	Description
Gateway	CUCM	69; then ephemeral UDP	TFTP
Gateway	CUCM	TCP 2000 – 2002	SCCP
Gateway	CUCM	UDP 2427	MGCP
Gateway	CUCM	TCP 2428	MGCP
Gateway	CUCM	TCP 2443	TLS
Gateway	CUCM	UDP 1719	H.225 RAS
Gateway	CUCM	TCP 1720	H225
Gateway	CUCM	Ephemeral/TCP	H.225 signaling services on gatekeeper-controlled trunk and H.245 signaling services for establishing voice, video, and data
Gateway	CUCM	TCP and UDP 5060	SIP
Gateway	CUCM	TCP and UDP 5061	SIP Secure (SIPS)
Gateway	CUCM	UDP 16384-32767	Real-Time Protocol (RTP) or Secure Real-Time Protocol (SRTP)
Gateway	CUCM	UDP 2427	Media Gateway Control Protocol (MGCP) gateway control
Gateway	CUCM	TCP 2428	Media Gateway Control Protocol (MGCP) backhaul
Gateway	CUCM	47, 50, 51	Generic Routing Encapsulation (GRE), Encapsulating Security Payload (ESP), and Authentication Header (AH)
Gateway	CUCM	UDP 500	IKE for IPSec

Ports Required Between CUPS and Other Applications and Endpoints

Table 8-5 lists the port usage between endpoints and applications and the CUPS server.

Table 8-5 *Applications and Endpoints to CUPS*

From (Sender)	To (Listener)	Destination Port and Protocol	Description
CUPS	CUPS	TCP 8061	SIP Proxy port used for Cisco IP Phone Messenger
Third-party client	CUPS	TCP 8062	Default Cisco Unified Presence HTTP Listener; used for third-party clients to connect
Third-party client	CUPS	TCP 8063	Default Cisco Unified Presence HTTPS Listener; used for third-party clients to connect
Browser, CUPC	CUPS	TCP 8443	Provides access to Cisco Unified Personal Communicator via SOAP
XMPP client	CUPS	TCP 5222	Client access port
IPVMS	CUPS	UDP 24576 - 32767	IP Voice Media Streaming Driver port; outgoing RTP streaming ports used for voice streaming. Inherited ports from Cisco Unified Communications Manager

Ports Required Between IP Phones and IP Telephony Servers

Tables 8-6 lists the ports that should be open between IP Phones and the voice equipment in the data centers.

Table 8-6 *Ports Required for Communication IP Phones and IP Telephony Servers*

From (Sender)	To (Listener)	Destination Port and Protocol	Description
Phone	CUCM (TFTP)	69; then Ephemeral UDP	Trivial File Transfer Protocol (TFTP) used to download firmware and configuration files.
Phone	CUCM	TCP 8080	Phone URLs for XML applications, authentication, directories, services, and so on. You can configure these ports on a per-service basis.
Phone	CUCM	TCP 2000	Skinny Client Control Protocol (SCCP).
Phone	CUCM	TCP 2443	Secure Skinny Client Control Protocol (SCCPS).

From (Sender)	To (Listener)	Destination Port and Protocol	Description
Phone	CUCM (CAPF)	TCP 3804	Certificate Authority Proxy Function (CAPF) listening port for issuing Locally Significant Certificates (LSC) to IP Phones
Phone	CUCM	TCP and UDP 5060	Session Initiation Protocol (SIP) phone
Phone	CUCM	TCP and UDP 5061	Secure Session Initiation Protocol (SIPS) phone
IP VMS	Phone	UDP 16384–32767	Real-Time Protocol (RTP), Secure Real-Time Protocol (SRTP) (Note: Cisco Unified Communications Manager uses only 24576–32767; although other devices use the full range.)
Phone	Voice Gateway	UDP 16384–32767	RTP, SRTP
Phone	Hardware Conference Bridge	UDP 16384–32767	RTP, SRTP
Phone	Unity	TCP 2000 or 2443	SCCP
Phone	Unity	UDP 22800–32767	RTP, SRTP

Ports Required Between End-User Workstations and IP Telephony Servers

In addition to the IP Phones, the end users also need to be allowed to access the IP Telephony solution using web browsers. The port requirements are detailed in Table 8-7.

Table 8-7 *End-User Station to CUCM Port Usage*

From (Sender)	To (Listener)	Destination Port and Protocol	Description
Browser	CUCM	TCP 80, 8080	Hypertext Transport Protocol (HTTP)
Browser	CUCM	TCP 443, 8443	Hypertext Transport Protocol over SSL (HTTPS)
User PC	CUCM	TCP 2912, 2748, 389	IPMA Console connection to CUCM, CTI, and LDAP

Subscribers can access the Cisco PCA. Thus, subscriber workstations must establish connections to the ports shown in Table 8-8 on Cisco Unity servers.

Table 8-8   *End-User Station to Unity Port Usage*

From (Sender)	To (Listener)	Destination Port and Protocol	Description
Browser	Unity Servers	TCP 80	IIS web server
Browser	Unity Servers	TCP 443	IIS web server (SSL certificate)
Browser	Unity Servers	TCP 135	WinRPC endpoint locator
Browser	Unity Servers	TCP/UDP 5000–5020	DCOM RPC range after restriction.

See the section on restricting DCOM ports at http://www.cisco.com/en/US/docs/voice_ip_comm/unity/8x/security/guide/8xcusec030.html#wp1067900.

Ports Required Between Management Stations and IP Telephony Servers

Finally, we consider the ports required for management stations to IP Telephony servers and devices for management purposes, as shown in Table 8-9.

Table 8-9   *Management Station to IP Telephony Servers and Device Port Usage*

From (Sender)	To (Listener)	Destination Port and Protocol	Description
Admin PC	CUCM, CUC, CUPS, IOS routers, and switches	TCP 22	SSH
Admin PC	IOS routers, and switches	TCP 23	Telnet
Admin PC	IOS routers, and switches	UDP 69	TFTP
Admin PC	IOS routers, and switches	TCP 20, 21	FTP
Admin PC	Cisco Unity	TCP 3389	RDP
Admin PC	Cisco Unity	TCP 5800, 5900	VNC
Admin PC	CUCM, CUPS, CUC, and Cisco Unity	TCP 80, 8080, 8443, 443	HTTPS, HTTPS
Admin PC	CUCM, CUPS, CUC, Unity, and IOS routers, and switches	UDP 162	SNMP
Admin PC	Cisco Unity	UDP 137, 138	NetBIOS
Admin PC	Cisco Unity	TCP 139, 445	NetBIOS

Telecommuters and Remote Workers

For telecommuters, a VPN solution needs to be provisioned because they will be coming over a public network (the Internet). The signaling, media, and other application traffic must be encrypted from the endpoint (Cisco IP Communicator running a PC) to the head end (Cisco ASA). When the encrypted traffic hits the Cisco ASA outside interface, it will be decrypted by the crypto-engine, and the decrypted stream will be sent to the destination server.

Finally, the Cisco ASA Firewall configuration results, as shown in Example 8-2.

Note This configuration assumes that along with IP Telephony services, other services, for example, DNS, SQL, CTI, LDAP, and so on (essentially third-party components) are allowed from outside to inside (provided the third-party components are placed along with IP Telephony servers).

Example 8-2 *Cisco ASA Perimeter Firewall Configuration*

```
IPTASA# show run
ASA Version 8.3(4)
!
hostname IPTASA
enable password <truncated> encrypted
passwd <truncated> encrypted
names
!
interface Management0/0
Description XYZ ASA Management interface
 nameif management
 security-level 90
 ip address 10.110.5.251 255.255.255.0 standby 10.110.5.253
 management-only
!
interface GigabitEthernet3/0
Description XYZ DC Outside
 nameif outside
 security-level 0
 ip address 10.105.5.251 255.255.255.0 standby 10.105.5.253
!
interface GigabitEthernet3/1
Description XYZ DC Inside
 nameif inside
 security-level 100
 ip address 10.101.5.251 255.255.255.0 standby 10.101.5.253
```

```
!
boot system disk0:/asa811-smp-k8.bin
ftp mode passive
clock timezone PST -8
dns server-group DefaultDNS
 domain-name IPTASA.com
!
object-group service Voice-Protocols-TCP tcp
Description TCP Voice Protocols
 port-object range 2427 2428
 port-object eq ctiqbe
 port-object range 2000 2002
 port-object eq www
 port-object eq https
 port-object eq 8080
 port-object eq 8443
 port-object eq sip
 port-object eq 5900
 port-object eq 135
 port-object range 1718 1720
 port-object range 1099 1129
 port-object eq 2443
 port-object eq 3129
 port-object eq smtp
 port-object eq ldaps
 port-object eq ldap
 port-object eq 2001
 port-object eq netbios-ssn
 port-object eq 115
 port-object eq 445
 port-object eq 1025
 port-object eq domain
 port-object eq 88
 port-object eq 3268
 port-object eq 1038
 port-object eq 691
 port-object eq 6970
 port-object eq 7161
 port-object eq 3804
 port-object eq 389
 port-object eq 2912
 port-object eq 2748
!
object-group service Voice-Protocols-UDP udp
Description UDP Voice Protocols
```

```
 port-object eq tftp
 port-object eq 6969
 port-object eq 53
 port-object eq 2427
 port-object eq 5060
 port-object eq domain
 port-object range 1718 1719
 port-object eq bootps
 port-object eq ntp
 port-object eq syslog
 port-object eq snmptrap
 port-object eq snmp
 port-object eq 161
 port-object eq 162
 port-object eq 1434
 port-object eq 389
 port-object eq 115
 port-object eq netbios-ns
 port-object eq netbios-dgm
!
object-group service Management-Protocols-UDP tcp
Description TCP Management Protocols
 port-object eq 138, 139
 port-object eq www
 port-object eq https
 port-object eq 5800, 5900
 port-object eq 8080
 port-object eq 8443
 port-object eq 1090
 port-object eq 1099
 port object eq 3389
 port-object eq 139
 port-object eq 445
!
object-group service Management-Protocols-UDP udp
Description UDP Management Protocols
 port-object eq 137, 138
!
object-group network IP Telephony
 network-object 10.101.5.0 255.255.255.0
!
object-group network Users
 network-object 10.105.5.0 255.255.255.0
!
object-group network ManagementAdmin
```

```
  network-object 10.110.5.0 255.255.255.0
 !
access-list permit-all extended permit ip any any log notifications
access-list deny-all extended deny ip any any log
access-list OUTSIDE extended permit tcp any object-group IP Telephony object-group
  Voice-Protocols-TCP
access-list OUTSIDE extended permit udp any object-group IP Telephony object-group
  Voice-Protocols-UDP
access-list OUTSIDE extended permit tcp object-group ManagementAdmin object-group
  IP Telephony object-group Management-Protocols-TCP
access-list OUTSIDE extended permit tcp object-group ManagementAdmin object-group
  IP Telephony object-group Management-Protocols-UDP
access-list OUTSIDE extended permit icmp any any
access-list OUTSIDE extended deny ip any any log
 !
pager lines 24
logging enable
logging timestamp
logging buffer-size 100000
logging console debugging
logging buffered notifications
logging trap warnings
logging asdm notifications
mtu outside 1500
mtu inside 1500
 !
no failover
 !
icmp unreachable rate-limit 1 burst-size 1
icmp permit any outside
icmp permit any inside
asdm image disk0:/asdm-611.bin
no asdm history enable
arp timeout 14400
access-group OUTSIDE in interface outside
route outside 0.0.0.0 0.0.0.0 1.1.1.2
route inside 0.0.0.0 0.0.0.0 10.101.5.1 1
timeout xlate 3:00:00
timeout conn 1:00:00 half-closed 0:10:00 udp 0:02:00 icmp 0:00:02
timeout sunrpc 0:10:00 h323 0:05:00 h225 1:00:00 mgcp 0:05:00 mgcp-pat 0:05:00
timeout sip 0:30:00 sip_media 0:02:00 sip-invite 0:03:00 sip-disconnect 0:02:00
timeout sip-provisional-media 0:02:00 uauth 0:05:00 absolute
dynamic-access-policy-record DfltAccessPolicy
aaa authentication ssh console LOCAL
aaa authentication telnet console LOCAL
```

```
http server enable
http 0.0.0.0 0.0.0.0 inside
no snmp-server location
no snmp-server contact
snmp-server enable traps snmp authentication linkup linkdown coldstart
service resetoutside
!
ip local pool vpnpool 192.168.100.1-192.168.100.254 mask 255.255.255.0
crypto dynamic-map telecommuters 65535 set pfs group1
crypto dynamic-map telecommuters 65535 set transform-set myset
crypto map mymap 65535 ipsec-isakmp dynamic telecommuters
crypto map mymap interface Outside
!
crypto ca trustpoint asa2
 enrollment terminal
 crl configure
crypto ca certificate chain asa2
 certificate ca a41ccd4a
!
    <certificate txt omitted>
  quit
!
crypto isakmp enable outside
crypto isakmp policy 1
 authentication pre-share
 encryption 3des
 hash md5
 group 2
 lifetime 86400
!
ssh 0.0.0.0 0.0.0.0 outside
ssh 0.0.0.0 0.0.0.0 inside
ssh timeout 60
console timeout 0
!
ntp server 10.101.5.10 prefer
username user password <omitted> encrypted privilege 15
!
class-map voice-traffic
 match dscp cs3  af31  ef
class-map inspection_default
 match default-inspection-traffic
!
policy-map voIP Telephonyraffic
 class voice-traffic
```

```
   priority
!
policy-map voipmap
  class inspection_default
  inspect h323 h225
  inspect h323 ras
  inspect rtsp
  inspect sip
  inspect mgcp
  inspect icmp
  inspect skinny
  inspect ftp
  inspect netbios
  inspect tftp
  inspect sqlnet
  inspect snmp
!
service-policy voIP Telephonyraffic interface outside
service-policy voipmap global
prompt hostname context
Cryptochecksum:<truncated>
: end
```

Equipped with the facts and knowledge about Cisco ASA, you should be able to set up the perimeter defense using Cisco ASA Firewall, deployed at the edge of your data center (where all entities, from the semi-trusted or untrusted environment converge to leverage IP Telephony services).

The earlier scenario provides comprehensive security to your IP Telephony data center. However, there's a concern when secure signaling and media are enabled, that is, TLS and SRTP (for signaling and media, respectively) are enabled. The Cisco ASA Firewall has SCCP and SIP inspection. However, if security is enabled on a cluster, the ALG features cannot see into the signaling as it is encrypted. In this case, the inspection feature cannot work (unless the whole range of UDP ports for RTP from 16384–32767 is opened). This is shown in Figure 8-8.

Figure 8-8   *TLS (Encrypted) Signaling Through Cisco ASA Firewall Without TLS Proxy*

So, what is the solution, you ask? Well, the solution is to enable the proxy features of the Cisco ASA Firewall so that the firewall proxies signaling streams between the CUCM and the IP endpoint. This decrypts the signaling at the firewall, and the firewall can inspect the contents so that the pinholes can be opened up dynamically between the sender and receiver. These concepts and their related configuration are explained in the ensuing sections:

■ Cisco ASA TLS proxy

■ Cisco ASA phone proxy

Introduction to Cisco ASA Proxy Features

The purpose of a proxy (server) is to terminate and re-initiate connections between a client and a server. Cisco ASA Firewall allows for signaling traffic decryption and re-encryption (by virtue of the TLS proxy feature), which enables the inspection engine to look into the packet contents to ensure it conforms to organization security policies. This enables the security and IP Telephony administrators to ensure that traffic coming from any endpoint is not malicious in nature, which would be otherwise dropped by the security appliance. The Proxy features of Cisco ASA are available in the following scenarios:

Phone proxy: Secures remote access for Cisco-encrypted endpoints and VLAN traversal for Cisco soft phones. This topic is covered in the "Phone Proxy" section.

TLS proxy: Enables decryption and inspection of encrypted signaling before Cisco ASA re-encrypts the signaling to chosen destination. This topic is covered in the next section.

Presence federation: Using Cisco ASA as a secure presence federation proxy, organizations can securely connect the CUPS servers to other Cisco or Microsoft presence servers, thereby enabling intra-enterprise and inter-enterprise communications. This topic is covered in Chapter 11, "Cisco Unified Presence Security."

Table 8-10 lists the default and maximum sessions for each Cisco ASA model.

Table 8-10   *TLS Default and Maximum Session per a Cisco ASA Platform*

Firewall	Default Sessions	Max Sessions
Cisco ASA 5505	10	80
Cisco ASA 5510	100	200
Cisco ASA 5520	1000	1200
Cisco ASA 5540	2000	4500
Cisco ASA 5550	3000	4500
Cisco ASA 5580	10,000	13,000

- Each TLS proxy session is composed of two SSL connections with mutual authentication.

- Default sessions: Default TLS proxy sessions.

- Max sessions: Increases the limit using the **tls-proxy maximum sessions** command.

Licensing for TLS (and phone) proxy is applicable to the following:

- Phone proxy

- TLS proxy for encrypted voice inspection

- Presence federation proxy

- Encrypted voice inspection

Licenses are sold in tiers: 25, 50, 100, 250, 500, 750, 1000, 2000, 3000, 5000, 10,000, as shown in Table 8-11.

Table 8-11   *Cisco ASA Proxy Licensing Scheme*

Firewall	Max Proxy Licenses	Tiers for Licenses
Cisco ASA 5505	25	25
Cisco ASA 5510	100	50, 100 plus above
Cisco ASA 5520	1000	250, 500, 750, 1000 plus above
Cisco ASA 5540	2000	2000 plus above
Cisco ASA 5550	3000	3000 plus above
Cisco ASA 5580	10,000	5000, 10,000 plus above

Note   The base license is two sessions per platform (refer to Table 8-11). Also, if you configure a phone with a primary and backup CUCM, there are two TLS proxy connections, so two UC proxy sessions are used.

In upcoming sections, you will comprehend the concept of Cisco ASA proxy, how it works, and where it is needed in your IP Telephony network.

Note   Cisco ASA Phone Proxy feature has limited compatibility with CUCM 8.x and later versions. Before implementing phone proxy, verify support for the CUCM version in your enterprise at http://www.cisco.com/en/US/docs/voice_ip_comm/cucm/srnd/8x/security.html.

Cisco ASA TLS Proxy

Cisco ASA TLS proxy, also known as secure inter-working, enables businesses to deploy encryption and firewall services within the campus or branch (hub/spoke topology) network environment to inspect and secure voice signaling and media traffic. In addition to protecting the IP Telephony data center perimeter, TLS proxy helps extend firewall services to include strong firewall policies for internal voice traffic by decrypting, inspecting, and re-encrypting signaling traffic and media, thereby ensuring that all traffic passing through the firewall is compliant with the organizational/IP Telephony Security policies.

Any Cisco Voice/video communications encrypted with SRTP/TLS can be inspected by Cisco ASA 5500 series by enabling the TLS proxy feature. This provides the following advantages over manually opening ports or configuring static statements on the Cisco ASA:

- It maintains integrity and confidentiality of the call while enforcing the security policy through advanced SIP/SCCP Firewall services.

- TLS signaling is terminated, inspected, and re-encrypted for the connection to the destination (leveraging integrated hardware encryption services for scalable performance).

- NAT/PAT is performed if needed.

- A dynamic port is opened for SRTP-encrypted media stream and automatically closed when the call ends.

Figure 8-9 shows TLS proxy functionality of a Cisco ASA.

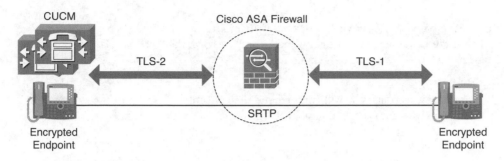

Figure 8-9 *Cisco ASA Firewall with TLS Proxy Enabled*

There are, however, a few questions, which may concern you about the working schema of TLS proxy. For example:

- How would a phone trust Cisco ASA?

- How would Cisco ASA trust a phone?

- How would CUCM trust the Cisco ASA?

- How would Cisco ASA trust CUCM?

Let's understand how the TLS sessions are set up before getting into the practicalities of configuring the same.

How Would a Phone Trust Cisco ASA?

The Certificate Trust List (CTL) is composed offline and stored on the phone. The phone trusts any certificate that is in the CTL. CUCM certificate and the self-signed proxy firewall certificate is in the CTL file.

Note Refer to Chapter 9 and Appendix A, "Cisco IP Telephony: Authentication and Encryption Essentials," for details on CTL and CAPF.

How Would Cisco ASA Trust a Phone?

The phone certificate is signed by CAPF (Locally Significant Certificate [LSC]). The CAPF certificate is installed in the Cisco ASA trust point store.

Note Refer to Chapter 9 and Appendix A for details on LSC.

How Would CUCM Trust the Cisco ASA?

Cisco ASA presents a certificate on behalf of the phone to the CUCM. The phone certificate is signed by Cisco ASA self-signed certificate on-the-fly with the name of the phone. CUCM has this ASA self-signed certificate in its trust store.

How Would Cisco ASA Trust the CUCM?

Cisco ASA has the self-signed certificate for the CUCM.

These questions and solutions are depicted in Figures 8-10 and 8-11.

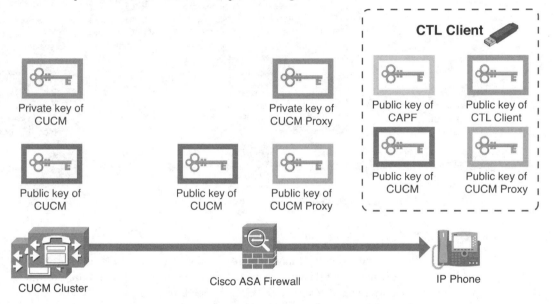

Figure 8-10   *TLS Proxy Server Authentication*

As you can see, the CUCM public key and the proxy (Cisco ASA) public key are brought together by the CTL client, which enables the CUCM signaling to be proxied through to IP Phone by Cisco ASA.

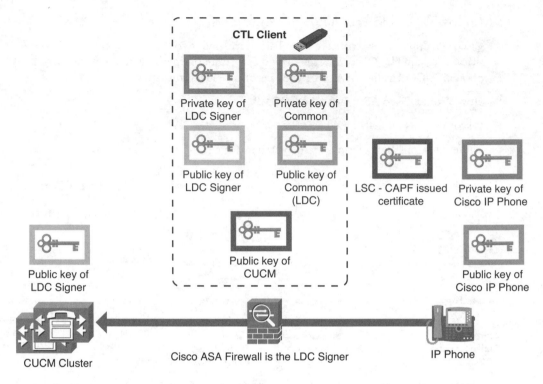

Figure 8-11 *TLS Proxy Phone Authentication*

When the IP Phone needs to communicate with CUCM, the signaling is again prox-ied by Cisco ASA, since the CTL client has the firewall in the trust list and the firewall presents the Locally Dynamic Certificate (LDC), which it represents as an IP Phone to the CUCM. The LDC is signed by the signer (Cisco ASA) on-the-fly, with CN=<phone-model>-<MAC address>, which enables a unique identification of the IP Phone to the CUCM.

In a nutshell, when the Cisco ASA receives the request from either the CUCM or IP Phone, it decrypts the signaling, inspects the content of the packet and re-initiates a new TLS session with the destination. The process is facilitated by CTL client as it brings together Cisco ASA, IP Phone, and call processing servers together and provides for a trust enabler.

Now that you have a handle on the basics of Cisco ASA TLS Proxy, you can start with the deployment of the same in your network with the help of the following configura-tion steps.

Step 1. Create the necessary RSA key pairs using the commands shown in Example 8-3.

Example 8-3 *Generating Cisco ASA RSA Keys*

```
IPTASA(config)# crypto key generate rsa label ccm_proxy_key modulus 1024
IPTASA(config)# crypto key generate rsa label ldc_signer_key modulus 1024
IPTASA(config)# crypto key generate rsa label phone_common modulus 1024
```

Step 2.   Create the proxy certificate for the CUCM cluster using the commands in Example 8-4.

Example 8-4 *Creating a Proxy Certificate for CUCM Cluster*

```
IPTASA(config)# crypto ca trustpoint ccm_proxy
IPTASA(config-ca-trustpoint)# enrollment self
IPTASA(config-ca-trustpoint)# fqdn none
IPTASA(config-ca-trustpoint)# subject-name cn=ASA5580 CCM Proxy
IPTASA(config-ca-trustpoint)# keypair ccm_proxy_key
IPTASA(config)# crypto ca enroll ccm_proxy
% The fully-qualified domain name will not be included in the certificate
% Include the device serial number in the subject name? [yes/no]: no
Generate Self-Signed Certificate? [yes/no]: yes
```

Step 3.   Create an internal local CA to sign the LDC for Cisco IP Phones using the commands shown in Example 8-5.

Example 8-5 *Cisco ASA LDC CA*

```
IPTASA(config)# crypto ca trustpoint ldc_server
IPTASA(config-ca-trustpoint)# enrollment self
IPTASA(config-ca-trustpoint)# proxy-ldc-issuer
IPTASA(config-ca-trustpoint)# fqdn myldcca.test.com
IPTASA(config-ca-trustpoint)# subject-name cn=LDC_SIGNER
IPTASA(config-ca-trustpoint)# keypair ldc_signer_key
IPTASA(config)# crypto ca enroll ldc_server
Would you like to continue with this enrollment? [yes/no]: yes
% The fully-qualified domain name in the certificate will be: myldcca.test.com
% Include the device serial number in the subject name? [yes/no]: no
Generate Self-Signed Certificate? [yes/no]: yes
```

Step 4.   Create a CTL provider instance in preparation for a connection from the CTL client using the commands shown in Example 8-6.

Example 8-6 *Cisco ASA CTL Provider Instance*

```
IPTASA(config)# ctl-provider my_ctl
IPTASA(config-ctl-provider)# client interface inside address 10.1.1.250
IPTASA(config-ctl-provider)# client username CCMAdministrator password <omitted>
```

```
    encrypted
IPTASA(config-ctl-provider)# export certificate ccm_proxy
IPTASA(config-ctl-provider)# ctl install
```

Step 5.   Create a TLS proxy instance using the commands shown in Example 8-7.

Example 8-7   *Cisco ASA TLS Proxy Instance*

```
IPTASA(config)# tls-proxy my_proxy
IPTASA(config-tlsp)# server trust-point ccm_proxy
IPTASA(config-tlsp)# client ldc issuer ldc_server
IPTASA(config-tlsp)# client ldc keypair phone_common
```

Step 6.   Enable TLS proxy for the Cisco IP Phones and Cisco UCM in Skinny or SIP inspection using the commands shown in Example 8-8.

Example 8-8   *Cisco ASA SCCP and SIP TLS Inspection*

```
IPTASA(config)# class-map sec_skinny
IPTASA(config-cmap)# match port tcp eq 2443
!
IPTASA(config)# class-map sec_SIP
IPTASA (config-cmap)# match port tcp eq 5061
!
IPTASA (config)# policy-map type inspect skinny skinny_inspect
IPTASA (config-pmap)# parameters
!
IPTASA (config)# policy-map global_policy
IPTASA (config-pmap)# class inspection_default
IPTASA (config-pmap-c)# inspect skinny skinny_inspect
IPTASA (config-pmap)# class sec_skinny
IPTASA (config-pmap-c)# inspect skinny phone-proxy asa_phone_proxy
IPTASA (config-pmap)# class sec_SIP
IPTASA (config-pmap-c)# inspect sip phone-proxy asa_phone_proxy
```

Step 7.   Export the LDC CA and import LDC CA into CUCM (see Example 8-9).

Example 8-9   *Cisco ASA LDC CA Export*

```
IPTASA(config)# crypto ca export ldc_server identity-certificate
The PEM encoded identity certificate follows:
-----BEGIN CERTIFICATE-----
MIICTjCCAbegAwIBAgIEJxKdSTANBgkqhkiG9w0BAQQFADA5MRYwFAYDVQQDFA1B
<truncated>
sPVxBHnQzCiPRHXCEK/7iiYe
-----END CERTIFICATE-----
```

Save the output to a .cer or .pem file and import the certificate on the CUCM into the Call Manage trust store, as shown in Figure 8-12.

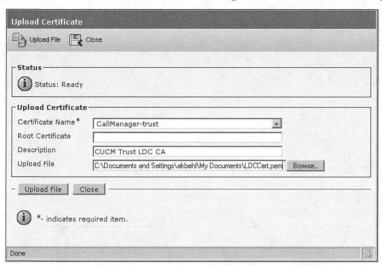

Figure 8-12 *Upload LDC CA Certificate to the CUCM Trust Store*

Step 8.   Run the CTL client application to add the server proxy certificate (ccm_ proxy) to the CTL file, and install the CTL file on the security appliance, as shown in Figure 8-13.

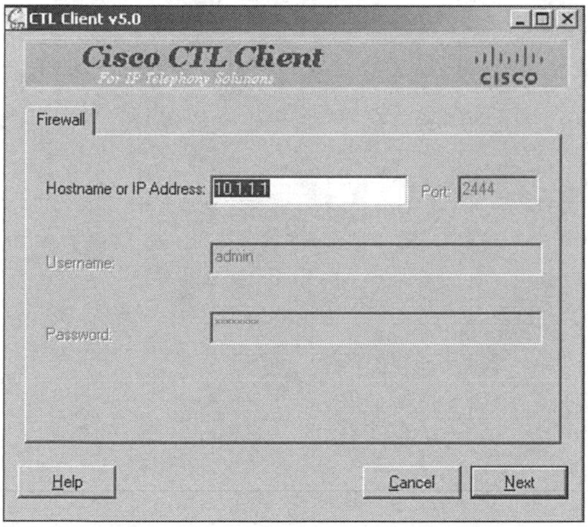

Figure 8-13 *CTL Client for Cisco ASA Proxy*

Examples 8-10, 8-11, and 8-12 display the **show** commands and respective outputs for the TLS proxy.

Example 8-10   show tls-proxy *Output*

```
IPTASA# show tls-proxy
Maximum number of sessions: 10
TLS-Proxy 'my_proxy': ref_cnt 1, seq# 1
  Server proxy:
    Trust-point: ccm_proxy
    Authenticate client: TRUE
  Client proxy:
    Trust-point: <unconfigured>
    Local dynamic certificate issuer: ldc_server
    Local dynamic certificate key-pair: common
    Cipher suite:  aes128-sha1 aes256-sha1
  Run-time proxies:
    Proxy 0xd4e567a8: Class-map: sec_skinny, Inspect: skinny
          Active sess 2, most sess 2, byte 10408
```

Example 8-11   show tls-proxy session detail *Output*

```
IPTASA# show tls-proxy session detail
2 in use (2 established), 2 most used
outside 192.168.0.2:40192 inside 10.1.1.250:2443 P:0xd4e55020(my_proxy) S:0xd4e24ec8
byte 9688
  Client: State SSLOK  Cipher AES128-SHA Ch 0xd3d07b98 TxQSize 0 LastTxLeft 0 Flags
  0x31
  Server: State SSLOK  Cipher AES128-SHA Ch 0xd3d07b78 TxQSize 0 LastTxLeft 0 Flags
  0x9
Local Dynamic Certificate
  Status: Available
  Certificate Serial Number: 2c
  Certificate Usage: General Purpose
  Public Key Type: RSA (1024 bits)
  Issuer Name:
    hostname=myldcca.test.com
    cn=ASA_LD_Signer
  Subject Name:
    cn=SEP001C58FBBE79
  Validity Date:
    start date: 11:16:17 UTC Feb 19 2011
    end   date: 11:16:17 UTC Feb 19 2012
  Associated Trustpoints:
```

Example 8-12   show service-policy inspect skinny *Output*

```
IPTASA# show service-policy inspect skinny
Global policy:
  Service-policy: global_policy
    Class-map: inspection_default
      Inspect: skinny skinny_inspect, packet 0, drop 0, reset-drop 0
        no enforce-registration
        SCCP MessageID greater than max value 0x181, drop 0
        SCCP Prefix length less than min value 4, drop 0
        Timeout, media 0:05:00 signaling 1:00:00
    Class-map: sec_skinny
      Inspect: skinny skinny_inspect tls-proxy my_proxy, packet 1145, drop 0, reset-
drop 0
              tls proxy: active sess 2, most sess 2, byte 24612
        no enforce-registration
        SCCP MessageID greater than max value 0x181, drop 0
        SCCP Prefix length less than min value 4, drop 0
        Timeout, media 0:05:00 signaling 1:00:00
```

The commands shown in Example 8-13 can be useful for troubleshooting issues with TLS proxy.

Example 8-13   *TLS-Proxy Troubleshooting Commands*

```
IPTASA# debug inspect tls-proxy events
IPTASA# debug inspect tls-proxy errors
IPTASA# logging enable
IPTASA# logging timestamp
IPTASA# logging list loglist message 711001
IPTASA# logging list loglist message 725001-725014
IPTASA# logging list loglist message 717001-717038
IPTASA# logging buffer-size 1000000
IPTASA# logging buffered loglist
IPTASA# logging debug-trace
```

Although TLS proxy is efficient at securing signaling and media streams, it is not designed to provide remote-access encryption services for IP Phones at remote sites, at outside campuses, or for telecommuters. Furthermore, TLS proxy is not intended to provide a solution in which the requirement is to provide secure data VLAN to voice VLAN traversal for softphone clients.

While for the former, IPSec-based VPN or VPN IP Phone services are more appropriate, for the latter Cisco ASA Phone Proxy is the appropriate solution.

> **Note** Cisco ASA Phone proxy also solves the issue of remote IP Phones traversing over an insecure medium and is a substitute for a VPN solution, depending on the situation.

In the next section, you learn about Cisco ASA Phone proxy, which is built on top of TLS proxy however, is much different in its design and usage.

Cisco ASA Phone Proxy

Cisco ASA Phone proxy feature enables remote Cisco IP Phones to use their existing encryption function (TLS/SRTP) as they connect back to a Cisco Unified Communications Manager (CUCM) cluster.

Now, you must be wondering, how is it different from TLS proxy? While phone proxy is considered as a superset of TLS proxy, that is, it is built on TLS proxy; it has some major differences as compared to TLS proxy as follows:

- It enables a user to plug a Cisco IP Phone directly into its home network and make secure calls through the centralized CUCM cluster via the Internet. This implies that the IP Phone may not be at one of the sites of the organization; however, it can be outside the campus or remote sites.

- Most important, it does not require changes to CUCM clusters or internal phones, that is, it provides interoperability between inside (Cisco ASA Firewall inside or a secure zone) an unsecured cluster and IP Phones with outside (Cisco ASA Firewall outside or an unsecure zone) secured IP Phones.

The Cisco ASA Phone proxy feature enables phones to establish secured communication channels directly with Cisco ASA Firewall. These secure communication streams terminate directly onto the firewall, and the firewall "proxies" the voice communication and signaling between the phone and the CUCM. The Cisco ASA Firewall acts as a secure phone media termination appliance, whereby the encrypted media streams terminate directly onto the firewall. The communication back to the CUCM may or may not be encrypted.

> **Note** Cisco ASA Phone Proxy feature does not support encrypted TFTP configuration file transfer and HTTPS communication for secure URLs. Refer to Chapter 9 and Appendix A for more information on secure TFTP file configuration transfer and HTTPS URL.

The concept of phone proxy (remote access) is illustrated in Figure 8-14.

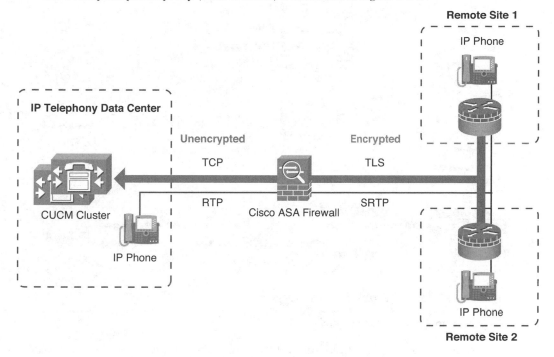

Figure 8-14 *Phone Proxy (Remote Access)*

As you can distinguish, the major difference between phone proxy and TLS proxy is that, phone proxy secures communication with internal phones that are unencrypted (or uses unregistered IP addresses). Although in TLS proxy, the requirement is to have encryption on both sides of the Cisco ASA (inside and outside), the phone proxy feature enables CUCM and internal phones to remain in a non-secure and unencrypted mode, respectively. This is a major advantage over TLS, if you do not want to convert your CUCM cluster into the mixed mode or have internally encrypted endpoints. As shown in the Figure 8-15, phone proxy leverages certificate-based authentication of devices to prevent rogue phone connections.

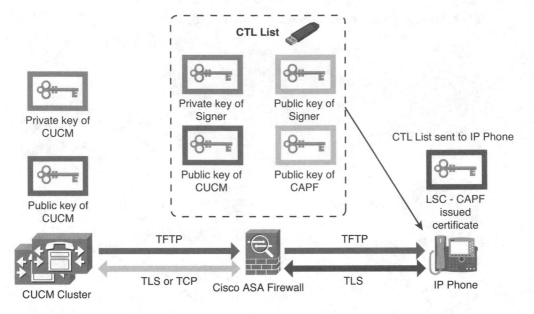

Figure 8-15   *Phone Proxy (Remote Access)*

Cisco ASA phone proxy works as follows:

■ It creates a new certificate trust list (CTL) file, which is used to perform certificate-based authentication with remote phones.

■ The phone trusts the Cisco ASA because it's present in the CTL file downloaded.

■ It modifies the IP Phone configuration file when it is requested via TFTP, (changes the security fields from non-secure to secure) and signs all files sent to the phone. These modifications secure remote phones by forcing the phones to perform encrypted signaling and media.

■ It terminates TLS signaling from the phone and initiates TCP or TLS to the CUCM (depending on whether the CUCM is in non-secure or in mixed mode).

■ Inserts itself into the media path by modifying the skinny and SIP signaling messages. It performs NAT if needed.

■ It terminates SRTP and initiates RTP/SRTP to the called party (inside IP Phone, depending on if the endpoint is non-secure or encrypted).

Phone proxy feature has yet another mode, VLAN traversal or VLAN bridging where it offers you the power to force any softphone client (for example, Cisco IP

Communicator) communication coming from data (native) VLAN to voice (auxiliary) VLAN. This feature can be deployed within the enterprise or branch campus to support softphone applications to securely traverse from the data VLAN to the phone VLAN. The advantages include protection of CUCM from rogue endpoints and attackers based on data VLAN. It also helps ensure a single, secure point of entry into the voice VLAN by forcing all soft client media to proxy via Cisco ASA (see Figure 8-16).

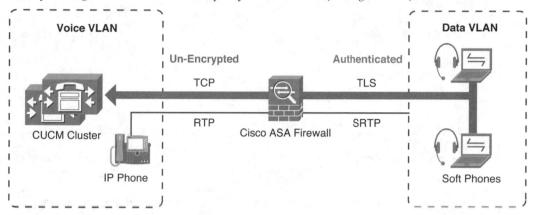

Figure 8-16   *Phone Proxy VLAN Bridging*

The process of phone VLAN bridging is explained as follows:

■ Phone proxy terminates TLS from outside on the Cisco ASA and initiates TCP to CUCM.

■ It enables softphones to call hardphones and vice versa without opening a wide range of ports between the two VLANs by performing inspection and dynamically opening pinholes.

■ It performs certificate-based authentication with the softphones.

Let's take a deep dive into the configuration required to enable phone proxy on Cisco ASA and CUCM. Since phone proxy, as discussed earlier, is a super set of TLS proxy, the CUCM cluster and internal phones can be in non-secure or secure mode (mixed-mode). These two topologies are shown in Figure 8-17 for reference.

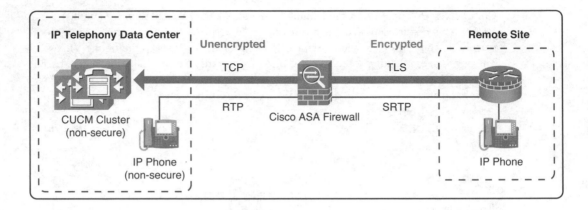

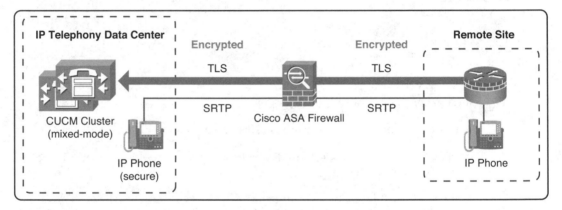

Figure 8-17 *Phone Proxy CUCM Non-Secure and Mixed Mode*

Both non-secure and mixed-mode cluster modes are covered in same configuration example, with steps explicitly marked for a mixed-mode cluster.

Step 1. This step is common to both non-secure and mixed-mode cluster setup. In this step the TFTP server is permitted through the Cisco ASA. (The TFTP server might need to be NAT'ed or PAT'ed as is on the inside of the network. See Example 8-14.)

Example 8-14 *TFTP Server Access*

```
IPTASA(config)# static (inside,outside) <outside IP> <inside IP> netmask
  255.255.255.255
IPTASA(config)# access-list permittftp extended permit udp any host <TFTP server IP>
  eq tftp
```

Step 2. This step is common to both non-secure and mixed-mode cluster setup. Here, the keys and trustpoints are generated (see Example 8-15).

Example 8-15   *Create Necessary RSA Key Pairs for Each CUCM*

```
IPTASA(config)# crypto key generate rsa label ccm_proxy_key modulus 1024
IPTASA(config)# crypto ca trustpoint ccm_proxy
IPTASA(config-ca-trustpoint)# enrollment self
IPTASA(config-ca-trustpoint)# fqdn none
IPTASA(config-ca-trustpoint)# subject-name cn=ASA-CCM-Proxy
IPTASA(config-ca-trustpoint)# keypair ccm_proxy_key
IPTASA(config-ca-trustpoint)# crl configure
!
IPTASA(config)# crypto ca enroll ccm_proxy
% The fully-qualified domain name will not be included in the certificate
% Include the device serial number in the subject name? [yes/no]: no
Generate Self-Signed Certificate? [yes/no]: yes
```

Step 3.   This step is required for mixed-mode cluster only. It is for creating the self-signed CA certificate to sign the LDC for phones (see Example 8-16).

Example 8-16   *Create Necessary RSA Key Pairs for CUCM, LDC Signer, and Common Phones*

```
IPTASA(config)# crypto key generate rsa label ccm_proxy_key modulus 1024
IPTASA(config)# crypto key generate rsa label ldc_signer_key modulus 1024
IPTASA(config)# crypto key generate rsa label phone_common modulus 1024
IPTASA(config)# crypto ca trustpoint ccm_proxy
IPTASA(config-ca-trustpoint)# enrollment self
IPTASA(config-ca-trustpoint)# fqdn none
IPTASA(config-ca-trustpoint)# subject-name cn=ASA-CCM-Proxy
IPTASA(config-ca-trustpoint)# keypair ccm_proxy_key
IPTASA(config-ca-trustpoint)# crl configure
!
IPTASA(config)# crypto ca enroll ccm_proxy
% The fully-qualified domain name will not be included in the certificate
% Include the device serial number in the subject name? [yes/no]: no
Generate Self-Signed Certificate? [yes/no]: yes
```

Step 4.   This step is specific for mixed-mode cluster. It creates the self-signed CA certificate to sign the LDC for phones (see Example 8-17).

Example 8-17   *Create Local CA (on Cisco ASA) to Sign LDC for IP Phones*

```
IPTASA(config)# crypto ca trustpoint ldc_server
IPTASA(config-ca-trustpoint)# enrollment self
IPTASA(config-ca-trustpoint)# proxy-ldc-issuer
IPTASA(config-ca-trustpoint)# fqdn my_ldc_ca.test.com
IPTASA(config-ca-trustpoint)# subject-name cn=LDC_SIGNER
```

```
IPTASA(config-ca-trustpoint)# keypair ldc_signer_key
!
IPTASA(config)# crypto ca enroll ldc_server
Would you like to continue with this enrollment? [yes/no]: yes
% The fully-qualified domain name in the certificate will be: myldcca.test.com
% Include the device serial number in the subject name? [yes/no]: no
Generate Self-Signed Certificate? [yes/no]: yes
```

Step 5. This step is common to both nonsecure and mixed-mode clusters. In this step the certificates will be imported by Cisco ASA (Example 8-18). Import the following certificates:

- CUCM certificate to authenticate the CUCM (required)

- Cisco_Manufacturing_CA if using MIC (depends on MIC or LSC)

- CAP-RTP-001 if using MIC (depends on MIC or LSC)

- CAP-RTP-002 if using MIC (depends on MIC or LSC)

- CAPF if using LSC (depends on MIC or LSC)

Example 8-18 *Create Trustpoint for Each Certificate Depending on Method Used*

```
IPTASA(config)# crypto ca trustpoint Cisco_manufacturing_CA
IPTASA(config-ca-trustpoint)# enrollment terminal
!
IPTASA(config)# crypto ca authenticate Cisco_manufacturing_CA
Enter the base 64 encoded CA certificate.
End with the word "quit" on a line by itself
```

Step 6. This step is common to both non-secure and mixed-mode cluster setup. It is required to create the CTL file instance (see Example 8-19).

Example 8-19 *Create CTL File Instance*

```
IPTASA(config)# ctl-file myctl
IPTASA(config-ctl-file)# record-entry capf trustpoint CAPF address <TFTP server IP
  address>
IPTASA(config-ctl-file)# record-entry cucm-tftp trustpoint ccm_proxy address <TFTP
  server IP address>
IPTASA(config-ctl-file)# no shutdown
```

Step 7. This step is common to both non-secure and mixed-mode cluster modes, with the exception of the **ldc issuer** and **ldc key-pair** commands. In this step, a TLS proxy instance is created (see Example 8-20).

Example 8-20 *Create a TLS Proxy Instance*

```
IPTASA(config)# tls-proxy my_proxy
IPTASA(config-tlsp)# server trust-point _internal_PP_myctl
IPTASA(config-tlsp)# client ldc issuer ldc_server
IPTASA(config-tlsp)# client ldc key-pair common
```

Step 8.   This step is common to both non-secure and mixed-mode cluster setup with
the exception of the **cluster-mode** command. It is required to create the
phone proxy instance (see Example 8-21).

Example 8-21 *Create Phone Proxy Instance*

```
IPTASA(config)# phone-proxy asa_phone_proxy
IPTASA(config-phone-proxy)# media-termination address <outside unique address>
IPTASA(config-phone-proxy)# tftp-server address <inside address> interface inside
IPTASA(config-phone-proxy)# tls-proxy my_proxy
IPTASA(config-phone-proxy)# cluster-mode mixed
IPTASA(config-phone-proxy)# ctl-file myctl
IPTASA(config-phone-proxy)# no disable service-settings
```

Step 9.   This step is common to both non-secure and mixed-mode cluster setup. In this
step, phone proxy in the SIP or SCCP inspection is enabled (see Example 8-22).

Example 8-22 *Cisco ASA SCCP and SIP TLS Inspection*

```
IPTASA(config)# class-map sec_skinny
IPTASA(config-cmap)# match port tcp eq 2443
!
IPTASA(config)# class-map sec_SIP
IPTASA(config-cmap)# match port tcp eq 5061
!
IPTASA(config)# policy-map type inspect skinny skinny_inspect
IPTASA(config-pmap)# parameters
!
IPTASA(config)# policy-map global_policy
IPTASA(config-pmap)# class inspection_default
IPTASA(config-pmap-c)# inspect skinny skinny_inspect
IPTASA(config-pmap)# class sec_skinny
IPTASA(config-pmap-c)# inspect skinny phone-proxy asa_phone_proxy
IPTASA(config-pmap)# class sec_SIP
IPTASA(config-pmap-c)# inspect sip phone-proxy asa_phone_proxy
```

Step 10. This step is explicit for mixed-mode cluster. In this step, the signer (LDC) certificate is exported from the Cisco ASA and uploaded to the CUCM (see Example 8-23).

Example 8-23 *Cisco ASA LDC Certificate Export*

```
IPTASA(config)# crypto ca export ldc_server identity-certificate
The PEM encoded identity certificate follows:
-----BEGIN CERTIFICATE-----
MIICTjCCAbegAwIBAgIEJxKdSTANBgkqhkiG9w0BAQQFADA5MRYwFAYDVQQDFA1B
<truncated>
sPVxBHnQzCiPRHXCEK/7iiYe
-----END CERTIFICATE-----
```

Save the output to a .pem file and import the certificate on the CUCM into the CallManager trust store.

The **show** commands in Examples 8-23, 8-24, and 8-25 are helpful to look into phone proxy configuration and session details.

Example 8-23 show phone-proxy *Output*

```
IPTASA# show phone-proxy
Phone-Proxy 'asa_phone_proxy': Runtime Proxy ref_cnt 1
  Cluster Mode: nonsecure
  Run-time proxies:
    Proxy 0xd8a64030: Class-map: sec_sccp, Inspect: skinny
```

Example 8-24 show phone-proxy secure-phones *output*

```
IPTASA# show phone-proxy secure-phones
asa_phone_proxy: 2 in use, 2 most used
          Interface     IP Address  Port MAC           Timeout Idle
            outside     192.168.0.20 29652 001c.58fb.be79 0:05:00 0:00:00
            outside     192.168.0.21 39433 001f.6c7f.31ea 0:05:00 0:00:23
```

Example 8-25 show phone-proxy signaling-sessions *Output*

```
IPTASA# show phone-proxy signaling-sessions
outside 192.168.0.21:39433 inside cucm6:2000
  Local Media (audio) conn: 192.168.0.21/31742 to 192.168.0.2/18248
    Local SRTP key set : Remote SRTP key set
  Remote Media (audio) conn: 192.168.0.2/18248 to 192.168.0.2/32110
outside 192.168.0.20:29652 inside cucm6:2000
```

```
   Local Media (audio) conn: 192.168.0.20/31750 to 192.168.0.2/32110
     Local SRTP key set : Remote SRTP key set
   Remote Media (audio) conn: 192.168.0.2/32110 to 192.168.0.2/18248
!
IPTASA# sh phone-proxy media-sessions
2 in use, 2 most used
Media-session: 192.168.0.2/32110 :: client ip 192.168.0.21/31742
  Lcl SRTP conn 192.168.0.2/32110 to 192.168.0.20/31750 tx_pkts 7097 rx_pkts 7098
Media-session: 192.168.0.2/18248 :: client ip 192.168.0.20/31750
  Lcl SRTP conn 192.168.0.2/18248 to 192.168.0.21/31742 tx_pkts 7098 rx_pkts 7099
```

You must consider some specifics before deploying the phone proxy feature in your IP Telephony network:

- If the existing CTL in the phone did not come from Cisco ASA, it needs to be erased and downloaded again.

- The media termination IP address cannot be the same as the outside interface; it must be a dedicated IP address on the outside interface range.

- If using MIC instead of LSC, you need to import Cisco_manufacturing_CA, CAP-RTP-001, and CAP-RTP-002 into Cisco ASA.

- Cisco ASA does not support multiple CUCM clusters; only one cluster is supported per firewall.

- The CUCM cluster can be composed of as many servers as can be listed in the CTL file sent to the phone. Although the limit as proposed by the Cisco IPCBU is 21, the real limiting factor is the size of CTL file, which must not be more than 32 KB.

- For each CUCM in the cluster, an additional license will be used. Therefore, the number of licenses required will be (Number_phones x Number_callmanagers).

- For each CUCM in the cluster, a new trustpoint must be configured on the Cisco ASA. In addition, a distinct CTL file entry must be created for each physical CUCM.

Following are the phone proxy-supported Cisco Unified IP Phone models:

7921, 7925, 7940, 7941, 7941G-GE, 7942, 7945, 7960, 7961, 7961G-GE, 7971, 7962, 7965, 7970, 7971, and 7975

CIPC for softphones (CIPC versions with authenticated mode only).

Note   For 7940 and 7960, only SCCP is supported, not SIP.

Now that you have a solid foundation of Cisco ASA Proxy services, it is time to consider the options you have for employees working from home and how you can provide them world-class Cisco IP Telephony services. More often than not, your organization's employees will be at a remote location, at home, at a small branch office, or on business travel. For them to leverage the IP Telephony services, it is essential to have a scalable yet easy-to-deploy solution. This requirement can be fulfilled by either Cisco VPN Phone or by Cisco VPN solution. While Cisco VPN Phone enables the telecommuters to plug-in the phone almost anywhere, to access corporate IP Telephony services, Cisco VPN solutions (for example, VPN Client or VPN client-server [hardware]) enables mobility, either at a remote location or on the move.

Cisco VPN Phone

Cisco VPN Phone is a VPN-enabled solution to extend the reach of your IP Telephony network outside the logical perimeter of your organization. It permits establishing secure connections from any location to your Intranet. It adds another option for the telecommuters or small branches office communications needs, in addition to regular IPSec based VPN hardware or software clients. Cisco VPN Client for IP Phones is easy to install, to use and to manage. It enables you to implement remote connectivity without extra hardware, other than an IP Phone, as shown in Figure 8-18.

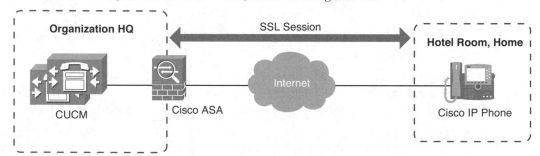

Figure 8-18   *VPN Phone Overview*

Although the VPN Phone feature compares with the Phone-Proxy feature, it has its own merits. For example, VPN Phone feature is supported with both Cisco ASA and Cisco IOS routers, whereas Phone Proxy is supported only with Cisco ASA. Moreover, VPN Phone can secure voice, video (depends on the IP Phone model), and IP Phone service traffic, whereas the Phone Proxy can secure only voice and IP Phone service traffic. In essence, it depends on your organization's business and technical requirements as to which remote-access solution works best for you.

Table 8-12 highlights the features of Cisco VPN Phone.

Table 8-12 *Cisco VPN Phone*

Cisco VPN Phone	
Deployment mode	IP Phone Remote Access
Services secured	Voice and Data (XML Phone services), video with 99XX/88XX IP Phones
Licenses	VPN Concentrator License and IP Phone DLUs
Supported VPN concentrators	Cisco ASA 5500 series and Cisco ISR with IOS SSL VPN
Encryption technology	Secure Socket Layer (SSL)
Deployment considerations	No additional hardware needed at remote location other than IP Phone

The end user has the following options to connect to VPN on an IP Phone:

■ The user can select whether the VPN client (mode) is enabled or disabled in a phone menu.

■ If the user disables the VPN client; the phone makes no attempt to create a VPN connection and proceeds with the standard startup sequence.

■ If the user enables the VPN client and auto-network detection is enabled, the phone tries to detect the type of network and attempts to create a VPN connection if appropriate.

■ If the user enables the VPN client and auto-network detection is not enabled, the phone attempts to create a VPN connection. This allows the VPN connection to be established within the secure enterprise network.

Cisco VPN Phone Prerequisites

Cisco VPN Phone client is supported on 7942G, 7945G, 7962G, 7965G, 7975G, and 99xx/89xx IP Phones. The minimum requirements are

■ CUCM 8.0.1 or above

■ IP Phone SCCP firmware version 9.0(2)SR1S or later

■ Cisco ASA IOS 8.0.4 or later

■ Anyconnect VPN Pkg 2.4.1012 or later

A Premium license and AnyConnect for Cisco VPN Phone license is required for Cisco ASA.

Implementing VPN Phone

This section details the various steps required to deploy VPN Phone in your Cisco IP Telephony network:

Step 1.   Configure Anyconnect VPN access on Cisco ASA to provide network access, as shown in Example 8-26.

Example 8-26   *Configuration for Anyconnect VPN Client*

```
IPTASA(config)# anyconnect enable
!
IPTASA(config)# group-policy GroupPolicy1 attributes
IPTASA(config-group-policy)# vpn-tunnel-protocol webvpn
!
IPTASA(config)# ip local pool VPN-Phone 10.10.1.100-10.10.1.254 mask 255.255.255.0
!
IPTASA(config)# tunnel-group VPNPhone type remote-access
!
IPTASA(config)# tunnel-group VPNPhone webvpn-attributes
IPTASA(config-tunnel-webvpn)# group-url https://IPTASA.orgXYZ.com/PhoneVPN enable
!
IPTASA(config)# tunnel-group VPNPhone general-attributes
IPTASA(config-tunnel-general)# address-pool VPN-Phone
IPTASA(config-tunnel-general)# default-group-policy GroupPolicy1
!
IPTASA(config)# webvpn
IPTASA(config-webvpn)# enable outside tls-only
IPTASA(config-webvpn)# svc image disk0:/anyconnect-win-2.4.5004-k9.pkg 1
IPTASA(config-webvpn)# svc enable
IPTASA(config-webvpn)# tunnel-group-list enable
```

Step 2.   Upload VPN certificates to CUCM from the OS admin page; choose **Security > Certificate Management**. The Cisco ASA self-signed certificate needs to be uploaded as Phone-VPN-Trust certificate, as shown in Figure 8-19.

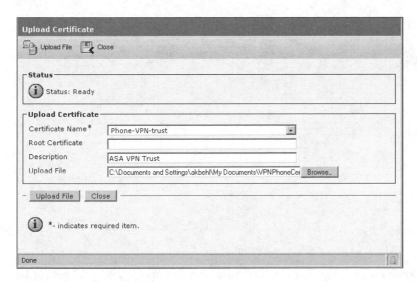

Figure 8-19   *Upload Cisco ASA Certificate to CUCM Trust Store*

Step 3.   Configure the VPN gateway on CUCM administrator page, under **Advanced Features > VPN > VPN Gateway**, as shown in Figure 8-20.

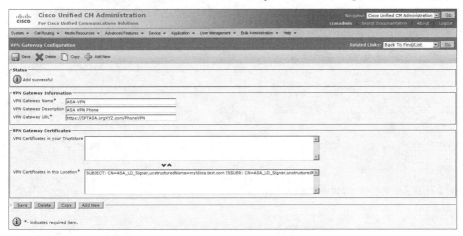

Figure 8-20   *CUCM VPN Gateway Configuration*

Step 4.   Create a VPN group in the **Advanced Features > VPN > VPN Group**, as shown in Figure 8-21.

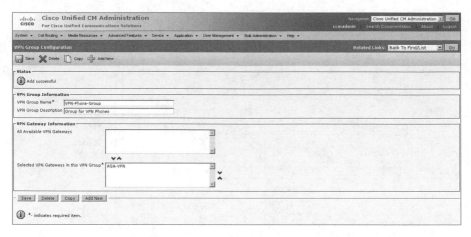

Figure 8-21   *CUCM VPN Group Configuration*

> **Step 5.**   Configure the VPN Profile under **Advanced Features > VPN > VPN Profile**, as shown in Figure 8-22.

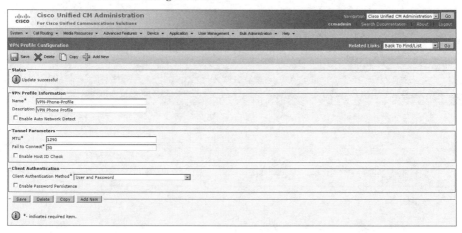

Figure 8-22   *CUCM VPN Profile Configuration*

> **Note**   Although as an IP Telephony Administrator you can force IP Phones for Auto-Network detect, it is recommended not to do so because with this option enabled, the IP Phone can connect only from outside your organization.

> **Step 6.**   Assign a VPN group and profile into the common phone profile. This is done under **Device > Device Settings > Common Phone Profile**, as shown in Figure 8-23.

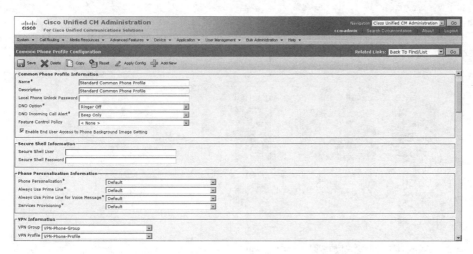

Figure 8-23 *CUCM Phone Profile Configuration*

Step 7.   Configure the IP Phone with a TFTP server manually. Register the phone internally before giving it to the telecommuter because it will ensure that the phone has the latest firmware and the ASA root certificate, and most important, it enables you to test and ensure that VPN works.

Step 8.   Apply the configuration on the IP Phone, that is, go to **Settings > Security Configuration > VPN Configuration.** Here you can enable VPN and use your Cisco IP Phone to establish a VPN connection.

At this time, you should be able to connect the IP Phones from within or outside of your organization's network, leveraging a fully functional remote-access solution based on Cisco Anyconnect technology.

Remote Worker and Telecommuter Voice Security

Remote and telecommuter voice solution can be broadly classified as

- Advance telecommuter solution (remote worker)

- Mobile telecommuter solution (on-the-move telecommuters)

Although for remote workers a small-sized firewall (for example, Cisco ASA 5505) or a wireless router (for example, an 800 series router) would work, for telecommuters on the go who are mobile most of the time, the Cisco IPSec-based VPN Client or Anyconnect client serves the purpose.

The advance telecommuter solution includes a wireless router at the home site of the teleworker. It delivers full IP telephony, wireless, and data services over an encrypted VPN channel, with dedicated quality-of-service (QoS). For on-the-move employees/ workers, Cisco VPN Clients and softphones (CIPC and CUPC) on the laptops allow telecommuters to leverage voice services anytime, anywhere. You have read about the

SSL VPN client on an IP Phone earlier in this chapter. Let's explore the IPSec VPN-based solution, which is equally applicable to both advance and mobile telecommuters. Figure 8-24 gives an insight to Telecommuter solutions.

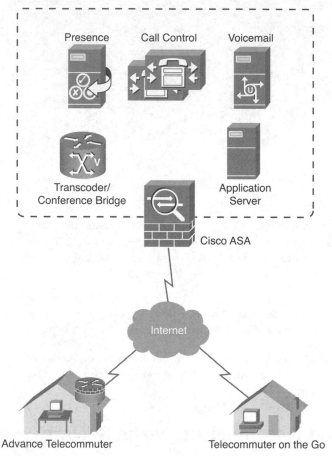

Figure 8-24 *CUCM Remote Worker and Telecommuter VPN Solution*

Example 8-27 shows the configuration of Cisco ASA to support the telecommuter voice IPSec solution.

Note   This example is based on Cisco ASA configuration.

Example 8-27 *Cisco ASA Head-End VPN Server Configuration*

```
IPTASA(config)# interface GigabitEthernet3/0
IPTASA(config-if)# description outside
IPTASA(config-if)# nameif outside
IPTASA(config-if)# security-level 0
IPTASA(config-if)# ip address 1.1.1.1 255.255.255.252
!
IPTASA(config)#interface GigabitEthernet3/1
IPTASA(config-if)# description inside
IPTASA(config-if)# nameif inside
IPTASA(config-if)# security-level 100
IPTASA(config-if)# ip address 10.10.10.251 255.255.255.0
!
IPTASA(config)# ip local pool vpnpool 192.168.100.1-192.168.100.254 mask
  255.255.255.0
!
IPTASA(config)# access-list 121 extended permit ip 10.10.10.0 255.255.255.0
  192.168.10.0 255.255.255.0
!
IPTASA(config)# crypto ipsec transform-set myset esp-des esp-sha-hmac
IPTASA(config)# crypto ipsec transform-set myset esp-des esp-md5-hmac
!
IPTASA(config)# crypto map mymap 1 match address 121
IPTASA(config)# crypto map mymap 1 set peer 2.2.2.2
IPTASA(config)# crypto map mymap 1 set transform-set myset
!
IPTASA(config)# crypto dynamic-map telecommuters 65535 set pfs group1
IPTASA(config)# crypto dynamic-map telecommuters 65535 set transform-set myset
IPTASA(config)# crypto map mymap 65535 ipsec-isakmp dynamic telecommuters
!
IPTASA(config)# crypto map mymap interface Outside
!
IPTASA(config)# crypto isakmp enable Outside
!
IPTASA(config)# crypto isakmp policy 10 authentication pre-share
IPTASA(config)# crypto isakmp policy 10 encryption 3des
IPTASA(config)# crypto isakmp policy 10 hash sha
IPTASA(config)# crypto isakmp policy 10 group 2
IPTASA(config)# crypto isakmp policy 10 lifetime 86400
!
IPTASA(config)# crypto isakmp policy 30 authentication pre-share
IPTASA(config)# crypto isakmp policy 10 encryption aes
IPTASA(config)# crypto isakmp policy 10 hash md5
IPTASA(config)# crypto isakmp policy 10 group 2
```

```
IPTASA(config)# crypto isakmp policy 10 lifetime 86400
!
IPTASA(config)# group-policy telecommuter internal
IPTASA(config)# group-policy telecommuter attributes
IPTASA(config)# vpn-tunnel-protocol IPSec
!
IPTASA(config)# username cisco password <omitted> encrypted privilege 0
!
IPTASA(config)# username cisco attributes
IPTASA(config)# vpn-group-policy telecommuter
!
IPTASA(config)# tunnel-group telecommuter type remote-access
IPTASA(config)# tunnel-group telecommuter general-attributes
IPTASA(config-tunnel-general)# address-pool vpnpool
IPTASA(config-tunnel-general)# default-group-policy telecommuter
!
IPTASA(config)# tunnel-group ipsec-l2l type remote-access
IPTASA(config-ipsec)# pre-shared-key *
!
IPTASA(config)# tunnel-group telecommuter ipsec-attributes
IPTASA(config-ipsec)# pre-shared-key *
```

Configuration example for Remote Worker IOS Router is shown in Example 8-28.

Example 8-28 *Remote Worker Cisco IOS Router Configuration*

```
RW800(config)# interface Ethernet0/0
RW800(config-if)# ip address 2.2.2.2 255.255.255.252
RW800(config-if)# crypto map remoteworker
RW800(config-if)# no shut
!
RW800(config)# access-list 101 permit ip 192.168.10.0 0.0.0.255 10.10.10.0 0.0.0.255
!
RW800(config)# crypto isakmp identity address
!
RW800(config)# crypto isakmp policy 1
RW800(config-isakmp)# encryption 3des
RW800(config-isakmp)# hash sha
RW800(config-isakmp)# authentication pre-share
RW800(config-isakmp)# group 2
RW800(config-isakmp)# lifetime 84600RW800(config-isakmp)# crypto isakmp key * address
  1.1.1.1
!
RW800(config)# crypto ipsec transform-set myset esp-des esp-sha-hmac
!
```

```
RW800(config)# crypto map remotewoker 100 ipsec-isakmp
RW800(config-crypto-map)# set peer 1.1.1.1
RW800(config-crypto-map)# set transform-set myset
RW800(config-crypto-map)# match address 101
```

The telecommuter VPN client configuration is shown in Figure 8-25.

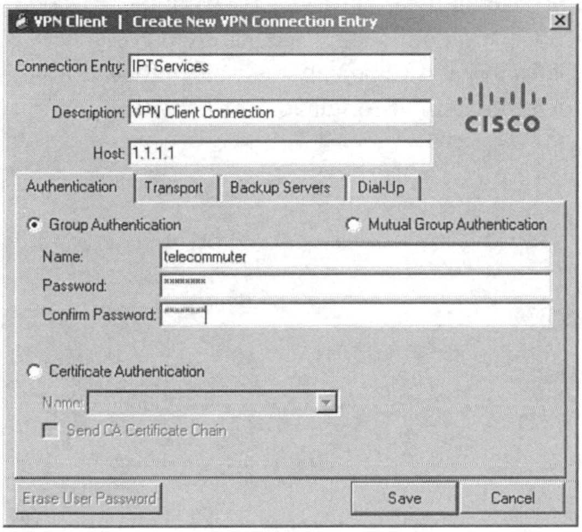

Figure 8-25   *Telecommuter VPN Client Configuration*

Summary

Every organization must defend its perimeter (both physical and logical) and the connections with the outside world to safeguard the data at rest and data in transit. Firewalls are the first line of defense. The design of the firewall system, the selection of the firewall solution that meets your enterprise requirements (including those of IP Telephony), and the configuration and management of the firewall is critical to guard entry and exit points.

Cisco ASA provides a range of enterprise-to-desktop security. It has much to offer for IP Telephony systems as well, acting as a perimeter firewall, a proxy firewall, and as a remote access solution. While the Cisco ASA inspection and filter engines help secure your IP Telephony network (data center) perimeter, its proxy (TLS and phone proxy) engines help ensure that encrypted signaling and media entering your IP Telephony domain are trustworthy. You can extend your IP Telephony network services far beyond the reach of your physical network, by giving telecommuters and remote workers a choice of VPN solutions that they can leverage on the move or from a base location.

This chapter built on the discussion of Cisco ASA Firewalls. Because the Cisco ASA Firewall forms the basis of any secure Cisco IP Telephony network security architecture, a thorough understanding of the topics covered in this chapter is crucial to ensure that you have a handle on the security of your IP Telephony data centers or deployments from a 360-degree perspective. Remember, security is only as strong as the weakest link. Firewalls can help make your enterprise security architecture a lot more formidable at the perimeter.

Next up is Part III, "Cisco IP Telephony Application and Device Security," which shows you how to protect your IP Telephony applications and devices. You will learn about the ways in which you can secure your IP Telephony applications for example, Cisco unified Communications Manager, Cisco Unity Connection, Cisco Unified Presence, Cisco Unified IP Phones, Cisco Voice Gateways and Gatekeeper, Cisco Unified Border Element, Cisco Unity Express, and so on against threats originating from within and outside of your network.

Part III

Cisco IP Telephony Application and Device Security

"Invincibility lies in the defense; the possibility of victory in the attack." –Sun Tzu

Chapter 9

Cisco Unified Communications Manager Security

The heart of any IP telephony network is the call control or call processing engine. Whether your organization is related to healthcare, retail, banking, financial, government, manufacturing, education, or any other business stream, if you are using Cisco IP Telephony, you are using Cisco Unified Communications Manager (CUCM) (or Cisco Unified Communications Manager Express) for call control, and it must be secured. Call control is the pivotal point for the entire IP Telephony architecture because it helps bring together the otherwise disparate pieces of a communication solution, for example, endpoints, voice messaging, presence, IP or PSTN calls, third-party communication devices ranging from PBXs to phones. Without secure and stable call control, all seems lost.

For a security system to be successful, it should protect against internal and external network attacks. It should also ensure privacy of all communications, at any place and any time. There are various mechanisms by which you can protect the integrity and privacy of your communication streams and at the same time also ensure the security of your IP PBX.

In this chapter, you will comprehend the following:

- CUCM platform security
- Certificate-based secure signaling and media
- Security by Default (SBD) Feature
- Deploying public PKI with CAPF
- Deploying public PKI with Cisco Tomcat
- Enabling Secure LDAP
- Securing IP Phone conversations
- Secure Tone feature

- CUCM trunk security

- Trusted Relay Point

- Preventing toll fraud

- Securing CTI/JTAPI connections

- Restricting administrative access

- Fighting Spam over Internet Telephony (SPIT)

- Security audit logs

- Single sign-on (SSO)

Cisco Unified Communications Manager (CUCM) Platform Security

Cisco Unified Communications Manager (CUCM) is the brain and heart of Cisco IP Telephony. The basic Cisco IP Telephony solution has CUCM at the center point, which performs the role of an IP PBX to bring together devices and applications such as Cisco Unified IP Phones, Cisco gateways, voice messaging, presence, and so on, in a single coherent system to deliver the value that Cisco IP Telephony has to offer. The CUCM application comes in a variety of flavors:

- A software that runs on a Microsoft Windows 2003 server on a Cisco provided (or third-party compatible) Media Convergence Server (MCS).

- A software that installs on a Cisco (or third-party compatible) MCS server with Linux as underlying operating system.

- An appliance that comes in the form of a Cisco MCS server, preloaded with Linux-based CUCM.

- A software running on top of VMware Hypervisor as a virtual machine, on a Cisco Unified Computing System (UCS) server.

Note   Throughout this chapter, all the configuration examples are based on CUCM 8.5(1) appliance version.

Windows version of CUCM is progressively being replaced by the appliance or Linux version. CUCM 4.x was the last major version to be released on the Windows platform. From CUCM 5.x onward, Linux has been the choice of an underlying operating system (OS) for both the appliance and UCS version.

Note   Because the CUCM Windows version is End of Life (EOL) and End of Support (EOS), Cisco highly recommends migrating windows-based CUCM installations to the latest, shipping version based on Linux OS.

In the following sections you will comprehend the Security for Linux version of CUCM, for platform (OS).

Note   Chapter 5, "Cisco IP Telephony Physical Security," addresses the physical security issues that apply equally to all IP Telephony servers, including CUCM whether it is MCS, appliance, or UCS.

CUCM Linux Platform Security

For the Linux version, the following security practices are highly recommended:

- **OS upgrade and patches: Install the latest Cisco provided OS and application updates (Service Units [SU]) when they are released. This ensures that all fixes offered in the software patch is available in your IP Telephony network to provide maximum protection from known threats. The updates are available at** http://www.cisco.com/cisco/software/navigator.html?mdfid=278875240

- **Cisco Security Agent (HIPS):** Although CSA is an integral component of a CUCM Appliance or server- (virtual and bare-metal) based implementation, it is highly recommended to have it active on your CUCM server. Cisco has developed a default CSA policy that enables all the correct processes, actions, and so on needed for CUCM server to function, while preventing known and unknown (0-day) attacks. CSA for Linux OS-based CUCM comes only in headless (standalone or unmanaged) version.

Note   To know the status of CSA on a CUCM server, enter the command **utils csa status**. CSA can be stopped or disabled by the CLI command **utils csa disable** and can be restarted or enabled with the CLI command **utils csa enable**. For CUCM version 8.6 and later, CSA is replaced by SELinux. See Appendix B, "Cisco IP Telephony: Firewalling and Intrusion Prevention," for details on SELinux.

- **Server hardening:** Following are the additional server hardening mechanisms that can help you evade any inside or outside attacks on you CUCM servers:
  - As a best practice ensure that all administrator passwords for CUCM server OS and application are strong (at least eight characters, if possible alphanumeric) passwords to evade any brute-force and dictionary-based attacks.

- Always ensure that the OS administrator and the CUCM application administrator passwords are unique, that is, the application and OS passwords are not the same. This is helpful in mitigating a possible dictionary-based attack and guess-work password breaking.

- OS and application passwords should be changed at least twice a year (or as defined by organizational or IP Telephony security policy).

- No access to the Internet should be allowed from CUCM cluster servers (or for that matter any IP Telephony application server). Having direct access to the Internet can be detrimental for the IP Telephony servers because it not only opens access from the outside the organization, but also enables a hacker to compromise the call control system by leveraging an exploit. Furthermore, if one IP Telephony server is compromised, it can become a hub to launch attacks on other neighbor servers.

- **Server firewall:** CUCM Linux edition (version 5.x onward) has a built-in firewall (IPTables) that protects the communication between servers within a cluster. It also protects servers from external attacks. Following are the salient features of the CUCM Linux Firewall:

  - Dynamic rules define the behavior of the firewall.

  - A cluster node list is maintained by the Cluster Manager.

  - All localhost traffic is allowed.

  - All outgoing traffic is allowed.

  - All established connections are allowed.

  - All ICMP traffic is allowed, but rate-limited to 10/sec with 5 burst.

  - All other traffic is dropped.

Certificate-Based Secure Signaling and Media: Certificate Authority Proxy Function

Cisco CUCM is a Public Key Infrastructure (PKI) Certificate Authority (CA) and can issue self-signed certificates. It can also accept certificates from other PKI CA authorities (external CA). To learn more about Cisco IP Telephony PKI, see Appendix A, "Cisco IP Telephony: Authentication and Encryption Essentials."

CUCM allows signaling authentication as well as signaling and media encryption. The Cisco Proxy Authentication Function (CAPF) and the Cisco Trust List (CTL) services help you enable encryption on your CUCM cluster.

Note Starting from Cisco Unified Communications Manager release 7.1(5) and later, CUCM is offered in two varieties to best meet the needs of all customers. Customers may order either the U.S. export "Restricted" or U.S. export "Unrestricted" versions of the product. The U.S. export Restricted version of CUCM provides all the encryption capabilities. The U.S. export Unrestricted version of CUCM does not provide signaling and media encryption; however, it is otherwise functionally equivalent (including the encryption of other types of data) to the U.S. export Restricted version of CUCM.

Before discussing CAPF and CTL, let's take a step back to understand the two major security modes of CUCM.

CUCM provides two security modes:

- Non-secure mode (default mode for any newly installed cluster)
- Mixed mode (enables security on a CUCM cluster)

The CUCM cluster (or server) when installed afresh is in default non-secure mode and cannot provide secure signaling or media services. In this mode the endpoints are all non secured and cannot communicate with each other or with call control on a Transport Layer Security (TLS) encrypted channel or using Secure Real Time Protocol (SRTP).

Note For more details on TLS, SRTP, certificates, and CTL client and PKI topologies, see Appendix A.

When the CAPF and CTL services (CAPF and CTL services on Publisher and CTL service on all other servers in the cluster) are activated, the cluster is ready to be changed into secured mode (better known as mixed-mode).

Note The reason it is known as mixed mode is that in this mode CUCM can support both secured as well as non-secured endpoints; that is, both encrypted and unencrypted endpoints are supported and interoperability, fallback to non-secure is maintained.

In the mixed mode, the cluster can support authenticated signaling and encrypted + authenticated signaling and media streams. When the endpoints are assigned their respective security profiles, they can exchange keys (public key) with call control and other devices or applications.

Cisco IP telephony offers you the capability to deploy authentication and encryption of communication channel (signaling and media) between devices, for example, Cisco Unified IP Phones, CUCM, voicemail ports, conference bridges, and so on by virtue of certificates. Secure signaling is achieved by using Transport Layer Security (TLS). The secure signaling encapsulates the Skinny Client Control Protocol (SCCP, or Skinny) or

Session Initiation Protocol (SIP) messages in TLS. Secure media transfer on the other hand provides confidentiality by encrypting the media stream between endpoints or an endpoint and an application. The call is considered a Secure RTP (SRTP) call.

Note   For more details on TLS, SRTP, keying mechanisms, Cisco IP Telephony PKI, and certificate format, see Appendix A.

With the context of CUCM encryption and authentication capabilities, following is a step-by-step example that explains how you can enable mixed-mode on your CUCM cluster.

Enabling CUCM Cluster Security: Mixed-Mode

Prerequisites for converting a non-secure cluster to a secure cluster are as follows:

- A PC or laptop with Windows XP® or 7OS
- At least two eTokens (four or more are preferred)
- CUCM cluster reach ability from Windows PC or laptop

Note   USB eTokens can be ordered with part number KEY-CCM-ADMIN-K9= or KEY-UCM-ADMIN2-K9=.

It is important for you to know that there are two different types of eTokens available today. They come from different vendors, namely

- Safenet
- ActivIdentity

If you order the eTokens on www.cisco.com, they have a different part ID:

- **Safenet:** KEY-CCM-ADMIN-K9= (Hardware Security Key for CCM Admin, Release 4.0 or greater)
- **ActivIdentity:** KEY-UCM-ADMIN2-K9= (CUCM Admin Security Token, 4.3, 6.0, or newer)

Safenet tokens are supported in all CUCM releases. Starting with 8.x, Both Safenet and ActivIdentity tokens are supported on CUCM.

Note   Among the older releases, only 7.1.5 has added support for ActivIdentity. CAPF issued certificates (self-signed) are valid for 5 years.

Following are the steps to install, run, and configure a CTL Client to convert a CUCM cluster or server from non-secure to mixed mode:

Step 1.   Turn on CAPF and CTL services on CUCM Publisher and CTL service on all CUCM subscribers, as shown in Figure 9-1.

Security Services		
Service Name		Activation Status
☑	Cisco CTL Provider	Activated
☑	Cisco Certificate Authority Proxy Function	Activated

Figure 9-1   *CAPF and CTL Services Activated*

Step 2.   Restart CCM and TFTP services on every node where these services are enabled.

Step 3.   From the CUCM Publisher (or any Subscriber) CCMAdministrator (application) web page, download and install the CTL Client plug-in for Windows. Go to **Application > Plugins**, as shown in Figure 9-2.

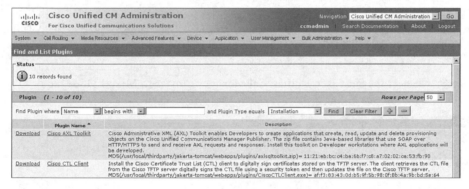

Figure 9-2   *CTL Client Plug-In Download*

Note   Ensure that the Windows system has the Smart Card Service enabled before installing the CTL Client. To ensure that this service is running, click **Start > Run > type services.msc**. Look for **Smart Card Service** and make sure it is enabled and started. The CTL Client plug-in downloaded from CUCM 8.5 or earlier release is only compatible with 32-bit Windows OS. With CUCM 8.6 and later releases, the CTL Client plug-in is compatible with 32 and 64-bit Windows OS.

Step 4.   Install the CTL Client application on your Windows PC or laptop. As the installation interface is quite intuitive, just follow the prompts.

Step 5.   After CTL Client is installed, launch it via the desktop shortcut. It asks you for an IP address, a username, and a password (see Figure 9-3). The IP address is the Publisher IP address, and the password is same as the application super-user (CCMAdministrator) password. Click **Next**.

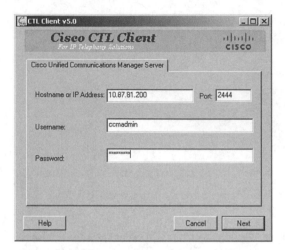

Figure 9-3   *CTL Client*

> **Note**   Keep the port to default 2444, unless you have changed it under **System > Service Parameters > Cisco CTL Provider service.**

Step 6.   Select the **Set Cisco Unified CallManager Cluster to Mixed Mode** radio button (see Figure 9-4). Click **Next.**

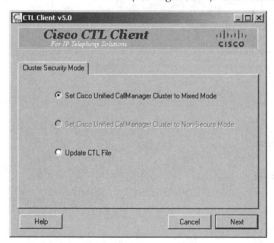

Figure 9-4   *Setting CUCM Cluster to Mixed Mode*

> **Note**   After the Cluster is secure, the other two options are your primary ones, that is, **Set CallManager Cluster to Non-Secure Mode** and **Update CTL File.** The former sets the cluster back to the non-secure mode, whereas the latter updates the CTL file if any server has been added or removed from the cluster or a firewall or a TFTP server needs to be added to the CTL file.

Step 7.   The CTL Client should now present you with a dialog box (see Figure 9-5) asking for a security token. Insert the USB eToken and click **OK**.

Figure 9-5   *CTL Client eToken Request*

Step 8.   You should now have a window that displays the certificate of the eToken (see Figure 9-6). Click **Next**.

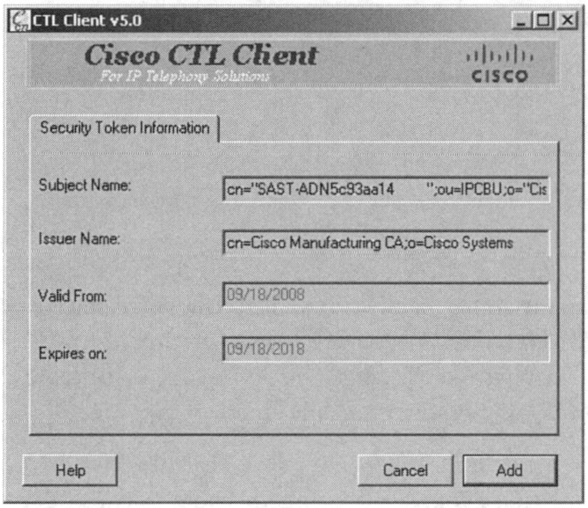

Figure 9-6   *eToken Certificate*

Step 9.   You should now see several pop-ups that come and go as CTL Client is downloading the certificates from all servers in the cluster.

Note   At times, it may seem like that the CTL Client is hung and becomes non-responding. Be patient, because it is running in the background.

Step 10.   Now you should see the screen shown in Figure 9-7. At this point, the CTL Client has downloaded the certificates from all servers. However, do not click Finish yet because you are not done. You need to add at least one more USB eToken to complete the process.

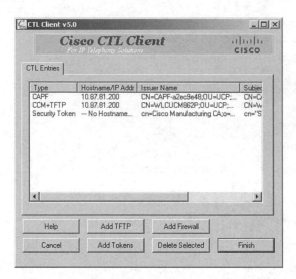

Figure 9-7 *CTL Client Certificate List*

Note Even if you click Finish, the CTL Client comes back with an error message stating Please Insert a Security Token. Click OK When Done. A second eToken is required for redundancy purposes, and you can use more than two eTokens. See Appendix A for more information on CTL client and eToken, and leading practices around them.

Step 11. **Click Add tokens.** Remove the first eToken if it is already there in your PC's or laptop's USB slot. Insert the second token (or consecutive tokens) and click **OK**. Again CTL Client shows the certificate for the second (or third or fourth) eToken. Click **Next** (in case you do not want to add any more eTokens).

Step 12. Now you should see a window similar to Figure 9-8, where you can see two (or more) eTokens in the CTL Client. Click **Finish**.

Figure 9-8 *CTL Client eTokens*

Note Make sure that there is only one eToken in your PC or laptop when you click Finish.

Step 13. You should be prompted for the password for the eToken. The default password is Cisco123 (without quotes). Enter the password and click **OK**.

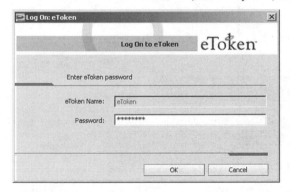

Figure 9-9 *eToken Password*

Note The password can be changed with the applet provided along with the eToken. The password is the root trust anchor of the whole IP Telephony PKI system and should be only known by authorized personnel. After 15 wrong attempts at guessing the password, the key will be locked and nothing will unlock it. In such a case, it is advisable to get another pair of keys from Cisco, and the recommendation is to have at least a single point of contact for the CTL and cluster security mode update rather than guessing the password.

Step 14. You see several pop-ups; the CTL Client creates a CTL List/File that contains the certificate of every server in the cluster and the certificate of all eTokens configured in CTL Client. The file is signed by the private key of the eToken in the USB port of your PC or laptop, as shown in Figure 9-10.

Figure 9-10   *CTL Client Signing Cluster Certificates and Creating a CTL File*

Note   Again, at times, it may seem like that the CTL Client is hung and becomes non-responding. Be patient, because it runs in the background.

Step 15. The CTL Client when finished with processing displays the window similar to Figure 9-11 wherein it displays certificates signed on each server. It also reminds you to restart the CCM and TFTP services on whichever servers they are configured. Click **Done**.

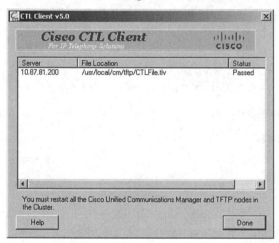

Figure 9-11   *CTL Client Wizard Completed*

Step 16. Restart the CCM and TFTP services on all servers where these are enabled and activated.

Step 17. Store the eToken pair(s) in a safe place, under lock and key.

With the aforementioned steps carried out, you should have successfully converted your cluster into mixed-mode.

Note After CAPF and CTL services are activated and the cluster is set to mixed mode, Cisco Unified IP Phones can no longer auto-register. Now, you must manually configure each phone or configure phones in bulk using the Bulk Administration Tool (BAT).

You can verify the same by going to **System > Enterprise Parameters**; look for **Cluster Security Mode**, which should be 1, as shown in Figure 9-12, indicating that the Cluster is in mixed mode and can support encrypted endpoints, trunks, gateways, voicemail ports, and much more.

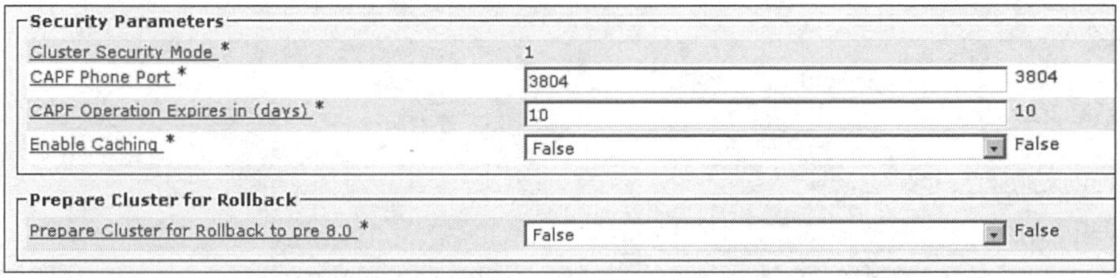

Security Parameters		
Cluster Security Mode *	1	
CAPF Phone Port *	3804	3804
CAPF Operation Expires in (days) *	10	10
Enable Caching *	False	False
Prepare Cluster for Rollback		
Prepare Cluster for Rollback to pre 8.0 *	False	False

Figure 9-12 *Enterprise Parameters Cluster Security Mode*

From this point onward, Cisco Unified IP Phones will download the CTL file as a part of the normal TFTP configuration download process. Depending on if the Cisco IP Phone has a security profile associated with it and the type of profile, the IP Phone can behave as a non-secure (unencrypted), authenticated, or encrypted (secure) endpoint. The information about the CTL file can be obtained by using the CUCM OS CLI command, as shown in Example 9-1.

Example 9-1 *CTL File Information*

```
admin: show ctl


Length of CTL file: 22183


The CTL File was last modified on Thu Jul 10 10:24:43 PDT 2011


Parse CTL File
----------------
Version:1.2
HeaderLength:304 (BYTES)


BYTEPOSTAGLENGTHVALUE
----------------------
3SIGNERID2117
4SIGNERNAME56cn="SAST-ADN5bbae514          ";ou=IPCBU;o="Cisco Systems
5SERIALNUMBER10DD:FC:14:00:00:00:8D:50:55:19
6CANAME42cn=Cisco Manufacturing CA;o=Cisco Systems
7SIGNATUREINFO215
```

```
8DIGESTALGORTITHM1

9SIGNATUREALGOINFO28

10SIGNATUREALGORTITHM1

11SIGNATUREMODULUS1

.

<output omitted>

.

14FILENAME12

15TIMESTAMP4


CTL Record #:1

         ----

BYTEPOSTAGLENGTHVALUE

---------------------

1RECORDLENGTH21180

2DNSNAME1

3SUBJECTNAME56cn="SAST-ADN5bbbeb14          ";ou=IPCBU;o="Cisco Systems

4FUNCTION2System Administrator Security Token

5ISSUERNAME42cn=Cisco Manufacturing CA;o=Cisco Systems

6SERIALNUMBER10A1:FE:14:00:00:00:7A:EF:70:19

7PUBLICKEY141

9CERTIFICATE895E3 B9 88 3C 33 A4 24 0C 26 1F D0 79 74 16 78 3A C1 74 65 E0 (SHA1
  Hash HEX)

10IPADDRESS4

This etoken was not used to sign the CTL file.


<output omitted>

CTL Record #:8

         ----

BYTEPOSTAGLENGTHVALUE

---------------------

1RECORDLENGTH21180

2DNSNAME1

3SUBJECTNAME56cn="SAST-ADN5bbae514          ";ou=IPCBU;o="Cisco Systems

4FUNCTION2System Administrator Security Token

5ISSUERNAME42cn=Cisco Manufacturing CA;o=Cisco Systems

6SERIALNUMBER10DD:FC:14:00:00:00:8D:50:55:19

7PUBLICKEY141

9CERTIFICATE89500 A1 49 4A E0 7C A1 D7 E6 76 60 EB 7E DC D5 2C 2E E3 18 2A (SHA1
  Hash HEX)

10IPADDRESS4

This etoken was used to sign the CTL file.


The CTL file was verified successfully.
```

For implementing security on endpoints, refer to the "Securing IP Phones" section. For information on how to enable security for trunks (inter-cluster trunk gatekeeper controlled, and non-gatekeeper controlled, H.323, H.225, and SIP trunks) at the gateway and gatekeeper end, refer to Chapters 12, "Cisco Voice Gateway Security," and 13, "Cisco Voice Gatekeeper and Cisco Unified Border Element Security."

Security by Default (SBD)

From CUCM version 8.0 onward, Cisco has introduced the concept of Security By Default (SBD) wherein, even without a CTL file, every endpoint gets an Initial Trust List (ITL) File. This file is similar to CTL; however, it does not need any security to be enabled (CAPF or CTL services or CTL Client).

Note   ITL is not a replacement for CTL. It's for initial security so that endpoints can trust the CUCM; however, to encrypt signaling or media, CTL is still required.

The ITL file is created automatically when the cluster is installed. The TFTP server's private key is used to sign the file. If the cluster is not in mixed-mode, only the ITL file is downloaded. However, if there is a CTL file, the CTL file is downloaded first, followed by the ITL file.

Behind the scene, the Trust Verification Service (TVS) is the core component of SBD feature. TVS runs on all CUCM servers in the cluster and authenticates certificates on behalf of the IP Phone. TVS certificates along with a few key certificates are bundled in the ITL file. Security By Default provides three basic functions for supported Cisco IP Phones:

- Default authentication of the TFTP downloaded files (configuration, locale, and so on).

- Optional encryption of the TFTP configuration files.

- Certificate verification for the phone initiated HTTPS connections using a remote certificate trust store on CUCM and TVS.

TFTP Download Authentication

When a CTL or ITL file is present, the Cisco Unified IP Phone requests a signed TFTP configuration file from the CUCM TFTP server. This allows the phone to verify the configuration file that came from a trusted source (authentication). With the CTL or ITL file present on phones, configuration files must be signed by a trusted TFTP server. This file comes with a special verification signature.

The phone requests **SEP<MAC Address>.cnf.xml.sgn** to get the configuration file with the special signature, as depicted in Figure 9-13.

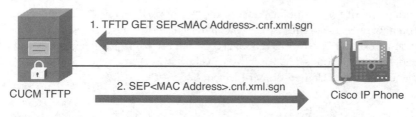

Figure 9-13 *ITL TFTP Authentication*

The signed file has a signature to authenticate itself; however, it is otherwise in clear text XML. The phone needs to verify the signature of the received file against the ITL file before this configuration file can be accepted.

Note TFTP configuration file authentication process is covered in Appendix A.

TFTP Configuration File Encryption

If TFTP configuration encryption is enabled in the associated Phone Security Profile, the phone requests an encrypted configuration file. This file is signed with the TFTP private key and encrypted with a symmetric key exchanged between the IP Phone and CUCM.

Note TFTP configuration file encryption process is detailed in Appendix A.

The phone requests **SEP<MAC Address>.cnf.xml.enc.sgn** to get the signed encrypted file, as shown in Figure 9-14.

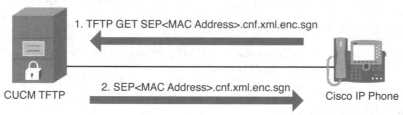

Figure 9-14 *TFTP File Encryption*

The encrypted configuration file has the signature at the beginning as well, but there is no plain text data after. The signer must be present in the ITL file before the phone can accept the file.

Trust Verification Service (Remote Certificate and Signature Verification)

Cisco Unified IP Phones contain a limited amount of memory (NVRAM). Instead of putting a full certificate trust store on each IP Phone (analogous to a browser where all trusted CA certificates are present), CUCM acts as a remote trust store via the Trust Verification Service (TVS). Any time an IP Phone cannot verify a signature or certificate via the CTL or ITL files, it refers to the TVS server for verification, as shown in Figure 9-15.

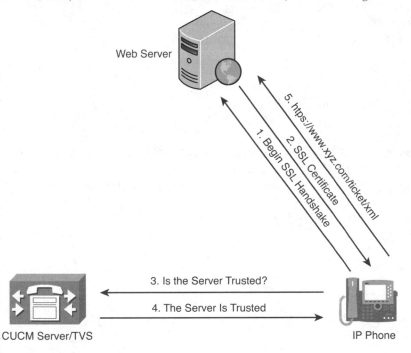

Figure 9-15 *Trust Verification Service for Endpoints*

Note   From a management perspective, too, the central trust store is easier to manage than if the trust store were present on all IP Phones.

If an IP Phone is set up to use an HTTPS URL for extension mobility, directories, or a ticker application, it refers to its TVS (CUCM call-processing subscriber or TFTP) and confirms the trust level of application server with the TVS server, before accepting any connections from the application hosting server.

To get information about the ITL file on your cluster, you can execute the command shown in Example 9-2 on CUCM OS CLI.

Example 9-2 *ITL File Information*

```
admin: show itl
Length of ITL file: 3564
The ITL File was last modified on Wed Sep 21 12:40:04 EDT 2011


        Parse ITL File
        ----------------
Version:        1.2
HeaderLength:   292 (BYTES)


BYTEPOS TAG              LENGTH  VALUE
------- ---              ------  -----
3       SIGNERID         2       107
4       SIGNERNAME       45      CN=CUCM851P;OU=UCP;O=Cisco;L=Wall;ST=NJ;C=US
5       SERIALNUMBER     8       35:08:03:83:C2:5E:1B:F4
6       CANAME           45      CN=CUCM851P;OU=UCP;O=Cisco;L=Wall;ST=NJ;C=US
7       SIGNATUREINFO    2       15
8       DIGESTALGORTITHM 1
9       SIGNATUREALGOINFO 2            8
10      SIGNATUREALGORTITHM 1
11      SIGNATUREMODULUS 1
.
<output omitted>
                  .
15      TIMESTAMP        4


        ITL Record #:1
               ----
BYTEPOS TAG              LENGTH  VALUE
------- ---              ------  -----
1       RECORDLENGTH     2       681
2       DNSNAME          2
3       SUBJECTNAME      45      CN=CUCM851P;OU=UCP;O=Cisco;L=Wall;ST=NJ;C=US
4       FUNCTION         2       TVS
5       ISSUERNAME       45      CN=CUCM851P;OU=UCP;O=Cisco;L=Wall;ST=NJ;C=US
6       SERIALNUMBER     8       01:58:BF:40:36:B1:D8:E6
7       PUBLICKEY        270
8       SIGNATURE        256
11      CERTHASH         20      55 7D C4 0F DD AD CC 94 98 0F 92 AE A8 C8 C4 DA 8C
B8 1E C6
12      HASH ALGORITHM   1       SHA-1
```

```
          ITL Record #:2

                ----

BYTEPOS TAG              LENGTH  VALUE
------- ---              ------  -----
1       RECORDLENGTH     2       1079
2       DNSNAME          2
3       SUBJECTNAME      45      CN=CUCM851P;OU=UCP;O=Cisco;L=Wall;ST=NJ;C=US
4       FUNCTION         2       System Administrator Security Token
5       ISSUERNAME       45      CN=CUCM851P;OU=UCP;O=Cisco;L=Wall;ST=NJ;C=US
6       SERIALNUMBER     8       35:08:03:83:C2:5E:1B:F4
7       PUBLICKEY        140
8       SIGNATURE        128
9       CERTIFICATE      680     E6 03 33 76 AC 24 0D 7A AB DB 61 4A
DA F1 16 14 91 FF D0 AE (SHA1 Hash HEX)
This etoken was used to sign the ITL file.


The ITL file was verified successfully.
```

Note If you upgrade from a pre 8.x CUCM to any 8.x version, and have to roll back to an earlier version for any reason, the ITL file still exists on all IP Phones that were registered to the cluster, and you must delete them manually. This overhead can be saved by enabling an enterprise parameter by going to **System > Enterprise Parameters > Prepare Cluster for Rollback to pre-8.0**. Set the value to **True**. After the roll back is completed, be sure to restart the TFTP services.

Using External Certificate Authority (CA) with CAPF

By now, you know what CAPF is and how it can help you achieve encrypted signaling and media conversations in your Cisco IP Telephony infrastructure. In most cases, organizations have a single trust entity through which the trust transitions are built. This entity can be an in-house CA for example, Microsoft Windows-based CA or an external CA, for example, VeriSign.

The following section outlines the steps to have the CAPF certificate signed by external CA:

Step 1.   Log in to Cisco Unified OS Administration. Go to **Security > Certificate Management**.

Step 2.   Click **Generate CSR**. Select CAPF from the pull-down, and click **Generate CSR** (see Figure 9-16).

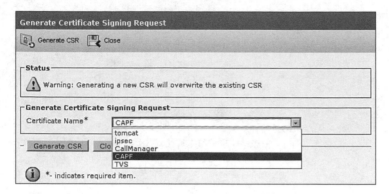

Figure 9-16   *Generating CAPF CSR*

Step 3.   On the Certificate Management page, you should see the **Download CSR** button. Click it and download the **CAPF.csr** file. The CSR is a text file, and the content looks something like that shown in Example 9-3.

Example 9-3   *CUCM CAPF CSR File*

```
-----BEGIN CERTIFICATE REQUEST-----
MIIB4zCCAUwCAQAwZjEWMBQGA1UEChMNY2lzY28gc3lzdGVtczELMAkGA1UECBMCbmMxD
DAKBgNVBAcTA3J0cDELMAkGA1UEBhMCVVMxFjAUBgNVBAMTDUNBUEYtMzJh
<output omitted>
atFtNeOY4Vbi4d3I0hpFAedwEBoWjV9bwJcIns7JapVglqIdrgVrqJe1ejFoogMuGrUZdfF1QA==
-----END CERTIFICATE REQUEST-----
```

Step 4.   Sign the CSR using an internal or external CA.

Note   Microsoft CA, VeriSign, and Keon are Cisco tested CAs. Ensure that the CSR should be signed (if using Microsoft CA) as a subordinate CA certificate.

Step 5.   After the certificate is issued, download it as a DER-encoded format. Rename the file from the default **certnew.cer** name (applicable to MS CA, the third-party or external CA will assign either a PKCS#12 value or a file with an extension as .cer) to a more meaningful name, for example, CAPF.cer. Also, download the CA root certificate and rename it to **CA-Root.cer**.

Step 6.   Upload the CA Root certificate in to **CAPF-Trust** store; it automatically creates .pem and .der versions of the certificate.

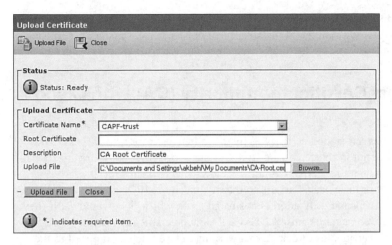

Figure 9-17 *Uploading CA Root Certificate*

    Step 7.   Upload the signed CAPF certificate in to the CAPF truststore (see Figure 9-18).

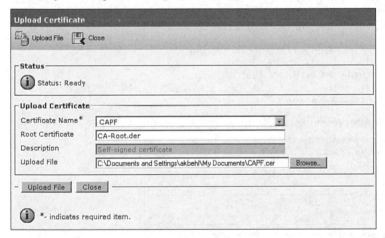

Figure 9-18 *Uploading Signed CAPF CSR*

As you upload the signed CAPF certificate, you must specify the Root certificate, which is the External CA Root certificate you uploaded in the previous step. In this example, the certificate filename is **CA-Root.der.** This automatically copies the External CA Root certificate into the CallManager trust store. The Certificate List will be updated again after you click **Close** on the Upload Certificate window.

    Step 8.   Run the CTL client using one of the same eToken keys you used before, and Update the CTL file.

    Step 9.   Reboot all nodes in the cluster.

Now, the endpoints should download the updated CTL file from TFTP (upon reset or new registration of the endpoint) and this CTL file will have the external CA certificate, which the endpoints will use for the CAPF (call signaling and media) encryption keys.

Using External Certificate Authority (CA) with Cisco Tomcat

Although CUCM has self-signed certificates by default enabled for https access (SSL), these certificates are not in the certificate store of your browser. Usually, organizations have either an internal or an external CA authenticate the certificates for its servers, whether for intranet or for extranet access so that the machines (PC, laptops, and mobile devices) do not get the name or IP address mismatch error, which they would get if they browse the CUCM web page. Because CUCM self-signed certificates are not by default in a user's machine's certificate store, it gives a warning before you can proceed to the CCMAdministrator, OSAdministrator, or CCMUser web pages.

The procedure to use the External CA with Tomcat is similar to using the External CA with CAPF. In the following section you will learn to secure your CUCM web, that is, application, and the OS Administration page access.

Step 1.   Log in to **Cisco Unified OS Administration**.

Step 2.   Go to **Security > Certificate Management**.

Step 3.   Click **Generate CSR**.

Step 4.   Select **Tomcat** from the pull-down, and click **Generate CSR** (see Figure 9-19).

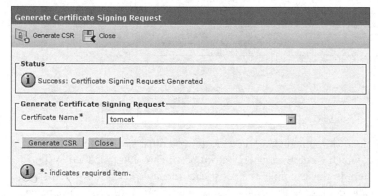

Figure 9-19   *Generating Tomcat CSR*

Step 5.   On the Certificate Management page, you should see the **Download CSR** button. Click it to download the **tomcat.csr** file. The CSR is a text file and the content should look something like what's shown in Example 9-4.

Example 9-4 *CUCM Tomcat CSR*

```
-----BEGIN CERTIFICATE REQUEST-----
MNIB4zCCAUwCAQAwZjEWMBQGA1UEChMNY2lzY28gc3lzdGVtczELMAkGA1UECBMCbmMxDDAKBgNVBAcT
A3J0cDELMAkGA1UEBhMCVVMxFjAUBgNVBAMTDUNBUEYtMzJh
<output omitted>
atFtNeOY4Vbi4d3I0hpFAedwEBoWjV9bwJcIns7JapVglqIdrgVrqJe1ejFoogMu
GrUZdfE1Q5==
-----END CERTIFICATE REQUEST-----
```

Step 6.   Sign CSR using an internal or external CA.

Note   If you use the Microsoft CA, ensure that the CSR should be signed using the template of the web server.

Step 7.   After the certificate is issued, download it as a DER-encoded format. Rename the file from the default **certnew.cer** name (applicable to the MS CA; the third party or external CA will assign either a PKCS#12 value or a file with the extension.cer) to a more meaningful name, for example, **tomcat.cer.** Upload the **root CA** certificate in **tomcat-trust store**, as shown in Figure 9-20.

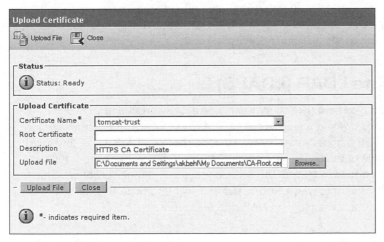

Figure 9-20 *Uploading CA Root Certificate*

The Certificate List will be updated automatically after you press **Close** on the Upload Certificate window.

Step 8.   Upload the signed tomcat certificate in the **tomcat trust-store** (see Figure 9-21), with the root CA certificate mentioned in the respective field.

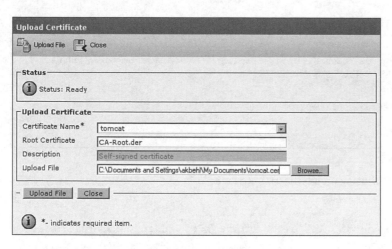

Figure 9-21 *Uploading signed Tomcat Certificate*

The Certificate List will be updated again after you press **Close** on the Upload Certificate window.

Step 9. Restart the Cisco Tomcat service via the CLI command: **utils service restart Cisco Tomcat.**

It is recommended to open the CUCM (application, OS, and CCMUser) web page to ensure that the signed tomcat certificate working as wanted, that is, you can get to the web page without any certificate authentication warning.

Enabling Secure LDAP (LDAPS)

More often than not, you have the end-user database already created in an external LDAP server, which you would import in the CUCM to associate the end users with their IP Phones and other applications. However, it is expected of MS AD or any LDAP administrator and that of the IP Telephony administrator to be paranoia about the security of the user information in transit. This section walks you through enabling secure LDAP on your CUCM cluster, which ensures that the user information exchanged between the call control agent and the LDAP server is secure.

Note This example considers that the LDAP directory is the MS Active Directory.

Enabling Secure LDAP Connection Between CUCM and Microsoft Active Directory

The prerequisites are as follows:

- Ensure that DNS is configured on the network and that CUCM is set to use DNS to resolve names, that is, DNS Client on the CUCM is active.

- A username for the CUCM connection to the LDAP server should be set up by the LDAP Administrator. It should have read rights to the directory.

The process to secure the LDAP connection between the CUCM and Microsoft AD is as follows:

Step 1. When the user for CUCM is created, note the fully distinguished name of the location where it was created. This information should include the CN, the OU(s) and the DCs.

Step 2. Export a Windows root certificate from a Domain Controller (preferably the one that has a copy of the Global Catalog).

Note You can do this by going to the Certificate Export Wizard and exporting a DER-encoded binary X.509 certificate.

Step 3. When the certificate is exported, it has a .cer extension. When a .cer certificate is imported into CUCM, it produces two certificates automatically, with .der and .pem extensions, respectively.

Note If you want to set up more than one LDAP server, certificates must be obtained from all of them.

Step 4. Go to CUCM OS **Administration page > Security > Certificate Management > Upload Certificate**.

Step 5. In the Certificate Name field drop-down, select **directory-trust** (pre CUCM version 8.x) or **tomcat-trust** (CUCM version 8.x and later). In the Upload File field, browse to the location where the certificate from LDAP server was saved, and click to upload the certificate, as shown in Figure 9-22.

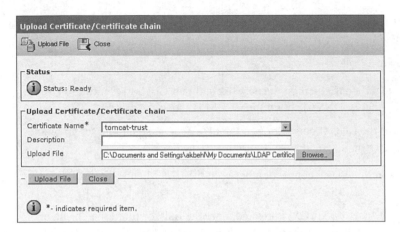

Figure 9-22   *Uploading the LDAP Certificate to CUCM Trust Store*

Note   Although the second field can remain blank, if the LDAP certificate is signed by an external CA or your internal CA, that certificate should be uploaded as well to CUCM under the previously explained heading and should be referred to as the root certificate. In the third field, it is always a good practice to have a description to identify the certificate among other certificates.

Step 6.   After the file has been successfully uploaded, click **Close**.

Note   If more than one certificate were obtained from more than one DC/GC server, repeat the previous two steps, and upload each certificate.

Step 7.   Repeat the previous steps on each of the Subscriber servers. All certificates from all LDAP servers that will be configured in the CUCM must be uploaded to the servers in the cluster.

Step 8.   After the certificate(s) has been uploaded to all nodes in the cluster, click the link for either the .pem or .der version of the certificates. This should open a window that shows the **FQDN/hostname** of the server that was issued the certificate.

Step 9.   Write down the CN just as it's listed, for example, if the name of the server says **CN=Publisher**, note this value; otherwise if it's listed as **CN=Publisher. XYZ.com**, then write down Publisher.XYZ.com. This will be used later when creating the CUCM LDAP Sync agreement.

Note   Remember that if there are than one LDAP servers configured, the "CN=" in each certificate will have to be noted.

Step 10. The CUCM servers should be ready for a secure connection to the MS AD. Now, you must configure the **LDAP System**, **LDAP Directory**, and **LDAP Authentication** in the CUCM Administration.

Step 11. Within the LDAP configuration pages in the CUCM Administration, enter the fully qualified name of the server. This name should be the same as what was noted in Step 9.

Note   CUCM and MS AD servers will only trust each other if they know the exact name (which is the CN) and it is for this reason that DNS entries should be defined correctly everywhere.

Step 12. After the server name is entered, the port number must be changed to the secure port (see Figure 9-23).

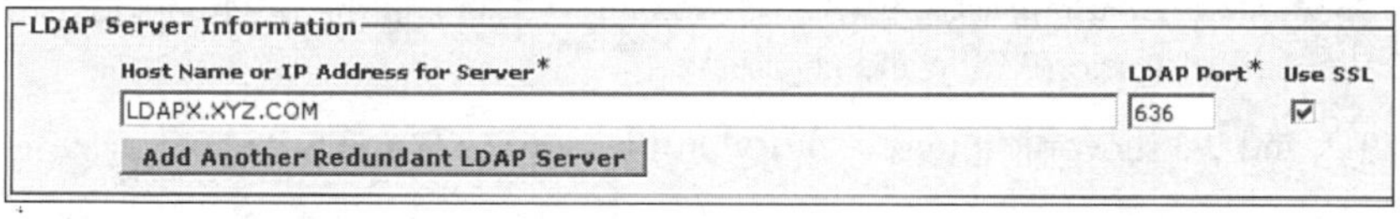

Figure 9-23   *Enabling Secure LDAP (Port and SSL)*

Note   For these settings, it is recommended to contact the MS AD administrator (or the person who issued the certificate). The secure port is usually 636 for a regular DC or 3269 for a GC.

Step 13. Check the **Use SSL** check box.

It is recommended to perform synchronization after the LDAP is configured. This ensures that the secure connection between the CUCM and MS AD works.

Note   If possible, schedule the sync to be performed during off-business hours to reduce the impact on bandwidth used for the contact sync, CPU, and memory of CUCM.

Securing IP Phone Conversation

You read earlier about how you can enable the CUCM secure mode or mixed mode. Once the CUCM Cluster is in mixed-mode, the IP Phones and trunks can be set up in encrypted, authenticated, or non-secure (unencrypted) modes.

Securing Cisco IP Phones

To secure a Cisco IP Phone, follow these steps:

Step 1.   Create a security profile for each model of the IP Phone that will support encrypted conversations. Go to **System > Security Profile > Phone Security Profile**, and click **Add New**.

Step 2.   In the Phone Security Profile Type drop-down, select the model number of the phone for which a profile needs to be created. Click **Next**.

Step 3.   Select the protocol the phone will use (SCCP or SIP), and click **Next**.

Step 4.   Give the profile a name and a description. The Name appears on the Device Security drop-down when a phone is created. In the Device Security Mode drop-down, select **Authenticated** if there is a requirement to authenticate the phone signaling. Select **Encrypted** if there is a requirement to encrypt the RTP and signaling streams.

Step 5.   In the Authentication Mode drop-down, the possible selections are **By Authentication String**, **By Null String**, **By Existing Certificate (Precedence to LSC)**, and **By Existing Certificate (Precedence to MIC)**. This states how encrypted communication happens between CUCM and the IP Phone. Set the Authentication Mode and click **Save**.

Tables 9-1, 9-2, and 9-3 show the phone security profiles for SCCP and SIP Phones.

Table 9-1   *6921 Phone Security Profile (SCCP)*

Parameter	Value
Product Type	6921
Device Protocol	SCCP
Name	Cisco 6921: Standard SCCP Encrypted Profile
Description	Cisco 6921: Standard SCCP Encrypted Profile
Device Security Mode	Encrypted
TFTP Encrypted Config	Unchecked
Authentication Mode	By Null String
Key Size	1024

Table 9-2 *7965 Phone Security Profile (SCCP)*

Parameter	Value
Product Type	7965
Device Protocol	SCCP
Name	Cisco 7965: Standard SCCP Encrypted Profile
Description	Cisco 7965: Standard SCCP Encrypted Profile
Device Security Mode	Encrypted
TFTP Encrypted Config	Unchecked
Authentication Mode	By Null String
Key Size	1024

Table 9-3 *9951 Phone Security Profile (SIP)*

Parameter	Value
Product Type	9951
Device Protocol	SIP
Name	Cisco 9951: Standard SIP Encrypted Profile
Description	Cisco 9951: Standard SIP Encrypted Profile
Device Security Mode	Encrypted
TFTP Encrypted Config	Unchecked
Authentication Mode	By Null String
Key Size	1024

Note   Using LSC is the most secure method. LSC is volatile and can be regenerated or re-installed if an existing certificate is compromised. Moreover, LSC has a default lifetime of 5 years, whereas MIC comes with a fixed lifetime of 10 years.

Step 6.   Repeat the aforementioned steps to create a profile for every model phone for which encryption will be configured. This can be done by copying the existing non-secure profile and creating the secure version of it.

Step 7.   Add a new phone (or go to an existing phone). Set the phone security profile to the wanted profile (non-secure or secure). Under the section Certificate Authority Proxy Function (CAPF) Information, click the drop-down for Certificate Operation and select **Install/Upgrade.** In the Authentication Mode drop-down, you can select **None** or **By Authentication String.**

Step 8.   Make sure the **Operation Completes By** setting is for some time in the near or distant future in which the download will be manually completed, for example, if you are not going to finish all phone provisioning and configuration downloads until Sunday, make sure the **Operation Completes By** setting reflects that.

Step 9.   After the phone registers, call another secure phone. After the call is answered, a **padlock icon** should show up next to the caller ID, confirming that the call is encrypted.

Identifying Encrypted and Authenticated Phone Calls

When security is implemented for a phone, you can identify authenticated or encrypted phone calls by icons on the screen on the phone. In an authenticated call, all devices participating in the establishment of the call are authenticated by the CUCM.

When a call in progress is authenticated, the Call Progress icon to the right of the call duration timer in the phone LCD screen changes to this icon:

In an encrypted call, all devices participating in the establishment of the call are authenticated by the CUCM. In addition, call signaling and media streams are encrypted. An encrypted call offers the highest level of security, providing integrity and privacy to the call. When a call in progress is being encrypted, the Call Progress icon to the right of the call duration timer in the phone LCD screen changes to an icon like this:

Note   If the call is routed through non-IP call legs, for example, PSTN, the call may be non-secure even though it is encrypted within the IP network and has a Lock icon associated with it.

Securing Third-Party SIP Phones

There may be a requirement in your network to have third-party SIP Phones (hard phones or softphones) and to secure them. At the onset of this section it is important to understand that the CUCM does not support Transport Layer Security (TLS) from or to third-party phones that are SIP based endpoints. Thus, SRTP and Secure Signaling is not an option with third-party IP Phones supporting SIP protocol as of today. The only available security option with a third-Party SIP phone is to use digest authentication credentials. Also, the third-party SIP Phones use their native configuration and do not leverage CUCM TFTP for downloading configuration files or firmware.

A CUCM server identifies a third-party SIP Phone using Digest credentials.

The REGISTER message includes the header shown in Example 9-5.

Example 9-5   *CUCM Third-Party Phone SIP Register Message Format*

```
Authorization: Digest
username="ciscouser",realm="ccmsipline",nonce="GBauADss2qoWr6k9y3hGGVDAqnLfoLk5",
    uri="
sip:10.100.100.100",algorithm=MD5,response="126c0643
a4923359ab59d4f53494552e"
```

Note   This is because third-party phones that run a SIP do not send a MAC address like Cisco IP Phones and must identify themselves by using a username.

Follow these steps to enable Digest Authentication for third-party SIP phones:

Step 1.   Go to **System > Security > Phone Security Profile**, and create a new Profile, for example, Third-Party SIP Phones. (You can copy the existing profile and create a new profile.)

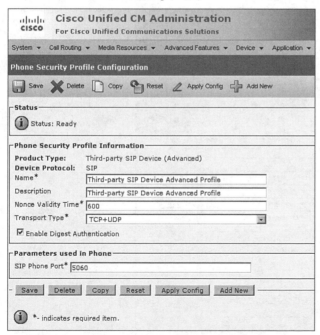

Figure 9-24   *Adding Third-Party SIP Device Security Profile*

Step 2.   Ensure that the **Enable Digest Authentication** check box is checked.

Note   In addition to providing Digest Authentication capability to the SIP Phone, it also prevents a malicious user from hijacking another user's SIP account.

Step 3.   **Click** Device > Phone and click **Add New.** In the drop-down list select the option for **Third Party SIP Device (Advanced or Basic).** Associate the SIP Trunk Security Profile created earlier with this device.

Note   While Third-Party SIP Device (Basic) supports one line and consumes three license units, the Third-Party SIP Device (Advanced) supports up to eight lines and video and consumes six license units.

Step 4.   Create an end user in the CUCM, assign a primary extension, and enter the password entered in the **Digest Credentials**. Also, associate the SIP Phone with this user (see Figure 9-25).

Note   This is the same password that will be entered in the SIP hard phone or softphone. This is required as per the Enable Digest Authentication box in the SIP Trunk Security Profile.

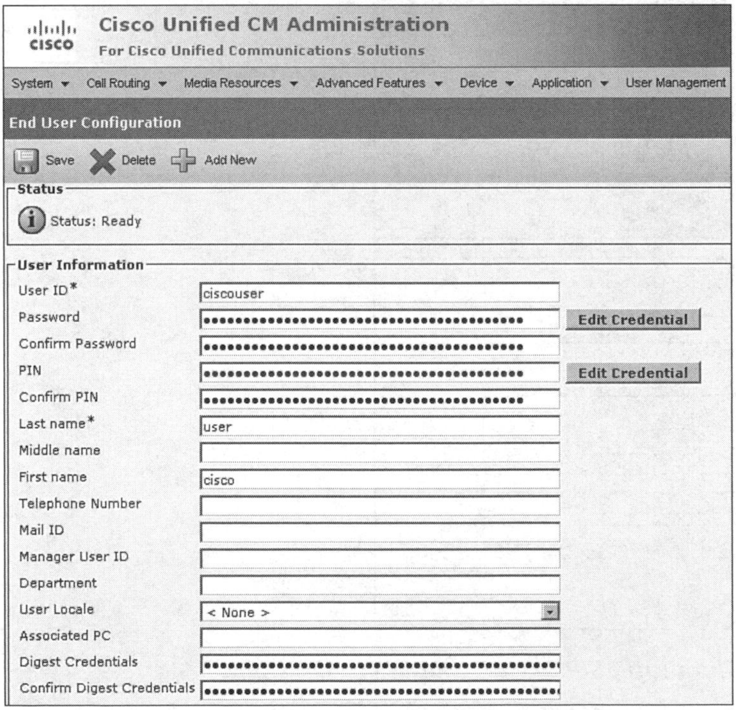

Figure 9-25   *User Configuration for Third- Party SIP Device Digest Credentials*

Step 5.   Associate the end user with the SIP Device (see Figure 9-26).

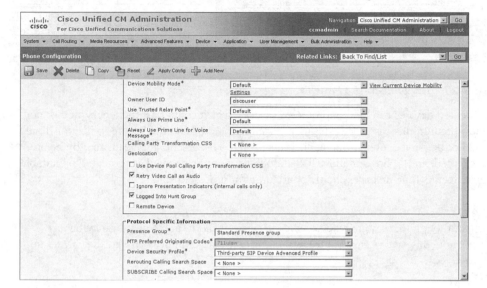

Figure 9-26   *Associating the End User with the Third-Party SIP Phone Device*

Configuring Third-Party SIP Phone

On the third-party SIP Phone (hard phone or softphone),

- Enter the **domain**, **authorization name**, and **password** (or their equivalent fields depending on SIP Phone provider's interface).

- The domain should be the IP address of the CUCM server, whereas the authorization name should match the name of the end user, and the password should match the Digest Credentials entered on the End User page.

Secure Tone

Cisco UCM provides an additional layer of security (and a sense of getting into a secure call) when a protected phone calls another protected phone. If the media is encrypted upon answering the call, both calling and called parties hear a 2-second secure indication tone at the beginning of the call, as shown in Figure 9-27. Both SCCP and SIP phones can be designated as protected phones.

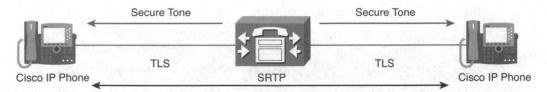

Figure 9-27 *IP Phone-to-IP Phone Protected Call with Secure Tone*

Protected devices can call nonprotected devices, which could be either encrypted or non-encrypted. In this case, the resulting call is nonprotected and the Secure Indication Tone will not be played, even if the media is encrypted. This essentially means that by being encrypted, an IP Phone or an MGCP endpoint cannot be deemed as protected or suitable for a Secure Tone unless explicitly configured for protected status.

Note Although this feature may seem to be an overhead to implement, it may be required in highly secure environments to have some sort of indication that the call set up is a protected call.

If a protected phone calls another protected phone, and the media is unencrypted, the call will be dropped. (An Encrypted Security Profile is necessary for protected status.)

The Secure Tone feature is also supported between IP phones and MGCP E1 PRI gateways, as shown in Figure 9-28. The MGCP gateway must be configured for SRTP encryption, that is, the SRTP Package must be enabled. The protected status is exchanged with the PRI gateway using the proprietary Facility IEs in the MGCP PRI Setup, Alert, and Connect messages. Although the CUCM plays only the secure indication tone to the IP Phone side, the tone to the other end is handled by a PBX in the network.

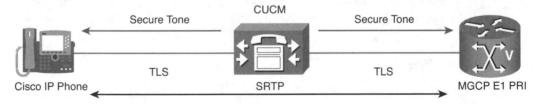

Figure 9-28 *IP Phone to MGCP E1 Gateway Protected Call with Secure Tone*

Note   The same rule applies in this case, too. If media between the IP Phone and the MGCP gateway is not encrypted, the call will be dropped.

Following are some facts about protected calls and endpoints:

- Multiline supplementary services such as call transfer, conference, and call waiting are disabled on protected phones.

- Extension Mobility and Join Across Line services are disabled on protected phones.

- Shared-line configuration is not available on protected phones.

- Hold/Resume and Call Forward All are supported for protected calls.

- Only intra-cluster IP-to-IP calls and IP-to-TDM calls through a voice (E1) gateway are supported.

- Only protected MGCP PRI E1 trunks are supported.

- Protected calls are supported only for voice calls, not video calls.

Note   A lock icon on an IP Phone display indicates only media encryption, not protection.

To enable Secure Tone on an IP Phone, follow the subsequent steps:

Step 1.   On the IP Phone CUCM GUI, configure the Soft key template to **Standard Protected Phone**, as shown in Figure 9-29.

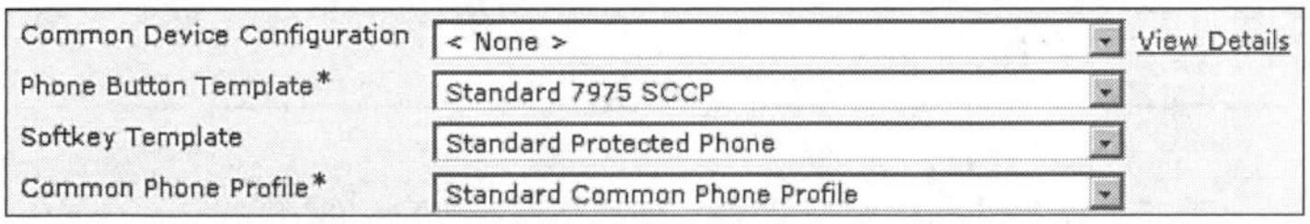

Figure 9-29   *IP Phone Protected Softkey Template*

Step 2.   Disable **Join Across Lines** option.

Step 3.   Check the check box labeled **Protected Device** **** (see Figure 9-30).

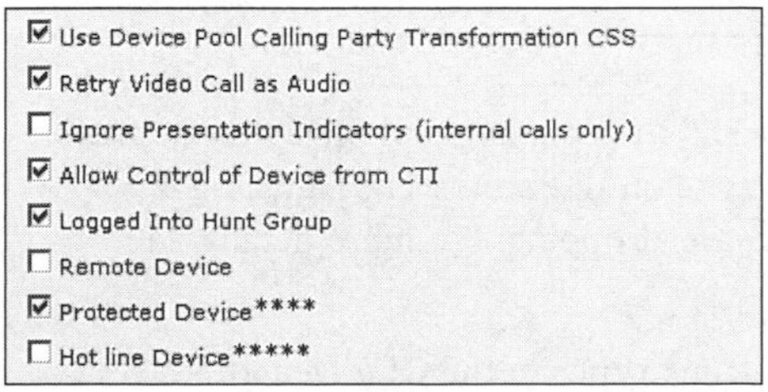

Figure 9-30   *Enabling Protected Device*

Step 4. Ensure that the IP Phone has an encrypted phone security profile applied to it.

> **Note** Without an encrypted security profile, you get an error if you try to save the phone configuration.

Step 5. Set the maximum calls and busy trigger to 1, under the directory number (DN) settings.

At this point, the IP Phone is set up for Secure Tone, in protected mode. The following section details how to configure the protected mode for MGCP PRI EURO (E1 PRI).

To configure MGCP gateway for supporting Secure Tone with a Protected IP Phone, the gateway should also support the Protected mode and SRTP. The following explains how this can be achieved.

Step 1. On an MGCP PRI E1 endpoint, the check box for **Enable Protected Facility IE** should be checked, as shown in Figure 9-31.

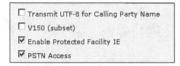

Figure 9-31 *Setting MGCP E1 PRI Gateway Endpoint for a Protected Facility*

Step 2. On the gateway, ensure that **SRTP package** is enabled, as shown in Example 9-6.

Example 9-6 *MGCP Gateway SRTP Package*

```
MGCPGW(config)# mgcp
MGCPGW(config)# mgcp call-agent 10.87.81.200 2427 service-type mgcp version 0.1
MGCPGW(config)# mgcp dtmf-relay voip codec all mode out-of-band
<output omitted>
MGCPGW(config)# mgcp package-capability srtp-package
MGCPGW(config)# no mgcp timer receive-rtcp
MGCPGW(config)# mgcp fax t38 inhibit
```

This enables the MGCP E1 endpoint to set up TLS for signaling and SRTP for media, which are required for Protected calls (Secure Tone on IP Phone). The signaling is still clear text and needs to be protected from eavesdropping. For more details, see Chapter 12.

In the next section, you discover the different trunk types in the CUCM and how to secure the signaling and media streams traversing the trunks.

CUCM Trunk Security

Trunks enable CUCM servers to communicate with other clusters, SIP gateways, and the gatekeeper. The four different types of trunks are as follows:

- Non-gatekeeper controlled inter-cluster trunk

- Gatekeeper (GK) controlled inter-cluster trunk

- H.225 trunk

- SIP trunk

A secure trunk could be an inter-cluster trunk (non GK or GK controlled), H.225 GK controlled, or a SIP trunk. The procedure to enable security on a trunk depends on the type of trunk.

> **Note**   MGCP, SIP, and H.323 gateway security is covered in Chapter 12, whereas gatekeeper and CUBE security is covered in Chapter 13.

ICT and H.225 (Gatekeeper Controlled) Secure Trunks

H.323 gateways and gatekeeper or non-gatekeeper controlled H.225/H.323/H.245 and Inter-Cluster trunks (ICT) support security. These devices can terminate SRTP (secure media) however, the signaling stream to CUCM is in clear text. The H.323, H.225, and H.245 devices generate the encryption keys, and these keys get sent to CUCM through the signaling path, which must be secured via IPSec, as shown in Figure 9-32.

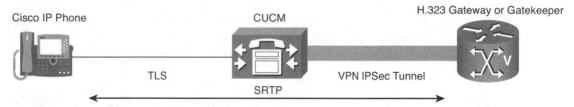

Figure 9-32   *IPSec Tunnel Between the CUCM and an H.323 Gateway or Gatekeeper*

Cisco recommends configuring IPSec tunnels with the device closest to the CUCM cluster, that is, a Layer 3 device capable to terminate IPSec tunnels and then send a clear text message to the CUCM. A suitable example is Cisco ASA Firewall, which can terminate IPSec tunnels from gateways, gatekeepers, and so on and then send a clear stream to the CUCM. This ensures that outside (non-trusted) and inside (trusted) zones are brokered by Cisco ASA and that CUCM server or cluster does not bear a rather unnecessary load of terminating IPSec tunnels. This topology is shown in Figure 9-33.

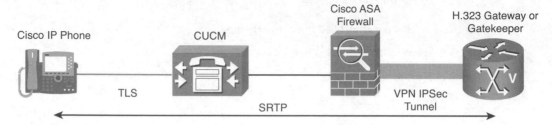

Figure 9-33 *IPSec Tunnel Offloaded to CUCM Trusted Next-Hop Cisco ASA Firewall*

The details of IOS configuration are covered in Chapter 13.

The **SRTP Allowed** check box must be checked in the device configuration window for an H.323 gateway, a H.225 trunk (gatekeeper controlled), the inter-cluster trunk (gatekeeper controlled), and the inter-cluster trunk (non-gatekeeper controlled) to have secure RTP established between an endpoint and the destination gateway.

Note The system can establish a secure media or signaling path with all devices (including originating and destination devices and midway trunks that support SRTP). If any device (originating endpoint or receiving endpoint or the trunk) does not support SRTP, the system uses an RTP connection, that is, SRTP-to-RTP fallback (and vice versa) occurs. This is applicable for transfers from a secure device to a non-secure device, conference bridge, transcoding, MoH, and so on.

For SRTP configured devices, such as endpoints and trunks, CUCM categorizes a call as encrypted if the SRTP Allowed check box is checked and if the SRTP capabilities for the devices are successfully negotiated for the call. If these criteria are not met, CUCM classifies the call as non-secure and reverts it to use RTP.

Note Faststart calls over a trunk or gateway are categorized as non-secure. SRTP does not interoperate with Faststart.

CUCM also enables gateways and trunks to transparently pass through the shared secret (DH key) and other H.235 data between two H.235 endpoints, to enable the two endpoints to establish a SRTP channel. This can be implemented by checking the passing **H.235 Pass Through Allowed** check box in the configuration settings of the following trunks and gateways:

- H.225 trunk

- ICT gatekeeper control

- ICT non-gatekeeper control

- H.323 gateway

SIP Trunk Security

SIP trunks support both encrypted signaling and media. To enable SIP trunk security, you must create a security profile like you did for IP Phones. The major difference is that this security profile is specific to SIP trunks and gives you many more options that a phone profile.

To configure the SIP trunk security profile, follow the subsequent steps:

Step 1.   Go to **System > Security Profile > SIP Trunk Security Profile**.

Step 2.   Set the device Security Mode as **Encrypted**, Incoming Transport Type to **TLS**, and Outgoing Transport Type to **TLS**.

Note There are many more options, such as digest authentication, unsolicited notification, and so on. Except for the former, you can enable a check box for almost everything else, that is, Accept Presence Subscription, Accept Out-of-Dialog REFER, Accept Unsolicited Notification, Accept Replaces Header, and Transmit Security Status.

Figure 9-34 shows an example of a SIP trunk security profile.

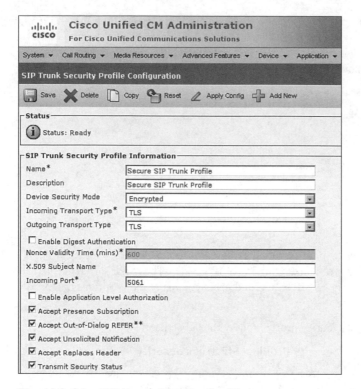

Figure 9-34   *SIP Trunk Security Profile*

Step 3.   After the SIP trunk security profile is configured, apply it to the SIP trunk. Go to **Device > Trunk > SIP Trunk**, and choose the trunk on which you want to enable secure signaling and media. Set SIP Trunk Security Profile to Secure Profile (see Figure 9-35).

Figure 9-35   *SIP Trunk Security Profile Applied to SIP Trunk*

Step 4.   Finally, check the **SRTP Allowed** check box in the trunk configuration (see Figure 9-36).

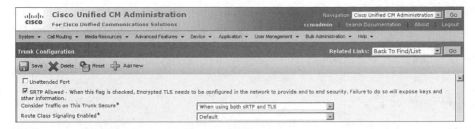

Figure 9-36 *SRTP Option Enabled for SIP Trunk*

> **Note** When selecting SRTP Allowed, the option Consider Traffic on This Trunk Secure is automatically set to When Using Both SRTP and TLS.

Using a secure profile for an SRTP-enabled trunk is highly recommended by Cisco so that keys and other security-related information do not get exposed during call setup. Also, to ensure that SRTP is supported for all calls, configure the SIP trunk for Delayed Offer.

Inter Cluster Trunk Security

In CUCM Inter Cluster Trunk (ICT), secure media (SRTP) can be configured just like it is in CUCM Inter Cluster Trunk Gatekeeper controlled trunk. When the SRTP Allowed check box is checked, the trunk supports SRTP capabilities, provided that the endpoints in both the originating and terminating cluster support SRTP capability. IPSec policies between the two clusters can be implemented to encrypt the signaling.

SME Trunk Security

CUCM Session Management Edition (SME) is a single front-end system via which, the multisite distributed call processing can be deployed. It acts as a single interface to interconnect numerous systems. SME is essentially a CUCM cluster dedicated for trunk interfaces only. It enables aggregation of multiple unified communications systems, referred to as leaf systems (thereby providing consolidation of Dial Plan). Although SME provides benefits of a single interface between contrasting entities, the media and signaling must be secured through the SME SIP trunks.

> **Note** The security of SME SIP trunks is not different from a regular SIP trunk and both signaling and media streams can be secured.

SME media encryption can be configured by checking the SIP trunk's SRTP Allowed check box. Figure 9-37 gives an overview of the CUCM SME SIP trunk security. However, this will allow the trunk to carry only SRTP traffic and does not encrypt the signaling traversing the trunk. Therefore, the session keys used to establish the secure media stream will be sent in the clear unless the signaling between CUCM and the destination SIP trunk device (SME cluster to leaf clusters or vice versa) is also encrypted, so that keys and other security-related information do not get exposed during call negotiations.

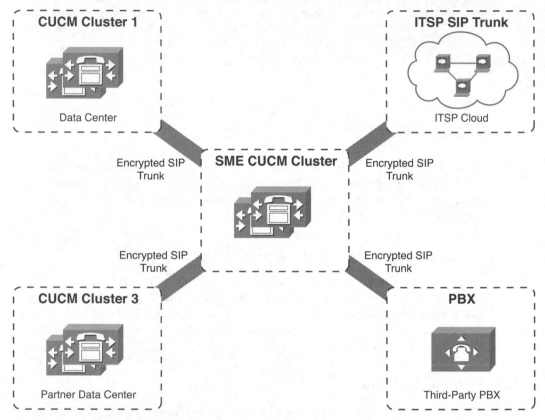

Figure 9-37 *SME SIP Trunk Security Overview*

SME SIP trunks use TLS for signaling encryption (just like any other SIP trunk). TLS is configured on the SIP Security Profile associated with the SIP trunk (as explained in the SIP trunk security section). TLS uses X.509 certificates to authenticate trunk devices and to enable signaling encryption. These certificates can be either imported to each CUCM node from every device that requires establishing a TLS connection or can be signed by a Certificate Authority (CA) so that all entities trust a common trust introducer, and there is no need to import the certificates of the remote devices because only the CA certificate needs to be imported.

Trusted Relay Point (TRP)

In any IP Telephony network design, as a best practice recommendation, you must have a clear segregation between data and voice traffic (VLANs) so that voice can get preferential treatment over data because of its nature of being real-time and non reproducible. Ideally, voice services will also be logically separated from data services and should also be logically separated from voice access devices, for example, logically separate call control, media providers, and voice endpoints.

Trusted Relay Point (TRP) is a software function that runs on Cisco network devices such as campus switches and routers (it can be compared to an MTP) and is dynamically inserted in the call flow by the call agent (CUCM) when requested. Effectively, it provides a trusted anchoring point for media to enable two fundamental functionalities:

- QoS enforcement
- Trusted VLAN traversal

For the Trusted QoS Enforcement, this mechanism can be applied equally to softphones (which are the natural target) and any endpoint incapable of marking QoS correctly, as long as it registers with CUCM. The topic of major interest from IP Telephony security standpoint here is the Trusted VLAN traversal. The current mechanisms today require opening up a wide range of ports just to allow media from the data VLAN (softphones) into the voice VLAN (VACLs or alternatively using the phone proxy with Cisco ASA (as explained in Chapter 8, "Perimeter Security with Cisco Adaptive Security Appliance").

Opening up a range of ports required for voice media traffic means that other untrusted and malicious applications running on host machine along with a softphone could also send traffic into the voice VLAN. TRP ensures that only media streams controlled by the CUCM will enter the voice VLAN, and thus these streams can be trusted from only the softphones registered with your CUCM cluster. TRP anchors or stitches the media streams together from softphones resident in data VLAN and Cisco IP Phones (wired or wireless) in voice VLAN, as shown in Figure 9-38.

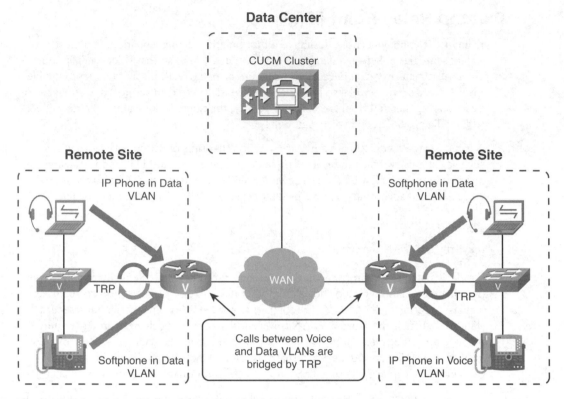

Figure 9-38 *Trusted Relay Point Secure VLAN Traversal Overview*

Following are the salient features of TRP for secure VLAN traversal:

■ TRP enables secure IP Phone connectivity by securely bridging only authorized media from data to voice VLAN.

■ TRP can also remark the QoS for authorized traffic from the softphones.

■ TRP concept was introduced in CUCM 7.0.

Let's now look into how to enable TRP in your network. In essence, TRP can be enabled for

■ Endpoints (anything that terminates media)

■ Media Termination Points (MTP)

To enable TRP for IP Phones, select the appropriate option from the IP Phone GUI, as shown in Figure 9-39.

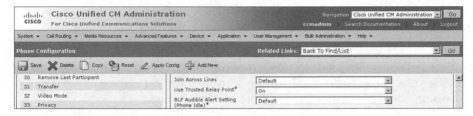

Figure 9-39 *Enabling TRP for IP Phone*

To enable TRP for MTP/Transcoder devices, enable the check box on the MTP/
Transcoder GUI.

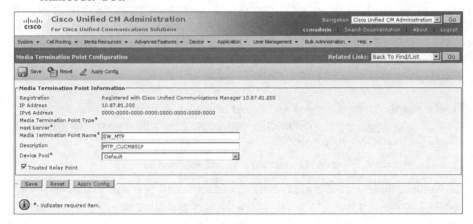

Figure 9-40 *Enabling TRP for MTP*

Note You can set the **Fail Call if Trusted Relay Point Allocation Fails** Parameter under
the CUCM service parameters to True or False. The call fails if no TRP resource is available
and if the parameter is set to True. The call proceeds regardless even if a TRP resource is
not available if this parameter is set to False.

Preventing Toll Fraud

To begin with, let's define toll fraud:

*Toll fraud is the unlawful use of a phone system or services to make long distance or
international calls.*

Toll fraud is a criminal activity analogous to computer hacking. Toll fraud is not a new
issue; it has been around since the Plain Old Telephony System (POTS) days. It is still relevant in IP Telephony, as it was in Traditional PBX systems. It is an industry wide crisis,

tallying over one billion dollars annually lost. Toll fraud can be in many forms, for example, calling local numbers, mobile phones, paid premium numbers, and long-distance (international) numbers. Now, you know the problem. So, what is the solution?

Cisco has various mechanisms via which you can restrain toll fraud and even stop it in its tracks. However, following your IP Telephony security policy is the foremost step while implementing steps and configuring CUCM to curtail toll fraud.

Partitions and Calling Search Spaces

Partitions and calling search spaces provide segmentation and access control to the number that can be called or can call someone. They are your primary lines of defense against rogue internal or external callers. By restricting calling privileges, you can be assured that no internal endpoint can call any internal or external destination unless the IP Telephony administrator assigns the appropriate calling privileges to that endpoint.

As a general rule:

- Call forward (All, Busy, No Answer) should be limited to internal partition only (unless as per the IP Telephony security policy, it is permitted for a certain class of users, for example, directors and above).

- Line logged out CSS should be restricted to internal partition.

- Adopting a line-device approach offers maximum flexibility in dial plan design as well as improved security by restricting at line level and allowing at device level (as specified by the IP Telephony security policy).

Time of Day Routing

Time of Day Routing allows certain partitions to be active during a pre-set time time-span during a day and post this period; these partitions become inactive automatically. Essentially, it allows or disallows a partition to be active during a certain predefined period during a day in a week. To create a Time of Day Routing schedule, follow the steps:

Step 1.   Explore the time period for which you want a partition to be active. This could be business hours, for example, Monday to Friday 9 a.m. to 5 p.m.

Step 2.   Group all time periods into one time schedule.

Note   If the time slots cannot be grouped into one time period, define multiple time periods.

Step 3.   Apply the time schedule to partitions.

Step 4.   Assign the partitions to respective calling search spaces (CSS).

Step 5.   Assign these CSS to the IP Phones.

Note Time of Day Routing can be applied to both internal and external destinations (numbers). If you want differential call treatment based on Time of Day Routing, you must define the same number twice, once in each partition, where one partition may be Time of Day Routing enabled partition, whereas the other is a normal partition. In this case, the Time of Day Routing enabled partition will be listed above the normal partition in the CSS.

Block Off-Net to Off-Net Transfers

There is a parameter in CUCM that allows or disallows off-net to off-net transfers. This is useful when your IP Telephony security policy does not permit off-net to off-net transfers to hold back toll fraud. This parameter is a cluster wide service parameter **Block OffNet to OffNet Transfer**. When enabled, it can block any off-net to off-net call transfers from endpoints thereby minimizing the risk of anyone misusing the feature for transferring local PSTN calls to international destinations.

Conference Restrictions

Toll fraud can also be committed using the conferencing capability of an endpoint. An attacker or a rogue user can conference a local call with an international number. While it can be stopped by restricting the CSS of the source endpoint, it does not prevent a user in a conference call (internal or external) user to invoke conference calls to long distance or international numbers, illegitimately. Ad hoc conference calls can optionally be dropped when the originator hangs up. This ensures that the other parties (such as external users) cannot initiate a call to another external number using your IP Telephony system.

Note The conference call can be dropped by setting a CUCM service parameter under **Clusterwide Parameters > Feature > Conference**, that is, Drop Ad Hoc Conference when conference controller leaves.

Calling Rights for Billing and Tracking

A Forced Authentication Code (FAC) can be used to control the access to international and long distance calls. When a call is routed through a route pattern where FAC is applied, CUCM plays a tone that is an indication for the user to enter the authorization code to proceed with the call. If the authorization code entered is within the level of authorization, the call matures; otherwise, the user gets a reorder tone. FAC associated calls are logged to the CUCM Call Detail Records (CDR). The CDR records can be used to track the usage for billing and tracking prohibited attempts.

Route Filters for Controlled Access

Route filters should be deployed to filter out any unwanted area codes and calls to known paid premium numbers. Route filters can help reduce the chances of people with unlimited access dialing the otherwise prohibited paid service numbers. Route filters make the system more flexible and easier to administer your outbound calling. They give you the ability to block certain area codes or country codes based on your requirement of not giving access to any user to dial these specific numbers. For example, a route pattern with 9.@ will cover all North American Numbering Plan (NANP) dial plan. To restrict premium numbers, for example, 900 numbers, you can create a route filter and assign it to the route pattern, which may not be very specific.

Note If you are not using a 9.@ route pattern and using specific route patterns, route filters may not be helpful. In this case, you can configure specific routing and blocking route patterns.

Access Restriction for Protocols from User VRF

Since Cisco IP Telephony has a clearly defined working model in which the end points (hard phones, softphones, or gateways) establish signaling with call control (that is, CUCM) unit and media with other endpoints (such as IP Phones and gateways), there is no reason for a user endpoint to send TCP to a gateway directly. Any such attempts should be blocked and logged.

Note There are third-party softphones and agents that can initiate SIP or H.323 signaling directly with IOS gateways enabling UA (SIP) or Client Server (H.323) relationship. This enables these endpoints to establish direct signaling and media channels by passing the actual legitimate call control (CUCM) therefore opening flood gates for toll fraud.

Social Engineering

An employee from within the organization can persuade an operator or a colleague with unrestricted calling access to the PSTN to conference a call with an international or a long distance number. Otherwise, someone from outside the organization can lure the operator (imitating an internal user) into connecting the call to an international number therefore resulting into toll fraud. These issues can be handled by clearly stating the Do's and Don'ts in the IP Telephony security policy. It is all about employee education and awareness that can curb social engineering or any imitation attempts.

Securing CTI/JTAPI Connections

In Cisco IP Telephony, Computer Telephony Integration (CTI) and Java Telephony Application Programming Interface (JTAPI) provide a means of communication between applications and clients to CUCM. CUCM enables you to secure the signaling connections and media streams between CTIManager and CTI/JTAPI/TAPI applications.

While considering securing CTI/JTAPI applications in your Cisco IP Telephony network, a prerequisite is having the CUCM cluster in mixed mode and that you configured security settings during the Cisco JTAPI/TSP plug-in installation on the client machine/server. The Cisco CUCM CTIManager process and the CTI application verify each other's identity through a mutually authenticated TLS handshake.

Note   When a TLS connection occurs, CTIManager and the application exchange Quick Buffer Encoding (CTIQBE) messages via the TLS port, port 2749.

To secure the user/application connection to CTIManager, you must add the application user or end users to the Standard CTI Secure Connection user group. If you want the application and CTIManager to secure the media streams, you must add the application user or end users to the Standard CTI Allow Reception of SRTP Key Material user group, as shown in Figure 9-41.

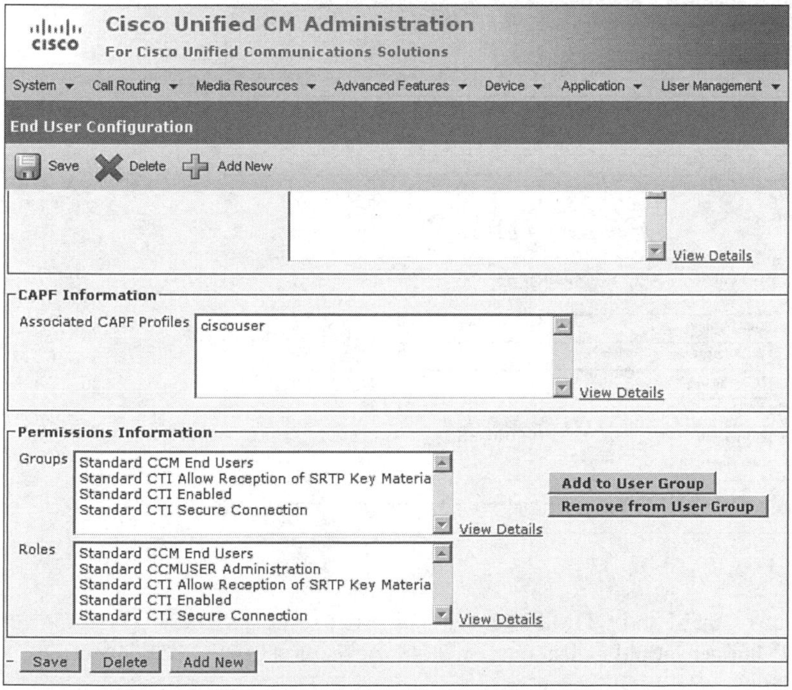

Figure 9-41   *End-User CTI Security Group Enrollment*

Note   You can assign a CTI application to either an application user or an end user.

To enable CTI security on your CUCM Cluster, follow these steps:

Step 1.   On the **Device > Phone** page check **Allow Control of Device from CTI** for the phone you want to monitor or control.

Step 2.   Associate your end user or application user with the phone.

Step 3.   Add the user to the groups **CTI Enabled**, **CTI Secure Connection**, and **CTI Allow Reception of SRTP Key Material**.

Note   Adding the user to the Secure CTI and SRTP Key Material groups means that this JTAPI user will be allowed to connect only on the secure port 2749.

Step 4.   Under **Users > End / Application User CAPF Profile**, select the certificate operation of **Install / Upgrade** for the JTAPI user (see Figure 9-42).

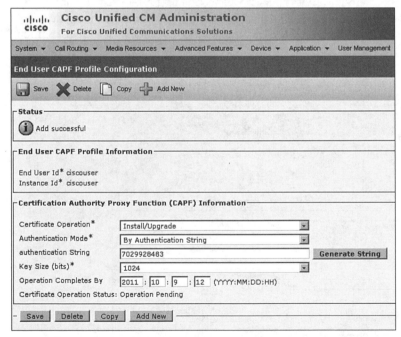

Figure 9-42   *End-User CAPF Profile*

Step 5.   Restart CUCM and CTIManager services. After restarting these services, CTIManager should be listening on 2749 for secure JTAPI/QBE connections.

JTAPI Client Config

Follow these steps to configure JTAPI client security on user endpoints:

Step 1.   Install the **Cisco JTAPI Client** on the server or client PC where JTAPI will be running. Make sure to download JTAPI for either Windows or Linux.

Step 2.   Under either the Start menu, or the JTAPITools directory, find **the JTAPI Preferences** tool.

Step 3.   Add **CUCM CTIManager server(s)** under **Cisco UCM** (see Figure 9-43).

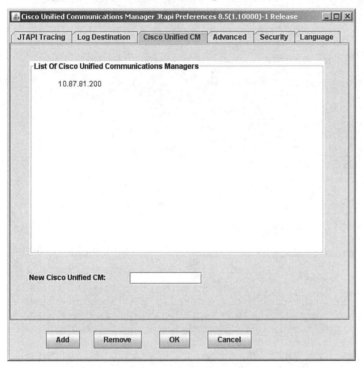

Figure 9-43   *JTAPI Client CUCM Servers*

Step 4.   On the **Security tab**, set the appropriate settings for your CUCM cluster, CAPF user, and so on, and click **Update Certificate** (see Figure 9-44).

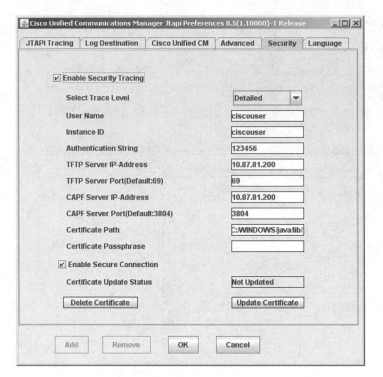

Figure 9-44 *JTAPI Client Security Configuration*

The Authentication String and Instance ID must match the User's CAPF Profile.

Note It is recommended to have the security traces enabled for JTAPI Client because it helps in troubleshooting the issues while connecting on a secure channel to CTIManager.

Application User CAPF Profile can be configured on same lines as the end-user CAPF profile. CUCM Manager Assistant, Cisco QRT, and Cisco Web Dialer services do not support encryption.

Restricting Administrative Access (User Roles and Groups)

Do you allow everyone in your network team full access to your network devices? The answer is probably no. Then, there is no reason why you would not like to have same the restrictive/privilege level access in your Cisco IP Telephony network.

Roles allow CUCM administrators (who have full administration privilege) to configure end users and application users with different levels of concession. This means that you have the ability to provide full read-write access or only read access to certain users (as defined by your organizational IP Telephony security policy). There are categories of users in CUCM:

CUCM End Users

These are users associated with a CUCM end user or administrative group. These users support interactive login.

CUCM Application Users

These users are associated with features or applications, for example, Cisco Unified Manager Assistant, Cisco Unified Attendant Console, and so on. These users serve only for integrating or authenticating the various Cisco and third-party applications with CUCM. These users are not intended to and cannot do an interactive login.

You must ensure that you have various categories for end users, which can be actual end user leveraging IP Telephony services or can be an administrative user managing and configuring the CUCM. Ideally, you should have a clear demarcation of full administrators versus partial (limited rights) administrators. Not everyone in your organization is equally skilled at managing the IP Telephony system or for the sake of becoming an administrator should have full rights. It is highly recommended to segregate the different classes of users based on your requirements and as driven by your security policy, for example:

- **CUCM Administrators:** Full read and write access

- **CUCM Power Administrators:** Partial write and full read access

- **CUCM Management Administrators:** Full read access, no write access

- **CUCM AXL Administrator:** Only AXL-related read/write access

- **CUCM End User:** Only standard CCM end-user access

And so on.

Note   This example is a hypothetical system management setup and is not to be taken as is or as a baseline. Every network has a different requirement driven by the security policy, business vision, and goals. Thus, you should decide on the requirements for your network based on the various aforesaid parameters.

Let's go over the process to add a user to CUCM DB and assigning privileges to it:

Step 1.   Go to **User Management > End User > Add New**.

Step 2.   Fill in the required information, for example, user name, password, PIN, and so on.

Step 3.   For assigning Roles/Permissions to the end user, click **Add to User Group** in the Permission Information section.

Step 4.   CUCM have multiple Groups for different types of users. Select the one required by this end user and click **Add Selected**; click **Save**.

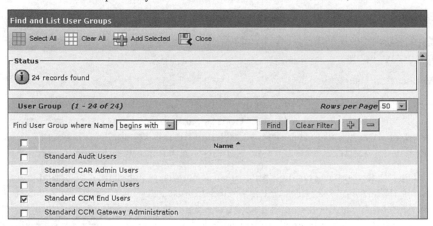

Figure 9-45   *Adding User Group/Roles*

Step 5.   The role(s) related to the group(s) selected should appear in the roles window.

Note   A CUCM Application user can be configured in the same way.

Having different classes of users ensures that the access rights are distributed clearly and that there is no redundancy in functionality (job and responsibility).

For more information on privilege-based access using groups and roles, go to http://www.cisco.com/en/US/products/sw/voicesw/ps556/products_tech_note-09186a00808c82d2.shtml.

Fighting Spam Over Internet Telephony (SPIT)

Spam over Internet Telephony (SPIT) is like just superfluous e-mail. Although latter is better known as SPAM, the former is known as Voice SPAM. As explained in Chapter 1, SPIT can cause a major aggravation to IP Telephony administrators and users alike since spam calls are disruptive to business. SPIT can lead to busy PSTN channels, high-processing load on the CUCM and voicemail and endpoints (IP Phones) unable to answer calls. Figure 9-46 gives an overview of SPIT in action.

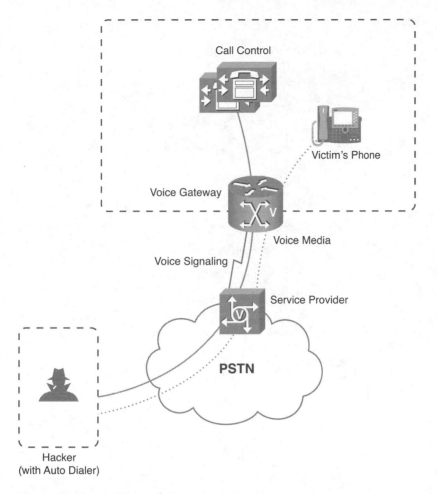

Figure 9-46 *SPIT Attack Overview*

The Cisco approach to address this threat is Malicious Call Identification service (MCID). MCID is a service by which a user that has received a malicious call from another network, typically the PSTN, may initiate a sequence of events that immediately notifies the on-net personnel (CUCM system administrator), flags the on-net (CUCM cluster) Call Detail Records (CDR), and notifies the off-net (PSTN) system or service provider of the malicious nature of the call to allow the off-net system to take actions, such as notifying legal authorities. This feature is supported in IOS gateways that terminate PSTN links. Figure 9-47 gives an insight to MCID implementation.

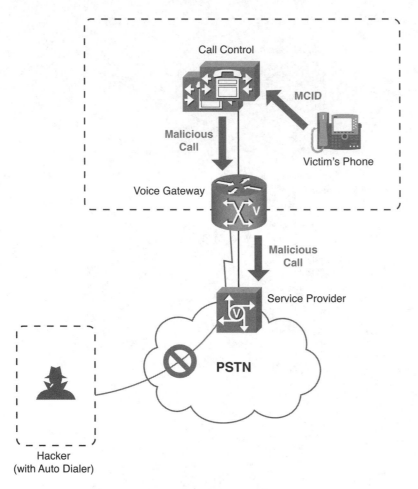

Figure 9-47 *MCID Helps in Thwarting SPIT*

The next section explores the audit capability support by Cisco UCM.

CUCM Security Audit (Logs)

In large organizations, there is customarily a need to log and report any and all changes happening in the network, so that if there is an issue reported related to human error, the same can be quickly identified and fixed. CUCM administrators have been given the power to perform an audit trail for administrative changes that occur in their CUCM cluster. The ability to enable auditing for administrative tasks has been introduced from CUCM version 7.1(2) and later. CUCM has several audit logs:

- Application

- Database

- Operating system

- Remote support account

Application Log

The application audit log can be used to track configuration changes and activities for the following applications and services:

- CUCM administrative web pages

- CUCM serviceability web pages

- Command Line Interface (CLI)

- Real Time Monitoring Tool (RTMT)

- Disaster Recovery System (DRS)

- CDR Analysis and Reporting (CAR)

Database Log

This log can track changes to the schema, updates, and reads. These logs can be accessed from RTMT using the Cisco Audit Logs/Informix audit logs subfolder.

Operating System Log

The CUCM appliance OS has functions and running routines in the background. The activities of these functions and routines can be tracked via the system's audit logging. The OS audit log shows you when a process was executed, and what was executed, the process ID, and so on. CUCM OS logs can be enabled or disabled by the commands shown in Example 9-7.

Example 9-7   *OS Log Audit Enable/Disable Commands*

```
admin:utils auditd enable
!
admin:utils auditd disable
```

The status of audit service can be discovered by the command shown in Example 9-8.

Example 9-8   *OS Log Audit Status Command*

```
admin:utils auditd status
```

These logs can be accessed from RTMT using the Cisco Audit Logs/vos subfolder.

Note   The vos folder does not display in RTMT unless the audit is enabled in the CLI.

Remote Support Accounting Log

If you have ever engaged with Cisco TAC and the TAC engineer requested remote access to your CUCM cluster, he accessed the root shell and look/touch/modify things that you cannot do. Remote support accounting log tracks the CLI commands issued by the TAC personnel.

Note   You cannot enable/disable this auditing feature because it is automatically enabled when the remote support account is enabled.

These logs can be accessed from RTMT using the Cisco Audit Logs/vos subfolder.

Enabling Audit Logs

By default, audit logs for administrative level tasks are enabled. To access this feature, you need to browse the audit log parameters from Cisco Unified Serviceability. The following procedures can be used to accomplish this task:

Step 1.   Go to **Cisco Unified Serviceability** on your CUCM server.

Step 2.   Go to **Tools > Audit Log Configuration**, as shown in Figure 9-48.

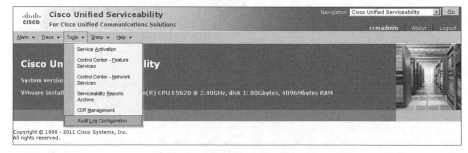

Figure 9-48   *Enabling CUCM Audit Logging*

Step 3.   Configure the **Audit Log** parameters, as shown in Figure 9-49.

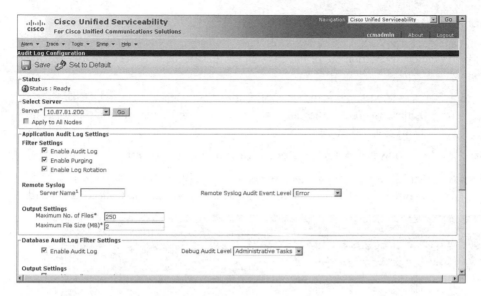

Figure 9-49 *Configuring CUCM Audit Log Parameters*

Step 4. Assuming that you have users identified for looking into Audit logs, assign
the Standard Audit Log Administration role to these predefined users/groups,
as shown in Figure 9-50.

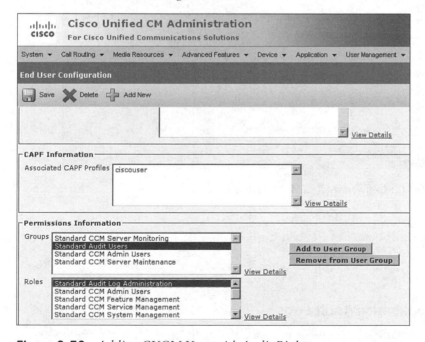

Figure 9-50 *Adding CUCM User with Audit Rights*

Collecting and Analyzing CUCM Audit Logs

You can access the Audit Logs using Real Time Monitoring Tool (RTMT). It is available as a plug-in under Application tab of CUCM. Follow these steps to collect and analyze audit logs.

Step 1. Load RTMT on your admin workstation, and connect to your CUCM cluster using a user ID that has the Standard Audit Log Administration role (or equivalent) assigned.

Step 2. Go to **System > Tools > Trace > Trace and Logs Central**.

Step 3. Under Trace and Logs Central, you have an option for Audit Logs (see Figure 9-51). Double-click the menu item to start the Log Collection Wizard.

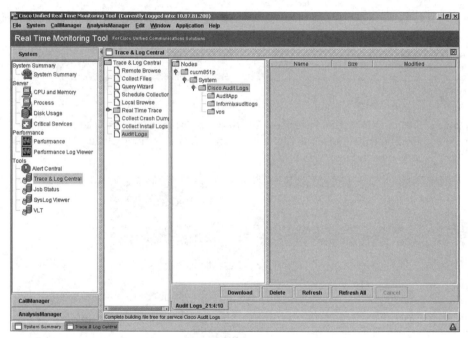

Figure 9-51 *RTMT: Collecting CUCM Audit Logs*

> **Note** You can either download the audit logs or browse them from the server using RTMT.

Analyzing Application Audit Logs

As Cisco IP Telephony administrator, an application audit log will have the most useful information for you. It tells you access and information accessed or changed from the

CCMAdministrator, RTMT, DRS, and so on web pages and applications. Also, it is this log that is presented in a decrypted form. A typical log is shown in Example 9-9.

Example 9-9 *CUCM Application Audit Log*

```
07:03:00.392 |LogMessage   UserID : ccmadmin  ClientAddress : 10.65.85.63
Severity : 5  EventType : GeneralConfigurationUpdate  ResourceAccessed: CUCMAdmin
EventStatus : Success  CompulsoryEvent : No  AuditCategory : AdministrativeEvent
ComponentID : Cisco CUCM Administration  AuditDetails :  record in table
securityprofile with key field name = Third Party SIP Phones added  App ID: Cisco
Tomcat Cluster ID:  Node ID: CUCM851P

10:52:28.337 |LogMessage   UserID : ccmadmin  ClientAddress : 10.65.80.107  Severity :
5  EventType : GeneralConfigurationUpdate  ResourceAccessed: CUCMAdmin  EventStatus :
Success  CompulsoryEvent : No  AuditCategory : AdministrativeEvent  ComponentID :
Cisco CUCM Administration  AuditDetails :  record in table enduser with key field
userid = ciscouser updated  App ID: Cisco Tomcat Cluster ID:
Node ID: CUCM851P
```

While the first one deciphers to a third-party SIP Security Profile added in CUCM DB, the second one refers to ciscouser details updated in CUCM DB. As you can notice, the audit logs clearly show the timestamp, source IP Address (of the machine which was used to access CUCM), the user ID that was used to access the CUCM, the table that was modified (securityprofile in the first snippet and enduser in second), and the information that was added or amended.

In the next section, you will learn about the new Single Sign-On application feature of Cisco UCM 8.5 and later releases.

Single Sign-On (SSO)

With so many IP Telephony applications that need user directory information and authentication, users end up asking the following:

Why do I need to provide credentials in every system that I use?

Why do I need to update all the applications when I change my password?

While it is an administrative nightmare to micromanage each user's credentials, it is even more stickier situation from a user perspective. To resolve these issues, Cisco developed a single sign-on (SSO) solution for IP Telephony applications.

This new feature is available in CUCM release 8.5(1) and later, and enables the IP Telephony administrator to allow a user to authenticate once and gain access to a variety of applications. Once SSO is enabled on a CUCM server, the end user will have the ability to authenticate once and gain access to applications and resources that otherwise would have required individual authentication.

For CUCM release 8.5, the CUCM user web page and CUCIMOC applications are available for SSO. It is important to understand that SSO is not a reduced Sign On or a simplified Sign On process.

SSO Overview

For SSO, the following applications are involved:

CUCM components:

- CCMUser WebApp (ccmui component)
- CTI Manager
- CCMCIP/UDS

Clients:

- Client PC Web Browser (for CCMUser web pages)
- CUCiMOC Application (CSF)

System Requirements for SSO

For enabling SSO in your organization, the following requirements must be met:

- Cisco Unified Communications Manager release 8.5(1) or later
- Microsoft Windows Server 2003 or 2008
- Microsoft Active Directory
- ForgeRock Open Access Manager (OpenAM) version 9.0

In addition, the non-Cisco (third-party) products must meet the following configuration requirements:

- Microsoft Active Directory must be deployed in a Windows domain-based network configuration, not just as an LDAP server.
- The OpenAM server must be accessible on the network to all client systems, and the Active Directory server, that is, share the user and the Microsoft application VRF.
- DNS must be enabled in the domain.
- CUCM server/cluster must be in the same domain as Active Directory (Domain Controller) server, Windows clients, and OpenAM.
- NTP should be configured, that is, the clocks of all the entities participating in SSO must be synchronized.

Figure 9-52 shows the SSO logical flow between an endpoint and the destination server.

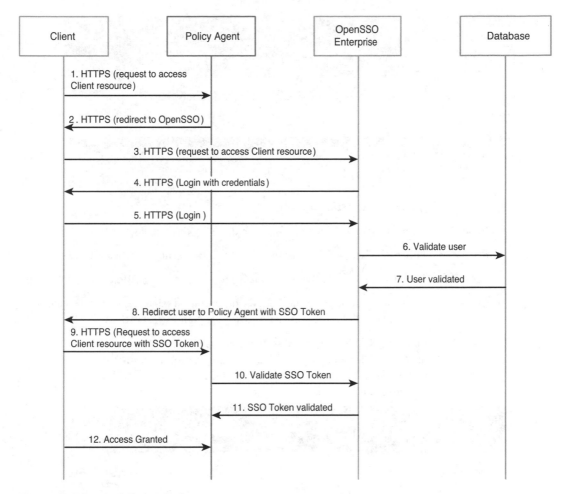

Figure 9-52 *SSO Logical Flow*

The next sections walk you through the configuration of the OpenAM SSO server and CUCM server to support the SSO process for end users.

Configuring OpenAM SSO Server

The following steps detail the process to configure the OpenSSO server for enabling SSO:

Step 1. Log in to the OpenSSO server with the **amAdmin** username and password (which was set during the initial setup).

Step 2. Go to the Access Control tab, and click /(**Top Level Realm**), as shown in Figure 9-53.

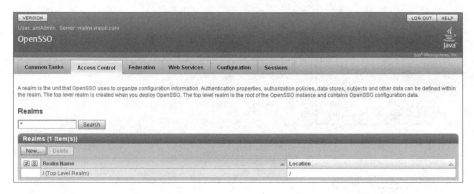

Figure 9-53 *OpenSSO: Access Control*

Step 3. Go to the **Authentication** tab. Click the **All Core Settings** option.

Step 4. Under All Core options, set the User Profile to **Ignored**. Click **Save**.

Step 5. Click **Go Back to Authentication**. Go to **Policies tab > Add a New Policy**.

Step 6. Create a new Rule from the Policy Configuration page. Select the service type as **URL Policy Agent (with Resource Name)**. Click **Next**.

Step 7. Enter the Rule Name and Resource URL as the Web Application URL. In this case, it will be the CUCM User application URL (https://<CUCM FQDN>:8443/*). Check the **GET** and **POST** check boxes. Click the **Finish** button (see Figure 9-54).

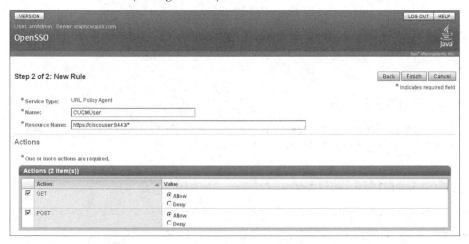

Figure 9-54 *OpenSSO: Defining URL Policy Agent Rule*

Step 8. Create another rule for the requests involving query patterns (*?*) in the Find and List pages of the CUCMUser application, as shown in Figure 9-55.

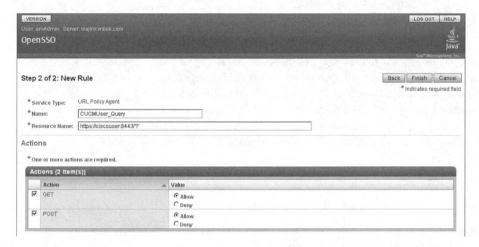

Figure 9-55 *OpenSSO: CUCM User Query Rule*

> **Step 9.** Click **New** button under Subjects on the Policy Configuration page. Select subject type as **Authenticated Users,** as shown in Figure 9-56.

Figure 9-56 *OpenSSO: Authenticated User*

> **Step 10.** Enter the Subject Name (for example, CUCMUser). Click **Finish**.

> **Step 11.** Click the **New** button under Conditions. Under Select Condition Type, select **Active Session Time**. Click **Next**. Set the session time to 60 minutes (or as defined by your organizational/IP Telephony security policy) (see Figure 9-57). Click **Save**.

Figure 9-57 *OpenSSO: Session Time*

Configuring Windows Desktop SSO Authentication Module Instance

The Windows Desktop SSO Authentication Module enables the OpenSSO Enterprise to work with Kerberos tokens. The user presents the Kerberos token, previously issued by a Kerberos Distribution Center, to the OpenSSO Enterprise using the SPNEGO protocol. The client browser sends back a SPNEGO token embedded with a Kerberos token. The OpenSSO Windows Desktop SSO Authentication module retrieves the Kerberos token and authenticates the user using the Java GSS API. If authentication is successful, the OpenSSO Windows Desktop SSO Authentication module returns an SSOToken to the client.

The process is

Step 1. Copy the keytab files to the OpenAM server.

Step 2. Log in to the OpenSSO Enterprise Administration; go to **Access Control > Default Realm > Authentication.**

Step 3. In the Module Instances page, click **New.**

Step 4. Enter a name for the new login module, and then select **Windows Desktop SSO.** Click **OK.**

Step 5. Configure the module as follows (see Figure 9-58):

- **Service Principal:** HTTP/ openAMhost.example.com@EXAMPLE.COM

- **Keytab File Name:** /root/keytab/openAMhost.HTTP.keytab

- **Kerberos Realm:** EXAMPLE.COM

- **Kerberos Server Name:** Kerberos.example.com

- If multiple Kerberos Domain Controllers exist for failover purposes, all Kerberos

- Domain Controllers can be set using a colon (:) as the separator.

- **Return Principal with Domain Name:** False

- **Authentication Level:** 22

Step 6. Restart the OpenSSO Enterprise server.

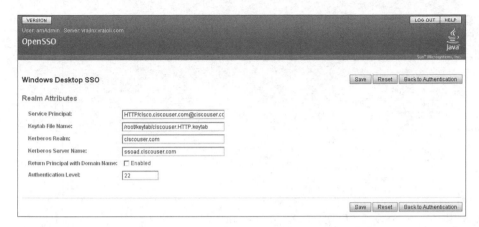

Figure 9-58 *OpenSSO: Windows Desktop SSO (Realm Attributes)*

Configure J2EE Agent Profile on OpenSSO Server

To configure the J2EE Agent Profile for Policy Agent, perform the following tasks in the OpenSSO Enterprise Console:

Step 1. Log in to OpenSSO Enterprise Console as Administrator. Go to **Access Control tab > /(Top Level Realm)**. Click the **Agents** tab.

Step 2. Click the J2EE tab. Click **New** in the agent section.

Step 3. Enter values for the following fields (see Figure 9-59):

■ **Name:** Enter the name or identity of the agent. This is the agent profile name, which is the name of the agent who logs into the OpenSSO Enterprise. Multibyte names are not accepted.

■ **Password:** Enter the agent password. However, it must be the same password entered in the agent profile password file used by the agentadmin utility to install the agent.

■ **Re-Enter Password:** Confirm the password.

■ In the Server URL field, enter the OpenSSO Enterprise server URL. For example: **https://<OpenAM FQDN>:8443/opensso**.

■ In the Agent URL field, enter the URL for the agent application. For example: **https://<CUCM FQDN>:8443/agentapp**.

■ Click **Create**.

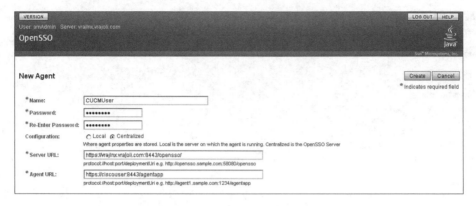

Figure 9-59   *OpenSSO: J2EE Agent Configuration*

Step 4.   The Console creates the agent profile and displays the J2EE Agent page again with a link to the new agent profile,

Step 5.   Click the J2EE agent. Go to **Application tab > Login processing > New Login Form URIs**, as shown in Figure 9-60:

■ **For CCMUser webapp:** /ccmuser/WEB-INF/pages/logon.jsp

■ **For UDS webapp:** /cucm-uds/WEB-INF/pages/logon.jsp

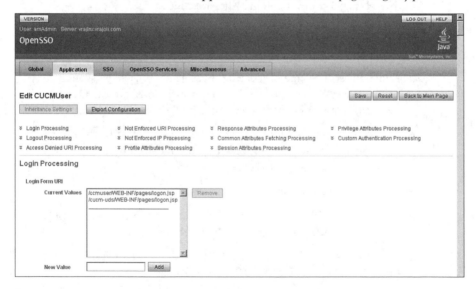

Figure 9-60   *OpenSSO: Login URIs*

Step 6.   Go to OpenSSO Services tab. Under Login URL, add the OpenSSO Login URL **https://<OpenAM FQDN>:8443/opensso/UI/ Login?module=CUCMUser**, as shown in Figure 9-61.

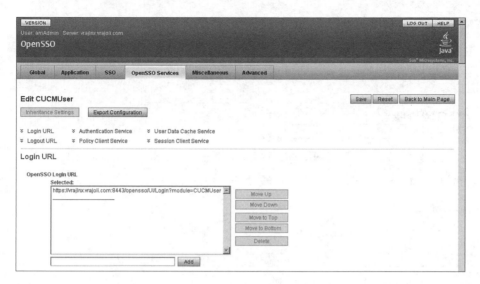

Figure 9-61   *OpenSSO — Login URL*

Configuring SSO on CUCM

You need to configure the CUCM to talk to OpenAM over https while enabling SSO. Thus, the CUCM must trust the OpenAM server, and you need to import an OpenAM server certificate into the Call Manager tomcat-trust store before enabling the SSO on the CUCM OS CLI.

> **Note**   Support for OpenSSO was introduced in CUCM version 8.5(1) and later and in Cisco Unity Connection version 8.6 and later.

To upload a certificate from OpenAM to the CUCM server, follow these steps:

Step 1.   Log in to the OpenAM URL (https://<OpenAMFQDN>:8443/opensso), click the Security icon at the bottom-right corner of your browser window.

Step 2.   Click the **Details** tab on the Certificate Viewer window, click the **Export** button, and save it to your desktop.

Step 3.   Log in to the CUCM OS Administrator GUI, and go to the **certificate management > upload certificate**.

Step 4.   In the Upload Certificate window, select the certificate trust store as tomcat-trust. Browse for the saved OpenAM certificate and upload it (see Figure 9-62).

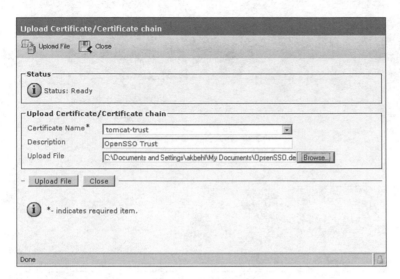

Figure 9-62 *CUCM: OpenSSO Certificate Upload*

> **Step 5.** Enable SSO by the CUCM OS CLI, as shown in Example 9-10.

Example 9-10 *SSO CUCM CLI Configuration*

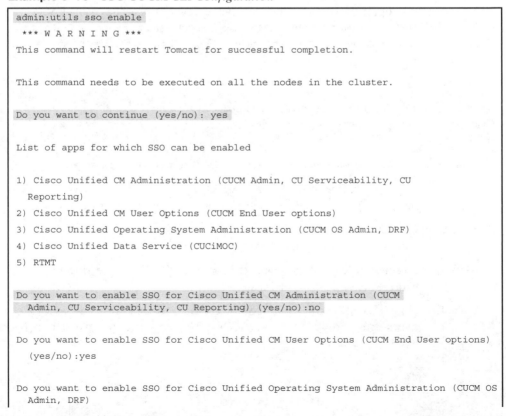

```
admin:utils sso enable

 *** W A R N I N G ***
This command will restart Tomcat for successful completion.


This command needs to be executed on all the nodes in the cluster.


Do you want to continue (yes/no): yes


List of apps for which SSO can be enabled

1) Cisco Unified CM Administration (CUCM Admin, CU Serviceability, CU
   Reporting)
2) Cisco Unified CM User Options (CUCM End User options)
3) Cisco Unified Operating System Administration (CUCM OS Admin, DRF)
4) Cisco Unified Data Service (CUCiMOC)
5) RTMT

Do you want to enable SSO for Cisco Unified CM Administration (CUCM
   Admin, CU Serviceability, CU Reporting) (yes/no):no


Do you want to enable SSO for Cisco Unified CM User Options (CUCM End User options)
   (yes/no):yes


Do you want to enable SSO for Cisco Unified Operating System Administration (CUCM OS
   Admin, DRF)
```

```
(yes/no):no

Do you want to enable SSO for Cisco Unified Data Service (CUCiMOC) (yes/no):no

Do you want to enable SSO for RTMT (yes/no):no

Enter URL of the Open Access Manager (OpenAM) server:
https://vrajlnx.vrajoli.com:8443/opensso

Enter the relative path where the policy agent should be deployed: agentapp

Enter the name of the profile configured for this policy agent: CUCMUser

Enter the password of the profile name: ********

Enter the login module instance name configured for Windows Desktop SSO: CUCMUser

Validating connectivity and profile with Open Access Manager (OpenAM) Server:
 https://vrajlnx.vrajoli.com:8443/opensso

Valid profile

Enabling SSO ... This will take upto 5 minutes

SSO Enable Success

Please make sure to execute this command on all the nodes in the cluster
```

Step 6.   You can verify the SSO by using the command, as shown in Example 9-11.

Example 9-11   *SSO Status Verification Command*

```
admin:utils sso status
SSO Status: Enabled

Primary Open Access Manager (OpenAM) server URL: https://vrajlnx.vrajoli.com:8443/
  opensso

Profile name: CUCMUser

Login module name: CUCMUser

List of apps for which SSO has been enabled
Cisco Unified CM User Options (CUCM End User options)
```

Configuring Client Machine Browsers for SSO

Standard browser clients such as Internet Explorer, Firefox, and Safari have the capability to handle HTTP 401: Negotiate.

Internet Explorer

Following are the steps to set up Internet Explorer for SSO:

> **Note**   The supported version is Internet Explorer 6.x onward.

Step 1.   In the Tool menu, go to **Internet Options > Advanced > Security.** Select the check box for **Integrated Windows Authentication.**

Step 2.   Go to **Tools > Internet Options > Security > Local Intranet.** Select Custom Level.

Step 3.   In the User Authentication/Logon panel/option, select the **Automatic Logon Only in Intranet Zone** option. Go to Sites and select all the options.

Step 4.   Click **Advanced > Add the OpenSSO Enterprise to the Local Zone** (if not added already).

Step 5.   For IE7 and IE8 browsers, go to **Tools > Internet Options > Security tab.** Uncheck the Enable Protected Mode check box (requires restarting Internet Explorer).

Step 6.   For windows machines (Windows7/Windows 2008 and other higher versions) with extended Protection for Authentication enabled, disable extended Protection for Authentication by creating a Registry entry Under the Registry key HKEY_LOCAL_MACHINE\SYSTEM\CurrentControlSet\ Control\LSA\. Add the DWORD value **SuppressExtendedProtection - 0x02.**

Mozilla Firefox

Following are the steps to set up FireFox for SSO:

> **Note**   Supported version 3.x onward.

Step 1.   Open the Firefox browser. In the address field, type **about:config.**

Step 2.   In the Filter, type **network.n.**

Step 3.   Double-click **network.negotiate-auth.trusted-uris.**

Step 4.   Enter a comma-delimited list of trusted domains or URLs, for example,
vrajoli.com.

For more information on SSO, visit http://www.cisco.com/en/US/docs/voice_ip_comm/
cucm/admin/8_5_1/ccmfeat/fssso.html.

Summary

This chapter has a plethora of information for securing your IP Telephony PBX, Cisco
Unified Communications Manager (CUCM), in various state of affairs. CUCM is the
brain and heart of voice communications in a Cisco IP Telephony environment. The
endpoints, end users, and all voice applications (for example, voice messaging, presence,
contact center applications, and so on) rely on call control to ensure that calls are managed properly and securely. This chapter showed how CUCM can be secured, from platform to application to end-user interface.

In this chapter, you were introduced to the various techniques by virtue of which you
can enable security on Cisco UCM to secure endpoint conversations (signaling and
media streams), CTI applications, end-user logon, security of the user data in transit
from LDAP to CUCM, and so on. While there are options that may be required in a
high-security environment, for example, Secure Tone, there are features such as CAPF
and TOMCAT third-party certificates, which are a given for maximizing productivity,
minimizing user intervention, and alleviating security issues, not every option or security
mechanism is required in every network.

This chapter showcased the various built-in and derived security features of CUCM.
Although your network may not demand all these to be implemented, it is you as the IP
Telephony administrator or security administrator who must decide what your organiza-
tion's corporate/IP Telephony security policy mandates as the minimum level of secu-
rity. Or it might be the need of the hour to enable a certain security feature on CUCM.
Either way, Cisco has empowered you to secure what is essential and central to your IP
Telephony network: the call control.

The next chapter introduces you to security constructs that you can deploy in your voice
messaging environment whether it is based on Cisco Unity or Cisco Unity Connection
voice messaging platform. You will learn about the attacks that can impact voice messaging when it comes to voice data in transit or at rest, and the ways in which you can
restrain them.

Chapter 10

Cisco Unity and Cisco Unity Connection Security

The CIO of XYZ Corporation was going through his agenda for the day when he got a call from his secretary about some visitors from ABC Corporation who were awaiting him in the boardroom. He said, "What? How come they are here without any prior notice?" The secretary replied that as per the ABC Corp. project manager, he did leave him a voicemail. The CIO dialed into his voicemail, and yes, indeed, there was the missing voicemail. However, the Cisco Unified IP Phone Message Waiting Indicator (MWI) was not on! How in the world could he have ever known if there were a voicemail? On further investigation by the IT team, it turned out that earlier last night the CIO's voicemail box was accessed from outside, and the voicemails were played out. Was XYZ Corporation under attack? Yes, without a doubt.

To avert such awkward instances and to safeguard the organization's communications "at rest" or "in transit," it's obligatory to have appropriate security deployed around a voice-messaging solution.

This chapter covers the following topics:

- Securing Cisco Unity/Unity Connection platform
- Securing Cisco Unity/Unity Connection web services
- Preventing toll fraud
- Secure voicemail ports
- Securing LDAP (LDAPS) for Cisco Unity Connection
- Securing Cisco Unity/Unity Connection accounts and passwords
- Cisco Unity/Unity Connection CoS
- Cisco Unity/Unity Connection secure messaging
- Cisco Unity/Unity Connection security audit
- Cisco Unity Connection single sign-on

Cisco Unity/Unity Connection Platform Security

Cisco Unity/Unity Connection Server is the premium voice messaging product for Cisco IP Telephony networks. Cisco Unity/Unity Connection fills in nicely for providing voice messaging services, for example, voicemail, IMAP support, Single Inbox with Exchange, or integration with Dominos, and much more. Cisco Unity application is a software application that runs on Microsoft Windows 2003/2008 Server on either MCS or UCS servers as following:

- Cisco provided (or third-party compatible) Media Convergence Server (MCS) 7800 series
- Cisco UCS B-series server

Cisco Unity Connection comes in two models:

- A software that installs on a Cisco (or third-party compatible) MCS server with Linux as the underlying operating system. (The application and operating system is bundled in the same DVD.)
- A software running on top of VMware virtual machine on a Cisco Unified Computing System (UCS) server (B or C series).

The following nomenclature is used for referring to the two platforms:

- **Cisco Unity:** When the discussion and configuration involves only the Cisco Unity platform
- **Cisco Unity Connection:** When the discussion and configuration involves only the Cisco Unity Connection platform
- **Cisco Unity/Unity Connection:** When the discussion and configuration applies to both Cisco Unity/Unity Connection platforms either directly or in that order

The next section discusses the security specifics of Cisco Unity Voice Messaging platform.

Note   Cisco has announced End of Life (EOL) for Cisco Unity 8.x and the software is End of Sale (EOS). The last date of support is 31 January 2015. Cisco recommends migrating from Cisco Unity to Cisco Unity Connection platform.

Note   Throughout this chapter, the configuration examples are based on Cisco Unity version 8.0(3) and Windows 2003 R2 as the operating system.

Cisco Unity Windows Platform Security

For Cisco Unity Server installed on Windows platform, the following security practices are highly recommended.

OS Upgrade and Patches

Install the latest Cisco provided MCS server OS upgrades and related patches as and when they are released on Cisco.com. This helps ensure that all fixes (issues found and fixed) in the software patch or new OS are enabled in your IP Telephony infrastructure, thus protecting you from known threats. As a matter of fact, Cisco has made Server Update Wizard software available for Cisco Unity server, which installs Cisco recommended Windows Server, Internet Explorer, and Microsoft SQL server updates. The operating system updates and patches are available at http://www.cisco.com/cisco/software/navigator.html?mdfid=278875240.

Note Cisco supports direct updates obtained from Microsoft; however, strongly recommends that these be applied in relevance with your security policy and software-maintenance policy.

Cisco Security Agent (CSA)

It is highly recommended to always have Cisco approved and supported Host Intrusion Prevention System (HIPS), such as Cisco Security Agent (CSA), installed and active on your Cisco Unity Windows server. Cisco has developed a default CSA policy that allows all the correct processes, actions, and so on needed for the Cisco Unity server to function, while preventing known and unknown (0-day) attacks. CSA comes in two flavors: managed and unmanaged. Although the latter helps curb any known or unknown attacks, managed CSA can send all the alarms from all the systems (all Cisco Unity servers) on one console (CSA Management console). At a minimum, you should install and run the unmanaged version of CSA.

You can download CSA at

http://www.cisco.com/cgi-bin/tablebuild.pl/cmva-3des

or alternatively from

http://www.cisco.com/cisco/software/navigator.html?mdfid=278875240&i=rp

Note CSA is not a substitute of antivirus software. Although it can prevent attacks on a system, it cannot remove infections from the system.

CSA is End of Life (EOL) and End of Sale (EOS) and is being replaced by SELinux in Linux-based operating systems from version Unity Connection 8.6 onward. However, for applications based on the Windows operating system, CSA will still be supported until December 31, 2013.

Antivirus

It is highly recommended to have a Cisco approved antivirus software installed and active on all Windows-based IP Telephony application servers. Cisco Unity is no exception and should have an antivirus installed and enabled. The antivirus software helps protect the Cisco Unity server from being infected with a worm or a virus, which could otherwise impact the processing capability of the Voicemail server and even worse, spread to other Windows-based servers reachable from the Cisco Unity server.

For information on supported antivirus software (or any other third-party software agents) for Cisco Unity, refer to the following link:

http://www.cisco.com/en/US/docs/voice_ip_comm/unity/8x/support/8xcusupp. html#wp469951

Note Antivirus software alone cannot protect the Cisco Unity system from attacks. It is highly recommended to install both CSA and antivirus software so that the system is secured from attacks as well as virus and worm infections.

Server Hardening

Following are the additional server hardening mechanisms that can help you evade any inside or outside attacks on your Cisco Unity servers:

- You can disable the unnecessary services in line with the Cisco best practice on a Cisco Unity server to make the exposure to any Microsoft service exploit. The following URL gives an overview of the services that can be changed from their default state:

  http://www.cisco.com/en/US/docs/voice_ip_comm/unity/8x/security/ guide/8xcusec010.html#wp1063058

Note Server hardening is strongly recommended. If your security policy does not cover server hardening, you should use the operating system hardening techniques to lock down the same more than what is provided in the default installation:

- As a best practice ensure that all administrator passwords for the Cisco Unity server operating system and application are strong (at least eight characters, if possible alphanumeric) passwords to evade any brute-force or dictionary-based attacks.

- No access to the Internet should be allowed from Cisco Unity server(s) or for that matter any IP Telephony server. Having direct access to the Internet can be detrimental for the IP Telephony servers because it not only opens access from outside the organization, but also allows any backdoor (which would have been otherwise dormant) to become a path for a hacker to compromise the server. Furthermore, if one IP Telephony server is compromised, it can become a hub to launch attacks on other neighbor servers.

■ It's recommended to change the OS and application passwords at least twice a year for improved security. Ideally, the time period to change passwords or to change them at all is something that your security policy should outline.

Cisco Unity Connection Linux Platform Security

Cisco Unity Connection (CUC) is a Linux (appliance or bare-metal) based application. The security of CUC operating system/platform is along the same lines as that of Cisco Unified Communications Manager (CUCM) discussed in Chapter 9, "Cisco Unified Communication Manager Security." Refer to Chapter 9 for details on securing CUC platform.

Note   Throughout this chapter, all the configuration examples are based on Cisco Unity Connection version 8.5(1).

Securing Cisco Unity/Unity Connection Web Services

This section addresses the security of Cisco Unity/Unity Connection to Client connections. Often, remote administration is a requirement, and doing so over an unsecure channel is definitely not a good idea. Moreover, client PCs connecting to Cisco Web Inbox (PCA) or using IMAP over a nonsecure channel is inviting trouble.

While Cisco Unity Connection gives you SSL protection for the aforesaid applications and utilities by default, Cisco Unity needs to be protected from internal and external reconnaissance and packet injection attacks. Still, the default CA certificate of a Cisco Unity Connection may not be suitable for use in your enterprise (because of various certificate name and address security warnings, even if the connection is secure). Thus, you may end up securing both Cisco Unity and Unity Connection voice messaging platforms with your internal or external CA certificates.

Securing Cisco Unity Web Services (SA, PCA, and Status Monitor)

Cisco Unity offers web administration and monitoring via the System Administrator (SA) and Status Monitor, respectively, and end-user message management via the Personal Communication Assistant (PCA). While all these utilities are very useful from an administration and end-user perspective, they do have a drawback because they do not provide SSL (HTTPS) support—by default, for information in transit that can be exploited by an attacker to intercept (eavesdrop) administration and end-user session passwords and activity.

To mitigate this issue you can have an internal or external CA signed certificate in Cisco Unity Internet Information Services (IIS) store so that it can enable administrator users and end users to use secure connectivity to SA and PCA, respectively. The following steps guide you through the process to enable SSL encryption for Unity SA and PCA:

Step 1.   Go to **Start > Programs > Administrative Tools > Internet Information Services (IIS) Manager**.

Step 2.   Expand the name of the Cisco Unity server. Expand **Web Sites**. Right-click **Default Web Site**; click **Properties**.

Step 3.   Go to the **Default Web Site Properties > Directory Security** tab, as shown in Figure 10-1.

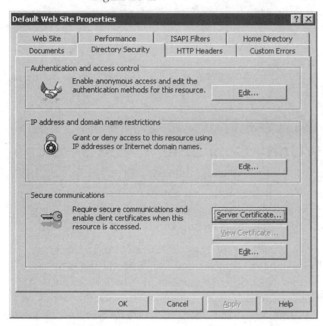

Figure 10-1   *IIS Manager–Default Website Properties*

Step 4.   Go to **Secure Communications > Click Server Certificate**. In the Web Server Certificate Wizard, you need to generate a CSR that will be signed by an internal or external CA. The following points give an insight to the process:

- Click **Next**.

- Click **Create a New Certificate**. Click **Next**.

- Click **Prepare the Request Now, but Send It Later**. Click **Next**.

- Enter the CSR name and bit length for the certificate. Click **Next**.

- Enter the required information. Click **Next**.

- Enter Cisco Unity server FQDN (which will be used for secure URL). Click **Next.**

- Enter the required information. Click **Next.**

- Enter CSR filename and location.

- Verify the request file information. Click **Next.** Click **Finish.**

Step 5.   Send the CSR to an internal or external CA for signing.

Step 6.   After you receive the signed CSR, go to (follow Steps 1 through 3) the Directory Security tab and click **server certificate.**

Step 7.   Click the option **Process the Pending Request and Install the Certificate,** as shown in Figure 10-2.

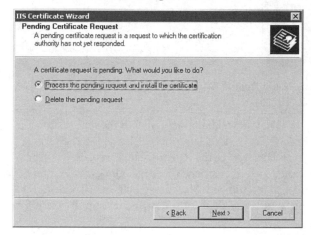

Figure 10-2   *IIS Manager—Installing CA Signed Certificate*

Step 8.   Enter the path to the received signed CSR (which is the identity certificate for Cisco Unity Server) and accept the default port 443.

Step 9.   Finish the wizard, and the identity the certificate should now be in the default website certificate store.

Note   You also need to import the CA root certificate into the Unity certificate store. Read the Microsoft article at http://technet.microsoft.com/en-us/library/cc754841.aspx for details on importing a CA certificate into the Cisco Unity Local Root Certificate Trust Store.

Step 10.   Go to **Default Web Site.** Right click and select **Properties.**

Step 11.   In the **Properties dialog box,** click the **Directory Security** tab.

Step 12. Under **Secure Communications**, click **Edit**. Check the **Require Secure Channel (SSL)** check box, and click **OK** (see Figure 10-3).

Figure 10-3 *IIS Manager – Enable SSL for Default Website and Underlying Components*

Step 13. When you click **Apply** or **OK**, you will be prompted with the dialog shown in Figure 10-4. Here, you can select or deselect options. This shows the various IIS dependent services that can leverage the Parent Default website CA certificate to provide SSL-based web interaction. These include SA, PCA, Status Monitor, Visual Voicemail, and optionally Blackberry Plug-In. Click **Select All** and click **OK** (unless you want to enable it for some services and disable it for others).

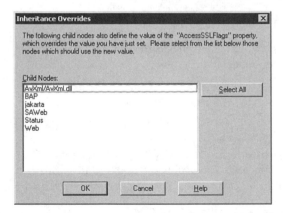

Figure 10-4 *IIS Manager – SSL Component Enablement Options*

Note If you do not get the prompt, you can go to individual dependencies under the default website, that is, AvXML/AvXML.dll, BAP, Jakarta, SAWeb, Status, VWMS, and the web and repeat the process defined in Steps 10–12, that is right-click each component of the default website to ensure these services use SSL instead of HTTP.

Securing Cisco Unity Connection Web Services (Web Administration, PCA, and IMAP)

As stated in the beginning of this section, Cisco Unity Connection (CUC) has self-signed certificates installed and enabled by default for https access (SSL) for connections originating from an administrator or end-user PC. However, because these certificates are not in the certificate store of your PC and the browser's trust store, it may not be in compliance with your organization's security policy. Organizations have either an internal or an external CA authenticate the certificates for its servers whether for Intranet or for extranet access so that the machines (PC, laptops, and mobile devices) do not get the name or IP address mismatch error, which they would get if they browse the CUC web page. Since CUC self-signed certificates are not by default in a user's machine's certificate store, it gives a warning before you can proceed to Cisco Unity Connection Administration, PCA, or OS Administration web pages.

The procedure to have CUC Tomcat certificates signed by an External CA is the same as the Cisco UCM Tomcat certificate signing process. Refer to Chapter 9 for details about the same.

Note If you use an in-house CA server, for example, a Microsoft-based CA server, ensure that the PC accessing CUC web pages has the CA server's root certificate installed in the web browser's trust store. For PCs that are part of a domain, this may already be the case.

Preventing Toll Fraud

Toll fraud needs no introduction, especially for those who have experienced it first hand or seen the effect of the same on an organization's monetary loss. Cisco Unity/Unity Connection voice messaging platforms are not immune to toll fraud, unless properly secured. You must secure Cisco Unity/Unity Connection voice messaging systems to prevent their misuse by any insider or someone from outside. Following are the best practices for curbing toll fraud initiating from voice-messaging servers in your IP Telephony network.

- Add a non-default call-restriction rule for calls, call transfers which denies everything starting with a number that is your outside (PSTN) access code. For example: In United States and many other regions worldwide, 9 is commonly used as an outside PSTN access code. Thus, create a restriction rule that denies everything starting with 9, that is, 9* (applicable to both Cisco Unity and Unity Connection). In Europe and some other countries, 0 is used as a PSTN access code; therefore, all the restriction rules must be changed to start from 0, and 0* should be denied from PSTN access.

Note This assumes the least permissive policy. Access to PSTN from a voice-messaging system may be necessary for intimation of new messages via SMS or outbound calls. Therefore, it really depends on your organization's security policy (or IP Telephony security policy) to define the level of PSTN exposure from voice messaging systems.

- In Cisco Unity, change the EAdmin (Example Admin, which is a default account and must not be deleted for proper functioning of Cisco Unity) Extension to a non-default, hard-to-guess extension and ensure that the password and PIN for EAdmin are difficult to guess (strong password and PIN). In addition, access to the EAdmin account using the Telephony User Interface (TUI) should be disabled.

- Add restriction table patterns to match appropriate trunk access codes for all phone system integrations.

- Restrict the numbers that can be used for system transfers and for AMIS message delivery.

Secure Voicemail Ports

Your organization may require encryption of signaling and media between endpoints and IP Telephony servers. For Cisco Unity/Unity Connection, you can have encryption enabled for voicemail ports (SCCP or SIP) between CUCM and Cisco Unity/Unity Connection such that an encrypted endpoint, that is, a Cisco Unified IP Phone, can initiate a secure conversation with Cisco Unity/Unity Connection voicemail servers.

Note All the following sections assume that CUCM is in mixed-mode. For information and configuration details on enabling encryption on CUCM by converting the cluster into mixed-mode, refer to Chapter 9. For in-depth detail on encryption and Cisco PKI, refer to Appendix A, "Cisco IP Telephony: Authentication and Encryption Essentials."

The configuration examples stated assume that the voicemail integration is set up and working before it is secured. Therefore, the specifics of configuring voicemail ports, pilot numbers, hunt-pilots, route patterns, and so on are not addressed.

Cisco Unity: Secure Voicemail Ports with CUCM (SCCP)

To secure Unity voicemail ports with Cisco UCM, follow these steps:

Step 1.   Open Cisco Unity Telephony Integration Management (UTIM) by browsing to **Programs > Cisco Unity > Manage Integrations**.

Step 2.   In the left pane, double-click **Cisco Unity Server**. The existing integrations with CUCM should appear. Select the desired integration.

Step 3.   Click the CUCM integration. In the right pane, click the cluster for the integration. Click the Servers tab. In the CUCM/CCM Cluster Security Mode field, click the **Encrypted** option. If you do not already have the TFTP.exe file in the C:\Windows\System32\ directory, you will receive an error, as shown in Figure 10-5.

Figure 10-5   *UTIM–TFTP Error*

You can obtain TFTP.EX_ from the Windows installation CD/DVD under the I386 folder. This file needs to be renamed to **TFTP.cab** and then you can extract TFTP.exe to System32 directory. (Depending on your installation, the path to windows\system32\ may vary.) When done, you can now set the mode to encrypted, and a new tab on UTIM appears, reading Security.

Note   The CUCM/CCM Cluster Security Mode setting for Cisco Unity voice messaging ports must match the security mode setting for the Cisco Unified CM ports. Otherwise, Cisco UCM authentication and encryption will fail.

Step 4.   In the add TFTP server dialog box, enter the IP Address of the primary TFTP server, and click **OK**. (Optional) Add the secondary TFTP server. Enter the IP address of the secondary TFTP server; click **OK** (see Figure 10-6).

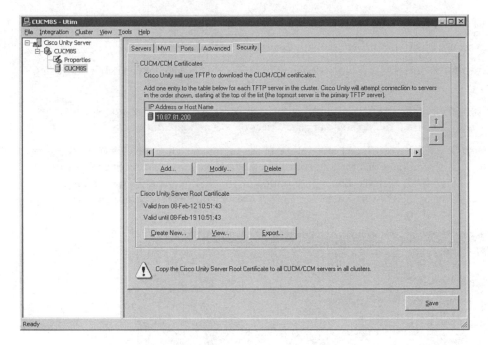

Figure 10-6 *Adding TFTP Hosts*

Step 5. Save the configuration. You have an option to create Unity certificate, which is required by the CUCM—CallManager truststore to establish TLS with Cisco Unity. Export the Cisco Unity server root certificate, and display the Export Cisco Unity Root Certificate dialog box. Note the filename of the exported Cisco Unity server root certificate. Click **OK** (see Figure 10-7). After clicking **Save**, Unity requests a restart of Unity services.

Figure 10-7 *Cisco Unity Root Certificate*

Step 6.   On the Cisco Unity server, browse to the **CommServer\SkinnyCerts** directory. Locate the Cisco Unity server root certificate file that was exported earlier. Right-click the file and click **Rename**. Change the file extension to **.pem**. Save the certificate on your PC.

Step 7.   Log in to the CUCM OS Administrator GUI, and go to **Certificate Management > Upload Certificate.**

Step 8.   On the Upload Certificate page, in the Certificate Name drop-down box, click **CallManager-trust**. In the Root Certificate field, enter **Cisco Unity Root Certificate**. Click **Browse** and browse to the **CommServer/SkinnyCerts** directory on the Cisco Unity server (or local folder on your PC where you saved the certificate), and select the Cisco Unity server root certificate file.

Step 9.   Click **Upload File**. Click **Close**.

Note   Steps 7–9 must be repeated on all CUCM servers running CallManager Service.

Step 10.   On CUCM, go to the **Serviceability page > Tools > Feature Services.** Restart the CAPF service.

Step 11.   On the Cisco Unity server, in the taskbar, right-click the Cisco Unity icon, and click Stop Cisco Unity. When Cisco Unity is stopped, in UTIM, left pane > Click the **CUCM cluster**. Click **servers**. Click **Verify Servers** to verify the connection to the Cisco Unified CM servers.

Note   You must stop Cisco Unity before verifying the connection. Otherwise, the test will fail. If the test is not successful, a dialog box appears that displays the location of the security logs, which provide troubleshooting steps. After troubleshooting, test the connection again.

Step 12.   On the Tools menu, click **Restart Cisco Unity** to restart the Cisco Unity services.

Cisco Unity: Authenticated Voicemail Ports with CUCM (SIP)

Cisco Unity version 8.x supports SIP integration with CUCM. However, with SIP voicemail integration, Cisco recommends only Digest Authentication and not encrypted calls (on SIP port 5061). This is primarily because of known issues with MWI and Dialouts from Cisco Unity. In this section, you will learn about the specifics of secure Cisco Unity—CUCM SIP Integration with Digest Authentication.

Step 1.   Log in to CUCM Administration GUI. Go to **System > Security > SIP Trunk Security Profile.**

Step 2.   Add a new SIP Trunk Security profile with the following parameters:

- **Name:** Any name you want to assign to the security profile, for example, Unity Authenticated SIP Trunk Profile
- **Description:** Any description you want to assign to this security profile, for example, Unity Authenticated SIP Trunk Profile
- **Device Security Mode:** Non-secure
- **Incoming Transport Type:** TCP+UDP
- **Outgoing Transport Type:** TCP
- **Check check box:** Enable Digest Authentication
- **Incoming Port:** 5060
- **Enable Check boxes:** Accept out-of-dialog refer, Accept unsolicited notification, and Accept replaces header

Step 3.   Add a SIP trunk with the security profile you just created, and point the destination address to the Cisco Unity server with destination port set as default 5060.

Step 4.   Reset the SIP trunk.

Step 5.   Create a new **SIP Realm** with Digest Credentials, which will be used for Unity SIP Digest credentials. (The username and password credentials should match the configured credentials in Unity server.)

Step 6.   Open Cisco Unity Telephony Integration Management (UTIM) by browsing to **Programs > Cisco Unity > Manage Integrations.** Run through the Integration Wizard, and select SIP as the Integration protocol.

Step 7.   When asked to enable authentication, check the check box labeled **Authenticate with the SIP Server,** and provide the username and password (should match those provided in SIP Realm in CUCM), as shown in Figure 10-8.

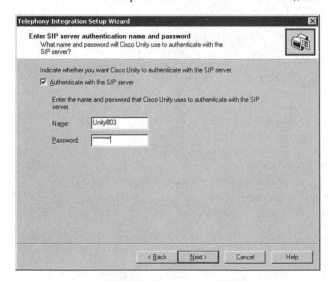

Figure 10-8   *Cisco Unity—SIP Authentication Credentials*

Cisco Unity Connection: Secure Voicemail Ports with CUCM (SCCP)

To configure secure voicemail ports on Cisco Unity Connection with CUCM integration based on Skinny (SCCP) protocol, follow these steps:

Step 1.   Log in to the Cisco Unity Connection (CUC) Administration GUI. Go to **Telephony Integrations > Security > Root Certificate**, as shown in Figure 10-9. On the link below the certificate that says Right Click, right-click and select **Save Target As**. Save the file with the .pem extension (instead of .htm or .0) to your PC.

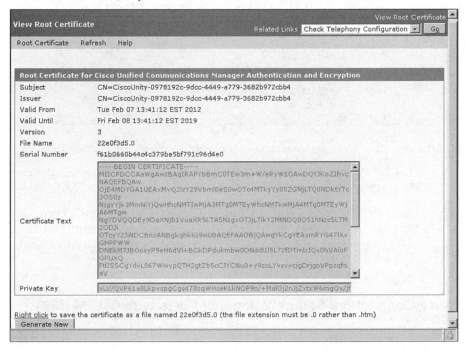

Figure 10-9   *Cisco Unity Connection—Root Certificate*

Step 2.   Log in to the CUCM OS Administration GUI. Go to **Security > Certificate Management**. Click the **Upload Certificate** button. Upload CUC certificate as CallManager-trust.

Note   This process must be repeated on all the servers running the CallManager service.

Step 3.   Log in to the CUCM Administration GUI. Go to voicemail ports. If the ports are already created, click the link for the first port, and set it as **Encrypted**. Click **Save and Apply**. Repeat this step for every voicemail port. If the ports are yet to be created, run the Voicemail Port Wizard, and be sure to set Device Security Mode to Encrypted for all the ports, as shown in Figure 10-10.

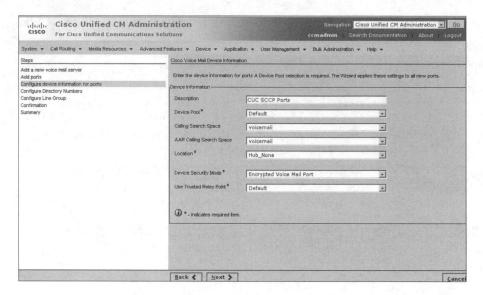

Figure 10-10   *Cisco Unified Communications Manager—Secure CUC Voicemail Ports*

Step 4.   On CUCM go to the **Serviceability Page > Tools > Feature Services.** Restart the CAPF service.

Step 5.   Log in to CUC Administration and go to **Telephony Integrations > Port.** Select each port and set the **Security Mode** to **Encrypted.** Alternatively, if you add new ports, ensure that the Security Mode is set to **Encrypted.** Click **Restart.**

Cisco Unity Connection: Secure Voicemail Ports with CUCM (SIP)

To secure CUC voicemail integration with CUCM using SIP Trunk, follow these steps:

Step 1.   Log in to CUCM Administration GUI. Go to **System > Security > SIP Trunk Security Profile.**

Step 2.   Add a SIP Trunk Security Profile with the following parameters:

- **Name:** Any name you wish to assign to security profile (e.g., CUC Secure SIP Trunk Profile)

- **Description:** A description you want to assign to this security profile, for example, CUC Secure SIP Trunk Profile

- **Device Security Mode:** Encrypted

- **Incoming/Outgoing Transport Type:** TLS

- **X.509 Subject Name:** CUC Name, for example, WLCUC85 (must match CUC SIP Certificate Subject Name)

- **Incoming Port:** 5061

- **Enable Check Boxes:** Accept out-of-dialog refer, Accept unsolicited notification, and Accept replaces header, as shown in Figure 10-11.

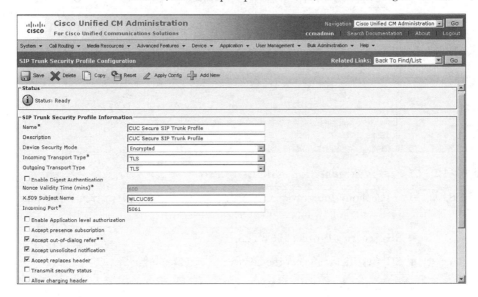

Figure 10-11 *Cisco Unified Communications Manager—Secure SIP Trunk Profile*

Step 3.   Add a SIP trunk with the security profile you just created, and point the destination address to the CUC server with the destination port set as 5061. Ensure that the **SRTP Allowed** check box is checked.

Step 4.   Reset the SIP trunk.

Step 5.   Upload CUC root certificate on all CUCM servers. Follow Steps 1–2 from the section, "Cisco Unity Connection: Secure Voicemail Ports (SCCP)."

Step 6.   Log in to Cisco Unity Connection Administration GUI. Go to **Telephony Integrations > Security > SIP Certificate.**

Step 7.   Click **Add New.** Generate a SIP certificate using the same X.509 name in the subject name field as in Step 2, for example, WLCUC85.

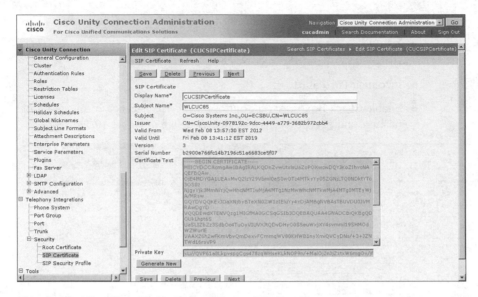

Figure 10-12 *Cisco Unity Connection—SIP Certificate*

Step 8. Go to **Telephony Integrations > Port group** (set up for SIP or create new port group). Set the following parameters:

- **SIP Security Profile:** 5061/TLS.

- **SIP Certificate:** Select the certificate you created in Step 7.

- **Security Mode:** Select **Encrypted**.

Check the check box marked **Secure RTP** (see Figure 10-13).

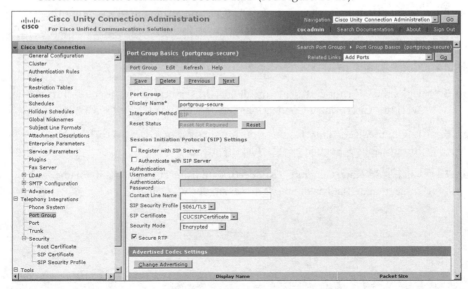

Figure 10-13 *Cisco Unity Connection—Enable SRTP (Port Group)*

Step 9.   Under **Edit > Servers**, add a TFTP server with the IP of the CUCM TFTP server (along with call processing CUCM servers). Reset the port group.

Secure LDAP (LDAPS) for Cisco Unity Connection

With the existing user base already created in your external LDAP (for example, Microsoft Active Directory Server, SunOne LDAP server, and so on), it becomes convenient to import the end users and associate them with their relevant voice-messaging accounts, extensions, rights, and so on. To secure the user information in transit, you can enable secure LDAP so that Cisco Unity Connection creates a Secure Socket Layer (SSL) channel between the CUC server and LDAP server. The process to enable secure LDAP between Cisco Unity Connection and Directory Server is addressed in Chapter 9. Refer to the process outlined for CUCM, which applies equally to CUC for enabling LDAPS. Be sure to restart the Cisco Dirsync and Cisco Tomcat services when certificates from LDAP/DC are uploaded on all members of the CUC Cluster.

Securing Cisco Unity/Unity Connection Accounts and Passwords

Cisco Unity/Unity Connection provide you with options to set the user account settings such as password strength, lockout period, and so on to help you set the system security behavior for user accounts inline with you organization or IP Telephony security policy. This section highlights the various options via which you can secure access via Telephony User Interface (TUI) and Graphical User Interface (GUI) in Cisco Unity/Unity Connection.

Cisco Unity Account Policies

To set the various options available under an account policy, follow these steps:

Step 1.   Go to Unity Web SA, and under Subscriber Heading, click **Account Policy**.

Step 2.   The default page is for Phone password restrictions (Figure 10-14). Here, you can change the following settings:

- Maximum Phone Password Age
- Phone Password Length
- Phone Password Uniqueness

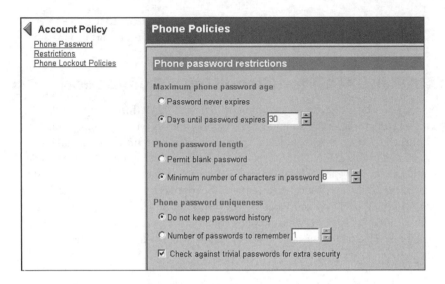

Figure 10-14 *Cisco Unity—Account Policies*

Set these inline with your organizational or IP Telephony specific security policy.

Step 3.   Under **Account** Policy, click the **Phone Lockout Policies** link (see Figure 10-15). Here, you can set up account lockout options, such as

- Lock Account After <number of> Invalid Attempts

- Reset Count After <minutes>

- Lockout Duration: Forever/Minutes

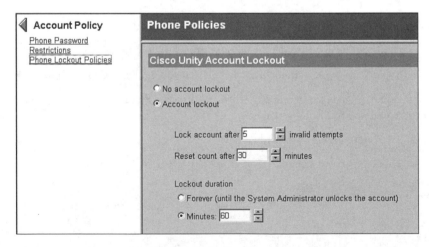

Figure 10-15 *Cisco Unity—Account Policies (Continued)*

Cisco Unity Authentication

Cisco Unity supports enforcing PCA and Status Monitor (only applied when logging in anonymously) login policies. These can be configured under **System > Authentication.** You can set the following parameters:

Cisco Unity PCA Settings

- Remember Logons For <number of days>

- Remember Passwords For <number of days>

- Session Duration <minutes>

- Disallow Blank Password <default is checked>

Cisco Unity PCA Lockout Policies

Lock Out Accounts (default is checked) (see Figure 10-16):

- Accounts are Locked Out for <minutes>

- Accounts Will Lock Out after <number of failed logon attempts>

- Reset Account lockout counters after <minutes>

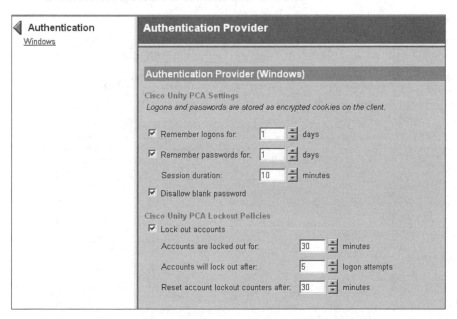

Figure 10-16 *Cisco Unity—Authentication (PCA)*

Cisco Unity Connection Account Polices

To set up the account policies in compliance with your organization's security policy or IP Telephony security policy, go to **Cisco Unity Connection Administration GUI > System Settings > Authentication Rules** (see Figure 10-17). You can either opt from existing web or Voice Authentication rules and edit them or create a new rule. You can set up the following options here:

- Display Name <name of rule>

- Failed Sign-In <number of attempts or no limit for failed sign-ins>

- Reset Failed Sign-In Attempts Every <minutes>

- Lockout Duration <minutes or Administrator must unlock>

- Minimum Duration Between Credential Changes <minutes>

- Credential Expires After <number of days or never expires>

- Expiration Warning Days <number of days>

- Minimum Credential Length <number of characters/digits>

- Stored Number of Previous Credentials <number>

- Check for Trivial Passwords <check box, default is checked>

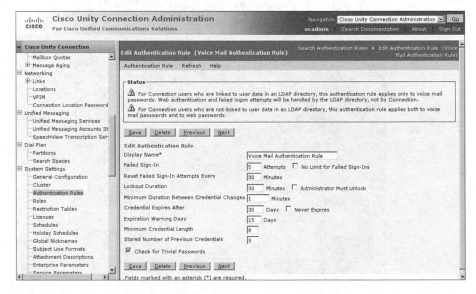

Figure 10-17 *Cisco Unity Connection—Authentication Rule*

Cisco Unity/Unity Connection Class of Service

Cisco Unity/Unity Connection Class of Service (CoS) controls some of the features that are available to users with voice mailboxes including Directory Listing, Secure Messaging, Call Transfer, Restriction Table, and so on. Unity Connection CoS defines limits and permissions for using Cisco Unity Connection features (see Figure 10-18).

Cisco Unity Class of Service (and Roles)

The leading practice is to have various CoS levels defined and provisioned in User Templates before creating or importing subscribers. This reduces overhead of associating already existing subscribers with the CoS defined later. Moreover having well-thought-out CoS levels would allow you to have granular control on who accesses what on Cisco Unity.

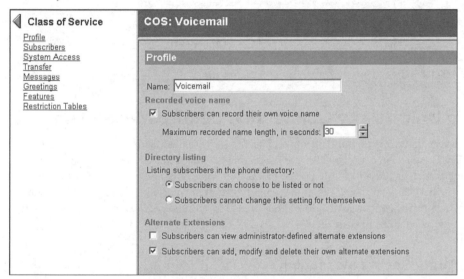

Figure 10-18 *Cisco Unity—CoS Settings*

Cisco Unity Connection Class of Service (and Roles)

Similar to Cisco Unity CoS, Cisco Unity Connection CoS can provide restricted rights to subscribers for access and administrative staff for the access and maintenance of system (voicemail and web CoS, respectively). You can fine-tune the settings and options as per each CoS setting pertinent per subscriber-group or individual subscriber. Moreover, leveraging roles, you can define what each administrator or delegate is allowed to do. Figure 10-19 gives an overview of CoS settings.

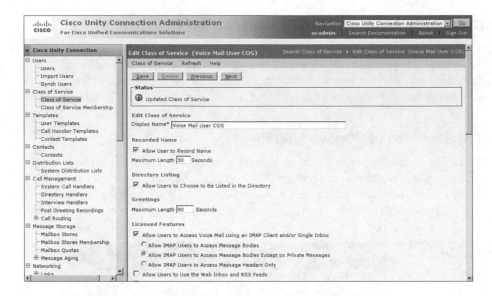

Figure 10-19 *Cisco Unity Connection—CoS Settings*

Cisco Unity/Unity Connection Secure Messaging

This section covers the fundamentals of secure (private) messaging on Cisco Unity/
Unity Connection platforms. Private messaging may be required under various circumstances such as providing a degree of privacy on voice messages so that only the intended
subscriber can hear them. This is particularly useful in environments in which stagnant
message privacy (privacy of information at rest) is required. For example, a government
agency or financial institution.

Cisco Unity Secure Messaging

The following steps detail the configuration of Cisco Unity to support secure (private)
messages.

> **Note** Configure the port and encryption type. Ensure that SSL is the only encryption
> type used and not TCP. This setting is manually done in Exchange 2003, but on Exchange
> 2007, SSL is the default.

Step 1. Enable secure messaging through the Cisco Unity System Admin Page. Go to
Subscribers > Subscriber Template > Features.

Step 2. Select the desired option in the Message Security: **When Sending a Message
list.** Click **Save** (see Figure 10-20).

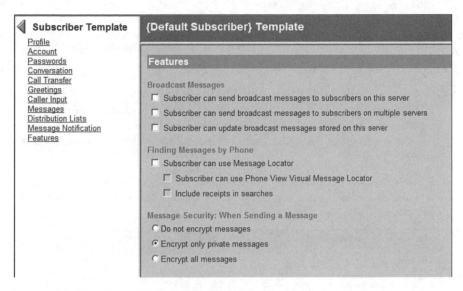

Figure 10-20 *Cisco Unity—Secure Messaging Options*

Note This setting can be applied to individual subscribers, too, if you want to have it applied only for selected subscribers.

Step 3.   Configure unidentified caller message security settings. Go to **System > Configuration > Message Security Settings**.

Step 4.   Select an option from the list on how messages should be secured from unidentified callers. Also, you can select the Message Aging option (see Figure 10-21). Click **Save**.

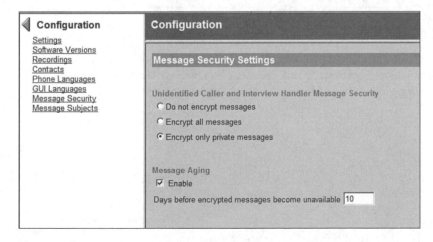

Figure 10-21 *Cisco Unity—Secure Messaging Setup*

Cisco Unity Connection Secure Messaging

The following steps define the procedure to enable CUC Secure (private) messaging:

Step 1.   Configure a CoS in CUC with IMAP enabled.

Step 2.   Check the **Allow Users to Use Unified Client to Access Voicemail Box** option. This enables access to port 7993 and TLS (for CUPC client support). Also, check the **Allow Users to Access Voicemail Using an IMAP Client Box** option, and select the **Allow Users to Access Message Bodies** button. Click **Save**.

Step 3.   Under the Message Options section of the CoS, select the **Private** next to the **Require Secure Messaging** option (recommended options are Always or Private) (see Figure 10-22).

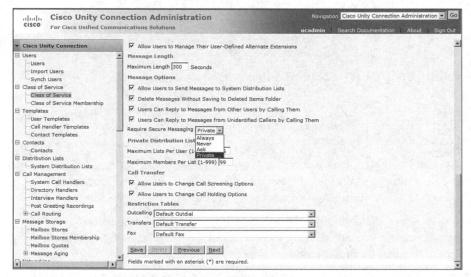

Figure 10-22   *Cisco Unity Connection—Secure Messaging Setup*

Step 4.   Edit unidentified caller message security settings, under **Users > Edit > Message Settings**. Check the check box marked **Mark Secure** in the Unidentified Caller Message Security section (see Figure 10-23).

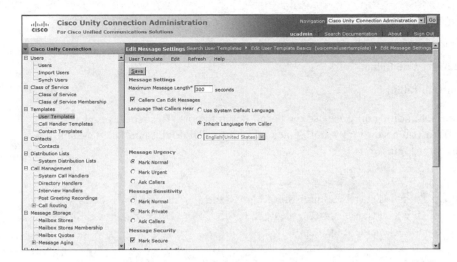

Figure 10-23 *Cisco Unity Connection–Message Security (Options)*

Note Under each subscriber voicemail account (including CUPC subscribers), ensure that the web application password is set for the user.

Cisco Unity/Unity Connection Security Audit (Logs)

This topic has been discussed from a call-control perspective in Chapter 9. Cisco Unity/Unity Connection platforms provide security auditing from a voice messaging platform perspective. This ranges from tracing activities of subscribers to changes in configuration by administrators. The following sections detail the auditing capabilities and relevant configuration for Cisco Unity/Unity Connection.

Cisco Unity Security Audit

Cisco Unity provides an option to generate two types of reports:

- Cisco Unity Subscriber Reports
- Cisco Unity System Reports

Cisco Unity Subscriber Reports

The following is a list of the different Subscriber Reports available on Cisco Unity platform:

- Subscribers
- Subscriber Message Activity

- Distribution Lists
- Failed Login
- Transfer Call Billing
- OutCall Billing

Of these, for auditing purpose use the Failed Login Report. This report provides the information you need to track both failed telephone (TUI) logins and failed system administrator logins.

Note To get the failed system administrator logins, auditing in Windows security policy must be enabled, which is done automatically in Cisco Unity version 8.x. For earlier versions, you need to enable it manually.

Here are items listed in the Failed Login report:

For each telephone login failure:

- Subscriber name
- Alias
- Caller ID (phone number called from)
- Subscriber DTMF
- Date and time of failure
- Maximum failures exceeded
- Failure number

For each System Admin login failure:

- Username
- Computer
- User domain
- Event ID
- Date and time of failure
- Failure number

Cisco Unity System Reports

The following is a list of the different System Reports available on Cisco Unity:

- Administrative Access Activity
- Event Log

- Port Usage

- System Configuration

- Unresolved References

- Call Handler Traffic

- AMIS Outbound Traffic

- AMIS Inbound Traffic

Of these reports, the report you would like to look for auditing administrative access and changes done from administrative accounts is the Administrative Access Activity Report. You have an option to run the report for all administrators or a selected one, from a particular date and time range. The report details on which data was created, deleted, or updated by whom. The depth of the report goes to each setting that was modified and the new value set for the same.

Note   Cisco Unity does not write system or security events. You can view this information using the Microsoft Windows Event Viewer.

Cisco Unity Connection Security Audit

Similar to CUCM, CUC enables you to audit the system for administrative tasks for the following logs:

- Application Log

- Database Log

- Operating System Log

- Remote Support Account Log

For details on each of these log types and to enable logging on CUC, refer to Chapter 9, the "Cisco Unified Communications Manager Security Audit" section. Moreover, you can also generate reports under Cisco Unified Serviceability. The reports of interest would be

- Phone Interface Failed Sign-In

- User Lockout

- Unused Voicemail Accounts

- System Configuration

Cisco Unity Connection Single Sign-On (SSO)

Single sign-on (SSO) is supported from Cisco Unity Connection version 8.6 onward. The topic of SSO was discussed in depth in Chapter 9. Refer to Chapter 9 for enabling SSO with OpenAM/LDAP and other dependencies for CUC subscribers.

Summary

Once they are in the voicemail system, perpetrators of cybercrime can listen to all your voicemails and even reset them as new to cover the trail. Even worse, they can forward particularly juicy voicemails to an e-mail address they enter. Or alternatively, an attacker can put in an alternate extension whereby listening to all voicemails. All it takes is just a few minutes and a poorly secured voice-messaging system for a skilled intruder to set this up.

Voice messaging being an integral part of your IP Telephony network needs to be safe-guarded from internal and external threats. Issues such as toll fraud can be curbed, eavesdropping of voice messages can be restrained, and misuse of voicemail solution can be deterred provided you have the right security controls in place. This chapter introduced you the threats that might threaten the integrity of your Cisco Voice Messaging platform(s). Cisco Unity/Unity Connection both possess powerful security mechanisms from simple password or account policies to complex secure voice messaging port encryption and authentication. Leveraging these security controls is easier than it may seem, provided you have chalked out a security plan well in advance (or even after the system is deployed and is functional).

You will learn about the threats that prowl around your Cisco Unified Presence Server and Client (Cisco Unified Personal Communicator) implementation in the next chapter and learn about the ways in which you can secure your presence infrastructure.

Chapter 11

Cisco Unified Presence Security

The presence concept has been in existence for a while. It helps users know the e-presence status of other users who connect to your (or partner) organization's (for example, organization XYZ) corporate network through a PC or a mobile device. Moreover, it gives the state of availability that the users are currently in real time. With all that said, did you ever wonder why the person you were trying to call was busy while the presence status shows available? Have you ever thought about how that ghost entry popped up in your IM client? Well, as simple as it is, organization XYZ's presence communications were being intercepted and now they are being exploited by an attacker.

When Unified Presence is a part of your organization's network, it is something that the end users will depend on, and you can't afford for someone rogue taking control of your presence infrastructure.

This chapter covers the following topics:

- Cisco Unified Presence Server platform security

- Securing Cisco Unified Presence Server integration with Cisco Unified Communications Manager

- Securing Cisco Unified Presence integration with LDAP

- Securing Presence Federation

- Securing Cisco Unified Personal Communicator

Securing Cisco Unified Presence Server Platform

Cisco Unified Presence Server (CUPS) is based on Cisco RHEL distribution and comes as an appliance version, that is an operating system (OS) software application bundled in a single package. Similar to CUCM and Cisco Unity Connection, CUPS is also available for installation on bare metal (Cisco or IBM MCS server) or a virtualized infrastructure (Cisco UCS with VMware hypervisor). In the following sections, you will grasp the basics for securing the CUPS platform (OS).

> **Note**   Chapter 5, "Cisco IP Telephony Physical Security," addressed the physical security mechanisms that apply equally to all IP Telephony servers, including CUPS whether it is MCS, Appliance, or UCS. Also, Chapter 9, "Cisco Unified Communication Manager Security," discussed CUCM Linux OS and platform hardening and security basics, which apply equally to CUPS, which however is reiterated here.

The following security practices are highly recommended for securing CUPS.

Application and OS Upgrades

Install the latest Cisco provided OS and application upgrades when they are released. This ensures that all fixes offered in the new release is available in your IP Telephony network, therefore, providing maximum protection from known threats. The updates are available at

http://www.cisco.com/cisco/software/navigator.html?mdfid=278875240

> **Note**   The application upgrade may be dictated by your organization's requirements or software management policy.

Cisco Security Agent (CSA)

CSA is an integral component of CUPS application. It is highly recommended to have it active always on your CUP servers. The Cisco default CSA policy enables all the correct processes, actions, and so on needed for CUP server to function while preventing known and unknown (0-day) attacks. CSA for CUP server comes only in the headless (stand-alone) version.

> **Note**   To know the status of CSA on a CUP server, enter the command **utils csa** status. CSA can be stopped or disabled by the CLI command **utils csa disable** and can be (re) started or enabled by the CLI command **utils csa enable**.

CSA is replaced by SELinux in Cisco IP Telephony applications starting from version 8.6 (CUCM, CUC, and CUPS). For more details on SELinux, refer to Appendix B, "Cisco IP Telephony: Firewalling and Intrusion Prevention."

Server Hardening

Following are the server hardening mechanisms that can help you avoid any inside and outside attacks on your CUP servers:

- As a best practice, ensure that all administrator passwords for a CUPS server OS and application are strong (at least eight characters, if possible alphanumeric) passwords to evade any brute force and dictionary-based attacks.

- The OS administrator and the CUPS application administrator passwords should be unique.

- OS and application passwords should be changed every 6 months (or as defined by your organization's security policy).

- No access to the Internet should be allowed from the CUP servers.

Securing CUPS Integration with CUCM

The key feature of CUPS is the ability to know the status of the people you want to interact with, whether they are away from their desk, in a meeting, on the phone, or just not available. This is a valuable piece of information to a business end user because it helps reduce costs and saves a lot of time. As simple as it may sound, if you can identify the status of a colleague prior to initiating a conversation, you can save time and reduce potential repeating of activities such as missed telephone calls, leaving voicemails, sending repeated e-mails, and so on. To summarize, presence offers the value of identifying who is available and who is not in an enterprise at a glance, not just on a client on a PC, but on a mobile device, in a MAC environment, or plugged into a third-party application. Figure 11-1 summarizes the CUPS architecture.

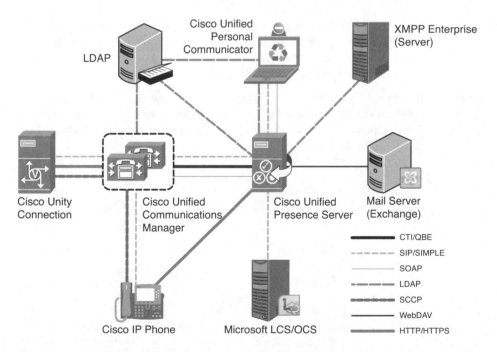

Figure 11-1 *CUPS Architecture*

Having presence functionality at your disposal is great! How about when an attacker can distort the presence status, and you call someone who is in an important meeting? Conversely, when that person is not available, and you keep trying to reach him/her, all efforts are in vain! Undoubtedly, not a pleasant experience at all. Let's understand how you can mitigate such a situation by securing the connection between Cisco Unified Presence Server (CUPS) and Cisco Unified Communications Manager (CUCM).

As shown in Figure 11-1, CUPS and CUCM communicate using CTI/QBE, SIP, and SOAP/AXL protocols. The following section details how you can secure the communication between CUPS and CUCM using certificates.

> **Note**   All configuration examples in this chapter are based on CUCM version 8.5(1), CUPS version 8.5(2), CUPC version 8.5(3), Microsoft OCS 2007, and Cisco ASA version 8.3(4).

Step 1.   Configure secure SIP Trunk Profile for CUPS. (Refer to the "SIP Trunk Security" section in Chapter 9.)

Step 2.   Apply the security profile on the configured CUPS SIP Trunk. Ensure that the SIP Trunk Device name is set as the CN of CUPS.

Step 3.   Export CUPS and CUCM self-signed certificates from the respective OS Administration GUI, by logging into **Cisco Unified OS Administration > Security > Certificate Management**. For CUPS cup.pem and for CUCM call-manager.pem certificates should be downloaded.

Step 4.   Import the CallManager.pem certificate in CUPS by selecting the import option under **Cisco Unified OS Administration > Security > Certificate Management**. The certificate should be uploaded in the **CUP-Trust** certificate store, as shown in Figure 11-2.

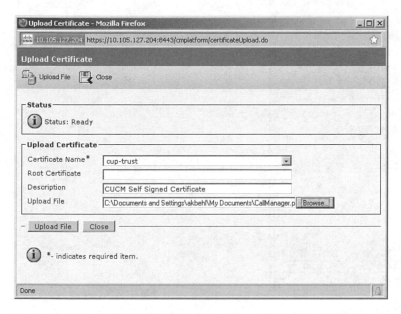

Figure 11-2 *CUCM Self-Signed Certificate Upload in CUPS*

Step 5. Go to **Cisco Unified Serviceability > Tools > Control Center - Feature Services** on the CUP server, and restart **Cisco UP SIP Proxy service**.

Step 6. Import the CUP.pem certificate in CUCM by selecting the import option under **Cisco Unified OS Administration > Security > Certificate Management**. The certificate should be uploaded in the CallManager-Trust certificate store.

Step 7. Go to **Cisco Unified Serviceability > Tools > Control Center - Feature Services** on CUCM server, and restart the CallManager service on CUCM.

Step 8. Go to **Cisco Unified Presence Administration > System > Security > TLS Peer Subjects**. Search for the CUCM CN for the certificate you uploaded from the CUCM. The TLS Peer Subject should be auto-created; ensure that the CN matches the CUCM name, as shown in Figure 11-3.

Figure 11-3 *TLS Peer Subject*

Step 9. If the TLS Peer were not created automatically, you must manually create the same. Click **Add New**. Enter the subject CN of the CUCM server and the name of the server in the Description field.

Step 10. Go to **Cisco Unified Presence Administration > System > Security > TLS Context Configuration**. Click **Find**. Select **Default_Cisco_UPS_SIP_Proxy_ Peer_Auth_TLS_Context**, and from the list of available TLS peer subjects, select the TLS peer subject that you configured. Ensure that this TLS peer subject is under selected TLS Peer Subjects, as shown in Figure 11-4.

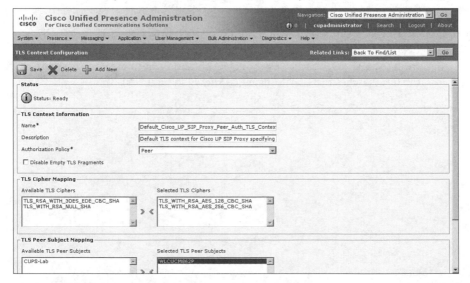

Figure 11-4 *TLS Context*

Step 11.   Go to **Cisco Unified Serviceability > Tools > Control Center - Feature Services** on the CUP server, and restart the Cisco UP SIP Proxy service.

At this point, CUPS and CUCM should have a TLS secured SIP (trunk) connection.

Securing CUPS Integration with LDAP (LDAPS)

CUPS can be integrated with LDAP servers. Since, by default, the connection is clear text, it is unsecure. If you are wary of someone snooping into the LDAP synchronization with CUPS, you need to implement LDAPS (secure LDAP), which leverages certificate-based encryption for contact synchronization between CUPS and LDAP. To secure your communications between CUPS and an LDAP server, you need to follow the same steps as CUCM LDAP secure integration, described in Chapter 9 (which is a specific example for Microsoft Active Directory).

Securing Presence Federation (SIP and XMPP)

Presence Federation is the ability for two (or more) businesses/organizations to collaborate and share presence information, even when they have different presence vendor solutions, for example, the Cisco Presence Federation with Microsoft's OCS or LCS solutions, as shown in Figure 11-5 intra-domain (intra-organization) and 11-6 inter-domain (inter-organization). Moreover, CUPS can also be deployed in a derived federation, that is, a CUPS-to-CUPS federation. Lastly, CUPS can federate with XMPP enterprises such as CUPS 8.x, GoogleTalk, Cisco WebEx Connect 6.0 or later, and IBM Sametime 8.x.

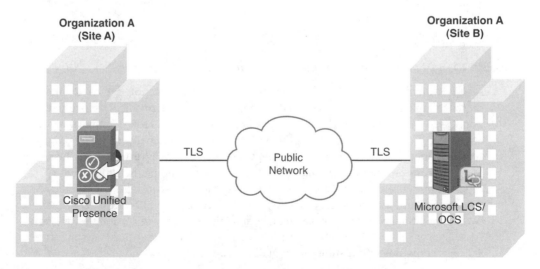

Figure 11-5   *Presence Intra-Domain SIP Federation (Within Enterprise)*

In this example, organization A has two main sites (or data centers) where CUPS and Microsoft OCS are used for a presence solution. Since here, the federation takes place within a trusted environment without any exposure to external world, you have an option to enable TCP or TLS for presence information exchange.

Note   If you federate with OCS across an enterprise boundary, you need Cisco ASA and Microsoft access edge proxy. If you plan to use inter-domain federation with OCS within your internal network (and therefore not crossing over the public network) you can set up a direct federation using static routes and do not need an ASA or Microsoft access edge proxy in that instance. The federation can be deployed using TCP or TLS. Figure 11-6 gives an overview of TLS based inter-domain federation.

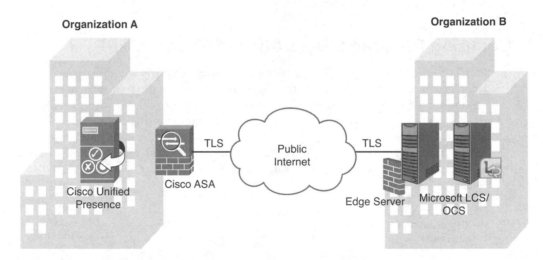

Figure 11-6   *Presence Inter-Domain SIP Federation (Between Enterprises)*

As it is evident from Figure 11-6, organization A has CUPS solution deployed for presence capability. On the other hand, organization B has Microsoft Presence solution. Cisco ASA security appliance acts as a proxy device (UC Proxy), terminating the encrypted TLS connection between the two organizations and between the two presence servers from different vendors. Essentially, Cisco ASA acts as a trusted broker between the two organizations representing one to the other while hiding the actual identity of either presence solution. Cisco ASA can apply inspection capabilities and policy enforcement around the presence traffic, which is actually the SIP traffic between these two entities. So, all the inherent capabilities and inherent security capabilities of Cisco ASA, such as the ability to enforce blacklists on what type of users, can communicate and share presence information can be applied here.

CUPS SIP Federation Security

The following sections detail intra-organization and inter-organization Cisco Presence and Microsoft OCS SIP federation configuration to support TLS.

Note   Office Communication Server 2007 (OCS) is the new version of Live Communication Server 2005 (LCS) with a different name to go with Microsoft® Unified Messaging portfolio.

Intra-Enterprise/Organization Presence SIP Federation

To enable presence federation within an enterprise/organization, follow the subsequent steps.

Note   This assumes that CUPS is correctly deployed with CUCM and other IP Telephony applications and that the OCS server is set up and working with Microsoft Office Client (MOC) software. For this example, configuration use Microsoft Windows® 2003 CA server (enterprise root).

Configuring CUPS for CA Certificates

Step 1.   If you have an internal or external CA server, download the root certificate of the CA server.

Step 2.   On CUP server, go to **Cisco Unified OS Administration > Security > Certificate Upload,** and upload the CA root certificate in the **cup-trust** store.

Step 3.   Under **Cisco Unified OS Administration > Security > Certificate Management,** click **Generate New CSR,** with the type as **cup.**

Step 4.   From Certificate Management select **Download/Generate CSR,** download the CSR.

Step 5.   Get the CSR signed by the CA server, and download the DER encoded file. Save the file as .pem extension.

Step 6.   On the CUP server, go to **Cisco Unified OS Administration > Security > Certificate Upload,** and upload the CSR in the **cup trust** store. Append the name of the root certificate from the CA that you uploaded earlier under the root certificate field.

Configuring OCS Server for CA Certificates

Step 1.   On OCS 2007, click **Start > Run >** type **http://<name of your Issuing CA Server>/certsrv.** Click **OK.**

Step 2. Click **Download a CA Certificate or Certificate Chain**.

Step 3. In the File Download dialog box, click **Save**. Save the file on your OCS server.

Step 4. Click **Start > Run > type mmc**, and click **OK**. On the File menu, click **Add/ Remove Snap-in**.

Step 5. In the Add/Remove Snap-in dialog box, click **Add**. In the list of Available Standalone Snap-Ins, select **Certificates**. Click **Add**.

Step 6. Select **Computer account** and click **Next**. In the Select Computer dialog box, ensure **Local computer** is selected, and click **Finish**. Click **Close**, and then click **OK**.

Step 7. In the left pane of the Certificates console, expand Certificates (Local Computer). Expand Trusted Root Certification Authorities.

Step 8. Right-click Certificates, point to **All Tasks**, and then click **Import**. Click **Next**.

Step 9. Click **Browse** and go to the folder where you saved the certificate chain (downloaded in Step 2). Select the **p7b** file, and click **Open**. Click **Next**.

Step 10. Leave the default value Place all certificates in the following store, and ensure that Trusted Root Certification Authorities appears under the Certificate store. Click **Next**. Click **Finish**.

Step 11. On OCS 2007 server open a web browser, and type the URL **http://<name of CA Server>/certsrv**. Click **Request a Certificate**.

Step 12. Click **Advanced Certificate Request**. Click **Create and Submit a Request to This CA**.

Note The name needs to match the OCS name, that is, FQDN.

Step 13. In the Type of Certificate Needed list, click **Other**. In the Name field of the Identifying Information section

- Enter the FQDN of the OCS server.

- Fill in the OID field (**1.3.6.1.5.5.7.3.1,1.3.6.1.5.5.7.3.2**).

- In Key Options click the Store Certificate in the Local Computer Certificate store check box. Enter a friendly name.

Click **Submit**.

Note   OID 1.3.6.1.5.5.7.3.1 stands for the server authentication, and in this object identifier, if you want to add an additional OID, for example, 1.3.6.1.5.5.7.3.2, to make the certificate eligible for computer or client and server authentication.

Step 14.   Assuming that the certificate was issued on the **subordinate CA server**, on the OCS server click **Start > Run > type http://<name of CA Server>/ certsrv**. Click **OK**.

Step 15.   From **Select a Task**, click **View the Status of a Pending Certificate Request**. From View the Status of a Pending Certificate Request, click your request. Click **Install This Certificate**.

Step 16.   From the OCS Admin Page, right-click the desired server, and select **Front-end Properties**. Click the **Certificate** tab, and click **Select Certificate** to choose the previously installed OCS certificate, as shown in Figure 11-7.

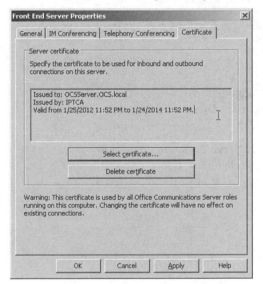

Figure 11-7   *OCS Front-End Server Certificate*

Step 17.   Click **Start > All programs > Administrative Tools > Internet Information Services (IIS) Manager**.

Step 18.   Expand the (local computer) tree, and right-click to select **Default Web Site Properties**. Right-click and select properties, as shown in Figure 11-8.

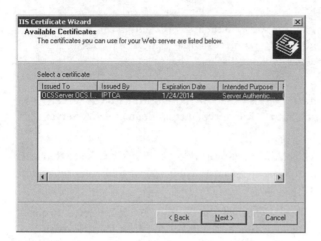

Figure 11-8 *IIS Certificate*

Step 19.   Click **Select Certificate** to launch the Certificate Wizard. Select the certificate that was installed for OCS.

Adding OCS Static Routers (with TLS)

Step 1.   Click **Start > All programs > Administrative Tools > Launch OCS 2007 Administrative Interface**. Right-click **OCS Server Pool**; go to **Properties**, and click **Front End Properties**.

Step 2.   Go to Routing tab and click **Add Static Route**. In the next hop, enter the CUPS hostname/FQDN, as shown in Figure 11-9.

Figure 11-9 *Static Route for CUPS (TLS)*

Note This should match with the Subject CN of CUPS certificate; otherwise, OCS cannot establish a TLS connection with CUPS. You can check the Subject CN of the CUPS certificate at **CUPS Platform GUI > Security > Certificate Management.** Click **CUPS.pem.**

- Select Transport TLS.

- Select Port 5062, which is the default CUPS port for peer authentication TLS connections.

- Check **Replace Host in Request URI.**

- Select the certificate that you configured previously. Look for the friendly name you gave to the certificate and select that.

Step 3. Go to the Host Authorization tab. Click **ADD.**

Step 4. Click **FQDN** and enter the CUP X.509 Subject Common Name as it appears in the CUPS certificate. Check the following check boxes, as shown in Figure 11-10.

- Throttle As Server

- Treat As Authenticated

Click **OK.**

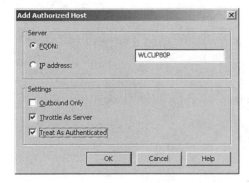

Figure 11-10 *CUPS as Authorized Host*

Step 5. Stop and start the server. The OCS server pool should display the outbound static route you have configured.

Configure OCS Computer to Send TLSv1 with Cipher Spec

Step 1. Go to **Start > Control Panel > Administrative Tools > Local Security Policy.**

Step 2. Select **Local Policies >Security Options**. In the right-side panel of Security Options, find the description and highlight it: **System Cryptography: Use FIPS Compliant Algorithms**, as shown in Figure 11-11.

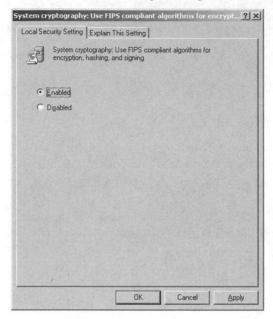

Figure 11-11 *Enable FIPS*

Note The FIPS compliant algorithm uses TLS_RSA_WITH_3DES_EDE_CBC_SHA cipher.

Step 3. Right-click and select **Properties**; then select **Enabled**. Click **Apply**. Click **OK**.

Step 4. Restart the OCS Front End Service.

Adding a Federated Domain

Step 1. Select **Cisco Unified Presence Administration > Presence > Inter Domain Federation**. Click **Add New**.

Step 2. Enter the federated domain name in the Domain Name field. Enter a description.

Step 3. From the Integration Type menu, select **CUP to LCS/OCS**. Click **Save**.

Configuring the Federation Routing Parameter

Step 1. Select **Cisco Unified Presence Administration > System > Service Parameters**. From the Server menu, select the **Cisco Unified Presence server**.

Step 2.   From the Service menu, select **Cisco UP SIP Proxy**. Enter the root FQDN value for the Federation Routing CUP FQDN parameter in the **Federation Routing Parameters** (Clusterwide) section.

Configure TLS Context on CUPS

Step 1.   Go to **CUPS Administration > Cisco Unified Presence Server > Security > TLS Peer > Subjects**.

Step 2.   Configure the Subject CN of OCS certificate and save.

Step 3.   Go to **CUPS Administration > Cisco Unified Presence Server > Security > TLS context**. Click **Find**.

Step 4.   Click **Default_Cisco_UPS_SIP_Proxy_Peer_Auth_TLS_Context**. Select **TLS_RSA_WITH_3DES_EDE_CBC_SHA** from Available TLS Cipher to Selected TLS Cipher.

Step 5.   Select the TLS Peer Subject you configured for OCS server, and ensure it is under **Selected TLS Peer Subjects**.

Note   Check the **Disable Empty TLS Fragments** check box. This is required for TLS to work between CUP and OCS (because OCS cannot handle 0 length TLS record).

Step 6.   Save the settings and restart **UP SIP Proxy** Service from CUPS Serviceability.

Configuring Transport Listener Port Settings

Step 1.   Select **Cisco Unified Presence Administration > System > Application Listeners**. Click **Find**.

Step 2.   Click the **Default Cisco SIP Proxy TLS Listener - Peer Auth** listener hyperlink.

Step 3.   Edit the Port value with a temporary value, for example, **506000**. This temporary value is required because you cannot have two listener entries with the same port value. Click **Save**.

Step 4.   Click the **Default Cisco SIP Proxy TLS Listener - Server Auth Listener** hyperlink. Edit the Port value to **5062**. Click **Save**.

Step 5.   Click the **Default Cisco SIP Proxy TLS Listener - Peer Auth Listener** hyperlink. Edit the Port value to **5061**. Click **Save**.

Configure Static Routes for TLS Exchange in CUPS

Step 1.   Configure static routes by selecting **CUP Administration > Presence > Routing > Static Routes**. When defining a static route for the foreign domain, ensure the following settings are implemented:

- The Destination Pattern value needs to be reversed. It must be in the following format: .local.cisco*

- The Next Hop value is the external Access Edge FQDN or IP address.

- The Next Hop Port number is 5061.

- The Route Type value is domain.

- The Protocol Type is TLS.

Inter-Enterprise/Organization Presence SIP Federation

This section details the configuration required to enable the inter-organization presence federation.

Note This configuration example assumes that CUPS is correctly deployed with CUCM and other IP Telephony applications, Cisco ASA is set up as an IP Telephony Firewall (see Chapter 8, "Perimeter Security with Cisco Adaptive Security Appliance," for details on Cisco ASA as IP Telephony Firewall), and that OCS server is set up and working with Microsoft Office Client (MOC) software and is configured for federation and Microsoft Edge Server is configured.

Configure Cisco ASA NAT and ACL

Step 1. Create a static NAT for the local domain (inside), which contains CUPS server to the outside. Also, configure access control lists (ACL) for permitting traffic between the CUPS and OCS, as shown in Example 11-1.

Note The following examples assume an internal IP subnet-facing CUPS in subnet 10.10.20.0 and external subnet between OCS and CUPS in subnet 10.10.10.0.

Example 11-1 *Cisco ASA NAT Configuration for CUPS-OCS Federation*

```
IPTASA(config)# object network CUPS_External
IPTASA(config)# description ASA Outside dedicated IP for federation
IPTASA(config)# host 10.10.10.200
!
IPTASA(config)# object network CUPS_Internal
IPTASA(config)# description CUPS Private IP for federation
IPTASA(config)# host 10.10.20.200
!
IPTASA(config)# object service TCP_5060
IPTASA(config)# service tcp destination eq sip
!
```

```
IPTASA(config)# object service TCP_5061
IPTASA(config)# service tcp destination eq 5061
!
IPTASA(config)# object service TCP_5062
IPTASA(config)# service tcp destination eq 5062
!
IPTASA(config)# object service TCP_5070
IPTASA(config)# service tcp destination eq 5070
!
IPTASA(config)# object service UDP_5070
IPTASA(config)# service udp destination eq 5070
!
IPTASA(config)# object service UDP_5060
IPTASA(config)# service udp destination eq sip
!
IPTASA(config)# object network OCS
IPTASA(config)# description OCS Edge Server address
IPTASA(config)# host 10.10.10.201
!
IPTASA(config)# access-list Inside extended permit ip any any
IPTASA(config)# access-list CUPS_OCS extended permit ip object CUPS_inside object OCS
IPTASA(config)# access-list OCS_CUPS extended permit ip object OCS object CUPS_External
IPTASA(config)# access-list OCS_CUPS extended permit ip object OCS object CUPS_Internal
IPTASA(config)# access-list Outside extended permit ip object OCS object CUPS_External
IPTASA(config)# access-list Outside extended permit ip object OCS object CUPS_Internal
!
IPTASA(config)# nat (inside,outside) source static CUPS_Internal CUPS_External destination
  static OCS OCS service TCP_5061 TCP_5061
IPTASA(config)# nat (inside,outside) source static CUPS_Internal CUPS_External destination
  static OCS OCS service UDP_5070 UDP_5070
IPTASA(config)# nat (inside,outside) source static CUPS_Internal CUPS_External destination
  static OCS OCS service TCP_5070 TCP_5070
IPTASA(config)# nat (inside,outside) source static CUPS_Internal CUPS_External destination
  static OCS OCS service TCP_5060 TCP_5060
IPTASA(config)# nat (inside,outside) source static CUPS_Internal CUPS_External destination
  static OCS OCS service TCP_5062 TCP_5062
IPTASA(config)# nat (inside,outside) source static CUPS_Internal CUPS_External destination
  static OCS OCS service UDP_5060 UDP_5060
IPTASA(config)# nat (inside,outside) source dynamic CUPS_Internal CUPS_External
```

Note   CUPS_OCS and OCS_CUPS ACLs will be used in class-maps for the inspection of SIP traffic.

The definition of NAT or Statics must be performed for each CUP Server (if using CUPS cluster)**Cisco ASA—CUPS Certificate Exchange**

Step 1. Generate a key pair and configure a trustpoint to identify Cisco ASA self-signed certificate for CUPS, as outlined in Example 11-2.

Example 11-2 *Cisco ASA RSA Keypair*

```
IPTASA(config)# crypto key generate rsa label cup_proxy modulus 1024
!
IPTASA(config)# crypto ca trustpoint cups_proxy
IPTASA(config-ca-trustpoint)# enrollment self
IPTASA(config-ca-trustpoint)# fqdn none
IPTASA(config-ca-trustpoint)# subject-name cn=<ASA inside interface ip address>
IPTASA(config-ca-trustpoint)# keypair cup_proxy
```

Step 2. Generate Cisco ASA self-signed certificate, as shown in Example 11-3.

Example 11-3 *Cisco ASA Self-Signed Certificate*

```
IPTASA(config-ca-trustpoint)# crypto ca enroll cups_proxy
% The fully-qualified domain name will not be included in the certificate
% Include the device serial number in the subject name? [yes/no]: no
Generate Self-Signed Certificate? [yes/no]: yes
```

Step 3. Export Cisco ASA Identity certificate, as illustrated in Example 11-4.

Example 11-4 *Cisco ASA – Export Self-Signed Certificate*

```
IPTASA(config)#crypto ca export cups_proxy identity-certificate
The PEM encoded identity certificate follows:
-----BEGIN CERTIFICATE-----
MIIBoTCCAQqgAwIBAgIEbYpDKzANBgkqhkiG9w0BAQQFADAVMRMwEQYDVQQDEwox
MC4xMC4xMC4xMB4XDTkzMDEwMTAwMDM1N1oXDTAyMTIzMDAwMDM1N1owFTETMBEG
<output omitted>
qocCvywgmJVC5lfldcDBrY+vx3LS6wimSyYsJxEPdGH2gCiqysd8t8SJ/OPIqEqi
GAmjmUEkIp3ANMSfgfwq7U0HsQYrMp9z+mJmZWKvSlOg9W+ztQ==
-----END CERTIFICATE-----
```

Save the text from ASA into a .pem file, say cups_proxy.pem.

Step 4. On the CUPS server go to **Cisco Unified Operating System Administration > Security > Certificate Management > Upload Certificate**. Select the **cup-trust** trust store, as shown in Figure 11-12.

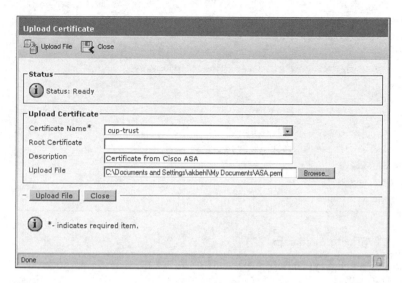

Figure 11-12 *Import Cisco ASA Self–Signed Certificate in CUPS*

Note Leave the Root Name field blank. It is recommended to give a meaningful description to identify the certificate.Browse for the cups_proxy.pem certificate file, and click **Upload File** to upload the certificate to CUPS as cup-trust.

Step 5. Generate CUPS certificate for enrollment in Cisco ASA Firewall. Go to **Cisco Unified Operating System Administration > Security > Certificate Management > Select cup-trust Certificate** (CUP self-signed certificate), which should have <CUP server name>.pem. Download and save the .pem file on your computer.

Step 6. Configure a trustpoint to identify CUPS self-signed certificate in Cisco ASA, as shown in Example 11-5.

Example 11-5 *Cisco ASA – Configure CUPS Trustpoint*

```
IPTASA(config)# crypto ca trustpoint cups_trust
IPTASA(config)# enrollment terminal
```

Step 7. Import the certificate that was downloaded in Step 5 from CUPS into Cisco ASA Firewall, as shown in Example 11-6.

Example 11-6 *Cisco ASA – Import CUPS Certificate*

```
IPTASA(config)# crypto ca authenticate cups_trust
Enter the base 64 encoded CA certificate.
End with the word "quit" on a line by itself
-----BEGIN CERTIFICATE REQUEST-----
MIIBtDCCAR0CAQAwEjEQMA4GA1UEAwwHQ1VQODA0UDCBnzANBgkqhkiG9w0BAQEF
```

```
AAOBjQAwgYkCgYEAoOjISjW5hKOPkBzsH7o/B3KxhFJUmbxVuRekdxwqaPJh+Xk+
sWgqc1U8DTtHYrXXkxA7hcVnuw1gMZLzOoFuijc9aU+/csRSCAJ50iwjMHAQgAhR
<output omitted>
H/JzY4zWFQdDl0O6n7keP/SH0yjJ0TCKzuSiDHhGutJv+qM48h1qD0fidgd1yVeV
B6dpq8GMZs0=
-----END CERTIFICATE REQUEST-----
quit
INFO: Certificate has the following attributes:
Fingerprint:    d71fb037 79238786 3f9eb3a3 d744d3ca
Do you accept this certificate? [yes/no]: yes
Trustpoint CA certificate accepted.
% Certificate successfully imported
```

Cisco ASA—CA Certificate Exchange

Step 1. Configure a new keypair and trustpoint for the CA Certificate, as shown in Example 11-7.

Example 11-7 *Cisco ASA – Generate CA Server Trustpoint*

```
IPTASA(config)#crypto key generate rsa label CA_Server modulus 1024
!
IPTASA(config)# crypto ca trustpoint CA_Server
IPTASA(config-ca-trustpoint)# enrollment terminal
IPTASA(config-ca-trustpoint)# fqdn cups.cisco.com
IPTASA(config-ca-trustpoint)# subject-name cn=cups.cisco.com
IPTASA(config-ca-trustpoint)# client-types ssl
IPTASA(config-ca-trustpoint)# keypair CA_Server
```

Step 2. Authenticate the CA server root certificate, as shown in Example 11-8.

Note For this configuration example, we use the Microsoft Windows 2003 CA Server. You can also use a third-party CA, for example, VeriSign.

Example 11-8 *Cisco ASA – Import CA Root Certificate*

```
IPTASA(config-ca-trustpoint)# crypto ca authenticate CA_Server
Enter the base 64 encoded CA certificate.
End with the word "quit" on a line by itself
-----BEGIN CERTIFICATE-----
MIIETDCCAzSgAwIBAgIQHznkdswFwYtBkARcTRA70jANBgkqhkiG9w0BAQUFADA8
MRUwEwYKCZImiZPyLGQBGRYFbG9jYWwxEzARBgoJkiaJk/IsZAEZFgNPQ1MxDjAM
BgNVBAMTBU1QVENBMB4XDTEyMDEwMjEyNTkyOFoXDTIyMDEwMjEzMDkwNVowPDEV
MBMGCgmSJomT8ixkARkWBWxvY2FsMRMwEQYKCZImiZPyLGQBGRYDT0NTMQ4wDAYD
```

```
<output omitted>
toU+ouFIgCGrlaNaV7HWMAYXSiSmXELzhp79Lil5gQnqq2PWd1EvYx7htn+mb/dD
CHRgDF/tea42y2ri3Cu55XOS+TWmHwlqeeOJYRQd2m2PRbCZa0tm3Bi7sSvFVe4F
7bwJmP685CWff3DBxIs7IwF/0W09Si9ghsWO1s3rAQo4L+0+mZwkORDloDCp/ex2
N6KD1hZGGvICeOGqFql3DenVG0RKmTGTKhvzUfmPiq0KI6JiysQVerQc8M97RuXF
-----END CERTIFICATE-----
quit
INFO: Certificate has the following attributes:
Fingerprint:      cf45bf45 6fd8b254 98362c0f 220b1fe2
Do you accept this certificate? [yes/no]: yes
Trustpoint CA certificate accepted.
% Certificate successfully imported
```

Step 3.   Create an enrollment request for the CA server, as shown in Example 11-9.

Example 11-9   *Cisco ASA – Generate CSR*

```
IPTASA(config)# crypto ca enroll CA_Server
WARNING: The certificate enrollment is configured with an fqdn
that differs from the system fqdn. If this certificate will be
used for VPN authentication this may cause connection problems.
Would you like to continue with this enrollment? [yes/no]: yes
% Start certificate enrollment ..
% The subject name in the certificate will be: cn=cups.cisco.local
% The fully-qualified domain name in the certificate will be: cups.cisco.local
% Include the device serial number in the subject name? [yes/no]: no
Display Certificate Request to terminal? [yes/no]: yes
Certificate Request follows:
-----BEGIN CERTIFICATE REQUEST-----
MIIBzjCCATcCAQAwUDEOMAwGA1UEChMFbG9jYWwxDjAMBgNVBAsTBWNpc2NvMQ0w
CwYDVQQDEwRjdXBzMR8wHQYJKoZIhvcNAQkCFhBjdXBzLmNpc2NvLmxvY2FsMIGf
<output omitted>
r70hMQRseT59m2dhMTQjREJXwj32gIvOo41Fv1L6TGcUHqiTZ64rMadO9i3rHZor
PjJSE5YJ4yJYbIE5c9MdOYMXUo60jqcjuR15PfxgClU+pQ==
-----END CERTIFICATE REQUEST-----
Redisplay enrollment request? [yes/no]:no
```

Save the Cisco ASA CSR request in a notepad file. Send the CSR to the CA authority for signing.

Step 4.   Import the CA signed certificate in Cisco ASA, as shown in Example 11-10.

Example 11-10   *Cisco ASA – Import CA Signed Certificate*

```
IPTASA(config)# crypto ca import CA_Server certificate
% The fully-qualified domain name in the certificate will be: cups.cisco.local
Enter the base 64 encoded certificate.
End with the word "quit" on a line by itself
-----BEGIN CERTIFICATE-----
MIIFHjCCBAagAwIBAgIKYWWTWwAAAAAADDANBgkqhkiG9w0BAQUFADA8MRUwEwYK
CZImiZPyLGQBGRYFbG9jYWwxEzARBgoJkiaJk/IsZAEZFgNPQ1MxDjAMBgNVBAMT
<output omitted>
3GIz9U6aCsqwPNIMpXPMYkFsTi0VrHog3hItO99vTtatzzg4nvSvvUsw42cWMAP4
xjq7cNAyCD/zoi8vd9UyW/tT
-----END CERTIFICATE-----
quit
INFO: Certificate successfully imported
```

Microsoft Access Edge Server—CA Certificate Exchange

Step 1.   For the CA root and signed (identity) certificate for Microsoft Access Edge Server follow the steps mentioned in the section, "Configuring OCS Server for CA certificates" (Steps 1 to 16).

Step 2.   Select the certificate that you wish to use for the External Access Edge Interface, and click Next. Click **Next**.

Step 3.   Click the Edge Server Private Interface check box, and click **Next**. Click **Next**. Click **Finish**.

Configure ASA TLS Proxy

Step 1.   Configure the TLS Proxy instances for TLS connections initiated by CUPS and by OCS (as connections may be initiated by CUPC client or MOC client, TLS Proxy instances should be bidirectional), as shown in Example 11-11.

Example 11-11   *Cisco ASA – Configure TLS Proxy Instance*

```
IPTASA(config)# tls-proxy OCS_CUPS
IPTASA(config-tlsp)# server trust-point CA_Server
IPTASA(config-tlsp)# client trust-point cups_proxy
IPTASA(config-tlsp)# client cipher-suite aes128-sha1 aes256-sha1 3des-sha1 null-sha1
  des-sha1
!
IPTASA(config)# tls-proxy CUPS_OCS
IPTASA(config-tlsp)# server trust-point cups_proxy
IPTASA(config-tlsp)# client trust-point CA_Server
IPTASA(config-tlsp)# client cipher-suite aes128-sha1 aes256-sha1 3des-sha1 null-sha1
  des-sha1
```

Step 2. Associate the OCS to CUPS and CUPS to OCS access-lists defined in section "Configure Cisco ASA NAT and ACL" (Step 1) with class-maps, and assign the class-maps to global policy-map, as shown in Example 11-12.

Example 11-12 *Cisco ASA – Configure Class-maps and Global-Policy*

```
IPTASA(config)# class-map CUPS_OCS
IPTASA(config-cmap)# match access-list CUPS_OCS
!
IPTASA(config)# class-map OCS_CUPS
IPTASA(config-cmap)# match access-list OCS_CUPS
!
IPTASA(config)# policy-map type inspect sip SIP_Inspect
IPTASA (config-pmap)# parameters
IPTASA (config-pmap-p)# max-forwards-validation action drop log
!
IPTASA(config)# policy-map global_policy
IPTASA (config-pmap)# class CUPS_OCS
IPTASA (config-pmap-c)# inspect sip SIP Inspect tls-proxy CUPS_OCS
IPTASA (config-pmap)# class OCS_CUPS
IPTASA (config-pmap-c)# inspect sip SIP_Inspect tls-proxy OCS_CUPS
!
IPTASA(config)# service-policy global_policy global
```

Configure OCS 2007 Server

Step 1. Go to **Administration GUI of OCS 2007**. Right-click on **OCS Server > Properties > Global Properties > Federation.**

- Check **Enable Federation** and **Public IM Connectivity**.

- Enter the FQDN, port number for the internal interface of Access Edge server (see Figure 11-13).

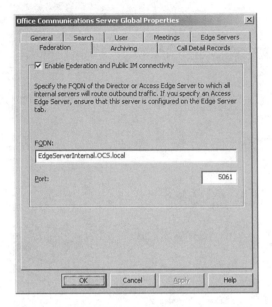

Figure 11-13   *Enable Federation and IM*

■ Go to **Edge Servers Tab**, Click **Add** under **Access Edge and Web Conferencing Edge Servers,** as shown in Figure 11-14.

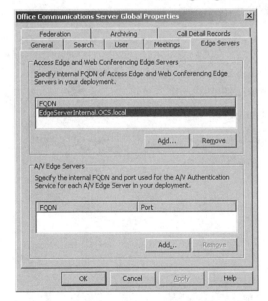

Figure 11-14   *Define Edge Server for OCS*

■ Enter the FQDN for the internal interface of the Access Edge server.

Step 2. Select **Properties > Front End Properties > Federation** in the front-end server branch in the left pane. Check **Enable Federation** and **Public IM Connectivity**

Step 3. Click **Start > Programs > Administrative Tools > Microsoft Office Communicator Server 2007**. Right-click the **Front End Server > Properties > Front End Properties**. Click the **Routing tab** > Click **Add**.

- Enter the domain for the Cisco Unified Presence server, for example **cisco.com**.

- Enter the IP of the Cisco Unified Presence server for the **Next Hop IP address.**

- Select **TCP** for the **Transport value.**

- Enter **5060** for the Port value.

- Click **OK.**

Configure Access Edge Server

Step 1. Go to **Start > Administrative Tools > Computer Management** on the external Access Edge server.

Step 2. Right-click Microsoft Office Communications Server 2007 in the left pane. Click the **IM Provider** tab. Click **Add** (see Figure 11-15).

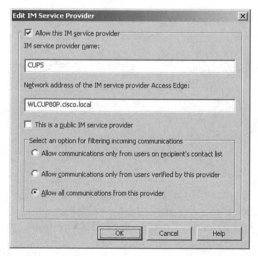

Figure 11-15 *Define Foreign IM Provider (CUPS)*

- Check **Allow the IM Service** Provider.

- Enter the IM service provider name, for example, **CUPS**.

- Enter the **FQDN** of the CUPS, for example, **WLCUP80P.cisco.local**.

■ Ensure that the IM Service Provider Public check box is not checked.

■ Enable **Allow All Communications** from this provider option.

■ Click OK.

Step 3.   Right-click Microsoft Office Communications Server 2007 in **MMC plug-in.** Click **Properties > Access Methods.** Enable **Federation,** as shown in Figure 11-16.

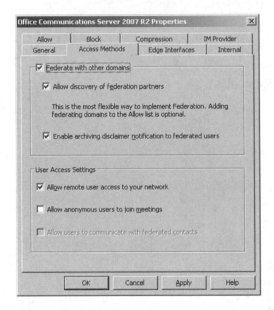

Figure 11-16   *Enable Presence Inter-domain Federation*

At this time, the Access Edge Server, OCS Server, Cisco ASA, and CUPS server should be ready for secure SIP inter-domain/organization federation.

CUPS XMPP Federation Security

To enable secure XMPP federation, follow these steps:

Step 1.   Go to **CUP Administration > Presence > Inter Domain Federation > XMPP Federation > Settings.** Select a security mode from the menu; for security the recommended options are **TLS Required** (preferred) or **TLS Optional** (falls back on dialback for DNS verification of other domain).

Note   Require client-side security certificates is enabled once you select **TLS Required** or an **optional** option. For XMPP federation with WebEx, do not check client-side security certificate option.

Step 2.   Check Enable SASL EXTERNAL on all incoming connections so that CUPS advertises support for SASL EXTERNAL on incoming connection attempts and will implement SASL EXTERNAL validation, as shown in Figure 11-17.

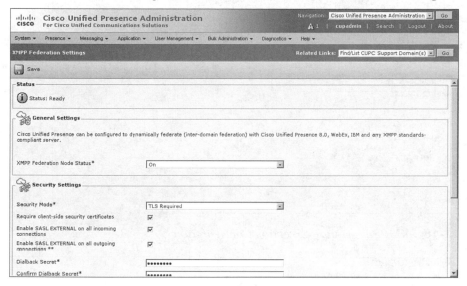

Figure 11-17   *XMPP Federation Settings*

Step 3.   Check **Enable SASL** on the outbound connections to ensure that the CUPS sends an SASL auth-id to the foreign domain in case foreign server requests SASL EXTERNAL.

Step 4.   If you set **TLS** to **Optional,** you should enter the **dialback secret**, which acts as a fallback to verify the identity of a foreign server attempting to connect to the CUP server, using DNS. Click **Save.**

Step 5.   Go to **CUP Administration > Presence > Inter Domain Federation > XMPP Federation > Policy.**

Step 6.   Define the **Allow or Deny** instance for allowed federated traffic from XMPP federated domains, as shown in Figure 11-18.

Note   By default, traffic from all federated domains is allowed, which is equivalent to IP ANY ANY ACL. If you want to restrict traffic, change the policy type to **Deny** and enter domains explicitly allowed.

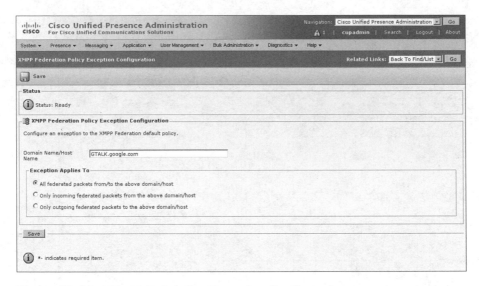

Figure 11-18 *XMPP Federation Exception Configuration*

- Click Add New.

- Enter domain name or the hostname of the foreign server.

- Specify the direction to apply the policy exception.

- Click **Save** in the Policy Exception window and then in Policy window.

Now, trust needs to be established between the CUPS and XMPP enterprise server(service). You can do this by either exporting and adding the CUPS Self-Signed Certificate to the XMPP server or leveraging the CA-Signed certificate where CA is a common trust provider for CUPS and XMPP server. Although the former method is a way to reduce any overheads initially, it is something that small enterprises can leverage. A CA-based certificate provides easy management and is suitable for large enterprises in which internal or external CA is leveraged for mutual trust establishment.

Using CUPS Self-Signed Certificate

Step 1. To export and add a CUPS self-signed certificate, go to **CUPS OS Administration > Certificate Management**. Click **Find**.

Step 2. Look for the **cup-xmpp-s2s** certificate, and download the cup-xmpp-s2s.pem file.

Note Generate (that is, regenerate certificate) for cup-xmpp-s2s from the Generate option, if you want to have a certificate valid from the current date for the next 5 years.

Step 3.   Send the certificate to remote/foreign enterprise so that it can be added as a trusted certificate on their XMPP server.

Using Third-Party CA Signed Certificate

Step 1.   Go to **CUPS OS Administration > Certificate Management**.

Step 2.   Click **Generate CSR > Select cup-xmpp-s2s** as the certificate type, as shown in Figure 11-19.

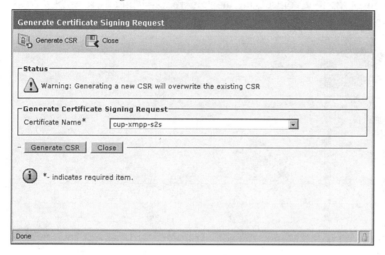

Figure 11-19   *Generate XMPP Certificate Signing Request*

Step 3.   Download the CSR file (named cup-xmpp-s2s.csr) to your PC. Open the file with Notepad or Word pad and copy the text (including **BEGIN CERTIFICATE REQUEST** and **END CERTIFICATE REQUEST**) and e-mail the text to (external) third-party and internal CA. Optionally, you can send the file to the CA.

Step 4.   When you get the signed certificate from the third-party (or Internal) CA, ensure that you upload the CA Root certificate before uploading the signed certificate (identity certificate).

Step 5.   Upload the CA Root certificate as **cup-xmpp-trust** followed by signed certificate, which should be uploaded to **cup-xmpp-s2s** trust store. (Mention the name of root CA certificate while uploading signed certificate.)

At this time, CUPS is ready for secure XMPP federation. The XMPP server also needs to get its certificate request signed and uploaded along with CA root certificate.

Note   Cisco ASA Firewall acts as a normal IP Telephony Firewall for the XMPP federation.

The next section highlights Cisco Unified Personal Communicator Security essentials.

Cisco Unified Personal Communicator Security

Cisco Unified Personal Communicator (CUPC) is a softphone client (see Figure 11-20), which acts as an endpoint for CUPS and is configured as the Cisco Services Framework endpoint in CUCM. CUPC interacts with LDAP, CUCM, and CUPS to deliver audio and video calling, IM, physical phone control, and much more to the end user.

Figure 11-20   *Cisco Unified Personal Communicator*

Note   The configuration examples pertinent to CUPC are based on CUPC version 8.5(3).

Securing CUPC LDAP Connectivity

For secure CUPC - LDAP communication, you can enable Enhanced Directory Integration (EDI).

Note   SSL connections can be initiated to either Global Catalog (GC) or Domain Controller (DC) servers. It requires TCP protocol and uses port 3269 for GC and 636 for DC.

To use SSL with LDAP server, you need a CA signed certificate (root certificate) in addition to an LDAP certificate, in the Windows certificate store. This certificate would be normally issued by the CA (internal or external), which signed the LDAP certificate. This in turn implies that LDAP server(s) should work in LDAPS mode, ready to accept incoming secure SSL sessions from PCs running the CUPC client.

However, when configured for EDI, secure connection is by default enabled, if you want to modify the connection to use SSL, you need to change and create the Registry key as follows:

> *HKEY_CURRENT_USER\Software\Cisco Systems, Inc.\Client Services Framework\Active Directory*

Create the new DWORD value named **UseSSL** with the value set to 1.

You need to export the LDAPS certificate (chain) and install it in the CSF directory on the CUPC PC.

Step 1.   Log in to **https://<LDAP_FQDN>** and click the **Security** icon at the bottom-right corner of your browser window.

Step 2.   Click the Details tab of the Certificate Viewer window, click the **Export** button, and save it to the following folder (Windows OS dependent):

Windows XP – drive:\Documents and Settings\username\Local Settings\ Application Data\Cisco\Unified Communications\Client Services Framework\certificates

Windows Vista / Windows 7 – drive:\Users\username\AppData\Local\ Cisco\Unified Communications\Client Services Framework\certificates

Both LDAP (AD) certificate and the CA root certificate should be placed in respective directories. On the CUP server, follow these procedure to configure LDAP with SSL support.

Go to **CUP Administration > Application > Cisco Unified Personal Communicator > LDAP Server**. Click **Add New** (see Figure 11-21).

- Enter the LDAP server name.

- Enter **FQDN** of the LDAP server.

- Specify the port number **636** used by the LDAP server for secure communication.

- Select **TLS** for the protocol type.

- Click Save.

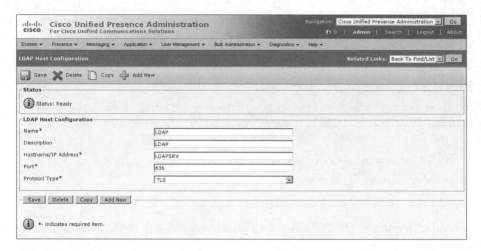

Figure 11-21   *LDAP Configuration in CUPS*

Securing CUPC Connectivity with Cisco Unified Presence

CUPC 8.x (CSF Client) supports secure connectivity with CUP Server. Although this is enabled by default using CUPS self-signed certificates, it can be made to use third-party CA (internal or external) signed certificates.

This can be established using a CA-signed certificate among the Cisco Unified Presence Server, Cisco Unified Communications Manager, and Cisco Unified Personal Communicator. The following steps walk you through the security enablement for CUPC leveraging a third-party CA.

Step 1.   On the CUCM, generate a CSR for Tomcat from the OS administration page, and get it signed by the internal (or external) CA server.

Step 2.   Upload the CA root certificate in the CUCM as **tomcat-trust** and the CA signed tomcat certificate as **tomcat**. Restart Tomcat Service on the CUCM.

Note   Refer to Chapter 9 for detailed steps to get CUCM Tomcat certificates signed and uploaded to a CUCM server.

Step 3.   On the CUPS Server, generate a CSR for CUP truststore from the OS administration page. Get the CSR signed by the internal (or external) CA Server.

Step 4.   Upload the CA root certificate in the CUPS as **cup-trust** and the CA signed cups certificate as **cup**. Restart the Cisco UP SIP Proxy service.

Note   The process to sign and upload the CUPS certificate is similar to that for CUCM Tomcat certificate.

Step 5. Ensure that the certificate mode in the CUPC profile in **CUPS Administration > Application > CUPC > CCMCIP Profile** is set to **keystore only**.

Step 6. Ensure that the CA signed CUP certificate and CA root certificate are placed in the certificates folder of the CUPC client workstations.

Note Delete any .cnf.xml files in the config folder on the CUPC client workstation. Ensure that the CUPC client is not running on the PC (in the background).

Securing CUPC Connectivity with CUCM

CUPC 8.5 is configured as a Client Service Framework (CSF) endpoint in the CUCM. Just like an IP Phone, the signaling and media can be secured by applying a CAPF profile. To enable TLS for signaling and SRTP for media for a CUPC client, follow these steps:

Step 1. Log in to Cisco UCM. Go to **System > Security > Phone Security Profile**.

Step 2. Click **Find**, and search for **Cisco Unified Client Services Framework - Standard SIP Non-Secure** profile. Click **Profile** and copy the same.

Step 3. Create a new profile, such as **CSF—Standard SIP Secure**, as shown in Figure 11-22.

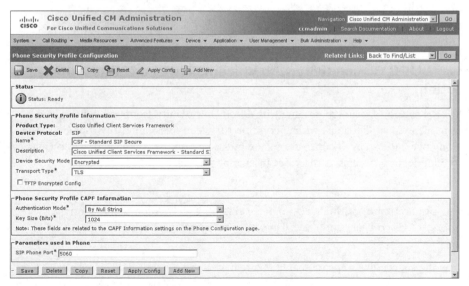

Figure 11-22 *Cisco Client Services Framework Secure Profile for CUPC 8.x*

Ensure that the device security mode is set to **Encrypted** and the Transport Type is set to **TLS**.

Step 4. Go to **Device > Phone > Add New Phone**. Select **Phone Type** as the Client Services Framework. If CSF is already added to the CUCM, go to the CSF page.

Step 5. Scroll down to the **Protocol Specific Information** section. Change the Device Security profile to **secure profile**. In addition, set Certificate Operation to **Install/Upgrade** under the CAPF information section, as depicted in Figure 11-23.

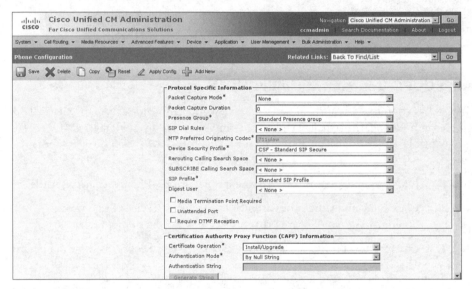

Figure 11-23 *CAPF for CUPC Client*

Securing CUPC Connectivity with Voicemail (Cisco Unity/Unity Connection)

CUPC 8.x supports secure messaging with Cisco Unity/Unity Connection voicemail systems. This capability helps with encryption for secure messaging environments. This section covers the steps to configure secure messaging on the CUPC with Cisco Unity/ Unity Connection systems as the voice messaging servers.

Note Configuration of private (secure) messaging on Unity/Unity Connection is covered in Chapter 10, "Cisco Unity and Cisco Unity Connection Security."

Follow the succeeding steps to enable secure messaging for the CUPC client:

Step 1. In CUPS GUI, go to **Application > Cisco Unified Personal Communicator > Voicemail Server** (see Figure 11-24). Click **Add New**.

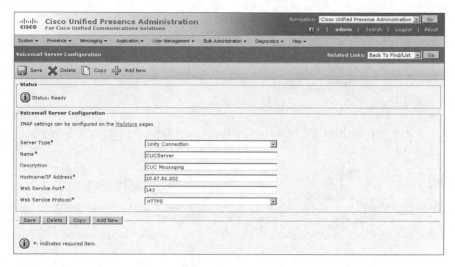

Figure 11-24 *CUPC Voicemail Server Configuration*

Step 2. Select **Unity** or **Unity Connection** in the server type:

- Enter the voicemail server name.

- Enter the FQDN hostname or IP address.

- If you chose **Cisco Unity Servers**, enter **443** for the Web Service Port. For Cisco Unity Connection Servers, enter port **143**.

- For Cisco Unity/Unity Connection Servers, select **HTTPS** for the Web Service Protocol.

- Click **Save**.

Step 3. Go to **Application > Cisco Unified Personal Communicator > Message Store** (see Figure 11-25). Click **Add New**.

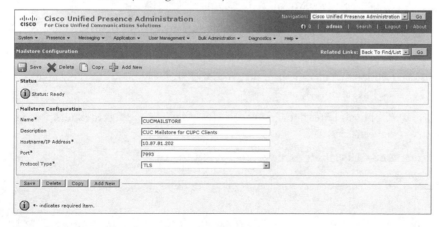

Figure 11-25 *CUPC Mailstore Configuration*

■ Enter the Mailstore server name.

■ Enter the FQDN hostname or IP address of the mailstore.

■ Enter the IMAP port number for CUPC connection to the mailstore server. Enter **143** for Unity. Enter **143** or **7993** for Unity Connection,

■ Click **Save**.

Step 4.   Go to **Application > Cisco Unified Personal Communicator > Voicemail Profile** (see Figure 11-26). Click **Add New**.

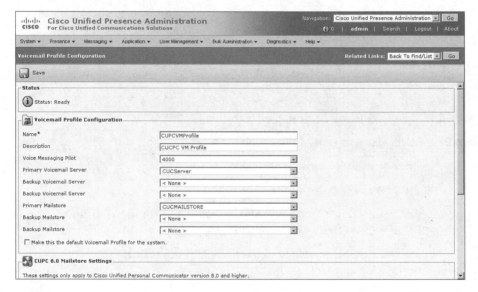

Figure 11-26   *Configuring CUPC Voicemail Profile*

■ Enter the Profile Name.

■ Select the Voice Message Pilot number.

■ Select the Primary (and if applicable secondary) voicemail server(s).

■ Select the Primary (and if applicable secondary) mailstore(s).

■ (Optional) You can make the voicemail profile default for the whole CUPS system.

■ (Optional) Enter details for the CUPC Mailbox settings (defaults preconfigured).

■ Add CUPC users to the profile.

At this point, CUPC clients are set to support encrypted messaging.

Summary

In today's competitive environment, customers seek secure and cost-effective presence solution to cater to their business requirements and to stay connected with their customers and colleagues. It is candid to think about e-presence working without secure bounds. In reality, it needs to be secured to mitigate internal and external threat exposure.

While Cisco Unified Presence Server enables you to leverage intra-enterprise and inter-enterprise presence solution(s) when integrating with existing XMPP or SIP presence infrastructure, it is important to secure the inter-communication between different entities of the presence ecosystem. In this chapter, you learned about the various tools available to secure your presence infrastructure from internal and external threats. For some environments, it can be as simple as securing the intra-domain or intra-organization presence communications, whereas for others it could mean securing presence information traversing unsecure WAN links. You were also introduced to the security of Cisco Unified Personal Communicator (CUPC), which is the presence client for CUPS. Armed with the knowledge to secure your presence infrastructure, you are prepared to deter any possible attacks on your organization's e-presence solution.

In next chapter, you will understand the security issues that pester the sanctity of voice gateways, with emphasis on major voice protocols viz. H.323, MGCP, and SIP. Since threats can be diverse it becomes vital to ensure your voice communications do not fall prey to attacks from within or outside of your organization.

Chapter 12

Cisco Voice Gateway Security

It is a peaceful morning and a fine day at the office. You are checking your e-mails, and there is one from your Telco helpdesk team about your organization XYZ's previous month's telephone bill. You open the e-mail, only to be shocked by the net payable amount of your PSTN bill! It shot through the roof, in the order of a five-digit figure. Stunned? Well, time to wake up to acknowledge that someone hacked your voice gateways and was spending hours chatting with his friends or talking with his fiancé overseas.

To dissuade such a situation, you must ensure that you implement the right security controls in your IP Telephony setup. Toll fraud has been an issue ever since the POTS days, and with the emergence of VoIP, it has found roots in IP-based systems as well. Although an attack may seem inevitable, you should be diligent enough to implement security measures to stop it in its tracks.

This chapter covers the following topics:

- Cisco voice gateway platform security
- Preventing toll fraud on Cisco voice gateways
- Securing conference resources
- Securing voice conversations on gateways
- Securing SRST
- Monitoring Cisco voice gateways

Cisco Voice Gateway Platform Security

As always, it is the physical security that comes at top of the charts. Without a proper physically secured environment (lockdown of equipment in racks, air conditioning, power backup, fire resistant walls and ceilings, and so on), because a security hole in any of the physical layer components can bring down the whole network.

Chapter 5, "Cisco IP Telephony Physical Security," covers the topic of physical security, and Chapter 7, "Cisco IP Telephony Layer 3 Security," covers Cisco IOS gateway logical security (Layer 3 and platform hardening). Refer to these chapters for respective physical and Layer 3 security and platform hardening mechanisms.

Preventing Toll Fraud on Cisco Voice Gateways

This month, your PSTN bill went through the roof! The reason, you ask? The voice gateways in your IP Telephony network were exploited to make long distance and international calls. Toll fraud is one big issue, which has become a pandemic, across all industry verticals. The scale of damage inflicted may vary; however, toll fraud continues to persist. This section details the preventive mechanisms you should implement not to become a victim of toll fraud.

Remember that in Chapter 1, "What Is IP Telephony Security and Why Do You Need It?," you read about toll fraud and some public examples in which hackers took advantage of security flaws or lack of implementation of basic security. Chapter 9, "Cisco Unified Communication Manager Security," covers the configuration of CUCM to restrain toll fraud, and Chapter 10, "Cisco Unity and Unity Connection Security," covers Cisco Unity and Unity Connection configuration to curb toll fraud. This is probably the only topic that continues to be in almost every chapter because of the magnitude of devastation it can inflict not only monetarily, but also reputation-wise to an organization.

Call Source Authentication

Cisco voice gateways enable calls from H.323 or SIP endpoints and peers without authentication. If your voice gateways are behind the corporate firewall, it may not present to a large extent risk of exploitation from external sources; however, it still presents a risk on the inside. (Do not forget that more than 80% of attacks originate from the inside.) Thus, limiting exposure to voice gateways from potentially untrusted networks or sources is imperative.

To do this, you can configure an ACL that can deny signaling traffic from all sources except legitimate call control, for example, CUCM. Example 12-1 shows the configuration (CUCM IP address is: 10.87.81.200) to accept signaling traffic only from CUCM. The signaling traffic includes SIP traffic (TCP and UDP ports 5060 and 5061), MGCP traffic (TCP 2427 and 2428), H.323 traffic (TCP 1720 and 1721), and SCCP traffic (TCP 2000–2002).

Example 12-1   *Access List-Based Call Control Traffic Filtering*

```
IPTRouter(confg)# ip access-list extended CUCMTraffic
IPTRouter(config-ext-nacl)# permit tcp host 10.87.81.200 any range 5060 5061
IPTRouter(config-ext-nacl)# permit udp host 10.87.81.200 any range 5060 5061
```

```
IPTRouter(config-ext-nacl)# permit tcp host 10.87.81.200 any range 1720 1721
IPTRouter(config-ext-nacl)# permit tcp host 10.87.81.200 any range 2427 2428
IPTRouter(config-ext-nacl)# permit tcp host 10.87.81.200 any range 2000 2002
IPTRouter(config-ext-nacl)# deny tcp any any range 5060 5061 log
IPTRouter(config-ext-nacl)# deny udp any any range 5060 5061 log
IPTRouter(config-ext-nacl)# deny tcp any any range 1720 1721 log
IPTRouter(config-ext-nacl)# permit ip any any
!
IPTRouter(config)# interface FastEthernet 1/0
IPTRouter(config-if)# ip access-group CUCMTraffic in
```

Voice Gateway Toll Fraud Prevention by Default

Cisco IOS voice gateways can stop toll fraud attempts in its steps by default. (Although this may sound like Security By Default [SBD] feature of CUCM, it certainly is somewhat close to it!) This new feature is Call Source Authentication, which has been introduced in IOS version 15.(1)2T and later, which is the default behavior of a toll-fraud prevention feature.

Note   Upgrading your IOS voice gateway to 15.1(2)T can block all inbound VoIP call setups until the gateway is properly configured to trust the call origination sources. This method to restrain toll fraud is somewhat an automation of what was mentioned in the previous section, "Call Source Authentication."

This feature is enabled by default, as shown in Example 12-2.

Example 12-2   *Toll Fraud APP Feature Enablement*

```
IPTRouter(config)# voice service voip
IPTRouter(conf-voi-serv)# ip address trusted authenticate
```

At this point, whenever you configure a VoIP dial-peer, the router automatically adds the destination IP address(es) that are defined as an IPv4 target in a VoIP dial-peer to the trusted source list. You can see the trusted source list contents in the output of commands, as shown in Example 12-3.

Example 12-3   *Trusted IP Address List*

```
IPTRouter# show ip address trusted list
IP Address Trusted Authentication
Administration State: UP
Operation State:      UP
IP Address Trusted Call Block   Cause: call-reject (21)
```

```
VoIP Dial-peer IPv4 Session   Targets:
Peer Tag          Oper State     Session Target
--------          ----------     --------------
160               UP             ipv4:10.87.81.200
180               UP             ipv4:10.87.81.201
```

Note   When the TOLLFRAUD_APP rejects a call, it generates a Q.850 disconnect cause value of 21. You can see this in the **debug voice ccapi inout** output.

Class of Restriction (COR)

The concept of Class of Restriction (COR) is identical to CUCM partitions and calling search spaces. The only difference is that in CUCM this is implemented for the end-points (IP Phones and analog endpoints), trunks, translation patterns, and route patterns (actually a lot of places), whereas in an IOS voice gateway, COR is implemented at either dial-peers or ephone-dns. The COR rules are used in H.323 and SIP gateways where the gateway is in control of call flows (unlike MGCP, where call control is with CUCM). Moreover, COR is used for implementing calling restrictions on a voice gateway when it goes in SRST mode. Because during SRST, any call restrictions defined within CUCM would not apply, COR comes to your aid. This section introduces the concept of calling restriction based on COR for toll fraud prevention.

To apply COR, there are two basic commands used to configure calling restrictions (outbound or inbound), and these commands are equivalent to CUCM partition and Call Search Space (CSS):

- **dial-peer cor custom** = partition
- **dial-peer cor list** = calling search space

Note   For a call to be controlled whether inbound or outbound, both an incoming and an outgoing COR list can exist. However, the outgoing COR list must be a superset of the incoming COR list.

Step 1.   As you would normally define internal, emergency, local, national, international, toll-free, services, and so on for partitions on CUCM, the same level needs to be defined on the IOS voice gateway (to have consistency in the overall dial plan). Example 12-4 outlines the definition of various partitions in a Cisco IOS router.

Example 12-4 *Define COR Custom (Partitions)*

```
IPTRouter(config)# dial-peer cor custom
IPTRouter(config-dp-cor)# name internal
IPTRouter(config-dp-cor)# name emergency
IPTRouter(config-dp-cor)# name local
IPTRouter(config-dp-cor)# name national
IPTRouter(config-dp-cor)# name international
```

Note The name for **cor custom dial-peer** can be anything. It is recommended to keep it short yet descriptive. The same applies to **cor list dial-peer**.

Step 2.   Define cor list = CSS and assign the desired cor custom = partitions, as shown in Example 12-5.

Example 12-5 *Define COR List (CSS)*

```
IPTRouter(config)# dial-peer cor list internal
IPTRouter(config-dp-corlist)# member internal
!
IPTRouter(config)# dial-peer cor list emergency
IPTRouter(config-dp-corlist)# member emergency
!
IPTRouter(config)# dial-peer cor list local
IPTRouter(config-dp-corlist)# member emergency
IPTRouter(config-dp-corlist)# member local
!
IPTRouter(config)# dial-peer cor list national
IPTRouter(config-dp-corlist)# member emergency
IPTRouter(config-dp-corlist)# member local
IPTRouter(config-dp-corlist)# member national
!
IPTRouter(config)# dial-peer cor list international
IPTRouter(config-dp-corlist)# member emergency
IPTRouter(config-dp-corlist)# member local
IPTRouter(config-dp-corlist)# member national
IPTRouter(config-dp-corlist)# member international
!
IPTRouter(config)# dial-peer cor list all
IPTRouter(config-dp-corlist)# member internal
IPTRouter(config-dp-corlist)# member emergency
IPTRouter(config-dp-corlist)# member local
IPTRouter(config-dp-corlist)# member national
IPTRouter(config-dp-corlist)# member international
```

Step 3.   After the cor lists have been defined, you must apply them to the respective **dial-peers**, as illustrated in Example 12-6.

Example 12-6   *Assign COR Lists to Voice Dial Peers*

```
IPTRouter(config)# dial-peer voice 10 pots
IPTRouter(config-dial-peer)# corlist incoming all
IPTRouter(config-dial-peer)# incoming called-number .
IPTRouter(config-dial-peer)# port 1/0/0:23
IPTRouter(config-dial-peer)# direct-inward-dial
IPTRouter(config-dial-peer)# forward-digits all
!
IPTRouter(config)# dial-peer voice 911 pots
IPTRouter(config-dial-peer)# corlist outgoing emergency
IPTRouter(config-dial-peer)# destination-pattern 911
IPTRouter(config-dial-peer)# port 1/0/0:23
IPTRouter(config-dial-peer)# forward-digits all
!
IPTRouter(config)# dial-peer voice 70 pots
IPTRouter(config-dial-peer)# corlist outgoing local
IPTRouter(config-dial-peer)# destination-pattern 9[2-9]......$
IPTRouter(config-dial-peer)# port 1/0/0:23
IPTRouter(config-dial-peer)# forward-digits 7
!
IPTRouter(config)# dial-peer voice 110 pots
IPTRouter(config-dial-peer)# corlist outgoing national
IPTRouter(config-dial-peer)# destination-pattern 91[2-9]..[2-9]......$
IPTRouter(config-dial-peer)# port 1/0/0:23
IPTRouter(config-dial-peer)# forward-digits 11
!
IPTRouter(config)# dial-peer voice 900 pots
IPTRouter(config-dial-peer)# corlist outgoing international
IPTRouter(config-dial-peer)# destination-pattern 9011T
IPTRouter(config-dial-peer)# port 1/0/0:23
IPTRouter(config-dial-peer)# prefix 011
```

While Examples 12-4 through 12-6 show the configuration for an H.323 or SIP voice gateway, you also need to consider SRST configuration during which local IP Phones should have same level of restriction as they had when CUCM was reachable. You need to define which devices will have what calling and called restrictions while in SRST (see Example 12-7). This is done under **call-manager-fallback**.

Example 12-7   *COR Configuration for SRST*

```
SRSTGW(config)# call-manager-fallback
SRSTGW(config-cm-fallback)# secondary-dialtone 9
SRSTGW(config-cm-fallback)# ip source-address 10.200.200.110 port 2000
SRSTGW(config-cm-fallback)# max-ephones 10
SRSTGW(config-cm-fallback)# max-dn 20
SRSTGW(config-cm-fallback)# transfer-system full-consult
SRSTGW(config-cm-fallback)# transfer-pattern 8...
SRSTGW(config-cm-fallback)# cor incoming local 1 8001
SRSTGW(config-cm-fallback)# cor incoming international 2 8002
SRSTGW(config-cm-fallback)# cor incoming internal  8003 - 8005
SRSTGW(config-cm-fallback)# cor outgoing internal  8001 - 8005
```

Calls from IP Phones to IOS Voice Gateway

Here, the incoming calls to the IOS voice gateway from the IP Phone (ingress to router) will be filtered based on the destination dialed by the IP Phone, as shown in Example 12-7:

- Directory number (DN) 8001 is allowed to call internal, emergency, and local because it has access to the cor list (equivalent to CSS) local.

- Directory number (DN) 8002 is allowed to call internal, emergency, local, national, and international because it has access to the cor list (equivalent to CSS) international.

- Directory number (DN) 8003, 8004, and 8005 (a range is selected) is allowed to call only internal because it has access to the cor list (equivalent to CSS) internal.

Calls to IP Phones from IOS Voice Gateway

The calls based on the criteria selected by dial-peer cor dictate whether a call can or cannot proceed to an IP Phone. Ideally, you would like all calls to reach the IP Phones (from other IP Phones or incoming calls from PSTN), for example:

- Directory number (DN) 8001–8005 (a range is selected) are allowed to be called by the voice gateway by the cor list internal.

Thus, by leveraging COR on IOS voice gateways, you can minimize the risk of unauthorized or unprivileged end users dialing international destinations or long distance (national) calls, thereby reducing the likelihood of toll fraud.

Call Transfer and Forwarding

In addition to calling restrictions, it is mandatory that call-forward and call-transfer capability is restricted so that the users can transfer and forward calls only internally or to predefined destinations while the gateway is in an SRST mode.

Ideally, for the least permissive access, call forwarding and transfers to all numbers except those on local IP Phones should be blocked. With that said, it is the ideal and the least permissive access. It depends on your organization's (IP Telephony) security policy. However, not disabling end-user functionality to forward to transfer calls to for example local-area code(s), you can allow transfers and call forward to non-internal numbers as well.

The **transfer-pattern** command enables the transfer of calls to PSTN. For call forward, the **call-forward max-length** command can be used to limit the maximum digits allowed for call forward. Example 12-8 shows the configuration of call forward and call transfer restriction.

Example 12-8 *Call Forward and Transfer Restrictions for SRST*

```
SRSTGW(config)# call-manager-fallback
SRSTGW(config-cm-fallback)# secondary-dialtone 9
SRSTGW(config-cm-fallback)# ip source-address 10.200.200.110 port 2000
SRSTGW(config-cm-fallback)# max-ephones 10
SRSTGW(config-cm-fallback)# max-dn 20
SRSTGW(config-cm-fallback)# transfer-pattern 9919....
SRSTGW(config-cm-fallback)# call-forward pattern 8...
SRSTGW(config-cm-fallback)# call-forward noan 8100 timeout 10
SRSTGW(config-cm-fallback)# call-forward busy 8100
```

The configuration shown in Example 12-8 restricts call forwarding to 8... (where . equals any number between 0 and 9), call forward busy, and no answer to an internal extension (could be an operator phone) 8100. Moreover, it pins down transfers to 9919XXXX, which are local calls for area code 919.

The next section covers the methods to secure voice conversation (media and signaling) as it pertains to Cisco voice gateways. Media encryption support for Cisco voice gateways is equivalent to Voice over Virtual Private Network (V3PN). It is particularly helpful to enhance the voice privacy on Cisco IP Phones in remote offices, while terminating media on local gateways before going out to PSTN and ITSP.

Securing Conference Resources

Cisco voice gateways provide the hardware (DSP) to enable secure conferencing facility. Secure conferencing is required when three or more secure IP Phones are in conference and the nature of the conversation must remain secure, that is, private (call privacy). Without a secure conference bridge, the call will be unsecured even if all the IP Phones in the conference are secure (that is, using TLS for signaling security and SRTP) because without all secure parties in a call (inclusive of IP Phones and conference bridge), the call falls back to an unsecure call. This section details the steps required to enable a secure conference bridge on a Cisco IOS voice gateway.

Note   The IOS version required to support secure conferencing is 12.4(11)T or later.

Step 1.   Ensure that the CUCM cluster is in mixed mode. Refer to the "Certificate-Based Secure Signaling and Media" section in Chapter 9 for detailed information about converting your cluster into the mixed mode to support encrypted and authenticated calls. The cluster security mode status can be verified by going to **System > Enterprise Parameters**. The security mode value should be 1.

Step 2.   Ensure that the clock is set on all IOS routers and on CUCM. Ideally, they should be synced with same NTP server. If the certificates have mismatched time stamps, there will be revocation issues in addition to certificate acceptance issues. The time zone and clock can be verified by using the following commands:

Cisco IOS routers: **clock set** and **clock timezone**

CUCM: Set the correct timezone in CLI using the command:

admin: set timezone <timezone number based on region/city or state>

For example: **admin: set timezone 150** (timezone 150 = America/New York)

Note   The time zone number can be determined by the CLI command **show timezone list**.

Step 3.   You can use an external CA, an internal CA, or an IOS CA. This example uses a dedicated router acting as a CA, as shown in Example 12-9. (Ensure that the http server is enabled on the CA router.)

Example 12-9   *CA Router Configuration*

```
CARouter(config)# crypto pki server CA
CARouter(cs-server)# database level complete
CARouter(cs-server)# grant auto
CARouter(cs-server)# database url nvram
CARouter(cs-server)# lifetime ca-certificate <number of days>
CARouter(cs-server)# lifetime certificate <number of days>
CARouter(cs-server)# no shut
```

Step 4. On the Secure CFB router, create a trust point used to retrieve and store the dspfarm certificate, as illsutrated in Example 12-11.

Example 12-11 *Secure Conference Router Enrollment with CA Router*

```
SecureCFB(config)# crypto pki trustpoint SecureCFB
SecureCFB(ca-trustpoint)# enrollment url http://<IP of CA Router>:80
SecureCFB(ca-trustpoint)# serial-number none
SecureCFB(ca-trustpoint)# fqdn none
SecureCFB(ca-trustpoint)# ip-address none
SecureCFB(ca-trustpoint)# subject-name cn=SecureCFB, ou=cisco, o=cisco
SecureCFB(ca-trustpoint)# revocation-check none
SecureCFB(ca-trustpoint)# rsakeypair SecureCFB
```

Note The name **SecureCFB** is also the name that dspfarm profile uses to register with CUCM because it is the CN for the IOS router certificate.

Step 5. Authenticate and enroll the secure conference bridge router's trust point with the CA router, as shown in Example 12-12.

Example 12-12 *CA Enrollment*

```
SecureCFB(config)# crypto pki authenticate SecureCFB
Certificate has the following attributes:
      Fingerprint MD5: 7EF1FD44 797C3317 BA4F9122 0520C72B
     Fingerprint SHA1: 41C3959D 349475A6 46D90C0C 6FBE70FA AC49BE03
% Do you accept this certificate? [yes/no]: yes
Trustpoint CA certificate accepted.
SecureCFB(ca-trustpoint)# crypto pki enroll SecureCFB
%
% Start certificate enrollment ..
% Create a challenge password. You will need to verbally provide this
   password to the CA Administrator in order to revoke your certificate.
   For security reasons your password will not be saved in the configuration.
   Please make a note of it.
Password:
Re-enter password:
```

```
% The subject name in the certificate will include: SecureCFB
% Include an IP address in the subject name? [no]:
Request certificate from CA? [yes/no]: yes
% Certificate request sent to Certificate Authority
% The 'show crypto pki certificate secdsp verbose' command will show
the fingerprint.
*Jun 19 19:45:34.855: CRYPTO_PKI:  Certificate Request Fingerprint
MD5: 3A6277A1 9D8BB4B5 6C0B132A FBAAF314
*Jun 19 19:45:34.855: CRYPTO_PKI:  Certificate Request Fingerprint
SHA1: A6443197 D197FA63 336FBD2F ED4BAEEF AA8DD07A
```

Step 6.   Copy the IOS root cert to the CUCM. There are two ways to do this. Either export the certificates to the router's Flash and then copy using TFTP, or export the certificates to the terminal, copy and paste them to a notepad file, and save them as .pem files. Or export them to terminal. Example 12-13 shows the flash method.

Example 12-13   *IOS Root CA and Identity Certificates Export*

```
SecureCFB(config)# crypto pki export SecureCFB pem url flash: SecureCFB
% Exporting CA certificate...
Destination filename [SecureCFB]?
Writing file to flash: SecureCFB.ca
% Exporting router certificate...
Destination filename [SecureCFB]?
Writing file to flash: SecureCFB.crt
```

Step 7.   Now you have the root CA certificate (SecureCFB.ca) and the identity certificate issues to the Secure CFB router (SecureCFB.crt). Both should be uploaded to CUCM as CAPF-Trust certificates; CA followed by the identity certificate (rename both file extensions to .cer or .pem extension), as shown in Figure 12-1.

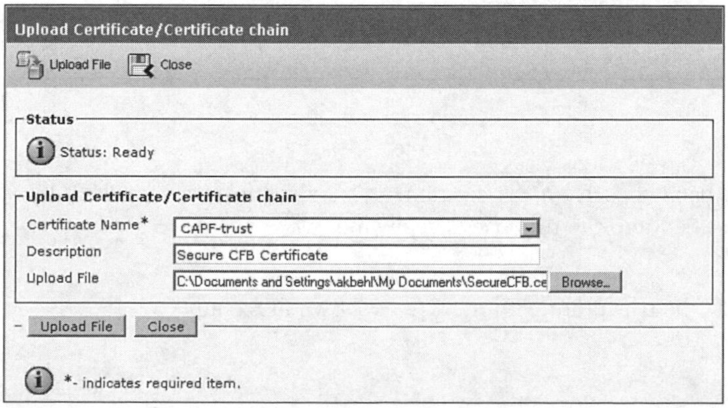

Figure 12-1   *Importing IOS (CA Root and Router Identity) Certificate in CUCM*

> **Note** Restart CUCM, TFTP, CAPF, and CTL services on all nodes running CUCM and TFTP services.

Step 8.   Download CallManager.pem certificate from certificate management. Go to **Cisco Unified OS Administration > Certificate Management.** Click the **CallManager.pem** certificate to download it. Ensure that you note the CN. This can be done by clicking the certificate and looking at the certificate details, as depicted in Figure 12-2.

Figure 12-2   *CUCM Self-Signed Certificate*

This CN will be used as the trustpoint name for the CUCM certificate when its created in the Secure CFB router.

Step 9.   Create a trustpoint to store the CUCM certificate, as shown in Example 12-14.

Example 12-14   *CUCM Enrollment with IOS Secure Conference Bridge*

```
SecureCFB(config)# crypto pki trustpoint WLCUCM862P
SecureCFB(ca-trustpoint)# enrollment terminal
SecureCFB(ca-trustpoint)# revocation-check none
```

> **Note** Since terminal has been chosen for the enrollment, it's essential that the CUCM certificate is copied and pasted into the router terminal window.

Step 10.   Authenticate the trustpoint with the CA, as shown in Example 12-15.

Example 12-15 *CUCM Enrollment with IOS Secure Conference Bridge (Cont'd)*

```
SecureCFB(config)# crypto pki authenticate WLCUCM862P
```

You are prompted to paste the base-64-format cert to the screen. Copy and paste the PKCS value from the certificate to the router terminal session to complete the authentication.

Note Step 10 should be repeated for each call processing server that references this conference bridge or hosts the IP Phones, which leverage the secure conference bridge.

Step 11. Configure the **dspfarm profile** for **conferencing**, as shown in Example 12-16.

Example 12-16 *Secure Conferencing Profile Configuration*

```
SecureCFB(config)# voice-card 1
SecureCFB(config-voicecard)# dsp service dspfarm
!
SecureCFB(config)# dspfarm profile 10 conference security
SecureCFB(config-dspfarm-profile)# trustpoint SecureCFB
SecureCFB(config-dspfarm-profile)# codec g711ulaw
SecureCFB(config-dspfarm-profile)# codec g711alaw
SecureCFB(config-dspfarm-profile)# codec g729r8
SecureCFB(config-dspfarm-profile)# maximum sessions 4
SecureCFB(config-dspfarm-profile)# associate application SCCP
```

Step 12. Configure the SCCP profile, as shown in Example 12-17.

Example 12-17 *SCCP Profile Configuration*

```
SecureCFB(config)# sccp local FastEthernet0/0
SecureCFB(config)# sccp ccm 10.87.81.200 identifier 1 version 7.0+
SecureCFB(config)# sccp ccm 10.100.100.200 identifier 2 version 7.0+
SecureCFB(config)# sccp
!
SecureCFB(config)# sccp ccm group 1
SecureCFB(config-sccp-ccm)# associate ccm 2 priority 1
SecureCFB(config-sccp-ccm)# associate ccm 1 priority 2
SecureCFB(config-sccp-ccm)# associate profile 101 register SecureCFB
```

Step 13. Configure the Conference Bridge in CUCM to complete the configuration (see Figure 12-3). Ensure that the CFB type is IOS Enhanced CFB. Register it with the same name (in this case, **SecureCFB**) as used in SCCP configuration.

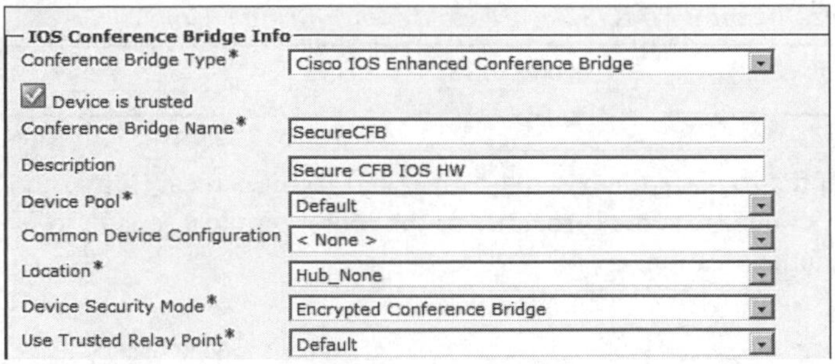

IOS Conference Bridge Info
Conference Bridge Type*: Cisco IOS Enhanced Conference Bridge
☑ Device is trusted
Conference Bridge Name*: SecureCFB
Description: Secure CFB IOS HW
Device Pool*: Default
Common Device Configuration: < None >
Location*: Hub_None
Device Security Mode*: Encrypted Conference Bridge
Use Trusted Relay Point*: Default

Figure 12-3 *Cisco IOS Enhanced Conference Bridge Configuration*

At this point, you should have an operational secure conference bridge. To test the same, engage three or more secured IP Phones in a conference call. (Ensure that the MRGL they are referencing directly or in the device pool have this secure conference bridge in its MRG.) All IP Phones should retain the lock symbol, which signifies a secure call. However, if there's an IP Phone that is not configured to make and receive encrypted calls or cannot support encryption, participating in a secure conference call, the entire conference call falls back to an unsecure conference.

Securing Voice Conversations on Cisco Voice Gateways

Let's set in motion with a real-world state of affairs. You have multiple remote sites where a small user population exists. The IP Telephony connectivity from Headquarters to remote sites can be via a public network (the Internet), a lease line, or an MPLS. Although your IP traffic (voice and data) traversing the WAN circuits can be encrypted with IPSec, how about the local IP Phone to the voice gateway traffic? By default, it will be in clear text unless you configure the voice gateways to support SRTP, failing which anyone on the inside can attempt to snoop into the voice conversations leaving your network, going out to PSTN or ITSP.

You must discern that the use of SRTP on a Cisco voice gateway has its own impact on the performance. Using the **codec complexity** of secure uses more DSP resources than using a codec without security. For example, setting **codec complexity secure** restricts the number of channels per NM-HDV network module from 4 to 2. Therefore, before you enable security on your Cisco voice gateways, you must ensure that the gateway's licenses, processing power, and the DSPs provisioned are sufficient to support SRTP and related security configuration.

The following sections detail the configuration of MGCP, H.323, and SIP gateways to support SRTP. It is worthwhile to note that unlike H.323 and MGCP, SIP voice gateways, CUBE, and so on support Transport Layer Security (TLS), which protects both signaling and media streams to and from CUCM. H.323 and MGCP gateways support only media encryption (if enabled) and the signaling is clear text. Thus, to protect signaling from reconnaissance attacks, it is highly recommended to leverage IPSec tunnels from CUCM to H.323 and MGCP gateways.

While the best practice is to have the tunnel from the voice gateway terminate on Cisco ASA Firewall acting as the default gateway for CUCM (or any IP Telephony server), both CUCM acting as the IPSec head-end and Cisco ASA acting as the IPSec head-end are covered. Chapter 9 briefly covers this topic. Figure 12-2 portrays these two options.

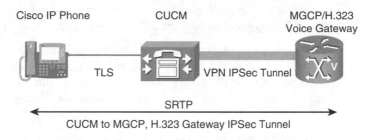

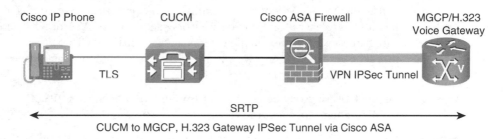

Figure 12-4   *CUCM to Voice Gateway IPSec Options*

> **Note**   CUCM IP addresses are 10.87.81.200/24 and 10.100.100.200/24, whereas the voice gateway address is assumed to be 10.100.200.180/24.

Configuring MGCP Support for SRTP

This section details the MGCP voice gateway configuration to support SRTP and secure signaling:

Step 1.   The MGCP Gateway should be configured to send and receive calls and the CUCM server (or cluster) should be in mixed-mode to support encryption between endpoints (IP Phones and Gateways).

Step 2.   Setting the encryption of RTP on the voice gateway requires only a single command, as illustrated in Example 12-18.

Example 12-18 *MGCP SRTP Package Enablement*

```
MGCPGW(config)# mgcp package-capability srtp-package
```

It takes some effort to ensure that the signaling between the CUCM and the MGCP Gateway is secured because by default it is sent in clear text.

Step 3. After the SRTP capability is enabled, issue **no mgcp** and then **mgcp** command. At this point, the secured IP Phone should establish an encrypted RTP stream between the IP Phone and the voice gateway, and the same can be confirmed by the presence of a lock icon, on successful completion of the call.

Step 4. To secure the encryption keys for the RTP stream, which are sent in clear text, an IPSec tunnel must also be configured between CUCM and the voice gateway. Now, there are two options: One is to have the IPSec tunnels terminate on the CUCM (not recommended for the performance reasons) and the other is to have a next-hop device (for example, Cisco ASA or IOS router with hardware encryption module) terminating tunnels for CUCM (recommended). For this example, we take the approach to configure the tunnels from the MGCP Gateway to the CUCM.

Step 5. On the CUCM, go to the **OS Administration GUI > Security > IPSEC Configuration**, and click **Add New**.

Step 6. Enter the IPSec Policy Name, and enter other information requested, such as the following:

- Pre-Shared Key (secure key that will be exchanged between CUCM and IOS router)

- Peer IP (destination address, IP of MGCP Gateway)

- Source Address (IP address of CUCM)

- Mode (Transport and Tunnel)

- Remote Port (Leave it at default 500)

- Protocol (TCP, UCP, or ANY)

- Encryption Algorithm (DES, 3DES, AES-128, and AES-256)

- Hash Algorithm (SHA1 and MD5)

- ESP Algorithm (optional, however recommended)

- Phase 1 and 2 DH Group Information

- Enable Policy (check the check box when the policy is configured, as shown in Figure 12-5)

Figure 12-5 *CUCM IPSec Policy Configuration*

Note If the voice gateway is configured to take calls on more than one interface, it is necessary to create an additional IPSec policy for each interface. Moreover, there must be a specific policy for each gateway and its interfaces. For all CUCM subscribers, IPSec policies should be configured with appropriate Source IP addresses with the mirror ACL on the voice gateway.

Step 7.   Configure the IPSec tunnel on the gateway (which is a mirror of the CUCM IPSec configuration), as shown in Example 12-19.

Example 12-19 *IOS Voice Gateway IPSec Tunnel Configuration*

```
MGCPGW(config)# access-list 110 permit ip host 10.100.200.180 host 10.87.81.200
!
MGCPGW(config)# crypto isakmp policy 10
MGCPGW(config-isakmp)# encryption 3des
MGCPGW(config-isakmp)# authentication pre-share
MGCPGW(config-isakmp)# encryption sha
MGCPGW(config-isakmp)# group 2
```

```
MGCPGW(config-isakmp)# lifetime 3600
!
MGCPGW(config)# crypto isakmp key cisco123 address 10.87.81.200 no-xauth
!
MGCPGW(config)# crypto ipsec transform-set mgcpset esp-3des esp-sha-hmac
!
MGCPGW(config)# crypto map mgcpmap 10 ipsec-isakmp
MGCPGW(config-crypto-map)# set peer 10.87.81.200
MGCPGW(config-crypto-map)# set transform-set mgcpset
MGCPGW(config-crypto-map)# set pfs group2
MGCPGW(config-crypto-map)# match address 110
!
MGCPGW(config)# interface FastEthernet 1/0
MGCPGW(config-if)# ip address 10.100.200.180 255.255.255.0
MGCPGW(configif)# crypto map mgcpmap
```

Step 8.   To ensure that the IPSec tunnel works, go to **CUCM OS Administration GUI > Services > Ping**, and try to ping the voice gateway. Ensure that the box marked **Validate IPSec** is checked. The response should say, "Successfully Validated IPSec Connection."

The next section covers the configuration details of SIP Gateways to support SRTP.

Configuring H.323 Gateway to Support SRTP

This section details the configuration of CUCM and H.323 gateway to support SRTP calls with secure signaling. You can configure TLS and SRTP at the global level or dial-peer level on the voice gateway. If TLS/SRTP is configured at the global level and dial-peer level, dial-peer takes preference. Cisco IOS release 12.4(6)T or later is required for H.323 SRTP support.

Almost similar to the MGCP gateway, the H.323 gateway also does a key exchange for the setup of the SRTP call in clear text. In H.323, it is the gateway that generates the SRTP keys and sends them along in the H.245 capabilities' exchange. Hence, certificate exchange between the gateway and CUCM is based on certificate exchange instead of a pre-shared key and must be secured with an IPSec tunnel. The following example gives an insight to configuration of an IPSec tunnel from an H.323 voice gateway to Cisco ASA, which acts as the default gateway for CUCM. This way, you follow the preferred method to terminate the IPSec tunnel to the nearest network device instead of terminating it on CUCM.

Step 1.   Configure the H.323 gateway to support SRTP. You can configure SRTP support at the global (see Example 12-20) or dial-peer (see Example 12-21) level.

Example 12-20 *Global Configuration for SRTP Support*

```
H.323GW(config)# voice service voip
H.323GW(conf-voi-serv)# srtp fallback
```

Example 12-21 *Dial-Peer Level Configuration for SRTP Support*

```
H.323GW(config)# dial-peer voice 101 voip
H.323GW(config-dial-peer)# destination-pattern 2…$
H.323GW(config-dial-peer)# session target ipv4:10.87.81.200
H.323GW(config-dial-peer)# srtp fallback
```

Step 2. Configure **codec complexity** to support secure calls (Example 12-22).

Example 12-22 *DSPFarm Configuration for Secure Codec*

```
H.323GW(config)# voice-card 1
H.323GW(config)# dspfarm
H.323GW(config)# dsp services dspfarm
H.323GW(config-voice-card)# codec complexity secure
```

Step 3. Configure Cisco ASA for IPsec tunnel termination, as shown in Example 12-23, so that the IPSec tunnel from H.323 gateway can terminate on the Cisco ASA Firewall.

Example 12-23 *Cisco ASA Security Appliance IPSec Configuration*

```
IPTASA(config)# access-list extended L2LGW permit ip host 10.87.81.200
  255.255.255.255
10.100.200.180 255.255.255.255
!
IPTASA(config)# nat (inside) 0 access-list L2LGW
!
IPTASA(config)# crypto isakmp enable outside
!
IPTASA(config)# crypto isakmp policy 10
IPTASA(config)# authentication pre-share
IPTASA(config)# encryption 3des
IPTASA(config)# hash md5
IPTASA(config)# group 2
IPTASA(config)# lifetime 3600
!
IPTASA(config)# tunnel-group 10.100.200.180 type ipsec-l2l
IPTASA(config)# tunnel-group 10.100.200.180 ipsec-attributes
IPTASA(config)# pre-shared-key cisco123
!
```

```
IPTASA(config)# crypto ipsec transform-set myset esp-3des esp-sha-hmac
!
IPTASA(config)# crypto map CUCMGW 10 match address L2LGW
IPTASA(config)# crypto map CUCMGW 10 set peer 10.100.200.180
IPTASA(config)# crypto map CUCMGW 10 set transform-set myset
IPTASA(config)# crypto map CUCMGW 10 set pfs group2
!
IPTASA(config)# crypto map CUCMGW interface outside
```

Step 4.   The mirror configuration at the H.323 gateway for the VPN tunnel will be same as that of MGCPGW, as illustrated in the earlier section, in Step 7, with the exception of the peer address that is now Cisco ASA Firewall's outside IP.

At this point, the H.323 gateway should establish the IPSec. In addition, when you use an H.323 gateway with a gatekeeper, you can authenticate the Registration, Admission, and Status Protocol (RAS) messages between the gateway and the gatekeeper. Chapter 13, "Cisco Voice Gatekeeper and Cisco Unified Border Element Security," covers the details and specifics.

Configuring SIP Gateway to Support SRTP

This section details the SIP voice gateway configuration to support SRTP and secure signaling. The process to configure the SIP TLS/SRTP is different from MGCP and H.323 configuration because for a SIP voice gateway, you configure a secure SIP Trunk (as detailed in Chapter 9 in the section, "SIP Trunk Security"), and the gateway undergoes certificate exchange with the CUCM.

The configuration of the voice gateway for the certificate exchange with the CUCM is much like that of a secure conference bridge. Refer to the "Configuring Secure Conferencing" section to review the process of:

- Enrolling an IOS voice gateway to an IOS CA server
- Generating IOS voice gateway certificates (trustpoint)
- Exporting IOS voice gateway certificates and importing them in CUCM
- Exporting CUCM certificates
- Enrolling CUCM with IOS voice gateway
- Importing CUCM certificates in IOS voice gateway

Follow Steps 1 through 10 as detailed in the section, "Configuring a Secure Conference Bridge." These are equally applicable for enabling SRTP support on a Cisco IOS SIP voice gateway. The only deviation is at Step 7, where the IOS certificate should be uploaded as CallManager-Trust instead of CAPF-Trust. In addition, it is recommended that the CN of the certificate is kept the same as the hostname of the router. The additional configuration steps that you need to enable SIP voice gateway for SRTP and TLS are as follows:

Step 1.   Configure the trustpoints (see Example 12-24) which will be used for certificate exchange with CUCM.

Example 12-24   *Trustpoint Definition*

```
SIPGW(config)# sip-ua
SIPGW(config-sip-ua)# crypto signaling remote-addr 10.87.81.200 255.255.255.255
  trustpoint SIPGW strict-cipher
```

Note   For multiple CUCM servers, as many entries must be defined under **sip-ua**. For this example, we assume that SIP Voice Gateway is enrolled with IOS CA router with trustpoint SIPGW.

Step 2.   Cisco IOS SIP Voice Gateways can have SRTP support enabled globally or on a VoIP dial-peer. When the SRTP is enabled globally (see Example 12-25), it applies to all dial-peers however, if the configuration is done at a dial-peer (see Example 12-26) level, then the dial-peer configuration supersedes the global configuration. The following examples illustrate how you can enable SIP SRTP support globally and at dial-peer level.

Example 12-25   *Global Configuration for SRTP*

```
SIPGW(config)# voice service voip
SIPGW(conf-voi-serv)# srtp
SIPGW(conf-voi-serv)# srtp fallback
SIPGW(conf-voi-serv)# sip
SIPGW(conf-serv-sip)# url sips
SIPGW(conf-serv-sip)# session transport tls
```

Example 12-26   *Dial-Peer Level Configuration for SRTP*

```
SIPGW(config)# dial-peer voice 51 voip
SIPGW(config-dial-peer)# destination-pattern 7...$
SIPGW(config-dial-peer)# session protocol sipv2
SIPGW(config-dial-peer)# session target ipv4:10.87.81.200
SIPGW(config-dial-peer)# session transport tcp tls
SIPGW(config-dial-peer)# voice-class sip srtp negotiate cisco
SIPGW(config-dial-peer)# dtmf-relay rtp-nte
SIPGW(config-dial-peer)# codec g711ulaw
```

Step 3. Apply the secure SIP Trunk profile on the trunk configured for the SIP gateway. This enables TLS for SIP signaling, and therefore no IPSec tunnel is required for the SIP voice gateway to CUCM. Configure the SIP trunk security profile, as shown in Figure 12-6.

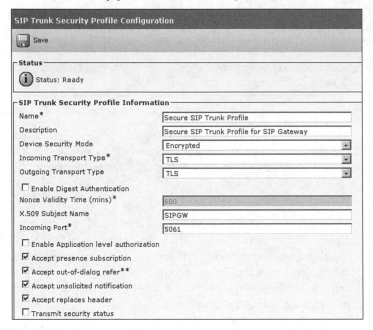

Figure 12-6   *CUCM SIP Trunk Security Profile for SIP Gateway*

Note   The X.509 Subject Name should match the CN configured on the voice gateway trustpoint.

Step 4. Enable SIP Trunk for SRTP. (See Chapter 9, section, "SIP Trunk Security," for details on setting up a secure SIP trunk for supporting SRTP/TLS.)

Note   SRTP keys are transported in Descriptors field in SDP.

Step 5. Configure CUCM to send the Asserted-Identity and accept Redirecting Diversion Header Delivery Inbound (under the "Call Routing" section of the SIP Trunk).

At this point, IOS SIP voice gateway should be ready to establish SRTP calls with encrypted IP Phones and TLS signaling with CUCM.

Securing Survivable Remote Site Telephony (SRST)

An organization can have a few to numerous remote sites with Cisco IP Phones and voice gateways. While the IP Phones may register to the Headquarters or main data center of the organization, it can also register to local gateway when it is configured as Cisco Unified Communications Manager Express (CUCME or Cisco Unified CME). Chapter 14, "Cisco Unified Communications Manager Express and Cisco Unity Express Security," covers CUCME security.

It is food for thought that, while the phones and communication with a gateway is secured in normal conditions when the link with CUCM is up, a hacker (or an insider) can take advantage that the IP Phones are prone to RTP/Signaling packet manipulation and eavesdropping because of unencrypted signaling and media when they lose connectivity with the main site and use the local router for call control. To prevent such a situation, Cisco has empowered you ensure that the IP Phones at remote sites can continue working in secure (encrypted) mode even when they use their local router for call control.

In this section, you will learn about the security of Cisco Survivable Remote Site Telephony (SRST) by which you can secure the IP Phone-to-IP Phone and IP Phone-to-voice gateway communication (SRTP for call media streams and TLS for signaling). This is when the remote site is segregated from your organization's headquarters (or IP telephony data center) because of a WAN failure or loss of connectivity between CUCM and the remote site voice gateway. The following steps will guide you through Secure SRST configuration:

> **Note** The following steps assume that the SRST gateway is enrolled with Cisco IOS CA with the trustpoint name SRSTGW. Refer to the section, "Securing Conference Resources," for the procedure to enroll an IOS voice gateway to IOS CA and upload the CA root and router identity certificate to CUCM.

Step 1. When the SRST router has its own certificate, you need to provide CUCM the certificate to enable secure SRST. This can be done by enabling the credentials' service (see Example 12-27), which enables CUCM to retrieve the secure SRST device certificate and make it part of the configuration file of the Cisco IP Phone.

Example 12-27 *SRST Credentials Service Configuration*

```
SRSTGW(config)# credentials
SRSTGW(config-credentials)# ip source-address 10.200.200.110 port 2445
SRSTGW(config-credentials)# trustpoint SRSTGW
```

Step 2.   From the CUCM Publisher server, download the following certificates:

- CAPF

- Cisco_Manufacturing_CA

- Cisco_Root_CA_2048

- CAP-RTP-001

- CAP-RTP-002

These must be copied to the SRST voice gateway under unique trustpoints. When downloaded, you can open the <certificate name>.pem file with Notepad to see the certificate contents in the base 64 encoded format.

Step 3.   Define a trustpoint for each certificate, as shown in Example 12-28.

Example 12-28   *CUCM Security Certificate Trustpoint Configuration*

```
SRSTGW(config)# crypto pki trustpoint CAPF
SRSTGW(ca-trustpoint)# enrollment terminal
SRSTGW(ca-trustpoint)# revocation-check none
!
SRSTGW(config)# crypto pki trustpoint CAP-RTP-001
SRSTGW(ca-trustpoint)# enrollment terminal
SRSTGW(ca-trustpoint)# revocation-check none
!
SRSTGW(config)# crypto pki trustpoint CAP-RTP-002
SRSTGW(ca-trustpoint)# enrollment terminal
SRSTGW(ca-trustpoint)# revocation-check none
!
SRSTGW(config)# crypto pki trustpoint Cisco_Manufacturing_CA
SRSTGW(ca-trustpoint)# enrollment terminal
SRSTGW(ca-trustpoint)# revocation-check none
!
SRSTGW(config)# crypto pki trustpoint Cisco_Root_CA_2048
SRSTGW(ca-trustpoint)# enrollment terminal
SRSTGW(ca-trustpoint)# revocation-check none
```

Step 4.   Authenticate each trustpoint defined. Example 12-29 highlights an example of a CAPF trustpoint, and the same should be repeated for each trustpoint where the actual base 64 encoded value (from certificates downloaded in Step 2) should be enrolled with the IOS SRST gateway.

Example 12-29 *CUCM Certificate Enrollment*

```
SRSTGW(config)# crypto pki authenticate CAPF
Enter the base 64 encoded CA certificate.
End with a blank line or the word "quit" on a line by itself
MIIDQzCCAiugAwIBAgIQX/h7KCtU3I1CoxW1aMmt/zANBgkqhkiG9w0BAQUFADA1
MRYwFAYDVQQKEw1DaXNjbyBTeXN0ZW1zMRswGQYDVQQDExJDaXNjbyBSb290IENB
<output omitted>
.
CYNu/2bPPu8Xs1gYJQk0XuPL1hS27PKSb3TkL4Eq1ZKR4OCXPDJoBYVL0fdX4lId
kxpUnwVwwEpxYB5DC2Ae/qPOgRnhCzU=
quit
Certificate has the following attributes:
Fingerprint MD5: 1951DA4E 76D79MAB FFB061C6 233C7E88
Fingerprint SHA1: 222891BE Z7B89B9A 447AB8E2 5831C2AB 25990998
% Do you accept this certificate? [yes/no]: yes
Trustpoint CAPF certificate accepted.
% Certificate successfully imported
```

Step 5. Configure SRST on the voice gateway (see Example 12-30) before moving to the CUCM for SRST configuration.

Example 12-30 *SRST (CallManager Fallback) Configuration*

```
SRSTGW(config)# call-manager-fallback
SRSTGW(config-cm-fallback)# secondary-dialtone 9
SRSTGW(config-cm-fallback)# ip source-address 10.200.200.110 port 2000
SRSTGW(config-cm-fallback)# max-ephones 10
SRSTGW(config-cm-fallback)# max-dn 20
SRSTGW(config-cm-fallback)# transfer-system full-consult
SRSTGW(config-cm-fallback)# transfer-pattern 8...
```

Note The configuration shown in Example 12-30 is the minimum recommended configuration to enable a voice gateway to support Cisco IP Phones.

Step 6. Configure the Secure SRST reference on CUCM. Go to **System > SRST** and configure the SRST gateway information. Ensure that **Is SRST Secure?** Check box is checked, as depicted in Figure 12-7.

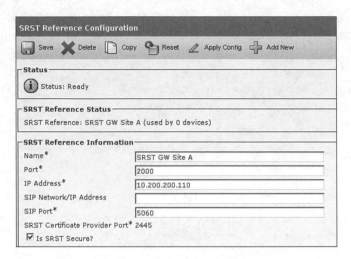

Figure 12-7   *CUCM Secure SRST Configuration*

Step 7.   Assign the secure SRST gateway as an SRST reference under a device pool. Do this by going to **Cisco Unified Communications Manager Administration > System > Device Pool**.

To test secure SRST, you can simulate a WAN link failure by shutting down the WAN interface of the SRST voice gateway. At this point, all the phones previously registered to CUCM (which have the SRST router being tested in their device pool as an SRST reference) should failover to the local gateway. When calling another phone within the same site, you should get a padlock on the IP Phones involved in the call, signifying that the call is an encrypted call.

Monitoring Cisco Voice Gateways

How crucial do you think it is to keep a check on your voice gateways and what is flowing through them? Moreover, how do you ensure that your voice gateways are not under attack? Without knowing about the state of health of any network equipment in your IP Telephony network, it is futile to expect a functional and delivering network. Thus, it is paramount that you have the right monitoring, logging, and security controls applied on the voice gateways.

The topic of monitoring and logging is covered comprehensively in Chapter 16, "Cisco IP Telephony Network Management Security," where you will learn about (secure) monitoring and logging using

- SNMP
- Syslog

On the other hand, you already covered the topic of controlled access to network equipment (applies equally to Cisco IOS voice gateways) in Chapter 7, using

- AAA
- ACLs
- Secure protocols for accessing Cisco network devices

Summary

Toll fraud, call hijacking, eavesdropping, and packet injection are some of the threats, which were highlighted in Chapter 1. This chapter helps build a foundation with the intention that you can counter them when it comes to your voice gateways and maintain the privacy of the conversation streams flowing through them.

In this chapter, you learned about the ways to secure RTP and signaling streams on MGCP, H.323, and SIP Gateways. In addition, you grasped the basics of secure conferencing and secure SRST. To build a secure IP Telephony network, every aspect should be duly considered including the voice signaling and media streams from call control to gateways and endpoints to gateways, respectively. With the right security controls and the right level of security in place, you can be confident that your voice gateways are less susceptible to attacks.

In the next chapter, you will comprehend security fundamentals of Cisco IOS Voice Gatekeeper and Cisco Unified Border Element (CUBE), which are the doorways to internal and external world connectivity with different systems, partners, and PSTN.

Chapter 13

Cisco Voice Gatekeeper and Cisco Unified Border Element Security

It's 9 p.m. Steve's cell phone rings. The call is from his credit card company's customer service representative. She reports numerous transactions made against his credit card and wants to confirm if he is the one initiating them. Steve's answer is obvious, "No, it's not me!" What in the world is going on? How could his credit card details be exposed when he didn't share them with anyone? Oh, yes! He did share the details on the phone with his kids, so they could order their school books online a couple days ago. Yet again, how could this be known to anyone?

The fact of matter is that Steve's conversation was eavesdropped on, on the way to the intended audience. The communication was in clear text channel to ITSP, which might not have been the only issue provided that the ITSP connectivity was secured. The major issue was that organization XYZ's IP-IP gateway (CUBE) is exposed to the outside world with minimal security deployed around it. If you think that securing voice within your network was sufficient, think again. Anything that holds certain value and is an asset within your premises may have greater value than you think outside the legit premises—even more so when your conversations are leaving the seemingly secure zone (your premises) and are exposed to un-secured outside.

This chapter covers the following topics:

- Physical and logical security of Cisco Gatekeeper and CUBE
- Cisco Gatekeeper security
- Cisco Unified Border Element security

Physical and Logical Security of Cisco Gatekeeper and Cisco Unified Border Element

The topic of physical security takes precedence over all other logical forms of security, for obvious reasons as described in Chapter 5, "Cisco IP Telephony Physical Security."

Refer to Chapter 5 for details about planning for effective physical security for all Cisco network devices and servers, including Cisco Gatekeeper and Cisco Unified Border Element (CUBE) routers.

The next important thing to physical security is secure Layer 2 connectivity, IOS services, platform, routing protocols, perimeter security, high-availability requirements, secure management, and so on. All these topics are addressed in Chapter 6, "Cisco IP Telephony Layer 2 Security," Chapter 7, "Cisco IP Telephony Layer 3 Security," Chapter 8, "Perimeter Security with Cisco Adaptive Security Appliance," and Chapter 16, "Cisco IP Telephony: Network Management Security."

Gatekeeper Security—What Is It All About?

Have you ever been in a situation in which you forgot the pass to an important convention? Gosh! It is not only frustrating, but also it may mean that you may lose a whole day at the convention. The security guards would not allow you, or for that matter anyone, to enter without a valid pass. An analogy to the guards is Cisco Voice Gatekeepers. In an H.323 network, the Cisco Voice Gatekeeper may be the single point of contact with which H.323 endpoints register and rely on call setup, link bandwidth management, call teardown, and address resolution. This implies that unless each endpoint is registered with a Cisco Gatekeeper (focal point in an H.323 network), it is not welcome in the network.

Note   Cisco Gatekeeper is one of the many components in an H.323 network that can be treated as an optional component in certain networks, whereas it's crucial in others.

With that said, a rogue endpoint getting access to your network or a hacker sniffing signaling streams going to the Gatekeeper can prove fatal for the voice network. As simple as it is, the attacker can initiate a DoS attack by sending a constant stream of forged H.225 RAS Admission Request (ARQ) messages. While these forged messages may fail the integrity check and be discarded by the Gatekeeper, nevertheless, the legitimate requests for admission will be swamped by continuous forged requests, thereby causing legitimate endpoints to be denied of the service. On the other hand, the attacker can sniff the signaling streams going to the Gatekeeper and find other potential targets (Call Control—CUCM, Voice Gateways, MCUs, and so on).

The following sections describe Cisco Voice Gatekeeper security methodology. Although some of the security mechanisms are derived from H.235, others are independent.

Securing Cisco Gatekeeper

Cisco Gatekeepers are the doorways to your IP Telephony network resources in an H.323 network and should be secured against any rogue endpoint or person trying to break into your voice domain and disrupt voice conversations. Cisco Gatekeepers enable a voice network to be divided in terms of zones and perform call routing between zones by translating an E.164 number to the destination IP address. In the next sections, you will learn about various ways to protect your Cisco Voice Gatekeeper infrastructure.

> **Note**   The terms Voice Gatekeeper and Gatekeeper will be used interchangeably. Cisco IOS version 15.2 is used for configuration examples throughout this chapter.

Restricted Subnet Registration

A Cisco Gatekeeper by default answers device registration requests from all subnets in its local zone. This saves administrative overhead in defining each endpoint in a local zone. but it is a lucrative option for an attacker or rogue gateway to send Discovery (GRQ) and Admission (ARQ) messages (an attack vector for DoS attack). To safeguard against rogue requests, you must restrict subnet registration by specifying which subnets are legible candidates for sending discovery and registration messages, by endpoints in those subnets, to the Gatekeeper. Example 13-1 gives an outline of the configuration of restricting subnets for registration with Gatekeeper.

Example 13-1   *Cisco Gatekeeper Subnet Restricted Registration*

```
GK(config)# gatekeeper
GK(config-gk)# zone local zonegk1 cisco.com 10.100.100.100
GK(config-gk)# zone local zonegk2 cisco.com
GK(config-gk)# no zone subnet zonegk1 default enable
GK(config-gk)# no zone subnet zonegk2 default enable
GK(config-gk)# zone subnet zonegk1 10.10.20.252/32 enable
GK(config-gk)# zone subnet zonegk2 10.20.40.240/32 enable
GK(config-gk)# gw-type-prefix 1#* default-technology
GK(config-gk)# no shutdown
```

In Example 13-1, the **no zone subnet <zone-name> default enable** command disables acceptance of the Gatekeeper discovery and registration messages from all subnets except those defined in the **zone subnet <zone-name> <ip address/subnet> enable** command. This helps curb rogue gateway and endpoint registration.

Gatekeeper Accounting

Cisco Gatekeeper empowers you to use accounting feature of AAA server (RADIUS) to log records for calls attempted via the Cisco Gatekeeper. This is a useful feature for investigating any malicious calls made or any unauthorized or rogue endpoints attempting calls to legitimate endpoints. Example 13-2 illustrates the configuration of Cisco Gatekeeper AAA-based accounting feature.

Example 13-2 *Cisco Gatekeeper AAA (RADIUS)–Based Accounting*

```
GK(config)# aaa new-model
GK(config)# radius-server host 10.100.100.250 auth-port 1645 acct-port 1646 key 7
  C1sc0123
GK(config)# aaa authentication login default group radius local
GK(config)# aaa authorization network default group radius local
GK(config)# aaa authorization exec default group radius local
GK(config)# aaa accounting connection H.323 start-stop group radius
!
GK(config)# username GK password C1sc0123
!
GK(config)# gatekeeper
GK(config-gk)# accounting
GK(config-gk)# security H.323-id
GK(config-gk)# security password default C1sc0123
```

The **start-stop** command starts the creation of an AAA record when a call starts and concludes the record when the call is terminated. You should configure the Gatekeeper endpoints, for example, Voice Gateways as AAA users in the RADIUS server (which can be configured in Cisco TACACS+ working in RADIUS mode) with their alias, that is, H.323-id, E.164, and so on as configured in the Gatekeeper. An alias however must be accompanied by a password. A default password can be configured for all devices registering with gatekeeper (refer to Example 13-1).

Essentially, you must perform a two-fold task on ACS:

- Create Cisco Gatekeeper as an AAA client defined by either the Gatekeeper name or IP address along with the password.

- Create Cisco Gatekeeper endpoints as AAA users with the H.323-id, for example, GW@cisco.com and password.

To create an AAA client on Cisco TACACS+, follow these steps:

Step 1. Log in to the Cisco ACS server; then go to **Network Resources > Clients >** Click **Add**.

Step 2. Enter the Gatekeeper IP address or hostname (hostname if DNS resolution is configured) and select the RADIUS option. Enter the Shared Secret as it is defined on the Gatekeeper in RADIUS configuration, as shown in Figure 13-1.

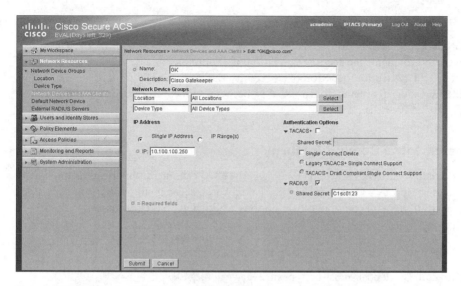

Figure 13-1 *Cisco TACACS+ (RADIUS)—Gatekeeper Client Configuration*

To create an AAA user on Cisco TACACS+, follow these steps:

Step 1. Log in to the Cisco ACS server. Go to **Users and Identity Stores > Users**. Click **Add**.

Step 2. Provide an endpoint name (for example, **GW@cisco.com**. It is essential to enter the full name as given in H.323-id. Enter the password that was defined in the Gatekeeper default, which should match the endpoint password, as shown in Figure 13-2.

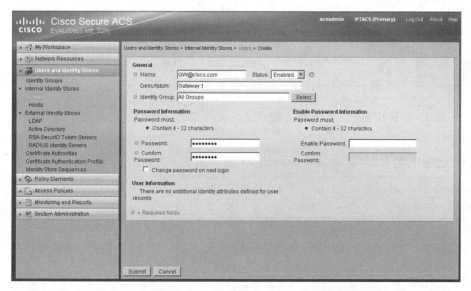

Figure 13-2 *Cisco TACACS+ (RADIUS)—User Configuration*

Gatekeeper Security Option

Cisco Gatekeeper allows various security options under the gatekeeper mode. These can be leveraged to enable the secure registration of endpoints or CUCM based on token or tokenless call authentication. Moreover, security can be enabled intra-domain (based on the H.235 standard) or inter-domain, that is, between two enterprises or enterprises and the IT Service Provider (ITSP).

Gatekeeper Intra-Domain Security

Intra-domain security is based on H.235, where H.323 calls are authenticated, authorized, and routed by a Cisco Gatekeeper. Token-based security authentication allows per call, registration, or all communication options. Following is an explanation of the various options:

- **Endpoint:** Authentication occurs only during registration.

- **Per-call:** Credentials must be sent on every call request.

- **All:** Both registration and per-call authentication.

Note   Token-based endpoint admission is only applicable for voice gateways and ATAs. CUCM cannot do token-based authentication, and tokenless authentication must be configured in such cases.

Example 13-3 shows the Cisco Gateway security token authentication.

Example 13-3   *Cisco Gateway Security Option*

```
H.323GW(config)# gateway
H.323GW(config-gateway)# security password <password> level [all | per-call | end-
   point]
```

Example 13-4 shows the Cisco Gatekeeper security token authentication configuration (pertinent to the Gateway configuration highlighted in Example 13-3).

Example 13-4   *Cisco Gatekeeper Token–Based Security*

```
GK(config)# gatekeeper
GK (config-gk)# security token required-for all
```

Example 13-5 shows the CUCM and Cisco Gatekeeper security tokenless authentication.

Example 13-5   *Cisco Gatekeeper Tokenless Security*

```
GK(config)# access-list 10 permit 10.87.81.200 0.0.0.255
!
GK(config)# gatekeeper
GK(config-gk)# security acl answerarq 10
```

Example 13-5 allows CUCM with the IP address 10.87.81.200 to register with the Cisco Gatekeeper. For tokenless call authentication, you must create an ACL, which should include permit statements for the IP addresses authorized to place call routing requests to the Cisco Gatekeeper. Admission requests (ARQ) received from endpoints that have IP addresses permitted by the ACL are answered, irrespective of a security token.

Note   Both security token and tokenless configuration can be done on the Cisco Gatekeeper simultaneously.

Gatekeeper Inter-Domain Security

Cisco Gatekeepers support authenticating and authorizing calls between different administrative domains, such as:

■ Two enterprises connecting via Cisco Gatekeepers

■ Connection to Internet Telephony Service Provider (ITSP)

The Inter-domain security is achieved by use of InterZone Clear Token (IZCT). IZCT validate calls from other networks. IZCT token travels in ARQ and LCF messages and ensures access control as well as secured connectivity. Figure 13-3 shows an overview of IZCT topology as it pertains to a typical gatekeeper-based ITSP (Inter-domain) connectivity. Moreover, Cisco Gatekeepers offer Gatekeeper-to-Gatekeeper authentication feature leveraging Cisco Access Token (CAT). A CAT verifies the adjacent gatekeepers so that they can authenticate each other before replying to Location Requests (LRQ).

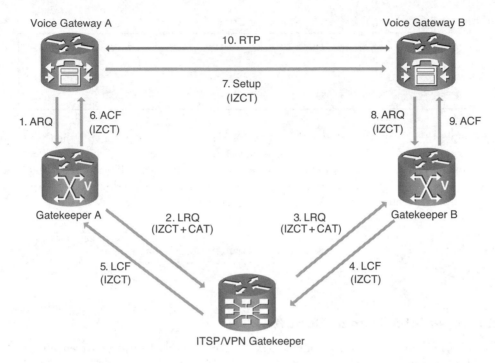

Figure 13-3 *Cisco Gatekeeper IZCT-CAT-Based Topology*

The following examples give you an insight into the configuration of IZCT and CAT deployment on Cisco Gatekeepers (refer to Figure 13-3). IZCT is configured with explicit command, whereas CAT is configured with the **security password-group** command and applied to a specific zone (must be adjacent to the Cisco Gatekeeper zone) with the **security zone** command. Example 13-6 highlights the IZCT-CAT configuration for Gatekeeper A.

Example 13-6 *Gatekeeper A Configuration*

```
GK(config)# gatekeeper
GK(config-gk)# zone local XYZ cisco.com 10.100.100.100
GK(config-gk)# zone remote ITSP cisco.com 10.10.200.200 1719
GK(config-gk)# zone prefix XYZ 408
GK(config-gk)# zone prefix ITSP *
GK(config-gk)# security izct password C1sc0123
GK(config-gk)# security password-group ITSP lrq receive C1sc0123
GK(config-gk)# security password-group ITSP lrq send C1sc0123
GK(config-gk)# security zone ITSP password-group ITSP
GK(config-gk)# gw-type-prefix 2#* default-technology
GK(config-gk)# no shutdown
```

Example 13-7 outlines the IZCT-CAT configuration for the ITSP gatekeeper.

Example 13-7   *ITSP Gatekeeper Configuration*

```
GK(config)# gatekeeper
GK(config-gk)# zone local ITSP cisco.com 10.10.200.200
GK(config-gk)# zone remote XYZ cisco.com 10.100.100.100 1719
GK(config-gk)# zone remote FGH cisco.com 10.200.200.200 1719 foreign-domain
GK(config-gk)# zone prefix XYZ 408
GK(config-gk)# zone prefix FGH 313
GK(config-gk)# security izct password C1sc0123
GK(config-gk)# security password-group XYZ lrq receive C1sc0123
GK(config-gk)# security password-group XYZ lrq send C1sc0123
GK(config-gk)# security password-group FGH lrq receive C1sc0123
GK(config-gk)# security password-group FGH lrq send C1sc0123
GK(config-gk)# security zone XYZ password-group XYZ
GK(config-gk)# security zone FGH password-group FGH
GK(config-gk)# lrq forward-queries
GK(config-gk)# no shutdown
```

Example 13-8 shows the IZCT-CAT configuration for Gatekeeper B.

Example 13-8   *Gatekeeper B Configuration*

```
GK(config-gk)# gatekeeper
GK(config-gk)# zone local FGH cisco.com 10.200.200.200
GK(config-gk)# zone remote ITSP cisco.com 10.10.200.200 1719
GK(config-gk)# zone prefix FGH 313
GK(config-gk)# zone prefix ITSP *
GK(config-gk)# security izct password C1sc0123
GK(config-gk)# security password-group ITSP lrq receive C1sc0123
GK(config-gk)# security password-group ITSP lrq send C1sc0123
GK(config-gk)# security zone ITSP password-group ITSP
GK(config-gk)# gw-type-prefix 1#* default-technology
GK(config-gk)# no shutdown
```

Gatekeeper HSRP Security

HSRP is one of the ways to provide redundancy for devices registering with Cisco Gatekeepers. You can configure your endpoints to register with the HSRP address, regardless of whichever router is the active Gatekeeper; all devices can successfully register (without knowing if the active gatekeeper is down).

Note   HSRP Gatekeepers do not share state tables; therefore if a failure occurs where the backup gatekeeper becomes active, all endpoints need to reregister with the newly active gatekeeper. Ensure that you consider this before enabling HSRP for gatekeepers. Another method to provide resiliency for endpoints is gatekeeper clustering.

Although HSRP gives your endpoints redundancy, it could also prove to be a weakness unless HSRP transactions between the Cisco Gatekeepers participating in HSRP are secured. An attacker can compromise the identity of a Gatekeeper and increase the standby priority with preempt whereby, causing the failover of endpoints. At this time, the attacker can either mimic as a gatekeeper (and provide services while eavesdropping the signaling, that is, performing a reconnaissance attack) or just let the clients trying to register and provide no services (DoS attack). To alleviate this situation, you must implement HSRP authentication, as explained in Chapter 7, in section, "Securing Hot Standby Routing Protocol."

Cisco Unified Border Element Security

Even though H.323 is the most widely deployed protocol to date, it is being replaced by SIP progressively. This is happening primarily because of the ease of deployment, management, and feature set of the SIP protocol. While enterprises are slowly moving from H.323 to SIP, the majority of ITSPs have already transitioned to SIP. Therefore, it becomes mandatory for IT and IP Telephony administrators to understand the basics of SIP Trunking with ITSP because you will be opening a new frontier in which all PSTN traffic flows via ITSP's SIP trunk to its soft switch. Although SIP trunking becomes attractive because of the higher ROI, easier configuration, and management, it is also lucrative for hackers to exploit a network via an open channel to the outside world.

Cisco Unified Border Element (CUBE) also known as Session Border Controller (SBC) is the Cisco-leading solution for terminating SIP trunks from ITSP and for intra-enterprise and inter-enterprise SIP traffic traversal. Although within an enterprise, this function may be fulfilled by Cisco Session Manager Edition (SME), CUBE has its own perks. The majority of organizations and security administrators might have serious concerns connecting a CUCM cluster (or SME cluster) directly to ITSP. CUBE comes to aid here because it can secure the SIP media and data traffic, can do address hiding, force media flow-through or flow-around, and much more.

Note   CUBE is a demarcation point for the enterprise that interoperates SIP or H.323 protocols with the ITSP's H.323 or SIP protocols.

Although CUBE is designed to protect your network from various possible threats, it needs to be secured to ensure that the edge of your network (logical domain) is out of harm's way. A number of means are available to safeguard CUBE from external and internal threats and misuse:

■ Access list-based filtering

■ Signaling and media encryption

■ Secure registration

■ SIP security features of CUBE

■ Firewalling

Note   The Cisco IOS version 15.2 is used for CUBE configuration examples.

A typical CUBE deployment in an enterprise could be either of the following topologies shown in Figure 13-4. These are not conclusive scenarios, and CUBE may be deployed in various ways depending on an organization's business and network requirements.

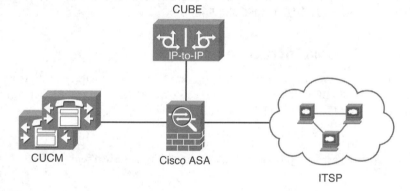

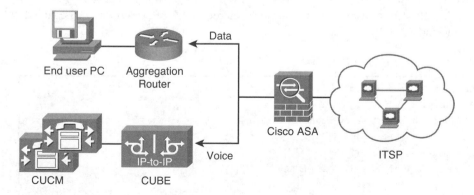

Figure 13-4   *CUBE Deployment Models*

The following sections detail various security options and mechanisms to safeguard CUBE from internal and external threats.

Filtering Traffic with Access Control List

The concept of access control list (ACL) based traffic filtering is not new; however, it's an effective one. It is a leading practice to limit the exposure of CUBE to the devices that can access your SIP trunk from the inside (assumingly a trusted zone) and outside (assumingly an untrusted zone) to block any or all requests from rogue endpoints and attackers on known SIP ports. CUBE should be set in a way so that it accepts connections only from the following:

- Service provider's SBC or soft-switch on the service provider side.

- Legitimate call control, devices, and applications, for example, voice gateways, CUCM, and SIP proxies (such as a Cisco Unified SIP Proxy Server) on the enterprise side.

The ACLs can be made even more specific so that they accept traffic over only known SIP and SIPS ports (TCP/UDP 5060 and 5061).

Signaling and Media Encryption

By using encryption, you can ensure that the signaling and media traversing from your network to ITSP SBC via CUBE are secure. Cisco SRTP supports the AES encryption algorithm as per IETF RFC 3711 standard.

Note It depends on ITSP to offer TLS/SRTP capability for SIP Trunks.

Refer to Chapter 12, "Cisco Voice Gateway Security," for information on setting up secure SIP Gateways with CUCM, which applies to CUBE as well. Example 13-9 illustrates the SIP security relevant configuration required on CUBE to support TLS-enabled signaling and SRTP for media.

Example 13-9 *CUBE TLS/SRTP*

```
IPTCUBE(conf)# voice service voip
IPTCUBE(conf-voi-serv)# srtp fallback
IPTCUBE(conf-voi-serv)# allow-connections sip to sip
IPTCUBE(conf-voi-serv)# sip
IPTCUBE(conf-serv-sip)# url sips
IPTCUBE(conf-serv-sip)# session transport tcp tls
!
IPTCUBE(conf)# sip-ua
IPTCUBE(config-sip-ua)# retry invite 10
```

```
IPTCUBE(config-sip-ua)# transport tcp tls
IPTCUBE(config-sip-ua)# crypto signaling default trustpoint <trust-point name>
  strict-cipher
```

In this example, SRTP fallback enables fallback to RTP for the endpoints, which cannot support SRTP. Under SIP-UA, transport TCP TLS defines that the signaling is based on TLS stack. In addition, by using strict-cipher you limit CUBE to an FIPS-approved security algorithm as per SIP RFC 3261, which includes TLS_RSA_WITH_AES_128_CBC_SHA.

Note   SRTP support can be enabled globally or for an individual dial-peer. Dial-peer settings take preference.

As CUBE can interoperate between RTP/SRTP,, you can unencrypt streams within your premises and have encrypted streams as they leave your premises. Again, the benefits can be reaped only if ITSP supports encryption. In addition, if you use H.323 within your organization and want to establish secure H.323 communications with CUBE, you can configure IPSec tunnel to CUBE for signaling and media protection. Refer to Chapter 12 for details on setting up secure H.323 gateway with CUCM.

Hostname Validation

CUBE supports hostname validation feature that can be leveraged to confine valid host-names to be accepted in the host portion (SIP URI) of a SIP INVITE. This is particularly useful when you not only want to filter the subnets or domains from which traffic can be accepted, but also limit the hosts from valid domains to curb any rogue endpoint reg-istration attempt. Example 13-10 shows the hostname validation process where only two hosts are allowed by SIP-UA.

Example 13-10   *Hostname Validation*

```
IPTCUBE(conf)# sip-ua
IPTCUBE(config-sip-ua)# permit CUBE1.internal.cisco.local
IPTCUBE(config-sip-ua)# permit CUBE2.external.cisco.local
```

Firewalling CUBE

When CUBE is the demarcation of your network from a service provider network, it becomes essential to protect CUBE from otherwise impending attack(s). Therefore, it is only viable to have CUBE protected by a firewall, for example, a Cisco ASA Security Appliance. Cisco ASA Firewall is the perfect companion for CUBE because it offers Application Level Gateway (ALG) Firewall capabilities with deep packet inspection. Moreover, Cisco ASA can inspect and block SIP and H.323 traffic based on various criteria. For more details on Cisco ASA Firewall's enhanced protocol inspection capabilities, refer to Appendix B, "Cisco IP Telephony: Firewalling and Intrusion Prevention."

Figure 13-5 highlights a layered approach to protect voice traffic traversing to and from CUBE. Here, the firewall acts as a generic traffic security device with ALG capability, and CUBE acts as a demarcation point between internal and external voice networks (where internal relates to an organization's IP Telephony network and external relates to an ITSP network).

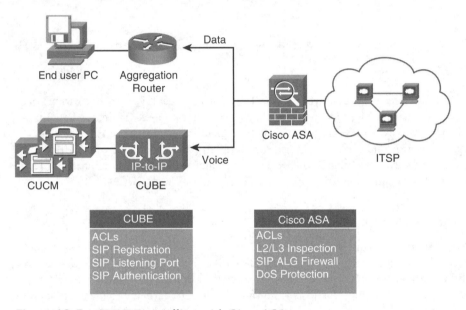

Figure 13-5   *CUBE Firewalling with Cisco ASA*

Refer to Chapter 8, "Perimeter Security with Cisco Adaptive Security Appliance," for facts about Cisco ASA as IP Telephony Firewall solution and Appendix B, for an insight into the Cisco ASA advance firewall functions.

Note   Cisco IOS CBAC or ZFW (which are discussed in Appendix B) can also be used to secure CUBE. CUBE functionality can be co-resident with an IOS Firewall in the same physical router.

CUBE Inherited SIP Security Features

SIP is popular protocol with some of its specifics, such as ports, well known to almost everyone in the IP Telephony world. Thus, when collaborating between enterprises or opting for ITSP SIP Trunks, it is only rational to have CUBE send and receive traffic on non-default SIP ports to increase security. Example 13-11 shows how you can set SIP ports in a non conventional manner.

Example 13-11 *SIP Listening Port Setting*

```
IPTCUBE(config)# voice service voip
IPTCUBE(conf-voi-serv)# sip
IPTCUBE(conf-serv-sip)# shutdown
IPTCUBE(conf-voi-serv)# sip
IPTCUBE(conf-serv-sip)# listen-port non-secure 50000 secure 50001
listen port Change will be effective once the SIP service is re-started
IPTCUBE(conf-serv-sip)# no shutdown
```

Note   The non standard SIP ports must be negotiated with ITSP, that is, ITSP must reconfigure the end with the same ports to send and receive non-encrypted or encrypted traffic.

CUBE supports SIP-UA registration and authentication. Some ITSPs offer registration sequence such that only their SBC or soft-switch can register with your CUBE. You can use SIP mechanisms to validate the originator of a SIP call and therefore provide a mechanism to reject SIP INVITEs that come from rogue endpoints. CUBE or ITSP can send a challenge to the INVITEs, and the instigator must reply with the right credentials for the call setup to proceed. Although both authentication and registration look alike, they have their own unique purpose. The former is required every time a call setup is initiated. On the other hand, the latter is required only once when the device initially registers with CUBE or SBC. Example 13-12 details the configuration required to enable CUBE registration and authentication.

Example 13-12 *SIP Registration and Authentication*

```
IPTCUBE(config)# sip-ua
IPTCUBE(config-sip-ua)# credentials username IPTCUBE password 7 C1sc0123 realm
  cisco.local
IPTCUBE(config-sip-ua)# authentication username IPTCUBE password 7 C1sc0123 realm
  cisco.local
```

Summary

Communication traffic is assumingly safe within an enterprise network, but not when it leaves your line of control to the public network/ITSP. In such cases, it becomes crucial to protect the communication streams at the boundary from internal and external threats.

In this chapter, you learned about Cisco Unified Border Element (CUBE) and Cisco Voice Gatekeeper security. You learned the ways to limit exposure to the IP-IP Gateways, enable limited device or endpoint registration, and authentication to assure that only legitimate devices leverage the Cisco Voice Gatekeeper or CUBE services. Also, you are now equipped with basic-to-advance mechanisms, which you can deploy in your Cisco IP Telephony network's edge to thwart attacks from outside and fraudulent attempts of calling (toll-fraud) or eavesdropping from inside. Multiple layers of security or a Defense-in-Depth approach is the way to go when considering securing your demarcation or virtual periphery with other organizations or ITSP.

Next chapter helps you understand and deploy security for the 'Express' version of call-control and voice messaging that is, Cisco Unified Communications Manager Express and Cisco Unity Express. You will comprehend the fundamentals to secure Cisco Unified CME and Cisco Unity Express platform and application.

Cisco Unified Communications Manager Express and Cisco Unity Express Security

It's a usual day at work so far. However, a critical task of a cutover of your organization XYZ's existing PBX to Cisco Unified Communications Manager Express router at the end of day awaits you. You log in to the router to double-check the configuration. The router seems to be a little sluggish and is acting odd. Moreover, certain things just weren't making sense. You see multiple changes to the configuration. You type in the **who** command. Holy Moly! Someone was logged in with a public IP! You clear the line, put an access-list on line VTY to allow only your management subnet and start to restore the configuration.

Before you rush to restore the configuration, the first thing you should do is determine how your router was hacked so that you can prevent it from happening again. This chapter is all about securing call control and voice messaging services provided by Cisco Unified CME and Cisco Unity Express, respectively.

This chapter covers the following topics:

- Cisco Unified Communications Manager Express platform security
- Preventing toll fraud on Cisco Unified Communications Manager Express
- Cisco Unified CME: AAA command accounting/auditing
- Cisco IOS Firewall for Cisco Unified CME
- Cisco Unified CME: Secure GUI access
- Strict ephone registration
- Disabling ephone auto-registration
- Cisco Unified CME: Call Logging (CDR)
- Cisco Unified CME: Securing Voice Traffic (TLS and SRTP)
- Securing Cisco Unity Express (CUE) platform

- Enabling AAA for Cisco Unity Express
- Preventing toll fraud on Cisco Unity Express
- Cisco Unity Express: Secure GUI access

Cisco Unified Communications Manager Express Platform Security

Cisco Unified Communications Manager Express (Cisco Unified CME) is a voice gateway running a special IOS with call-control capability. Hence, it is not entirely different from a voice gateway router, and the same fundamentals as those of IOS voice gateway security (physical and logical) apply to Cisco Unified CME. Chapter 5, "Cisco IP Telephony Physical Security," discusses the topic of physical security in depth. Chapter 7, "Cisco IP Telephony Layer 3 Security," covers Cisco IOS gateway logical (Layer 3 and platform hardening) security. Refer to these chapters for respective physical and Layer 3 security specifics and platform-hardening mechanisms.

Preventing Toll Fraud on Cisco Unified Communications Manager Express

As its counterparts CUCM and voice gateways, Cisco Unified CME is not immune from toll fraud either, unless appropriate security controls are applied. This section details some of the best practices methodologies, which you should put into operation to evade toll fraud.

> **Note**   All Cisco Unified CME configuration examples in this chapter are based on Unified CME version 8.6 with IOS 15.1(4)M.

After-Hours Calling Restrictions

Just like CUCM offers Time of Day Routing, Cisco Unified CME also offers the same in the form of after-hours call blocking. Cisco Unified CME enables you to configure toll restriction policies based on time and date. You can configure calling policies so that the users are not allowed to make calls to predefined numbers during certain hours of the day or for that matter, all the time. Example 14-1 illustrates **after-hours** in action. Here, national and international numbers in the United States are blocked outside of business hours, Monday through Friday, before 8 a.m. and after 8 p.m., and all day on Saturday and Sunday. In addition, calls to premium numbers, for example, 900 numbers, are blocked all the time irrespective of the day.

Example 14-1 *After-Hours Configuration*

```
CME(config)# telephony-service
CME(config-telephony)# after-hours block pattern 1 91900 7-24
CME(config-telephony)# after-hours block pattern 2 91
CME(config-telephony)# after-hours block pattern 3 9011
CME(config-telephony)# after-hours day Mon 20:00 08:00
CME(config-telephony)# after-hours day Tue 20:00 08:00
CME(config-telephony)# after-hours day Wed 20:00 08:00
CME(config-telephony)# after-hours day Thu 20:00 08:00
CME(config-telephony)# after-hours day Fri 20:00 08:00
CME(config-telephony)# after-hours day Sat 12:00 12:00
CME(config-telephony)# after-hours day Sun 12:00 12:00
```

Call Transfer Restriction

Call transfer to all numbers except those local to Cisco Unified CME are blocked by default. You can allow transfers to VoIP (WAN) or POTS (PSTN) numbers explicitly; however, this may open doors for toll fraud. There are tools you can use to secure Cisco Unified CME from toll fraud.

The transfer-pattern command enables the transfer of telephony calls from Cisco SCCP IP Phones to phones other than Cisco IP Phones, such as external PSTN calls or phones on another CME system. You can use the transfer pattern to limit the calls to internal extensions only or perhaps limit calls to PSTN numbers in a certain area code. Example 14-2 shows how to use the **transfer-pattern** command to limit calls to numbers in area code 919 and bar transfers to any other numbers.

Example 14-2 *Restricting Transfer Pattern*

```
CME(config)# telephony-service
CME(config-telephony)# transfer-pattern 91919.......$
```

You can also prevent individual phones from transferring calls to numbers that are otherwise at a global level enabled for transfer. The command transfer-pattern blocked overrides the **transfer-pattern** command and disables call transfer to any destination (POTS or VoIP). This ensures that individual phones do not incur toll charges when calls are transferred outside the Cisco Unified CME system. Moreover, the **transfer max-length** command specifies the maximum number of digits a user can dial when a call is transferred. This command over-rides the **transfer-pattern** command and enforces maximum digits allowed for the transfer destination.

In Example 14-3, ephone 10 is not allowed to use **transfer-pattern** (defined globally) to transfer calls, whereas ephone 20 can transfer only calls to four-digit extensions.

Example 14-3   *Transfer Pattern and Max Length Configuration*

```
CME(config)# ephone-template 1
CME(config-ephone-template)# transfer-pattern blocked
!
CME(config)# ephone-template 2
CME(config-ephone-template)# transfer max-length 4
!
CME(config)# ephone 10
CME(config-ephone)# ephone-template 1
!
CME(config)# ephone 20
CME(config-ephone)# ephone-template 2
```

Note   **transfer-pattern blocked** and **transfer max-length** commands can also be used in global mode under **telephony-service.**

Call Forward Restriction

For an attacker, the most convenient way to exploit a phone system for toll fraud is to have an insider do a **call-forward** to a certain destination. To restrict the number of digits that can be dialed by Cisco Unified CME system, you can use the **call-forward max-length** command. This command can be issued either at the **ephone-dn-template** level, as shown in Example 14-4, or per the **ephone-dn** level.

Example 14-4   *Restricting Call-Forward*

```
CME(config)# ephone-dn-template  10
CME(config-ephone-template)# call-forward max-length 4
!
CME(config)# ephone-dn  1  dual-line
CME(config-ephone-dn)# number 1001
CME(config-ephone-dn)# ephone-dn-template 1
!
CME(config)# ephone-dn  2  dual-line
CME(config-ephone-dn)# number 1002
CME(config-ephone-dn)# call-forward max-length 4
```

Alternatively, **no forward local-calls** command can be programmed in ephone-dn configuration mode such that the specific Directory Number (DN) does not have ability to do any call-forward at all, as shown in Example 14-5.

Example 14-5 *Restricting Call-Forward (No Local Calls)*

```
CME(config)# ephone-dn  50
CME(config-ephone-dn)# number 1001
CME(config-ephone-dn)# no forward local-calls
```

Class of Restriction

The concept of Class of Restriction (COR) in Cisco Unified CME is identical to voice gateways. Refer to Chapter 12, "Cisco Voice Gateway Security," on details about COR, cor entities, that is, **cor custom** (equivalent to partition), **cor list** (equivalent to CSS), and usage of COR at dial-peer level. The only deviation in Cisco Unified CME is that cor list can also be applied to **ephone-dn** in addition to dial-peers.

Example 14-6 describes how you can apply **cor lists** to **ephone-dn**'s (based on the cor definition in Chapter 12).

Example 14-6 *Call-of-Restriction (COR) Implementation*

```
CME(config)# ephone-dn  10
CME(config-ephone-dn)# number 1001
CME(config-ephone-dn)# cor incoming internal
CME(config-ephone-dn)# cor outgoing local
```

Cisco Unified CME: AAA Command Accounting and Auditing

The commands in Example 14-7 use a Cisco TACACS+ server for command accounting and auditing purposes.

Example 14-7 *Cisco Unified CME AAA-Based Command Accounting*

```
CME(config)# aaa new-model
!
CME(config)# ip tacacs source-interface Loopback 0
CME(config)# tacacs-server host 10.100.100.250
CME(config)# tacacs-server key C1sc0123
CME(config)# tacacs-server timeout 5
!
CME(config)# aaa authentication login default tacacs+ local
CME(config)# aaa authentication enable default tacacs+ local
CME(config)# aaa accounting exec CME start-stop group tacacs+
```

Note   Cisco Unified CME AAA authentication and authorization is similar to a normal Cisco IOS router. This specific topic is covered in Chapter 7.

Cisco IOS Firewall for Cisco Unified CME

Just as any other network equipment, Cisco Unified CME also requires protection from external threats, originating from the Internet and from other sites of organization. This is where the IOS Firewall can help you protect your communication streams and information flowing through Cisco Unified CME. You can enable Context-Based Access Control (CBAC) or Zone-Based Policy Firewall (ZFW) on Cisco IOS routers that are running K9 (security-enabled) image.

Firewalling Cisco Unified CME using an IOS Firewall can be done in two ways:

- Run IOS Firewall on same router as Cisco Unified CME (co-resident).
- Run IOS Firewall on another (WAN) router to which Cisco Unified CME is connected for WAN access.

Moreover, if you have multiple remote sites leveraging Cisco Unified CME call control and converging onto a main site (aggregation site), going out to a WAN, you could have a dedicated IOS router for firewalling all Cisco Unified CME routers at once, at data center periphery. You could also have Cisco ASA security appliance to frontend all Cisco Unified CME routers, offloading all firewall functions to a dedicated firewall.

For more details on Cisco ASA security appliance as an IP Telephony Firewall, refer to Chapter 8, "Perimeter Security with Cisco Adaptive Security Appliance," and Appendix B, "Cisco IP Telephony: Firewalling and Intrusion Prevention." For a detailed insight to Cisco IOS CBAC or ZFW, see Appendix B.

Cisco Unified CME: Securing GUI Access

SSL for HTTP (HTTPS) provides server authentication, encryption, and message integrity to allow secure HTTP communications. SSL also provides HTTP client authentication. It is highly recommended to have Cisco Unified CME GUI interface secured with HTTPS access.

However, not all Cisco Unified IP Phones support HTTPS. If HTTPS is enabled on the Cisco Unified CME router, some Cisco Unified IP Phones may still attempt to connect to port 80. This may lead to issues with the display of local directory and system speed-dials. The workaround for this is to enable both HTTP and HTTPS, as shown in Example 14-8.

Example 14-8 *Enabling Cisco Unified CME HTTPS*

```
CME(config)# crypto key generate rsa exportable label httpkeys usage-keys 1024
!
CME(config)# ip http server
CME(config)# ip http secure-server
CME(config)# ip http secure-port <port number>
!
CME(config)# ip http authentication AAA | TACACS | local
```

Note The default HTTPS port is 443, which can be changed to a higher port (non 0–1024 port) number.

If you want to have the IOS certificates signed by the Cisco IOS CA router, refer to Chapter 12 for the IOS CA server and client configuration specifics.

Cisco Unified CME: Strict ephone Registration

Cisco Unified CME should be configured to enable only Cisco Unified IP Phones in the trusted domain (inside zone) for registration. You can use the **strict-match** option in the **ip source-address** command, so that only locally attached IP Phones can register to Cisco Unified CME router and leverage telephony services, as shown in Example 14-9.

Example 14-9 *Restricting IP Phone Registration*

```
CME(config-telephony)# ip source-address 10.87.104.162 port <2000/5060> strict-match
```

In addition, block TCP ports 2000–2002 and 5060 from the WAN to prevent external SCCP/SIP Phones registering with Cisco Unified CME. You can add the ACL, as shown in Example 14-10, to outside interface.

Example 14-10 *Deny External Traffic on Well-Known Voice Signaling (Registration) Ports*

```
CME(confg)# ip access-list extended BlockTraffic
CME(config-ext-nacl)# deny tcp any any range 2000 2002
CME(config-ext-nacl)# deny tcp any any eq 5060
CME(config-ext-nacl)# permit ip any any log
!
CME(confg)# interface FastEthernet 1/0
CME(confg-if)# ip access-group BlockTraffic in
```

Cisco Unified CME: Disable ephone Auto-Registration

Cisco Unified CME enables auto-registration of ephones by default. This implies that new Cisco Unified IP Phones that try to register with Cisco Unified CME are auto-registered with DN auto-assigned (if configured) and are able to make calls immediately. You can disable auto-registration by using the **no auto-reg-ephone** command, as shown in Example 14-11. This augments the strict registration described in the preceding section.

Example 14-11   *Disable Auto-Registration*

```
CME(config)# telephony-service
CME(config-telephony)# no auto-reg-ephone
```

For Cisco SIP IP Phones, you must configure the system so that the SIP endpoints must authenticate with a username and password before they can be admitted to the system, as shown in Example 14-12.

Example 14-12   *Restricting SIP Phone Auto-Registration*

```
CME(config)# voice register global
CME(config-register-global)# mode cme
CME(config-register-global)# source-address 10.87.104.162 port 5060
CME(config-register-global)# authenticate register
```

Cisco Unified CME: Call Logging (CDR)

You can configure the Cisco Unified CME system to capture CDR and log the same to the router flash, an external FTP server, external Syslog Server, or a AAA (Cisco TACACS+) server. CDR records can then be used to retrace calls to see if abuse by internal or external parties has occurred. Example 14-13 outlines the configuration of Cisco Unified CME call logging. Here the RADIUS server is reachable via IP 10.100.100.250 and is configured with the security key value of **C1sc0123**.

Example 14-13   *Cisco Unified CME Call Logging*

```
CME(config)# aaa new-model
!
CME(config)# aaa authentication login h323 group radius
CME(config)# aaa authorization exec h323 group radius
CME(config)# aaa accounting connection h323 start-stop radius
CME(config)# aaa session-id common
!
CME(config)# gw-accounting aaa
!
CME(config)# radius-server host 10.100.100.250 auth-port 1812 acct-port 1813
```

```
CME(config)# radius-server key C1sc0123
CME(config)# radius-server retransmit 30
CME(config)# radius-server vsa send accounting
CME(config)# radius-server vsa send authentication
```

Note Using AAA server has one disadvantage over other methods, that is, most of the time the AAA server is located at the main site (Headquarters) and on WAN disruption, remote sites with Cisco Unified CME cannot log CDR.

Cisco Unified CME: Securing Voice Traffic (TLS and SRTP)

Analogous to Cisco UCM support for secure voice signaling (TLS) and media (SRTP), Cisco Unified CME also supports TLS for signaling and SRTP for bearer media. Enabling TLS/SRTP on Cisco Unified CME implies that your signaling and media are less susceptible to eavesdropping and pack manipulation attacks.

There are, however, some restraints associated with Cisco Unified CME TLS/SRTP for signaling and media, respectively:

■ Cisco Unified CME does not boast a secure conference bridge; therefore, secure software conferencing is not supported. An SRTP call falls back to RTP when joined in a conference.

■ Calls to Cisco Unity Express (CUE) are not secure because CUE does not support encrypted calls.

■ Music on Hold (MOH) and video calls are not secure.

■ Secure Cisco Unified CME supports only H.323 trunks, and SIP trunks are not supported. This further implies that SRTP supports secure supplementary services in both H.450 or non-H.450 Cisco Unified CME networks.

■ Secure calls are supported only in the default session application.

The following section outlines the steps required to enable TLS/SRTP on your Cisco Unified CME router.

Step 1.   Enable the IOS CA server. The CA server can derive certificates for encryption of signaling and media traffic. An IOS CA server can be created on a dedicated IOS router (acting as the IOS CA for your organization, which becomes a centralized point of interaction for certificates and allows for ease of managing certificates) or on the same router that runs Cisco Unified CME software.

Note Example 14-14 enables the CA server on the same IOS router as Cisco Unified CME. SRTP fallback can be configured to support IP Phones or devices that do not support encryption.

Example 14-14 *Enable IOS CA Server*

```
CME(config)# crypto pki server CAServer
CME(cs-server)# database level complete
CME(cs-server)# grant auto
CME(cs-server)# lifetime certificate 1825
CME(cs-server)# lifetime ca-certificate 1825
CME(cs-server)# database url nvram:
CME(cs-server)# no shutdown
%Some server settings cannot be changed after CA certificate generation.
% Please enter a passphrase to protect the private key
% or type Return to exit
Password:

Re-enter password:
% Generating 1024 bit RSA keys, keys will be non-exportable...[OK]
% Exporting Certificate Server signing certificate and keys...
% Certificate Server enabled.
```

CA server will issue certificates for the following:

- **Cisco Unified CME:** Certificate for TLS sessions with phones
- **TFTP/HTTPS:** A key pair and certificate for signing configuration files
- **CAPF:** Certificate for TLS sessions with phones
- **SAST (equivalent to eToken):** Required for signing the CTL file

Step 2. Make sure that the HTTP server is enabled on the router because it is required for enrollment with the CA and the certificate grant from the CA, as shown in Example 14-15.

Example 14-15 *Enable Cisco Unified CME HTTP Server*

```
CME(config)# ip http server
```

Step 3. Create a trustpoint (see Example 14-16) for Cisco Unified CME call control. This will be used for the call control and CAPF.

Example 14-16 *CME Trustpoint Definition*

```
CME(config)# crypto pki trustpoint CME
CME(ca-trustpoint)# enrollment url http://10.87.104.162:80
CME(ca-trustpoint)# chain-validation stop
CME(ca-trustpoint)# revocation-check none
CME(ca-trustpoint)# rsakeypair CME
```

Step 4. Authenticate and enroll Trustpoint CME with the CA, as outlined in Example 14-17.

Example 14-17 *Trustpoint Authentication*

```
CME(config)# crypto pki authenticate CME
Certificate has the following attributes:
        Fingerprint MD5: 92A5A072 3A816D6C 3334FCB0 154C29B4
        Fingerprint SHA1: AF0790F3 742A76E5 A55F7613 250FB79E D70CA253

% Do you accept this certificate? [yes/no]: yes
Trustpoint CA certificate accepted.
!
CME(config)# crypto pki enroll CME
%
% Start certificate enrollment ..
% Create a challenge password. You will need to verbally provide this
  password to the CA Administrator in order to revoke your certificate.
  For security reasons your password will not be saved in the configuration.
  Please make a note of it.


Password:
Re-enter password:

% The subject name in the certificate will include: CME
% Include the router serial number in the subject name? [yes/no]: no
% Include an IP address in the subject name? [no]: no
Request certificate from CA? [yes/no]: yes
% Certificate request sent to Certificate Authority
```

Step 5. Create trustpoints for SAST1 and SAST2. Authenticate and enroll with the CA, as shown in Example 14-18.

Example 14-18 *Trustpoint Definition for SAST1 and SATS2*

```
CME(config)# crypto pki trustpoint SAST1
CME(ca-trustpoint)# enrollment url http://10.87.104.162:80
CME(ca-trustpoint)# chain-validation stop
```

```
CME(ca-trustpoint)# revocation-check none
CME(ca-trustpoint)# rsakeypair SAST1
!
CME(config)# crypto pki authenticate SAST1
<output omitted>
!
CME(config)# crypto pki enroll SAST1
<output omitted>
!
CME(config)# crypto pki trustpoint SAST2
CME(ca-trustpoint)# enrollment url http://10.87.104.162:80
CME(ca-trustpoint)# chain-validation stop
CME(ca-trustpoint)# revocation-check none
CME(ca-trustpoint)# rsakeypair SAST2
!
CME(config)# crypto pki authenticate SAST2
<output omitted>
!
CME(config)# crypto pki enroll SAST2
<output omitted>
```

Note We will use CME trustpoint for call control (CME), TFTP, and CAPF.

> **Step 6.** Configure CTL (IOS) Client.

Note Similar to CUCM, you can use a minimum of two eTokens, namely SAST1 and SAST2 for primary and backup purpose. However, unlike CUCM, you do not have the option to use eTokens; therefore, the tokens are created using IOS CA certificates (as previously defined in Step 5). The configuration for enabling these eTokens is shown in Example 14-19.

Example 14-19 *CTL Client Configuration*

```
CME(config)# ctl-client
CME(config-ctl-client)# server capf 10.87.104.162 trustpoint CME
CME(config-ctl-client)# server tftp 10.87.104.162 trustpoint CME
CME(config-ctl-client)# server cme 10.87.104.162 trustpoint CME
CME(config-ctl-client)# sast1 trustpoint SAST1
CME(config-ctl-client)# sast2 trustpoint SAST2
CME(config-ctl-client)# regenerate
```

Step 7. Configure the Cisco Unified CME CAPF server, as shown in Example 14-20.

Example 14-20 *CAPF Server Definition*

```
CME(config)# capf-server
CME(config-capf-server)# trustpoint-label CME
CME(config-capf-server)# cert-enroll-trustpoint CAServer password 0 C1sc0123
CME(config-capf-server)# phone-key-size 1024
CME(config-capf-server)# port 3084
CME(config-capf-server)# auth-mode null-string
CME(config-capf-server)# source-addr 10.87.104.162
```

Step 8. Configure the Cisco Unified CME Telephony Service for supporting signaling and media encryption and TFTP file authentication (signing files), as shown in Example 14-21.

Example 14-21 *Telephony Service Configuration to Support Security*

```
CME(config)# telephony-service
CME(config-telephony)# secure-signaling trustpoint CME
CME(config-telephony)# tftp-server-credentials trustpoint CME
CME(config-telephony)# server-security-mode secure
CME(config-telephony)# device-security-mode encrypted
CME(config-telephony)# cnf-file perphone
CME(config-telephony)# cnf-file location flash:
```

Step 9. Configure ephones for supporting TLS/SRTP, as outlined in Example 14-22.

Example 14-22 *ephone Configuration to Support Secure Signaling and Media*

```
CME(config)# ephone 10
CME(config-ephone)# device-security-mode encrypted
CME(config-ephone)# cert-oper upgrade auth-mode null-string
```

Note Optionally, you can have an authentication string defined under the ephone that must be entered by the end user before the IP Phone can be registered with Cisco Unified CME.

Step 10. Regenerate the CTL file and CNF files followed by the ephone reset, as shown in Example 14-23.

Example 14-23   *Subsequent Steps Required to Enable ephone Secure Mode*

```
CME(config)# ctl-client
CME(config-ctl-client)# regenerate
!
CME(config)# telephony-service
CME(config-telephony)# create cnf-files
!
CME(config)# ephone 10
CME(config-ephone)# reset
```

Example 14-24 lists some verification commands.

Example 14-24   *Cisco Unified CME Security—Verification Commands*

```
CME# show telephony-service security-info

Skinny Server Trustpoint for TLS: CME
TFTP Credentials Trustpoint:
Server Security Mode: Secure
Global Device Security Mode: Encrypted

CME# show ctl-client
CTL Client Information
----------------------
        SAST 1 Certificate Trustpoint: SAST1
        SAST 2 Certificate Trustpoint: SAST2
        List of Trusted Servers in the CTL
                CAPF    10.87.104.162    CME
                TFTP    10.87.104.162    CME
                CME     10.87.104.162    CME
```

Following are some useful debugs for troubleshooting:

- **debug crypto pki transactions**
- **debug crypto pki server**
- **debug capf-server all**
- **debug ephone register**
- **debug tftp events**

Securing Cisco Unity Express Platform

Cisco Unity Express (CUE) complements Cisco Unified CME call control as voicemail. This section highlights the security controls that should be implemented around CUE in your *Express* call control and voice messaging environment to safeguard the voice messaging platform.

Cisco Unity Express is a service-module running on top of the IOS engine. Just as any other IOS-based platform, it also needs to be protected from platform-level intrusion attempts by internal and external attackers.

Note   All Cisco Unity Express configuration examples in this chapter are based on Cisco Unity Express version 8.6.

Telnet to CUE (SSH is not supported at this time) can be done in two ways:

■ From Cisco Unified CME using the **service-module service-Engine <module slot> session** command

■ From a PC directed toward a specific port (as per the slot in which the CUE module is installed)

While the first method is presumably safe (provided that the attacker has not compromised the Cisco Unified CME), the second method opens up CUE for intrusion from within your network infrastructure. To prevent direct access to CUE from Cisco Unified CME or from outside, access must be secured using line TTY login and password. This is demonstrated in the following steps:

Step 1.   To find out the line TTY on which CUE can be accessed, issue the command shown in Example 14-25.

Example 14-25   *Checking CUE Service Module Status—TTY Port Number*

```
CME# service-module service-Engine 1/0 status
Service Module is Cisco Service-Engine1/0
Service Module supports session via TTY line 66
Service Module is in Steady state
Service Module heartbeat-reset is enabled
```

Step 2.   Enable the line TTY login and password so that CUE authenticates a user whether logging in from Cisco Unified CME or from outside using the port number, as shown in Example 14-26.

Example 14-26 *Restricting TTY Login*

```
CME(config)# line 66
CME(config-line)# password C1sc0123
CME(config-line)# login
```

At this time, when you try to log in to CUE from a PC or from Cisco Unified CME, it should ask for the login password (see Example 14-27). From Cisco Unified CME you get the following prompt:

Note A login banner can be configured from CLI or GUI (by going to **System > Login Banner**).

Example 14-27 *Log In from Cisco Unified CME*

```
CME# service-module service-Engine 1/0 session
Trying 10.76.104.21, 2066 ... Open

User Access Verification

Password:
Password OK
*************************************************************************
WARNING!  This router is the property of XYZ Corporation.
It may be accessed only by authorized users. Unauthorized use of this
system is strictly prohibited and may be subject to criminal prosecution.
*************************************************************************
CUE#
```

From PC when you login, you see what's shown in Example 14-28.

Example 14-28 *Login from PC*

```
C:\>telnet 10.76.104.21 2066
Trying 10.76.104.21, 2066 ... Open

User Access Verification

Password:
Password OK
```

```
*************************************************************************
WARNING!  This router is the property of XYZ Corporation.
It may be accessed only by authorized users. Unauthorized use of this
system is strictly prohibited and may be subject to criminal prosecution.
*************************************************************************
CUE#
```

Enabling AAA for Cisco Unity Express

To further augment CUE platform security, you can have CUE authenticated by AAA with Cisco TACACS+. This further reduces the probability of someone attacking the system because the passwords are not local to the system, and thus the attacker cannot log in unless TACACS+ is compromised.

You can enable AAA (Authentication) by going to https://<ip address of cue>. Log in and go to **Configure > AAA > Authentication**, as shown in Figure 14-1.

Note   By default, CUE supports only HTTP for GUI. CUE GUI HTTPS configuration is covered in the next section.

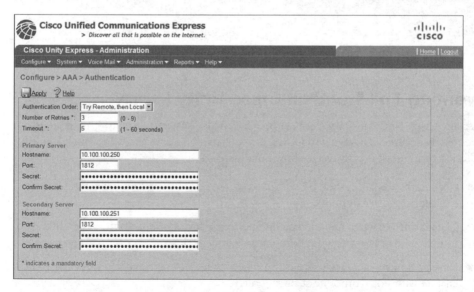

Figure 14-1   *Cisco Unity Express—(AAA) Authentication Configuration*

You can also enable CUE accounting, which logs login, exec, configuration, failed-attempts, and so on so such that, you can have AAA server generate logs or alerts when someone tries to brute-force CUE. The settings and all options are portrayed in Figure 14-2.

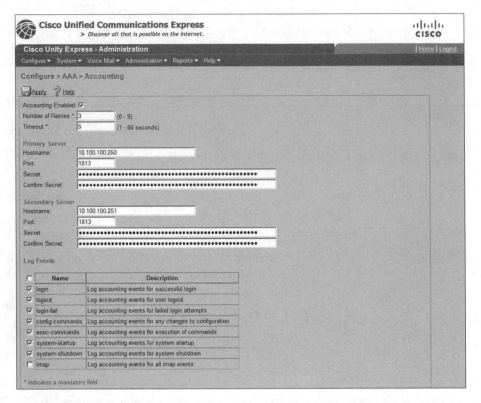

Figure 14-2 *Cisco Unity Express—(AAA) Accounting Configuration*

Preventing Toll Fraud on Cisco Unity Express

Just like Cisco Unity or Unity Connection, CUE is also susceptible to toll fraud unless adequately secured. To safeguard CUE from toll fraud, observe the following leading practice configurations, which are shown in Figure 14-3:

- Change the default system password, ping, and account lockout behavior. Go to **Configure > User Defaults.**

- Change the password and pin (maximum length, history depth, auto-generation, and so on) to be in line with your corporate security policy.

- Have account temporary lockout, maximum failed attempts, and so on parameters change with your corporate security policy.

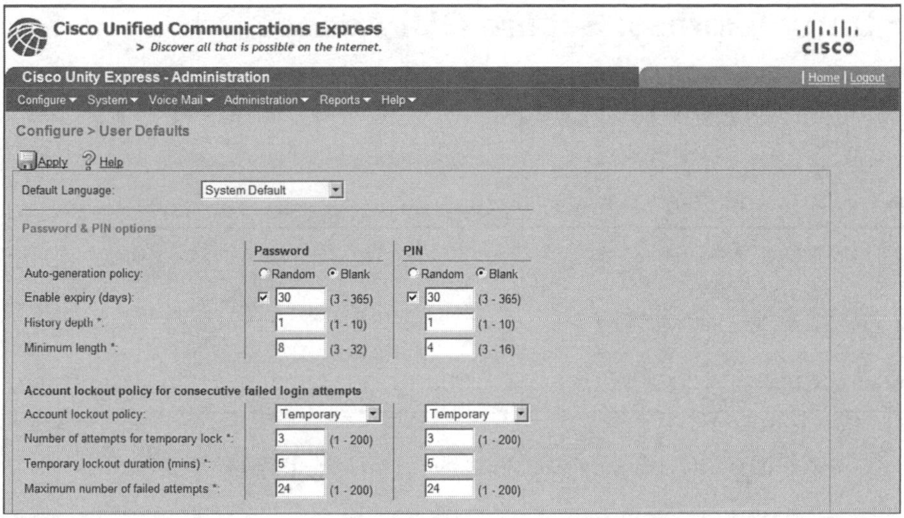

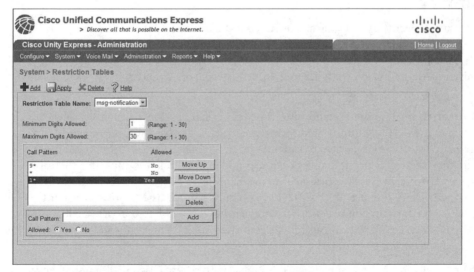

Figure 14-3 *Cisco Unity Express—System User Defaults*

Change the restriction tables to disallow any calls out-dialed to PSTN. Go to **System > Restriction Tables** (see Figure 14-4). Disable the default restriction table "*" by selection allowed as **None**, and provide the specific destination number as per your dial plan. (In Figure 14-4, only patterns starting with 1 will be reachable, which are internal extensions.)

Figure 14-4 *Cisco Unity Express—Restriction Tables*

Note The out-dial Auto Attendant by default blocks the transfer to external (PSTN) numbers.

Cisco Unity Express: Secure GUI Access

Similar to Cisco Unified CME, you can enable HTTPS (SSL) for CUE module as well to protect the administrative and end-user sessions from prying eyes. Example 14-29 details the process.

Example 14-29 *CUE HTTPS Configuration*

```
CUE(config)# crypto key generate
Key generation in progress. Please wait...
The label name for the key is CUE
!
CUE(config)# web session security keyLabel CUE
```

You can access CUE GUI securely by pointing your browser to https://<ip address of CUE>.

Note   Since this will be a CUE self-signed certificate; you may be prompted to accept the same. At present, CUE does not support third-party signed certificates.

Summary

It has never been easy to evade any intended malicious attacks when the attacker is determined and motivated. Yet, it never meant that you can let your defenses down or not be prepared for the inevitable attack. In this chapter, you learned about Cisco Unified CME and Cisco Unity Express security (which are counterparts to CUCM and Cisco Unity/Unity Connection for smaller sites).

More often than not, the remote sites connect to headquarters or main site(s) via public network (the Internet), and this connectivity is exposed to outside world (unless adequately secured). Needless to say, if your communications are disrupted, nothing will come to avail when it involves customer and internal relationships. It is therefore important to realize the various security mechanisms to protect Cisco Unified CME and Cisco Unity Express. In this chapter, you grasped the basic to advance security design and configuration necessary to safeguard Cisco IOS-based express call-control and voice-messaging solution against threats originating from within and outside of your organization.

The next chapter helps you build solid foundation to secure Cisco IP Telephony endpoints. It is user-facing devices and endpoints, which are directly exposed to threats originating from malicious insiders and outsiders. You will comprehend security specifics for Cisco Unified IP Phones (wired and wireless) and Cisco IP Communicator.

Cisco IP Telephony
Endpoint Security

XYZ is a large corporation with a state-of-the-art Headquarters and receives many visitors daily. One day, one such visitor, Mr. X, pays a visit to the CTO of XYZ Corp. (who happens to be his close friend) to invite him to an upcoming security conference. After calling the CTO, who will meet him in the lobby, he turns his attention to the shiny piece of hardware, which a moment ago he used to call his friend. Well, does it look too technical for him to sort out what it is? Maybe not! Mr. X is a seasoned White-Hat hacker and today he is onto something. Mr. X starts playing around with the Cisco Unified IP Phone and reaches the Network Configuration menu. To his surprise, the settings are unlocked! He opens the IP address of the IP Phone in a web browser from his laptop plugged into the PC port of the IP Phone (yet another crucial security setting that should have been toggled off). Surprise, surprise! He has sufficient information that a hacker would need to begin his attack!

If it were not for Mr. X being friendly and a White-Hat hacker, but for someone with malicious intentions, XYZ's network is begging to be exploited! It does not matter if it has firewalls, IPS, or state-of-the-art security mechanisms if someone from inside can initiate an attack. As vital it is to secure network equipment (physical security), perimeter, links, applications, and conversation streams, end-to-end security is achieved only when user endpoints are also part of the overall security plan.

This chapter covers the following topics:

- Why is endpoint security important?
- Securing Cisco Unified IP Phones
- Securing Cisco Unified Wireless IP Phones
- Securing Cisco Softphones (Cisco IP Communicator)

Why Is Endpoint Security Important?

Take a step back and think about the various threats you have come to know about untill now, that can pester your IP Telephony network, and the ways in which you can mitigate them. While all the groundwork has been at the network, application, and related device end, you should not forget that it is the endpoints that enable the end user to leverage the power of Cisco IP Telephony. It does not help when every other resource is secured and endpoints are exposed to threats. It is only rational to have the endpoints secured and hardened to minimize the risk of voice streams being hijacked or replayed, or an IP Telephony infrastructure being played with because of a weakness at the end device.

To recap, when you started the journey to achieve secure IP communications, you confronted the various threats that possibly can disrupt the sanctity of your Cisco IP Telephony network. For the ease of access, following are the threats reiterated from Chapter 1, "What Is IP Telephony Security and Why Do you Need It?"

- **Identity spoofing:** Impersonation exploits, in which a hacker steals a legitimate user's identity so that the hacker's phone calls appear legitimate

- **Eavesdropping (man-in-the-middle attack):** Passively sniff the data (voice packets and data packets) during a voice conversation or transfer of information from one endpoint to another

- **Toll fraud:** Internal or external 'malicious' users placing unauthorized toll (long distance and international) calls via the corporate telephone system

- **Denial of Service (DoS):** Hurl a deluge of irritant traffic to IP Phones, call-processing servers, or IP Telephony infrastructure so that the authorized users cannot leverage critical communication resources

Before taking a deep dive into Cisco Unified IP Phone and Softphone security, it is crucial that CUCM settings must be appropriately configured to protect against toll fraud attacks, as the same cannot be implemented at the user end, and must be provisioned at the call-control end (relevant to SRST and CME as well). The most common culprit leading to toll fraud is the improper configuration of the following settings:

- Call-Forward (All, Busy, and No Answer)

- Transfer (Blind and Consultative)

- Conference

In essence, a proper dial plan design is a prerequisite to fend off toll fraud attempts.

Following are some of the key security threats relevant to Cisco Unified IP Phones (equally applicable to wired and wireless IP phones):

- Identity impersonation

- Tampering of TFTP file or configuration file transfer

- Network Access Compliance

- Eavesdropping or manipulation of conversations

- Rogue phone registration

The following sections for wired and wireless Cisco Unified IP Phones cover the stated security issues along with details on threat mitigation mechanisms.

Cisco Unified IP Phone Security

Since the time when IP Telephony has been in existence, because of its very nature of dependency on the underlying data network, it has shared the strengths and weaknesses of the same. This legacy extends right from the user-facing access layer to the distribution layer to the core layer to the data center access. While, most of the times, if not all, the security efforts are concentrated on applications, network devices, and perimeter it is the endpoints facing the end-users which are forgotten, which leads to the downfall of all other security controls.

This section discusses Cisco Unified IP Phone security for wired IP Phones. The security for wired IP Phones is a multiple step process:

- Hardening the wired endpoints against imminent threats from malicious end users

- Securing admission to network

- Protecting voice conversations

- Securing file transfers from TFTP (firmware, configuration, and so on)

The following sections cover these topics in detail.

Wired IP Phone: Hardening

Cisco Unified IP Phones (endpoints) and Cisco Unified Communications Manager (CUCM) offer built-in features to secure the user-facing endpoints. These features can be enabled or disabled on a phone-by-phone basis to increase the security of an IP Telephony deployment. Because the end-user layer is where most of the attacks (internal or external) originate from, it is sensible to have some simple tasks carried out to harden the endpoints so that the otherwise impending attacks are counteracted. These tasks can be performed from the CUCM.

Note   You have the option to disable or restrict certain settings, for example, phone settings. It is recommended to follow your security policy so that the security applied is in line with business requirements.

To harden a Cisco Unified IP Phone, you can modify the settings, as shown in Figure 15-1, from their default settings to a more secure configuration.

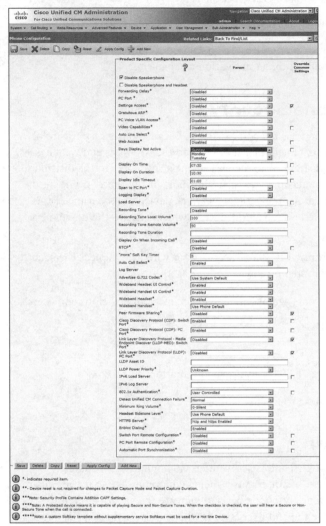

Figure 15-1 *Cisco Unified IP Phone Hardening*

Speakerphone

Insiders (malicious users) can eavesdrop the conversations on speakerphone. You can disable speakerphones, for example, on a per user or job function basis, by enabling the check box to disable the speakerphone.

PC Port

PC ports enable a daisy-chained PC to connect to the corporate network. Malicious users can exploit this feature as an access point into the IP Telephony network. It is strongly recommended to have this feature turned off in phones that are placed in public-facing areas of an organization (for example, the lobby, elevator, break rooms, and so on) and when an employee does not need hardwire connectivity to the network.

Note   The PC port must be turned on for some applications to work properly, for example, for Cisco Unified Video Advantage to operate properly, both the PC port and video capabilities must be enabled.

It is important to understand that there is no point to disable the phone's PC port if an end user can simply plug directly into the switch port of the wall jack and gain data VLAN access and try to perform a VLAN hopping attack. Therefore, for end-to-end security, 802.1x should be deployed for endpoint secured network access.

Settings Access

Details about the network infrastructure could be compromised with access to the settings button of the IP Phone. Each Cisco Unified IP Phone has a network settings page that lists many of the network elements and detailed information needed for the phone to operate. This information could be used by an attacker to start a reconnaissance on the network. Access to the Settings button can be completely disabled, or just the network settings can be disabled, leaving the ring types and contrast options available for end users to access (in restricted mode).

Gratuitous Address Resolution Protocol ARP (GARP)

First, you should know why gratuitous ARP (GARP) is dangerous, particularly in an IP Telephony environment. Network devices use GARP packets to announce their presence on the network. Although this may seem like a useful functionality (and in some cases it might be), it can be exploited by an attacker who claims to be the default router, thereby leading the network device into sending all information the attacker (performing a man-in-the-middle [MITM] attack). By default, Cisco Unified IP Phones accept GARP packets. By disabling the IP Phone to respond to GARP packets, you can prevent MITM attacks.

PC Voice VLAN Access

This functionality acts like a two-edged sword. On one hand, it enables the network administrators to capture voice traffic, which aids in troubleshooting any voice-related issues. However, on other hand it can be exploited by hackers and attackers to sniff the voice traffic off the IP Phone. The sniffed streams can be reconstructed and replayed to hear conversations. By disabling this feature, the IP Phone can stop forwarding voice traffic to the PC Port. This functionality should be disabled and should be temporarily enabled only for troubleshooting.

Video Capabilities

The Video capabilities are meant for supporting Cisco Unified Video Advantage (CUVA) on the client PC and Cisco VT Camera and should be disabled if you are not going to use video with an endpoint. In other words, this setting should be selectively enabled if an IP Phone user can leverage CUVA-based video calls.

Web Access

Just like settings access, if the web server on the phone is turned on, a potential hacker can point a web browser at the phone's IP address and data mine much of the information from the web pages that are served from the phone (see Figure 15-2). Disabling the web server functionality for the phone blocks access to the phone internal web pages, which provide statistics and configuration information. Features, such as the Cisco Quality Report Tool, do not function properly without access to the phone web pages. Disabling the web server also affects any serviceability applications, such as CiscoWorks and Cisco UCAT tool that relies on web access.

CISCO	**Network Configuration**	
	Cisco Unified IP Phone Cisco Communicator (SEP00247EDA3DEC)	
Device Information	DHCP Server	171.68.10.69
Network Configuration	Host Name	SEP00247EDA3DEC
Network Statistics	IP Address	10.55.82.46
Device Logs	TFTP Server 1	10.105.127.216
Status Messages	Default Router 1	
Debug Display	Default Router 2	
Streaming Statistics	Default Router 3	
Stream 1	Default Router 4	
Stream 2	Default Router 5	
Stream 3	Unified CM 1	10.105.127.216 Active
Stream 4	Unified CM 2	
Stream 5	Unified CM 3	
	Unified CM 4	
	Unified CM 5	
	Information URL	http://NGEPLOS-XCUM-PUB01:8080/ccmcip/GetTelecasterHelpText.jsp
	Directories URL	http://NGEPLOS-XCUM-PUB01:8080/ccmcip/xmldirectory.jsp

Figure 15-2   *Cisco Unified IP Phone Web Server—Network Configuration*

Span to PC Port

The span-to-PC port functionality is somewhat similar to PC Voice VLAN access. It allows spanning one port to another (just like in a Cisco Catalyst switch) to enable all the traffic from one or more VLANs to go out a port on the PC port (such as the Voice VLAN) using the IP Phone's internal switch. This functionality should be enabled only when you have a situation in which you need to troubleshoot any voice-related issue.

> **Note**   To use this feature, PC Voice VLAN access must be enabled.

Logging Display

This setting enables logging and generation of log files on a console or on a downstream port, that is, a PC port. Again, this option is for debugging any voice-related or device-related issue and should be enabled only when such a requirement exists.

Peer Firmware Sharing

In a distributed site model where the main site is segregated by low-speed WAN links, Peer Firmware Sharing (PFS or PPID) is a recommended option so that the root phone can distribute firmware to local phones, taking the load off the WAN bandwidth. However, the same feature can be a compromising factor when an attacker emulates an IP Phone and requests for firmware. The load type and characteristics can aid in attacking the network. Even worse, if an attacker can compromise the identity of the root phone, the rest of the local phones would be at the attacker's mercy. To elevate this issue and use PPID functionality, use of CAPF and LSC is highly recommended so that the identity of a phone is not disclaimed.

Link Layer Discovery Protocol: Media Endpoint Discover (LLDP-MED) Switch Port

Unless you have third-that do not support CDP (Cisco Catalyst switches and other endpoints support CDP for device identification and assignment to Voice and Auxiliary VLAN), it is worthwhile to disable LLDP-MED feature. LLDP is a vendor-neutral protocol (similar to CDP that is Cisco-proprietary) used by network devices for advertising their identity and capabilities to the network.

Link Layer Discovery Protocol (LLDP) PC Port

The logic explained in LLDP-MED applies equally to devices connected on a PC port and should be disabled unless you have a requirement to support third-party devices.

There are other options, such as 802.1x Authentication, HTTPS Server, Switch Port Remote Configuration, PC Port Remote Configuration, and an Automatic Port Synchronization, which are set to a default and could be changed as per your organization's corporate and IP Telephony Security policy. However, for most of these, the default settings on a Cisco IP Phone should provide sufficient security.

Configuring Unified IP Phone Hardening

To configure Cisco Unified IP Phone hardening, follow these steps:

Step 1.   Go to **Cisco Unified Communications Manager Administration > Device > Phone**.

Step 2. Click **Find** to list the IP Phones, and click the phone you want to set the settings for hardening the same.

Step 3. Scroll down to locate the product-specific parameters.

Step 4. Choose Disabled for each parameter you want to disable. (It depends on your organization's corporate or IP Telephony Security policy as to which settings you want to disable or restrict for the end user's access.) Click **Save**. Click **Reset**.

Wired IP Phone: Secure Network Admission

You must secure IP Phone network admission and registration with Cisco Unified Communications Manager. It is vital to understand the extent of damage that rogue IP Phones can inflict on your IP Telephony network. It could scale from toll fraud to network to DoS attacks. Therefore, it is strongly recommended to implement 802.1x network access control on IP Phones to ensure that only legitimate endpoints can get access to the network and leverage IP Telephony services. The topic of secure network access using 802.1x is covered in depth in Chapter 6, "Cisco IP Telephony Layer 2 Security."

In addition, when communicating with CUCM over a timidly unsecure network, it is always a good idea to use the secure service (HTTPS) URL instead of a non-secure URL to evade meddlesome listeners. This helps shun (MITM attacks and eavesdropping and promiscuous scans.

Wired IP Phone: Voice Conversation Security

With Cisco unified IP Phone (wired endpoint) hardened and securely admitted to the network, half the battle is won. Now, you need to ensure that endpoint conversation is secured with other endpoints and CUCM. By default, Cisco Unified IP Phones communicate to CUCM and other endpoints or gateways over an unencrypted or unsecure channel. Therefore, the conversation is still vulnerable to eavesdropping, packet-manipulation, and DoS attacks. To safeguard signaling and media streams from IP Phones, CUCM supports security features such as SRTP for media encryption and TLS/SSL for signaling encryption. By encrypting the signaling and media streams, voice conversations are secure and less vulnerable to attacks.

After securing the IP Phone and its conversation, you are sure to win the battle (or at least put your digital-age foes on a back foot). For details on how you can secure IP Phone conversations using encrypted media (SRTP) and signaling (TLS), refer to Chapter 9, "Cisco Unified Communications Manager Security."

Refer to the following URL to confirm if your IP Phone model supports SRTP/TLS: http://www.cisco.com/en/US/docs/voice_ip_comm/cucm/srnd/8x/endpnts.html.

Wired IP Phone: Secure TFTP Communication

As discussed in Chapter 9, TFTP encryption is one of the available options in the security profile of Cisco IP Phones and available for both SCCP and SIP security profiles. IP Phones can communicate with a CUCM TFTP server to download device images and configuration. When a security profile on the IP Phone is enabled, the IP Phone uses certificate exchange with the CUCM TFTP server to establish a TLS encrypted channel. This makes the task of even a talented and experienced hacker extremely difficult, that is, to sniff the TFTP streams, manipulate the packets, or spoof the identity of TFTP server. For more details on configuration of encrypted TFTP file transfer, refer to Chapter 9 and Appendix A, "Cisco IP Telephony: Authentication and Encryption Essentials."

Cisco Unified Wireless IP Phone Security

If an attack surface is large for wired endpoints, it becomes colossal for wireless endpoints. This is primarily because of the reach of wireless network. The attacker does not need to be physically on the premises where wireless signal is available to launch an attack. It is much easier for a hacker to initiate wardrives, conduct eavesdropping, or indulge in unauthorized network access while being invisible, beyond the physical bounds of your network. The power of mobility provided by wireless networks can become the con point, if not secured adequately. There are tools such as NetStumbler, MiniStumbler, Vistumbler, and various Linux Live Wireless Hacking CDs that make it trivial to identify and exploit inadequately secured wireless networks.

Note If your enterprise wireless network is not adequately secured, it is as good as a Switch outside your organization's premises, allowing anyone to connect, access, or monitor your network.

Before discussing the security of wireless endpoints, it is essential to understand that endpoint security by itself is not sufficient, and the whole underlying network must be secured both physically and logically. Physical security has been discussed in Chapter 5, "Cisco IP Telephony Physical Security." This section discusses the security of supporting a wireless infrastructure, that is, Wireless LAN Controller (WLC), Wireless Access Point (WAP), and so on.

Note The security configuration on Cisco WLC is discussed from the perspective of establishing a secure communication channel with Cisco Unified Wireless IP Phone models 7921G, 7925G, 7925-EX, and 7926G.

Cisco Wireless LAN Controller (WLC) Security

Figure 15-3 illustrates the connectivity and communication scheme in a typical Cisco Unified Wireless IP Phone to WLC to RADIUS setup.

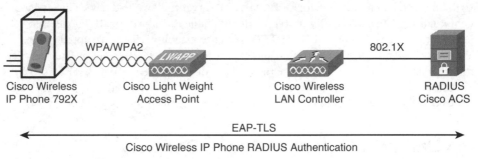

Figure 15-3 *Cisco Unified Wireless IP Phone—Secure Communication with the Network*

More details on the same will be discussed in subsequent sections.

From Cisco wireless endpoint security perspective, the best practice is to segment wireless voice and data into separate SSIDs, each with its QoS, access control, and security policy well outlined. A Secure Voice SSID and a dedicated profile for voice communication is depicted in the Figure 15-4. The SSID CiscoVoice will be used only with Cisco Unified Wireless IP Phones.

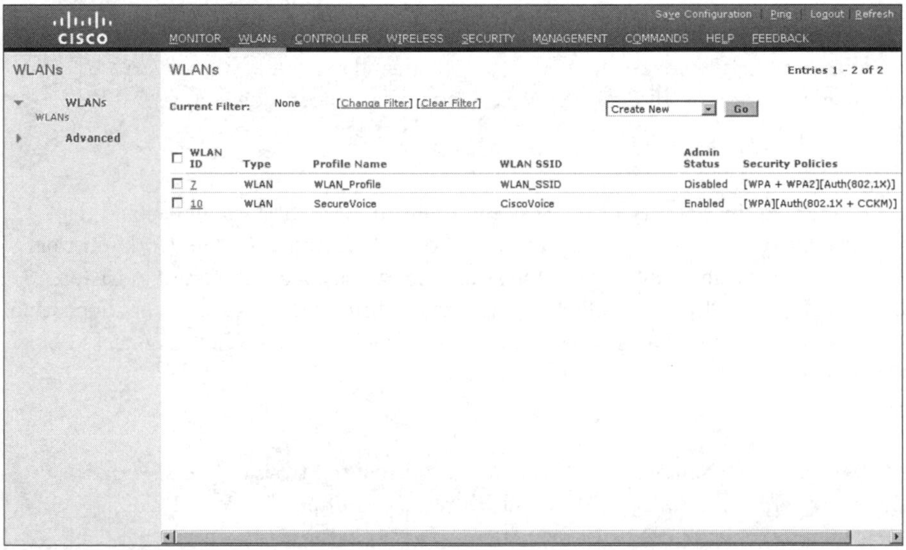

Figure 15-4 *Cisco Wireless LAN Controller—Voice WLAN Configuration*

As shown in Figure 15-5, **Cisco WLC WLAN > General** tab shows the parameters configured for profile SecureVoice with SSID CiscoVoice.

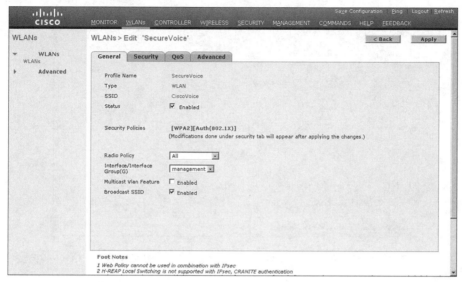

Figure 15-5 *Cisco Wireless LAN Controller—Voice WLAN Configuration (General)*

When using 802.1X authentication with WPA/TKIP, it is recommended to implement Cisco Centralized Key Management (CCKM) for authentication because the 802.1x-only mode can introduce delay during roaming due to its requirement for full re-authentication. Enable WPA policy with TKIP to use CCKM, when 802.1x authentication is used, as shown in Figure 15-6.

Note When WPA+WPA2 is enabled with 802.1x+CCKM-only wireless endpoints, which are Cisco Compatible Extensions (CCX), version 5 or later will support WPA2 with CCKM (for example, 7925). Other non-CCX 5.x-compatible devices will use opportunistic key caching, which is not supported with Cisco Wireless LAN Controller (WLC) resulting in a full re-authentication during roaming. If using devices that are not CCX version 5-compatible, it is recommended to allow only WPA/TKIP.

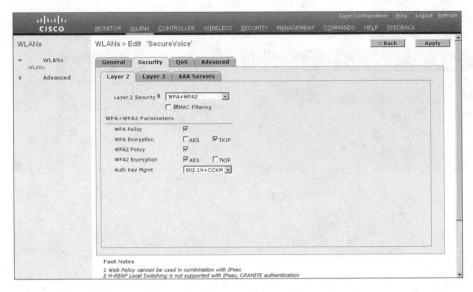

Figure 15-6 *Cisco Wireless LAN Controller—Voice WLAN Configuration (Security Layer 2)*

Under the **Security** tab, you can enable 802.1x authentication for the controller (see Figure 15-7), associated APs, and clients. This will be used for EAP-TLS authentication by wireless endpoints. (EAP-TLS is the most secure EAP standards available today.)

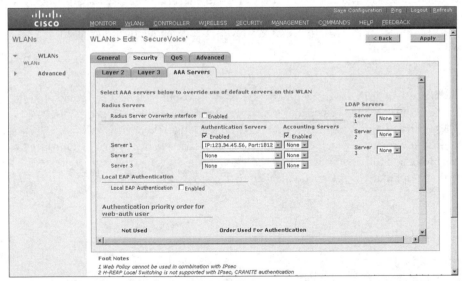

Figure 15-7 *Cisco Wireless LAN Controller—Voice WLAN Configuration (AAA)*

The QoS tab enables you to set up QoS properties for Voice WLAN endpoints. Cisco Wireless LAN supports Wi-Fi Multi Media (WMM), a QoS system based on the IEEE

802.11e draft (published by Wi-Fi Alliance). The Wireless LAN controller supports four levels of QoS:

- Platinum/Voice

- Gold/Video

- Silver/Best Effort *(default)*

- Bronze/Background

Voice traffic WLAN should be configured to use Platinum QoS, as shown in Figure 15-8.

Note   The Allowed option signifies that the Voice WLAN allows both WMM and non-WMM clients.

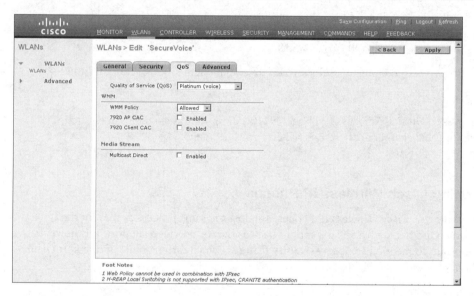

Figure 15-8   *Cisco Wireless LAN Controller—Voice WLAN Configuration (QoS)*

Following are a few best practices from a Voice WLAN deployment point of view:

- Avoid use of VLAN 1 for any purpose whatsoever, and ensure that switch port security is applied on access and if your security policy mandates, on distribution switches, in case the Wireless LAN Controllers (WLC) or Autonomous Access Points (AP) are connected to the latter.

- Ensure that Public Secure Packet Forwarding (PSPF) is not enabled for the voice VLAN because this can prevent clients from communicating directly when associated to the same access point.

- Cisco recommends disabling TKIP Countermeasure on Voice SSIDs.

■ Management of the wireless infrastructure (WLC and AP) should be done from a dedicated management subnet (In-Band or Out-of-Band) and management over wireless network from clients should be disabled.

Cisco Wireless Unified IP Phone Security

For wireless endpoint security, securing a Cisco Unified Wireless IP Phone (models 7921G, 7925G, 7925-EX, and 7926G) is a multistep process, just like wired equivalent endpoints:

■ Hardening of a wireless endpoint

■ Securing a wireless endpoint

■ Securing access to a network

The following sections address these mechanisms and walk you through the configuration steps. Refer to following URL for information on security features supported by Cisco Unified Wireless IP Phone models:

http://www.cisco.com/en/US/docs/voice_ip_comm/cucm/srnd/8x/endpnts.html

Note   Cisco Unified Wireless IP Phone 7921G configuration examples illustrated throughout this chapter are based on SCCP Firmware version 1.3(4)SR2.

Hardening Cisco Wireless IP Phones

Hardening of Cisco Wireless IP Phones is almost the same process as that for the wired endpoints, with a few exceptions such as that of no video support. It is however important to mention some key security features, which differ from wired or soft client phones, as shown in Figure 15-9.

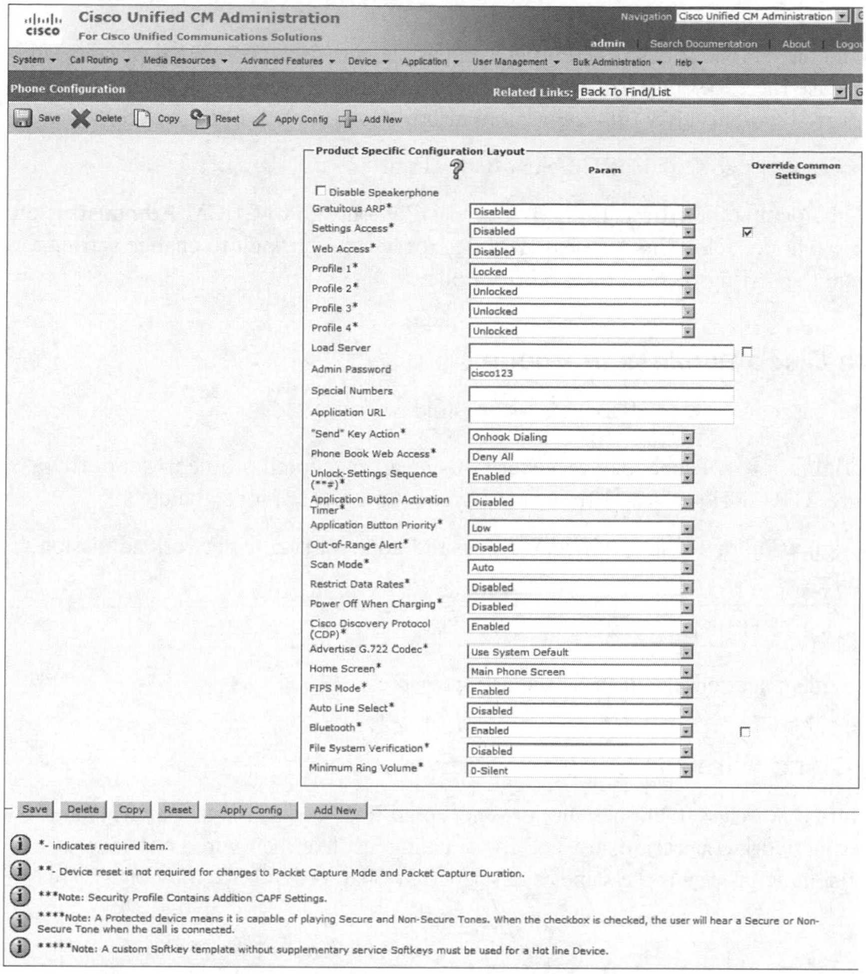

Figure 15-9 *Cisco Wireless Unified IP Phone Hardening*

Profile

The Profile option indicates whether WLAN Profile <number> can be modified by the end user. If the profile is locked, the user cannot modify it. It is recommended to set this setting for locked if strict access control is required however to restricted when the user is allowed to change the username and password.

Admin Password

This is the password that you can set to authenticate a user accessing the Wireless IP Phone web page (GUI). The defaults are **username: admin** and **password: Cisco**, and as such, it is recommended to change the same to non-default values to minimize the chances of any unauthorized user probing in the IP Phone GUI.

FIPS Mode

This parameter sets the Wireless IP Phone (compatible with 7921G, 7925 all variants, and 7926G) to use the Federal Information Processing Standards (FIPS) mode for the phone. The supported mode is FIPS 140-2. For more information on FIPS 140-2, go to

http://csrc.nist.gov/groups/STM/cmvp/index.html

To enable hardening for a Cisco Unified Wireless IP Phone, go to **CUCM Administration > Device > Phone.** Select the Wireless IP Phone for which you want to change settings, and change the settings as per your security policy.

Securing a Cisco Wireless IP Phone

Securing a Cisco Wireless IP Phones is a three-fold process:

- Configuration of Phone (device) security using an encrypted profile to support secure RTP (SRTP) calls and Transport Layer Security (TLS) for signaling

- Configuration of a Cisco Unified Wireless IP Phone for secure network admission (802.1x)

- Securing TFTP communication

The subsequent sections detail these security measures.

Securing Cisco Wireless Endpoint Conversation

Cisco Unified Wireless IP Phones support encrypted RTP media stream via SRTP and encrypted network connections via TLS for signaling just like their wired counterparts. The provisioning process is the same as described in Chapter 9 for SCCP Phones.

> **Note**   A prerequisite before configuring encryption for media and signaling is to have the CUCM cluster in secure mode (aka mixed-mode).

- Configure an SCCP Security Profile with the device security set to encrypted.

- Optional, select an encrypted TFTP configuration.

- Configure the Wireless IP Phone and apply the security profile on the phone.

- Configure the CAPF information to generate a device-specific certificate (LSC).

For detailed steps, refer to Chapter 9.

Securing Cisco Wireless Endpoint Network Admission

This section details the process to enable EAP-TLS support for Cisco Unified Wireless IP Phones. Cisco Wireless Security Suite (CWSS) provides authentication based on an IEEE 802.1X admission control standard using an upper-layer Extensible Authentication Protocol (EAP). Several EAP options are available:

- **EAP-TLS:** EAP Transport Layer Security uses pre-issued digital certificates to authenticate a user to the network. This requires certificates and public key infrastructure (PKI) management on both RADIUS servers and WLAN clients (considered the most secure of all EAP options).

- **PEAP:** Protected EAP is a hybrid authentication protocol that creates a secured TLS tunnel between the WLAN user and the RADIUS server to authenticate the user to the network. This requires certificates and PKI management only for the RADIUS servers, alleviating the effort to install and manage certificates on WLAN clients.

- **EAP-TTLS:** EAP Tunneled Transport Layer Security is similar to the PEAP method; it requires certificates and PKI management only for the RADIUS servers.

- **EAP-FAST:** EAP Flexible Authentication with Secure Tunneling is an authentication protocol that creates a secure tunnel without using certificates.

The EAP-TLS method of authenticating and permitting Cisco Unified Wireless IP Phones into a network (which is the most secure of all the EAP options previously listed) is discussed next. In the next section, you will comprehend the EAP-TLS deployment using third-party certificates. This option gives flexibility and ease of deployment by using the established (internal or external) certificate authority in your organization.

Note   Configuration steps detailed in this section are applicable to Cisco Unified Wireless IP Phone models 7921G, 7925G, 7925-EX, and 7926G.

Using Third-Party Certificates for EAP-TLS

Follow these steps to leverage third-party CA certificate for Cisco Unified Wireless IP Phone authentication using EAP-TLS.

Note   The Certificate Authority (CA) should already be configured to be trusted by the Cisco ACS. The ACS server should have an identity certificate (in the local certificate store for EAP) signed by the same CA and the CA root certificate (loaded in the CA Certificate store).

Step 1.   Connect to the Wireless IP Phone via either the wireless network or a USB cable to your PC.

Step 2. If the IP Phone is on wireless, open the GUI by typing the assigned static or DHCP IP address. (Cisco Unified Wireless IP Phones have a built in HTTPS server and can be connected with the assigned IP address.) If you connect via USB to your PC, assign an IP in the 192.168.1.0/24 subnet to the virtual adaptor, which Cisco Unified Wireless IP Phone driver creates since Cisco Unified Wireless IP Phone has a default static IP of 192.168.1.100/24 for wired connection.

Step 3. Log in to the wireless IP Phone Administration web page by using default credentials (unless changed earlier):

- **Username:** admin

- **Password:** Cisco

Step 4. Browse to the phone and select the Certificates menu. Click the User Installed option (click install), as shown in Figure 15-10.

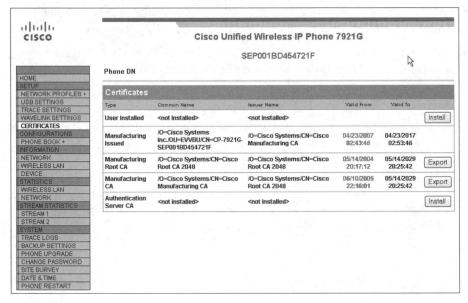

Figure 15-10 *Cisco Wireless Unified IP Phone—Certificate Overview*

Step 5. Type the information required to generate a CSR. Upload the CA root certificate (see Figure 15-11).

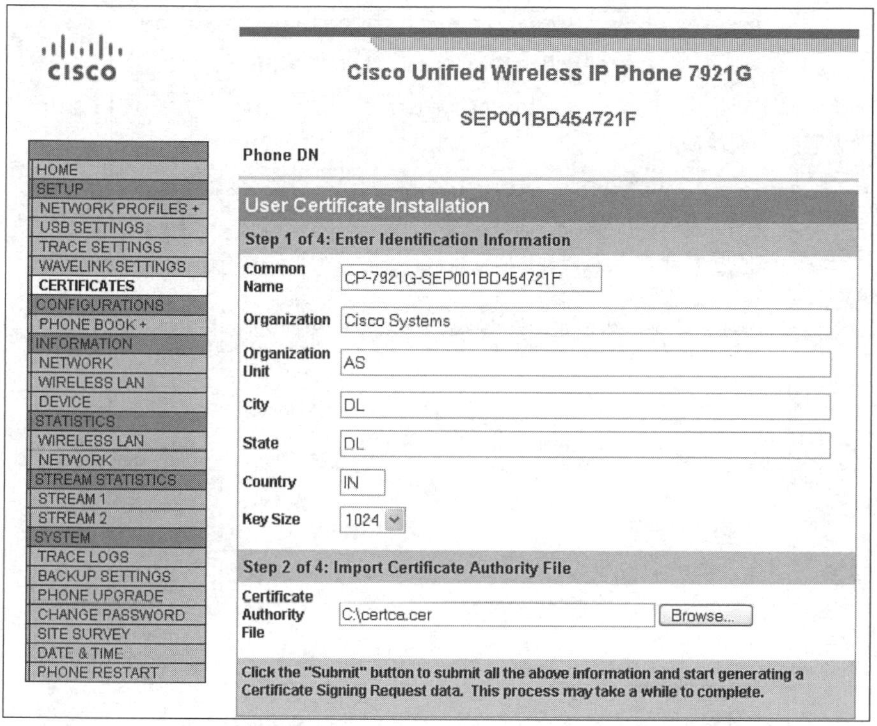

Figure 15-11 *Cisco Wireless Unified IP Phone—Generating CSR*

Step 6.   Generate a Certificate Signing Request (CSR).

Step 7.   Copy and paste the CSR text (including Begin and End request statements) in a notepad file. and save as .cer or .pem file. Get the CSR signed by your (internal or external) CA server.

Note   In this example, Microsoft Windows 2003 server is used as CA.

Step 8.   Load the signed CSR into the Wireless IP Phone, as shown in Figure 15-12.

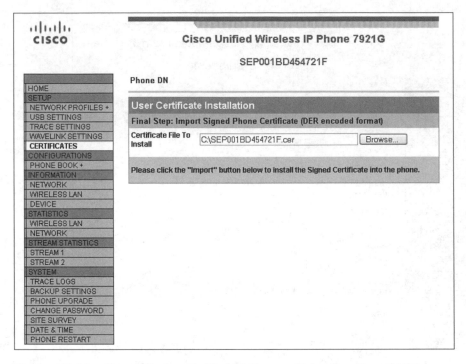

Figure 15-12   *Cisco Wireless Unified IP Phone—Uploading Signed CSR*

At this time, both the root CA and signed (identity) certificate should show under the certificate menu, as shown in Figure 15-13.

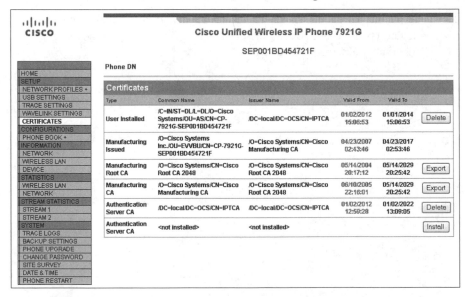

Figure 15-13   *Cisco Wireless Unified IP Phone—CA Root and IP Phone Identity Certificates*

Step 9. Create a user account in ACS with the username that corresponds to the CN of the uploaded (identity) certificate. A user account must be created in the format of **CP-7921G-SEP<MACADDRESS>** to allow that device to authenticate successfully, as shown in Figure 15-14.

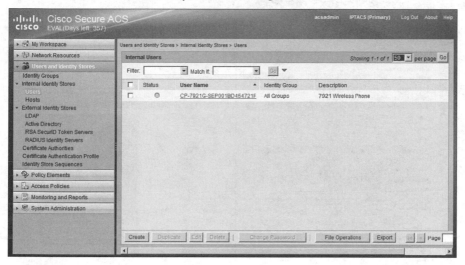

Figure 15-14 *Cisco Access Control Server (ACS)—IP Phone Configured as User*

Note Even though you need to configure a password for this user, it will not be checked during the EAP-TLS handshake because the mutual authentication is based on certificates.

Step 10. On the Wireless IP Phone, configure the WLAN Security Mode to EAP-TLS for the target Network Profile. Select **User Installed** certificate under Certificate Options for EAP-TLS, as shown in Figure 15-15.

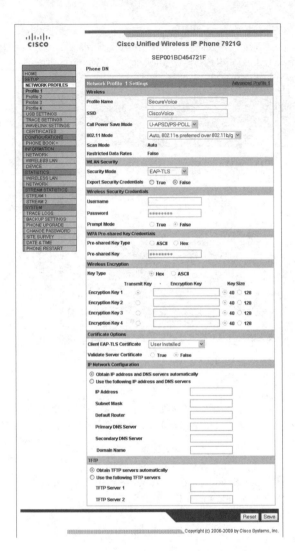

Figure 15-15 *Cisco Wireless Unified IP Phone—Setting EAP Mode and Certificate Option*

Step 11. If the Cisco Unified Wireless IP Phone has not been registered to a Cisco Unified Communications Manager yet, you must manually configure the date and time for the first time by going to **System > Date & Time**. After registration is successful, the date and time will be written to flash periodically. If the Wireless endpoint uses SCCP for CUCM registration, it leverages CUCM for Date/Time. For SIP, the CUCM NTP source will be used.

The Cisco Wireless Unified IP Phone should EAP-TLS authenticate with the Cisco ACS server.

Finally, as it was with wired IP Phones, leverage the secure service URLs to defend the XML transactions (revealing call control and other application IP addresses and DNS names) from eavesdropping and MITM attacks.

Wireless IP Phone: Secure TFTP Communication

The security of the TFTP file transaction using CAPF certificates is similar to wired IP Phones. This topic is discussed in section, "Wired IP Phone: Secure TFTP Communication." For configuration details, refer to Chapter 9.

Securing Cisco IP Communicator

Cisco IP Communicator (CIPC) is a Softphone. It is basically a software client installed on a user's PC that functions as an IP Phone (with MIC and speakers or a headset for communication), as shown in Figure 15-16. A CIPC installed on a PC becomes part of Data Network (Data VLAN), which is separate from the Voice network (Voice VLAN) and thus, securing CIPC becomes indispensable.

Figure 15-16 *Cisco IP Communicator Overview*

Many enterprise users use softphones on their laptop when traveling, working from home, or even at work. Although this solution can result in significant savings when compared to the use of cellular phones for Closed User Group (CUG) and external calls, a compromised laptop can spell disaster for the IP Telephony network. It can be used as a hub to launch attacks and inject worms, Trojans, and malware into the corporate network, not to mention, become hub for reconnaissance, MITM, and DoS attacks. Such an exploited, exposed PC and laptop is as good as an unmonitored channel into the corporate network.

Note   CUG here refers to calls within the users of the same enterprise using VoIP instead of PSTN access.

The security focus in this section is around CIPC, as an application and the security of voice traffic (media and signaling) from and to CIPC. Because CIPC becomes part of the Data VLAN, it is difficult to apply the same security policies for it, as you would like to apply for the Voice VLAN. This exposes CIPC to various spoofing, reconnaissance, conversation manipulation, and DoS attacks.

Note   Cisco IP Communicator version 8.6(1) has been used for all softphone security configuration examples in this chapter.

Following are some of the key security concerns for softphones:

- Softphone spoofing or user impersonation
- Softphone configuration protection
- Network access compliance
- Secure connectivity: Encryption and authentication
- Rogue phone registration
- VLAN traversal: Media from the data to the VLAN

The following section discusses the specifics—the whats, hows and whys for attaining a secure CIPC (from the client, network, and CUCM perspective) deployment in your enterprise.

Hardening the Cisco IP Communicator

Cisco IP Communicator (CIPC) should be hardened by disabling certain default settings on CUCM. Start by accessing the CUCM web administration page; then, go to **Device**

> Phone > CIPC, which you have configured. Under Product Specific Configuration Layout (see Figure 15-17), change the following settings:

- Setting Access

- Web Access

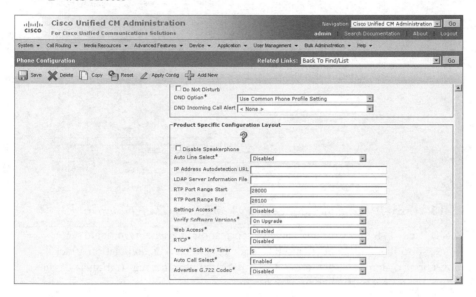

Figure 15-17   *Cisco IP Communicator Hardening*

In addition, you can limit the RTP port range for CIPC to a specific UDP port range (between 16384 to 32767) so that the RTP traffic for a certain endpoint is contained within a known port range (For example, the RTP port range has been restricted to 28000–28100, as shown in Figure 15-17.) This can help shield the endpoints from a wide range of port scans and help with the diagnosis of an attempted attack as well as attack correlation.

Encryption (Media and Signaling)

Use secure profile and Locally Significant Certificates (LSC) with CIPC to avoid eavesdropping of call media and signaling. This also mitigates the threat of MAC spoofing because the certificate issued to a client (user PC) is unique and cannot be repudiated. The security can be further strengthened by using an authentication string so that the end user must feed in the preconfigured authentication string to authenticate and enroll CIPC with CUCM (see Figure 15-18).

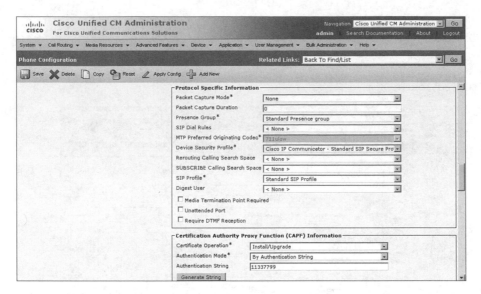

Figure 15-18   *Cisco IP Communicator Security Profile and CAPF Information*

Using SRTP and TLS for media and signaling correspondingly helps mitigate recon- naissance, spoofing, fake identity, and RTP code injection and manipulation attacks. Moreover, it also aggravates any rogue Cisco IP Communicator registration since the LSC is unique for each valid endpoint registered.

Note   CUCM version 6.1.2 and earlier-only support an authenticated profile for CIPC. CUCM version 6.1.3 and later also support the option for an encrypted profile for CIPC.

Enable Extension Mobility for CIPC

It might sound a little off the beaten path, but enabling Extension Mobility (EM) for a softphone client can ensure that only when logged in can you receive appropriate calling rights. In a nutshell, without an EM profile, the user gets access to only internal numbers, whereas with a proper EM profile and when logged in, the user gets access to PSTN numbers as mandated by his profile.

This would ensure that even if an attacker gets unauthorized access of CIPC and mimics himself as a legitimate user, he still cannot use it until he logs in with the right EM pro- file username and password. This mechanism helps confine toll fraud. With HTTPS for an EM service, the credentials can be exchanged between an endpoint and CUCM in a TLS-encrypted channel.

Note   CIPC 8.6 does not support secure EM (HTTPS login for EM).

Lock Down MAC Address and Device Name Settings

In case a CAPF (secure media and signaling) profile is not possible due to the load on the cluster or sizing issues, you can secure CIPC by using a device name instead of a Mac address.

Note   This procedure does not secure RTP and signaling.

However, because the device name can still be compromised, you can follow these recommendations to overcome the same:

Locking the settings down via the device page in CUCM locks only the phone settings and the TFTP option in the Network preferences. If you do not want an end user to fiddle with the DEVICENAME option, you can set the Windows Registry keys to the following values:

- NetworkTabUI = 0

- AlternateDeviceName = 0

These Registry keys can be found under HKEY_LOCAL_MACHINE\SOFTWARE\Cisco Systems, Inc.\Communicator, as shown in Figure 15-19.

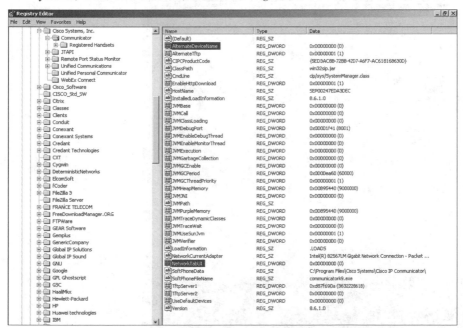

Figure 15-19   *Restrict Cisco IP Communicator Device Name Change by Registry Edit*

Note The location of the Registry entry is valid for default installation only and may change depending on where CIPC is installed.

As shown in the Figure 15-20, the CIPC is locked down to no choice of the device name; hence, the administrator defined device nomenclature is enforced at the end user side.

Note When used with CIPC, the phone proxy does not support end users resetting their device name in CIPC (**Preferences > Network tab > Use This Device Name Field**) or Administrators resetting the device name in the Cisco UCM Administration console (**Device menu > Phone Configuration > Device Name Field**). To function with the phone proxy, the CIPC configuration file must be in this format: SEP<mac_address>.cnf.xml. If the device name does not follow this format, CIPC cannot retrieve its configuration file from CUCM via the phone proxy, and CIPC will not function.

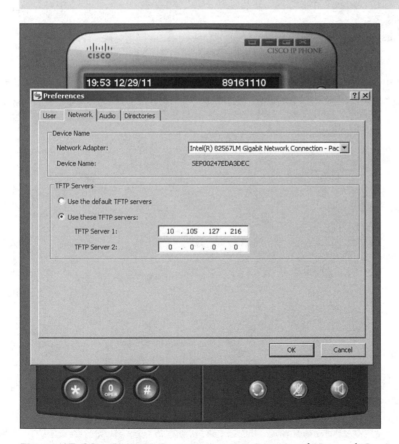

Figure 15-20 *Cisco IP Communicator—Restricted Network Settings*

Network Access Control (NAC)-Based Secured Network Access

From a Network Access Control perspective, Cisco NAC can be configured to have as coarse or fine-grained policies as required. This ensures that the end-user machine (PC, MAC, and so on) with a soft client installed is secured.

For example, softphone end-user machines are authorized to access only the network if their state is healthy:

- Antivirus (A/V) installed and running

- A/V update with the latest signature

- A/V on-access scan enabled

The Cisco NAC Agent (also known as Clean Access Agent) ensures that a machine connecting to the network has the essential and bare minimum security software (or patches), as defined in the NAC policy, before admitting it into the network. This in turn provides security from a user layer perspective to stop malicious code or software entering the IP Telephony network.

Refer to following URL for details on Cisco NAC solution:

http://www.cisco.com/en/US/products/ps6128/index.html

VLAN Traversal for CIPC Voice Streams

Because CIPC becomes part of the Data VLAN (by virtue of its nature of deployment as a soft client on an end-user PC), all the voice traffic (signaling and media) flows via the Data VLAN. This can be detrimental for the voice streams from a quality (QoS) perspective and from a security perspective. Although not many people may be aware of hacking a Voice VLAN, they can certainly disrupt the Data VLAN traffic.

Thus, it becomes important to consider the possibility to force Voice Traffic into Voice VLAN or at least safeguard it from an inquisitive audience. This issue can be addressed in two ways:

- Using ASA Phone Proxy for VLAN Traversal

- Using CUCM TRP

Both of these tools and techniques have been discussed in Chapter 8, "Perimeter Security with Cisco Adaptive Security Appliance," and Chapter 9, respectively.

Summary

You would not like someone fiddling with your personal stuff, which applies to your IP Telephony network. Whether it is the Cisco IP Telephony servers, applications, network devices, or endpoints, you want them controlled, owned, and operated by yourself and not a hacker or malicious insider. Deployment of a Cisco IP Telephony solution, similar to other network devices, must account for security of the end-user-facing device underlining the risk about how it can be used to attack the network as a whole.

In this chapter, you learned about the importance of endpoint security. Also, you were introduced to various security issues relevant to Cisco Unified IP Phones (wired and wireless) and CIPC, and the ways to mitigate the same. IP Phone hardening is only one aspect of securing Cisco Unified IP Phones (wired or wireless) or Softphones. A complete security plan should include securing the data network and the communication streams (signaling and media) off the IP Phones. By using Secure Real-Time Transport Protocol (SRTP), encrypted phone loads, configurations, and TLS secured signaling, Cisco Unified IP Phones, Softphones and CUCM can be defended from intrusive efforts. On the other hand, secure network admission of Cisco Unified IP Phones and Softphones help pin down any rogue device registration, block point of entry for malicious software, viruses, worms, and so on and helps keep the sanctity of your IP Telephony network intact.

Part IV, "Cisco IP Telephony Network Management Security," which shows you how to protect your IP Telephony network management construct. You will learn about the ways in which you can secure your management network communications and management protocols against threats originating from within and outside of your IP Telephony network.

Cisco IP Telephony Network Management Security

"By failing to prepare, you are preparing to fail." –Benjamin Franklin

Cisco IP Telephony: Network Management Security

A few days ago, you were logged into one of the voice gateway (one of many in your organization XYZ's network) to configure some new dial-peers. Today, when you log in again, you see some major changes in the configuration. The POTS dial-peers are now pointing to some international numbers. Surprised? Did you reckon that you were using Telnet to manage the router and that a smart insider attacker was sniffing the traffic? Waiting for you to log off to show his magic!

Having a secure IP Telephony network in place does not mean that you can take the management aspect of it for granted. Managing an IP Telephony network includes everything that touches or is involved in voice media or signaling, that is, network equipment (routers, switches, and firewalls), IP Telephony network equipment (voice gateways), IP Telephony servers (applications), and endpoints. Moreover, without secure management processes and practices in place, you can never be sure if someone on the inside or outside is sniffing your management sessions, waiting to unleash a flurry of attacks.

In this chapter, you will learn about:

- Secure IP Telephony network management design
- Securing network management protocols
- Managing security events

Secure IP Telephony Network Management Design

Network management is an art in itself and if properly implemented, it can not only give you power to control your network in the best possible way, but also enable you to look into what goes in your network. This section shows how the protocols used for network management and monitoring can be deployed on a security-sensitive IP Telephony network.

> **Note** Always remember that it is your security and corporate policies that will help drive the type of secure management network you wish to deploy.

Following are three options to pick from when you chose to manage your IP Telephony network:

- In-band network management
- Out-Of-Band (OOB) network management
- Hybrid network management

The following sections detail each of these network management deployment options.

In-Band Network Management

In-band network management is the most apprehensive management option available today. Moreover, it is this management option majorly used by most of the organizations. In-band management infers that all management traffic travels across the same logical links as the production network traffic, as shown in Figure 16-1.

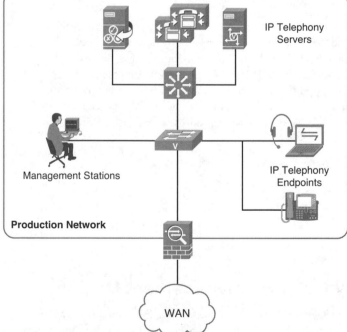

Figure 16-1 *In-Band Management Overview*

By default, many of the management protocols are clear text; not only are passwords sent in the clear, but so are configuration details and alarm data when they pass between the management stations or Network Management Systems (NMS) and the managed devices.

Securing In-Band Management Deployment

Following are some of the best practices to secure the management traffic when using in-band management:

- RFC 2827 filtering should be implemented throughout your network to curb any spoofing attacks.

- Identify a specific IP address or range of IP addresses that are allowed to access a particular management interface using the ACL's or device's built-in management process.

- Layer 2 port security (and other security mechanisms) should be deployed to minimize the chances of spoofing or MITM attacks.

- Host-hardening using HIPS and antivirus products should be implemented.

- A firewall brokering connections from managed devices to a management station can help with restricting spoofing, packet manipulation, and injection attacks, by virtue of deep packet inspection.

- Traffic should be restricted to required protocols (for example, SSH, SNMP, HTTP, and so on) using port-based ACLs.

- Using a strong authentication mechanisms for human interface is preferable, for example, a Cisco TACACS server for authentication and authorization of any network staff.

- Use of encrypted protocols (for example, SNMPv3, SSH, and HTTPS) to mitigate MITM attacks.

- Use IPSec or TLS tunnels from managed devices to NMS if the management protocol does not support encryption.

Out-of-Band (OOB) Network Management

As the name suggests (and in contrast to in-band management), in OOB management, the management traffic is sent on a separate logical or physical network, as shown in Figure 16-2. This is the most secure form of management, and this alleviates many of the security issues found in management networks.

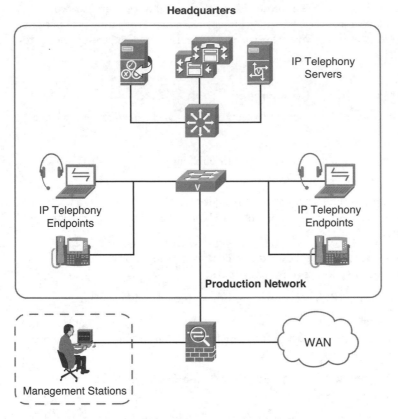

Figure 16-2 *Out-of-Band Management Overview*

OOB management is both a recommended and common practice in secure environments where production traffic flows on a dedicated interface, whereas management traffic flows on a separate dedicated management VLAN, sourced from dedicated interfaces. This is like having a special subnet only for managing the various IP Telephony and network devices. This management interface is typically on a separate management VLAN or separate physical network.

Use of management network on a separate channel, in other words logical or physical network allows for securing the management servers (NMS) and the management traffic. This prevents the management channel from being used to allow an exploited managed device to attack another device through the management network.

Securing OOB Management Deployment

Following is a list of mechanisms or protocols that you can implement to secure the OOB management traffic:

■ Implement filtering as per RFC 2827 and use dedicated RFC 1918 private addresses for the OOB network.

- Configure outbound and inbound distribution lists on all devices running routing protocols, route filters, ACLs, and firewalls between the production network and OOB management network at the transition points.

- All managed devices should still allow predetermined IP addresses to connect on the dedicated OOB management interface.

- For additional security, use of secure protocols (SSH, HTTPS, and so on) is highly recommended.

Hybrid Network Management Design

You may have an existing network with no explicit in-band or out-of-band management structure. It is perfectly normal to have that prevail in most of the organizations, since most networks do not have the explicit goal of using only one type of management infrastructure.

However, the overall goal is to make network management as secure as possible bearing a few facts, such as

- Management protocols used

- Capabilities of the devices to support OOB management

- Network topology and architecture

Most networks end up with either of the defined management architectures or a combination of both. So, if you use the in-band and OOB management, you are using a hybrid management structure.

Securing a Hybrid Network Management Deployment

- Clear text management protocols should be avoided wherever possible.

- Use encryption for remote management stations (which are outside the trusted zone).

- Enable Layer 2 and Layer 3 security for in-band management endpoints and for transition points for OOB management.

- Always use a firewall between the management network and other devices (managed or end user).

- If possible, deploy a Network Intrusion Detection System (NIDS) or better yet, a Network Intrusion Prevention System (NIPS) where possible, to detect any traffic anomaly or intrusion attempt.

- Filter RFC 2827 addresses and be sure to use nonpublic, internal (RFC 1918) addresses for NMS.

- Install Host Intrusion Prevention System (HIPS) where possible on managed servers and NMS.

The next section introduces various popular network management protocols and you will comprehend the techniques and mechanisms by which you can ensure secure management of your IP Telephony network.

Securing Network Management Protocols

There is a wide range of distinct protocols that are commonly used for network management. Although some have major security issues about their use, others provide a minimum level of security whether inherent or via a workaround. This section outlines the main protocols used in management and monitoring of a Cisco IP Telephony solution. The focus is the security consideration for the protocol's use and deployment best practices.

> **Note**   The various protocols described in this chapter are not endorsed by Cisco.

It is highly recommended that you use these protocols in their secure form wherever possible. Proper testing should be conducted in a lab environment before implementing management or monitoring protocols or tools in a production environment.

Following are two broad classes of network management:

- Network configuration management

- Network monitoring and logging

You will learn about how to secure both monitoring and logging and configuration management in your IP Telephony milieu. You will learn about the deployment, configuration, and best practices to secure the following:

- Simple Network Management Protocol (SNMPv3)

- Syslog

- Secure Shell (SSH)

- HTTP/HTTPS

- Virtual Network Computing (VNC)

- Remote Desktop Protocol (RDP)

- Trivial File Transfer Protocol (TFTP), Secure File Transfer Protocol (SFTP), and Secure Copy (SCP)

It is your IP Telephony network, and it is you who should be in control of how it is managed or configured, not a hacker or attacker. It is time to be empowered by enabling security of the management protocols to ensure that management data in transit is safe from inquisitive eyes.

Secure Network Monitoring with SNMPv3

Simple Network Management Protocol (SNMP) is an application layer protocol. SNMP is UDP-based and runs on port 161 for most functions and 162 for SNMP traps. It can help network administrators manage, find, and solve network problems. Although it is primarily used for monitoring, SNMP can also be used for making configuration changes.

SNMP protocol comes in three different editions (versions):

SNMP Version 1: The oldest and most basic version of SNMP, which is supported by most devices that are SNMP-compatible; it is simple to set up. However, the serious limitation is on the security front because it uses only a simple password, that is, a community string, and data is sent in clear text. Also, it supports only 32-bit counters, which is not enough for monitoring gigabit networks.

SNMP Version 2c: This is next in line to v1 and has support for 64-bit counters and therefore supports bandwidth monitoring in gigabit networks. The protocol is still clear text, that is, no support for encrypted messages from an agent to a management console and station.

SNMP Version 3: This version is the latest in breed and adds authentication and encryption support. It offers user accounts and authentication for multiple users (optional support for encryption of data packets.)

Table 16-1 lists the various options available with SNMPv3 on Cisco IP Telephony network.

Table 16-1 *SNMPv3 Authentication Options (Hashing and Encryption)*

Level	Authentication	Encryption	Key Information
noAuthNoPriv	Username	No	Uses username match for authentication
authNoPriv	MD5 or SHA	No	Authentication based on the HMAC-MD5 or HMAC-SHA hashing algorithms
authPriv	MD5 or SHA	DES, 3DES, AES-56, AES-128	Authentication based on the HMAC-MD5 or HMAC-SHA hashing algorithms
			Privacy (encryption) based on DES, 3DES, AES-56, or AES0128 bit standards

As you can distinguish, the earlier two versions of SNMP i.e. v1 and v2c do not support encryption, whereas the v3 has full support for authentication (hash) and privacy (encryption). For this reason, you should consider enabling SNMPv3 in IP Telephony applications, namely:

- Cisco Unified Communications Manager
- Cisco Unity Connection
- Cisco Unified Presence Server
- Cisco IOS Routers and Switches
- Cisco ASA Security Appliance

Cisco IP Telephony Applications with SNMPv3 Support

The IP Telephony applications that support SNMPv3 are as follows:

- Cisco Unified Communications Manager
- Cisco Unity Connection
- Cisco Unified Presence Server

Note   All these applications support SNMPv3, and their configuration steps are similar. Cisco Unity however does not support SNMPv3, and secure private and public community strings should be used to provide snooping protection for Cisco Unity server.

Following are the (common) steps to configure SNMPv3 for aforesaid Cisco IP Telephony applications (CUCM, CUC, and CUPS):

Step 1.   Log in to **Cisco Unified Serviceability > Go to > SNMP > v3 > User**, as shown in Figure 16-3.

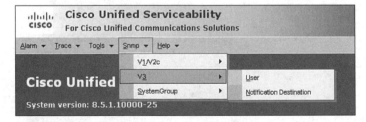

Figure 16-3   *Configuring CUCM SNMPv3*

Step 2.   To add a new SNMP user, click the **Add New** button.

Step 3.   Fill in the required information (see Figure 16-4):

- **Server:** Where SNMP will be enabled, it can be changed to all nodes by checking the check box at the end of page.

■ **User:** The username of the SNMP user, which will be configured in the SNMP management console.

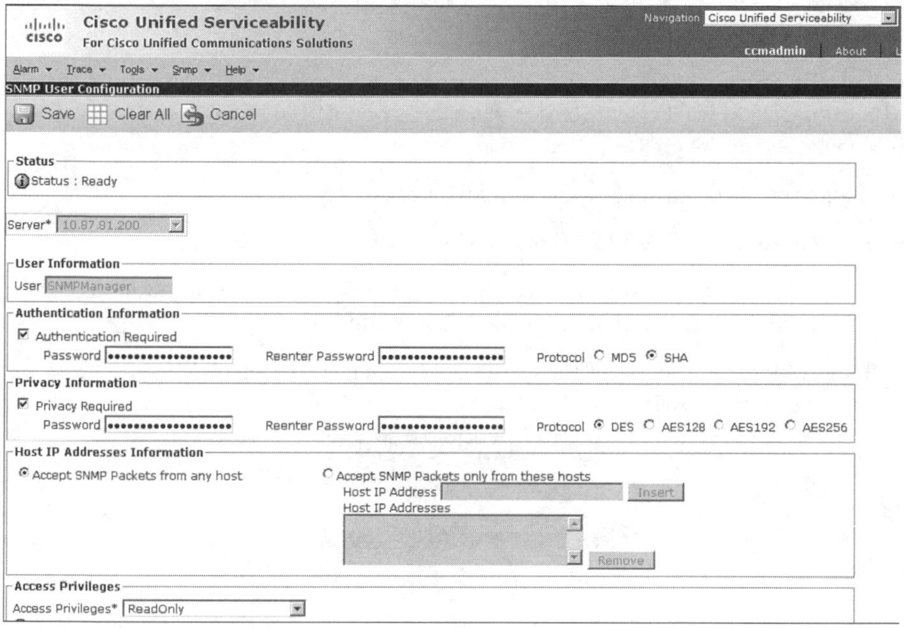

Figure 16-4   *SNMPv3 User Configuration*

■ **Authentication Required:** Check this box if you want to enable hash for the data transmitted from agent (CUCM) to server (Management console).

■ **Privacy:** Checking this option enables encryption for the data between agent and server.

■ **Accept SNMP Packets:** You can either trust any host in your network to accept SNMP requests from, or to be more restrictive define specific IP addresses (for example, management subnet IPs) by enabling Accept SNMP Packets only from these hosts option.

■ **Access level:** It defines the level of access of this user (ReadOnly, ReadWrite, ReadWriteNotify, NotifyOnly, ReadNotifyOnly, and None).

■ This step is relevant only to the CUCM cluster and not to Cisco Unity Connection or CUPS. You can check the check box that enables the same user (recommended) on all nodes of the cluster.

Step 4.   When you finish configuring the user and save it, the system prompts you to restart the SNMP master agent.

Note It is recommended to wait for the SNMP configuration steps to finish before restarting the aforementioned service.

Next, you configure the SNMP server, that is, the host where the SNMP notifications or TRAPS from CUCM will be sent. This destination is popularly known as the Network Management Server (NMS).

To configure the NMS (destination server), follow these steps:

Step 1. Go to **SNMP > V3 Configuration > Notification Destination**.

Step 2. From the drop-down list box, choose the server for which you want to configure the notification destination. Click **Add New**.

Step 3. Add the IP Address of the Network Management Server (NMS) (see Figure 16-5).

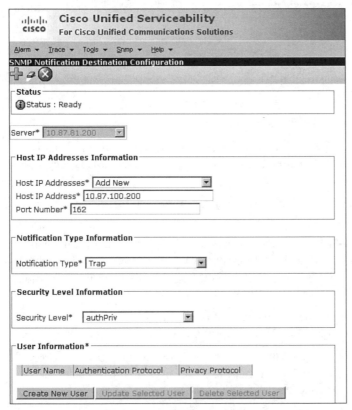

Figure 16-5 *SNMPv3 Notification Destination Configuration*

■ In the Port Number field, enter the notification receiving port number on the destination server. (It is usually UDP 162 unless your NMS server is configured to listen at a different port.)

- Choose the appropriate notification type as TRAP or Inform.

- Depending on your previous choice between TRAP and Inform, from the Remote SNMP Engine Id drop-down list box, choose **Add New**, and enter the ID in the Remote SNMP Engine Id field. (This should match with the SNMP Engine ID on your NMS server.)

- From the Security Level drop-down list box, choose the appropriate security level for the user: noAuthNoPriv, authNoPriv, or authPriv (recommended).

Step 4. Either associate an existing user or add a new SNMP user from the User Information group box.

Step 5. To apply the notification destination to all nodes in the cluster, check the **Apply to All Nodes** check box.

Step 6. A message prompt indicates that changes will not take effect until you restart the SNMP master agent. The SNMP master agent needs to be restarted for these changes to take effect. Restart the SNMP master agent after all the configuration changes are completed. Restarting the SNMP Master Agent also restarts the Host Resources Agent if it is running. The Master agent restart takes approximately 1 minute.

Step 7. Press **OK** to restart the SNMP master agent now or **Cancel** to restart later. Click **OK**.

Depending on the level of authentication and privacy chosen, your SNMPv3 connection to the NMS will be authenticated and encrypted, respectively. It is highly recommended to encrypt your SNMP session in case it is leaving the IP Telephony VRF and going to a Management VRF, outside the Cisco ASA deemed secure zone. (To learn more about ASA perimeter security, refer to Chapter 8, "Perimeter Security with Cisco Adaptive Security Appliance.")

Note Here, Virtual Routing and Forwarding (VRF) is used as an analogy to a logical domain.

SNMP for Cisco IOS Routers and Switches

SNMP v3 is supported on Cisco network equipment, which forms the basis of Cisco IP Telephony. Cisco SNMP version 3 (SNMPv3) is supported since the version 12.0.3T of the IOS; therefore, it's recommended to have the latest (non-deferred) release of IOS on your Cisco network equipment (not only for SNMP however, but for new security features).

Example 16-1 shows the commands used to enable SNMPv3 on Cisco IOS devices.

Example 16-1   *Cisco IOS SNMP Configuration*

```
SNMPRouter(config)# snmp-server engineID local 00000009020000013C096
!
SNMPRouter(config)# snmp-server group NETWORK v3 priv read NETWORK write NETWORK
SNMPRouter(config)# snmp-server group TRAPS v3 priv
!
SNMPRouter(config)# snmp-server user NETWORK NETWORK v3 auth sha Cisco123 priv des56
  Cisco123
SNMPRouter(config)# snmp-server user TRAP TRAPS v3 auth sha Cisco123 priv des56
  Cisco123
!
SNMPRouter(config)# snmp-server enable traps snmp linkup linkdown
SNMPRouter(config)# snmp-server host 10.10.10.250 traps version 3 priv TRAP
```

The SNMP ID 00000009020000013C096 is unique to this router. (It should be a minimum of 10 hexadecimal characters.) Here, we created an SNMP group called NETWORK and a user called TRAP attached to the group, with authentication set as HMAC SHA and encryption set to DES 56 bit. Whenever a link flaps (status up or down) an SNMP trap will be sent to the NMS host at 10.10.10.250.

Example 16-2 show commands help you verify the SNMP v3 configuration.

Note   SNMPv3 users do not appear in the running configuration for security reason; however, you can see some information using the **show snmp users** command.

Example 16-2   show *Commands to Verify SNMP Configuration*

```
SNMPRouter# show snmp user

User name: TRAP
Engine ID: 00000009020000013C096
storage-type: nonvolatile active
Authentication Protocol: SHA
Privacy Protocol: DES
Group-name: TRAPS

User name: NETWORK
Engine ID: 00000009020000013C096
storage-type: nonvolatile active
Authentication Protocol: SHA
Privacy Protocol: DES
Group-name: NETWORK
!
```

```
SNMPRouter# show snmp group
groupname: TRAPS                              security model:v3 noauth
readview :            writeview:
notifyview: *tv.FFFFFFFF.FFFFFFFF.FFFFFFF0F
row status: active


groupname: NETWORK                            security model:v3 priv
readview : NETWORK                            writeview: NETWORK
notifyview:
row status: active
```

SNMP Deployment Best Practices

It is recommended to use SNMP where it adds considerable value. Follow these best practices to ensure that your IP Telephony network can leverage SNMP to the maximum, keeping security in mind:

- Use an ACL on the SNMP process (network equipment toward the SNMP monitored device) to limit the addresses that can send SNMP commands to the IP Telephony devices.

- For IP Telephony applications, accept the incoming requests limited by the IP addresses within the SNMPv3 user configuration.

- Treat the community strings (if using SNMP v1 or v2c) like strong passwords, and change them as your security policy mandates (for example, every 6 months).

- While DES may not be the right encryption protocol for your network (as per your security policy or guidelines) it is the minimum you should enable to leverage the power of SNMPv3.

You can download the SNMP Management Information Base (MIB) for Cisco IP Telephony applications and Cisco network gear at http://tools.cisco.com/Support/SNMP/do/BrowseMIB.do

Syslog

Syslog protocol collects the alarms, notifications, and other network data (for example, CPU Spike, memory overflow counters, and so on). As defined in RFC 3164, a network device can send Syslog messages on UDP port 514 to a Syslog collector. Syslog is used in a wide variety of ways in network management.

Almost every security device is ideally expected to send some kind of Syslog information to a collector. It is interesting to know that even though Syslog is often used in a security role to send and collect logs, the protocol is not secure by itself, that is, it does not inherent security and needs to be made secure.

> **Note**   Syslog uses UDP without authentication and has no mechanism to ensure the delivery of a message.

Essentially, Syslog is a fire and forget system, that is, the devices generating Syslog send a message, and after a message is sent, they never know if the messages were delivered at the destination (because Syslog is a UDP-based protocol). This fact can become an attack vector for an attacker to launch a MITM or DOS attack. This way, messages can be changed on the way to the collector. Worse, the attacker can leave the network congested by the DoS attack, so the communication between Syslog generator and collector is out of order.

In the subsequent sections, you will learn about how you can secure the Syslog connections between various IP Telephony applications, underlying network devices, and the Syslog server.

Secure Syslog for IP Telephony Applications

In case of Cisco Unified Communications Manager (CUCM or Cisco UCM), Cisco Unity Connection (CUC), and Cisco Unified Presence Server (CUPS), the Syslogs are sent to the monitoring station on which the Real Time Monitoring Tool (RTMT) is installed. The connection between any IP Telephony application and the endpoint can be secured by checking the optional check box, which enables security for RTMT data being pulled from the server, as shown in Figure 16-6.

Figure 16-6   *RTMT Secure Connection*

You may get a warning on the management station (depending on whether the CUCM self-signed certificates are used or if the Cisco Tomcat certificates on CUCM are signed by your internal or external and third-party CA), as shown in Figure 16-7.

Figure 16-7 *RTMT Certificate Prompt*

You can click **View** to view the certificate details (shown in Figure 16-8).

Certificate Details: CUC851Shared	
Issued To	
Common Name (CN) :	CUC851Shared
Organization (O) :	Cisco
Organizational Unit (OU) :	UCP
Email Address :	<Not Specified>
Issued By	
Common Name (CN) :	CUC851Shared
Organization (O) :	Cisco
Organizational Unit (OU) :	UCP
Validity	
Issued On :	Fri Apr 15 05:13:59 IST 2011
Expires On :	Fri Apr 15 05:13:59 IST 2016
Fingerprints	
SHA1 :	c5b7 12f6 cb73 c774 ba52 ebed 8838 c463 2f82 bc92
MD5 :	af9b bf8c 0b98 cef3 0331 e0a4 969a 6c3f
Others	
Serial Number :	5471747892105140258
Signature Algorithm :	SHA1withRSA
Public Key Algorithm :	RSA
OK	

Figure 16-8 *RTMT Certificate Details*

Figure 16-9 gives an overview of the Syslog option in RTMT.

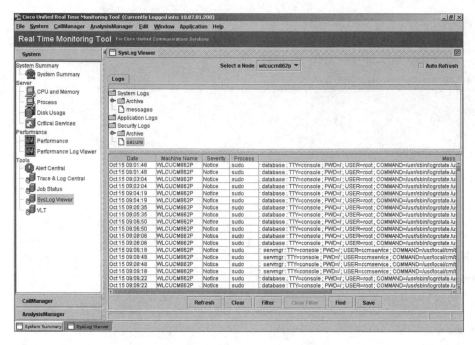

Figure 16-9   *RTMT—Syslog Overview*

Configuring Syslog in Cisco Network Devices (Cisco IOS Devices and Cisco ASA)

To enable Syslog functionality in a Cisco network, you must configure the built-in Syslog client within the Cisco IOS routers and Cisco ASA Firewall. Cisco devices use various severity levels for warnings through emergencies to generate error messages to log software or hardware malfunctions. The debugging level displays output of various debug commands. The Notice level displays interface up or down transitions and the system restart messages. The informational level displays the reload requests and low-process stack messages.

For more information on the Syslog messages, level of logging, and messages to the log, see http://www.cisco.com/web/about/security/intelligence/identify-incidents-via-syslog.html.

Cisco IOS Devices Syslog

Cisco IOS devices (routers and switches) have the capability to send Syslog messages to a Syslog server. Although the connection is not secure by default, Syslog can be made to run on UDP, TCP, or BEEP (which is a generic application protocol framework for connection-oriented, asynchronous interactions). Moreover, to secure the Syslog messages in transit (if doing in-band management), the channel can be protected using an IPSec tunnel.

The configuration of IOS Syslog is shown in Example 16-3.

Example 16-3 *Configuring Syslog on IOS Router*

```
IPTRouter(config)# logging trap notifications
IPTRouter(config)# logging console critical
IPTRouter(config)# logging 10.10.10.230
IPTRouter(config)# service timestamps debug datetime localtime show-timezone msec
IPTRouter(config)# logging enable
IPTRouter(config)# logging source-interface Loopback 0
IPTRouter(config)# hidekeys
IPTRouter(config)# notify syslog
IPTRouter(config)# logging facility local3
IPTRouter(config)# exit
```

Here, all Syslog logging data is sent to the Syslog server (or NMS) running at IP 10.10.10.230 from the loopback interface 0.

Note   The **hidekeys** command will not send passwords in the Syslog messages.

The **show** command in Example 16-4 illustrates the output of the IOS Syslog configuration.

Example 16-4   **show** *command to Verify Syslog Configuration*

```
IPTRouter # show logging
syslog logging: enabled (0 messages dropped, 0 flushes, 0 overruns)
    Console logging: level debugging, 79 messages logged
    Monitor logging: level debugging, 0 messages logged
    Buffer logging: disabled
    Trap logging: level warnings, 80 message lines logged
        Logging to 10.10.10.230, 97 message lines logged
```

Cisco ASA Firewall Syslog

Somewhat similar to IOS Syslog, Cisco ASA Security Appliance can also be configured for Syslog messages. Example 16-5 outlines the Syslog configuration on Cisco ASA Firewall.

Example 16-5   *Cisco ASA Firewall Syslog Configuration*

```
IPTASA(config)# logging on
IPTASA(config)# logging time
```

```
IPTASA(config)# logging host 10.10.10.250
IPTASA(config)# logging facility 21
IPTASA(config)# logging trap warnings
IPTASA(config)# no logging message 111005
```

Example 16-6 has the **show** command for looking at the Syslog configuration.

Example 16-6   show *Command to Verify Syslog Configuration*

```
IPTASA# show logging
Syslog logging: enabled
    Facility: 21
    Timestamp logging: enabled
    Standby logging: disabled
    Console logging: disabled
    Monitor logging: disabled
    Buffer logging: disabled
    Trap logging: level warning, 6 messages logged
        Logging to inside 10.10.10.250
    History logging: disabled
    Device ID: disabled
```

For increased security of Syslog in Cisco ASA, you can set up a Syslog process to use TCP connections instead of UDP (see Example 16-7).

Example 16-7   *Cisco ASA Firewall Syslog Configuration to Support TCP*

```
IPTASA(config)# logging host inside 10.10.10.250 tcp/1500
```

This command forces Cisco ASA to use TCP protocol for Syslog messages on port 1500.

Syslog Deployment Best Practices

Syslog is a scalable and useful source for network events and logs. Ideally, all Syslog messages and communication should be done OOB (discussed earlier) to increase the security of the message in transit from the log generator to the collector.

Also, the performance impact of Syslog should be considered because some hardware-based forwarding engines may be significantly slowed by logging. As Syslog messages may be huge in numbers, it may take a toll on the system's performance. Thus, it is wise to examine the capabilities of your devices before you turn on logging.

Secure Shell (SSH)

If you have ever logged into an IOS (Cisco) router or switch, there is a good chance that you have used the non console access, that is, Telnet or SSH. Telnet or SSH enable a remote device (such as your PC or laptop) to log in to a server or a router and manage the same without being physically present near the device, that is, using the IP connectivity. While the server could be a Linux-based machine, in terms of IP Telephony application (OS) management, it can be a Cisco switch, router, firewall, IDS/IPS, VPN concentrator, or almost anything else with an IP address. The typical use cases for Telnet or SSH include but are not limited to interactive configuration changes, enabling the device for a software upgrade, or to run a script against a network device.

Although Telnet and SSH both use TCP, the former is a clear text protocol, whereas the latter is an encrypted protocol (RSA). For Telnet, all the commands, usernames, and passwords are sent as clear text between the client and the server and are susceptible to MITM attacks. SSH is superior to Telnet from a security perspective because cryptographic protection is provided for the session.

When you SSH to a remote device or server such as CUCM, CUPS, or a Cisco IOS router or switch, you get the following message, as shown in Figure 16-10.

Figure 16-10 *SSH RSA Key Fingerprint Security Prompt*

Now, it is entirely up to you as an IP Telephony or network administrator if you want to continue connecting to the device. Although in a high-security environment it is not too difficult to distribute these fingerprints to all your management stations, it should be done as a practice. Otherwise, all management stations must be strictly on an OOB management network to accept unknown RSA signatures, from managed devices, provided they are hooked up on a dedicated management port.

Note By selecting **Yes** without validating the fingerprint, you take a calculated risk that you or the server are not the victims of an MITM attack.

When connected to the destination server, now you have a secure tunnel for the data in transit between the management station and destination device.

SSH is supported with the following Cisco IP Telephony applications:

- Cisco Unified Communications Manager (OS CLI)

- Cisco Unity Connection (OS CLI)

- Cisco Unified Presence Server (OS CLI)

- Cisco Unified Contact Center Express (OS CLI)

In addition, SSH is supported by the following Cisco network equipment:

- Cisco IOS routers

- Cisco Catalyst switches

- Cisco ASA Firewall

- Cisco IDS/IPS

These Cisco IP Telephony applications support SSH by default on the CLI, and no additional configuration is required to enable the same. On Cisco network devices however, while some support it natively, others support it only when configured for. This depends on the RSA keys generated on the device to support SSHv2. Cisco ASA, IPS, IDS, and other security modules and components have RSA keys generated by default and need configuration only for it to be accessible, for example from a certain interface.

Configuring SSH on IOS Devices

To configure SSH on a Cisco IOS device (router and switch), follow these steps:

Note To use SSH for terminal access, you must have an image that supports encryption, that is, a K9 image.

Step 1. Check for the status of SSH on an IOS device (see Example 16-8).

Example 16-8 *Establish SSH Status*

```
IPTRouter# show ip ssh
SSH Disabled - version 1.99
%Please create RSA keys to enable SSH (and of atleast 768 bits for SSH v2).
Authentication timeout: 120 secs; Authentication retries: 3
Minimum expected Diffie Hellman key size : 1024 bits
IOS Keys in SECSH format(ssh-rsa, base64 encoded): NONE
```

Step 2. As SSH is disabled and you want to enable it, configure a domain name on the IOS device, as shown in Example 16-9.

Example 16-9   *Configure Domain Name*

```
IPTRouter(config)# ip domain-name XYZ.com
```

Step 3.   Configure the version of SSH on the IOS device (see Example 16-10).

Example 16-10   *Configuring SSH Version*

```
IPTRouter(config)# ip ssh version 2
```

Step 4.   Configure crypto RSA keys (minimum recommended modulus length is 1024 for SSHv2), as shown in Example 16-11.

Example 16-11   *Generating Crypto RSA Keys*

```
IPTRouter(config)# crypto key generate rsa usage-keys exportable modulus 1024 label
  SSHKeys
The name for the keys will be: SSHKeys

% The key modulus size is 1024 bits
% Generating 1024 bit RSA keys, keys will be exportable...
[OK] (elapsed time was 2 seconds)
% Generating 1024 bit RSA keys, keys will be exportable...
[OK] (elapsed time was 2 seconds)
```

Note   The command shown in Example 16-11 enables exportable keys named SSHKeys so that you can export the keys and import them in the management workstations, so they do not need to take the leap of faith "blindly".

Step 5.   Enable the SSH timeout and number of connection retries (see Example 16-12).

Example 16-12   *Configure SSH Timeout and Authentication Retries*

```
IPTRouter(config)# ip ssh time-out 60
IPTRouter(config)# ip ssh authentication-retries 2
```

Step 6.   Now, you must enable the line inputs (line VTY) to accept SSH connections (see Example 16-13).

Example 16-13   *Configure Line VTY to Accept SSH Sessions*

```
IPTRouter(config)# line vty 0 4
IPTRouter(config-line)# login local
IPTRouter(config-line)# transport input ssh
```

Step 7.   At this point, your IOS device should be ready to accept an SSHv2 RSA encrypted session from the management stations. To confirm the same, you can issue the command shown in Example 16-14.

Example 16-14   *Confirm SSH Status*

```
IPTRouter# show ip ssh
SSH Enabled - version 2.0
Authentication timeout: 60 secs; Authentication retries: 2
Minimum expected Diffie Hellman key size : 1024 bits
IOS Keys in SECSH format(ssh-rsa, base64 encoded):
ssh-rsa AAAAB3NzaC1yc2EAAAADAQABAAAAgQDB9wFHeFfNF1+xl+RY/IVl3c7lq2f9iPrIobjnP71W
lvswpfXJLGi7R9oGaRLD5FwxXLNA5KhYybZLsDlSnBxxImOwYccEnlmDm4cxkdPVKPhD8
T5lcYv5E46H/grKVeJc7uFA+t4A+cW2KLyVf5yTZEBGbfdosTNHxjk7o7e/rw==
```

Step 8.   To further lock down the IOS device access, to accept connections from only intended IP Addresses, create an ACL and apply it on the line VTY, as shown in Example 16-15.

Example 16-15   *Restricted Access to VTY*

```
IPTRouter(config)# access-list 51 permit 10.100.100.250
IPTRouter(config)# access-list 51 deny any any log
IPTRouter(config)# line vty 0 4
IPTRouter(config-line)# access-class 51 in
```

Enabling SSH Access on Cisco ASA

On Cisco ASA Firewall, SSH RSA keys are pre-generated. (You can regenerate them by first removing the existing keys.) Basically, you need to configure a username and password, the location where the Cisco ASA should look for this user (LOCAL is on the firewall), and the interface to which SSH access is allowed, as illustrated in Example 16-16.

Example 16-16   *Configuring SSH on ASA*

```
IPTASA(config)# aaa authentication ssh console LOCAL
IPTASA(config)# username cisco password C1$c0!@# privilege 15
IPTASA(config)# ssh 10.100.100.250 255.255.255.0 inside
IPTASA(config)# ssh timeout 60
```

If you want to remove the existing RSA keypair, you need to remove the keys manually by using the commands shown in Example 16-17.

Example 16-17 *Deleting and Re-Creating RSA Keys*

```
IPTASA(config)# crypto key zeroize rsa noconfirm
IPTASA(config)# crypto key gen rsa general-keys mod 1024 noconfirm
```

Note The **noconfirm** option will not prompt for any yes or no options however will do what the command is supposed to automatically without any further intervention.

SSH Deployment Best Practices

Following are the best practices that you should follow when implementing SSH in your IP Telephony network:

- As a general rule, use SSH wherever possible, and disable Telnet when necessary.

- When using SSH, it is useful to limit access to an SSH daemon from the IP addresses that can access it. This can be enforced by the security policy.

- Change the SSH passwords at least once per 3 months or as directed by the security policy.

- Limit the time for which a management station can be connected to a device being idle (idle timeout).

HTTP/HTTPS

Analogous to Telnet and SSH respectively, HTTP and HTTP Secure (HTTPS) are both used for static configuration modifications and software upgrades of servers and network devices. Some network devices offer variants of either Telnet or SSH that are equivalent for a graphical user interface (GUI).

The typical use of HTTP and its secure variant HTTPS are commonly used in CUCM, Unity, Cisco Unity Connection, UCCX, and CUPS applications for

- Provisioning

- Making configuration changes

- Checking system status and reporting

Again, as an analogy, the security difference between HTTP and HTTPS are on same lines as those between Telnet and SSH. HTTP, like Telnet, is clear text and runs over TCP. HTTPS, like SSH, is encrypted using the application layer (Layer 7) protocol—Secure Sockets Layer (SSL) or Transport Layer Security (TLS) for security.

Although HTTPS is by default enabled on the various Cisco IP Telephony applications, it is not enabled on all underlying and supporting network devices such as a Cisco IOS router or catalyst switch, and so on.

When you attempt to establish the connection to CUCM, CUC, or CUPS servers, if you initiate the session on HTTP, it is redirected to HTTPS on port 8443 automatically to ensure that the session is safe from hijacking and MITM attacks. This redirection and HTTPS functionality is supported by the underlying Cisco TOMCAT Service Daemon.

Note   All Cisco IP Telephony applications on a Linux-based platform have self-generated and self-signed certificates for secure HTTPS access and OS CLI SSH access.

You can have an enterprise wide CA certificate used for HTTPS access to avoid any security warnings or errors on client machine. The process to generate CSR from an OS GUI and uploading the signed CSR along with a CA root certificate has been covered in respective IP Telephony application security chapters. For Cisco network components such as IOS routers and Cisco ASA Firewalls, there are HTTP servers (supports HTTPS as well) built in the device that you can use to deploy the security management software such as the following:

- Cisco Configuration Professional (Cisco CP) for Cisco IOS routers
- Cisco Adaptive Security Device Manager (ASDM) for Cisco ASA

Both Cisco CP and ASDM leverage the SSL or TLS protocols to establish secure connection with the device, and the administrator can then manage these devices remotely over a GUI Interface, securely.

Enabling Cisco CP for Cisco IOS Routers

There are two different editions of Cisco CP: the full Cisco CP package and the Cisco CP Express package. The former contains a number of modules and options for your router's configuration including voice modules, whereas the latter is essentially a trimmed-down version containing the core modules.

Note   Cisco CP was introduced to replace Cisco Security Device Manager (SDM) and has Cisco SDM capabilities along with many additional functions. Similar to Cisco SDM, Cisco CP also runs on a Java plug-in.

You can find the full Cisco CP on the CD that came with your router, or alternatively, you can download it from www.cisco.com. However, the Cisco CP Express package may also come preinstalled on your router's flash memory.

To enable Cisco CP support on IOS router, follow these steps:

Step 1.   On the Cisco IOS router, issue the command shown in Example 16-18 to ensure that Cisco CP express is not installed on the current system.

Example 16-18   *Establish Cisco CP Express Status*

```
IPTRouter# show flash:
-#- --length-- -----date/time------ path
1     53722384 Aug 9 2010 13:59:52 +00:00 c2800nm-spservicesk9-mz.150-1.M3.bin
2         1038 Aug 9 2010 14:09:46 +00:00 home.shtml
3       122880 Aug 9 2010 14:09:54 +00:00 home.tar
4       527849 Aug 9 2010 14:10:04 +00:00 128MB.sdf
5      1697952 Aug 9 2010 14:10:20 +00:00 securedesktop-ios-3.1.1.45-k9.pkg
6       415956 Aug 9 2010 14:10:32 +00:00 sslclient-win-1.1.4.176.pkg
7     66483320 Sep 21 2011 09:19:54 +00:00 c2800nm-adventerprisek9-mz.151-3.T.bin
```

Step 2.   Download the cisco-config-pro-exp-k9-2_5-en.zip or full package from the Cisco website.

Note   To download any security or K9 image, you need to have CCO access, that is, these images cannot be downloaded as guest user.

Step 3.   Copy the downloaded **cpconfig*.cfg** file from the zip file, within your router's flash for your version of the router (using TFTP or SCP client).

Step 4.   You can confirm the presence of the file using the command **show flash.**

Step 5.   Run the **setup.exe** from the zip. Install the file on the management station.

Note   Although you have an option to install the file on both a PC and Cisco IOS router, for performance reasons, install it only on a PC or management station.

Step 6.   Enter the commands shown in Example 16-19 on your router to enable Cisco CP access.

Example 16-19   *Enable HTTPS (IOS) Server*

```
IPTRouter(config)# ip http server
IPTRouter(config)# ip http secure-server
IPTRouter(config)# ip http authentication local
IPTRouter(config)# username <username> privilege 15 password 0 <password>
```

Note It is assumed that RSA key pair has been generated to support HTTPS.

Step 7. Open https://<ip address of router>. It should launch Cisco CP for you, as shown in Figure 16-11.

Figure 16-11 *Cisco Configuration Professional (Express)*

Enabling Cisco ASA ASDM

Cisco Adaptive Security Device Manager (ASDM) is the equivalent of IOS SDM for Cisco ASA. It also leverages SSL/TLS for connection to Cisco ASA Firewall. Following are the steps to enable ASDM on Cisco ASA Firewall:

Step 1. Download the ASDM code from Cisco.com, and copy to flash on Cisco ASA.

Note To download any security or K9 image, you need to have Cisco.com access. These images cannot be downloaded as guest user.

Step 2.   Taking the example of your management group being on subnet
10.100.100.0/24, the commands shown in Example 16-20 can enable ASDM
access from an inside (or a dedicated management) network.

Example 16-20   *Configuring Cisco ASA ASDM*

```
IPTASA(Config)# interface ethernet3
IPTASA(Config-if)# nameif management
IPTASA(Config-if)# ip address 10.100.100.1 255.255.255.0
IPTASA(Config-if)# security-level 90
IPTASA(Config-if)# no shutdown
!
IPTASA(Config)# http server enable
IPTASA(Config)# http 10.100.100.0 255.255.255.0 management
IPTASA(Config)# asdm image flash:asdm635.bin
```

At this point, your Cisco ASA Firewall should be accessible from a PC or laptop in the
management network. Open your web browser, and then enter the address **https://<ip
address of your ASA>/admin** (see Figure 16-12).

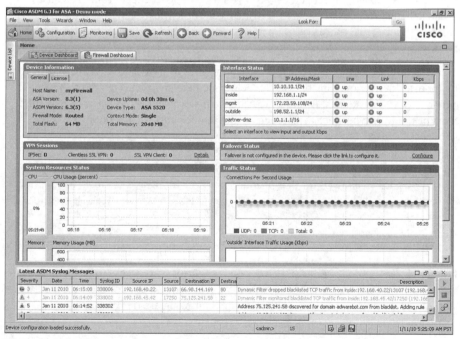

Figure 16-12   *Cisco Adaptive Security Device Manager*

HTTPS Deployment Best Practices

Following are the HTTPS deployment best practices:

- HTTPS should be preferred over HTTP wherever possible.

- Layer 3 filtering should limit who can establish connections to the application server by TCP port 443, 8443, and 8080.

- For enterprise wide compatibility, enroll the CUCM, CUC, CUPS, and Unity server (platform, administration, and user access GUI) certificates with internal CA or with third-party CA.

Securing VNC Management Access

If you have been in the IT world for some time, there is a good chance that you have used Virtual Network Computing (VNC) software to manage or control remote desktops. VNC Protocol enables you to remotely manage a desktop environment on a PC or server and interact with that desktop from your local machine. Although VNC is versatile and gives a feel of being physically on the desktop, it lacks security, and the data is sent in clear text unless the version of VNC you use supports encryption. VNC uses a random challenge-response system to provide basic authentication. However, the traffic between the viewer and the server is unencrypted and could be sniffed by an attacker on its way.

There are various solutions to this issue. One solution is to have a VNC client and server that supports encryption. This option can help remediate any issues related to eavesdropping and MITM attacks. Another solution to this problem is leveraging a SSH tunnel to encrypt the traffic between your machine and remote host (IP Telephony server).

Note   It is not recommended to run any third-party software unless it has been certified by the Cisco Business Unit (BU) for that product to be run alongside the main application on the same server (collocated). In certain cases, to get support with a Cisco application, Cisco Technical Assistance Center (TAC) engineer may ask you to uninstall any non-supported third-party software.

Although the first option is easy and gives you straightforward access to encrypted management traffic via a VNC, it also means that you may have to pay for the commercial version of encryption supporting VNC software. Following are the various popular VNC software available:

- **RealVNC:** It supports AES encryption in VNC Viewer Plus and Personal and Enterprise editions (not the free version). The RealVNC products provide security in the form of TLS, providing protection from VNC connection snooping, MITM attacks, and packet-tampering. RealVNC is available with free and commercial licenses (http://www.realvnc.com).

- **TightVNC:** It is not secure by default and gives only an option to assign a port for connection and the IPs to filter. TightVNC does not encrypt the data in transit. It is available in GPL license and commercial license (http://www.tightvnc.com).

- **TurboVNC:** It is a sequel of TightVNC and carries the deficiency from its parent product, that is, it is not secure and you cannot have encrypted communication between the host and remote machines unless you allow secure SSH or do a VNC-based login on an IPsec VPN. TurboVNC is open source code and is free for personal or commercial use (http://www.virtualgl.org/Downloads/TurboVNC).

- **UltraVNC:** This VNC software provides security for information in transit by using the optional DSM encryption. It enables the administrator to ensure that the communication between the viewer and the server is secure, thereby reducing the possibility of MITM attacks, which would enable a hacker to see the remote screen. UltraVNC is a freeware provided under GNU (http://www.uvnc.com).

To conclude, each type of VNC software has its strengths and weaknesses. Thus, whatever flavor of VNC you use, ensure that you understand its limitations and test it in a lab setup before deployment in production.

VNC Deployment Best Practices

Following are some of the best practices that you should implement in your network while deploying VNC to manage Windows based voice application servers:

- Always enable encryption at the server and at the client level (if supported by the VNC software you use).

- On VNC server, limit the IP addresses from which connections can be initiated to the server.

- Enable password authentication of the client, using a strong password.

- It is highly recommended to enable VNC server logging.

Securing Microsoft Remote Desktop Protocol

Microsoft Remote Desktop Protocol (RDP) is the Microsoft's proprietary protocol for Windows Terminal Services. Microsoft's Windows Terminal Services, built into Windows server 2000, 2003, and 2008) and the RDP client provide an easy and convenient way for network administrators to connect to their XP desktops from a remote computer and run applications or access files. By default, RDP client does not provide a secure connection to Windows Terminal Services and provides little to no protection for data in transit during management sessions.

To remediate this issue, using encryption provided by SSL provides an extra layer of encryption for data confidentiality and also enables the client to verify the identity of the server. This is particularly useful against MITM attacks.

Note   If the client doesn't trust the Certification Authority (CA) that issues the SSL certificate to the server or server name can't be verified, the client displays a warning before connecting to the server.

Using SSL to insist on server identity check and data encryption for RDP is different from RDP over HTTP. The latter can initiate connection to a Windows Terminal Services server via RDP through port 443 (SSL). By using a regular RDP client, TCP Port 3389 is still required to establish a terminal server session in Windows 2003 SP1 and later.

Note   It is not recommended to run any third-party software unless it has been certified by the Cisco Business Unit (BU) for that product to be run alongside the main application on same server (colocated). In certain cases, to get support with Cisco application, Cisco Technical Assistance Center (TAC) engineer may ask you to uninstall any nonsupported third-party software.

Version 5.2 of the Remote Desktop Connection client has a new Security tab, which you can use to specify whether the client should check the server's certificate before establishing a connection with the server. You can choose from three options:

■ **No authentication:** The client won't attempt to check the server certificate before a connection is made. If the server requires SSL authentication, the client cannot connect.

■ **Require authentication:** The client checks the server certificate before it connects with the server. If the client can't determine the identity of the server, it won't establish a connection with the server.

■ **Attempt authentication:** The client checks the server certificate before connecting with the server. The client can connect to the server with or without SSL authentication, depending on the configuration of the server, even if the client can't fully verify the server identity.

Configuring IP Telephony Server for Accepting Secure RDP Connections

This section covers the process to enable Secure RDP using certificates. Follow these steps:

Step 1.   On your IP Telephony (running Windows 2003 SP1 or later) server, go to **Administrative Tools > Terminal Services Configuration**.

Step 2.   Double-click RDP-TCP to configure the properties of Terminal Services using the RDP protocol. Under the General tab to the right of the word certificate, click **Edit**. Choose the installed certificate that you want to associate with the Terminal Services connection over RDP, as shown in Figure 16-13, and click **OK**.

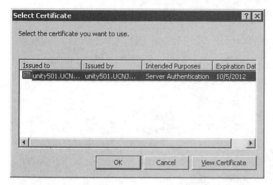

Figure 16-13   *RDP-TCP Certificate*

Note   This assumes that you have already requested a certificate from an internal or external CA. To know more about the various options to get a certificate for Terminal Services, see Microsoft KB article 895433 at http://support.microsoft.com/kb/895433.

Step 3.   On the General tab, you can now choose SSL for the Security Layer (see Figure 16-14). This is what ultimately requires the use of certificates for the RDP communication on the server side.

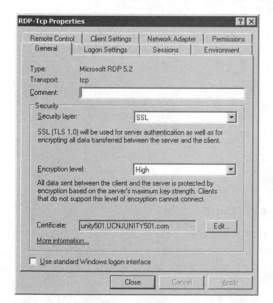

Figure 16-14   *RDP-TCP Properties*

You are done on the IP Telephony Server end, and now you must configure the RDP Client on the management station (PC or laptop) for using TLS, as explained in the next section.

Configuring RDP Client for Initiating Secure RDP Session

The following steps cover the necessary steps to enable TLS on RDP Client PC / Laptop:

Step 1.   Ensure that on the management PC (Client), RDP Client version 5.2.3790.1830 is installed.

Note   If the required version of RDP Client is not installed, you can install it from a server running at minimum Windows Server 2003 SP1. The installation files are located on the server in c:\windows\system32\clients\tsclient directory. (For your implementation the path may vary depending on where the Windows directory is located.)

Step 2.   Open the Remote Desktop Connection client. Click **Options**, and click the **Security** tab. Choose Require authentication in the pull-down box, as shown in Figure 16-15.

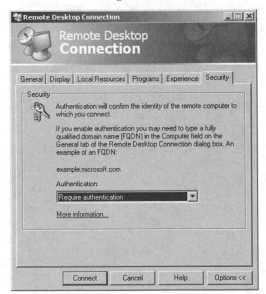

Figure 16-15   *Remote Desktop Client Security Configuration*

Step 3.   Click the **General** tab. Enter the FQDN name of the IP Telephony (Windows) server you want to connect to (see Figure 16-16). Enter the FQDN name because certificates use a hostname as the CN.

Figure 16-16 *Connection Using the FQDN of the IP Telephony Server*

> **Step 4.** You may receive a warning shown in Figure 16-17. Click the **View Certificate** button. Install the certificate by following the prompts.

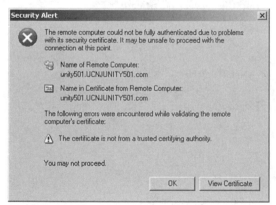

Figure 16-17 *Certificate Error*

Note Choose the option for Automatic Certificate Store assignment.

> **Step 5.** Click **OK** and the Remote Desktop Connection closes.
>
> **Step 6.** When you re-open RDP Client and try to establish a secure encrypted Remote Desktop Connection from the client to the IP Telephony server, your connection will be allowed (because now the certificate is in the trust store

and the client can authenticate the server's identity). If you connect in full screen mode, you see the SSL lock symbol next to the push pin in the yellow toolbar, as shown in Figure 16-18.

Figure 16-18   *Secure RDP Connection*

Step 7.   Click the padlock sign to bring up the server's certificate.

Note   Even if you have a certificate issued by your intranet CA or a third-party CA, such as VeriSign, SSL cannot be used to ensure that only known or trusted clients connect via RDP to the IP Telephony server(s). Client certificate requests are not supported. An IPSec VPN or SSH tunnel is the preferred method to provide enhanced security to endpoints connecting for management in such cases.

RDP Deployment Best Practices

Following are the leading practices for secure RDP deployment:

■ Change the port at which the RDP client connects to the server. You can do this by changing the Registry key at HKEY_LOCAL_MACHINE\SYSTEM\CurrentControlSet\Control\Terminal Server\WinStations\RDP-Tcp\PortNumber.

Note   The setting is in Hex by default; you must change to decimal for exact numeral digits. You need to specify the port when you connect to your system, that is, abc.com:<port>.

- If the server runs Windows Firewall, add the IP addresses allowed in the White List. You can do this by going to **Control Panel > Windows Firewall > Exceptions tab**, and then check the check box for Remote Desktop.

Note If you have changed the default port from 3389 to any other port number, you must add the new port the server's firewall should listen for RDP by selecting the **Add Port** option.

Enable RDP Certificate-based security wherever possible as per your security policy guidelines.

TFTP/SFTP/SCP

The three protocols in discussion have almost the same function, that is, to enable a device to get its configuration file(s) from a known source or to pull the configuration of the Cisco IP Telephony and network device for backup and archive.

Trivial File Transfer Protocol (TFTP) is a UDP-based (port 69) protocol, which is clear text and supports no authentication or encryption by default. It is most commonly used for transferring images for network devices and IP Telephony endpoints, for example, Cisco IOS routers, switches, and Cisco Unified IP Phones.

Although the TFTP protocol is non-secure by default, there are ways to make it secure by working around the network and devices to provide security. For Cisco IOS devices, TFTP sources can be limited (based on UDP port 69) using ACLs. Furthermore, the access to any image should not be from the local network but from a trusted management subnet. The same logic applies for the Cisco ASA Firewall as well.

Cisco IP Telephony endpoints, that is, IP Phones, support encrypted TFTP file transfers for firmware, the configuration file, and other file downloads. This topic is covered in Chapter 9, "Cisco Unified Communications Manager Security," and in Appendix A, "Cisco IP Telephony: Authentication and Encryption Essentials."

SFTP is an interactive file transfer like traditional FTP. SFTP, or Secure FTP, is a program that uses SSH to transfer files. It encrypts both commands and data thereby preventing passwords and sensitive information being transmitted in the clear over the network. SFTP protocol uses port TCP 22. Just like TFTP, the function of SFTP is to upload or download the configuration and files to or from a platform, respectively.

Cisco IP Telephony applications, for example, CUCM, CUC, and CUPS support SFTP by default for Disaster Recovery System (DRS) that is, database and configuration backup and restore.

On the other hand, Cisco IOS devices and Cisco ASA support it when configured for SSH, with Secure Copy (SCP). SCP is a secure way to transfer configuration files and image files to and from Cisco routers, switches, and Cisco ASA Firewall. Comparable to SFTP, SCP also works on SSH protocol on port 22.

> **Note** To configure SCP on your router or firewall, you need to ensure SSH works, that is, SSH is a prerequisite for SCP.

To configure SCP on Cisco IOS devices, issue the following command:

ip scp server enable

To enable SCP server on a Cisco ASA Firewall, issue the subsequent command:

ssh scopy enable

> **Note** On the receiving end, you need to have a SCP server running, which can connect to an IOS device or Cisco ASA Firewall to either pull the configuration file or put the configuration file, for example, in flash.

TFTP/SFTP/SCP Deployment Best Practices

Following are the best practices for using TFTP, SFTP, or SCP protocols:

- Always try to use a secure file transfer protocol.

> **Note** It is often not possible because many network management systems (NMS) still require clear text protocols such as TFTP to function. Moreover, many devices do not support encryption for initial firmware or configuration load.

- Filter the IP addresses that are allowed to access the file transfer process.

Managing Security Events

Before we understand security event management, there's need to understand the same that is:

What is a Security Event Management System and why do you need it?

The Problem

Let's admit, that you really do not know, all the time, what is happening in your IP Telephony network. This can be intimidating because things can happen behind your back, and you would have no trace of them. The network perimeter becomes blurry when your employees, partners, and vendors connect to your network. Insider attacks happen all the time; however, they are easy to conceal.

The Solution

Security Event Management System (SEMS) is the key to effectively manage critical network and IP-based communication systems. A SEMS solution can benefit a network Security Operations (SOC) team responsible for monitoring infrastructure security. SEMS can be used both in a real-time monitoring, correlating as well as in post-mortem fashion, for an investigation to determine how the attack was carried out.

Figure 16-19 shows the conceptual view of a SEMS system.

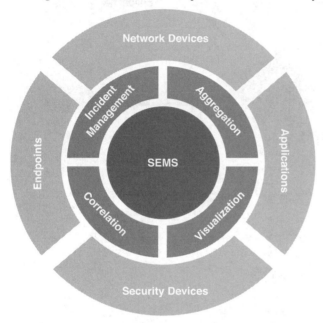

Figure 16-19 *Security Event Management Methodology Overview*

In addition to security devices such as firewalls and IPS/IDS, most systems on an IP Telephony network can generate security events (SNMP logs and Syslogs). Examples of security events include authentication events, audit events, intrusion events, and so on. As a best practice, you need to have the various applications and network systems monitored by the SEM system, as shown in Figure 16-20.

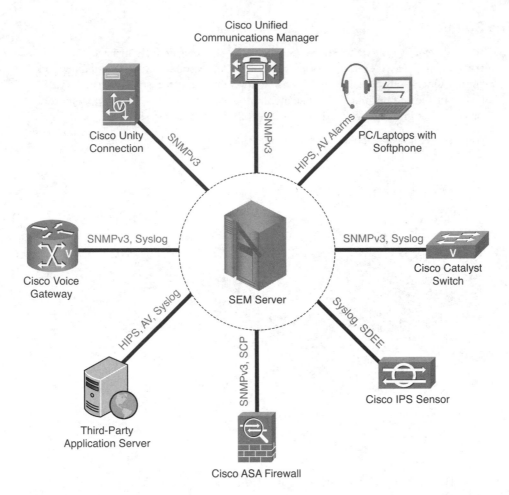

Figure 16-20   *SEM System Overview*

This is where Risk Assessment gives you a lead as to which systems are critical for your network or your IP Telephony network to continue functioning (refer to Chapter 4, "Cisco IP Telephony Security Framework," for more details on risk assessment). After the review is completed, a standard for logging configurations can be created for each type of IP Telephony and network device. Standardization is important to ensure that devices are logging common information. In addition to defining a standard logging configuration, it is important to ensure that all monitored devices and systems, and especially the SEM servers, are synchronized with a reliable and accurate time source, such as an internal authenticated NTP server.

When security events reach the SEM server, they may be stored on a physical disk for some period of time, as directed by your corporate policy, security requirements, and business requirements. Also, these records should be encrypted using software or hardware to avoid any unpleasant exposure to curious audience.

Usually, there will be some type of secure or cryptographic connection used to transmit events between devices and the SEM server. This is where the protocol level and device level security capability play a major role. This might be limited to various choices depending upon the capability of a device or the management protocol to transmit information in a secure manner.

These can range from

- SNMPv3 encrypted notifications or TRAPS

- TLS/SSL encrypted management channels

- SCP or SFTP based file and configuration transfer

- Syslog from identified sources, on TCP

It is a leading practice to have different sets of encryption keys for each managed device so that compromising of one system does not lead to compromising the whole SEM infrastructure. Also, a fault redundant system (redundant SEMS system) is preferable in a critical production environment.

As a leading practice, SEM systems should have fault tolerance built in to detect and recover from failures such as system or network outages. This is important to ensure integrity and completeness of the collected events.

For Cisco IP Telephony, there's no single system that can harmonize a SEM system. However, there are two different systems that form the basis of SEM and allow Security Event Management, monitoring, recording, and correlation of events from the following two layers:

- Network layer

- Application layer

At the network layer, it is Cisco Security Manager (CSM) software that connects to and gets information from various network and security devices. At the application layer, it is the Cisco Unified Communication Management Suite.

CSM software provides SEM capability for the following network devices:

- IOS-based devices (routers and switches)

- Cisco ASA firewall

- Cisco IPS sensors

- Cisco AnyConnect client solution

Figure 16-21 illustrates the CSM console in action.

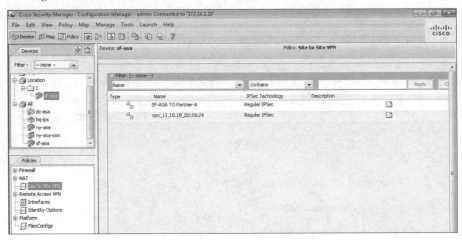

Figure 16-21   *Cisco Security Manager Console*

Note   CSM is not a substitute for Cisco MARS, which is now EOL/EOS.

On the Cisco IP Telephony front, you have the Cisco IP-PBX Management Suite (better known as Cisco Unified Communications Management Suite, which is a part of Cisco Prime portfolio) providing all-in-one capability to monitor, provision, manage, and log events.

Cisco Prime Unified Communication Management Suite (UCMS) is a collection of four applications:

■ Cisco Prime Unified Operations Manager (CUOM)

■ Cisco Unified Service Statistics Manager (CUSSM)

■ Cisco Prime Unified Service Monitor (CUSM)

■ Cisco Prime Unified Provisioning Manager (CUPM)

This suite is designed to provide full product lifecycle management, from pre-assessment to post-deployment. It enables the IP Telephony administrator to pull the statistics out and dump them into another analytical package for further review. Although Unified Provisioning Manager is for provisioning endpoints and IP Telephony servers, the first three form the SEM system for Cisco IP Telephony applications and devices.

Cisco Prime Unified Operations Manager (CUOM)

Cisco Unified Operations Manager (see Figure 16-22) is used for general IP-PBX management, troubleshooting, and fault notification.

Figure 16-22   *CUOM Dashboard*

Note   CUOM is equivalent to a typical NOC application with a dashboard view that shows where you can set up service levels for specific groups of phones, call-control servers, voice-messaging servers, gateways, and so on.

The system can issue alerts in a number of ways, including e-mails and audible tones. It uses Cisco Discovery Protocol (CDP) to show which devices connect to each other and provides performance statistics, such as how many calls were handled and how many trunks are up. There is a device center that can do an SNMP walk to communicate with devices at a management level and pull pertinent information from them, with the following options:.

■ Options for diagnostics to set up tests to occur on scheduled and periodic basis

■ Tab for reporting

■ Tab for notification services

■ Device tab that activates a network search for telephony devices

■ Administrative tab where you set up users and overall operations

Cisco Prime Unified Service Monitor (CUSM)

The Unified Service Monitor is used for reporting, configuration of thresholds, and monitoring of those thresholds for voice quality, as shown in Figure 16-23. It does this by looking at either

■ Cisco Voice Transmission Quality (VTQ) readings

or

■ Cisco 1040 probes that can be installed at remote sites. The Unified Service Monitor keeps track of all the phones physically deployed and the associated licenses.

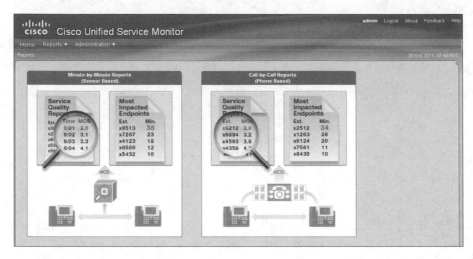

Figure 16-23 *CUSM Dashboard*

Note Unified Service Monitor can be launched directly from Cisco Unified Operations Manager, and it can feed findings to the Cisco Unified Service Statistics Manager.

Cisco Unified Service Statistics Manager (CUSSM)

CUSSM application essentially does historical reporting, analysis, and trending. It starts with a dashboard view (see Figure 16-24) that can be customized with your specific reports, such as bandwidth, trunk utilization, and quality and call volume.

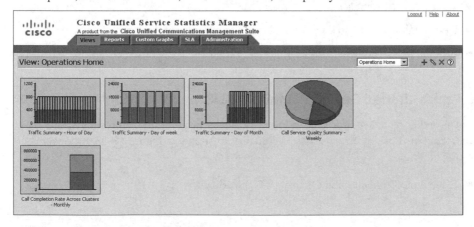

Figure 16-24 *CUSSM Dashboard*

Cisco Prime Unified Provisioning Manager (CUPM)

As the name implies, Cisco Unified Provisioning Manager (shown in Figure 16-25) is designed for deployment scenarios of new IP-PBX installations. It can set up devices such as call processors, endpoints, presence, and other unified communication units. CUPM also sets up deployment for configuration of domains and service areas and helps with batch deployments. It can also track inventory, and IP Telephony administrators can define employee roles and telephony rights.

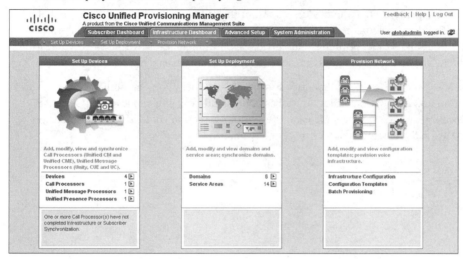

Figure 16-25   *CUPM Dashboard*

Summary

Ahoy, I have a notification! That was the purpose of this chapter: to introduce you to a diverse set of information on management network design, protocols, and tools pertinent to Cisco IP Telephony. You learned the best practices to design your management network, adopting any one of the three models: in-band, out-of-band or hybrid design. It is important to realize that the management requirements of every network are different. Moreover, every device in your Cisco IP Telephony network may need you to pick and chose the management functions and put a bare minimum design around it that meets the business and technical requirements. With all of this, keep in mind the best practices to securely monitor and manage the Cisco IP Telephony and underlying network devices.

After you understand which security controls you want to deploy and where, you can start putting things in order and alter the network management design as required. Deciding on various security protocol options you have to enable for the management functions has an impact on both the type of information you get as well as the capability of the device to handle the protocol. For example, you have various methods to configure an IOS router or CUCM using remote management tools (for example, SSH, HTTPS, or HTTP) however, the ones you choose is dependent on your organization's business requirement and the level of access, ease, and security a particular protocol/tool can offer you.

After determining the protocols and design options, how you plan to aggregate network security events, leveraging a SEMS approach, is entirely dependent on the system you have in place, that is, Cisco Security Manager (CSM) for network devices and Cisco Prime Unified Communications Management Suite (UCMS) for IP Telephony.

You must clearly define the devices you want to get logs, notifications, alerts, and alarms from. Building a secure management solution is neither a one-day job nor a one-time process; it takes time, planning, and participation from all levels within the organization's IT hierarchy to set up a successful, secure, and resilient management system.

Part V, "Cisco IP Telephony Security Essentials," will help you comprehend the authentication and encryption basics, as well as understand how you can leverage Cisco ASA Firewall, Cisco 4200 series Intrusion Prevention/Detection, and Cisco Host Intrusion Prevention System technologies to your advantage.

Cisco IP Telephony Security Essentials

"The only real security that a man can have in this world is a reserve of knowledge, experience, and ability." –Henry Ford

Cisco IP Telephony: Authentication and Encryption Essentials

Have you ever thought when you share information with someone over the phone or via e-mail if all the information you send is received in its entirety at the destination—always? On second thought, did the information transmitted even reached the intended destination or was it hijacked and changed on the way? This scenario can be intimidating particularly for private conversations or business conversations in which apart from the genuine sender and receiver, a third party (our old foe hacker) becomes involved.

Throughout this book, you learned about the attacks that can be launched against your IP Telephony network and their mitigation techniques. Authentication and encryption mechanisms were used many times from CUCM security profiles to secure conference bridges to SRTP to Cisco ASA IPSec tunnels. Let's explore the nuts and bolts of authentication and encryption as it applies to Cisco IP Telephony.

This appendix covers the following topics:

- Introduction to cryptography
- PKI overview
- Cisco IP Telephony PKI fundamentals
- Cisco IP Telephony authentication basics
- Cisco IP Telephony encryption basics

Introduction to Cryptography

Before we get started with nuts and bolts of authentication and encryption, it is imperative that you have a solid grasp of some basic concepts, which will be referred often. You should ideally know about four key concepts before dwelling deep into authentication and encryption schemes for Cisco IP Telephony. These are as follows:

Identity: Means of authentication by which the authority to perform certain functions is granted, in other words:

- Authentication is the process in which identity is provided and verified.

- Authorization is the process in which an entity of a known identity is granted a privilege within the system.

Integrity: Maintains an authenticated link to guarantee:

- A packet originated from a trusted entity who shares your secret.

- The message contents haven't changed in transit.

Privacy: Implies encrypting the contents of a packet to ensure that it cannot be interpreted by someone else during transit.

Non-repudiation: This is an extension to the identification and authentication service. It implies that all parties involved in a transaction must be confident that the transaction is secure; that the parties are who they say they are (authentication); and that the transaction is verified as final. (That is, a party cannot subsequently reject a transaction.)

Based on these building blocks, let's understand the two mechanisms that help protect your data and voice communication, in transit or at rest, before delving into the details of authentication and encryption for Cisco IP Telephony.

Authentication

Authentication functions provide for integrity and non-repudiation. Authentication can be implemented by mechanisms that provide integrity checks based on a secret key are usually called Message Authentication Codes (MAC), as explained in RFC 2104. The most common method of hashing is Hash-based Message Authentication Code (HMAC), leveraging cryptographic hash functions or digital signatures. The sender adds the hash to the actual payload. The receiver checks the verification data added by the sender by hashing the data again and comparing it with the stored hash. If the results match, the authenticity is confirmed.

The two most commonly used hash functions are Message Digest (MD5) and Secure Hash Algorithm (SHA). MD5 (RFC 1321) takes an arbitrarily sized block of data as input and produces a 128-bit hash. On the other hand, SHA's output is a 160-bit hash. SHA was developed by NSA and standardized by NIST.

Note: MD5 is comparatively weaker than SHA.

With the bare bases covered, let's go over an example to solidify the concept of authentication.

In this example, two entities, A and B in that order, decide to exchange information over a rather insecure medium. Both entities are concerned that the information sent or received may be intercepted, and on the way someone can change the contents of the information exchanged. Both entities have agreed on a common authentication method, as shown in Figure A-1.

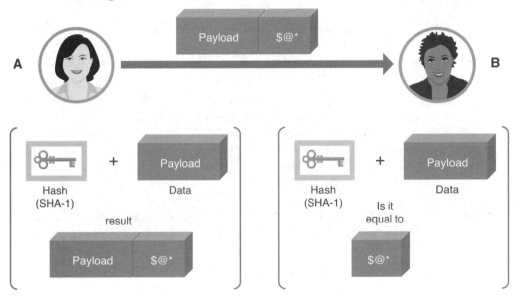

Figure A-1 *Authentication Process Overview*

- Before transmitting the information, entity A uses SHA-1 hashing method and appends the actual information (payload) with hash.

- Upon reception of the packet (Payload + Hash), the entity B reruns SHA-1 hash on the payload again.

- If the hash matches the appended hash, B can be certain that the information was not changed during the transit and that it is authentic.

- On the other hand, if the hash does not match the appended hash, the information is either malformed or was manipulated on the way.

While authentication alone can solve identity and integrity issues, it cannot ascertain that someone has not read the contents of the packet exchanged with a remote entity. Thus, there is still a risk of exposing information even though the packet reaches its destination intact.

Many tools are available to sneak-peak into the contents of the packet (most popular being sniffers). On the other hand, you can ensure that these tools cannot succeed for the very purpose they were built for and this mechanism is known as encryption. In the next section, you will learn the essentials of encryption. Later, you will gain knowledge of encryption and authentication as they apply to Cisco IP Telephony.

Encryption

Confidentiality is an instrument for protecting privacy. In other words, confidentiality means that information cannot be access by unauthorized parties. Confidentiality functions are provided by encryption. Encryption is the process of scrambling a message so that only the intentional recipient can interpret it.

Encryption can be done using various protocols, of which the most common ones are Data Encryption Standard (DES) and Advance Encryption Standard (AES). DES is available in two flavors: DES, which has 56-bit key size, and Triple DES (3-DES), a stronger variant of DES with 168-bit key size (RFC 2405). AES is available in three flavors: AES-128, AES-192, and AES-256-bit key size (RFC 3268).

Note: AES is a preferred choice over DES algorithm because it's not only significantly more secure than DES, but also faster than DES when deployed in software or hardware.

Following are two different methods of encryption:

- **Same key encrypts and decrypts data:** Symmetric encryption algorithms
- **Different keys encrypt and decrypt data:** Asymmetric encryption algorithms

Symmetric (secret-key) encryption:

The same key encrypts and decrypts, and the (single) key must be kept secret, as shown in Figure A-2.

Same Encryption and Decryption Keys

Figure A-2 *Symmetric Encryption Process*

The process of symmetric encryption is faster than asymmetric encryption.

Asymmetric (public-key) encryption:

Different keys are required for encryption and decryption. Each entity (person, system, and phone) has its own pair of keys: a public key and a private key. While one key can be distributed to the outside world (encryption key or public key), one key must be kept secret (decryption key or private key). Figure A-3 details the asymmetric encryption process.

Figure A-3 *Asymmetric Encryption Process*

This process is slower than symmetric encryption because of the involvement of two keys.

In Cisco IP Telephony, all these concepts play a major role to protect the vital information traversing a possibly, rather insecure infrastructure from prying eyes and overhearing ears. To be more precise, in the Cisco IP Telephony network,

- Authentication and integrity are applicable to calls (media), signaling, configuration, and firmware.

- Encryption or privacy is applicable to media, signaling, and configuration.

Note: It is important to realize that encryption and authentication go hand-in-hand to create a secure environment.

Public Key Infrastructure (PKI) Overview

Public Key Infrastructure (PKI) is a collection of hardware, software, policies, and procedures required to create, use, manage, distribute, and if required, revoke digital certificates. PKI is based on a trusted third-party entity. It provides a secure and scalable public-key distribution method. X.509 v3 (certificates) is the standard for PKI data formats and protocol.

In general, there are some rules associated with PKI:

- PKI enrollment must be performed securely.
- Some form of PKI revocation is always required.

Encryption with PKI

Let's understand the process of information encryption with PKI. Figure A-4 shows two entities, A and B, which share information over an insecure medium. They want the information to be securely delivered to the destination.

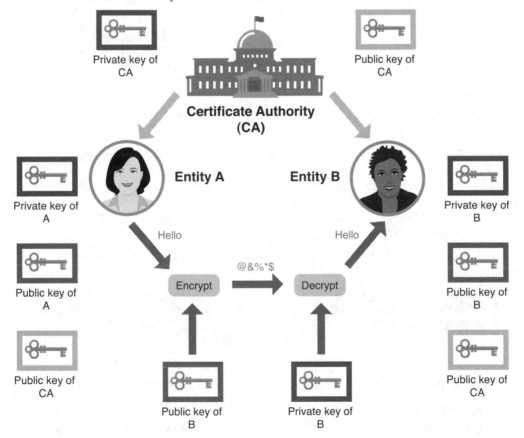

Figure A-4   *PKI-Based Encryption Process*

A and B have decided to use certificates and PKI to solve the issue of any MITM, reconnaissance, spoofing, or data manipulation attacks. The various events in chronological order are as follows:

- Entities A and B trust the CA.

- Entities A and B enroll their public keys with the CA.

- CA signs their public keys with its private key and issues them their respective signed keys. This becomes A's and B's certificates (identity certificates).

- A gets B's certificate, which contains B's public key.

- A check that the certificate is trusted (as it is signed by the trusted CA).

- A encrypts the message with B's public key from the certificate.

- The message goes as ciphertext to B.

- Because it is garbled, even if an attacker sniffs the message, it will be all gibberish.

- Only B can decrypt message using its private key.

In the following section, you will go over the different Cisco IP Telephony PKI topologies to understand the differences and similarities. This will help you build a high-level view of how an IP Telephony PKI works and its various constituent components.

Cisco IP Telephony PKI Fundamentals

Cisco IP Telephony is a self-contained PKI solution. However, Cisco IP Telephony PKI is not a single PKI system; instead, it has various bits and pieces to it:

- Each server in a CUCM cluster is capable of being a CA (including Publisher, Subscriber, and TFTP).

- Each server has its own unique private key and public key (asymmetric keys).

- CUCM server certificates are self-signed by default and can be signed by an external CA.

- Manufacturing Installed Certificates (MIC) on Cisco IP Phones are signed by the Cisco Manufacturing CA.

- Locally Significant Certificates (LSC) on IP Phones are signed by CUCM CAPF (service that runs on Publisher server in a cluster).

- CUCM cluster and other IP Telephony applications, for example, Unity, CUC, CUPS, and so on can all have their certificates signed and trusted by an external CA.

With all these pieces, the IP Telephony (CUCM) PKI system is still unrelated. A single trusted introducer to bring all entities together is missing.

Note: This is done intentionally because if the trusted introducer were part of the system from inception, the PKI could be manipulated by simply manipulating the trusted introducer.

Cisco IP Telephony Self-Signed Certificates PKI Topology

Each CUCM server has a self-signed certificate but can also have it signed by an external CA. All of them act as their own PKI root. However, because there is no trust enabler is among all these independent PKI authorities, these systems do not trust each other and remain isolated, as depicted in Figure A-5.

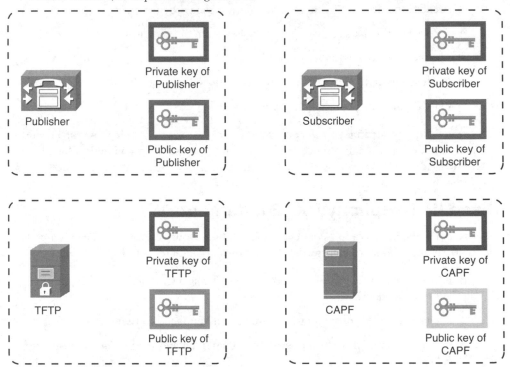

Figure A-5   *Cisco IP Telephony Self-Signed Certificate PKI Topology*

Cisco IP Telephony External CA Signed Certificates PKI Topology

Taking this model one step further, the different PKI roots can have their certificates signed by an external (trusted) CA. Figure A-6 shows all entities (CUCM Publisher, TFTP, CAPF, and so on) have their public keys signed by an external CA.

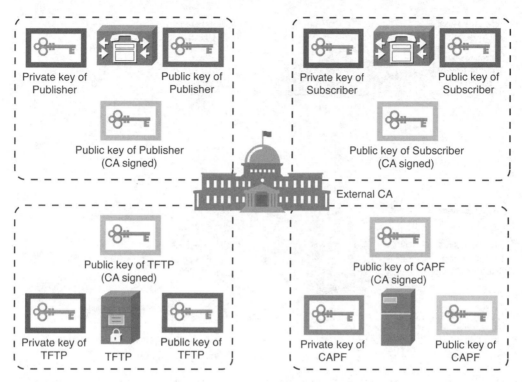

Figure A-6 *Cisco IP Telephony CA-Signed Certificate PKI Topology*

However, the CUCM implementation doesn't rely on CA trust.

Cisco IP Telephony MIC PKI Topology

Cisco IP Phones have a public and a private key pair, a Manufacturing Installed Certificate (MIC) for the phone, and a Cisco Manufacturing CA certificate installed. These certificates are installed in non-volatile, non-erasable memory. Certificates of the IP Phone are signed by the Cisco Manufacturing CA, as shown in Figure A-7.

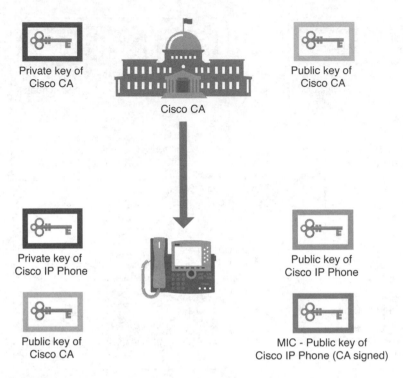

Figure A-7   *Cisco IP Telephony MIC PKI Topology*

Note: Cisco Manufacturing CA is the PKI root for all MICs.

Cisco IP Telephony LSC (CAPF) PKI Topology

As mentioned earlier, Cisco IP Phones have a public and a private key pair, a Manufacturing Installed Certificate (MIC) for the phone, and a Cisco Manufacturing CA certificate installed. In addition to these certificates, Cisco IP Phone can also support another type of certificate, that is, Locally Significant Certificate (LSC). This certificate is not Cisco Manufacturing CA installed; however, it is a CAPF-generated certificate. CAPF service runs co-resident with CUCM Publisher. LSC certificates are installed in erasable memory. Figure A-8 gives an overview of the LSC PKI topology.

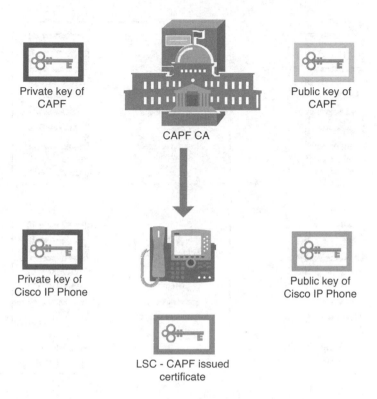

Figure A-8 *Cisco IP Telephony LSC PKI Topology*

Note: CAPF is the root for all LSCs.

Cisco CTL Client PKI Topology

Cisco IP Telephony PKI topology is an incongruent topology since, no common trust introducer is available to glue it together. This is done deliberately by Cisco to ensure that no rogue certificates or external entities can be trusted by default, as shown in Figure A-9.

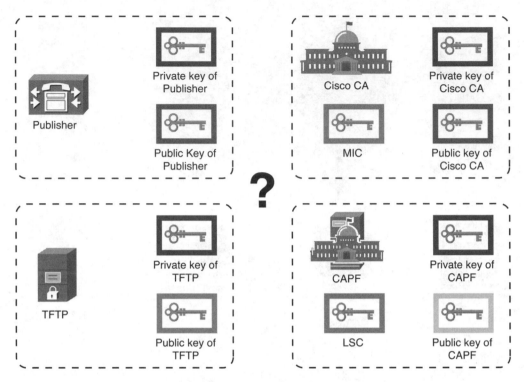

Figure A-9   *Cisco IP Telephony Disparate PKI Topology*

Even though it may look like it is not a disorder, this is intentionally done to avoid any rogue device signing the certificates from various PKI roots and entities. There is an indigenous solution for this incongruence by Cisco. The key lies in the fact that, there must be an entity that can enable a trust relationship between all the aforesaid topologies and bring them together so that each entity (PKI root) can trust the other. This function is taken care of by Cisco Trust List Client (CTL Client), as portrayed in Figure A-10.

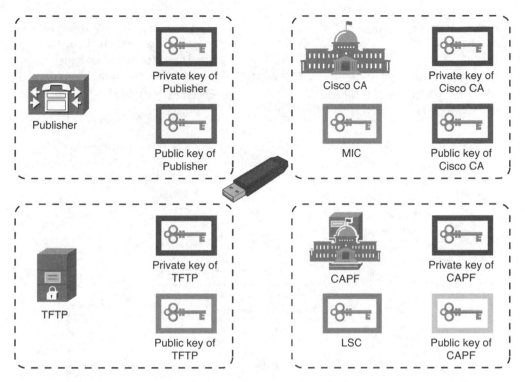

Figure A-10 *Cisco IP Telephony CTL Client-Based Unified PKI Topology*

The CTL Client is a software plug-in that you can download from the CUCM plug-in's web page (only available for Windows platform). It contains a private key and a public key. The public key is signed by Cisco Manufacturer CA. The private key is securely stored on a hardware token (USB eToken) and is not exportable but accessible by the CTL Client only.

Note: Each USB security token has its own private and public key.

As a general rule, at least two security eTokens are required for CTL Client to sign the certificates from PKI entities. This is a deliberate mechanism introduced for redundancy reasons by Cisco so that if after signing certificates and creating a CTL file, even if an eToken is lost, it does not hold back you from using the other eToken to re-create or re-sign the CTL file. After the CTL files have been pushed to the phone, they can be updated and replaced only if signed by a security token contained in the previous CTL file.

Note: Although the number of eTokens required to sign or create a CTL file is set to two by Cisco, it's a best practice to have more than two eTokens at a minimum to sign or re-create a CTL file. (The recommended value is four.) This is for safety reasons. Moreover, these eTokens should be kept in pairs separately at two locations under lock and key. This can provide for disaster recovery in case a set of eTokens is lost because of an artificial (human-induced) or natural catastrophe.

CTL Client has a certificate issued by the Cisco CA (CAP-RTP-001 subordinate to Cisco Root CA 2048). It obtains certificates of all certificate-issuing instances (PKI roots) and creates a list (CTL) containing all obtained certificates and signs the list, as shown in Figure A-11.

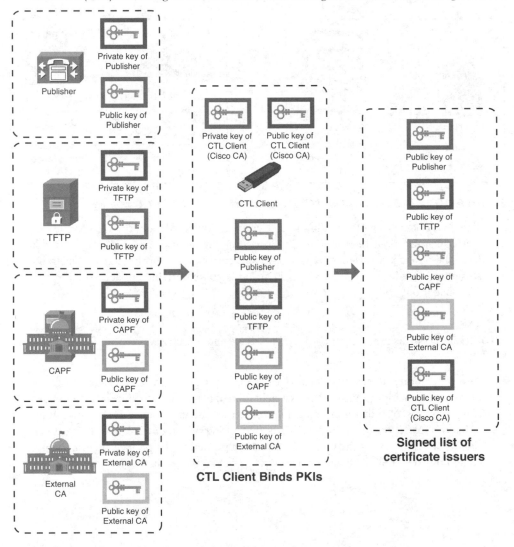

Figure A-11 *Cisco CTL Client as the Trust Introducer*

Note: An eToken (USB) is only a pictographic representation of the CTL Client. The actual CTL Client is software installed on Windows PC with Smart Card service enabled.

Cisco Unified IP Phone Certificates

Have you ever wondered where the certificates on your Cisco IP Phone come from? It is Cisco manufacturing that programs the certificates in the IP Phones.

The phone certificates come in two flavors:

■ Manufacturing Installed Certificate (MIC)

■ Locally Significant Certificate (LSC)

Cisco manufacturing is the source for Manufacturing Installed Certificates (MIC):

■ Installed by Cisco in non-erasable, non-volatile memory

■ Rooted in Cisco Certificate Authority

■ Used in all new phone models

CAPF is the source for Locally Significant Certificates (LSC):

■ Runs co-resident with Publisher

■ Installed by the IP Telephony administrator in erasable phone memory

■ Self-Signed Certificate Server bundled with CAPF

■ Can be signed by an organization's Certificate Authority or an external trusted CA, for example, Microsoft Certificate Services Manager, VeriSign, and Thwate

■ Can be used with all new phone models

Note: CAPF acts as a proxy for the external CA Authority signing process. It's a root for LSC.

X.509 v3 Certificates

When talking about Cisco IP Telephony PKI and its various implementations, it is important to know the basic construct for this PKI model, that is, the X.509 v3 certificate. This certificate format is what you find on Cisco IP Phones, CAPF, CUCM servers, and all those devices where you can possibly enable encryption.

At the core, the X.509 v3 certificate is a *digital document* that establishes the *identity* of a subject and provides the public encryption key issued by a trusted Certificate Authority.

An X.509 v3 certificate has the format shown in Figure A-12. All the fields have been explained alongside the actual certificate fields.

Version	V3	Certificate Version
Serial Number	5B74 F440 66CC 70CD B972 4C5B 7E20 68D1	Certificate ID
Signature Algorithm	md5RSA	Encryption Algorithm
Issuer	CN = VeriSign Class 1 CA Individual Subscriber-Persona Not Validated OU = www.verisign.com/repository/RPA Incorp . By Ref.,LIAB.LTD (c)98 OU = VeriSign Trust Network O = VeriSign, Inc.	Certificate Authority
Valid From	Thursday, June 20, 2000 8:00:00 PM	Certificate Validity
Valid To	Saturday, June 23, 2001 7:59:59 PM	
Subject	E = security@cisco.com CN = Securing Cisco IPT OU = Persona Not Validated OU = www.verisign.com/repository/RPA Incorp . by Ref.,LIAB.LTD (c)98 OU = VeriSign Trust Network O = VeriSign, Inc.	Certificate UserID
Public Key	3481 8B02 9181 01AC AF8B ...	RSA 1024 Bit Public Key
Thumbprint	7A52 28D0 1A0C FFD6 859A ...	Digital Signature

Figure A-12 *X.509 v3 Format*

For more details on the X.509 v3 certificate format, refer to RFC 3280.

Following are the salient features of this certificate format in relevance to Cisco IP Telephony:

- Every Device in Cisco IP Telephony has a unique certificate since, it is via certificates that a device advertises its Public Key, as shown in Figure A-13.

- The certificate may be signed by a trusted Certificate Authority to establish validity (for example, VeriSign)

- Certificates come from a variety of sources:

  - CUCM self-signed

  - MICs installed by Cisco manufacturing

  - LSCs from CAPF

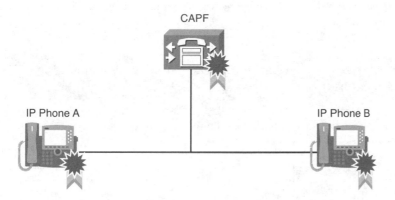

Devices with their X.509 v3 certificates

Figure A-13   *X.509 v3 Device Certificates*

Transport Layer Security (TLS)

Formerly known as Secure Sockets Layer 3.0 (SSL), TLS Protocol (RFC 2246 TLS v1.0, RFC 4346 TLS v1.1, and RFC 5246 TLS v1.2) is a client/server-based protocol, which allows client/server applications to communicate across a network so that eavesdropping and tampering issues are evaded. The TLS client and server negotiate a stateful connection by using a handshaking procedure. The client/server agree on various parameters used to establish the connection's security during this handshake.

TLS protocol is composed of two layers: the TLS Record Protocol and the TLS Handshake Protocol. While the former provides connection security with an encryption method such as DES, the latter enables the server and client to authenticate each other and to negotiate an encryption algorithm and cryptographic keys before data is exchanged.

TLS is used for secure signaling between Call Control and endpoints/applications as follows:

■ Bidirectional exchange of certificates for mutual authentication.

■ RSA signatures.

■ Encryption of the session keying material.

■ HMAC-SHA-1 authentication tags ensure packet integrity.

■ AES-128-CBC encryption protects session keys, DTMF tones and other data.

In addition, if an IP Phone is configured with a security profile for encryption, it creates an SHA-1 key and an AES key after the two-way authentication in TLS. The IP Phone encrypts both keys using the public RSA key of the Call Control server and then sends them to the server. The server decrypts the message (using its private key) so that the

IP phone and the server can exchange signaling messages over an authenticated and encrypted channel using TLS.

Note: In Cisco IP Telephony, encryption requires authentication so that the authenticity of the encrypted TLS packets is ensured.

Figure A-14 gives an overview of a TLS packet structure.

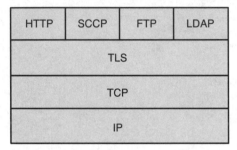

Figure A-14 *TLS Packet Format*

Secure Real Time Protocol (SRTP)

SRTP is a security contour for RTP, which adds confidentiality, message authentication, and replay protection to RTP protocol and to the control traffic for RTP (RTCP).

SRTP protocol has following prominent features:

- IETF RFC3711 for transport of secure media
- Uses AES-128 for both authentication and encryption
- High-throughput, low-packet expansion

In Cisco IP Telephony, media streams are encrypted by SRTP. CUCM generates the SRTP session keys for media authentication and media encryption, and sends them to the IP Phones inside signaling messages. This process is covered in the Cisco IP Telephony encryption basics section of this appendix.

SRTP Packet Format

As shown in Figure A-15, the SRTP packet (header and body) is similar to the RTP packet.

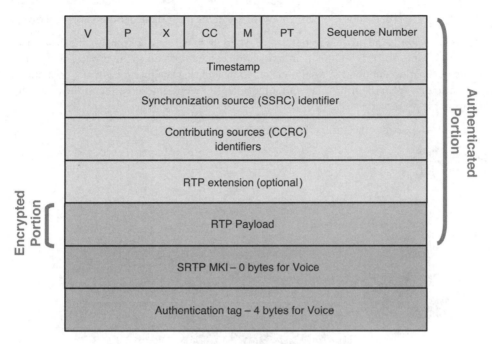

Figure A-15 *SRTP Packet Format*

The major difference is that the RTP payload is encrypted, and a 4-byte SHA-1 authentication tag is added to the packet. The authentication tag is a truncated fingerprint since; it holds the first 32 bits (4 bytes) of the 160-bit (20 bytes) SHA-1 hash digest computed from the RTP header and the encrypted voice payload. As you can infer from the figure, everything, including the encrypted RTP payload, is authenticated; although, only the RTP payload is encrypted.

Note: RTP encryption is performed before computing the hash.

SRTP is ideal for defending VoIP traffic because it can be used in concurrence with the header compression and has no effect on the QoS.

Cisco IP Telephony Authentication Basics

At the onset of this section, let's understand the meaning of authentication, as it pertains to Cisco IP Telephony. Answer the following questions:

What is authentication?

What is authentication in perspective of IP Telephony?

Although various definitions for authentication exist, the most basic definition is as follows:

Authentication is the process to determine whether someone is who he or she claims to be. In relevance to IP Telephony, authentication can be defined as the process to ensure if the destination endpoint is what it claims to be and that the integrity of the communication stream from the source (an endpoint or an IP Telephony server) until the intended endpoint is preserved.

Figure A-16 portrays the authentication process.

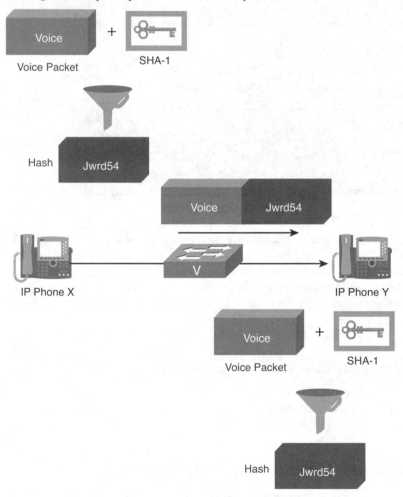

Figure A-16 *Authentication Process Overview*

In a Cisco IP Telephony environment, authentication is applicable to the following processes:

- Device firmware authentication
- Device configuration authentication
- Authentication and integrity of signaling messages

Note: Authentication of calls does not hash the media. It applies only to signaling. For firmware image authentication, the process is independent of Cisco PKI.

Cisco Unified IP Phone Firmware Image Verification

How does a phone know if an image was manipulated during transit, even if it were from a trusted source?

The answer to this question is in the heart of the solution that Cisco has established to ensure that the IP Phones cannot be distorted with a malicious TFTP server or a manipulated firmware image. Cisco provides signed firmware images. Cisco IP Phones support image authentication on all IP Phone models. Cisco manufacturing signs the images using a private key and affixes the signature to the firmware image. The third-generation Cisco IP Phones already include the public key supplied by Cisco manufacturing to verify that the signature is truthful.

This process is as follows:

- The administrator installs a new Cisco-signed phone image on the TFTP server.
- The IP Phone verifies the signature using the corresponding public key already embedded in the phone.

This is illustrated in Figure A-17.

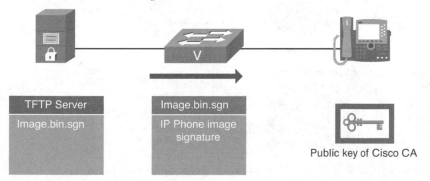

Figure A-17 *Authenticated IP Firmware Transfer Process*

As previously mentioned, IP Phone image authentication is independent of the Cisco IP Telephony PKI and it is not required for the CUCM cluster to be in mixed mode.

Authentication of Cisco Unified IP Phone Configuration Files

This process enables IP Phones to ensure that the configuration file is from a trusted source and has not been fiddled with on the way from the TFTP server. This helps restrain MITM attacks on the Cisco IP Phone configuration files, which could possibly direct the IP Phone to a rogue CUCM call-processing server.

The whole concept of configuration file authenticity is based on Cisco PKI. The configuration files are signed by the Cisco TFTP server's private key. The IP Phone leverages the public key of the TFTP server to verify the integrity of the configuration file. Once, authenticated, the configuration is applied on the Cisco Unified IP Phone. This process helps skirt the tampering of the files in transit and the identity of the TFTP server.

Note: Authentication of configuration files implies Cisco PKI is involved in the process; Cisco Unified IP Phone is configured for the authenticated or encrypted mode; and that CUCM cluster is in mixed mode.

The process of obtaining authenticated configuration files is as follows:

■ Configuration files are signed by the TFTP server (private key).

■ Cisco Unified IP Phone verifies the signature before applying a configuration (using TFTP server's public key).

Figure A-18 illustrates this process.

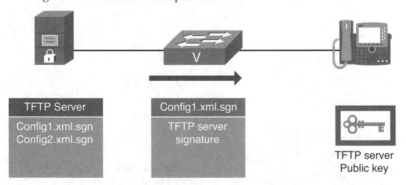

Figure A-18   *Authenticated IP Phone Configuration Transfer Process*

Authentication and Integrity of Voice Call Signaling

CUCM allows authenticating the signaling for an IP call between the call-control agent and the endpoints (signaling in Cisco IP Telephony exists between the Call Control and endpoints only while RTP flow is between endpoints). The following scheme is used for authentication:

- Device authentication for the phone and the server is provided using device certificates and digital signatures (asymmetric keys).

- Authentication and integrity of signaling messages is provided using TLS SHA-1 HMAC (symmetric keys).

Note: Enabling merely authentication for an IP Phone (by the security profile) enables authentication for signaling only; RTP is still clear text and unprotected.

The process of authenticated call signaling uses Cisco PKI. It requires the cluster to be in mixed-mode. Figure A-19 details the call flow.

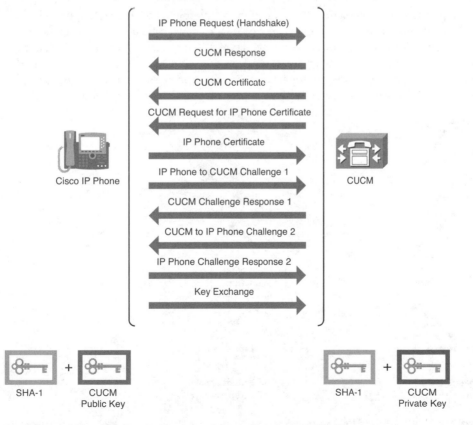

Figure A-19 *IP Phone Authenticated Signaling Setup Call Flow*

The authenticated call (signaling) process follows:

- The phone sends a random challenge to the server and demands that the server signs it.
- The server signs the random challenge with its RSA private key and returns it to the phone.
- The phone verifies the signature using the RSA public key of the server (available locally in the CTL).
- The server sends a random challenge to the phone and demands that the phone signs it.
- The phone signs the random challenge with its RSA private key and returns it to the server.
- The server verifies the signature using the RSA public key of the phone just received over the network (in the certificate).
- If configured only for authentication, the phone generates a session key for SHA-1 hashing, encrypts it using the public RSA key of the server, and sends it to the server.
- The server decrypts the message and now the phone and the server can start signing signaling messages (signaling channel integrity).

Cisco IP Telephony Encryption Basics

As described earlier in section, "Introduction to Cryptography," encryption provides confidentiality of data. Encryption is the process of converting cleartext to ciphertext. Decryption is the process of converting ciphertext to cleartext. Only authorized entities can decrypt data. The capability to encrypt and decrypt data depends on the knowledge of encryption and decryption keys. These keys can be symmetric or asymmetric. Figure A-20 shows a high-level overview of the encryption and decryption process.

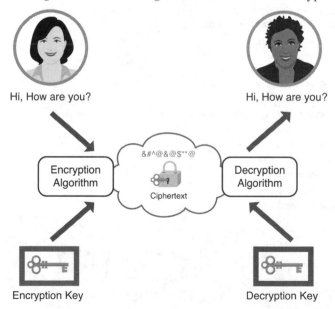

Figure A-20 *PKI-Based Encryption Process*

In a Cisco IP Telephony environment, encryption is applicable to the following processes:

■ Device configuration encryption (for Cisco IP Phones)

■ Encryption for signaling and media

Cisco TFTP server allows encrypting of configuration files, as depicted in Figure A-21, which helps prevent exposure of sensitive phone configuration settings from curious audience.

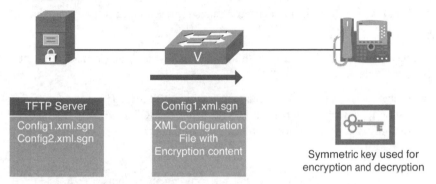

Figure A-21   *TFTP Encrypted IP Phone Configuration Transfer*

The process to enable encrypted configuration files follows:

■ After the phone profile is set for a TFTP encrypted configuration, the TFTP server deletes the unencrypted configuration files and generates an encrypted version of the same.

■ A configuration file encrypted by a TFTP server is transmitted to the IP Phone. The TFTP server encrypts the symmetric key using the IP Phone's public key (for supported phones) and appends it to the configuration file.

■ The IP Phone decrypts the configuration file before applying the configuration using the symmetric key.

Note: You have to manually enter keys for IP Phones that do not support public and private keys, that is, 7905/7912 and 7940/7960 (SIP only).

CUCM enables the encryption of voice calls (signaling and media) with the subsequent scheme:

■ For signaling messages using TLS encryption with AES 128-bit encryption.

■ For media transfer using SRTP AES 128-bit encryption.

- The signaling and media channel between two parties will be protected using symmetric cryptography (HMACs and encryption).

- For symmetric algorithms, the two parties share secret session keys (one for HMAC and one for encryption).

- Symmetric key distribution for signaling is done using asymmetric cryptography.

- Asymmetric cryptography relies on Public Key (Certificate) distribution via PKI.

The process for an authenticated and encrypted call is represented as follows and shown in Figure A-22:

- The sender hashes the RTP payload with its SHAXY key, and the (truncated) result is appended to the RTP payload.

- The receiver hashes the received payload again with its Rx SHA-1 key and compares it to the embedded (truncated) hash. If it is the same, the RTP payload is coming from a trusted source and has not been distorted in transit.

Note: SHA-1 exchange is done using symmetric keys. Only 32-bit hash (out of original 160-bits hash result) is added to the packet.

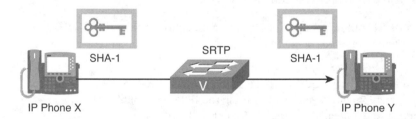

Figure A-22 *SRTP Call Authentication Overview*

Encryption provides confidentiality to RTP payloads. AES algorithm with 128-bit secret session keys is used only for a single call, as shown in Figure A-23.

Note: At least three parties have access to keys for a call: two phones and the CUCM.

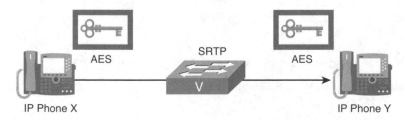

Figure A-23 *SRTP Call Encryption Overview*

- The two phones share secret symmetric keys (provisioned by the CUCM).

- The sender AES-encrypts the RTP payload with its Tx AES key.

- The receiver AES-decrypts the received payload with the same (Rx) session key.

This process is detailed in Figure A-24.

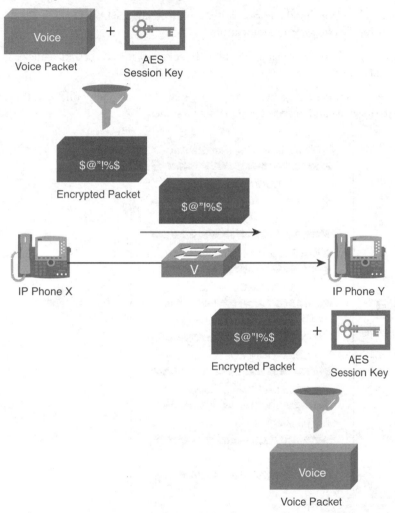

Figure A-24   *SRTP Call Encryption Process*

SRTP Call Flow Overview

This section offers an insight to SRTP call flow. Figure A-25 depicts the SRTP call flow between CUCM and an endpoint (signaling).

Following are some of the characteristics of SRTP calls:

■ If configured for encryption, the phone will not only create a SHA-1 key, but also an AES key after the two-way authentication.

■ The phone encrypts both keys using the public RSA key of the server and sends them to the server.

■ The server decrypts the message (using its private key) and now the phone, and the server can start signing and encrypting signaling messages.

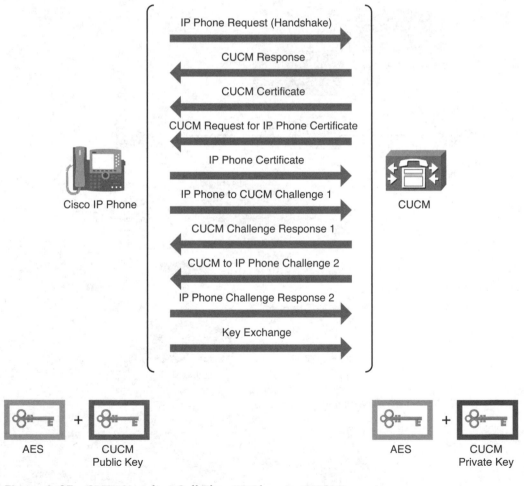

Figure A-25   *SRTP Signaling Call Flow (IP Phone to CUCM)*

Following is the SRTP call flow, as shown in Figure A-26, insight including two IP Phones registered with CUCM, using Secure SCCP (TLS) for signaling and configured for encryption (SRTP).

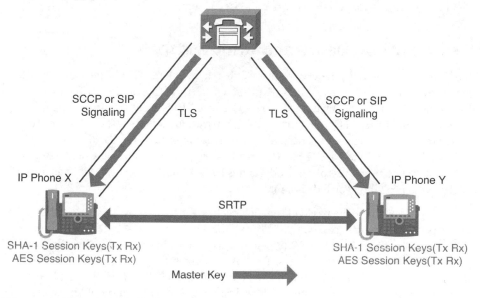

Figure A-26 *SRTP Call Flow (TLS, SRTP)*

Step 1.   Phones and CUCM exchange certificates.

Step 2.   Phones and CUCM authenticate each other.

Step 3.   Phones create TLS session keys for SHA-1 authentication and AES encryption.

Step 4.   Phones encrypt session keys with CUCM public key and send the keys to CUCM. CUCM decrypts them with its private key.

Step 5.   CUCM shares TLS keys with each phone and starts secure exchange of signaling messages.

Step 6.   CUCM creates session keys for SRTP SHA-1 authentication and SRTP AES encryption.

Step 7.   CUCM distributes the session keys to both phones across the encrypted and authenticated signaling link.

Step 8.   Phones share keys and start secure media exchange.

Impact of Encryption on IP Telephony Network

This section provides information on the impact of enabling encryption in Cisco IP Telephony infrastructure on the network and Call Control.

SRTP Impact on Delay and Bandwidth

SRTP has a delay of 15 microseconds (μs). With a delay budget of 150 milliseconds, 15 microseconds is almost immaterial. As explained in section, "Secure Real Time Protocol," SRTP adds a 4-byte authentication tag to every packet. Packets using the default G.711 codec with 20 millisecond packet timers are 160 bytes, including the TCP header. Add 4 bytes to that and you are looking at a 2.5% increase in bandwidth. Packets using G.729 codec are 40 bytes, and if the TCP headers are compressed using Compressed RTP (CRTP) they're only 24 bytes. Add 4-bytes for a 16.66% bandwidth hit in an area in which you're probably worried about it.

When SRTP is enabled, the payload for each packet is increased by 4 bytes. At the default packetization rate of 20 ms, SRTP VoIP packets have a 164-byte payload for G.711 or a 24-byte payload for G.729. The IP header is 20 bytes, the UDP header is 8 bytes, and the RTP header is 12 bytes. The link header varies in size according to the Layer 2 media used. Thus, we can conclude that enabling SRTP in your IP Telephony infrastructure may not impact bandwidth or delay in a way that you should be worried about it.

It is recommended that you understand the impact to enable SRTP in your IP Telephony network, on a per protocol, per codec basis. This information is detailed in CUCM 8.x SRND at http://www.cisco.com/en/US/docs/voice_ip_comm/cucm/srnd/8x/netstruc. html#wp1165070.

The next section details the effect of enabling encryption on CUCM servers in a cluster.

TLS Performance Impact on CUCM

Generally, phones running TLS use 36K more memory and 3% to 5% more CPU than phones not running TLS. Obviously, a large number of phones running TLS require more servers in the solution. Thus, it is advised to use the CUCM sizing tool provided by Cisco to ensure that your cluster is scaled to the right capacity to support encrypted endpoints. This tool is available at http://tools.cisco.com/cucst/.

Note: The CUCM sizing tool can distinguish between phones running TLS and phones not running TLS, thus providing you with the right number of servers required in the cluster to support them.

Summary

In this appendix, you were introduced to the following concepts:

- Device identity

- Signaling integrity

- Signaling privacy

- Media integrity and privacy

- CUCM PKI

- Protocols that are pillars of IP Telephony Security: TLS, SRTP, and SHA

This chapter discussed the concepts of authentication and encryption as they pertain to Cisco IP Telephony. Cisco IP Telephony leverages authentication and encryption mechanisms to challenge the threats that creep around your IP Telephony network. These include (and are not limited to) eavesdropping, IP Phone firmware and configuration file tampering, MITM attacks, DoS attacks, call hijacking, and information injection attacks. While, authentication provides for data integrity, encryption provides privacy by scrambling data. Cisco PKI is a fully established PKI system that is unrelated and can be brought together with the help of the CTL Client. Cisco IP Phones can use preinstalled certificates from Cisco manufacturing or use LSCs issued by the CUCM CAPF, or use both for enablement of authentication and encryption of signaling and media. TLS helps you encrypt the signaling stream while SRTP ensures that the media packets are secured.

Armed with these facts and concepts, you can know that, Cisco has gone an extra mile to ensure that your IP Telephony networks built on Cisco technology are world-class and secure, robust, and resilient to attacks.

Cisco IP Telephony: Firewalling and Intrusion Prevention

Firewalls, Network Intrusion Prevention Systems (NIPS), and Host Intrusion Prevention System (HIPS) continue to be the agents that defend the data and voice streams from external and internal attacks. As the topology of the enterprise network continued to change dramatically over the past few years, firewalls, Intrusion Prevention and Detection systems also continue to evolve. With the evolution of Unified Threat Management (UTM) systems and self-defending networks, Cisco has empowered you to safeguard the core of almost every successful business in existence: communications.

This appendix introduces the best practices to defend your IP Telephony network with Cisco Adaptive Security Appliance (ASA). In addition, you can comprehend the fundamentals of IOS-based firewall solutions. You learn about Cisco Intrusion Prevention Systems (NIPS and HIPS) that help ensure your IP Telephony network remains a secure and trustworthy service.

This appendix covers the following topics:

- Cisco ASA Firewall: Best practices for IP Telephony security

- Cisco IOS Firewall solution (CBAC and Zone-Based Policy Firewall)

- Cisco Network Intrusion Prevention System (NIPS)

- Cisco Host Intrusion Prevention System (HIPS)

Cisco ASA Firewall: Best Practices for Securing Voice Communications

Chapter 8, "Perimeter Security with Cisco Adaptive Security Appliance," discusses Cisco ASA security appliance in detail. This section walks you through the fundamentals of securing Cisco IP Telephony network, leveraging leading practices for Cisco ASA Firewall-based solution(s). In addition, you will realize some of the not-so-well-known facts about the Cisco ASA IP Telephony protection capabilities.

Cisco ASA Failover

Communications is one of the top priorities of every modern-day organization. You cannot afford your organization's communication streams going down. In today's world, when businesses are open 24 X 7 X 365 by virtue of the Internet, contact centers, and so on, a lapse in customer interaction could mean a shift of the customers' focus from your brand to another, where they get uninterrupted support. In a nutshell, to be successful with your customers, it is crucial that you are connected with them. In context of IP Telephony, voice calls, voice messages, IM, and presence, which are some of the most commonly used utilities by enterprise and SMB customers, must always be available, uninterrupted so business can continue as usual.

If you have a data center or any remote or large site where IP Telephony resources are located, you must ensure the high-availability (HA) of connectivity to these resources. In context of WAN this could mean redundant WAN links by the same or a different Internet service provider (ISP). In context of your network's fringe, it means the high-availability of Cisco ASA Firewalls. In such case, LAN-based failover should be used for ASA Primary and Secondary Firewalls.

For Cisco ASA failover implementation, the following points provide best practice recommendations:

- Active/Standby failover is the recommended and supported approach to support voice traffic (to avoid asymmetric routing issues encountered in Active/Active failover or a load-balancing scenario that can lead to one-way audio). Active/Standby Failover allows a standby Cisco ASA to take over the functionality of a failed unit. When the active unit fails, it changes to the standby state while the standby unit changes to the active state. The unit (which was previously standby before failover) that becomes active assumes the IP addresses and MAC addresses of the failed unit (previously primary) and begins to pass traffic. Because network devices see no change in the MAC-to-IP address pairing, no ARP entries change or time out anywhere on the IP Telephony network. The unit can fail if one of these events occurs:

  - The unit has a hardware failure or a power failure.

  - The unit has a software failure or one or more monitored interfaces fail.

  - The **no failover active** command is entered on the active unit, or the **failover active** command is entered on the standby unit.

- Stateful failover should be enabled using a dedicated stateful failover interface. When stateful failover is enabled, the active unit continually passes per-connection state information to the standby unit. After a failover occurs, the same connection information is available at the new active unit. Supported end-user applications are not required to reconnect to keep the same communication session. The state information passed to the standby unit includes the following:

  - TCP connection states

  - UDP connection states

- ARP table

- HTTP connection states

- ISAKMP and IPSec SA table

Example B-1 and Example B-2 illustrate the Cisco ASA Stateful Failover configuration for both the Primary and Secondary Firewalls.

Note: Cisco ASA IOS version 8.3(2) is used for the configurations examples.

Example B-1   *Cisco ASA Primary Unit Stateful Failover Configuration*

```
IPTASA(config)# interface GigabitEthernet3/0
IPTASA(config)# description ASA Outside
IPTASA(config)# nameif outside
IPTASA(config)# security-level 0
IPTASA(config)# ip address <outside ip> <subnet> standby <standby ip>
!
IPTASA(config)# interface GigabitEthernet3/1
IPTASA(config)# description ASA Inside
IPTASA(config)# nameif inside
IPTASA(config)# security-level 100
IPTASA(config)# ip address <inside ip> <subnet mask> standby <standby ip>
!
IPTASA(config)# interface GigabitEthernet3/2
IPTASA(config)# description STATE Failover Interface
!
IPTASA(config)# interface GigabitEthernet3/3
IPTASA(config)# description LAN Failover Interface
!
IPTASA(config)# failover
IPTASA(config)# failover lan unit primary
IPTASA(config)# failover lan enable
IPTASA(config)# failover key <key>
IPTASA(config)# failover replication http
IPTASA(config)# failover lan interface HEART GigabitEthernet3/3
IPTASA(config)# failover polltime unit 1 holdtime 5
IPTASA(config)# failover polltime interface 1 holdtime 5
IPTASA(config)# failover link STATE GigabitEthernet3/2
IPTASA(config)# failover interface ip HEART <ip address> <subnet mask> standby
   <standby ip>
IPTASA(config)# failover interface ip STATE <ip address> <subnet mask> standby
   <standby ip>
```

Example B-2   *Cisco ASA Secondary Unit Failover Configuration*

```
IPTASA(config)# failover
IPTASA(config)# failover lan unit secondary
IPTASA(config)# failover lan enable
IPTASA(config)# failover key <key>
IPTASA(config)# failover replication http
IPTASA(config)# failover lan interface HEART GigabitEthernet3/3
IPTASA(config)# failover polltime unit 1 holdtime 5
IPTASA(config)# failover polltime interface 1 holdtime 5
IPTASA(config)# failover link STATE GigabitEthernet3/2
IPTASA(config)# failover interface ip HEART <ip address> <subnet mask> standby
  <standby ip>
IPTASA(config)# failover interface ip STATE <ip address> <subnet mask> standby
  <standby ip>
```

Cisco ASA: IP Telephony Application Clustering over WAN

You may have a requirement to cluster your call control, voice or unified messaging, or other IP Telephony services over WAN, distributed in two or more data centers for resiliency or as per your network design. More often than not, these Data Centers will be protected by Cisco ASA Firewall(s) against external threats.

In such a case, you can sway away from opening port-based signaling and media exchange between the entities in the data centers (which allows least permissive access, however, may turn out to be a management and administrative overhead in the longer run with various versions of applications or newer applications leveraging different ports). Instead, you can create an IPSec tunnel between the data centers for IP Telephony server-to-server subnets whereby, the traffic goes unfiltered, un-natted, and un-inspected. Moreover, if your organization's security policy and compliance program, for example, PCI compliance permits, you can also allow the IP Telephony server-to-server (similar PCI defined security zones), subnet-to-subnet traffic between two or more data centers at an IP level, thereby bypassing port level configuration. These solutions are particularly useful when you have multiple data centers and various IP Telephony servers, for example, CUCM servers exchanging ICCS traffic amid various servers within the cluster, across the data centers over WAN and MAN, as shown in Figure B-1.

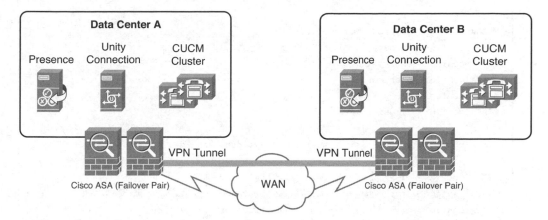

Figure B-1 *Cisco ASA: Seamless IP Telephony Server-to-Server Traffic via IPSec LAN-to-LAN Tunnel*

Example B-3 illustrates the configuration of a LAN-to-LAN IPSec VPN tunnel between Cisco ASA Firewalls at Data Center A and B, respectively, for passing through IP Telephony Server subnet traffic, without NAT, port-based ACLs, and inspection.

Note: Only IPSec VPN point-to-point tunnel details are enlisted. The configuration is equally applicable to Firewalls at data center A and B.

Example B-3 *Cisco ASA IPSec LAN-to-LAN Tunnel Configuration*

```
IPTASA(config)# interface GigabitEthernet3/0
IPTASA(config)# description ASA Outside
IPTASA(config)# nameif outside
IPTASA(config)# security-level 0
IPTASA(config)# ip address <outside ip> <subnet mask> standby <standby ip>
!
IPTASA(config)# interface GigabitEthernet3/1
IPTASA(config)# description ASA Inside
IPTASA(config)# nameif inside
IPTASA(config)# security-level 100
IPTASA(config)# ip address <inside ip> <subnet mask> standby <standby ip>
!
IPTASA(config)# access-list L2L extended permit ip <local-IP-Telephony-server-sub-
    net>
<subnet mask> <remote-IP-Telephony-server-subnet> <subnet mask>
!
IPTASA(config)# crypto isakmp enable outside
```

```
!
IPTASA(config)# crypto isakmp policy 10
IPTASA(config)# authentication pre-share
IPTASA(config)# encryption 3des
IPTASA(config)# hash md5
IPTASA(config)# group 5
IPTASA(config)# lifetime 86400
!
IPTASA(config)# crypto ipsec transform-set voipset esp-3des esp-md5-hmac
!
IPTASA(config)# crypto map voipmap 10 match address L2L
IPTASA(config)# crypto map voipmap 10 set peer <outside-IP-of-remote-ASA>
IPTASA(config)# crypto map voipmap 10 set transform-set voipset
!
IPTASA(config)# crypto map voipmap interface outside
!
IPTASA(config)# tunnel-group outside-IP-of-remote-ASA ipsec-attributes
IPTASA(config-tunnel-ipsec)# ikev1 pre-shared-key <key>
IPTASA(config-tunnel-ipsec)# isakmp nat-traversal
IPTASA(config-tunnel-ipsec)# isakmp identity address
!
IPTASA(config)# class-map myvoip
IPTASA(config-cmap)# match access-list L2L
!
IPTASA(config)# policy-map myvoipmap
IPTASA (config-cmap)# class myvoip
IPTASA(config-pmap-c)# set connection random-sequence-number disable
!
IPTASA(config)# service-policy myvoipmap global
```

With benefits of non port-based ACLs and seamless traffic transition from one data center to another, comes the limitation of doing so per your WAN Link Speed. It is important to observe delay for packets from one IP Telephony server subnet to another through the IPSec VPN tunnel to ensure that the Round Trip Time (RTT) is well under the limits specified by Cisco SRND and Design Guides for CUCM, Unity Connection, and CUP Server intra cluster traffic. Following are the RTT values for different IP Telephony applications:

- For CUCM 8.x and later, the RTT value is maximum 80 ms. In addition, 1.544 Mbps should be reserved for each CUCM server deployed remotely.

- For Cisco Unity 8.x, a maximum of 10 ms RTT between primary and secondary servers. In addition, you must dedicate a minimum of 1 Gigabit of bandwidth between the primary and secondary server. (GCDC must be colocated with Unity servers.)

- Cisco Unity Connection 8.x and later has a tolerance for 150 ms, with a requirement for 7 Mbps for every 50 ports (Active/Active HA pair).

- Cisco Unified Presence Server 8.x and later requires a maximum of 80 ms RTT with a minimum 5 Mbps of bandwidth for each Cisco Unified Presence subcluster.

Any bandwidth less than the Cisco recommended values can adversely impact performance.

Cisco ASA: QoS

In relevance to perimeter firewall, voice bearer traffic should be accepted only from telephony devices. Voice bearer traffic should be allocated to a low latency queue (LLQ) to ensure that jitter is minimized. Although, voice signaling traffic does not have the same jitter constraints as voice bearer, it must be forwarded in a timely fashion. Finally, data traffic should be allocated to one or more queues and policed to limit excessive traffic volumes.

The best practice is to have devices mark traffic or traffic classification done as close as possible to the voice server and endpoint (that is, source of traffic). Cisco ASA Firewalls would then follow the QoS markings set by CUCM and other IP Telephony applications, endpoints to remote sites, home workers, and telecommuters. The QOS DSCP markings as per leading practices are as follows:

- Voice Media Traffic will be classified as DSCP EF and should be assigned to LLQ.

- Voice Signaling Traffic will be classified as DSCP CS3 or AF31 and should be assigned to LLQ.

- The rest of the traffic will be considered as nonmission critical and gets best effort treatment.

The configuration in Example B-4 summarizes the QoS for voice on Cisco ASA with the assumption that voice signaling and media traffic is properly marked and classified before it reaches the firewall.

Example B-4   *Cisco ASA QoS for Voice*

```
IPTASA(config)# priority-queue outside
!
IPTASA(config)# class-map Media
IPTASA(config-cmap)# match dscp ef
!
IPTASA(config)# class-map Signaling
IPTASA(config-cmap)# match dscp cs3
IPTASA(config-cmap)# match dscp af31
!
IPTASA(config)# policy-map Voip
IPTASA(config-pmap)# class Media
```

```
IPTASA(config-pmap-c)# priority
IPTASA(config-pmap)# class Signaling
IPTASA(config-pmap-c)# priority
IPTASA(config-pmap)# class class-default
IPTASA(config-pmap-c)# police output 500000
!
IPTASA(config-pmap)# service-policy Voip interface outside
```

Cisco ASA: Enhanced Inspection for Voice Protocols

Cisco ASA security appliance offers inspection feature for some of the most popular and widely used protocols. However, what may remain as an infamous piece of information is that it also offers customized inspection for protocols. This section explores the enhanced inspection capability of Cisco ASA for voice protocols, namely:

- SIP
- H.323
- MGCP
- SCCP

Note: Enabling multiple inspects on a Cisco ASA Firewall can be CPU-intensive and can impact the throughput speed. Hence, it is recommended to follow your organization's security policy or IP Telephony security policy as a guideline to enable inspects selectively.

Example B-5 exhibits the commonly used voice and network protocols which are supported with inspect **policy-map**.

Example B-5   *Cisco ASA Enhanced Inspection Options*

```
IPTASA(config)# policy-map type inspect ?
configure mode commands/options:
  dns                 Configure a policy-map of type DNS
  smtp                Configure a policy-map of type SMTP
  ftp                 Configure a policy-map of type FTP
  h323                Configure a policy-map of type H.323
  http                Configure a policy-map of type HTTP
  im                  Configure a policy-map of type IM
  mgcp                Configure a policy-map of type MGCP
  netbios             Configure a policy-map of type NETBIOS
  rtsp                Configure a policy-map of type RTSP
  sip                 Configure a policy-map of type SIP
  skinny              Configure a policy-map of type Skinny
```

The following sections discuss the implementation of voice protocol enhanced inspection capabilities of the Cisco ASA security appliance.

Enhanced SIP Inspection

Cisco ASA SIP Application Inspection Control (AIC) functions are designed to prevent attacks and restrict or deny certain applications. These include the following:

- Prevent DoS attacks using SIP ports

- Prevent non-RFC-compliant SIP packets

- Prevent buffer over flow attacks

- Disallow black-listed users from using IM over SIP

- Prevent exploitation of SIP endpoints or servers

- Disable Instant Messaging

- Prevent unrecognized SIP messages

- Prevent SIP packets arriving out of state

- Prevent non-RTP traffic through the media pinholes

- Drop SIP packets with invalid max-forwards field

- Block rogue callers

- Limit SIP traffic to specific domains

- Restrict content length and type of SIP messages

The **match-request method** keyword can be used to take specific actions such as drop, drop-connection, log, or reset on the following SIP messages, as shown in Example B-6.

Example B-6   *Cisco ASA SIP AIC—Match Request-Method Options*

```
IPTASA(config-pmap)# match request-method ?
mpf-policy-map mode commands/options:
  ack              Method ACK
  bye              Method BYE
  cancel           Method CANCEL
  info             Method INFO
  invite           Method INVITE
  message          Method MESSAGE
  notify           Method NOTIFY
  options          Method OPTIONS
  prack            Method PRACK
  publish          Method PUBLISH
  refer            Method REFER
  register         Method REGISTER
```

```
subscribe           Method SUBSCRIBE
unknown             Method UNKNOWN
update              Method UPDATE
```

In addition, the **parameters** keyword enables you to define certain SIP-related parameters, which can be used to deter attack attempts. Example B-7 gives an insight to the various parameters available.

Example B-7   *Cisco ASA SIP AIC—Parameters Options*

```
IPTASA(config-pmap)# parameters
IPTASA(config-pmap-p)# ?
MPF policy-map parameter configuration commands:
im                       Enable or disable Instant Messaging
ip-address-privacy       Enable or disable IP address privacy
max-forwards-validation  Check if the value of Max-Forwards header is zero
rtp-conformance          Check RTP packets flowing on the pin-holes for protocol
  conformance
software-version         Inspect the SIP endpoint software version as specified in
  User-Agent and Server headers
state-checking           Enable or disable SIP state checking
strict-header-validation Enable or disable strict validation of SIP messages based
  on RFC 3261
traffic-non-sip          Allow or disallow non-SIP traffic on SIP port
uri-non-sip              Check a non-SIP URI in SIP message
```

Example B-8 illustrates DoS attack prevention by rate limiting SIP INVITE message to ten messages per second. If the number of INVITE messages exceeds ten messages per second on an interface, the connection will be dropped. This feature can be used to protect internal servers and endpoints from being flooded by INVITE messages, thereby causing a DoS attack.

Example B-8   *Cisco ASA SIP AIC—Rate Limit*

```
IPTASA(config)# policy-map type inspect sip SIPMAP
IPTASA(config-pmap)# match request-method invite
IPTASA(config-pmap-c)# rate-limit 10
!
IPTASA(config)# policy-map global_policy
IPTASA(config-pmap)# class inspection_default
IPTASA(config-pmap-c)# inspect sip SIPMAP
!
IPTASA(config)# service-policy global_policy global
```

> **Note:** The default **inspect sip** statement must be removed before applying the new **sip inspect policy-map**; otherwise, you get following error:
>
> ERROR: Inspect Configuration of This Type Exists, First Remove That Configuration and Then Add the New Configuration

Example B-9 describes how to prevent unrecognized messages on SIP ports. This configuration disallows any non-SIP traffic attempted on known SIP ports.

Example B-9 *Cisco ASA SIP AIC—Non-SIP Traffic Restriction*

```
IPTASA(config)# policy-map type inspect sip SIPMAP
IPTASA(config-pmap)# parameters
IPTASA(config-pmap-p)# no traffic-non-sip
!
IPTASA(config)# policy-map global_policy
IPTASA(config-pmap)# class inspection_default
IPTASA(config-pmap-c)# inspect sip SIPMAP
!
IPTASA(config)# service-policy global_policy global
```

The next section gives you an insight to Cisco ASA Firewall's enhanced inspection capabilities for the Cisco proprietary SCCP protocol.

Enhanced Skinny Inspection

Cisco ASA Firewall's SCCP AIC functions are designed to prevent attacks and restrict or deny certain applications based on SCCP (Skinny Protocol). These include the following:

- Enforce registration to prevent rogue phone calls.

- Prevent buffer over flow attacks.

- Restrict services on endpoints.

- Prevent unrecognized SCCP messages.

- Prevent potential misuse of idle media connections.

The **match** keyword can be used to take specific actions, as shown in Example B-10.

Example B-10 *Cisco ASA SCCP AIC—Match Options*

```
IPTASA(config-pmap)# match ?
mpf-policy-map mode commands/options:
  message-id    Match StationMessageID field in SCCP messages
```

The **parameters** keyword can be used to take specific actions, as shown in Example B-11.

Example B-11   *Cisco ASA SCCP AIC—Parameters Options*

```
IPTASA(config-pmap-p)# ?
MPF policy-map parameter configuration commands:
  enforce-registration    Enforce registration before calls can be placed
  message-id              Set maximum SCCP StationMessageID allowed
  rtp-conformance         Check RTP packets flowing on the pin-holes for protocol
  conformance
  sccp-prefix-len         Set maximum and minimum SCCP prefix length value allowed
  timeout                 Configure timeout value for signaling and media connections
```

Example B-12 describes the configuration to implement RTP conformance. In addition to pinhole conformance, it also checks for sequence number validity and prevents spoofing of RTP packets on an existing session. This example describes the configuration required to enable SCCP-enhanced inspection.

Example B-12   *Cisco ASA SCCP AIC—RTP Conformance*

```
IPTASA(config)# policy-map type inspect SCCPMAP
IPTASA(config-pmap)# parameters
IPTASA(config-pmap-p)# rtp-conformance enforce-payloadtype
!
IPTASA(config)# policy-map global_policy
IPTASA(config-pmap)# class inspection_default
IPTASA(config-pmap-c)# inspect skinny SCCPMAP
!
IPTASA(config)# service-policy global_policy global
```

Enhanced H.323 Inspection

The H.323 AIC functions are designed to prevent attacks and restrict or deny certain applications based on your security policy or organization's requirements. These include the following:

- Restrict call duration.
- Block rogue callers.
- Prevent RAS/H.225 packets arriving out of state.
- Restrict H.323 services that can be used.
- Media-type data control.
- H.225 tunneling control.

- Allow or disallow video or audio.

- State check.

- Phone number filtering.

- HSI routed call setup.

The **match** keyword can be used to take specific actions, as shown in Example B-13.

Example B-13 *Cisco ASA H.323 AIC—Match Options*

```
IPTASA(config-pmap)# match ?
mpf-policy-map mode commands/options:
  called-party             Match a Called-party
  calling-party            Match a Calling-party
  media-type               Match Media type
```

The **parameters** keyword can be used to take specific actions, as shown in Example B-14.

Example B-14 *Cisco ASA H.323 AIC—Parameters Options*

```
IPTASA(config-pmap)# parameters
IPTASA(config-pmap-p)# ?
MPF policy-map parameter configuration commands:
  call-duration-limit      Configure the call duration for H.323 call
  call-party-numbers       Enforce sending call party numbers during call setup
  h245-tunnel-block        Blocking H.245 tunnelling
  hsi-group                Define hsi group
  rtp-conformance          Check RTP packets flowing on the pin-holes for protocol
  conformance
  state-checking           Enforcing state checking for H.323
```

Example B-15 demonstrates how you can block an H.323 video call using H.323 AIC.

Example B-15 *Cisco ASA H.323 AIC—Block Video Calling*

```
IPTASA(config)# policy-map type inspect h323 H323MAP
IPTASA(config-pmap)# match media-calltype video
IPTASA(config-pmap-c)# drop
!
IPTASA(config)# policy-map global_policy
IPTASA(config-pmap)# class inspection_default
IPTASA(config-pmap-c)# inspect h323 H323MAP
!
IPTASA(config)# service-policy global_policy global
```

As illustrated in Example B-15, H.323 AIC is set to drop any video call attempted through Cisco ASA. This could be useful when your organization does not warrant use of video calls on H.323 protocol and some rogue endpoint tries to negotiate video capabilities with an H.323 server or another endpoint.

Enhanced MGCP Inspection

The MGCP AIC functions are designed to prevent attacks and restrict or deny certain applications based on leveraging MGCP protocol.

The **parameters** keyword can be used to take specific actions, as shown in Example B-16.

Example B-16   *Cisco ASA MGCP AIC—Parameters Options*

```
ASA(config-pmap)# parameters
ASA(config-pmap-p)# ?
MPF policy-map parameter configuration commands:
  call-agent                Add a call-agent
  command-queue             Configure a Command Queue
  gateway                   Add a Gateway
```

Example B-17 details the configuration to limit the commands allowed in MGCP command queue, thereby rate limiting the source (possible attacker) to queue MGCP commands and averting the possibility of a DoS attack.

Example B-17   *Cisco ASA MGCP AIC—Command Queue Limit*

```
IPTASA(config)# policy-map type inspect mgcp MGCPMAP
IPTASA(config-pmap)# parameters
IPTASA(config-pmap-p)# command-queue 100
!
IPTASA(config)# policy-map global_policy
IPTASA(config-pmap)# class inspection_default
IPTASA(config-pmap-c)# inspect mgcp MGCPMAP
!
IPTASA(config)# service-policy global_policy global
```

Cisco IOS Firewall

While Cisco ASA security appliance is the de-facto standard for enterprise firewalling, for smaller organizations or remote branches of an enterprise, Cisco offers the IOS Firewall solution. Cisco IOS Firewall comes in two flavors:

- Cisco IOS Context-Based Access Control (CBAC)
- Cisco IOS Zone-Based Firewall

The subsequent section details the Cisco IOS CBAC Firewall feature.

Cisco IOS CBAC Firewall

Similar to Cisco ASA Firewall inspect feature, Cisco IOS CBAC Firewall solution delivers stateful packet inspection for TCP and UDP sessions and consequently dynamically modifies ACLs to permit or deny traffic, that is, CBAC can inspect traffic for sessions that originate from either side of the firewall (that is, from inside to outside or outside to inside). CBAC can open pinholes for connections traversing through the IOS router. CBAC inspects packets when the packet is permitted through a relevant ACL under subsequent circumstances:

- An inbound ACL from the protected (internal) network

- An outbound ACL to the unprotected (external) network

Figure B-2 shows the behavior of an IOS CBAC Firewall.

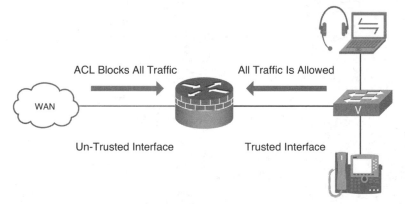

Figure B-2   *IOS CBAC Firewall Overview*

CBAC has a number of benefits compared to regular IOS ACL-based filtering, such as

- Stateful packet inspection offers deep-packet inspection thereby, reducing chances of a packet going through with a malformed payload, which regular ACL-based access-control cannot offer and thereby assists in blocking DoS attacks plus packet injection attacks.

- Alert and audit trail attributes enable a detailed logging facility.

On the flip side, CBAC also has some limitations:

- Unlike Cisco ASA, CBAC cannot replicate session states to a standby firewall, thereby reducing CBAC capability to be supported by a single IOS router (single point of failure).

- CBAC does not offer proxy features such as Cisco ASA; that is, it cannot terminate and re-originate an encrypted TLS session for voice.

- Because CBAC is an add-on to the IOS capability set, it does impact system performance. You should ensure that the router has enough processing power and memory before enabling CBAC on your network routers.

Various application layer protocols can be inspected. The following list details voice (signaling, media, and network dependency) protocols, which can be inspected by CBAC firewall:

- dns

- h323

- http

- https

- icmp

- imap

- ldap

- ntp

- pop3

- radius

- rpc

- rsvp-encap

- rtsp

- sip

- skinny

- smtp

- tacacs

- tftp

You can leverage the IOS CBAC Firewall feature set at remote sites or branches where traffic load is nominal and it is not possible to place a Cisco ASA security appliance. However, before you enable CBAC, you should ensure that your network design supports the same and that the IOS router has sufficient processing power (CPU and memory) to support inspection of traffic flowing through the router. The following examples illustrate the configuration of CBAC on an IOS router.

Note: IOS firmware 15.1(3)T ADVENTERPRISEK9-M is used for the CBAC configuration examples.

Step 1. Deny all or select traffic from external (untrusted) interface so that only traffic originating from an internal (trusted) interface can be accepted, as shown in Example B-18.

Example B-18   *ACL Definition*

```
IPTRouter(config)# ip access-list extended OUTSIDE
IPTRouter(config-ext-nacl)# deny ip any any
!
IPTRouter(config)# interface GigabitEthernet0/0
IPTRouter(config-if)# ip access-group OUTSIDE in
```

Step 2. Create **inspect** named instance to define the protocols to be inspected, as shown in Example B-19.

Example B-19   *Voice Protocol Definition for Inspection*

```
IPTRouter(config)# ip inspect name VOIP sip
IPTRouter(config)# ip inspect name VOIP skinny
IPTRouter(config)# ip inspect name VOIP http
IPTRouter(config)# ip inspect name VOIP https
```

Note: You must repeat the named instance statement for all protocols you want to define.

Step 3. Implement the **inspect** instance on egress traffic on untrusted interface, as shown in Example B-20.

Example B-20   *Application of Inspect to Untrusted Interface*

```
IPTRouter(config)# interface GigabitEthernet0/0
IPTRouter(config-if)# ip inspect VOIP out
```

Step 4. (Optional) Enable **inspect audit trail** and logging, as shown in Example B-21.

Example B-21   *Audit Trail and Logging Configuration*

```
IPTRouter(config)# ip inspect audit-trail
!
IPTRouter(config)# ip inspect log drop-pkt
```

You can define various audit, alert, and timeout options per protocol. Every supported protocol has common options in addition to its own set of unique options, as shown in Example B-22.

Example B-22 *Inspect Options*

```
IPTRouter(config)# ip inspect name VOIP sip ?
  alert       Turn on/off alert
  audit-trail Turn on/off audit trail
  timeout     Specify the inactivity timeout time
!
IPTRouter(config)#ip inspect name VOIP http ?
  alert       Turn on/off alert
  audit-trail Turn on/off audit trail
  java-list   Specify a standard access-list to apply the Java blocking. If
              specified, MUST appear directly after option "http"
  timeout     Specify the inactivity timeout time
  urlfilter   Specify URL filtering for HTTP traffic
```

Cisco IOS Zone-Based Policy Firewall

Cisco IOS Zone-Based Policy Firewall (ZFW) employs CBAC technology and offers you everything you had there and more. The major difference between CBAC and ZFW is that the former is built upon inspection at specific interfaces, whereas the latter defines zones for (grouping of) interfaces with similar functions, for example, IP Telephony server-facing interface, CUBE-facing interface, and so on, and inspection in a single direction from one zone to another. The goal of ZFW is to provide an intuitive policy design approach for multiple interfaces of a router just like you would define zones in Cisco ASA Firewall. A ZFW integrates the functions of dropping packets inside policy definitions, enabling more granularity in a configuration and policy enforcement, as shown in Figure B-3.

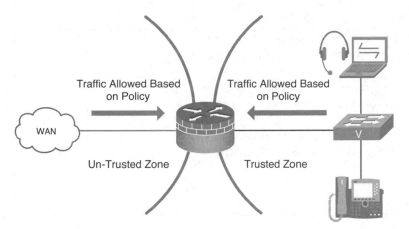

Figure B-3 *IOS Zone-Based Policy Firewall Overview*

Note: Refer to Chapter 8 for details about a Cisco ASA security appliance interface and zone concepts.

Cisco strongly advocates that before you create zones you must think about what should constitute the zones. In other words, think about what goes in those zones and why you would create a zone. As shown in Figure B-3, you need to define at a minimum two zones, one of which will be a trusted and the other will be an untrusted network, just as you would do in case of a Cisco ASA security appliance. At the end of day, your organization's security policy or IP Telephony network-specific security policy should define the number of zones you need and what type of traffic is allowed to traverse through ZFW. This is important because if you end up creating too many zones, you are bypassing the need for additional firewall(s)/ZFW's which can be disadvantageous in the longer run as your router may end up being oversubscribed and doing more firewall functions than it was initially designed for.

To configure ZFW, at a high-level you need to define zones, class maps, policy maps, and finally define zone pairs and apply policy maps to them. Possible actions for traffic moving between zones is inspect, drop, police, or pass. IOS inspect monitors traffic moving between zones if inspect is in action. If set to pass, the traffic can move between zones with no inspection whatsoever. If set to drop the traffic is dropped when moving from one security zone to another. Lastly, if set to option police the traffic can be subjected to policing rates between 8000–2,000,000,000 bps. The following steps walk you through the configuration of IOS ZFW.

Step 1.   Define security zones as per your security policy and associate zones with respective interfaces, as shown in Example B-23.

Example B-23 *ZFW Security Zone Definition*

```
IPTRouter(config)# zone security INSIDE
IPTRouter(config-sec-zone)#description Trusted Zone
!
IPTRouter(config)# zone security OUTSIDE
IPTRouter(config-sec-zone)#description Un-Trusted Zone
!
IPTRouter(config)# interface GigabitEthernet0/0
IPTRouter(config-if)# zone-member security OUTSIDE
!
IPTRouter(config)# interface GigabitEthernet0/1
IPTRouter(config)# zone-member security INSIDE
```

Step 2. Define the class maps that identify traffic that will be permitted between zones, as shown in Example B-24.

Example B-24 *Class-map Definition*

```
IPTRouter(config)# class-map type inspect match-any INOUT
IPTRouter(config-cmap)# match protocol sip
IPTRouter(config-cmap)# match protocol h323
IPTRouter(config-cmap)# match protocol skinny
```

Step 3. Configure a **policy map** that specifies the action for the class map, as illustrated in Example B-25.

Example B-25 *Policy-map Configuration*

```
IPTRouter(config)# policy-map type inspect INOUT
IPTRouter(config-pmap)# class type inspect INOUT
IPTRouter(config-pmap-c)# inspect
```

Step 4. Configure the zone pair and apply your policy, as outlined in Example B-26.

Example B-26 *Zone Pair and Policy Configuration*

```
IPTRouter(config)# zone-pair security INOUT source INSIDE destination OUTSIDE
IPTRouter(config-sec-zone-pair)# service-policy type inspect INOUT
```

The next section gives you with an insight of Cisco IPS best practices, design, and configuration for Cisco IP Telephony network.

Network Intrusion Prevention System (NIPS)

A Network Intrusion Prevention System (NIPS) is a device or software application that monitors network for malicious activities or policy violations or both, and takes the necessary action to stop the attack in its tracks. Cisco Network Intrusion Detection/ Prevention Systems (NIDS and NIPS) are primarily focused on identifying possible incidents, logging information about them (when they occur), and reporting malicious activity. In addition, an IPS system can be leveraged to identify problems with security policies and dissuade individuals from violating security policies.

Cisco NIPS and NIDS can typically log attack events, send alerts on IPS monitoring tools and SNMP alerts, produce reports, and respond to a detected threat by attempting to prevent it from succeeding by changing the security environment, for example, reconfiguring a firewall (Shun connections) or IOS router (dynamic ACLs), block source of attack, and much more. Cisco IPS is available in many flavors for various deployment and network types:

- Cisco IPS 4200 series appliance

- Cisco ASA Security Appliance AIP-SSM module

- Cisco Catalyst IDSM2 module

- Cisco IOS Router IPS-AIM and IPS-NME modules

The schematic in Figure B-4 provides an overview of various Cisco IPS solutions available to cater from small to large organizations.

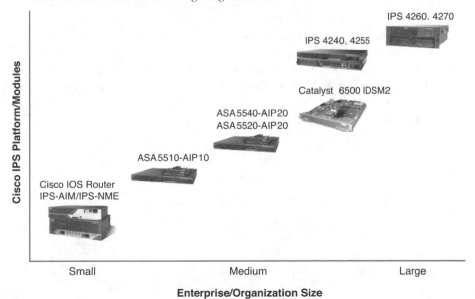

Figure B-4 *Cisco IPS Product Portfolio*

Cisco IPS Deployment for IP Telephony Networks

This section is dedicated to design and deployment of Cisco IPS sensor specifically catering to a Cisco IP Telephony environment. The focus is on Cisco IPS 4200 series appliance model because it provides maximum scalability and a rich feature set for enterprises.

Cisco IPS 4200 series appliance can be deployed in one of the following modes:

- Promiscuous mode

- Inline interface pair mode

- Inline VLAN pair mode

- Inline VLAN group mode

An IPS sensor can be deployed either in inline mode or promiscuous mode. In inline mode, the sensor analyzes the traffic live and therefore can actively block or drop any malicious packets before they reach their destination. This however, can be detrimental for time sensitive traffic, for example, RTP, SQL, and so on as each packet is analyzed for attack signature or profile, which introduces delay. In promiscuous mode, the sensor receives a copy of the data for analysis, whereas the original traffic still makes its way to its destination. Hence, there's no impact on network traffic (including voice traffic) however, it may allow malicious traffic to reach the destination (before blocking or dropping of malicious traffic post sensing can begin).

For an IP Telephony network, the promiscuous mode is the recommended option to minimize the impact on voice signaling and media streams, in terms of delay and jitter. The original packets are forwarded unchanged to their original destinations as; the IPS sensor is sent a copy of traffic (mirroring traffic). In addition, it does not require re-addressing the network and does not impact the network if the sensor is down (for example, because of hardware failure). Figure B-5 illustrates this mode of operation.

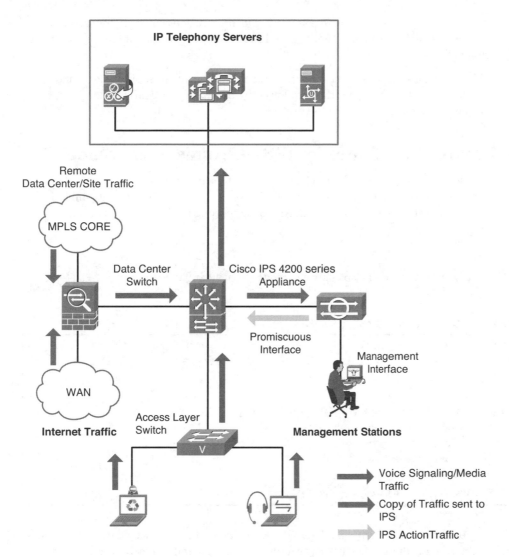

Figure B-5 *Cisco IPS 4200 Series Appliance—Promiscuous Setup for IP Telephony Network*

Cisco IPS 4200 Series sensors can use their sensing interfaces in promiscuous mode to leverage Switched Port Analyzer (SPAN) or Remote SPAN (RSPAN) to capture traffic off the VLANs or interfaces. Typically, for centralized deployment of an IPS 4200 series sensor, you would use SPAN mode off the data center switch so that the attack traffic flowing from within the headquarters (or main site) and from remote sites to the most likely targets(that is, IP Telephony servers) can be analyzed at the aggregation point. It enables attack analyses and mitigation by an IPS sensor deployed in promiscuous mode.

As portrayed in Figure B-5, an IPS sensor has its promiscuous interface connected to the data center switch (with no IP address) and has a second interface only for management connected to management subnet.

The following sections detail the configuration of the switch to support SPAN and RSPAN to an IPS sensing interface, followed by the IPS sensor configuration for the promiscuous mode.

Infrastructure Setup for IPS—Promiscuous Mode

This section concentrates on infrastructure setup to support the Cisco IPS 4200 series appliance promiscuous mode. Example B-27 gives an insight to the configuration of Cisco Catalyst Switch for enabling SPAN for supporting the IPS sensor in promiscuous mode.

Note: The configuration examples are based on the Catalyst Switch IOS version 12.2(44)SE5.

Example B-27   *Cisco Catalyst Switch Configuration for SPAN*

```
SW3750(config)# monitor session 1 source interface FastEthernet 1/0/8 rx
SW3750(config)# monitor session 1 destination interface FastEthernet 1/0/10
encapsulation dot1q ingress vlan 100
!
SW3750(config)# Interface FastEthernet 1/0/10
SW3750(config)# switchport mode access
SW3750(config)# no ip address
SW3750(config)# speed auto
SW3750(config)# duplex full
SW3750(config)# spanning-tree portfast
```

As you can see in Example B-27, the IPS sensing interface is connected to Switch 3750's interface FastEthernet 1/0/10 (destination interface). All traffic received from interface FastEthernet 1/0/8 (source interface) is sent to IPS sensor for monitoring and taking a legitimate action when a signature is fired. The traffic direction can be chosen from rx, tx, or both. Example B-28 outlines the configuration of the Cisco Catalyst Switch to support RSPAN. This is particularly useful while spanning traffic from a remote switch to a data center switch so that the IPS sensor can analyze the traffic flowing in remote sites.

Example B-28   *Cisco Catalyst Switch (with IPS Sensing Interface) Configuration for RSPAN*

```
SW3750(config)# vlan 900
SW3750(config-vlan)# remote-span
!
SW3750(config)# monitor session 2 source remote vlan 900
SW3750(config)# monitor session 2 destination interface
FastEthernet 1/0/10 encapsulation dot1q ingress vlan 100
```

Example B-29 shows a remote switch configuration.

Example B-29   *Cisco Catalyst Switch (Remote Switch) Configuration for RSPAN*

```
SW3550(config)# vlan 900
SW3550(config-vlan)# remote-span
!
SW3550(config)# monitor session 2 source vlan 100 rx
SW3550(config)# monitor session 2 destination remote vlan 900
```

Examples B-28 and B-29 describe the configuration required for Remote SPAN such that, remote switch (SW3550) VLAN traffic can be re-routed to the sensing interface port of the data center access layer switch (SW3750). Essentially, traffic received from VLAN 100 on SW3550 will be monitored by the IPS sensing interface connected on interface FastEthernet 1/0/10 on SW3750 by virtue of RSPAN VLAN 900.

Cisco IPS Setup

To set up Cisco IPS in promiscuous mode, you need to assign a physical interface to the virtual sensor. The following step-by-step procedure walks you through assigning one of your IPS's interfaces to act as a promiscuous interface and to take certain actions when a violation occurs.

Note: This assumes that you have already run through the initial IPS setup. For information on initializing an IPS system, refer to following URL: http://www.cisco.com/en/US/docs/security/ips/7.0/configuration/guide/cli/cli_initializing.html.

Step 1.   Go to https://*<ip address of IPS>*. Click **Run IDM** (see Figure B-6), which launches a Java plug-in, install it in your PC, and you will be prompted for a username and password. Enter the username and password that you set up during the IPS sensor initialization.

Figure B-6 *Cisco IDM Overview*

Note: If you have multiple IPS sensors, you can use Cisco IPS Manager Express (IME) to manage up to five sensors from a single dashboard. Cisco IME can be downloaded from the following URL: http://www.cisco.com/cisco/software/type.html?mdfid=282052550& flowid=4444.

Step 2. When logged in, you should be presented with the home screen, that is, the System Health Dashboard. At the top of the window, click **Configuration**.

Step 3. Go to **Configuration > Interfaces > Summary**, where you can see the various interfaces of the IPS 4200 series appliance and their current mode. For this example, we are going to use a single interface GigabitEthernet 0/1 for promiscuous monitoring (see Figure B-7) and sending resets or carrying out other actions upon the triggering of an IPS signature.

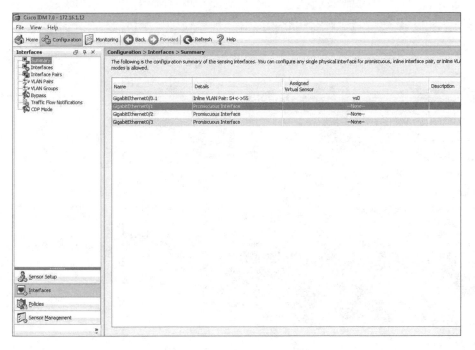

Figure B-7   *Cisco IPS 4200 Series Appliance—Interfaces*

Step 4.   Under Configuration go to **Policies > IPS Policies**, where you can see the default Virtual Sensor vs0 assigned by default. Here, you can add an interface for promiscuous monitoring of your IP Telephony network.

Step 5.   Click **Add Virtual Sensor**. It shows you the available interfaces that you can assign to a new virtual sensor. Select the interface you want to add as a promiscuous interface (see Figure B-8). You can also adjust the properties for the interface, for example, signature definition, event action rules, anomaly detection, and so on.

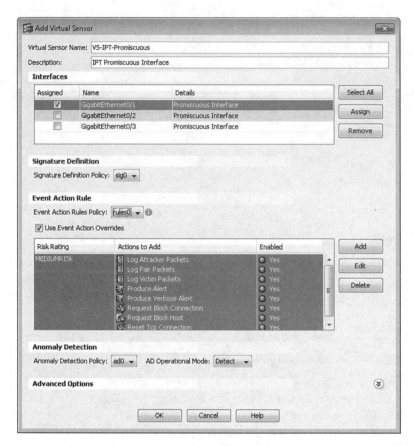

Figure B-8   *Cisco IPS 4200 Series Appliance—Virtual Sensor Configuration*

At this point, you are all set with the IPS promiscuous interface assigned to the newly created virtual-sensor and ready to deflect external and internal threats. The next step is to select and fine-tune actions taken by IPS signatures specifically designed for IP Telephony. These may be required in your organization for conformance requirements.

Cisco IPS Signatures for IP Telephony Network

Cisco IPS has a dedicated category of signatures for IP Telephony applications under the category of UC Protection. This signature class is active by default; however, individual signatures may need to be enabled as per your requirements. As depicted in Figure B-9, most of the signatures for commonly seen attacks are enabled and active, except a few that you can enable if the need be. The signatures can be modified however, that requires expertise on signature development. With that said, you can set the action of a signature when it fires (a language of IPS signature being activated on a preset event is known as the firing of the signature) for alerts, logs, and actions.

The following example walks you through modifying IPS signatures and tuning them as per your network requirement or conformance to your organization's security policy:

Step 1.   Log in to IDM. Go to **https://***ip-address-of-IPS.*

Step 2.   Go to **Configuration > Signature Definitions** (on left pane). Click **UC Protection**. This shows all available signatures under the selected signature set in the right pane, as shown in Figure B-9.

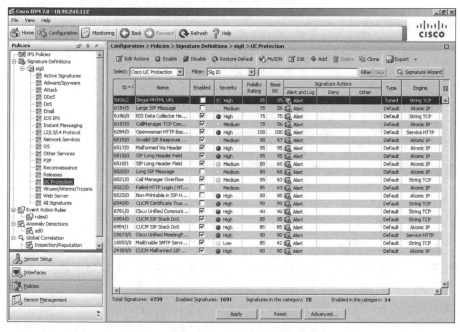

Figure B-9   *Cisco IPS 4200 Series Appliance—Signatures*

Step 3.   Right-click the signature you want to edit, and click **Edit Actions**.

Step 4.   You have an assortment of Alert and Log action options. For this example, the following was chosen:

- Produce Alert

- Produce Verbose Alert

- Log Attacker Packets

- Log Victim Packets

In addition, for other actions the selected options are (as shown in Figure B-10):

- Reset TCP Connection

- Request Block Connection

- Request Block Host

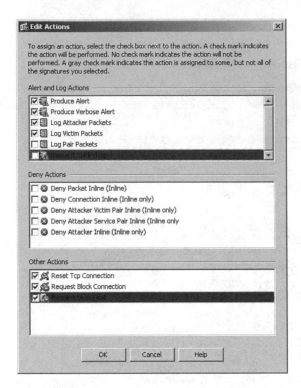

Figure B-10   *Cisco IPS 4200 Series Appliance—Tweaking Signatures (Continued)*

Note: Setting the signature to reset the TCP connection works only if the traffic is TCP-based.

Step 4.   After selecting the desired options, click **OK**. You should now see the selected options for the signature, as shown in Figure B-11.

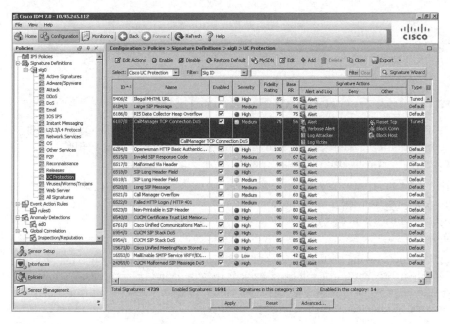

Figure B-11   *Cisco IPS 4200 Series Appliance—Tweaked Signature Overview*

Step 5.   To see the signatures firing and performing desired actions or logging, go to **Monitoring > Sensor Monitoring > Events**. Select the desired options, and click **View**, as shown in Figure B-12.

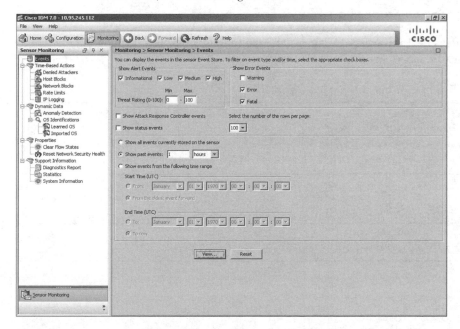

Figure B-12   *Cisco IPS 4200 Series Appliance—Monitoring Events*

Note: Only when a signature is fired, that is, an attack event is matched to a signature, you can see the signature in monitoring view, as well as see the actions taken by the signature.

Host Intrusion Prevention System (HIPS)

Cisco IP Telephony Linux-based distribution software DVD contains the OS and application bundled into the same package. In the same package there is also a HIPS agent installed by default. This HIPS agent is Cisco Security Agent (CSA).

Note that CSA is replaced by Security Enhanced Linux (SELinux) in Cisco IP Telephony application version 8.6 onward. SELinux is a Linux feature that provides a variety of security policies through the use of Linux Security Modules (LSM) in the Linux kernel.

SELinux incorporates the same security policy as CSA. The major difference that you as an IP Telephony administrator will experience is the command-line options. With version 8.6 and later, when you issue a CSA command, the system reverts with an equivalent command for SELinux, as shown in Example B-30.

Example B-30   *CSA to SELinux Command Mapping*

```
admin:utils csa status
utils csa status is no longer supported, please use:
utils os secure status
```

Examples B-31 through B-34 demonstrate the various commands that you can use to enable, disable, or know the status of SELinux.

Example B-31   *SELinux Command Options*

```
admin:utils os secure
    utils os secure enforce
    utils os secure permissive
    utils os secure status
```

Example B-32   *Disable SELinux*

```
admin:utils os secure permissive
OS security mode changed to Permissive
```

Example B-33   *Enable SELinux*

```
admin:utils os secure enforce
OS security mode changed to Enforcing
```

Example B-34   *Determine SELinux Status*

```
admin:utils os secure status
OS Security status:            enabled
Current mode:                  enforcing
```

Summary

Cisco offers next-generation security solutions for businesses leveraging Cisco IP Telephony solution to deliver protection for voice signaling, media, critical applications, and data. Cisco ASA security appliance, IOS Firewall, and Network and Host Intrusion Prevention Systems offers protection against a multitude of VoIP threats, including DoS attacks, session hijacking, eavesdropping, session replay, and Spam over Internet Telephony (SPIT).

In this appendix, you learned about Cisco network firewall and Intrusion Prevention and Detection portfolio. As more and more businesses move to converged networks, the requirement for security to safeguard voice and data communications becomes ever more critical. The Cisco ASA Firewall presents a high-performance, dedicated firewalling solution for today's IP Telephony networks. On the other hand, for small businesses and remote sites of enterprises, Cisco IOS Firewall provides an option for sustainable yet cost-effective protection of IP Telephony assets. To complement firewalls at the perimeter or protecting data centers, Cisco IPS solution is a perfect match, which can detect malicious activity or attacks, and stop them in their tracks.

Glossary

3DES (Triple DES)   A mode of the DES encryption algorithm that encrypts data three times. Three 64-bit keys are used, instead of one, for an overall key length of 192 bits. (The first encryption is encrypted with the second key, and the resulting cipher text is again encrypted with a third key.)

AA (Automated Attendant)   Voice processing system that provides callers with a recorded message and directs them to specific extensions based on their responses to various prompts.

AAA (authentication, authorization, accounting)   Services provided by Cisco TACACS+ or any RADIUS server for authentication, command, or privilege level authorization, and command or usage accounting for users or call setup-related events.

access layer   The layer at which user workstations, IP Phones, and servers connect in the Cisco three-layer hierarchical design model. Servers connect not at the user access layer, however, at the data center access layer.

ACL (access control list)   A permit or deny list for ingress or egress connections to devices such as routers, switches, gateways, and servers defining who or what is allowed to access certain types of resources in a network.

AES (Advanced Encryption Standard)   A symmetric-key encryption standard that can use 128-, 192-, and 256-bit key lengths.

AIC (Application Inspection and Control)   Provides advanced application layer (OSI Layers 5 to 7) filtering that provides a more granular level of control for voice signaling, media, and other traffic.

AIM (Advanced Integration Module)   A hardware accelerator that can be added to the Cisco router that can offload cryptographic functions from the router's main CPU.

AH (authentication headers)   Encapsulation for authentication of user traffic, which is almost no longer in use. Provides data integrity, data origin authentication, and protection against replay.

ARP (Address Resolution Protocol)   Used to find the matching IP-to-MAC assignment.

ASA (Adaptive Security Appliance)   Provides perimeter security services with integrated IPS, firewall, VPN technology, and voice security services with TLS Proxy and Phone Proxy to secure a converged Communications solution.

asymmetric encryption   Uses a public and a private key to encrypt and decrypt data.

AutoSecure   A statement command used in the Cisco command-line interface to secure the router. It replaces an individual configuration for each item you want to secure with a Cisco recommended best practice configuration.

BGP (Border Gateway Protocol)   Performs inter domain routing in Transmission-Control Protocol/Internet Protocol (*see* TCP/IP) networks. BGP is an Exterior Gateway Protocol (EGP), which means that it performs routing between multiple autonomous systems or domains.

BPDU (Bridge Protocol Data Unit)   Exchanged by STP-supporting switches to discover and announce Layer 2 topology information.

CA (certificate authority)   An entity trusted by disparate parties that want to communicate with each other. Provides a common trust relationship.

CAM (Content Addressable Memory) table   Contains the discovered MAC address-to-port assignments on a switch.

CAPF (Certificate Authentication Proxy Function)   A service that runs on a CUCM Publisher server and acts as a central point of contact for the cluster for signing and distribution of certificates when a cluster is in mixed mode.

CBAC (Context-Based Access Control)   Cisco IOS feature that provides a stateful packet inspection on routers.

CDP (Cisco Discovery Protocol)   Cisco proprietary, Layer 2 protocol used to exchange information between Cisco network devices in an IP network.

CIPC (Cisco IP Communicator)   Client application, a softphone for the PC/laptop. It's a full scale soft IP Phone, which enables users to dial within or outside an enterprise, checks voice-mails, and so on.

COR (Class of Restriction)   Enables inbound or outbound restrictions for receiving or placing calls, respectively. Applicable to dial-peers and ephones.

core layer   The layer at which high-speed routing and switching occur in the Cisco three-layer hierarchical design model.

CoS (Class of Service)   Defines limits and permissions for using Cisco Unity/Unity Connection. It defines how users can interact with the system and what they are allowed to do in the system.

CSR (certificate signing request)   A block of text sent to the CA requesting an identity certificate to be generated, that is, signed CSR.

CTL (Certificate Trust List) A file that contains the IP addresses of members of Cisco Unified Communications Manager (*see* CUCM) cluster enabling the endpoints to trust the members of the cluster for signaling or media communication. Signaling can be secured using TLS and media using SRTP if encryption is enabled.

CUBE (Cisco Unified Border Element) Business-to-Business UA, which provides a demarcation between the two or more networks to mask one from the other for security issues. Although demarcation is only one of many features, CUBE is used for SIP trunking between an internal call control and a service provider switch.

CUC (Cisco Unity Connection) Cisco IP voicemail solution. It integrates with CUCM to provide enterprise voicemail solution.

CUCM (Cisco Unified Communications Manager) Cisco IP Call Control solution. It has the dial-plan intelligence and enables endpoints such as IP Phones and Voice Gateways to register and leverage telephony features.

CUCME (Cisco Unified Communications Manager Express) Cisco Express IP Call Control solution. Similar to CUCM however scaled for IOS platform. It is suitable for smaller sites or small-sized phone deployment at remote sites.

CUE (Cisco Unity Express) Cisco voicemail express solution. It is based on a module on a Cisco IOS router where a service engine can serve as an Auto Attendant (*see* AA) and serves as express voicemail for CUCME.

CUOM (Cisco Unified Operations Manager) Comprehensive monitoring and diagnostics solution for the Cisco IP Telephony system.

CUPC (Cisco Unified Personal Communicator) Client application that enables users to share presence information, use Instant Messaging (*see* IM), check voicemail, and dial other IP Phones or external numbers by using a controlled or an associated IP Phone.

CUPM (Cisco Unified Provisioning Manager) A provisioning application for Cisco Unified Communications initial deployments and implementations. It provides comprehensive provisioning, monitoring, and troubleshooting capabilities for Cisco Unified Communications Solution.

CUPS (Cisco Unified Presence Server) Cisco Presence Server that enables an enterprise user to see the presence status of another user, use Integrated Messaging, and allows federation with other presence solutions.

CUSM (Cisco Unified Service Monitor) Provides a reliable way to continuously monitor active calls supported by the Cisco IP Telephony System.

CUSSM (Cisco Unified Service Statistics Manager) Provides a variety of easy-to-use, yet advanced executive and operational reports, enhancing capacity planning and budgeting.

DAI (Dynamic ARP Inspection) Security feature used to prevent man-in-the-middle (*see* MITM) attacks.

DDoS (distributed denial of service) Occurs when multiple systems flood the bandwidth or resources of a targeted system, usually one or more web servers. These systems are compromised by attackers using a variety of methods.

DES (Data Encryption Standard)   A symmetric-key encryption standard that uses a 56-bit key.

DHCP (Dynamic Host Configuration Protocol)   Protocol used to dynamically allocate and assign IP addresses to devices in a network, for example, computers or IP Phones. DHCP enables easy administration and allocation of IPs to devices in a large IP network.

DHCP snooping   A security feature available on Cisco Catalyst LAN switches that prevent rogue DHCP servers on an IP network.

Dial-Peer   Defines the mapping of a telephone number to a voice port or IP address.

Distribution layer   The layer at which routing redistribution, network policies, and Internet access may occur in the Cisco three-layer hierarchical design model.

DID (Direct Inward Dial)   Enables an external caller to dial a business's internal extension number without needing to go through an operator or automated attendant.

DoS (denial of service)   An attack in which a user or organization is deprived of the services of a resource normally accessible.

Dot1q   Also called 802.1q, is an IEEE-based virtual LAN (*see* VLAN) standard that provides common interoperable solutions to the establishment of VLAN-bridged infrastructures.

double-tagging   Attack vector that involves an additional 802.1Q tag to an already tagged packet for the purpose of hopping from one VLAN to another.

DSP (digital signal processor)   Processes a voice signal, samples it into segments, and packs it into frames for transmission over a packet network.

DTP (Dynamic Trunking Protocol)   Protocol used to negotiate the status of a trunk between Layer 2 switches.

EAP (Extensible Authentication Protocol)   Authentication method used by 802.1x and RA-DIUS and Cisco TACACS+ server.

EAP-FAST   Authentication protocol that does not require digital certificates; supports a variety of user and password database types, supports password expiration and change, and is flexible, easy to deploy, and easy to manage.

EAP-MD5   Enables a RADIUS server to authenticate a connection request by verifying an MD5 hash of a user's password. The server sends the client a random challenge value, and the client proves its identity by hashing the challenge and its password with MD5. This EAP method is vulnerable to man-in-the-middle attacks.

EAPOL (Extensible Authentication Protocol over LAN)   Used between the supplicant and the authenticator.

EAP-TLS protocol   Performs mutual SSL authentication for both the supplicant (the end user's machine) and the authentication server (the RADIUS server) via a certificate. Each side is required to prove its identity to the other using its certificate and its private key for a better security.

EIGRP (Enhanced Interior Gateway Routing Protocol)   An enhanced version of IGRP (latter being the Cisco Interior Gateway Routing Protocol). Although EIGRP is regarded as an Interior Gateway Protocol (IGP), it is used extensively as an EGP for inter domain routing.

encapsulation   The technique used by layered protocols in which a layer adds header information to the protocol data unit (PDU) from the layer above.

encryption   The conversion of information into a scrambled form that helps effectively disguising it to prevent unauthorized access.

ESP (Encapsulating Security Protocol)   Provides data integrity, data origin authentication, protection against replay, and confidentiality to user traffic.

eToken   USB eToken enables Cisco Unified Communications Manager (*see* CUCM) conversion from nonsecure to mixed mode and simplifies the security feature deployment and configuration. eToken is a digital certificate (X.509) footprint containing public and private keys required to sign the CUCM CTL file. For Cisco Unified CME (*see* CUCME) it is a soft token in IOS.

extranet   Private network that uses Internet to securely share part of a business's information. Used often between partner organizations.

Firewall   A hardware appliance (for example, Cisco Adaptive Security Appliance) or software application that shields a business's internal network from external attacks, such as through the Internet. This is accomplished by allowing only certain types of traffic to enter the internal network.

FTP/TFTP (File Transfer Protocol/Trivial File Transfer Protocol)   Protocols used to transfer files from one machine to another over a network, for example, firmware and other files from TFTP server to IP Phones.

gatekeeper   An H.323 device that provides bandwidth management and address translation and that controls access for H.323 devices. H.323 devices register with a gatekeeper, easing the provisioning, installation, and management of a large H.323 service provider or enterprise networks.

H.323   A standard developed by the International Telecommunication Union (ITU) that specifies techniques to compress and transmit real-time voice, video, and data between a pair of videoconferencing workstations.

hacker   A person who investigates the integrity or security of a network or operating system. Hackers can be White Hat or Black Hat. Although the former is a person who helps find out weaknesses or exploits in a network or operating system, the latter does it for malicious purposes, such as financial gain.

hash   A function that takes an arbitrary block of characters and outputs a fixed-size bit string. This accounts for the integrity of messages from source to destination provided the hash recalculation produces same checksum at the source as it produced at source.

HIPS (Host Intrusion Prevention System)   An IPS (*see* Intrusion Prevention System) written specifically for an operating system to protect endpoints, for example, servers from malicious code execution and 0-day attacks.

HMAC (Hash-based Message Authentication Code)   A cryptographic hash function used to protect a message's integrity and authenticity.

HSRP (Hot Standby Routing Protocol)   Cisco proprietary redundancy protocol for establishing a fault-tolerant default gateway, described in detail in RFC 2281. Active/Standby election and link failover is established with Hello, Coup, ARP Reply packets and timers.

HTTP (Hypertext Transfer Protocol)   The protocol used by web browsers on client machine and web servers to transfer files data, images, and text files on the World Wide Web or a web server.

HTTPS (Secure Hypertext Transfer Protocol)   Secure version of HTTP protocol used to provide security between clients and server using Secure Socket Layer (*see* SSL) or Transport Layer Security (*see* TLS).

ICMP (Internet Connection Messaging Protocol)   Error reporting and diagnostic protocol used by routers, intermediary devices, or hosts for communicating updates and error information to other like devices.

ICT (Inter Cluster Trunk)   Used to connect CUCM clusters across an IP network.

IDS (Intrusion Detection System)   It is used by virtue of forwarding a copy of all received traffic to it so that it can analyze for potential attacks. An IDS is reactive in nature.

IKE (Internet Key Exchange)   A framework that provides policy negotiations and key management processes in a virtual private network (see VPN).

IM (Instant Messaging)   Instant Messaging enables two or more people to communicate in real time by typing their messages in a software messenger (for example, CUPC) thereby eliminating the need for e-mails or voice calls.

in-band network management   An in-band management involves managing devices through the common protocols such as telnet or SSH, using the underlying network as a media.

IP (Internet Protocol)   The Internet protocol suite is the set of communications protocols used for the Internet and other similar networks. It is the basis of the existence of today's networks.

IPS (Intrusion Prevention System)   It is used inline having all traffic forwarded through it to analyze for potential attacks. An IPS is proactive in nature.

IPSec (Internet Protocol Security)   IPSec is a suite of protocols for securing network connections. It uses cryptographic security services to protect communications over Internet Protocol (IP) networks. IPSec supports network-level peer authentication, data origin authentication, data integrity, data confidentiality (encryption), and replay protection.

IPT (Internet Protocol Telephony)   Technology that uses the Internet Protocol's packet-switched connections for exchange of voice, fax, and other forms of communication information using an underlying IP network.

ISL (Inter-Switch Link)   Cisco proprietary switch trunk negotiation protocol.

ITL (Initial Trust List)   A leaner version of Certificate Trust List (*see* CTL), which provides initial trust between an endpoint and the cluster. It does not enable encryption however, only enables trust between device and cluster.

LEAP (Lightweight Extensible Authentication Protocol)   Authentication protocol used in Cisco wireless environments and uses username/passwords for authentication.

MD5 (Message Digest Algorithm 5)   Works by creating a one-way hash out of a shared secret and sending this hash between the source and destination. The destination then calculates the hash from its configured shared secret and verifies the source authenticity. Because this is a one-way process, the process cannot be reversed to determine the originating shared secret.

MGCP (Media Gateway Control Protocol)   VoIP developed by Cisco described in IETF RFC 2705. It is a gateway signaling protocol where the gateway has minimal intellect and all call control intelligence lies with CUCM (*see* Cisco Unified Communications Manager).

MIB (Management Information Base)   A virtual information storage location that contains collections of managed objects. Within the MIB, there are objects that relate to different defined MIB modules.

MITM (man-in-the-middle) attack   An attack in which the attacker intercepts communications between two or more systems and captures data from each of the victim systems. The victims believe they are still communicating to their original, legitimate peer.

MOC (Microsoft® Office Client)   Client for end user PCs that is similar to Cisco Unified Personal Communicator (*see* CUPC) and used for IM, voicemail, and calls via Microsoft OCS.

MQC (Modular Quality of Service)   Provides a modular method to configure several different features on Cisco equipment, including quality of service (*see* QoS).

MTP (Media Termination Point)   Provides a termination and re-origination anchor point in the middle of the media path of a call. Often used to change IP addresses for security reasons on different segments of the call.

MWI (Message Waiting Indicator)   Unity/Unity Connection notification to alert a user when a voice mail message is waiting. Typical MWI alerts include a light and a phone display icon.

NAC (Network Admission Control)   A security framework designed to regulate who accesses a network. It leverages identity management system (based on unique criteria, for example, MAC address).

NAT (Network Address Translation)   A way to translate an IP address from an RFC 1918 (or private address) to a public address or vice versa. This is typically used to preserve public IP space and to hide internal IP addresses.

NOC (Network Operations Center)   A place from which administrators supervise, monitor, and maintain a telecommunications network.

OCS (Office Communication Server)   Microsoft's UC solution including IM, Audio, Video, Web Conferencing, and Presence.

OOB (Out of Band) Network Management   An out-of-band solution is to have an access server or dedicated network connected to a management port of each managed device.

OSI (Open Systems Interconnection)   Reference model published by International Organization for Standardizations (ISO) as a framework to build a systems of open systems protocols. OSI layers contain seven layers that are more often referred to by number than by name. The layers are Layer 1 (physical layer), Layer 2 (data link layer), Layer 3 (network layer), Layer 4 (transport layer), Layer 5 (session layer), Layer 6 (presentation layer), and Layer 7 (application layer).

OSPF (Open Shortest Path First)   A link state protocol that bases its path descriptions on link states that take into account additional network information. It uses a shortest path first algorithm to build and calculate the shortest path to all known destinations. OSPF routing domains are known as areas.

PAT (Port Address Translation)   Used when many internal addresses need to access an external network and few external addresses are available. It is also known as NAT overloading.

PBX (Private Branch Exchange)   Small telephone switch that an organization may deploy for its internal calls and connection to PSTN. A traditional PBX is analog in nature, whereas a modern PBX is usually IP-based, for example, CUCM or CUCME.

phreaker   An individual who has extensive knowledge of telephone networks and switching equipment and has malicious intents to leverage the same.

PKI (Public Key Infrastructure)   A set of hardware, software, and policies that manage certificates for use in identity validation and authentication.

POE (Power over Ethernet)   Technology for wired LANs (*see* LAN) that enables the electrical current, necessary for the operation of each device, to be drawn from the switch port.

POTS (Plain Old Telephone Service)   An alternative term for PSTN.

private address   IP addresses reserved and blocked on the Internet (also known as RFC 1918 addresses) so that they can be used on private networks.

proxy   A device in a Session Initialization Protocol (SIP) network that terminates a connection, accepts requests from a user, potentially authenticates a user, and then either passes on the requests or processes them.

proxy server   Used to access the Internet or other applications by the computers in an organization's network. All information requested for by internal clients is relayed via proxy server.

PSTN (Public Switched Telephone Network)   Public telephone service.

QoS (quality of service)   Differential treatment of priority data and information over non critical information traversing the same link. QoS has many tools, for example, marking, classification, queuing, policing, shaping, and so on.

RADIUS (Remote Authentication Dial In User Service)   A standard first used for dial-in users. It can now be generally used for any kind of remote access system for authentication.

RDP (Remote Desktop Protocol)   Microsoft proprietary protocol that provides a user with a graphical interface to another computer or server. Used for remote management.

reconnaissance attack   An attack designed not to inflict immediate damage to a system or network, however, only to map out the network and discover which address ranges are used, which systems are active, and so on.

RIP (Routing Information Protocol)   A distance-vector protocol that uses hop count as its metric. It performs routing within a single autonomous system. Exterior gateway protocols, such as the Border Gateway Protocol (*see* BGP), perform routing between different autonomous systems.

root bridge   The bridge in the network with the lowest - priority value. It is elected by exchanging Bridge Protocol Data Units (*see* BPDU) with all the other switches in the network.

RSPAN (Remote Switched Port Analyzer)   An advanced feature of a switch that is used to monitor source ports available all over in the switched network. All SPAN features are typically supported in RSPAN.

RTCP (RTP Control Protocol)   The transport of an RTP session is augmented by a control protocol (RTCP) to enable monitoring of the voice packet delivery.

RTP (Real Time Transport Protocol)   IP Telephony protocol used for delivering audio and video streams. It is media bearer protocol, which is delay-sensitive.

SA (security association)   A set of security algorithms and technologies that will be agreed upon and used to securely transmit data between two IP Security (*see* IPSec) endpoints.

SBD (Security By Default)   Using Initial Trust List (*see* ITL) this service enables initial security service for endpoints.

SCCP (Skinny Client Control Protocol)   VoIP signaling protocol used by CUCM and CUCME to exchange messages between the call agent and an IP Phone to the control phone and call state. It is a Cisco-proprietary protocol.

SCEP (Simple Certificate Enrollment Protocol)   Lightweight certificate enrollment protocol.

SCP (Secure Copy Protocol)   Typically uses SSH (TCP port 22) to securely transfer files between two hosts.

security cycle   A continuous reiterating security wheel that defines an organization's commitment to ensure secure network architecture deployment.

Security Framework   Defines a security construct to address risks and security issues in the way that business and information technology systems are designed, built, operated, and managed.

SHA (Secure Hash Algorithm)   Cryptographic hash function published by National Institute of Standards and Technology (NIST). Has various versions starting namely, SHA-0 (original version 160-bit hash function), SHA-1 (160-bit hash function resembles MD5), SHA-2 (consists of two similar hash functions, with different block sizes, that is, 256 and 512), and SHA-3 (proposed, still in development).

SIP (Session Initialization Protocol)   A protocol developed by an IETF Working Group as an alternative to H.323. Its advantages are simplicity, flexibility, and capability to work alongside a host of other different protocols, and the ease with which it can be embedded in end-user devices and Internet technologies.

SIP UA (SIP User Agent)   A device that transmits SIP packets over IP.

SNMP (Simple Network Management Protocol)   Used for standard operations and maintenance protocol for the network devices such as routers, switches, and servers. Typically uses
the well-known UDP port 161.

SNMP Agent   The component run directly on the device and maintains data and reports the
data to the SNMP manager.

SNMP Manager   The component used to control and monitor the devices within the network
using SNMP. Information is gained from SNMP agents.

SPAN (Switched Port Analyzer)   Also sometimes called port mirroring or port monitoring.
Selects network traffic for analysis by a network analyzer.

SPIT (Spam over IP Telephony)   A security threat with the potential to fill voicemail boxes
with unwanted messages and impact the normal operation of PBX and end users (by overloading resources). Also known as VoIP spam.

spoofing   Illegal act to send a packet labeled with a false address to deceive network security
mechanisms such as access lists (*see* ACL).

SRST (Survivable Remote Site Telephony)   A feature available in Cisco IOS voice gateways
that provides redundant call control for remote sites and branch offices. If a WAN link failure
occurs, the remote site and branch IP Phones can register with the SRST gateway that acts as a
call control until the WAN is restored.

SRTP (Switched Port Analyzer)   Secure form of RTP (*see* RTP) where RTP packets are encapsulated in TLS.

SSH (Secure Shell)   Network protocol that enables data to be exchanged using a secure channel between two networked devices. TCP port 22 has been assigned for the SSH protocol.

SSL (Secure Socket Layer)   A cryptographic protocol that provides security for transmis-
sions of public transports such as the Internet.

SSO (single sign-on)   Also known as Enterprise Single Sign On, gives the ability to a user
to enter the same id and password, once, and to log on to multiple applications within an
enterprise.

stateful inspection   A stateful inspection engine permits the firewall to track the state of
TCP/IP sessions by monitoring the three-way handshake that happens at the beginning of a
session and permits only inbound traffic from hosts with already internally established sessions. This concept has been extended in Cisco ASA to not only track TCP/IP sessions, but
also to monitor UDP/IP traffic. Also, using AIC it provides a deep inspection engine used for
Layer 5 through Layer 7 traffic monitoring and control.

STP (Spanning Tree Protocol)   Protocol used to prevent loops in a Layer 2 network (on
switches).

supplicant   Software on the client that performs the 802.1X client-side activities when
requesting authentication.

TACACS+ (Terminal Access Controller Access-Control System)   A remote authentication protocol used to communicate with an authentication server to authenticate, authorize, and account for clients trying to access a network resource. TACACS+ uses the Transmission Control Protocol (*see* TCP).

TCP (Transmission Control Protocol)   Transport layer protocol, which is a connection-oriented protocol. It requires a three-way handshake before delivery of information can start.

TLS (Transport Layer Security)   A method to provide security for communications, TLS is commonly used to secure web pages. It is the successor to the Secure Socket Layer protocol (*see* SSL).

transcoder   Enables the ability to modify the codec of a VoIP call midstream between devices that support different codecs.

TRP (Trusted Relay Point)   An anchor to the voice stream such that the endpoints to call-control (for example, CUCM) can get preferential QoS treatment in voice VLAN and for secure traversal from data to voice VLAN.

TVS (Trust Verification Service)   A primary component of Security By Default (*see* SBD). It runs on a CallManager server or a dedicated server that authenticates certificates on behalf of phones and other endpoints. It associates a list of roles for the owner of the certificate, for example, TFTP.

UCS (Unified Computing System)   Platform composed of hardware compute, storage, switching fabric, and virtualization support. Available in B-Series and C-Series.

UDP (User Datagram Protocol)   A Layer 4 connectionless protocol. Time-sensitive applications are usually UDP-enabled, for example, Real Time Protocol (*see* RTP).

unity   Cisco voice messaging solution (similar to Cisco Unity Connection (*see* CUC). Integrates with CUCM or CUCME to provide enterprise voice messaging.

UTM (Unified Threat Management)   Designed to provide a range of security solutions in a single appliance thus reducing costs and simplifying the whole process of security systems management, reporting, and installation.

Vishing   A technique that involves using a phone call to gather user information for further attacks.

VLAN (virtual local-area network)   Used to provide a virtually separate network within a single physical LAN.

VNC (Virtual Network Computing)   Technology for remote desktop sharing, enabling the desktop display of one computer to be remotely viewed and controlled. Similar to Remote Desktop Protocol (*see* RDP), however, a nonproprietary protocol.

VoIP (Voice over IP)   Used to provide a voice call/conferencing facility between two or more parties using the Internet Protocol.

VPN (virtual private network)   Used to provide a secure connection over an insecure network, typically the Internet. The VPN provides a secure "tunnel" that enables traffic to be sent from source to destination without being vulnerable to traffic eavesdropping.

WAN (wide-area network)   A network or several LANs that connect computers and sites across a wide geographic area.

WLAN (wireless LAN)   Local-area network (*see* LAN) service to wireless clients (computers, IP Phones and so on) without the limitation of requiring a physical connection.

WLC (wireless LAN controller)   Responsible for system wide wireless LAN functions, for example, security policies, radio frequency management, quality management, and increased wireless network availability.

WPA (Wi-Fi Protected Access)   A popular standard for wireless network security. Two versions exist: WPA and WPA2.

X.509   A well-known standard that defines the basic PKI data formats such as the certificate and the Certificate Revocation List (CRL) formats to enable basic interoperability.

zeroize   A command used with RSA crypto keys on the router. Zeroize removes any previous keys that might have been present.

ZFW (Zone-Based Policy Firewall)   Assigns router interfaces to security zones, and firewall inspection policy is applied to traffic moving between the zones. Zone-Based Policy Firewall enforces a secure inter zone policy by default, such that a given interface cannot pass traffic to interfaces in other security zones until an explicit policy allowing traffic is defined.

Index

O

X

Z

FREE
Online Edition

Your purchase of *Securing Cisco IP Telephony Networks* includes access to a free online edition for 45 days through the **Safari Books Online** subscription service. Nearly every Cisco Press book is available online through **Safari Books Online**, along with thousands of books and videos from publishers such as Addison-Wesley Professional, Exam Cram, IBM Press, O'Reilly Media, Prentice Hall, Que, Sams, and VMware Press.

Safari Books Online is a digital library providing searchable, on-demand access to thousands of technology, digital media, and professional development books and videos from leading publishers. With one monthly or yearly subscription price, you get unlimited access to learning tools and information on topics including mobile app and software development, tips and tricks on using your favorite gadgets, networking, project management, graphic design, and much more.

Activate your FREE Online Edition at
informit.com/safarifree

STEP 1:   Enter the coupon code: TPYREAA

STEP 2:   New Safari users, complete the brief registration form.
Safari subscribers, just log in.

If you have difficulty registering on Safari or accessing the online edition,
please e-mail customer-service@safaribooksonline.com